Michel St-Yves

The Psychology of Criminal Investigations:

The Search for the Truth

Revision of English text by Steven Sacks

(Chapters 1, 6-10, 12-13, 16-17, 19-Conclusion, front matter, and selected sections of Chapters 11 and 18)

Translated by Jeffrey Miller, B.A., M.A., LL.B.

CARSWELL®

A cataloguing and record for this publication is available from Library and Archives Canada.

Translation of: Psychologie de l'enquête criminelle.
Includes bibliographical references and index.
ISBN 978-0-7798-1676-7

HV8073.P7813 2008 **363.3501′9** **C2008-903248-9**

Composition: Computer Composition of Canada Inc.

THOMSON REUTERS

CARSWELL, A DIVISION OF THOMSON REUTERS CANADA LIMITED

One Corporate Plaza
2075 Kennedy Road
Toronto, Ontario
M1T 3V4

Customer Relations
Toronto 1-416-609-3800
Elsewhere in Canada/U.S. 1-800-387-5164
Fax 1-416-298-5082
www.carswell.com
Online www.carswell.com/email

In his search for the truth and defence of human rights, he brought nobility to the Sheriff of Nottingham. I dedicate this work to my friend, the late, lamented Tom Williamson.

Michel St-Yves

For a generation Madeleine Giauque has influenced my thought and personal growth: Her generosity with her time and judicious advice, as both prosecutor and friend, have steered me along a rewarding path. I thank my lucky stars that I found her!

Michel Tanguay

FOREWORD

Robert Roy*

Ethics, Truth, and Criminal Investigations

Truth, truth, truth is a handful of fine sand
Truth, Truth, Truth that slips between my fingers
There's no rest but for him that finds
There's no rest but for him that seeks
And then it's time to begin again.

Raôul Duguay

Many fundamental principles of our justice system relate more or less explicitly to the truth or, at the very least, are animated by the desire to discover the truth. The presumption of innocence invites us not to convict a person only on appearances. Oath-taking by witnesses — "Do you swear to tell the truth, the whole truth, and nothing but the truth?" — is meant to guarantee the quality of information submitted for consideration by the court. The principle of reasonable doubt requires us to assume the risk of allowing a criminal to escape rather than convicting an innocent person.

This last principle is crucial to a better understanding of the position that truth occupies in our justice system. The Supreme Court of Canada has specified how a judge must present reasonable doubt to the jury,[1] and its decision defines an unbreakable link between is principle and the presumption of innocence. The court has stipulated that doubt can be established only where there is a logical link with the evidence or lack of it. It has emphasized that the norm, while requiring more than a probability of guilt, does not require proof to an absolute certainty. The standard is not proof beyond all doubt, but the relevant doubt must not be imaginary or frivolous.

---

* The author is an Associate Professor in the Applied Ethics Chair at the University of Sherbrooke. In 1977, he began his career as an instructor of philosophy. Since 1999, he has devoted his energies to the development of applied organizational and institutional ethics in Quebec and Europe. His publications, conference presentations, and research concern police, organizational, and educational ethics, as well as concepts of democracy.

1 *R v. Lifchus*, [1997] 3 S.C.R. 320 at para. 36.

In short, according to the high court, a conviction or acquittal does not equate with absolute certainty as to guilt or innocence. The concept of reasonable doubt ensures that convictions or acquittals are not based on such certitudes, but rather on juries' confidence, supported logically by the evidence, that their verdicts are correct.

Traditionally, certainty has been associated with truth-finding — if we convict without absolute certainty, does it follow that we convict without knowing the truth? What, moreover, is evidence that fails to produce certainty? These two questions are crucial for anyone who must conduct a criminal investigation whose very nature consists of assembling evidence and shedding light on the circumstances of the crime in question.

To understand the wisdom of the Supreme Court's view which appears, at first glance, astonishing, a detour into the philosophy of truth might prove helpful.[2]

For millennia humans have tried to understand the world in which they live. We have made the heavens, the planet, life, and, more recently, human personal and social relationships objects of study. We have deployed sundry methods for understanding reality. Our desire to know presupposes a gap between reality and our representation of it. In traditional thought, when we believe we have reduced that gap to zero, we are certain that our representation conforms with reality. It is precisely this correspondence between our representation and reality that defines the classic vision of truth.

Over time, philosophy and the sciences have questioned the value of the various means used to represent reality. As a result, today they uphold a very different conception, in which truth is defined by a representation that is rigorously logical and effective in predicting the results of certain operations.

Fundamentally, truth is still knowledge with the power to induce human conviction, but there is a major difference between the two concep-

---

2 Concerning the views expressed here on truth and modes of knowing, I am indebted to Georges A. Legault, "La délibération éthique: Aspects Théoriques" in *Professionalisme et délibération éthique: Manuel d'aide à la décision responsable"* Presses de l'Université du Québec, Collection "Éthique" no. 8, 1999, pp. 225-271, and to Jean-François Malherbe, "Éthique et vérité" *Ethica,* vol. 9, no. 2, volume 1, 1997, pp. 214-226.

tions: in the classical model, certainty is present; in the modern view, uncertainty subsists. It is this latter conception of the truth that informs the Supreme Court in its formulation of reasonable doubt.

The majority of police investigators follow the classic conception of truth — in which "proof" is synonymous with absolute certainty — creating significant problems in their work. We will now attempt to see proof in a more modern view. To that end, we must look more deeply into the nature and limits of different modes of human knowledge.

Empiricism

For empiricists, the direct experience of humans, in which the senses are paramount, is the main mode of knowing. But, as we will discuss, while this mode is often used, a rather limiting weakness is inherent in it.

Empiricism figures profoundly in police work. For example, if a suspect says, "last night I worked between 8 and 11," the police officer's first step will be to verify this claim. He or she will collect statements from the suspect's colleagues at work, and investigate the nature of the suspect's relationship to those witnesses — are they friends, enemies, mere acquaintances? If all the testimony concurs, the officer will probably conclude that the suspect is telling the truth. But this conclusion is somewhat premature, given that empiricism carries six fundamental shortcomings.

First, lies are a fact of life — which is why we must corroborate statements with the help of witnesses who are as impartial as possible. But does such corroboration produce absolute certainty regarding the suspect's statement? No. While falsehood is different than truth, it is more than simple negation. What matters with lies is not only that they represent a disconnect with the facts, but also that they harbour an intention to mislead investigators. This is why we speak of "lies by omission," of failing to say what one knows so as to mislead. But where a statement does not accord with the facts and there is no intention to mislead, this is a mistake, not a lie. In fact, adopting a tone or attitude meant to mislead, while making a statement that conforms to the facts is also lying.

The second fundamental problem with empiricism is that language is always a matter of interpretation. When an investigator poses a question to a suspect, victim or witness, the interviewee responds based on their understanding of the query. In my career as a researcher, I have observed the work of numerous police officers over periods of many weeks. During the first two days of each observation, I explain to the officers that I am investigating police ethics and, each time, a malaise sets in. At last I understood that, while I was using "investigate" in the scientific sense, the officers hear it in the police context.

Empiricism's third problem is that reality changes. Between the moment people observe something and the time they speak to investigators, the situation can alter radically.

The fourth problem is that perception is subjective, varying according to the perceiver. Not everyone shares the same visual and auditory acuity. It is completely possible that a person who is slightly hard of hearing will hear absolutely no suspicious noise in a neighbouring apartment while another, who has particularly good hearing, is able to describe the sound in detail. The same is true with other senses. For example, who among us has not recognized a familiar face, only to discover that, on a closer view, it belongs to a complete stranger? Emotions can modify perception considerably. The cashier robbed at gunpoint tends to remember the weapon as larger than it actually is.

The fifth problem with empiricism stems from the fact that saying is choosing. Each witness chooses to say what that witness sees as important. The selection is partially subjective, as a function of what the witness judges to be most important.

The last (but not the least) problem with empiricism is that all witness statements involve two types of radically different operations: describing and explaining. According to Jacques Rancière, an explanation is always subjective.[3] Given that all explanations interpret what has happened, a given explanation might seem plausible, but does it really describe what happened?

Interpretation establishes logical links between different perceptions. Based on our personal knowledge or experience, we can judge links plausible and, by extension, accord a certain credibility to an interpretation. But our certainty has nothing to do with whether this interpretation is correct.

It is therefore important not to confuse the plausible, the probable, the credible, and the true. Plausibility belongs to the ambit of possibility. While

---

3 J. Rancière, "La raison des égaux" in *Le maître ignorant : cinq leçons sur l'émancipation intellectuelle*, Fayard, 1995, (first ed., 1987), pp. 77-124.

the words "plausible" and "probable" are often used as synonyms, I would say that insofar as "probable" implies "probably true," this gives it more force. "Probable" (or "likely") evokes probability more than it does simple possibility. The more an assertion or representation is plausible or probable, the more it tends toward credibility. But this does not at all mean that it conforms to reality.

For all these reasons, we can state that empirical knowledge provides us no objective certainty. All worldly representation is, in part, subjective.

Pragmatism

Pragmatism is a mode of knowledge centered on the effects and consequences of a reality. Effectiveness here holds pride of place over truth, as is well expressed in the saying, "if it works, it must be right."

Conventional wisdom is often the fruit of pragmatism. In medicine, for example, years of trial and error have proven the therapeutic effectiveness of certain plants or minerals. Chinese and Aboriginal medicine, naturopathy and chiropractic were, at first, based on pragmatism. Today, some of these forms of medicine explain their efficacy in scientific terms.

The sciences are partly based on pragmatism, although by itself pragmatism does not suffice to confer scientific status on any given theory. For a theory to become scientific, it must not only be effective but must also be based on coherent explanations. Science elaborates explanations on the functioning of reality and verifies the validity of these explanations by making predictions on reality's behaviour. The validity of a rigorous theory is confirmed when several experimenters succeed, separately, in obtaining the predicted results while using the same methods under the same conditions.

It is very important not to confuse "validity" with "truth" in the classic sense of the term. Even where a theory is effective, nothing guarantees that the theoretical model explaining that interpretation will be coherent or will reflect reality comprehensively.

Even an effective theory supported by a coherent explanation of its efficacy is not guaranteed to conform to reality. If a theory totally and perfectly represented reality, the sciences would not evolve — but they do. Consider this example from astronomy: For many centuries, astronomers used Ptolemaic theory to predict astronomical phenomena. For a theory elaborated in the second century A.D., the Ptolemaic view was remarkably effective. It allowed accurate prediction of when the next lunar and solar eclipses would take place, as well as — several months in advance — the position of the planets in the sky. It contained, however, a small error: Ptolemy was convinced that the sun rotated around the earth. His theory was effective, and logically and mathematically rigorous, yet false. A valid theory, of course, comprises much truth, but it is always difficult to know exactly how much.

Modern science always relies in part on the pragmatic model of knowledge, but does so in a contemporary framework of truth — truth in which scientific theory claims nothing more than to be a logical and effective interpretive model of reality. Modern science does not claim to give us direct access to the laws of nature. It has given up the paradigm of conformity with reality to more modestly propose interpretive models of reality whose validity has been tested.

The same is true of statistics which, at base, is simply a form of pragmatism that makes explicit the margin of uncertainty in its prediction. When doctors tell their patients that they have a 90% chance of surviving an operation, they are saying that the result of the surgery proposed is uncertain. However, on the basis of past experience, this intervention has generated positive results 90 times out of 100. Probability theory uses a pragmatic model of knowledge and a contemporary conception of truth.

How is this distinction between truth and validity useful to the police officer? Regularly, on the basis of working experience, the officer constructs valid explanations. During a training session, an officer declared (based on working experience) that members of the Hell's Angels criminal organization have distinctive tattoos. On the strength of this observation, verified on several occasions, the officer considered all persons so tattooed as potentially dangerous. Undoubtedly this theory has some validity (even if it lacks the rigour of a full-blown science of tattooing) but it would be absolutely unfounded to conclude that anyone with the tattoos in question is necessarily dangerous. This theory certainly partly conforms to reality and is very useful to the officer who made these observations. This pragmatism does not harm the quality of police work as long as the officer remains conscious that the theory does not amount to an absolute truth. In other words, police officers can, like scientists, rely on pragmatism as long as they (like scientists) do not claim that the result conforms to reality — unless they endorse past notions of the truth.

Rationalism

One part of human knowledge does not arise from direct observation of the real but from logical deduction based on premises judged acceptable.

What guarantees the value of information thus obtained is the rigour of the deductions carried out and the strength of the premises. Unfortunately we have a tendency to forget that the value of conclusions so drawn is linked to the value of the reference system used.

In fact, rationalism is essential to investigative work. Using diverse indices and testimony, the investigator constructs a logical interpretation of what has happened at the moment of the crime. The clues and statements serve as deductive premises that lead the investigator to build an explanation of the events to be verified by rigorous proof. "Reasonable doubt" about the evidence consists of attacking the validity of the premises or the logical deductions drawn from them.

Scientific knowledge

Scientific knowledge draws its strength from the fact that it utilizes all the previously mentioned modes of knowing. In the collection of observations it depends on empiricism. On that basis, it resorts to rationalism to construct a logical representation of how reality functions. With the help of this representation, it attempts to logically predict how reality will conduct itself. In other words, it conceives experience. If empirical results confirm the prediction, pragmatism permits us to conclude that our representation conforms to reality. We have the truth in the contemporary sense of that term: effective, logical, based on empirical observation, but always partly uncertain and subjective.

Conclusion

Absolute certainty remains beyond the reach of human knowledge. Despite ever increasing recourse to science and new techniques, a police investigation remains a representation of events which, even if very credible, can never be absolutely certain and purely objective. An investigator does not collect proof; using rigorous logic, he or she constructs it, relying on testimony and related material elements with the goal of presenting a valid and impartial representation of the events in question.

All the same, adopting such a vision of the truth engenders new requirements. On the one hand, police must act with special vigilance in collecting statements and interviewing witnesses. Credible statements can prove false, improbable statements can prove true, and contradictory statements can each contain an element of truth.

On the other hand, given that proof is partly a subjective construction, police officers must mistrust their conviction that they have uncovered the truth. Anyone who harbours such certainty considers that they have nothing to learn and is less open to differing opinion while more susceptible to tunnel vision. Moreover, when two people working with the same certainty have opposed opinions, the risk of confrontation and even violence grows considerably.

In any event, dialogue contributes greatly to mutual respect among those working together, as well as to the quality of the proof and therefore to the fairness of the trial.

PREFACE

Robert R. "Roy" Hazelwood[1]

Popular views of crime largely emanate from three primary sources: the imagination of fiction writers in the publishing, film and television industries; media and Internet accounts of the more sensational offences and; the perceptions of victims fortunate enough to have survived their encounter with violent offenders. Michel St-Yves and Michel Tanguay, the editors of this book have assembled some of the best informed and most current information available, and the result is a book which professionally and effectively discusses a very diverse and complex topic.

I would like to emphasize several strong points of this book. First, it is edited by practitioners who are currently working in the field, and in my opinion the difference between knowledge and wisdom is experience. Author experience is an essential feature of any book that proposes to provide strategies and techniques applicable to specific tasks. To assist them in their task, the editors solicited contributing authors who are well known experts within their individual fields. This vast amount of experience ensures the book will appeal to readers from the many disciplines which have an interest in offenders and their crimes.

Another excellent feature is that this text greatly expands upon, topics that are much more commonly dealt with in single chapters. For example, the editors of this text have accumulated such a wealth of information on false allegations that they were able to subdivide the subject into four chapters which not only address various types of false reports (rape, child sexual abuse, false 911 calls) but also provide the reader with valuable information on the analysis of such complaints. The value of this informative

---

1 Robert R. "Roy" Hazelwood holds a Bachelor of Science degree in Sociology and a Masters degree in Counseling Psychology. He also attended a one-year fellowship in forensic medicine at the Armed Forces Institute of Pathology. He has published more than 45 articles, 10 book chapters, and 5 books. He has been assistant professor at the University of Virginia, and affiliate professor of administration of justice at George Mason University, He has taught at the University of Pennsylvania, the FBI Academy and the U.S. Army Military Police (CID) School. Mr. Hazelwood has testified as an expert witness in both criminal and civil trials and currently serves on the editorial review board of four professional journals.

expansion to the criminal investigator, lecturer, and researcher cannot be overstated. The same is true with another strong section, "Risk and Threat Assessment." Again, the editors have examined the subject in five comprehensive and practical chapters, each of which deals with the assessment of commonly encountered investigative situations (crisis negotiations, stalking, homicide and suicide) and frequently encountered types of criminals (psychopaths and authors of anonymous threats).

Equally informative are the remaining two sections, "Investigative Interviewing" and "Sex Crimes and Criminal Profiling." The former provides an in-depth examination of the use of information collected from witnesses and the impact of social and cognitive influences on that process. It also addresses the issue of eyewitness memory enhancement, non-verbal communication, and the psychology underlying police interrogations. The latter deals with a subject which is constantly before the public and has been sensationalized beyond all reason — "criminal profiling." In this book however, the editors have gone to great lengths to present readers with factual *and* useful information. Three chapters are dedicated to providing the reader with an accurate overview of criminal profiling the application of profiling to sexual crimes, and the analysis of crime scenes. The remaining chapters in this section address the motivations and lifestyle of sexual offenders and the profile of consumers of child pornography on the Internet.

The close study of crime always reveals that it is much more complex than was assumed at first glance. Michel St-Yves and Michel Tanguay have certainly provided evidence of this through a wonderfully informative and richly practical book. I congratulate them on making a definitive contribution to the literature and it is with a great deal of professional pleasure that I recommend this text to the reader.

ACKNOWLEDGMENTS

During one's life there are unexpected or singular encounters, innocuous at first blush, that turn out to be gifts of destiny.

Hector Bianciotti

We would like to offer all our co-authors our profound gratitude for sharing their passion, ideas, and professional and scientific skills. This work would not have been possible without their generosity.

Our most sincere thanks are also due the Sûreté du Québec (the Quebec provincial police force), particularly the *Service de l'analyse du comportement* (behavioural analysis service), for their support and encouragement in the production of this book; the staff at the SQ's Documentation Centre, and especially Francis Durocher, for their generosity with their time and their unfailing courtesy; and to Francis Brabant for his judicious advice.

We would also like to thank Benjamin Chaignon for having produced a picture worth a thousand words (the cover of this book).

We owe a debt of gratitude, as well, to everyone at Éditions Yvon Blais (the publishers of the original, French edition), and particularly to Louis Bossé and Johanne Forget, for the confidence and respect they have accorded all our caprices, as well as to Steven Sacks for supplemental translation and editing.

Finally, these acknowledgments would be incomplete unless we mentioned the inestimable contribution of all those who have inspired us and shaped our world views, as well as the way we conduct criminal investigations. We thank all of you whom space precludes us from naming individually.

CONTRIBUTORS

Michel St-Yves

Michel St-Yves has been a forensic psychologist with the *Service de l'analyse de comportement* (behavioural analysis service) of the Sûreté du Québec since 2002. He works as a critical-incident specialist and is actively involved in criminal investigations both in the preparation of psychological profiles and the preparation of interrogations. Since 1997, he has taught the psychology of interrogation at the *École nationale de police du Québec* (Quebec police academy); more recently, he has taught crisis negotiations at that institute. As well, since 2002 he has been a lecturer at the Université de Montréal's School of Criminology. He worked at the Correctional Services of Canada from 1988 to 2002, first, in risk assessment of adult offenders, and later in research on sexual offenders. His publications and papers focus on sexual assault, crisis negotiation, and police interrogation. He is the author of *Psychologie des entrevues d'enquête: de la recherche à la pratique* (*The psychology of investigative interviews: from research to practice*), published in 2004 by Éditions Yvon Blais.

Michel Tanguay

Michel Tanguay was a lieutenant in the Sûreté du Québec and chief of the criminal analysis and profiling unit in that force's *Service de l'analyse de comportement* (behavioural analysis service). He holds a Bachelor of Arts degree from the Université de Sherbrooke and has 35 years of experience with the Sûreté du Québec — 13 with the crimes against persons unit of the major crimes division. He was a consultant on investigative strategies, a crisis-negotiation trainer at the *École nationale de police du Québec* (Quebec police academy), and a guest speaker at the Université de Montréal. Passionate and generous with his learning, his contribution to the police community has been remarkable. Now retired from the Sûreté du Québec, this book represents his legacy to his colleagues and friends.

Eric Beauregard

Eric Beauregard is an assistant professor in the School of Criminology at Simon Fraser University. He is a graduate of the Université de Montréal's School of Criminology, where his doctorate research was on the hunting (predation) tactics of serial sexual aggressors. From 1997 to 2005 he worked at Correctional Services Canada, first in the assessment of sexual preferences, then in research on sexual aggressors. His publications and research mainly concern the modus operandi of sexual aggressors, sexual homicide, and geographic profiling.

Michel Bézénech

Michel Bézénech studied medicine, then specialized in forensic pathology, occupational medicine, and, finally, psychiatry. He also studied law and in 1973 obtained his doctorate in criminal sciences. He was associate professor in forensinc medicine at the Université de Bordeaux II and in private law at the Université de Bordeaux IV. He practised for ten years at the *Unité pour malades mentaux dangereux et criminels* (unit for dangerous and criminal mental patients) at the *Hôpital psychiatrique de Cadillac*, near Bordeaux, and for the subsequent 23 years was director of the regional medico-psychological service for Bordeaux's penitentiary region. He is the author of more than 450 scientific publications and the co-author of some 30 medical monographs. He was awarded the *Médaille pénitentiaire* in 1999 and the *Palmes académiques* in 2000.

Dominique Blais

Dominique Blais is a student at the Université du Québec à Trois-Rivières. Her master's thesis is entitled *Appel 911 — une analyse conversationnelle* ["911 Calls: A conversational analysis]. Under the direction of linguistics professor Marty Laforest, and with the support of Michel St-Yves, forensic psychologist of the Behavioural Analysis Service at the Sûreté du Québec, her research derives, *inter alia*, from linguistic theory, particularly that of discourse analysis. Since 1996, she has also participated, as an actor in training at the *École nationale de police du Québec* (Quebec police academy).

Chantal Blanchette

Chantal Blanchette holds a bachelor's degree in psychology from the Université du Québec à Montréal and has completed her master's degree in criminology at the Université de Montréal. She currently works as a researcher on recidivism among sexual aggressors. An intern at Montreal's Institut Philippe-Pinel, she is interested in studying the lifestyle of offenders, particularly sexual aggressors.

Guy Bruneau

Guy Bruneau has been a police officer since 1976. During his 18 years as a detective sergeant he specialized in taped interviews of child victims of sexual and physical abuse. He has taught for 18 years at the *École nationale de police du Québec* (Quebec police academy) and consults on criminal investigations for numerous training programs. Since 2004, he has been captain of the research and development section of the Longueuil, Quebec, police force.

Peter I. Collins

Peter I. Collins is director of the Forensic Psychiatry Unit, Investigative Support Bureau, Ontario Provincial Police, and a consultant in forensic psychiatry for the Assistant Director of Behavioural Sciences at the Royal Canadian Mounted Police. He also works with the psycholegal program at the Centre for Addiction and Mental Health and is an assistant professor in the University of Toronto's Department of Psychiatry.

Mireille Cyr

Mireille Cyr holds a doctorate in psychology, and for 18 years has been a full professor in the psychology department at the Université de Montréal. She works with the *Centre de recherche interdisciplinaire sur les problèmes conjugaux et les agressions sexuelles* (Centre for interdisciplinary research on domestic disputes and sexual assault) and the Marie-Vincent Inter-University Research Chair on Childhood Sexual Abuse. For 10 years, her research projects have concentrated on these topics. She is particularly interested in the after-effects of sexual assaults in children and adolescents, determinants of parental support, and investigative interviews of young children who are suspected of being sexual-assault victims. Her research, conducted in collaboration with members of the police and child-welfare communities, has been reported in numerous publications in French and English.

Ronald P. Fisher

Ronald P. Fisher is a professor of psychology at Florida International University (Miami), and director of that institution's legal psychology program. Dr. Fisher is the co-creator of the cognitive interview (CI) method, designed to stimulate witness memory. He has published several works on CI and conducted numerous training seminars for diverse police and other investigative services (FBI, British police, NASA, Israeli air force, NTSB, etc.). He was a member of the United States Department of Justice's planning committee and technical working group, which set up national directives for evidence collection from eyewitnesses. His research also includes studying the cognitive principles related to lie detection.

Francis Fortin

Francis Fortin holds a master's degree in criminology and has worked with the Sûreté du Québec since 1999. He joined the cyber-surveillance unit shortly after its creation in October 2002. He specializes in the analysis of Internet crime. In addition to providing regular training to various members of the justice community — police, police cadets, probation officers, prosecutors, etc. — he teaches at the Université de Montréal and the École polytechnique de Montréal. His research focuses on computer crime and child pornography.

Groupe d'Analyse Comportementale, Gendarmerie nationale française (Behavioural science unit)

The Groupe d'Analyse Comportementale (GAC) is an operational unit of the Gendarmerie nationale française, an armed forces group reporting to the French Ministry of Defence. The GAC is also available to the Minister of the Interior and Regional Development for internal security operations. Created in 2002, the GAC today is composed of five military officials who are also police officers in the national criminal investigation division — Captain Pascal Thys and Captain Pierre Chaignon (investigators), Lieutenant Marie-Laure Brunel, Lieutenant Elen Vuidard, and Lieutenant Stephanie Le Maoût (analysts). Combining practical experience in police work and expertise in the social sciences (criminal psychology and psychiatry, sociology, forensic science, forensic medicine, criminal law, criminal procedure, criminology, victimology), the GAC's behaviour analysts directly support investigations of serial (homicides, rapes, sexual assaults, kidnappings, arson), and single-occurrence (unusual violent crimes with no apparent motive) offences. The GAC prepares criminal profiles, devises interview strategies for suspects with complex personalities, and assists on missing-persons cases.

Robert Hare

Robert Hare is an emeritus professor of psychology at the University of British Columbia, where he taught and directed research projects for 35 years. He is president of Darkstone Research Group Ltd., a company that provides research and consultancy services in the field of forensic medicine. He devoted the major part of his academic career to research on the nature, assessment, and implications for mental health and criminal justice of psychopathy. He is author of *Without Conscience: The Disturbing World of the Psychopaths Among Us*, and co-author (with Paul Babiak) of *Snakes in Suits: Why Psychopaths Go to Work*. He has published numerous works on psychopathy, conceived the *Psychopathy Checklist Revised* (PCL-R), and co-authored the related *Psychopathy Checklist: Screening Version; Psychopathy Checklist: Youth Version*; and *Antisocial Process Screening Device*. He works as a consultant with various police services, including the FBI and RCMP, is a research consultant to the FBI Child Abduction and Serial Murder Investigative Resources Center, and is a member of the International Criminal Investigative Analysis Fellowship. He has received numerous awards for his research and contributions to forensic psychology and psychiatry.

Marty Laforest

Marty Laforest is a professor of linguistics in the Department of Humanities and Social Communication at the Université du Québec à Trois-Rivières. Her main fields of research are discourse analysis, sociolinguistics, and pragmatics. In recent years, she has been particularly interested in conflict discourse and in negotiation as a means of interaction. Her most recent work concerns workplace interactions.

Éric Latour

Éric Latour has been a lieutenant with the *Service de l'analyse du comportement* (behavioural analysis service) of the Sûreté du Québec since

2004. From 2000 to 2004, he served as an investigator with the *Services des enquêtes sur les crimes contre les personnes* (crimes against persons investigative services). He is completing the International Criminal Investigative Analysis Fellowship's (ICIAF) training program in criminal profiling. Before joining the ranks of the Sûreté du Québec, he was a lawyer with the Syndic's Office of the Barreau du Québec (Quebec Bar Association) and Quebec's Office of the Ombudsman. Sgt. Latour is also a trainer with the *École nationale de police du Québec* (Quebec police academy), a guest speaker at the Université de Montréal, and a member of the ICIAF and the International Homicide Investigators Association.

Marc Lépine

Marc Lépine has been a sergeant with the *Service de l'analyse du comportement* (behavioural analysis service) of the Sûreté du Québec since 2004. He is completing the International Criminal Investigative Analysis Fellowship's (ICIAF) training program in criminal profiling. He has been a police officer since 1988, and has 15 years of experience as an investigator. He has investigated major crimes, notably arson and crimes against persons. He teaches at the Canadian Police College and supervises specialized training in interrogation at the *École nationale de police du Québec* (Quebec police academy). He is also a guest speaker at the Université de Montréal, and is a member of the ICIAF and the International Homicide Investigators Association.

Matt Logan

Matt Logan is a staff sergeant with the Royal Canadian Mounted Police. From May 1999 to November 2001 he worked as a psychologist with the Correctional Service of Canada, where he undertook risk assessment for the National Parole Commission and therapy for sexual predators. As a psychologist with the RCMP's Major Crimes Section, he works as a consultant on serious crime, undercover operations, investigative interviews, and crisis-situation negotiation. He prepares risk and threat assessments concerning persons suspected of serious crime, and is an expert witness on violent behaviour and sexual deviance. He conducts training seminars on psychopathy and on lie detection and truth assessment with Robert Hare and Paul Ekman, respectively.

Patrick Michaud

Patrick Michaud holds a master's degree in criminology from the Université de Montréal. His research, conducted in conjunction with the *Science de l'analyse du comportement* (behavioural analysis service) of the Sûreté du Québec, concentrated on unlawful confinement and hostage situations in Québec, and more particularly on risk assessment of auto-aggressive and hetero-aggressive behaviours. Since 2005, he has assessed the sexual preferences of federally incarcerated sexual aggressors for the Correctional Services of Canada.

Micheline Milot

Micheline Milot is a professor in the Department of Sociology at the Université de Québec à Montréal. Her fields of research are the sociology of religion, and the political and legal regulation of religion. She is a member of the *Centre d'études ethniques des Universités Montréalaises* (Montreal Universities Centre for Ethnic Studies) and of *Groupe Sociétés, Religions et Laïcité-* (Societies, Religion, and Secularism Group) (CNRS, Paris). Her publications include *Laïcité dans le Nouveau Monde: Le cas du Québec* (Secularism in the New World: The Case of Quebec), Brepols Publishers (2002), and "Religions minoritaires, droits et citoyenneté" ("Minority Religions, Rights, and Citizenship"), in *Appartenance, institutions et citoyenneté*, (Noreau and Woehrling (eds.), Montreal: Wilson and Lafleur, 2005).

Pierre Nezan

Pierre Nezan has 22 years of experience as a police officer with the Royal Canadian Mounted Police. For several years he was an investigator with a major crimes unit in British Columbia and, since 2001, he has been a criminal profiler certified by the ICIAF. He is manager of the RCMP's criminal profiling program and teaches at the Canadian Police College.

Gary L. Plank

For 22 of his 27 years with the Nebraska State Patrol, Gary L. Plank has worked in the criminal investigation division. In 1991 he obtained his diploma from the Police Fellowship Program on Criminal Investigative Analysis (profiling). He has specialized in behavioural analysis for 15 years and holds a bachelor's degree in criminal justice as well as a master's degree in mental-health counselling. He is an assistant professor in the master's program in forensic medicine at Wesleyan University in Nebraska.

Jean Proulx

Jean Proulx is a professor at the School of Criminology, Université de Montréal. He is also a clinical psychologist and researcher at the Institut Philipe-Pinel in Montreal and at the Université de Montréal's International Centre for Comparative Criminology. During the last 20 years, he has published five books and more than a hundred papers in the fields of criminology and sexual offences.

Joe Navarro

For 25 years, Joe Navarro, M.A. (Special Agent, ret.) worked in counter-espionage and counter-terrorism at the Federal Bureau of Investigation. He was a founding member of the behavioural analysis program of the National Security Division and still teaches interview techniques and behaviour assessment at the FBI academy in Quantico, Virginia. Joe Navarro is a member of the Institute for Intergovernmental Research. As well, he is an assistant professor at Saint Leo University in Florida, where he specializes in the psychopathology of extremist groups. He is co-author, with John Schafer, of *Advanced Interviewing Techniques* (Charles C. Thomas), and author of *Hunting Terrorists: A Look at the Psychopathology of Terror* (both Charles C. Thomas) and of *What Everybody Is Saying: An Ex-FBI Agent's Guide to Speed Reading People* (Harper Collins).

Kim Rossmo

Kim Rossmo is a professor in the Criminal Justice Department, Texas State University at San Marcos. He is also the director of the Center for Geospatial Intelligence and Investigation. During his career of more than 20 years as a police officer, he served as an inspector in charge of the geographic profiling section of the Vancouver police department. He holds a doctorate in criminology from Simon Fraser University. His publications and research principally concern police, criminal profiling, and environmental criminology (geocriminology).

Julie Roy

Julie Roy holds a master's degree in criminology from the Université de Montréal. Her master's research, conducted in collaboration with the Sûreté du Québec, concerned the personal characteristics of individuals prosecuted for the possession and distribution over the Internet of child pornography. Currently she is a human relations agent with the *Centre jeunesse de la Mauricie* (Mauricie Youth Centre) — *Centre du Québec.*

Mario J. Scalora

Mario J. Scalora obtained his doctorate in clinical and forensic psychology from the University of Nebraska in 1989, and has been a professor at that institution since 1997. His research interests include sex crimes, violence in the workplace, threats against political figures, and risk assessment, as well as aspects of terrorism and counter-terrorism. He works with local, state, and federal police in the area of risk assessment, evaluating risk factors associated with threats of violence against political figures and institutions.

Katherine A. Schoeneman

Katherine Schoeneman, M.A., is a doctoral candidate in clinical and forensic psychology at the University of Nebraska-Lincoln. She became a member of Psi Chi in 2000 at Lewis and Clark College in Portland, Oregon, where she obtained her bachelor's degree in psychology the same year. Ms. Schoeneman's research includes the risk assessment of threats against public representatives and institutions. In August 2005, the Association of Threat Assessment Professionals awarded her its Dr. Hatcher Memorial Scholarship.

Peter Smerick

Peter Smerick holds a bachelor's degree in political science from Penn State University and a master's degree in education from the University of Virginia. He was a combat photography officer with the American army in Vietnam, and has been a special agent with the Naval Investigative Service, a special surveillance agent with the Federal Bureau of Investigation (FBI), a certified investigator of suspect documents and photographic evidence for the FBI (for 24 years), a professor and instructor in forensic sciences at the FBI academy, and a specialist in criminal profiling and a violent-crimes analyst for the FBI's National Center for the Analysis of Violent Crime in Quantico, Virginia. Currently he is president and executive director of the Academy Group, Inc., a consulting company specializing in behavioural and forensic sciences, and staffed by retired FBI and Secret Service agents, as well as by criminal profiling agents from the Virginia State Police in Manassas, Virginia.

Jim Van Allen

Detective Sergeant Jim Van Allen is the senior criminal-profiling specialist in the Behavioural Sciences Section of the Ontario Provincial Police, in Orillia, Ontario. He works regularly with many police services in Canada on special investigations involving the profiling of unidentified criminals, crime-scene analysis and reconstruction, analysis of suspicious deaths, special search warrants, and interview strategies. He is a member of the International Criminal Investigative Analysis Fellowship and a conference convener at the University of Toronto, Laurentian University, Sir Sandford Fleming College, and Georgian College, as well as at various police-training academies. As well, he has participated in seminars all over Canada, and in the United States and the Netherlands. Det.-Sgt. Van Allen has also been an expert witness in numerous court proceedings in Ontario.

Tom Williamson

Tom Williamson enjoyed an exceptional career. He was a police commander at New Scotland Yard and, from 2001, Assistant Chief Constable for Nottinghamshire, U.K. He held a doctorate from the University of Kent — his doctoral research having been on investigative interviews — and was one of the creators of PEACE, the investigative-interview model in the U.K. He was also a forensic psychologist and, until recently, lecturer at the Institute of Criminal Justice Studies, University of Portsmouth. He is the author of the book, *Investigative Interviewing: Rights, Research, Regulation*, published in 2006 by Willan Publishing. His passion for police practices permitted him to complete several works before his recent passing, including the forthcoming *International Development in Investigative Interviewing* (Willan Publishing) and *Handbook of Psychology and Investigative Interviewing: Current Developments and Future Directions.* The police community at large has profited greatly from his devotion to the discipline of investigative interviewing, the search for the truth, and his respect for human rights.

Rachel M. York

Rachel York holds a doctorate in legal psychology from Florida International University. Her primary research interest concerns jury-making. She is a member of the American Psychology-Law Society. (AP-LS) and the American Society of Trial Consultants (ASTC). Ms. York has presented several research papers at annual AP-LS conferences, as well as at other psychology- and law-oriented conferences. In 2007, she co-authored an article on the "CSI effect" in the Judicial Notebook section of the American Psychological Association's publication *Monitor on Psychology*. Ms. York is currently a senior research consultant at a trial-consulting firm in the Washington, D.C., area.

TABLE OF CONTENTS

PART II: FALSE ALLEGATIONS

PART III: RISK AND THREAT ASSESSMENT

PART IV: SEX CRIMES AND CRIMINAL PROFILING

INTRODUCTION

There are three main tasks in the search for the truth:
to discover it, to show it,
and, when one possesses it, to distinguish it from the false.

Blaise Pascal

Illegality, immorality, shameful acts, however one views crime, it fascinates us. It feeds neighbourhood and office chat and — particularly if it is lurid or "perfect" — inspires journalists, novelists, and filmmakers. But crime is neither fictional nor a matter of news snippets. It is a drama that touches all society every day, a tragedy at whose heart we find victims and their families, witnesses, suspects... and the police. The latter are usually the first called to the scene, the ones who must undertake to secure it, and protect the public from further risk and ensure that no one disturbs clues left by the offender.

Thus begins the police investigation, with crime-scene analysis, statement collection, and victimology. Over the course of days, weeks, sometimes years, investigators meet with witnesses, neighbours, and various experts, attempting to solve the crime. To better conduct their investigation, they must consider Lacassagne's maxim: "Open your eyes, shut your mouth, observe carefully, and inform yourself fully before reaching conclusions."[1]

All police investigations seek the truth — the essence of justice. In so doing, police depend on increasingly effective technologies and methods that are more objective and scientific than ever before. Today is the era of "forensic science," including DNA analysis, ballistics, fingerprinting, forensic entomology, forensic anthropology, polygraphy and, more lately, forensic psychology. The goal is to understand why and how these tragedies arise and who the individuals involved are. Derived from the Latin *investigare*, "investigate" means to "search out" — hunt down clues and other evidence, collect material data, check alibis, etc. But to investigate also means to seek out an understanding — human understanding, of the criminal, victim, witness. Each of them holds part of the sought after truth.

1 Antoine Lacassagne (1843-1924), father of criminal anthropology, devoted his life to studying criminals. This quotation is taken from *Wilfrid Derome, expert en homicides*, p. 30, Jacques Côté, Les Éditions du Boréal (2003).

This book summarizes the experience of experts who work in the criminal-investigation field or perform related research. They include Europeans as well as North Americans, police officers and researchers, all seeking the truth, albeit sometimes by different paths — the implication being that there is no single route leading to the truth, and perhaps no single truth at all.

Our book includes 20 chapters, divided into four parts. Part I concerns investigative interviews. Films and television shows — such as *Crime Scene Investigation* (CSI) — have warped public perception of police work, overemphasizing technology to the detriment of real police work, which most often involves knocking on doors and interviewing witnesses. Studies show that investigators collect technical evidence such as fingerprints and DNA in 10% of cases at best. Usually, therefore, evidence is made up of statements, including those of the suspect. Hence the significance of investigative interviews.

We devote six chapters to this first part. The first concerns police interrogation, covering the nature and risks of the principal persuasive methods used in North America. The chapter asks specifically whether the search for a confession is compatible with the search for the truth. Chapter 2 considers the cognitive interview, a technique that facilitates access to the witness's memory. The chapter presents all the basic ingredients for successful witness interviews, including how the interview should be conducted. Chapters 3 and 4 concern cognitive and social influences on the creation and collection of witness statements. These two sections transport us into the complex and fascinating universe of human perception and information processing. Chapter 5 discusses non-verbal communication. Its author reveals that almost everything in our minds is reflected in our non-verbal behaviour. And we end this first part with the psychology of extreme beliefs (Chapter 6), which preoccupy our world more than ever. The author explains how fanatical beliefs can lead an individual to compromise the lives and safety of others. The believer does not believe that he *believes,* he believes that he *knows.* Therefore the investigation involves two opposing planes of truth — conventional rationality as expressed in the investigator, and religious belief that justifies the believer.

The second part of this book concerns a lesser-known, even taboo, phenomenon, false allegations of crime. One would have to be naive to believe that all crimes reported to police are well founded. People report all sorts of false crimes for various reasons. A woman might say she was raped to extricate herself from an embarrassing situation. A man might call police to say he's found his wife hanged in his garage — when in fact he has strangled her and attempted to cover his tracks. Then again, someone might report their motor vehicle stolen so as to collect insurance benefits. According to the Canadian Coalition Against Insurance Fraud, this type of crime is the second most profitable in North America, after the sale of illegal drugs.

Four chapters consider "crimes" that don't exist, which are, in fact, public mischief. Chapter 7 concerns false allegations of sexual assault by women. The extent of the problem, the principal motivations for it, the difficulty of detecting it and the delicate nature of the investigation are examined.

Chapter 8 discusses the phenomenon of false allegations by children. The stakes are high here. To disbelieve a child who has been harmed, or to believe a child who has not, can have enormous consequences for that child, the supposed assailant, as well as social services workers, the police and the administration of justice. The chapter considers tools for separating the facts from manipulation and fabrication.

Chapter 9 concerns false crime reports to emergency services such as 911. We examine the results of a promising exploratory study that seem to be useful for the early detection of calls made by persons attempting to manipulate police or hide a crime from them. The final chapter in this part (Chapter 10) concerns the analysis, collection and investigative uses of written statements.

Part III discusses risk and threat assessment. Since September 11, 2001, we hear daily about these concerns, probably because they have become synonymous with terrorism, a global concern. But risk and threats — directly related concepts — have always existed and can take more discreet forms: a man barricaded somewhere with a firearm who threatens suicide; an anonymous letter which says, unequivocally, "You're going to die"; a man head over heels with unrequited love for a woman he harasses, spying on her and even becoming violent. The fact that someone is a psychopath can itself constitute a risk for society. We devote five chapters to the assessment of these matters.

The first (Chapter 11) discusses pathological harassment, commonly known as stalking. The principal types and motivations of stalkers are presented, followed by strategies for managing the risk such individuals represent. The chapter also considers a rare yet important phenomenon, false claims of harassment.

Chapters 12 and 13 concern negotiation and risk assessment in crisis situations. Chapter 12 describes the police-intervention process in such situations, and particularly the role of police negotiators. The authors explain how such crises arise and suggest appropriate intervention methods. As well, they describe the SINCRO model, conceived by the Sûreté du Québec and taught at *l'École nationale de police du Québec* (Quebec police academy). The subsequent chapter discusses the main risk factors in crisis situations and in assessing the risk of "auto-" and "hetero-aggressive" behaviour. Predicting risk is a complex task that itself carries risks, including being wrong.

Chapter 14 discusses the assessment of anonymous threats. The authors explore how anonymous communications can reveal the risk that the sender will move from words to action. Most of those who make threats do not act on them, and most of those who commit crimes do not make threats.

Chapter 15 examines criminal psychopathy. The term "psychopath" immediately evokes thoughts of terrifying characters such as Hannibal "the Cannibal" Lecter in *The Silence of the Lambs,* or "celebrity" killers such as Jack the Ripper or Ted Bundy. However, psychopaths are not exclusively sadistic murderers. Psychopaths represent about 1% of the general population and 25% of incarcerated offenders. In this last chapter of the third part, the authors explain the nature of criminal psychopathy and the risks associated with this personality disorder. They then propose police negotiation and interrogation strategies.

Finally, the fourth part, comprising five chapters, concerns sex crimes and criminal profiling. Although sex crimes often make the newspapers, they represent only about 1% of all crime reported to police. Insofar as they are seen as odious, they incite public emotion. To apprehend these "predators," police use all sorts of investigative methods, including those drawn from the behavioural sciences. The relevant criminal profiling, also called psychological profiling, consists of using crime-scene analysis, material evidence, and witness statements to outline the offender's profile.

Chapter 16 considers sexual assailants (rapists and paedophiles) and their motivations and modus operandi, as well as a new and useful aspect of criminal profiling — profiling offenders on the basis of their daily habits and living conditions. Chapter 17 discusses a phenomenon that is recent but evolving with the speed of the Internet — cyberpaedophilia. The authors explore the history of this new phenomenon and create portraits of consumers and collectors of juvenile pornography. Chapter 18 describes the North American approach — established by the FBI — to criminal profiling. The authors define the discipline, then discuss its techniques in serial sex-crime investigation and crime-scene analysis, including the detection of "staged" scenes. Chapter 19 considers behavioural analysis of crime scenes. The authors provide a protocol they have developed in their work with *La Gendarmerie Nationale Française*, the French national police. The fourth part closes with geographic profiling and hunting-tactic (predation) analysis of serial sexual offenders (Chapter 20). The authors show what crime locales can teach us about the environment inhabited by a crime's author.

While this book was written to assist police in their investigations, it is also addressed to all those who work in the field of criminal investigation or are interested in that endeavour — legal scholars, social workers, criminologists, psychologists and other mental-health professionals, as well as students hoping to contribute to research in the area.

We hope that this text can assist all readers in performing their work with increased objectivity — the first step on the long journey that leads to the truth.

PART I

INVESTIGATIVE INTERVIEWS

CHAPTER 1

The Psychology of Interrogation:

A Quest for a Confession or a Quest for the Truth?

Michel St-Yves and Michel Tanguay

There is no such source of error as the pursuit of absolute truth.

Samuel Butler

At law, a confession is a person's admission of the truth of an allegation made against that individual (Bénézech, 1995: 63). Historically this *mea culpa* has been considered absolute proof and led directly to a conviction. Not until the nineteenth century did courts begin to question certain methods used to obtain confessions and their admissibility as evidence. Today, even though the confession does not reign supreme as evidence, it remains for many police investigators the principal objective of interrogation. This is understandable given that confessions resolve between 25% and 30% of crime investigations (Baldwin and McConville, 1980; Cassell, 1999; Phillips & Brown, 1998; Stephenson and Moston, 1994).

The quest for a confession often entails the use of strategies or methods that are controversial by virtue of their illegality (e.g. torture), the risks they entail, or the ethical questions they raise (e.g. certain techniques of persuasion). According to Gudjonsson (1992; 2003), the use of such methods can limit the suspect's[1] rights and create fertile ground for false confessions. Indeed, the line between persuasion and oppression can be thin. What to do, then, when the genuinely guilty will walk free where, absent a confession, there is insufficient evidence to convict them? This is a classic problem

1 In this book we use the word "suspect" to mean any person suspected of having participated in a crime. In Canadian law, police cannot make an arrest unless they have reasonable and probable grounds to believe the person detained participated in the crime which is the subject matter of the arrest. Upon detention, police must inform the detainee of his or her rights — the right to counsel and the right to silence. Moreover, the arresting officer must ensure that the person has understood this information.

arising in nearly a third of police files (Irving and McKenzie, 1989; Leo, 1996; Moston, Stephenson and Williamson, 1992).

The debate about interrogation methods extends not only to coercive methods such as torture but also to methods of persuasion used in many Western countries. The debate raises questions such as: Is the use of persuasive methods and tricks acceptable? Are the methods themselves coercive? Are they truly effective? Do they present real risks? Is the quest for a confession compatible with the quest for truth?

In this chapter we consider what motivates people to confess to or deny their crimes, or to exercise their right to remain silent. Understanding the psychology of confessions helps us to better grasp the use of effective interrogation strategies. We also closely examine the use of certain persuasive techniques and the risks associated with them. We end with five fundamental rules essential to successful investigative interviewing:

(1) Keep an open mind and remain objective

(2) Build up a rapport

(3) Pay attention

(4) Keep a professional attitude

(5) Know how to conclude

Such rules permit police investigators to better fulfil their mandate — of determining the truth, not just guilt.

A. WHY SOME OFFENDERS CONFESS TO THEIR CRIMES

A confession is a dynamic process influenced by the interaction of several individual factors — social, emotional, cognitive, and situational (Gudjonsson, 2003; Irving and Hilgendorf, 1980; Moston, Stephenson and Williamson, 1992; St-Yves, 2004a). Those interviewed by police find themselves in a complex decision-making situation: Talk or remain silent? Speak truthfully or lie? Tell the whole truth or just part of it? Suspects decide these matters according to how they view the choices available at the moment, the subjective probability of consequences arising from that decision, and the utilitarian value or related advantages of the decisions (Irving and Hilgendorf, 1980). Threats and promises, even if they are subtle, can also influence the suspect's decision to confess (Irving and Hilgendorf, 1980; Kassin and McNall, 1991).

1. The Quality of the Evidence

Though confession as a phenomenon is linked to a combination of factors (Gudjonsson, 2003; St-Yves, 2004a), the suspect's perception of police evidence is certainly the determining factor in trying to obtain a confession (Deslauriers-Varin and St-Yves, 2006; Gudjonsson and Petursson, 1991). Williamson (1990) reported that on perceiving the police had solid proof, two suspects in three (66.7%) admitted their crimes, compared to one in three (36.4%) when the quality of the evidence seemed unexceptional, and one in ten (9.9%) when the evidence was weak. Gudjonsson and his colleagues have observed that nearly 70% of offenders admitted they would never have confessed had they not been police suspects, and that between 55% and 60% confessed because they were certain that police possessed sufficient evidence to charge them and have them convicted (Gudjonsson and Bownes, 1992; Gudjonsson and Petursson, 1991; Sigurdsson and Gudjonsson, 1994). Recently, Deslauriers-Varin and St-Yves (2006) observed that the rate of convictions almost doubled (from 31.4% to 55.6%) when suspects perceived the evidence against them to be relatively strong. The principle is clear: overwhelming proof renders denial futile. In such cases, suspects have only two choices: remain silent or provide a version of the story that allows the suspect to explain themselves or save face.

2. Internal Pressures

Internal pressure in an individual arises from feelings of guilt and remorse, as well as from a compulsive (irrepressible) need to confess. According to psychoanalytic theory, when the superego remains silent or transgresses a social rule or norm, it develops a strong sense of guilt and a need for self-punishment (Freud, 1916). "Confession is an attempt at reconciliation that the superego undertakes in order to settle a quarrel between the ego and the id" (Reik, 1973, p. 216).

Confession secures a feeling of freedom that has a significant cathartic effect (Berggren, 1975). Almost 40% of suspects who confess report a feeling of relief thereafter, while a comparable number affirm they confessed because they felt guilty about their crimes (Gudjonsson and Bownes, 1992; Gudjonsson and Petursson, 1991; Gudjonsson and Sigurdsson, 1999; Sigurdsson and Gudjonsson, 1994; St-Yves, 2002). In a study of individuals convicted of sexual crimes, we have observed that a little more than half (52%) of subjects who reported feelings of guilt or remorse had nonetheless failed to admit their crimes to police (St-Yves, 2002). This suggests that feelings of guilt alone are not sufficient to motivate a confession. According to Inbau, Reid, and Buckley (1986), very few confessions result from feelings of guilt unprovoked by interrogation.

3. External Pressures

"External pressures" generally refer to persuasive methods and certain kinds of pressure, such as promises and threats, police sometimes use. The term can also connote coercive measures such as torture. Police cautions, such as that used in the United Kingdom, can also become, or be perceived as, external pressure: "You do not have to say anything. But it may harm your defence if you do not mention when questioned something which you later rely on in court. Anything you do or say may be given in evidence" (Code of Practice C, 10.1; Burke, T., Street, R. and Brown, D., 2000; p. 27). In other words, "It's now or never," which amounts to the kind of pressure that is felt when a shop announces that the sale ends today.

B. WHY CERTAIN PEOPLE DO NOT ADMIT THEIR CRIMES

Despite all efforts made to facilitate a confession, and despite overwhelming evidence against them, some people persist in denial or do not confess. The principal reason for this is fear of the consequences, which themselves fall into two major categories: concrete consequences and personal consequences (Gudjonsson and Bownes, 1992; Gudjonsson and Petursson, 1991; Sigurdsson and Gudjonsson, 1994). These inhibiting factors act like corks blocking the flow of a confession. In other words, even if suspects feel deeply guilty and believe police have sufficient evidence against them, they can persist in denying their crime or in remaining silent.

1. Concrete Consequences

Concrete consequences are consequences that occur to or preoccupy suspects during interrogation for crimes they have committed. Among the most commonly feared of such consequences is penal sanction (Gudjonsson, 2003). Individuals never before in trouble with the law can strongly fear being saddled with a criminal record and, above all, the fallout from the record, such as losing, or having trouble finding, a job. Fear of sanctions is associated with the loss of liberty (imprisonment) and, in some countries, with the death penalty. Generally, the more serious the crime, the more severe the punishment (Eysenck and Gudjonsson, 1989), and the more serious the crime, the more likely it is that the perpetrator will deny or resist admitting it (Moston, Stephenson and Williamson, 1992; St-Yves, 2002). Some suspects also fear the consequences they could suffer if their confession incriminates others. In such situations, the consequences can be more unpleasant than the penal sanction.

Other probable consequences feared by suspects include: losing those close to them (spouses, children, family, friends), a worry more pronounced in those suspected of sexual crimes; and losing their jobs, particularly in cases of workplace theft. Fear of financial loss is another concern, notably with arson or large-scale fraud. These consequences can be quite real, which is why they can inhibit the flow of a confession, but they are never immediate. The suspect can hope that their spouse will be understanding, that their employer won't dispense with his services, that the judge will show them leniency.

2. Personal Consequences

Because personal consequences are immediate and touch on a person's sense of integrity and self-esteem, they are often more daunting than those regarded as concrete. Personal losses are experienced instantaneously. As soon as suspects admit their crime, they lose face, first in their own eyes, then in the eyes of those around them — beginning sometimes with the investigator confronting them. This is particularly true in cases of sexual crimes (Holmberg and Christianson, 2002). Sometimes investigators themselves become inhibiting factors by virtue of their attitude (St-Yves, 2004b; Deslauriers-Varin and St-Yves, 2006).

3. Police Cautions

A suspect's perception of the quality of police evidence is the determining factor in the decision to confess. But it is the possibility of exercising their right to retain counsel (constitutionally guaranteed in Canada, as in many other countries) that explains why many individuals do not confess or cooperate with police.[2]

---

2 Contrary to practice in the United States and the United Kingdom, Canadian law does not accord a right to have counsel present in the interrogation room. It recognizes only the obligation to inform suspects of their rights to silence and to consult a lawyer without delay, which latter right is generally afforded by telephone. However, where the interviewee is an adolescent (aged 12 to 18 years), the *Youth Criminal Justice Act* provides for the presence of counsel during interviews. With adults, police retain a discretionary power to permit

In Canada, the police caution has these two elements — the right to silence and counsel. While the precise formulation varies from jurisdiction to jurisdiction, the following caution, used by the Sûreté du Québec, is representative:

> You have the right to remain silent. We must inform you that we are police officers. You are not obliged to say anything but you must understand clearly that if you wish to say anything, whatever you do say may be taken down in writing and be given in evidence. Do you fully understand?
>
> You have the right to retain and instruct counsel of your choice without delay. Regardless of your financial status, you also have a right to free and immediate preliminary legal advice from a duty counsel.
>
> - Do you fully understand?
> - Do you wish to consult a duty counsel or any other lawyer?

Consultation with counsel by the suspect, police officers find, is often an obstacle to cooperation in an investigation (Leiken, 1970; Walsh, 1982). Several studies have lent credence to these concerns, insofar as suspects who exercise their rights to silence and counsel confess less often to police (Deslauriers-Varin and St-Yves, 2006; Leo, 1996; Moston, Stephenson and Williamson, 1992; Phillips and Brown, 1998). Nevertheless, Moston, Stephenson and Williamson (1992) have observed that suspects who invoke their right to silence are more likely to be convicted than are those who deny their crimes during questioning. Invoking the right to silence is thus not always advantageous for the suspect.

C. INTERROGATION: POLICE AND ACADEMIC PERSPECTIVES

Interrogate derives from the Latin *interrogare*, meaning "to question someone on a precise point or points that they are supposed to know about and concerning which they must respond." By definition, interrogation is a form of imposed conversation, as suggested by the phrases "submit to

---

attendance by counsel, in which case the lawyer becomes a witness and can later be called to testify, should the interviewee's statement be contested on a *voir dire* in court.

questioning," "undergo interrogation," "worm something out of someone." This type of constraint, which one finds in almost all interrogation, explains why interrogation is so often perceived as being more or less oppressive.

Two principal factors determine how police conduct interrogations. The first is the legal framework in which the interview takes place. The second is respect for any constitutional rights that may apply. In the United Kingdom, the law permits no ruses or persuasive techniques. At the beginning of the interview, it is also forbidden to discuss anything other than the crime in question, which makes it more difficult to establish a rapport with the suspect. In Canada, as in the United States, courts accept the use of certain ruses and persuasive techniques.[3] In a Supreme Court of Canada decision, Justice Antonio Lamer has said:

> [T]he investigation of crime and the detection of criminals is not a game to be governed by the Marquis of Queensbury rules. The authorities, in dealing with shrewd and often sophisticated criminals, must sometimes of necessity resort to tricks or other forms of deceit and should not through the rule be hampered in their work. What should be repressed vigorously is conduct on their part that shocks the community.[4]

Context can also influence the conduct of police interviews. The struggle against terrorism has militarized criminal justice and changed the rules. "Suspects are interrogated by the military in ways that would never be accepted by ordinary courts with criminal suspects" (Williamson, 2006a, p. 5).

1. Preparation

Planning and preparation will dictate how the interview progresses (Baldwin, 1992; St-Yves and Landry, 2004). It is at this point that the interviewer determines the objectives, the best time to question the suspect, and the strategies to employ. Before proceeding, investigators should always ask themselves three questions: 1) How will the interview assist the investigation? 2) What is known about the person to be questioned? 3) What remains to be established? The answers to these questions will help set out the objectives to be reached. It is not always necessary to count on a confession. Sometimes eliciting a misleading version of the facts (such as an unfounded alibi) or some compromising information will suffice.

---

3 See *R. v. Oickle*, [2000] 2 S.C.R. 3.

4 *R. v. Rothman*, [1981] 1 S.C.R. 640.

2. The Pre-interrogation Interview

Inbau et al. distinguish clearly between interviewing and interrogating a suspect (see Buckley, 2006). An interview is non-accusatory and its principal objective is to make certain the suspect is in fact the author of the crime in question. Interrogation, on the other hand, is an accusatory process, the object of which is not confession but the persuasion of the suspect to tell the truth (Buckley, 2006).

The aim of the pre-interrogation interview is to collect information concerning both the suspect and the circumstances of the crime which they presumably have committed. This allows the interviewer to evaluate the mental state — the operating mind — of the person being interrogated (see Perron, 2004). As well, the interviewer can establish a rapport with the suspect and create a climate of confidence favourable to a confession. The quality of the relationship between the suspect and interviewer is undoubtedly one of the most significant influences on the interrogation's outcome (Deslauriers-Varin and St-Yves, 2006; Holmberg, 2004; St-Yves, Tanguay and Crépault, 2004; St-Yves, 2006). Obviously, another goal of the interview is to learn the suspect's version of the facts — their own, unforced version, free of contamination by the interviewer. To obtain this, the investigator must use open questions such as, "tell me everything that happened last Saturday." This type of question elicits richer and more detailed responses (Fisher and Geiselman, 1992; Griffiths and Milne, 2006). Subsequently, to establish additional detail, the investigator can ask more intrusive questions (generally beginning with, "Who? Where? When? How? Why?") followed by so-called "closed" questions ("Did you hit this man more than once?") that produce short and to-the-point "yes" or "no" answers (Griffiths and Milne, 2006: 182).

Resorting to specific or closed questions at the wrong moment is often problematic in examining suspects. The same is true of leading or suggestive questions ("Do you usually get aggressive when you drink?"), questions that intimidate or force choices ("Did you hit or push this woman?") or inquiries based on personal views, for example, "I think you hit this person" (Griffiths and Milne, 2006: 183). Such tactics are not only unproductive but increase the risk that the interviewer will contaminate the witness. The interviewer ends up distancing himself from the truth.

3. Bait Questions

Inbau et al. (2001) suggest that the interviewer turn to so-called "bait questions," after the suspect has been offered the opportunity to give their version of the facts. These are usually personalized and prepared in advance. They are introduced progressively, working from more general and non-accusatory questions to questions of greater concern to the suspect. The latter would include queries such as, "What sort of person do you suppose would act like this? Why would somebody do something like this? How do you think such a person would feel today concerning these actions? Would it be important for them to explain themselves?" The goal of such questions is to create verbal and non-verbal reactions, allowing the interviewer to evaluate the responses and determine whether the suspect is indeed the perpetrator of the crime. Even though the responses are often interesting and sometimes assist the development or refinement of interrogation themes, they do not allow objective evaluation of whether the suspect is lying, let alone a determination of whether they are the perpetrator. Numerous studies concerning lie detection show that personal opinion is often wrong and based on subjective indicators without scientific foundation (Vrij, 2000; Vrij, 2004). Kassin and Fong (1999) have observed that police officers using the Reid Technique are less accurate than students untrained in lie detection, yet more confident in their results.

Usually the last question in such a series suggests the implication of the suspect in the crime under investigation. This question, commonly called "the bait," is intended to improve the apparent value of the evidence and make the suspect wonder if they might have misspoken or compromised themselves. For example: "Is there any reason why a witness would tell us they saw you there at the time when the crime was committed?" Given that using non-existent or fabricated evidence can help render a confession inadmissible in court, the investigator poses the question as strictly hypothetical.[5] Some authors have strongly criticized manipulation of the suspect's understanding of the evidence (through exaggeration or deliberate misrepresentation) on the basis that it can lead to false confessions (Kassin and Kiechel, 1996; Kassin and Gudjonsson, 2004; Redlich and Goodman, 2003).

---

5 *R. v. Oickle*, *supra* at para. 61.

4. Confrontation: The Nine Steps of the Reid Technique

The Oxford English Dictionary defines "confront" as "to compel (someone) to face or consider something, especially by way of accusation." To assist investigators faced with suspects who lie or persist in denying their role in a crime, Inbau et al. (1986; 2001) have developed a strategic interview process aimed at breaking down the suspect's resistance, minimizing the relevant consequences, and permitting the suspect to save face, thereby making it easier for them to confess. This technique, commonly called the Reid Technique, comprises nine steps:

Step One: Positive confrontation

This first step consists of confronting the suspect by accusing them of the crime in question: "Our investigation indicates clearly it was you who committed this crime." At this point, it is no longer a question of discovering whether the suspect actually committed the crime, but rather why they committed it. It is often easier for the interviewee to explain what motivated their behaviour (the why) than to talk about the behaviour itself, which is frequently perceived as being more reprehensible. The problem at this stage is that the investigator often has no objective basis for deciding conclusively that the accused in fact committed the crime. According to Buckley (2006), before using this confrontation technique, the investigator must be reasonably certain of the suspect's guilt (p. 193). In making that assessment, investigators must often rely essentially on their "hunches" and their appreciation of the verbal and non-verbal indicators of lying. However, a number of studies have shown that the rate of success in detecting lies rarely exceeds 50%, the same odds when one flips a coin (Mann, Vrij and Bull, 2004; Vrij, 2000).

Step Two: Theme development

The "theme" is the probable or possible reason which explains the suspect's criminal act. Themes[6] permit suspects to confess their crimes without losing face or even with the impression that the confession will work in their favour. They allow suspects to morally excuse themselves or justify their behaviour. Throughout this phase, the investigator can minimize the gravity of the crime, provide the suspect with an excuse

---

6 In a recent work, Senese (2005) explains the usefulness of such themes and proposes more than 1,600 crime-specific themes.

by redirecting blame onto others (the victim, an accomplice, society) and appeal to the suspect's pride. The investigator often unfolds the theme in a long monologue which not only describes the motivation for the crime, but sometimes suggests a hypothetical scenario explaining how the suspect was impelled to act and may actually suggest the crime script the suspect followed. This carries certain risks, notably suggestion and witness contamination, which can lead to false confessions, particularly where the suspect is intellectually vulnerable (Clare and Gudjonsson, 1995). The theme is meant to reflect the reasons underlying the suspect's commission of the crime, but often better reflects the investigator's perspective. Gudjonsson (2003) summarizes the Reid Technique this way:

> According to the model, it seems that the success of the interrogation depends on the extent to which the interrogator is successful in identifying psychological vulnerabilities, exploiting them to alter the suspect's belief system and perceptions of the consequences of making self-incriminating admissions, and persuading them to accept the interrogator's version of the truth (p. 120).

Steps Three and Four: Handling denials and overcoming objections

If the suspect still resists, Inbau et al. (2001) suggest investigators overcome denials ("No, I didn't do it") (Step Three) as well as objections ("I couldn't have done it; I don't have a gun) (Step Four), by either a hand gesture or facial expression (e.g. looking away) signifying that the suspect's arguments are futile. In so doing, investigators must be careful, as they run the risk of overlooking important information and, falling prey to their tunnel vision. As Justice Peter Cory mentioned:

> "Tunnel vision is insidious. It can affect an officer or, indeed, anyone involved in the administration of justice, sometimes with tragic results [...] Anyone, a police officer, counsel or judge, can become infected by this virus" (Williamson, 2006b).

Step Five: Gaining or regaining a suspect's attention

When suspects become withdrawn or unresponsive, investigators must gain or regain their attention; this can often be done by establishing visual or physical contact.

Step Six: Handling the suspect's passive mood

At this stage, the suspect is usually more relaxed, and may even be resigned. He or she listens to the themes developed by the investigator and may even weep. The investigator generally focuses on a particular theme, stating it precisely in one or two sentences and underlining its essential elements.

Step Seven: Presenting an alternative question

The investigator presents the suspect with two versions of the crime, one desirable and the other undesirable. Frequently the alternative question minimizes the gravity of the act and makes it more acceptable to save face; for example: "Was this the first time (the more positive alternative) or has it happened several times before?" The suspect is encouraged to choose the positive alternative.

This strategy is undoubtedly one of the most controversial as the suspect has no choice but to incriminate himself or herself, which increases the risk of a false confession (Gudjonsson, 2003). Buckley points out that one should not lose sight of a third option: the suspect is innocent (St-Yves and Landry, 2004: 19).

Minimizing the act at issue — for example, by presenting it as accidental or provoked — can obfuscate the intention behind the crime or its objective seriousness. It can also be perceived as a sort of tacit promise. Kassin and McNall (1991) decry the use of such techniques (maximization and minimization), in which investigators exaggerate the quality of the evidence and the seriousness of the crime (maximization), and offer suspects sympathy and a dignified way out, often blaming the victim or diminishing the gravity of the charges. Inbau et al. (2001, p. 235) warn investigators against any minimization of moral blameworthiness that relieves suspects of their criminal responsibility. While such tactics might be effective for securing a confession, they increase the risk of false ones (Russano et al., 2005).

Steps Eight and Nine: Getting the suspect to talk about the offence and converting the confession into a written statement

The first objective is to obtain an admission from the suspect and, following that, a confession — an authentic confession, corroborated by the investigation. Ofshe and Leo state that there are at least three ways to determine the validity of a confession (Ofshe and Leo, 1997a; Leo and Ofshe, 1998): (1) *Does the confession lead to the discovery of evidence previously unknown to police?* — for example, the confession allows investigators to recover the weapon used and the objects stolen. In such instances, the facts corroborate the confession. (2) *Does the confession include unusual details, unknown to the public, about the crime?* — for example, the suspect explains how and why he used a knife to cut a star of David into the victim's abdomen. (3) *Has the suspect provided a precise description of crime-scene details unknown to the public?* — for example, the suspect describes what the victim wore or the room (which he certainly could not have visited afterwards) where the crime took place. It is important to make certain the suspect has not been contaminated , that is, learned crime-scene details from third parties such as the media, the police, crime-scene photos, or the actual perpetrator (Ofshe and Leo, 1997a; Leo and Ofshe, 1998). As Cassell (1999) points out, establishing a person's innocence can prove just as difficult as establishing their guilt.

5. Audio-visual Recording of Interrogations

In the United Kingdom and Canada, investigators usually record or videotape the questioning of those suspected of major crimes (St-Yves, 2004c; St-Yves and Lavallée, 2002). In the United States, more and more states are doing the same (Buckley and Jayne, 2005). The use of this technology has no negative effect on the number of confessions obtained; what is more, the videotaping of interviews seems to produce a much greater number of answers and more incriminating information than do written statements (Geller, 1992; Grant, 1987). Moreover, in addition to providing a verbatim record of the interrogation,[7] audiovisual recording encourages investigators to conduct better interrogations[8] and protects them from unjustified criticism (Pitt, Spiers, Dietz and Dvoskin, 1999). Several courts have remarked that "recording provides objective documentation by which the judge can determine whether a confession is free and voluntary and

7 In *Stephan* (1985), the Supreme Court of Alaska suggests several other benefits, notably: 1) Human memory is often defective, and people forget certain facts, or reconstruct or interpret past incidents differently. Taping mitigates this. 2) It helps trial and appeal courts to determine the truth (L'enregistrement audiovisuel des interrogatoires des suspects ou des accusés: Rapport d'étape, 1996).

8 In *Scales* (1994), the Supreme Court of Minnesota also sets out a list of advantages, including: (1) Reduction in the number of recantations and objections to warnings given; (2) Greater professionalism in law enforcement.

assess the circumstances in which it was made, as well as its content, rather than having to rely on the subjective and self-serving statements of the protagonists."[9]

Audiovisual recording also permits the assessment of the climate surrounding the interrogation, and of the protagonists' attitudes and body language. Finally, it helps prevent miscarriages of justice. Overall, audiovisual recording is the most reliable witness record of the interrogation process.

D. FALSE CONFESSIONS

The number of wrongful convictions is difficult to estimate. One estimate puts the percentage related to serious crime at less than 1% (Huff, Rattner and Sagarin, 1986). Although false confessions do occur, they are not the leading cause of miscarriages of justice — erroneous identification by witnesses leads the list by a wide margin (Borchard, 1932; Brandon and Davies, 1973; Rattner, 1988). Despite the difficulty in estimating the frequency of false confessions, research on the subject and the number of documented cases suggest there is cause for concern (Gudjonsson, 2003; Kassin and Wrightsman, 1985; Leo and Ofshe, 1998). All the same, Cassell (1999) and Buckley (2006) are skeptical of the importance of the problem, and believe that the statistics on false confessions are exaggerated. In Quebec, in any event, the number of wrongful convictions arising from the thousands of interrogations conducted each year show the problem to be very marginal. Nonetheless, the rarity of the phenomenon makes it all the more insidious.

False confessions are often made to protect another person (a spouse, a friend, an accomplice), or, particularly when police use persuasive and coercive methods, as a result of police pressure (Gudjonsson and Sigurdsson, 1994; Kassin and Wrightsman, 1985; Leo and Ofshe, 1998). A false confession can be made freely or be coerced (see Bénézech, 1995; Gudjonsson, 1992, 2003; Kassin and Wrightsman, 1985; Leo, 1998; Leo and Ofshe, 1998; St-Yves, 2004c; Wrightsman and Kassin, 1993). Kassin and Wrightsman (1985) identify three main types of false confessions:

(1) Voluntary false confessions, made without pressure from the police. Those who make such statements often do so to attract attention or

9 L'enregistrement audiovisuel des interrogatoires des suspects ou des accusés: Rapport d'étape, 1996, p. 51.

notoriety (Kassin and Wrightsman, 1985; Radelet, Bedau and Putnam, 1992). This was probably the case with John Mark Karr, whose photo was in the news around the world, following his claim to have killed JonBenet Ramsey, the young beauty queen murdered in Colorado in 1996. Following the kidnapping and murder of Charles Lindbergh's baby in the 1930s, more than 200 people came forward to confess the crime.

(2) Compliant false confessions, made following police questioning and pressure. The principal reason for such confessions is to achieve an immediate instrumental gain, such as to stop torture or threats, or to end an interrogation (Gudjonsson, 1992; Kassin and Wrightsman, 1985; Wrightsman and Kassin, 1993). The classic example is the suspect who, following 12 hours of questioning, admits to the crime under investigation by giving a version of events suggested to him by investigators.

(3) Internalized false confessions, which arise when the suspect comes to believe during the interrogation that they committed the crime under investigation. Gudjonsson and MacKeith (1982) associate this type of false confession with "memory distrust syndrome," which occurs, in some instances, when the suspect has no memory of the crime alleged, let alone of their role in it. In other instances, suspects who, at the beginning of questioning, are sure that they did not commit the crime begin to doubt their own recollection of events because of the interviewer's manipulation and influence (Ofshe and Leo, 1997a, 1997b).

Kassin (1997) contends that this phenomenon is directly linked to: (1) *the suspect's vulnerability*, especially the malleability of their memory, their naiveté, their suggestibility, their intellectual level (those with intellectual deficits being more suggestible than others: Clare and Gudjonsson, 1995), their level of stress and fatigue, and the extent to which intoxicants have altered their mental state; (2) *interrogation methods*, often highly suggestive and containing false evidence.

E. EFFECTIVENESS OF PERSUASIVE METHODS

Some authors claim that persuasive methods have little effect on a person's decision to confess; others go so far as to say that such methods are useless or at least not altogether necessary for the securing of confessions (Baldwin, 1993; Bull, 2006; Evans, 1993; Irving and McKenzie, 1989; Moston, Stephenson and Williamson, 1992; Pearse and Gudjonsson, 1996; Pearse *et al.*, 1998). Baldwin (1993) observed that only 20 of 600 suspects interrogated changed their stories during the course of questioning, and that persuasive techniques were responsible for these changes in only 9 of these 20 cases. Pearse and Gudjonsson (1996), who observed the same phenomenon, state that the suspects in their study had already made their decision to confess or deny their crimes before interrogation started. In a recent study of tactics used by British police in interviewing 80 suspects, Bull (2006) noted that only 16% (5 out of 31) had confessed at the beginning of the interview. Inbau et al. (2001), on the other hand, believe that the vast majority of suspects at first intend to deny any involvement in the crime, although a great percentage of them change their minds and confess during the course of questioning, thanks to investigators' techniques.

Along the same lines, Deslauriers-Varin and St-Yves (2006) observed that 25% of convicted suspects changed their initial position during questioning. Out of this number, nearly half (46%) said they had intended to confess but changed their minds. This shows that the decision-making process can be influenced one way or another. Deslauriers-Varin (2006) also noted that 43.5% of those who confessed their crimes to police reported that they had been disposed to do so from the outset of questioning. On the other hand, 31.5% stated they had not been at all disposed to confess at the beginning of interrogation. What made them change their mind? Was it the quality of the evidence? Remorse? The investigators' attitude? Persuasive techniques?

Despite all the effort expended in trying to obtain confessions, the level of success remains modest. The average is about 60% in the United Kingdom (Baldwin and McConville, 1980; Clark and Milne, 2001; Irving and Mackenzie, 1989; Mitchell, 1983; Moston and Stephenson, 1992; Pearse et al., 1998; Phillips and Brown, 1998; Softley, 1980; Zander, 1979) and about 50% in North America (Cassel and Hayman, 1998; Deslauriers-Varin and St-Yves, 2006; Neubaher, 1974; Leo, 1996; St-Yves and Lavallée, 2002). The difference between the percentage of confessions in the United Kingdom and North America is largely attributable to the judicial systems under which the interrogations take place (Gudjonsson, 2003). Nonetheless, we believe that police success in the United Kingdom can also be explained by other factors, such as the exceptional quality of witness and victim interviews, which permits investigators to improve the quality of the evidence. After all, such testimony is often closer to the truth than the suspect's version.

F. PSYCHOLOGY OF RAPPORT: FIVE FUNDAMENTAL RULES

It is possible that persuasive techniques — whose effectiveness is difficult to measure — are overrated, and that the importance of the attitude of the person conducting the interrogation is underrated. Indeed, a number of authors believe the success of suspect interviews depends on the quality of the rapport established between the two parties (Baldwin, 1992; Holmberg and Christianson, 2002; Shepherd, 1991; St-Yves, 2006; St-Yves, Tanguay and Crépault, 2004).

The practice and teaching of investigative interviews has led us to identify five rules that are essential to a successful interrogation, and to the better management of the risks associated with such interrogations: (1) Keep an open mind and remain objective; (2) Build up a rapport; (3) Pay attention; (4) Keep a professional attitude; (5) Know how to conclude (St-Yves, 2006; St-Yves, Tanguay and Crépault, 2004).

Rule One: Keep an open mind and remain objective

The initial contact with the interviewee is often a determining factor. It is at that time that the two parties form an impression of each other. That first impression builds upon the initial information the investigator has learned about the interviewee — from a statement, the testimony of associates, an expert's report, a criminal record, a photograph. It is possible, therefore, that the interviewer forms an impression of the interviewee even before meeting that person. This subjective perception, which is often wrong, will markedly affect the interview process. Asch (1987) has shown that we quickly form an impression of others from the first things we perceive about them, and it is thereafter difficult for us to disabuse ourselves of those impressions, particularly when they are wrong. The tendency is to try to justify our initial impression rather than remain open to new ideas. Sometimes called the Pygmalion Effect, this phenomenon is better known as the Rosenthal Effect (Rosenthal and Jacobson, 1968).

A lack of objectivity can also result in the formulation of suggestive questions or in "scotomization" — the formation of blind spots due to the elimination of challenging information (Abric, 2003). To better establish a relationship with a witness, a victim, or a suspect, it is therefore necessary to break through the preconceptions we carry from our personal and professional experience, ignore stereotypes, and set aside our prejudices. Investigators must exercise the same caution in protecting their perceptions that they would apply in protecting a crime scene; once they are contaminated it is often too late. "First impressions are the cancer of objectivity."[10] Between the investigator and the person under interrogation, only one of them was at the scene of the crime. Only that person knows what happened.

Rule Two: Build up a rapport

We create rapport by attending to the needs and preoccupations of others, as well as taking the time to create a climate in which trust and confidence can grow as we remain open to the other person's feelings and beliefs. With authentic rapport, the investigator knows when and how to ask a question or make a comment — when to say, "I see," or "mm-hmm," at what moment to put a hand on the interviewee's shoulder by way of support, when and how to confront the interviewee with contradictions or evidence. This capacity for analysis and timing is sometimes called "emotional intelligence" (see Goleman, 1995) and is typical of good interviewers. Rapport is the heart of an interview, and learned techniques are only complementary. Rapport doesn't require particular technique, but to be effective, technique requires rapport. "A person reveals no secret without rapport" (Schafer and Navarro, 2003: 39). Even with terrorists, establishing rapport is more effective than relying on a coercive or an aggressive approach (Gelles, McFadden, Borum and Vossekuil, 2006).

Rule Three: Pay attention

Hearing is not necessarily the same as listening. Listening denotes paying attention to and participating actively in what another person says. A French study has revealed that more than 85% of officers in criminal investigation units interrupt interviewees' statements soon after they begin to speak (Ginet and Py, 2001). On average, these interruptions arise 7.5 seconds into the narrative (Fisher and Geiselman, 1992: 21). They disrupt interviewees' concentration, causing them, little by little, to become passive and unmotivated; this in turn commensurately diminishes the quality of their narrative (Py, Demarchi and Ginet, 2004; Jou and Harris, 1992).

The work of Carl Rogers (1902-1987) has demonstrated that active listening amounts to reading what the interviewee expresses. The listener attends to the interviewee's words and behaviour and stimulates the inter-

---

10 Jean-Michel Wyl. *Québec Banana State.*

viewee to speak their mind without interruption. The principal ingredients of such active listening are:

- ***Encouragement.*** To encourage, the listener indicates that they are truly listening to what is said, without interruption. The signals can be visual (facial expressions, nodding one's head, posture) or vocal ("Okay," "I see," "Mm-hmm"). Lack of encouragement can block expression, insofar as the interviewee can interpret it as a lack of interest and attention. Encouragement can increase fourfold the amount of information provided (Wainwright, 1993).
- ***Paraphrasing.*** There are several forms of paraphrase, including reformulation (restatement of what the interviewee says in the investigator's own words) and reflection, commonly called "echoing" (repeating the subject's last words). Paraphrasing stimulates discussion, facilitates rapport, and reassures the speaker that their words are being heard and understood.
- ***Identifying emotions.*** Giving verbal expression to the speaker's emotions shows that the listener is empathetic. It also assists the speaker's self-awareness, commonly called insight.
- ***Open questions***. Avoid closed questions — i.e. those that require solely a yes or no answer. Open questions stimulate richer answers and reduce the risk of contamination and suggestion.
- ***Tolerate silence.*** Rather than improvising clumsily in a search for words to stimulate or reassure the speaker, it is preferable to keep quiet. "It is only silence if no one is listening."[11] Silence frequently turns out to be advantageous. Among other things, it permits the interviewer to reflect and take a break. But bear in mind that silence, too, can be suggestive.

Rule Four: Keep a professional attitude

Moston and his colleagues have observed that confrontation and the persuasive approach are the most common styles of police interviews (Moston and Engelberg, 1993; Moston and Stephenson, 1993). Typically in such cases, the investigator accuses the suspect of having committed the crime, advises them of the evidence the police have against them, then asks them to confirm the allegations. If the interviewer encounters denial or silence, they likely will repeat the question more loudly and aggressively, or will

---

11 Réjean Ducharme. *L'Oceantume*.

simply conclude that the suspect is lying. Faced with such resistance, the investigator doesn't always have the ability to negotiate with the suspect, and the suspect maintains their denial until the end of the interview (Moston and Engelberg, 1993; Moston and Stephenson, 1993).

Holmberg and Christianson (2002) have observed that denial is associated with a dominating style of interviewing, while a humane style is associated with confessions. According to Baldwin (1992), the worst sort of interviewer uses a macho style and is incapable of seeing how counterproductive it is. A humane attitude including active listening, empathy, openness, respect, and willingness to discover the truth — as opposed to an attempt to get a confession at all costs — plays a crucial role in the investigative interview process (Deslauriers-Varin and St-Yves, 2006; Shepherd, 1991; St-Yves, Tanguay and Crépault, 2004; Williamson, 1993).

Rule Five: Know how to conclude

The end of an interrogation often produces strong emotions linked to fatigue, among other things. The suspect can be exasperated by the investigator's questions, and the latter might feel themselves at a loss in the face of persistent denial. In such contexts, investigators who are quick-tempered are most susceptible to encounter problems. They feel a sense of failure, which can lead them to openly express frustration or show impatience and make disagreeable remarks. In such cases, the atmosphere inevitably becomes oppressive. Such an approach is not only fruitless, but also puts paid to all further attempts at questioning. In indulging their temper, investigators risk hobbling the investigative process. A more sensible strategy is to take a break or give the suspect a business card to use if they decide to provide more information.

Knowing when to conclude also means making certain all the points have been covered, that the suspect has nothing to add, and that the suspect has been advised of what will now happen to them. Investigators must remain professional, whether one has obtained a confession or not. "Concluding" includes making oneself available in the future, and it provides the opportunity for the interviewer to make a good final impression. It also means leaving the interviewee an open door to confessing — in an hour, tomorrow, or sometime later — and possibly to someone other than the interviewer. "Concluding" is also recalling that there are five rules and that they are the same for everyone.

CONCLUSION

While evidence is the determining factor in securing a confession, it is not always enough to accuse or charge a suspect. Some studies reveal that evidence such as fingerprints and DNA are collected in 10% of cases at most (Bottomley et Coleman, 1980 ; Horvath and Meesig, 1996). Evidence generally is based on testimony, including that of the suspect.

The quest for a confession usually leads to the use of persuasive techniques, but such methods are controversial, as they can compromise the truth and carry risks that can lead to wrongful convictions. It should however be recalled that the majority of such miscarriages of justice are attributable to misstatements by witnesses — wilful or otherwise — and not to false confessions (St-Yves, in press).

Today, interrogation continues to allow numerous crimes to be resolved, even though confession is no longer the pre-eminent form of evidence. The methods used to obtain confessions are varied, but in North America the most popular are persuasive methods, particularly the Reid Technique. While controversial, these methods are acceptable to Canadian courts, and their audio-visual recording is becoming more and more widespread. Although interrogations cannot always be counted upon to produce the truth, audio-visual recording at least allows us to accurately assess the methods used to obtain confessions.

The quest for a confession most definitely carries risk — that of finding guilt instead of the truth. But without this quest for the confession, we would never convict a large number of criminals and the truth would remain unknown. To better manage the risks associated with police interrogations, we propose five basic rules: (1) Keep an open mind and remain objective; (2) Build up a rapport; (3) Pay attention; (4) Keep a professional attitude; (5) Know how to conclude. As long as these rules are respected, no method — not even persuasive ones — will appear or become oppressive. Rather, the rules will incline interviewers to proceed respectfully and protect the dignity of the interviewee. When this is achieved, the search for a confession takes on an entirely different meaning, becoming a search for the truth.

REFERENCES

Abric, J.-C. (2003). *Psychologie de la communication: théories et méthodes [Psychology of communication : Theories and methods.]*, Armand Colin.

Asch, S.E. (1987). *Social Psychology*. Oxford, England: Oxford University Press.

Baldwin, J. (1993). Police interviewing techniques. Establishing the truth or proof? *The British Journal of Criminology*, 33, 325-352.

Baldwin, J. (1992). *Video taping police interviews with suspects — An evaluation*. Police Research Group – Police Research Series, paper 1. Home Office, London.

Baldwin, J. and McConville, M. (1980). *Confessions in Crown Court Trials*. Royal Commission on Criminal Procedure Research Study No. 5. London : HMSO.

Bénézech, M. (1995). Splendeur et misère de l'aveu criminel. Esquisse médico-légalale et psychopathologique. In *La garde à vue en question. L'aveu, reine des preuves?* [Questioning detention. Confession, queen of evidence?] Actes du colloque de Bordeaux, December 3-4, 1994. ACAT document, Paris.

Berggren, E. (1975). *The Psychology of Confessions*. Leiden: Brill.

Borchard, E.M. (1932). *Convicting the Innocent: Sixty-Five Actual Errors of Criminal Justice*. Garden City, NY: Doubleday.

Bottomley, A.K. and Coleman, C.A. (1980). Police effectiveness and the public: the limitations of official crime rates. In R.V.G. Clarke and J.M. Hough (eds.), *The Effectiveness of Policing*. Farnborough: Gower.

Brandon, R. and Davies, C. (1973). *Wrongful Imprisonment*. London: Allen and Unwin.

Buckley, D.M and Jayne, B.C. (2005). *Electronic Recording of Interrogations*. John E. Reid and Associates.

Buckley, J.P. (2006). The Reid Technique of interviewing and interrogation. In T. Williamson (ed.), *Investigative Interviewing: Rights, Research, Regulation*. Devon: Willan, 190-206.

Bull, R. (2006). *Research on the Police Interviewing of Suspects*. Paper presented at Séminaire d'échanges de bonnes pratiques sur les auditions de police judiciaire [Seminar on best practices of judicial police hearings], Jan. 23-26, 2006, Paris.

Burke, T., Street, R. and Brown, D. (2000). *The Right of Silence: The Impact of the Criminal Justice and Public Order Act 1994*. A Research, Development and Statistics Directorate Report. Research Study 199. London: Home Office.

Cassell, P.G. (1999). The guilty and the "innocent": An examination of alleged cases of wrongful conviction from false confessions. *Harvard Journal of Law and Public Policy*, 22, 523-603.

Cassell, P.G. and Hayman, B.S. (1998). Police interrogation in the 1990s: an empirical study on the effect of Miranda. In R.A. Leo and G.C. Thomas III (eds.), *The Miranda Debate, Justice and Policing*. Boston: Northeastern University Press, 222-235.

Clare, I.C.H. and Gudjonsson, G.H. (1995). The vulnerability of suspects with intellectual disabilities during police interviews: A review and experimental study of decision-making. *Mental Handicap Research*, 8, 110-128.

Clark, C. and Milne, R. (2001). *National Evaluation of the PEACE Investigative Interviewing Course*. Police Research Award Scheme. Report No. PRAS/149. London: Home Office.

Deslauriers-Varin, N. (2006). *Les facteurs determinants dans le processus d'aveu chez les auteurs d'actes criminels*. [Determinant factors in the confession process of authors of criminal acts]. Master's thesis. Université de Montréal.

Deslauriers-Varin, N. and St-Yves, M. (2006). *An empirical investigation of offenders' decision to confess their crime during police interrogation*. Paper presented at the Second International Conference on Investigative Interviewing, Portsmouth (UK), July 5-7.

Evans, R. (1993). *The Conduct of Police Interviews with Juveniles.* Royal Commission on Criminal Justice Research Report No. 8. London: HMSO.

Eysenck, H.J. and Gudjonsson, G.H. (1989). *The Causes and Cures of Criminality.* New York: Plenum Press.

Fisher, R.P. and Geiselman, R.E. (1992). *Memory-Enhancing Techniques for Investigative Interviewing.* Springfield, Illinois: Charles Thomas.

Geller, W.A. (1992). *Police Videotaping of Suspects Interrogations and Confessions: A Preliminary Examination of Issues and Practices.* Report to the National Institute of Justice. Washington: Police Executive Research Forum.

Gelles, M.G., McFadden, R., Borum, R. and Vossekuil, B. (2006). Al-Qaeda-related subjects: a law enforcement perspective. In T. Williamson (ed.), *Investigative Interviewing: Rights, Research, Regulation.* Devon: Willan, 23-41.

Ginet, M., and Py, J. (2001). A technique for enhancing memory in eyewitness testimonies for use by police officers and judicial officers: the cognitive interview. *Le Travail Humain*, 64, 173-191.

Goleman, D. (1995). *Emotional Intelligence.* New York, USA: Bantam Books.

Grant, A. (1987). *The Audio-Visual Taping Interviews with Suspects and Accused Persons by Halton Regional Police Force, Ontario, Canada: An Evaluation, Final Report.* Ottawa: Law Reform Commission of Canada.

Griffiths, A. and Milne, B. (2006). Will it all end in tiers? Police interviews with suspects in Britain. In T. Williamson (ed.), *Investigative Interviewing: Rights, Research, Regulation.* Devon Willan, 167-189.

Gudjonsson, G.H. (2003). *The Psychology of Interrogations and Confessions. A Handbook.* Chichester: John Wiley and Sons.

Gudjonsson, G.H. (1992). *The Psychology of Interrogations, Confessions and Testimony.* Chichester: John Wiley and Sons.

Gudjonsson, G.H. and Bownes, I. (1992). The reasons why suspects confess during custodial interrogation: data for Northern Ireland. *Medicine, Science and the Law*, 32, 204-212.

Gudjonsson, G.H. and MacKeith, J.A.C. (1994). Learning disability and the Police and Criminal Evidence Act 1984. Protection during investigative interviewing: a video-recorded false confession to double murder. *Journal of Forensic Psychiatry*, 5, 35-49.

Gudjonsson, G.H. and MacKeith, J.A.C. (1982). False confessions: psychological effects of interrogation. A discussion paper. In A. Trankell (ed.), *Reconstructing the Past: The Role of Psychologists in Criminal Trials*. Deventer: Kluwer, 253-269.

Gudjonsson, G.H. and Petursson, H. (1991). Custodial interrogation: Why do suspects confess and how does it relate to their crime, attitude and personality? *Personality and Individual Differences* 12, 295-306.

Gudjonsson, G.H. and Sigurdsson, J.F. (1999). The Gudjonsson Confession Questionnaire — Revised (GCQ-R): factor structure and its relationship with personality. *Personality and Individual Differences*, 27, 953-968.

Holmberg, U. (2004). *Police Interviews with Victims and Suspects of Violent and Sexual Crimes: Interviewees' Experiences and Interview Outcomes*. Doctoral dissertation, Stockholm University.

Holmberg, U. and Christianson, S.A. (2002). Murderers' and Sexual Offenders' Experiences of Police Interviews and Their Inclination to Admit or Deny Crimes. *Behavioral Sciences and the Law,* 20, 31-45.

Horvath, F. and Meesig, R. (1996). The Criminal Investigation Process and the Role of Forensic Evidence: A Review of Empirical Findings. *Journal of Forensic Science*. November 1996.

Huff, C.R., Rattner, A. and Sagarin, E. (1986). Guilty until proven innocent: wrongful conviction and public policy. *Crime and Delinquency*, 32, 518-544.

Inbau, F.E., Reid, J.E. and Buckley, J.P. (1986). *Criminal Interrogation and Confessions*. Third edition. Baltimore: Williams and Wilkins.

Inbau, F.E., Reid, J.E., Buckley, J.P. and Jayne, B.C. (2001). *Criminal Interrogation and Confessions.* Fourth edition. Gaithersburg, Maryland: Aspen Publication.

Irving, B. and Hilgendorf, L. (1980). *Police Interrogation: The Psychological Approach.* Research Studies, No. 1, London: HMSO.

Irving, B. and McKenzie, I.K. (1989). *Police Interrogation: The Effects of the Police and Criminal Evidence Act.* London: HMSO.

Jou, J., and Harris, R.J. (1992). The effect of divided attention on speech production. *Bulletin of the Psychonomic Society*, 30, 301-304.

Kassin, S.M. (1997). The Psychology of Confession Evidence. *American Psychologist*, 52, 221-233.

Kassin, S.M. and Fong, C.T. (1999). I'm innocent! Effects of training on judgments of truth and deception in the interrogation room, *Law and Human Behavior*, 23, 499-516.

Kassin, S.M. and Gudjonsson, G.H. (2004). The Psychology of Confessions: A Review of the Literature and Issues. *Psychological Science in the Public Interest*, 5, 33-67.

Kassin, S.M. and Kiechel, K.L. (1996). The social psychology of false confessions: Compliance, internalization, and confabulation. *Psychological Science*, 7, 125-128.

Kassin, S.M. and McNall, K. (1991). Police interrogations and confessions. *Law and Human Behavior*, 15, 233-251.

Kassin, S.M. and Wrightsman, L.S. (1985). Confession evidence. In S.M. Kassin and L.S. Wrightsman (eds.), *The Psychology of Evidence and Trial Procedures.* London: Sage, 67-94.

L'enregistrement audiovisuel des interrogatoires des suspects ou des accusés: Rapport d'etape. [Audio-visual rercording of interrogations of suspects or accused individuals: Interim report] Report to the Minister of Public Security, Serge Ménard. Working group charged with examining criminal investigative practices within Quebec police forces. Montreal, January 25, 1996.

Leiken, L.S. (1970). Police interrogation in Colorado: the implementation of Miranda. *Denver Law Journal*, 47, 1-53.

Leo, R.A. (1998). Miranda and the problem of false confessions. In R.A. Leo and G.C. Thomas III (eds.), *The Miranda Debate, Justice and Policing*. Boston, MA: Northeastern University Press, 271-282.

Leo, R.A. (1996). Inside the Interrogation Room. *Journal of Criminal Law and Criminology*, 86, 2, 266-303.

Leo, R.A. and Ofshe, R.J. (1998). The consequences of false confessions: deprivations of liberty and miscarriages of justice in the age of psychological interrogation, *Journal of Criminal Law and Criminology*, 88, 429-96.

Mann, S., Vrij, A. and Bull, R. (2004). Detecting true lies: Police officers' ability to detect suspects' lies. *Journal of Applied Psychology*, 89, 137-149.

Mitchell, B. (1983). Confessions and police interrogation of suspects. *Criminal Law Review*, September, 596-604.

Moston, S. and Engelberg, T. (1993). Police questioning techniques in tape-recorded interviews with criminal suspects. *Policing and Society*, 6, 61-75.

Moston, S. and Stephenson, G.M. (1993). The changing face of police interrogation. *Journal of Community and Social Psychology*, 3, 101-115.

Moston, S. and Stephenson, G.M. (1992). Predictors of suspect and interviewer behaviour during police questioning. In F. Loesel, D. Bender and T. Bliesener (eds.), *Psychology and Law: International Perspectives*. Berlin: De Gruyter, 212-218.

Moston, S., Stephenson, G.M. and Williamson, T.M. (1992). The effects of case characteristics on suspect behaviour during police questioning. *British Journal of Criminology*, 32, 23-40.

Neubauer, D.W. (1974). Confessions in Prairie City: Some causes and effects. *Journal of Criminal Law and Criminology*, 65, 103-112.

Ofshe, R.J. and Leo, R.A. (1997a). The decision to confess falsely: rational choice and irrational action. *Denver University Law Review*, 74, 979-1122.

Ofshe, R.J. and Leo, R.A. (1997b). The social psychology of police interrogation. The theory and classification of true and false confessions. *Studies in Law, Politics and Society*, 16, 189-251.

Pearse, J. and Gudjonsson, G.H. (1996). Police interviewing techniques at two South London police stations. *Psychology, Crime and Law*, 3, 63-74.

Pearse, J., Gudjonsson, G.H., Clare, I.C.H. and Rutter, S. (1998). Police interviewing and psychological vulnerabilities: predicting the likelihood of a confession. *Journal of Community and Applied Social Psychology*, 8(1), 1-21.

Perron, M. (2004). Les aspects juridiques de la confession. [Judicial aspects of confessions]. In M. St-Yves and J. Landry (eds.), *Psychologie des entrevues d'enquête: de la recherche à la pratique [The psychology of investigative interviews: from research to practice]*. Cowansville: Éditions Yvon Blais, 373-413.

Phillips, C. and Brown, D. (1998). *Entry into the Criminal Justice System: A Survey of Police Arrests and Their Outcomes*. London: Home Office.

Pitt, S.E., Spiers, E.M., Dietz, P.E. and Dvoskin, J.A. (1999). Preserving the integrity of the interview: The value of videotape. *Journal of Forensic Sciences*, 44, 1287-1291.

Py, J., Demarchi, S. and Ginet, M. (2004). Comment placer les témoins dans des conditions optimales de restitution de leurs souvenirs d'une scène criminelle? [How to place witnesses in optimal conditions to restore their recall of crime scenes] In M. St-Yves and J. Landry (eds.), *Psychologie des entrevues d'enquête: de la recherche à a pratique [The psychology of investigative interviews: from research to practice]*. Cowansville: Éditions Yvon Blais, 169-179.

Radelet, M.L., Bedau, H.A. and Putnam, C.E. (1992). *In Spite of Innocence. Erroneous Convictions in Capital Cases*. Boston, MA: Northeastern University Press.

Rattner, A. (1988). Convicted but innocent. Wrongful conviction and the criminal justice system. *Law and Human Behavior*, 12, 283-293.

Redlich, A.D. and Goodman, G.S. (2003). Taking responsibility for an act not committed: The influence of age and suggestibility. *Law and Human Behavior*, 27, 141-156.

Reik, T., (1961). *The Compulsion to Confess: On the Psychoanalysis of Crime and Punishment* (New York: Grove Press.

Rosenthal, R. and Jacobson, L. (1968). *Pygmalion in the classroom*. New York: Holt, Rinehart and Winston.

Russano, M.B., Meissner, C.A., Narchet, F.M. and Kassin, S.M. (2005). Investigating true and false confessions within a novel experimental paradigm. *Psychological Science*, 16, 481-486.

Schafer, J.R. and Navarro, J. (2003). *Advanced Interviewing Techniques*. Springfield, Illinois: Charles C. Thomas.

Senese, L.C. (2005). *Anatomy of Interrogation Themes. The Reid Technique of Interviewing and Interrogation*. John E. Reid and Associates.

Shepherd, E. (1991). Ethical interviewing. *Policing*, 7, 42-60.

Sigurdsson, J.F. and Gudjonsson, G.H. (1994). Alcohol and drug intoxication during police interrogation and the reasons why suspects confess to the police. *Addiction*, 89, 985-997.

Softley, P. (1980). *Police Interrogation: An Observational Study in Four Police Stations*. Home Office Research Study, No. 61. London: HMSO.

Stephenson, G.M. and Moston, S.J. (1994). Police Interrogation. *Psychology, Crime and Law*, 1.

St-Yves, M. (in press). Police interrogation in Canada: From the quest for confession to the search for the truth. In Tom Williamson, Becky Milne and Steve Savage, International Developments in Investigative Interviewing, Devon: Willan.

St-Yves, M. (2006). The psychology of rapport: five basic rules. In T. Williamson (ed.), *Investigative Interviewing: Rights, Research, Regulation.* Devon: Willan, 87-106.

St-Yves, M. (2004a). La psychologie de l'aveu [The psychology of the confession]. In M. St-Yves and J. Landry (eds.), *Psychologie des entrevues d'enquête: de la recherché à la pratique [The psychology of investigative interviews: from research to practice].* Cowansville: Éditions Yvon Blais, 31-52.

St-Yves, M. (2004b). L'aveu chez les auteurs de crimes sexuels [Confessions by the authors of sexual crimes]. In M. St-Yves and J. Landry (eds.), *Psychologie des entrevues d'enquête: de la recherche à la pratique [The psychology of investigative interviews: from research to practice].* Cowansville: Éditions Yvon Blais, 85-103.

St-Yves, M. (2004c). Les fausses confessions: comprendre et prévenir [False confessions: understanding and preventing]. In M. St-Yves and J. Landry (eds.), *Psychologie des entrevues d'enquête: de la recherche à la pratique [The psychology of investigative interviews: from research to practice].* Cowansville: Éditions Yvon Blais, 105-133.

St-Yves, M. and Landry, J. (2004). La pratique de l'interrogatoire de police [The conduct of police interrogations]. In M. St-Yves and J. Landry (eds.), *Psychologie des entrevues d'enquête: de la recherche à la pratique [The psychology of investigative interviews: from research to practice].* Cowansville: Éditions Yvon Blais, 7-30.

St-Yves, M., Tanguay, M. and Crépault, D. (2004). [La psychologie de la relation: cinq règles de base [The psychology of relations : five basic rules]. In M. St-Yves and J. Landry (eds.), *Psychologie des entrevues d'enquête: de la recherche à la pratique [The psychology of investigative interviews: from research to practice].* Cowansville: Éditions Yvon Blais, 135-153.

St-Yves, M. (2002). Interrogatoire de police et crime sexuel: profil du suspect collaborateur [Police interrogations and sexual crimes: a profile of suspects who collaborate]. *Revue internationale de criminologie et de police technique et scientifique.* 81-96.

St-Yves, M. and Lavallee, P.R. (2002). *L'interrogatoire video: État de la situation à la Sûreté du Québec.* [video interrogations: State of the situation at the Sûreté du Québec]. Direction conseil et développement en enquêtes criminelles [Criminal investigation advisory and development directorate]. Sûreté du Québec. Unpublished.

Vrij, A. (2004). Guidelines to catch a liar. In P.A. Granhag and L.A. Stromwall (eds.). *The Detection in Forensic Contexts*. Cambridge: Cambridge University Press.

Vrij, A. (2000). Detecting Lies and Deceit. *The Psychology of Lying and the Implications for Professional Practice*. Chichester, United Kingdom: John Wiley and Sons.

Wainwright, G.R. (1993). *Teach Yourself Body Language*. London: Hodder Headlines.

Walsh, D.P.J. (1982). Arrest and interrogation: Northern Ireland 1981. *Journal of Law and Society*, 9, 37-62.

Walters, S.B. (1995). *Principles of Kinesic Interview and Interrogation*. CRC Press.

Williamson, T.M. (2006a). Investigative interviewing and human rights in the war on terrorism. In T. Williamson (ed.), *Investigative Interviewing: Rights, Research, Regulation*. Devon: Willan, 3-22.

Williamson, T.M. (2006b). Towards greater professionalism: minimizing miscarriages of justice. In T. Williamson (ed.), *Investigative Interviewing: rights, research, regulation*. Willan, 147-189.

Williamson, T.M. (1993). From interrogation to investigative interviewing: Strategic trends in police questioning. *Journal of Community and Social Psychology*, 3, 89-99.

Williamson, T.M. (1990). *Strategic Changes in Police Interrogation: An Examination of Police and Suspect Behaviour in the Metropolitan Police in order to Determine the Effects of New Legislation, Technology and Organizational Policies*. Unpublished PhD Thesis, University of Kent.

Wrightsman, L.S. and Kassin, S.M. (1993). *Confessions in the Court-Room*. Newbury Park, CA: Sage.

Zander, M. (1979). The investigation of crime: a study of cases tried at the Old Bailey. *Criminal Law Review*, 203-219.

CHAPTER 2

Enhancing Eyewitness Memory with the Cognitive Interview

Ronald P. Fisher and Rachel M. York

In popular television police shows, handsome and beautiful investigators and their white-smocked laboratory colleagues solve crimes by conducting high-tech computer-assisted analyses of paint samples, cloth fibers, burn patterns and the like. In reality, ordinary-looking police solve crimes by asking victims and witnesses, "what happened?" Indeed, police investigators agree that eyewitnesses usually provide central leads in their investigations (Berresheim and Weber, 2003; George and Clifford, 1992; Kebbell and Milne, 1998; Kebbell and Wagstaff, 1997). Police lament, however, that witnesses rarely provide sufficient information (Kebbell and Milne, 1998). How might police improve the quality of eyewitness evidence? In the ideal world, intelligent and perceptive witnesses would observe crimes under optimal viewing conditions, would have detailed and accurate recollections of the crimes, and would voluntarily and accurately communicate these recollections on request. Although ideal, police cannot control these factors (estimator variables; Wells, 1978) and, as such, they represent more wishful thinking than effective police investigative technique. A more productive approach would be to concentrate on those factors that police can control (system variables). Of those, the most important, and the focus of this chapter, is how they interview witnesses.

We start by illustrating a typical police interview of a cooperative witness. We then examine some of the scientific research on interviewing witnesses, specifically with an eye toward developing better techniques. There is consensus among researchers about several interviewing techniques, and these have formed the core elements that appear in many interviewing protocols. We focus on one specific interviewing protocol, the Cognitive Interview (CI), which incorporates these core elements along with several unique techniques to facilitate witness recollection. Much of the scientific research that tests specific interviewing protocols examines the CI, and we briefly review the laboratory and field research. To complement this scientific research, we examine some practical issues associated with the CI and witness interviewing, and explore some real-world cases in which the CI was used by police and other investigative agencies. Finally, we address some of the legal ramifications of using the CI.

A. CURRENT POLICE INTERVIEWING PRACTICES

Although the police interview is a central element in eliciting detailed, accurate witness reports, we know relatively little about how police actually conduct interviews with cooperative witnesses. Two decades ago Fisher, Geiselman, and Raymond (1987) and George and Clifford (1992) described typical interviewing protocols used by American and British police, respectively. The results were surprisingly uniform and discouraging. Following a perfunctory effort to establish rapport, police interviewers generally began interviews by making an open-ended request to the witness: "Tell me what happened." After listening to an initial outburst of crime-related facts, often no more than just a few seconds, the interviewer interrupted the witness's narrative response and asked a series of direct, short-answer questions, on the order of: How tall was he? How much did he weigh? Did he have a weapon? These questions, which reflect generically salient crime facts, were often asked in the same order to all witnesses. In addition to these neutral questions, police often asked leading or suggestive questions: Was he wearing a red shirt? If a witness did not provide the requested details, the police interviewer did little or nothing to assist the witness. We note, with a sigh of renewed discouragement, that similar patterns of poor interviewing procedures have been found in more recent interviews conducted by German (Berresheim and Weber, 2003) and American police (Schreiber and Fisher, 2005).

We were discouraged by the poor quality of police interviews, in part, because forensic research scientists have known for a while how to conduct interviews effectively. Of these techniques, the best known are the Cognitive Interview, Conversation Management, the Memorandum of Good Practice, and the Step-wise method. Each of these protocols is composed of many specific techniques that have generally been found to (a) increase the amount of information gathered, and/or (b) decrease the likelihood of a recalling an event incorrectly. Common to all of these protocols are several core elements, including (a) developing rapport with the witness, (b) asking open-ended questions primarily, (c) asking neutral questions and avoiding leading or suggestive questions, and (d) funneling the interview, beginning with broader questions and narrowing down to more specific questions. We shall focus here on the CI procedure because it is more encompassing than the others and it has been the focus of extensive scientific testing.

B. THE COGNITIVE INTERVIEW

The following is a thumbnail sketch of the CI (for a complete description, see Fisher and Geiselman, 1992). The core elements of the CI are organized around three basic psychological processes: memory and cognition, social dynamics, and communication. In addition, we describe the sequential structure of the CI.

1. Memory and Cognition

Witnesses can do little to prepare themselves initially to perceive crimes effectively. For cognitive theory to be useful in an eyewitness memory task, it must therefore focus on the retrieval phase of memory, after the crime has occurred. Second, both the witness and the interviewer are engaged in demanding cognitive tasks: The witness is attempting to recall and describe in detail a complex event; the interviewer is listening for details and subtleties within the witness's response, generating and testing hypotheses about the crime, formulating questions, and notating the witness's answers. Because these tasks are demanding, the witness's and interviewer's cognitive resources must be used efficiently.

a) Context reinstatement

Retrieving information from memory is most efficient when the context of the original event is recreated at the time of recall (Tulving and Thomson, 1973). Interviewers should therefore instruct witnesses to mentally recreate their physiological, cognitive and emotional states that existed at the time of the original event. Context reinstatement might also be implemented by conducting the interview at the scene of the crime or accident.

b) Limited mental resources

People have only limited mental resources to process information (Baddeley, 1986; Kahneman, 1973). Performing a task therefore suffers when we engage in several other difficult tasks at the same time. For instance, witnesses may search through memory only superficially, because they are concurrently occupied with listening to the interviewer's questions. For the same reason, interviewers may fail to process subtle nuances within a witness's response, because they are concurrently occupied with formulating questions. Interviewers can minimize overloading witnesses by refraining from asking questions while witnesses are searching through memory, and, in general, by asking fewer, but more open-ended, questions. Asking fewer questions, but rather encouraging witnesses to narrate their story in an uninterrupted fashion, also makes the interviewer's task easier — by not having to formulate many questions — and frees the interviewer to listen more effectively to the witness's narration.

Interviewers can also promote more efficient use of witnesses' limited mental resources by encouraging them to close their eyes when recalling (Bekerian and Dennett, 1997). Doing so, however, requires that the interviewer has developed a good rapport with the witness. Interviewers can also assist witnesses to focus their mental resources more effectively by minimizing physical distractions, such as phone calls during the interview.

c) *Witness-compatible questioning*

Each witness's mental record of an event is unique. Some witnesses may have focused on the perpetrator's face, whereas others may have focused on the weapon. Similarly, witnesses differ in their personal interests and/or perceptual skills. For instance, some witnesses may notice vehicles whereas others notice clothing. Interviewers should tailor their questions to the interests and perceptual skills of each particular witness instead of asking all witnesses the same set of questions. Interviewers often violate this rule by using a standardized checklist to guide their questioning of all witnesses (Fisher et al., 1987).

Within each witness, the accessibility of event details varies systematically throughout the course of the interview. Memory for the perpetrator's face, for instance, should be more accessible when the witness is thinking about the perpetrator than when the witness is thinking about the getaway car. In general, event details will be most accessible when they are perceptually related to the witness's current mental image (Pecher, Zeelenberg, and Barsalou, 2003). Interviewers therefore should try to be aware of the witness's currently active mental image, so as to time their questions most efficiently. This may require interviewers to defer asking questions about investigatively relevant details until later in the interview, when the questions are compatible with the witness's current mental image. For instance, if the interviewer needs to learn about the license tag of the getaway car, but the witness is currently thinking about the robber's face and not about the getaway car, then the interviewer should defer asking the witness to describe the license tag until the witness is thinking about the getaway car.

d) Multiple and varied retrieval

The more often witnesses search through their memories about the crime, the more new details they will recall. Interviewers can make use of this principle by (a) asking the witness to describe the critical event several times within the interview, and by (b) interviewing the witness on two or more occasions. Interviewers should instruct the witness to continue thinking about the crime even after the interview has terminated. Interviewers should then speak to the witness a few days later and ask about any new recollections since the interview.

If witnesses attempt to recall the target event repeatedly, they should be directed to think about the event in various ways, since different retrieval cues may activate different aspects of a complex event (Anderson and Pichert, 1978). For instance, witnesses might think about an event in terms of its temporal properties (when things happened) and also its spatial properties (where things were located) (Gilbert and Fisher, 2006). Similarly, events may be represented both semantically (e.g., robber was angry) and also in terms of their sensory properties (e.g., robber's face was red: Paivio, 1971). Witnesses should be encouraged to describe an event in terms of its semantic, meaningful properties and also its various sensory properties. In general, the more different ways witnesses think about an event, the more details they should recall.

e) Accuracy of responding

Witnesses can recall events accurately if they refrain from guessing (Koriat and Goldsmith, 1996). To promote high accuracy in recall, interviewers should explicitly instruct witnesses not to guess, but, preferably, to indicate that they "don't know." Furthermore, interviewers should refrain from applying social pressure on witnesses or otherwise encouraging them to answer questions they are uncertain of. In general, witness recall is much more accurate when answering open-ended questions (describe the robber's appearance) than closed questions (did the robber have dark or light hair?). These principles are particularly important when interviewing children.

f) Minimizing constructive recall

At times, memory is a constructive process, whereby the rememberer incorporates information from other (non-crime) sources to construct the crime episode (Bartlett,1932; Bransford and Franks, 1971; Loftus and Palmer, 1974). A witness, for instance, might incorporate knowledge gathered from other witnesses or the media to help construct his or her memory of a crime. Interviewers should therefore warn witnesses not to expose themselves to these sources. More important, witnesses may also acquire and use information from the interviewer, based on his or her verbal or non-verbal behavior (Ceci and Bruck, 1995). Interviewers should therefore be careful about not leaking information to witnesses either non-verbally (smiling or paying increased attention when the witness makes a particular statement) or verbally by asking leading or suggestive questions.

2. Social Dynamics

Witnesses and victims are often asked to describe unpleasant experiences to people whom they do not know. Two critical features mark this social interaction. First, witnesses must be psychologically comfortable with the interviewer *as a person* to go through the mental effort and emotional distress of describing crime-related details. Second, there are social and knowledge-based inequalities between the witness and the interviewer: The interviewer (e.g., police officer) generally has higher social or expert status, which normally dictates that that the interviewer should control the interview; however, the witness has more first-hand knowledge of the crime, which dictates that the witness should control the interview. Resolving this apparent conflict is critical for a successful interview.

a) Developing rapport

Witnesses, and especially victims, are often asked to give detailed descriptions of intimate, personal experiences to police officers, who are complete strangers. If anything, the police investigator's official appearance (badge, uniform, gun) may create a psychological barrier between the police officer and the witness. To overcome this natural barrier, police interviewers should invest time at the outset of the interview to develop meaningful, personal rapport with the witness (Collins, Lincoln and Frank, 2002), a feature often absent in police interviews (Fisher et al., 1987).

b) Active witness participation

The witness has extensive first-hand information about the target event. Therefore the witness, and not the interviewer, should be doing most of the mental work during the interview. In practice, however, police interviewers often dominate the social interaction with the witness by asking many questions, and by asking questions that elicit only brief answers. This relegates the witness to sit passively waiting for interviewers to ask questions (Fisher et al., 1987). To compound the problem, police interviewers often discourage witnesses from taking active roles by interrupting them in the middle of a narrative response. Interviewers can induce witnesses to take more active roles by (a) explicitly requesting them to do so, (b) asking open-ended questions, (c) not interrupting witnesses during their narrative responses, and (d) constructing the social dynamic so that witnesses perceive themselves to be the "experts" and therefore the dominant person in the conversation. This last point is especially important when interviewing children (McCauley and Fisher, 1995).

3. Communication

For police interviews to be effective, investigators must communicate their professional investigative needs to the witness. Witnesses must also communicate their knowledge of the crime to the investigator. Ineffective communication will lead witnesses to withhold valuable information or to provide irrelevant, imprecise or incorrect answers.

a) Promoting extensive, detailed responses

Police interviews require witnesses to describe people, objects and actions in more detail than civilians normally do in casual conversation. Inducing such an extraordinary level of description requires that police convey this goal explicitly, which they rarely do. To compound the problem, witnesses often withhold information because they do not know what is relevant for a police investigation. To minimize witnesses' withholding information, interviewers should instruct witnesses to report everything they think about, whether it is trivial, out of chronological order, or even if it contradicts a statement made earlier.

Police investigators generally direct witnesses to provide relevant information by asking many specific, short-answer questions about investigatively relevant topics, e.g., perpetrator's age, height, weight, clothing, weapon. (Fisher et al., 1987). This questioning style minimizes irrelevant information, but at the cost of (a) minimizing unsolicited, but relevant, information, (b) reducing the depth and precision of witnesses' responses, and (c) sometimes inducing incorrect responses. Rather than asking many specific, detailed questions interviewers should explicitly instruct witnesses on the importance of describing events in great detail.

b) Code-compatible output

Interviewers and respondents often exchange ideas using only the verbal medium. Some people, however, are more expressive non-verbally, and some events are better described non-verbally (Leibowitz and Guzy, 1990). Ideally the response format should be compatible with the witness's mental record of the event, thereby minimizing the need to transform the mental record into an overt response (Greenwald, 1970). If an event is inherently spatial, (e.g., the location of objects within a room) then witnesses should respond spatially, by drawing a sketch of the room or by placing model objects within a (model) room. As a general rule, encouraging witnesses to sketch out the crime scene should promote more extensive recall.

C. SEQUENCE OF THE COGNITIVE INTERVIEW

The CI follows a designated order intended to maximize the effectiveness of the individual techniques. The general strategy is to guide the witness to those memory records that are richest in relevant information and to facilitate communication when these mental records have been activated. The recommended questioning sequence, which is common to the Stepwise method (Yuille, Hunter, Joffe, and Zaparniuk, 1993) and the Memorandum of Good Practice (Home Office, 2002), is to progress from asking open-ended questions to more specific follow-up probes.

The CI is divided into five sections:

1. Introduction

The introduction establishes the appropriate psychological states and interpersonal dynamics to promote efficient memory and communication during the remainder of the interview. The interviewer attempts to (a) develop rapport with the witness, (b) convey his or her investigative needs for extensive, detailed information, and (c) encourage the witness to play an active role by volunteering information.

2. Open-ended Narration

The initial open-ended narration permits the interviewer to infer the witness's overall representation of the event and to develop an efficient strategy for probing the various memory records. The interviewer notes the witness's "mental images" of the crime (e.g., perpetrator, weapons), and develops a preliminary plan about which images to probe, in what order, and which questions to ask when probing each image. If the initial narrative is not interrupted, witnesses will convey a large portion of their total knowledge during this segment (e.g., Roberts and Higham, 2002).

3. Probing

In the probing stage, the interviewer guides the witness to the richest sources of knowledge ("mental images") and thoroughly exhausts these sources of their contents. The interviewer might direct the witness to close his or her eyes and to think about the best view he or she has of the perpetrator, and then to describe that image in extensive detail. Follow-up questions related to the image are asked to elicit additional information. Crime-relevant information that is not associated with a specific image (e.g., perpetrator's self-assurance or anxiety) is also gathered during the probing stage.

4. Review

Reviewing the information already notated allows the interviewer to check on its accuracy. It also provides the witness with an opportunity to recall additional information. During the review stage, the interviewer clarifies any uncertainties or discrepancies (e.g., contradictions) that occurred earlier in the interview. The interviewer should read his or her notes back to the witness at the end of the interview and ask the witness to (a) correct any errors or omissions in the interviewer's notes, and (b) inform the interviewer of any new recollections. The interviewer should also point out in a non-challenging way any ambiguities or contradictions within the witness's statement and ask the witness to clarify these matters, even if that means to indicate that the witness is not certain about the matter.

5. Closing

When closing the interview, the interviewer fulfills any official police requirements associated with the investigation, e.g., collecting background information about the witness. The interviewer should also encourage the witness to contact him or her several days later when the witness thinks of new information.

Although this is the conventional sequence, interviews invariably deviate from this plan, as unexpected information arises. Interviewers must be flexible to adapt to unexpected conditions. In that regard, the CI is more of a general guideline or a collection of tools than it is a recipe for conducting an interview.

D. EMPIRICAL TESTING OF THE COGNITIVE INTERVIEW

The CI has been examined in close to 100 laboratory tests, many of which were conducted in the United States, England, Germany and Australia. In these tests, volunteer witnesses (typically, but not always, college students) observe either a live, non-threatening event or a film of a simulated crime. Several hours or a few days later, the witnesses participate in a face-to-face interview, which is either the CI or a control interview. The control is either a "standard" police interview or a "structured interview" that incorporates generally accepted principles of interviewing minus those unique to the CI. The interviews are tape recorded, transcribed, and then scored for the number of correct statements and incorrect statements. Across these studies, the CI has typically elicited between 25 to 100% more correct statements than Standard or Structured interviews. The effect is extremely reliable: Of the 55 experiments in Koehnken Milne, Memon, and Bull's (1999) meta-analysis, 53 experiments found that the CI elicited more information than did the comparison interview (median increase 34"). Equally important, accuracy was as high or slightly higher in the CI interviews (accuracy rate = .85) than in the comparison interviews (.82). (for reviews, see Bekerian and Dennett, 1993; Fisher and McCauley, 1995 and Fisher and Schreiber, 2007).

1. Non-standard Witnesses

Since the late-1990s, many studies have examined whether the CI could be used effectively with children and other "non-standard" witnesses. In some of these studies, the experimental witnesses were young children (from 7-12 years of age: e.g., Geiselman and Padilla, 1988; Milne and Bull, 1996; Larsson, Granhag, and Spjut, 2003; McCauley and Fisher, 1995; Saywitz, Geiselman and Bornstein, 1992), in some studies, the witnesses were older people (Mello and Fisher, 1996; McMahon, 2000), and in some studies, the witnesses were young adults with learning disabilities or some other cognitive deficit (Milne, Clare, and Bull, 1999; Brown and Geiselman, 1990). The patterns of results are remarkably similar to those found with "normal" adults, namely, the CI elicits considerably more information than the control interview, and at comparable or slightly higher accuracy rates.

In addition to the laboratory studies, two field studies that examined interviews with victims and witnesses of real crime found the advantage of the CI to hold equally well. In Fisher, Geiselman, and Amador (1989), 16 experienced detectives from the Metro-Dade (Florida) Police Department tape recorded several interviews, mainly from victims or witnesses of purse snatchings or commercial robbery. The detectives then were divided into two equivalent groups based on their supervisors' evaluations and on their objective performance (number of statements elicited on the tape recorded interviews). One of the two groups received training on the CI, and the other did not. Although the two groups were comparable before training, the trained group of detectives elicited 63% more information than the untrained group after training. Furthermore, the trained detectives elicited 48% more facts after training than before training. Of the seven trained detectives, six improved dramatically (34 to 115%). Only the one detective who did not change his interviewing style failed to improve.

A parallel field study was conducted in England by George and Clifford (1992, 1996) in which experienced police investigators tape recorded interviews before and after training (or no training for some). The investigators' questioning styles changed dramatically as a result of CI training. Compared to the untrained group, and also to themselves before training, the CI-trained group (a) asked fewer questions, (b) asked a higher proportion of open-ended questions, (c) asked fewer leading questions, and (d) injected more pauses. These changes in questioning style were also accompanied by an increase in the amount of information elicited. The CI group elicited 55% more information after than before training, and 14% more information than did the untrained group.

In overview, the CI effect has been found repeatedly by different researchers, with different witness populations, and in a variety of settings. The CI elicits considerably more information than the typical police interview, and the accuracy of the information is as high as or slightly higher with the CI than with conventional police interviews.

E. PRACTICAL APPLICATION OF THE COGNITIVE INTERVIEW: POLICE INTERVIEWERS' FEEDBACK

Given the success of the CI in laboratory and field experiments, how does it fare in real-world investigations? Geiselman and Fisher (1997) reported several instances in which the CI was used successfully to solve real-world cases, ranging from a witness to a kidnapping, to a child molestation victim, to a witness of a politically motivated bombing. Recently, an investigator from the U.S. Bureau of Alcohol, Tobacco, and Firearms reported conducting an extended (3-day) CI with a 38-year-old woman who had witnessed a homicide as a 4-year-old child. The interview elicited many recollections, most of which were corroborated by police records established at the time of the crime (e.g., location of objects and furniture at the crime scene). We have also received some encouraging feedback from the National Transportation Safety Board, whose investigators received training on the CI and shortly thereafter conducted extremely effective interviews of crew members of the USS Greenville, the American submarine that collided at sea with a Japanese fishing boat in February, 2001. Of course, we recognize that these are merely anecdotes, which are subject to many biases. Offsetting these successes, British police reported that the complete CI was sometimes difficult to implement (Kebbell, Milne, and Wagstaff, 1999; Kebbell and Wagstaff, 1996). Officers interviewed by these researchers reported that they found it difficult to communicate some of the CI's mnemonic instructions to witnesses. Specifically, British police reported that they were uncomfortable to use — and only rarely did use — the Varied Retrieval and Imagery techniques. Other researchers have noted that officers in the field often do not use the cognitive interview mnemonics at all, or use only one or two of them (see George, 1991; see also Memon, Holley, Milne, Kohnken and Bull, 1994). Kebbell and Wagstaff (1996) note, however, that it may be possible to overcome these problems with suitable training.

Police officers interviewed about their experiences with the CI have also reported that using the complete CI often requires more time than is available (Fisher, Geiselman and Amador, 1989; Kebbell, Milne, and Wagstaff, 1999). In response to this practical concern, Davis, McMahon, and Greenwood (2005) set out to create a shorter version of the CI that would still capture most of the information gathered by the complete CI. Their laboratory-based research demonstrated that a pared-down version of the CI, deleting the Varied Retrieval technique, saved considerable time and yet was almost as effective as the complete CI. We find this a healthy development in the CI research, trying to make it more efficient and sensitive to real-world conditions.

F. LEGAL CONCERNS

Although the CI has been found reliably to enhance recollection, might it be unacceptable for forensic use? As with any innovative technique, we expect the CI to be challenged in the courts. On what grounds might it be challenged, and how well does it stand up to these attacks?

We can think of five possible lines of attack against the CI (cf. hypnosis, Wrightsman, 1987): (a) the CI may generate unreliable information; (b) it may render witnesses overly suggestible to leading or misleading questions; (c) it may alter the witness's confidence; (d) it may unduly influence the perceptions of decision-makers involved in the case; and (e) it may alter the effectiveness of ensuing interviews or other procedures conducted with the witness.

We can dismiss the first two concerns, as (a) we have already noted that CI-elicited recollections are as accurate or slightly more accurate than those from conventional interviews, and (b) we have shown elsewhere (Fisher, Brennan, and McCauley, 2002) that the CI does not render witnesses overly suggestible to leading questions. If anything, witnesses are less suggestible when interviewed with the CI. We focus now on the remaining arguments and then examine two legal cases in which the CI was at issue.

1. Witness Confidence

Even if the CI does not directly affect the testimony itself, it may elevate witnesses' confidence in their testimony, which might inflate their influence on various decision-makers (Cutler, Penrod, and Dexter, 1989; Cutler, Penrod, and Stuve, 1988; summarized in Cutler and Penrod, 1995). This would be particularly disturbing if witnesses were unduly confident after an incorrect recollection (cf. hypnosis, Sheehan and Tilden, 1983). Five experiments have examined the effects of the CI on witness confidence (measured either by self-rating scales or as inferred by trained judges). Of these, two experiments found no reliable differences in confidence between the CI and a control interview (Mello and Fisher, 1996; McCauley and Fisher, 1995); one found a slight increase in confidence for the CI, but this was a harmless effect, as it occurred only for correct responses — there was no difference for incorrect responses (Geiselman et al., 1984); one found a slight increase in confidence (Gwyer and Clifford, 1997); and one found a slight decrease in confidence for the CI (Koehnken, Schimmossek, Aschermann, and Hofer, 1995). On balance, the evidence appears to suggest that the CI does not unduly increase witnesses' confidence in their recollections.

2. Perceptions of Decision Makers

Thus far, all of the studies have examined the effect of conducting a CI on the witness's behavior or on the testimony itself. However, since the ultimate decision maker is someone other than the witness (e.g., police officer, attorney, juror, or judge), we also need to be concerned with their impressions. How do these decision makers perceive the CI and the resulting testimony? Do they assign either greater or lesser credibility to witnesses who have been interviewed with a CI?

Two recent studies examined these issues. Kebbell, Wagstaff, and Preece (1998) presented transcripts to jurors in a mock trial (burglary) and informed them that the witnesses' testimony was elicited either by an innovative technique (CI) or by a procedure typically used by British police (asking the witness to "try again" to recall additional information). The jurors were instructed about the various components of the CI. After reading the transcripts, the jurors answered several questions about the quality of the interviewing techniques. For our purposes, the critical questions focused on whether the techniques increased the likelihood of eliciting incorrect information and whether they should be used by the police. The jurors also made a guilty/not guilty verdict. The results showed that the jurors' evaluations of the CI and control techniques were indistinguishable on all dimensions, including verdict.

In a second study, participants actually listened to tape recordings (taken from an earlier CI experiment) of witnesses being interviewed with a CI or with a conventional police interview (Fisher, Mello, and McCauley, 1999). The listeners then rated the credibility of the witnesses on several dimensions (e.g., accuracy of memory, confidence, intelligence, trustworthiness). In two separate experiments, one in which the witnesses were children and the second in which the witnesses were adults, there were no differences in perceived credibility. These non-differences were apparently not due to insensitivity of the data, as other differences were observed: specifically, CI interviewers were perceived to be less manipulative than were conventional interviewers. This was a serendipitous finding, but, with the benefit of hindsight, not all that surprising given that CI interviewers ask fewer questions, ask fewer leading questions, and in general play a more passive role in the interview than do conventional interviewers. On balance, these results suggest that, if anything, the CI should be *more*, not less, acceptable as an interview procedure — assuming, of course, that it is desirable for an interviewer not to manipulate the witness's testimony.

3. Court Cases

We know of only two court cases, one in England and one in the United States, in which the CI was at issue. In *R v. Hill* (1995, as described in Milne, 1997, and Ray Bull, personal communication), which was heard by the National Court of Appeal in London, a convicted murderer claimed that he did not commit the crime, but that his friend did. The friend then participated in a CI interview and provided a very detailed account of the murder episode. The Court then received a report reviewing the published CI research written by the appellant's expert. Eventually, the Court overturned the original conviction, claiming that the (original) eyewitness evidence could have been mistaken. The Court did not mention the CI in its ruling, thus we do not know whether the Court viewed the CI favorably or unfavorably. The Court's decision, however, was compatible with the information elicited by the CI and incompatible with the original eyewitness testimony.

A second case entailed a pre-trial hearing in California, in which the defendant was charged with vehicular homicide (*People v. Tuggle*, 1995). Some of the evidence used by the prosecution had been elicited from witnesses by a police officer trained to use the CI. The defense attorney challenged the use of the CI, claiming that it was similar to hypnosis and that it promoted inaccurate eyewitness testimony. After listening to expert witnesses from both sides testify about the CI and related issues, the judge ruled against the defense's objection to the CI and permitted the CI-elicited testimony to stand.

Admittedly, these are only two cases, and we do not know if other cases will bring more potent arguments against the use of the CI. As matters stand now, though, the CI has not been challenged successfully, and CI-elicited testimony has been accepted by the courts.

We expect the CI to be challenged in the future by attorneys, simply because of their obligation to question any innovative procedure used by the opposition. In our thinking, challenges should be directed toward the specific components of the CI — a particular instruction given by the interviewer or a specific question — and not toward the technique as a whole. At some level, the CI is just a collection of individual techniques, and its acceptability should be based on the component techniques, not on whether the collection of techniques is unified under one label (the "Cognitive Interview"). Furthermore, a proper challenge needs to demonstrate that the offensive instruction or question had actually been implemented during the interview, and not merely that the interviewer was trained to use the technique or that the offensive technique was technically a component of the CI. This is critical because, in most cases interviewers use only a fraction of all the CI techniques (George and Clifford, 1992; Kebbell et al., 1999; Memon, Holley, Milne, Koehnken, and Bull , 1994). Finally, an effective challenge needs to present a compelling reason to believe that a particular CI technique promotes incorrect recollection. Of the techniques that are regularly used by CI-trained police interviewers in actual investigations (see George and Clifford 1992; Kebbell, et al., 1999) none are known to promote increased errors. Nevertheless, it will be interesting to see how challenges to the CI materialize in the future.

CONCLUSION

A myriad of studies over the past two decades have demonstrated clearly that the CI reliably enhances witness descriptions under a variety of event and test conditions. We think the next major areas of progress will be to (a) train investigators to learn the procedure more efficiently, (b) streamline the procedure so that police can use it more efficiently in field situations, where resources are often limited, (c) develop new component techniques to expand the CI, and (d) explore the CI's utility in other (non-criminal) investigations. To end this chapter on a positive note, we are happy to report that considerable progress has been made along these lines. For instance, Powell, Fisher and Wright (2005) explored various methods to improve training; Davis et al. (2005) have examined ways to streamline the interview for time-constrained situations; and Chapman and Perry (1995) have examined how the CI might be used to investigate a car accident. We encourage others to advance the interviewing research in similar directions.

REFERENCES

Anderson, R.C. and Pichert, J.W. (1978). Recall of previously unrecallable information following a shift in perspective. *Journal of Verbal Learning and Verbal Behavior, 17,* 1-12.

Baddeley, A. D. (1986). *Working memory.* Oxford: Oxford University Press.

Bartlett, F. C. (1932). *Remembering: A study in experimental and social psychology.* London: Cambridge.

Bekerian, D. A., and Dennett, J. L. (1993). The cognitive interview technique: Reviving the issues. *Applied Cognitive Psychology, 7,* 275-298.

Bekerian, D. A., and Dennett, J. L. (1997). Imagery effects in spoken and written recall. In D. Payne and F. Conrad (Eds.), *Intersections in basic and applied memory research* (pp. 279-289). Mahwah, NJ: Erlbaum.

Berresheim, A. and Weber, A. (2003). Die Strukturierte Zeugenvernehmung und Ihre Wirksamkeit [Structured witness interviewing and its effectiveness]. *Kriminalistik, 57,* 757-771.

Bransford, J. D. and Franks, J. J. (1971). The abstraction of linguistic ideas. *Cognitive Psychology, 2*, 331-350.

Brown, C. L., and Geiselman, R. E. (1990). Eyewitness testimony of mentally retarded: Effect of the cognitive interview. *Journal of Police and Criminal Psychology, 6*, 14-22.

Ceci, S. J. and Bruck, M. (1995). *Jeopardy in the courtroom: A scientific analysis of children's testimony.* Washington, DC: American Psychological Association.

Chapman, A. J., and Perry, D. J., (1995). Applying the cognitive interview procedure to child and adult eyewitnesses of road accidents. *Applied Psychology: An International Review, 44*, 283-294.

Collins, R., Lincoln, R., and Frank, M. G. (2002). The effects of rapport in forensic interviewing. *Psychiatry, Psychology and Law, 91*, 69-78.

Cutler, B. L., and Penrod, S. D. (1995). *Mistaken identification: The eyewitness, psychology, and the law*. New York: Cambridge University Press.

Cutler, B. L., Penrod, S. D., and Dexter, H. R. (1989). The eyewitness, the expert, and the jury. *Law and Human Behavior, 13*, 311-332.

Cutler, B. L., Penrod, S. D., and Stuve, T. E. (1988). Juror decision making in eyewitness identification cases. *Law and Human Behavior, 12*, 41-55.

Davis, M. R., McMahon, M., and Greenwood, K. M. (2005). The efficacy of mnemonic components of the cognitive interview: Towards a shortened variant for time-critical investigations. *Applied Cognitive Psychology, 19*, 75-93.

Fisher, R.P., Brennan, K.H., and McCauley, M.R. (2002). The cognitive interview method to enhance eyewitness recall. In M. Eisen, G. Goodman, and J. Quas (Eds.), *Memory and suggestibility in the forensic interview* (pp. 265-286). Mahwah, N.J.: Erlbaum.

Fisher, R. P. and Geiselman, R. E. (1992). *Memory-enhancing techniques in investigative interviewing: The cognitive interview*. Springfield, IL: C.C. Thomas.

Fisher, R.P., Geiselman, R.E. and Amador, M. (1989). Field test of the Cognitive Interview: Enhancing the recollection of the actual victims and witnesses of crime. *Journal of Applied Psychology, 74*, 722-727.

Fisher, R. P., Geiselman, R.E., and Raymond, D.S. (1987). Critical analysis of police interviewing techniques. *Journal of Police Science and Administration, 15*, 177-185.

Fisher, R. P., and McCauley, M. L. (1995). Information retrieval: Interviewing witnesses. In N. Brewer and C. Wilson (Eds.) Psychology and policing, Hillsdale, NJ: Erlbaum. (pp. 81-99).

Fisher, R. P., Mello, E., and McCauley, M. L. (1999). Are jurors' perceptions of eyewitness credibility affected by the cognitive interview? *Psychology, Crime and Law, 5*, 167-176.

Fisher, R. P., and Schreiber, N. (2007). Interviewing protocols to improve eyewitness memory. In M. Toglia, R. Lindsay, D. Ross, and J. Reed

(Eds.), *The handbook of eyewitness psychology: Volume One. Memory for events*. Mahwah, NJ: Erlbaum Associates, 53-80.

Geiselman, R. E, Fisher, R. P., Firstenberg, I., Hutton, L. A., Sullivan, S. J., Avetissian, I. V., and Prosk, A. L. (1984). Enhancement of eyewitness memory: An empirical evaluation of the cognitive interview. *Journal of Police Science and Administration, 12*, 74-80.

Geiselman, R. E., and Fisher, R. P. (1997). Ten years of cognitive interviewing. In D. G. Payne and R. G. Conrad (Eds.), *A synthesis of basic and applied approaches to human memory* (pp. 291-310). Hillsdale, NJ: Erlbaum.

Geiselman, R. E., and Padilla, J. (1988). Cognitive interviewing with child witnesses. *Journal of Police Science and Administration, 16*, 236-242.

George, R. C. (1991). A field evaluation of the cognitive interview. Unpublished Masters Thesis, Polytechnic of East London.

George, R. C. and Clifford, B. (1992). Making the most of witnesses. *Policing, 8*, 185-198.

George, R. C. and Clifford, B. R. (1996). The Cognitive Interview - Does it work? In S. Lloyd-Bostock and G. Davies (Eds.), *Psychology, Law and Criminal Justice: International developments in research and practice* (pp.146-154). Oxford: de Gruyter.

Gilbert, J. and Fisher, R. P. (2006). The effects of varied retrieval cues on reminiscence in eyewitness memory. *Applied Cognitive Psychology*, 20, 723-839

Greenwald, A. G. (1970). Sensory feedback mechanisms in performance control: With special reference to the ideo-motor mechanism. *Psychological Review, 77*, 73-99.

Gwyer, P., and Clifford, B. R. (1997). The effects of the cognitive interview on recall, identification, confidence and the confidence/accuracy relationship. *Applied Cognitive Psychology, 11*, 121-145.

Home Office (2002). *Achieving best evidence in criminal proceedings: Guidance for vulnerable or intimidated witnesses, including children*. London: Her Majesty's Stationery Office. (Also available on the World

Wide Web at <http://www.cps.gov.uk/publications/prosecution/bestevidencevol1.html> Access date January 31, 2005).

Kahneman, D. (1973). *Attention and effort*. Englewood Cliffs, NJ: Prentice-Hall.

Kebbell, M. R. and Milne, R. (1998). Police officers' perception of eyewitness performance in forensic investigations. *Journal of Social Psychology, 138*, 323-333.

Kebbell, M. R., Milne, R. and Wagstaff, G. F. (1999). The Cognitive Interview: A Survey of its Forensic Effectiveness. *Psychology, Crime and Law, 5*, 101-115.

Kebbel, M. R., and Wagstaff, G. F. (1996). Enhancing the practicality of the cognitive interview in forensic situations. *Psycoloquy, 7(16)*, witness-memory.3.kebbell.

Kebbell, M. R., and Wagstaff, G. F. (1997). Why do the police interview eyewitnesses? Interview objectives and the evaluation of eyewitness performance. *The Journal of Psychology, 131*, 595-601.

Kebbell, M. R., Wagstaff, G. F., and Preece, D. (1998). The effect of knowledge that testimony was elicited with a cognitive interview on jurors' judgments of guilt. *Psychology, Crime and Law, 14*, 17-25.

Koehnken, G., Milne, R., Memon, A., and Bull, R. (1999). The cognitive interview: A meta-analysis. *Psychology, Crime and Law, 5*, 3-27.

Koehnken, G., Schimossek, E., Aschermann, E., and Hofer, E. (1995). The cognitive interview and the assessment of the credibility of adults' statements. *Journal of Applied Psychology, 80*, 671-684.

Koriat, A., and Goldsmith, M. (1996). Monitoring and control processes in the strategic regulation of memory accuracy. *Psychological Review, 103*, 490-517.

Larsson, A. S., Granhag, P. A., and Spjut, E. (2003). Children's recall and the Cognitive Interview: Do the positive effects hold over time? *Applied Cognitive Psychology, 17*, 203-214.

Leibowitz, H. W., and Guzy, L. (1990). Can the accuracy of eyewitness testimony be improved by the use of non-verbal techniques? Paper presented at the American Psychology-Law Society, Williamsburg, VA.

Loftus, E.F. and Palmer, J.C. (1974). Reconstruction of automobile destruction: An example of the interaction between language and memory. *Journal of Verbal Learning and Verbal Behavior, 13*, 585-589.

McCauley, M. R., and Fisher, R. P. (1995). Facilitating children's recall with the revised cognitive interview. *Journal of Applied Psychology, 80*, 510-516.

McMahon, M. (2000). The effect of the enhanced cognitive interview on recall and confidence in elderly adults. *Psychiatry, Psychology and Law, 7*, 9-32.

Mello, E. W. and Fisher, R. P. (1996). Enhancing older adult eyewitness memory with the cognitive interview. *Applied Cognitive Psychology. 10*, 403-417.

Memon, A., Holley, A., Milne, R., Koehnken, G., and Bull, R. (1994). Towards understanding the effects of interviewer training in evaluating the cognitive interview. *Applied Cognitive Psychology, 8*, 641-659.

Milne, R. (1997). *Analysis and application of the cognitive interview. Volume 3: Discussion, References and Appendices.* Unpublished Ph.D. Dissertation, University of Portsmouth, Portsmouth.England.

Milne, R., and Bull, R. (1996). Interviewing children with mild learning disability with the cognitive interview. In N. Clark and G. Stephenson (Eds.), *Investigative and forensic decision making* (pp. 44-51). Leicester: British Psychological Society.

Milne, R., Clare, C. I. W., and Bull, R. (1999). Using the cognitive interview with adults with mild learning disabilities. *Psychology, Crime and Law, 5*, 81-99.

Paivio, A. (1971). *Imagery and verbal processes.* New York: Holt, Reinhart, and Winston.

Pecher, D., Zeelenberg, R., and Barsalou, L.W. (2003). Verifying different-modality properties for concepts produces switching costs. *Psychological Science, 14*, 119-124.

People v. Tuggle (1995).

Powell, M. B., Fisher, R. P., and Wright, R. (2005). Investigative interviewing. In N. Brewer and K. Williams (Eds.), *Psychology and Law: An empirical perspective* (pp. 11-42). New York: Guilford.

R. v. Hill (1995).

Roberts, W. T., and Higham, P. A. (2002). Selecting accurate statements from the cognitive interview using confidence ratings. *Journal of Experimental Psychology: Applied, 8*, 33-43.

Saywitz, K.J., Geiselman, R.E. and Bornstein, G.K. (1992). Effects of cognitive interviewing and practice on children's recall performance. *Journal of Applied Psychology, 77*, 744-756.

Schreiber, N., and Fisher, R. P. (2005). Police interviewing techniques: Types of questions, positive and negative techniques in a South Florida sample. Paper presented at the American Psychology-Law Society, La Jolla, CA.

Sheehan, P. W., and Tilden, J. (1983). Effects of suggestibility and hypnosis on accurate and distorted retrieval from memory. *Journal of Experimental Psychology: Learning, Memory, and Cognition, 9*, 283-293.

Tulving, E, and Thomson, D. M. (1973). Encoding specificity and retrieval processes in episodic memory. *Psychological Review, 80*, 352-373.

Wells, G. L. (1978). Applied eyewitness testimony research: System variables and estimator variables. *Journal of Personality and Social Psychology, 36*, 1546-1557.

Wrightsman, L. S. (1987). *Psychology and the legal system.* Belmont, CA: Brooks/Cole.

Yuille, J. C., Hunter, R., Joffe, R., and Zaparnuik, J. (1993). Interviewing children in sexual abuse cases. In G. S. Goodman and B. L. Bottoms (Eds.), *Child victims, child witnesses. Understanding and improving testimony* (pp. 95-115). New York: Guildford Press.

CHAPTER 3

Human Information Processing:

The Cognitive Influences that Shape the Construction of Testimony

Tom Williamson

The ideal purpose of an investigation is to seek the truth and as a result move from a state of uncertainty to one of certainty that a true account of what happened can be given. Information is the lifeblood of any inquiry and success or failure in satisfactorily resolving uncertainty will depend on the accuracy of the information acquired. An examination of the investigative process would reveal how information is collected and then worked on to turn it into intelligence, evidence or knowledge. The outcome of an investigation results from this process of construction and the "truth" that emerges from an inquiry is a constructed truth (Innes, 2006). The information obtained from victims (if they are still alive), witnesses and suspects is important in determining what is accepted as the truth. Despite recent advances in forensic science, such as the greater use of DNA, information obtained by investigators from interviews remains a primary means of progressing an inquiry. The courts are heavily dependent on the narrative that emerges from these interviews and, in adversarial systems of justice, on oral testimony at trial. Although considerable progress is being made in disseminating a wider knowledge of good investigative interviewing practice (see Williamson, 2006), there remain a number of problems that we shall address in this chapter which reflect a lack of understanding of the role of cognitive processes involved in the construction of our memory for events.

One problem is that investigators, lawyers and judges frequently receive no teaching on psychology as part of their training and so they remain in ignorance of some basic psychological processes regarding how the account is generated. This gap in their knowledge and understanding will affect their attitude towards interviewees, their decision-making and can affect the outcome of the investigation or trial leading on occasions to miscarriages of justice. If the object of an inquiry is to collect accurate and reliable information – and all too frequently this is not the objective, as investigators can be prone to "tunnel vision" (Cory, 2006), there is an additional problem. Memory for events is a very malleable process which means that the "truth" emanating from interviews is a process of construction. The encouraging news is that research points to ways in which investigators can improve their interviewing techniques through a better understanding of the processes that affect memory. Given the malleability of these processes the way in which testimony is collected needs to be treated with the same careful attention that we give to preserving trace evidence, such as fingerprints and DNA samples, from contamination (Wells, 1995).

In this chapter we will begin by considering the cognitive psychological processes involved in the construction of testimony and demonstrate that a greater understanding of these processes will lead to more effective investigations and better justice.

A. CONSTRUCTING TESTIMONY

1. From Experiencing an Event to Providing an Account

Human information processing is a term used to describe the whole process that leads to the identification and interpretation of sensory stimuli. It focuses on how information from the external world is processed to produce our conscious perceptions and guide our actions. It is assumed to include a sensory phase where the sensation is first registered, an interpretive phase, and a memory phase. This concept attempts to integrate sensation, perception and cognition within a common theoretical framework.

The study of sensation is concerned with the first contact between the organism and the environment such as how electromagnetic radiation (light) is registered by the eye. It involves looking at the physical structure of the sense organ in order to establish how sensory experiences are related to physical stimulation of receptor cells and their physiological functioning. These studies also investigate the subsequent psychological experience such as how we perceive brightness, colour or loudness and our conscious experience of objects such as, identifying the object, calculating how far away it is and how large it is. These studies explain how witnesses form a conscious representation of an event in their outside environment and how accurate that representation is.

One theoretical approach which may have originated with Helmholtz in 1867 is that the final conscious impression may involve combining a number of different factors to "construct" the final perception, and so they are called constructive theories (Coren, Ward and Ens, 2004: 8-11). The biological events which are triggered when our senses are stimulated occur almost simultaneously with the psychological process involved in interpreting the stimulus. One of the brain's most important features is that in addition to taking in information through the senses it is constantly sending messages back from its highest levels of interpretative processing to the earliest stages of sensory processing. It is now understood that many cognitive processes involve almost simultaneous bottom-up perceptual and top-down intellectual processing, that do not work in isolation. This means that the feedback system modifies the way sensory input is processed affecting how that which we become aware of is constructed and interpreted (Rolls 2000). It is this constructed and interpretive version of reality that is then stored in the memory of witnesses, that investigators have to rely on to establish the truth.

An example demonstrating the link between effective perceptual processes and cognition or intellectual functioning was demonstrated in one experiment that examined the assumed correlation between ageing and reduced intellectual functioning. People aged 25 to 103 years of age were tested on five different cognitive tests used to measure intelligence and then averaged into a composite "intellectual functioning" score. This demonstrated as expected the decrease in mental ability with age. However, if the effects of decreasing visual and hearing abilities of older people are taken into account the decline in mental ability with age is relatively small, indicating that it is the ageing sense organs that are not allowing the ageing mind to perform at the level of which it is capable (Baltes and Lindenberger, 1997).

Generally speaking our sensory modalities can be remarkably accurate and sensitive (Gallanter, 1962). These sensitivities vary across the species, with many species having far greater sensitivity than humans. Dogs can smell substances in concentrations 100 times lower than those that can be detected by humans. In this case, our relative lack of sensitivity is due to our having fewer olfactory receptors, by about a factor of 100, roughly 10 million receptors for humans versus 1 billion for dogs (Marshall, Blumer and Moulton, 1981). The German psychologist Gustav Teodor Fechner (1801-1887) assessed the sensitivity of the senses through experiments using the concept of the "absolute threshold" which is the minimum magnitude of a stimulus that can be reliably detected from no stimulus at all and which he described as lifting the sensation over the threshold of conscious awareness. These values were then used to measure the relationship between the physical magnitude of some stimulus, such as the physical intensity of light or sound, and the resulting psychological response that was experienced, such as how bright the light is or how loud the sound appears to be.

In deciding whether something makes it into conscious awareness there will be occasions where people report something when nothing is present. To take account of these variations in the accuracy of what is detected, a theory of "signal detection" has been developed, which acknowledges that any stimulus must be detected against a background of ongoing random noise in the environment. Correctly detecting a signal that is present is called a hit and a false alarm is the response of incorrectly responding yes when only noise but no signal is present. People process sensory information rather like that proposed in signal detection theory in that the brain often gets a "hit" by correctly identifying a signal but it can also incorrectly identify a signal. The cost of employing this type of discrimination when sensory information is processed and interpreted is that there will inevitably be false-alarms. There is an in-built frailty to human information processing. Examining the conditions under which these false-alarms occur can help us in understanding how information may be getting processed. A 20th century American psychologist, S.S. Stevens was able to demonstrate that there appears to be a law that the perceived psychological magnitude of a stimulus is a power function of its physical magnitude (Stevens, 1975).

There is also a trade-off between speed and accuracy in correct identification of sensory information. Where making a choice between a pair of stimuli is really more difficult than between another pair, the more difficult pair will result in both lower average response accuracy and longer average response times. This is relevant to the testimony of witnesses who may have had to make difficult discriminations about an event that has occurred quickly. The more information one has in order to make the discrimination and the longer one has to attend to it the more likely it is that the identification will be accurate. Making the right decision is always a problem when presented with a large number of possible alternatives.

Psychologists in the 1950s began to borrow from communication theory in order to better understand these identification problems (Shannon and Weaver 1949). They observed that whether the final decoded message reflects the original message depends on the ability of the system to transmit information without distortion which is what is meant by the fidelity of the system. When stimuli are presented to an observer through one of the sensory systems, and this information is then decoded in the central nervous system, the extent to which the identification corresponds to the actual stimulus will be affected by the ability of the sensory system to handle the stimulus input without distortion. Psychologists use the term veridical to mean accurate perception. Since people do not process sensory information using high fidelity channels of communication the possibility of error is inevitable and the account provided by a witness is unlikely to be entirely veridical.

Measuring the fidelity of a communications channel draws upon information theory where information is defined as the reduction of uncertainty and where uncertainty reflects our need to guess because we don't have enough information to be sure (Coren *et al.*, 37). Information theory goes some way to explaining why what reaches our consciousness is the product of a constructive process.

2. Visual and Auditory Neural Transmission Channels

The basic building block of the communication channels that make up our nervous system is a neuron. This is a single cell that can communicate in a binary (on/off) way with its neighbouring single cell structures using a combination of electrical and chemical means. When a neuron is unstimulated or at rest the inside is electrically negative to the outside. When a neuron is stimulated the electrical potential changes across the cell membrane in a process called depolarisation. The abrupt change in a cell's state is called an action potential and takes only a few milliseconds. The speed at which information can be transmitted along these neural communications channels can reach 120 metres per second.

Neural functioning has been examined in two ways. First, by examining the function of a single neuron usually using anaesthetised animals and microelectrodes inserted into the brain that allow changes in electrical activity in one brain cell to be recorded. The rate at which the cell responds to stimuli can then be monitored. When the firing rate increases with a specific stimulus it means that the neuron is being excited by that stimulus. Other stimuli may cause a decrease in the firing rate.

The second method of studying neural functioning is through examining the function of regions of the brain. Some of this research is conducted on animals which have undergone a lesion operation to remove neurons and supporting cells from the brain, but the results are often difficult to interpret. Similarly, one can observe changes in the behaviour of humans who have been involved in an accident in which some part of the brain has been destroyed. More recently there have been developments using modern technology that studies the functioning of the brain without being invasive. The electroencephalogram (EEG) measures electrical brain activity, called evoked potentials, in response to brief sensory stimuli that allows researchers to infer what part of the brain is most active during various tasks. Another technique involves the injection of a radioactive form of glucose which is the major fuel for brain activity. This is picked up by the part of the brain needing it for continued activity and this is monitored through positron emission tomography (PET) which allows maps to be developed of the regions of the brain that are active during certain tasks. We will now briefly consider how these various research methodologies demonstrate that the decoding of physical stimuli by the brain is a process of construction.

Our eyes contain light sensitive receptors. There are two types of photoreceptors in the eye; rods that are achromatic and help us in poor light conditions and cones that enable us to see colour. The eye conducts visual information to the brain along the optic nerve and we know from brain imaging techniques that parts of the brain begin to create visual maps that preserve relative distances and directions between points of light. There are estimated to be over 100 million neurons in the visual cortex of the brain. Single cell research has demonstrated that the cells appear to respond to particular stimuli such as a spot or the edge of an object (Hubel and Weisel, 1962). Various areas within the visual cortex of the brain have been studied and they appear to deal with creating maps for form and local movement; a map for colour; and a map for global motion. The brain needs to coordinate the information from these various maps that are being constructed, and different parts of the brain are involved in this process. It would appear that the parietal lobes have developed a system for establishing where an object is, and the temporal lobes a system for inferring what it is. In the upper regions of the temporal lobe neurons have been found with a remarkable degree of specificity. Neurons in this region in monkeys have been found to respond selectively to faces and the strongest responses are given to the most monkey-like faces (Bruce, Desimone and Gross, 1981).

Remember that the function of the visual system is *not* to re-create a veridical image of the outside world in the brain; it is not analogous to a video-recorder. Instead it processes the sensory information to form hypotheses that assist it to recognise objects, to locate them in space, and to assist the organism to respond appropriately to objects and events in its environment.

Auditory processing appears to be similar. Sound is a series of changes in the mechanical pressure in an elastic medium such as air and is the result of a wave of mechanical energy. The French scientist J.B.J. Fourier (1768-1830) proved that any periodic waveform can be represented by a set of simple sine (translated from Arabic for bosom) waves, sometimes known as Fourier components. Sounds can be analysed into their Fourier components. It transpires that the ear performs a mechanical Fourier analysis on complex sounds. To understand how this works we will consider the cochlea which fills a space of only two cubic centimetres in the ear but has over one million moving parts (Hudspeth, 1985). The ear is an extremely complex biological system. The cochlea, whose name means shell, is similar in appearance to a coiled snail-shell structure that contains two different types of hair cells with specialised functions. The outer ear channels sound waves into the ear canal until they encounter the eardrum that vibrates in phase with the incoming sound waves. The vibrations are transmitted to a mechanism in the cochlea by three tiny bones in the middle ear, the malleus (or hammer) the incus (or anvil) and the stapes (or stirrup). The stapes amplifies the soundwaves so that fainter sounds can reach the threshold of hearing. Inside the cochlea mechanical vibrations in the ear are changed into electrochemical fluctuations through a process of transduction which happens when the mechanical pressure causes the hair cells to bend. Each auditory neuron has a characteristic frequency for which its neural absolute threshold is lowest. Each neuron appears to be connected to a hair cell and to be involved in a process of tuning sounds (Liberman, 1982). There are principal regions of the cortex responsive to sound and they appear to be grouped into areas dealing with "what" and "where" subsystems (Rauschecker and Tian 2000). The findings that sound frequencies are spatially mapped into regions of the cortex has been confirmed in humans by using brain-imaging techniques (Cansino, Williamson and Karron, 1994). It has been suggested that there may be a similar common set of functional principles which underlies all primary sensory areas (Shamma, 2001).

The implications for investigative interviewers from the research on how people process sensory information means that the account provided by a witness will be constructed and affected by the conditions attending the event. They should consider the context including:

- Was the light poor or good when something was observed?
- How loud was any noise that was heard?
- How much time did the witness have to make observations?

- Were there many or few alternative explanations of what could have been observed?
- Does the witness suffer from any impairment in the senses, including hearing and sight?

3. Attention and Conscious Awareness

The account that a witness is able to provide will also be affected by the amount of attention that they paid at the time. In this section we will consider the theories and research evidence about how the brain attends to, selects and filters out information registered by the senses for further processing; how sensory perception gives rise to consciousness and how we process more sensory information than that of which we are consciously aware.

At any time our sensory organs are being bombarded with a vast amount of information from the environment. As we are normally not aware of all of this sensory information it would imply that the sensory systems and the brain have some mechanism to screen the incoming information. How the brain filters out some and selects other information to bring into our consciousness forms the area of psychological study known as "attention." When we attend to stimuli it is called the orienting response which is where our attention is drawn to a source of sudden change in our sensory world. For example, it is possible to identify and trace a persons eye movements when they orient towards an object. A practical application of this kind of research has been into weapon focus, that is, where a person pays rapt attention to a weapon in a scene. Victims of armed crime are often able to provide a detailed description of the weapon but seem to know relatively little about other aspects of the scene such as the appearance of the person holding the weapon. Laboratory experiments showed that eye fixations occurred on the critical object compared with the rest of the scene (Loftus, Loftus and Messo, 1987).

Filtering out information is necessary in order to allow us to concentrate on only one of many available sources of information. Although you could say that attention actually determines what reaches our conscious awareness (Taylor, 2002) it may make more sense to consider attention as selecting from among already conscious experiences those we will be able to report about and to which we can devote special processing (Lamme, 2003). Lamme implies that there is additional (visual) information about which we are unaware. Research studies have examined tasks that involve paying attention to a single event (focussed attention) or dividing it among several (divided attention), and more information appears to be retained if we are focussed on a single event.

Attention is multimodal. It can move within a modality say from one visual stimulus to another, or between modalities. Sudden stimuli in one modality can capture attention in another modality, for example, a pistol shot will capture our visual attention and this happens for all combinations of modalities that have been tested so far (Spence and Driver, 1997).

Overt orienting is the response to sudden changes in the environment accompanied by focussed attention on the event or object that elicited the reflex, whereas covert orienting refers to situations in which attention is focussed on a particular object or event but an overt orienting response is absent. A way of conceptualising covert orienting is attentional gaze or the "mind's eye" by which metaphor we can imagine that our attention can "gaze" independently of where our eyes are looking. The fact that our mind's eye or attentional gaze can be shifted without accompanying eye or head movement suggests that there are two systems working. Studies have shown that attentional gaze can reach a stimulus much faster than the eye (Remington, 1980). Three aspects of attentional gaze are important in processing sensory information. Attention may be described as having a locus, an extent and a detail set. When attention is focussed at a particular place, processing is better. The extent of the area over which attention is spread can be changed, and processing efficiency is less the greater the area over which attention is spread. Research into the detail set seems to suggest that observers can focus selectively on either the more global aspects or the relatively smaller aspects of the stimuli. Presented with a large stimulus made up of smaller distinct components, attention can either be directed to the large figure or to its smaller components. When focussed on one level of detail processing features in the other is poorer as in weapon focus (Hoffman, 1998).

Filtering sensory information occurs when we exclude information except that which relates to the spatial location or object that we are attending to. A well known example relating to auditory attention is the "cocktail party" effect, first described by Cherry in 1953, which is where the sounds of many voices bombard our ears yet we are able to pick out one voice and attend to it (Cherry, 1953). We may hear a number of conversations around us but remember little of what we do not attend to. This is known as selective listening and occurs in the early stages of recognition and after the message's meaning has been determined. This has been studied using a technique called shadowing where information is presented to the observer through two channels, for example, both ears, and the observer has to attend to and follow and repeat the information presented in just one channel. In one experiment where a powerful stimulus such as the observers name is presented in the unshadowed ear, it was only detected by 34% of the listeners (Wood and Cowan, 1995). Similar results have been found in an experiment where observers were shown a film of two different teams playing basketball with either a woman with an umbrella walking across the floor or someone in a gorilla suit. Even when the gorilla had stopped and thumped its chest, many viewers failed to notice its presence (Simons and Chabris, 1999). Quite dramatic stimuli can pass by unnoticed if attention is directed elsewhere. This has been called unattentional blindness (Mack and Rock, 1998). It means that although a witness may categorically deny observing an aspect of an event, that aspect may still have occurred.

A similar phenomenon is where a scene is presented for a brief period followed by a blank and then the original scene is represented with something missing, such as a picture of an aircraft with one engine missing. The sequence is repeated until the observer notices the missing item. Unless attention alights on the engine that is missing, the change is not apparent to the observer although they will have physically processed the same sensory information and so "seen" it. This has led researchers to argue that much of our visual experience is not as solid as it seems. Attention may act to solidify only a part of a rather volatile and dynamic representation of the world and only as long as that part is attended to. According to this view, attention is not filtering out unattended material, rather, it is giving life to the material which is attended to (Rensink, 2002). Divided attention tasks become easier with extensive practice. A skilled typist can type at a high rate and shadow a message at the same time with almost no loss of efficiency at either task (Shaffer, 1975). Automatic processing requires less attention than does controlled processing allowing more attention to be allocated to the less automatic skill.

A major part of maintaining attention is the degree of physiological arousal that gives us the feeling of concentrating whenever we want to be vigilant. The relationship between arousal and performance is demonstrated by the well-known Yerkes-Dodson law (Yerkes and Dodson, 1908). Overall performance of any task peaks at an intermediate level of arousal. The level is lower for difficult tasks, which suggests that difficult tasks are best performed under low levels of arousal.

Our past experience enables us to prepare and predict when an important stimulus event may take place. We use our experience to create an expectancy about the event, and we prepare for the event by aligning our attention with the location and timing of the anticipated event. Detection of sounds is more difficult if they are not what was expected, for example, where they are not of the expected frequency, so that a low pitched male voice may not be detected when a higher pitched female voice was expected (Scharf et al., (1987).

The divided attention experiments seem to suggest that there are attentional resources that can be used up by a task. If there is more demand than resources, performance suffers. Events are often sudden and cause the observers to orient their attention to a particular location and, therefore, they may not be able to supply other vital information needed by the investigator as they may not have attended to it. We should note that much of our visual experience is not as solid as it seems. Attention may act to solidify only a part of a rather volatile and dynamic representation of the world, and only as long as that part is attended to. Therefore, matters of particular interest to an investigator may have been missed by the witness. The investigative interviewer can address the issues raised by the attention research by considering the following:

- What was the orienting event that attracted the witness's attention?
- Did it receive the witness's focussed attention?
- Or, did the witness have to cover a wide area and take in a lot of information quickly in which case detailed information may have been lost?
- What else was happening that would have distracted the witness and meant that they had to divide their attention?
- Did attention fluctuate between two or more events which would result in only partial processing of sensory information?
- What was the witness thinking about, or their "mind's eye" attending to, at the time?
- Was the witness consciously filtering out anything, e.g., background noise, other conversations?
- If the witness's attention was directed elsewhere could this account for them missing relevant and even dramatic aspects (unattentional blindness)?

- How aroused was the witness feeling at the time; under or over arousal affects performance?
- Was the arousal associated with negative emotion?
- Has the witness experienced the event before and if so what was their expectation of what was going to happen next? Could the anticipated event have influenced the account they gave?

4. Conscious Awareness

We will now examine how perception gives rise to consciousness and whether unconscious perception is possible. We can start by distinguishing between conscious and unconscious states, such as between being awake and being asleep. Even this neat distinction is complicated by the existence of ambiguous states such as sleeping, sleepwalking and hypnosis. A working definition is that consciousness includes everything that you can report about your world and your experience at any moment in time.

We are not aware for most of the time of information coming to us through our sensory receptors. For example, when reading this sentence you were probably not consciously aware of the weight of your body resting in your chair, but as soon as your attention is drawn to it, you immediately do become aware of it. As we do not go through the world aware of the gaps in our conscious perception we have an illusion of complete perception. William James, described our constantly changing perceptions using the metaphor of a "stream of consciousness" (James, 1890). James argued that the stream of consciousness is made up of substantive states that occur where our consciousness is occupied with a perceptual object or even a thought, and transitive states when our consciousness is in a state of change but we are not aware of any particular object or thought. James considered that consciousness was a process not a "thing." A later psychologist, Block, considered that there were four different types of consciousness. First, access consciousness, which is where the mental contents of consciousness are available for either report or other actions. Secondly, phenomenal consciousness, which refers to our psychological experience of the stimuli, such as the particular colour, sound, taste, smell or type of pain. Thirdly, monitoring consciousness that occurs when our thoughts about these experiences are distinct from the experience itself. Fourthly, self-consciousness is the awareness of your "self" that is distinct from the rest of the world (Block, 1995).

Experimental methods demonstrate that our conscious awareness of a situation can change even though there are no changes in the stimuli that are reaching our sensory receptors. One method of examining this alternating consciousness is binocular rivalry. The view from each eye is slightly different because the eyes are separated by a few centimetres and so view the world from different angles. Perceptual mechanisms integrate these two slightly different views resulting in a single view in consciousness with stereoscopic depth perception. If the two views are very different such as horizontal stripes to the left eye and vertical stripes to the right eye, the brain refuses to merge the two views. Instead the two eyes seem to fight for control of consciousness. The view of one eye will be dominant and visible in consciousness, while the other eye's view will be suppressed. Then the views will switch over. This is called binocular rivalry. The amount of time that a stimulus is in view can be affected by its psychological strength. In one experiment subjects were presented with faces that had strong emotions (especially negative emotions) to one eye, and a face that had neutral or weak emotions to the other eye, the face with the stronger emotions was visible more of the time (Coren and Russell, 1992).

Other experiments have shown that the fluctuations in consciousness may have nothing to do with binocular rivalry but depend instead on the information we posses at the time to interpret what we are seeing. This can be demonstrated through using multistable figures which are representations that can have different interpretations. If individuals look at a stimulus and find that there is a consistent interpretation in consciousness, even though the figure is multistable, ambiguous, or reversible, there will be no fluctuations in consciousness. However, if they are informed that there is an alternative way of seeing the figure then attention will begin to redistribute over the figure and bring into focus new details and construct a new representation that will begin to fluctuate in consciousness. The brain appears to be actively interpreting the physical stimuli in order to form some sort of sensible working hypothesis.

Other experiments have addressed the question of whether there is perception without conscious awareness. These have involved experiments where one stimulus is masked or blocked by the introduction of another one. If a stimulus is masked and we are not consciously aware of it, then no information from the stimulus should be available to influence our subsequent behaviour. In experiments where the duration of the first word presented to subjects and the timing of the masking stimulus made the first word virtually unidentifiable, it was found that there was an influence from the unconscious prime word. For example, if the prime word was meaningfully related to the target word (e.g., prime = dog, target = puppy) participants were able to identify the word more rapidly than when the prime word was unrelated in meaning (e.g., prime = sky, target = puppy). This suggests that perceptions do not have to be conscious to have an influence on our actions.

Other experiments of this kind have been used to demonstrate that the information from unseen prime stimuli do make their way into the brain and influence behaviour despite the fact that there is no conscious awareness of it. It transpires that what directs our attention and so determines what is in consciousness can be a stimulus that never makes it into consciousness itself. Patients with a lesion in the right parietal lobe in the brain can detect a stimulus in their left visual field when it is presented alone, but if it is presented at the same time as another stimulus in their right visual field, they are no longer conscious of the stimulus in the left field. When information is presented to the neglected visual field that patients claim to be unaware of, they respond more quickly to a target even though they are not consciously aware of it. The consciously unseen stimulus seems to be still influencing behaviour. In experiments subjects are asked to look at an illuminated target and then touch it with their hand. On some trials the target is flashed on and then, just as the eye has begun to move, the target is displaced to another location. Although the subject is consciously unaware that the target has moved, they make quick corrective eye movements suggesting that the information was registered, and even more revealing, the arm movements took the displacement into account and helped the subject to accurately reach the target, even though the observer was consciously unaware that the target had moved from one place to another (Fectau et al., 2001).

Further evidence of this kind of active unconscious processing comes from studies with patients who have suffered from brain damage, who demonstrate a phenomenon known as blindsight, in which a person can act appropriately towards visual objects even in the absence of any perceptual awareness of aspects of these objects or even of their existence. One patient could not name objects or provide a report of their physical attributes, yet when asked to perform visually guided actions toward the object, she could do so correctly. If she was asked to indicate the size of a block from a distance by using her thumb and forefinger to indicate its dimensions, her indicated dimensions were unrelated to its actual dimensions. However, if asked to reach out and grasp the block, she was able to reach the correct distance and to position her thumb and fingers appropriately to pick it up. If she had used the dimensions she had indicated originally she would have been unable to grasp the block correctly (Weiskrantz 1986: 1997). Consciousness works to integrate perceptual information and construct a global interpretation. It combines all of the information from the various sensory streams and various locations in the brain to resolve conflicts that might arise between different processes and to construct a global hypothesis as to the objects, and what relationships among objects are (Baars, 1997). Consciousness seems to be the glue that makes sense of all this electrical and chemical neuronal activity, and the picture that is constructed is the perceptual universe we inhabit.

A witness should only be able to provide an account about what was registered in their consciousness. It may be the case that other sensory information was processed at an unconscious level, but it is not clear whether or how this information could be accessed. More research is needed. The result is that we have to concentrate on what can be recovered from the conscious experience stored in memory.

B. WORKING MEMORY AND LONG-TERM MEMORY

The purpose of this section is to provide knowledge and understanding of how memories are formed and demonstrate that they are the result of an active process of construction that can be explained by the concept of working memory which is an active cognitive process that integrates and interprets information from sensory stores.

Research on human memory began to blossom in the late 1950s as psychologists began to examine the organisation of memory and propose memory models. They frequently found that material was altered during memory, for example, by people's previous knowledge. Behaviourist principles such as "reinforcement" could not explain these alterations (Bargh and Fergusson 2000). At this time researchers began speculating that human thought processes could be understood as analogous to communication and computer science which led to the development of the information processing approach (Palmer 1999). It was considered that mental processes can best be understood by comparing them with the operations of a computer and that a single mental process can be interpreted as information progressing through the system in a series of stages, one step at a time (Groome, 1999).

It was originally considered that memory can be broken down into three discrete stages; encoding, storage and retrieval (Melon 1963). Encoding is when environmental information is translated into and stored as a meaningful entity. The storage stage is where this information is maintained over time. The third stage, retrieval, is where an attempt is made to pull from memory information that was previously encoded and stored.

The three memory stores were described in a theory put forward by Atkinson and Shiffrin as the basis of different memories corresponding to different time intervals, and it achieved such an outstanding level of popularity and influence that it became known as the "modal model" (Atkinson and Shiffrin, 1971). According to this model, stimuli from the environment first enter a sensory memory store which records information from each of the senses with considerable accuracy, but this highly accurate (veridical) record, degrades very quickly. Research into visual sensory memory (iconic memory) or auditory sensory memory (echoic) demonstrated that the information is stored for 2 seconds or less and then most of it is forgotten. The model proposed that some information from the sensory store passes on to what was called short-term memory the function of which is to contain the small amount of information that we are actively working on. Memories held in the short-term memory store are fragile and can be lost within 30 seconds unless the information is rehearsed by repeating it. Information that has been rehearsed passes on to long-term memory that has an enormous capacity. It contains all our memories acquired during our existence. Information stored here is relatively permanent. The model dominated memory research for many years but its influence has diminished, as have information processing models to an extent since research has indicated that more complex models are required to account for human thinking.

More recently the short-term store in which information is attended to, has been called working memory which appears to have two distinct stores, a phonological buffer storing acoustic information and a visual-spatial sketch pad storing visual or spatial information (Baddeley, 1986, 1990). Baddeley realised from the extensive research on short-term memory that the researchers had overlooked an important question which was, "what does short-term memory accomplish for our cognitive processing?" The major function of working memory was to hold several interrelated bits of information in our mind, all at the same time, so that this information could be worked with and then used. Hence, the expression "working memory" was coined by Alan Baddeley and his colleague Graham Hitch (Baddeley and Hitch, 1974). The working memory approach proposes that our immediate memory is part of a system that temporarily holds and manipulates information as we carry out cognitive tasks. In its current design the model consists of the phonological loop, the visuospatial sketchpad, a central executive and the episodic buffer, a feature that was added more recently to function as an integrative component (Baddeley, 2001b).

Perhaps the most striking aspect of working memory is that it is very limited in capacity, most normal adults have a capacity of seven items, or chunks of information plus or minus two items (Miller, 1956; Baddeley, 2000). A chunk is a grouping of several components that are strongly associated with each other, for example, your area telephone code. Cowan has argued that without chunking, the real capacity of short-term memory is only four plus or minus one (Cowan, 2001).

In order to study the capacity of short-term memory, subjects were asked to study three letters and then count backwards for a short period that prevented people from rehearsing the stimuli. These studies demonstrated that after a 5-second delay people had forgotten approximately half of what they had seen and after 18 seconds about 80 per cent of what they had seen which demonstrated the fragility of material stored for just a few seconds. Another technique demonstrated that there was a serial position effect in that people had a better recall for items at the end of the list which was called the recency effect, and to a lesser extent better recall for items at the beginning of the list called the primacy effect. Capacity was also influenced by the acoustic properties of the stimuli. These studies provided support for a cognitive approach to the study of memory and to human information processing models (Bower, 2000), but it also highlights the difficulties that witnesses may experience in providing an accurate account. In particular, it shows the impossibility of being able to provide an accurate verbatim account of a conversation either had or heard.

Research into the capacity of working memory showed that it was influenced by the pronunciation time. People are better at recalling items they can pronounce within 1.5 seconds. People could accurately recall an average of 4.2 words from a list of countries with short names, but only 2.8 words from a list of countries with long names. This was also tested using numbers in four different languages. The names for English numbers can be spoken rapidly whereas Spanish, Hebrew and Arabic take longer and have more syllables. The number of items recalled was greater in English than in the other languages (Naveh-Benjamin and Ayers, 1986).

There is also a semantic similarity effect in that the meaning of words can have an effect on the number of items that can be stored in working memory. If people are given a list to remember and then asked to recall other similar items in that category they have great difficulty in recall because the new lists appear to interfere with what is in memory, but if they are presented with information from a different semantic category, they have a higher recall (Wickens et al., 1976). Baddeley and Hitch proposed that working memory is not a passive storehouse but a process where new material is constantly being worked on and transformed. It holds both new material and draws on old material that has been accessed from storage in long-term memory. When they asked subjects to perform a mental reasoning task (rehearsing a list of up to eight items) and simultaneously a spatial reasoning task the subjects performed well on both tasks indicating that they may have been using different processes, one involving verbal rehearsal and one that required spatial judgements. It was concluded that working memory was not unitary and four components for working memory were proposed (Baddeley, 2000c). The phonological loop stores a limited number of sounds for a short period of time. The pronunciation time effect can be explained by the fact that it appears to have a limited capacity. People also confuse similar sounding letters and numbers. Research using brain-imaging techniques has shown that the phonological tasks are associated with the frontal lobe and the temporal lobe in the left hemisphere of the brain (Baddeley, 2000c).

The visuospatial sketchpad stores visual and spatial information but also stores visual information that has been encoded from verbal stimuli; for example, when we are being told a story and start to visualise the scene. This is an important finding as witnesses may subsequently confuse what they have seen and what they have visualised contrary to what they were told. Like the phonological loop the capacity of the visuospatial sketchpad is limited. It is very difficult to conduct two visuospatial tasks simultaneously (Baddelely, 1999). Most real world tasks involve utilising spatial and visual components, and the notion of an episodic buffer is proposed as a temporary storehouse where we can gather and combine information from the phonological loop, the visuospatial sketchpad and long term memory. This enables us to interpret the new information in the context of our earlier experiences and to solve problems and plan future activities. It has a limited capacity.

The central executive, as the name implies, plays a critical role in the overall functions of working memory; it plans and coordinates, but does not store information. It has a limited ability to work on two things at once. The various components in working memory function in ways that are complex, flexible and strategic and more elaborate than envisaged in the earlier short-term memory models (Baddeley, 2001a). Working memory appears to be related to verbal fluency and language skills. Rosen and Engle divided students into two groups depending on their performance on tests of working memory. Those with a high working memory score were able to list 50% more items than those with a low working memory score (Rosen and Engle, 1997). Other studies have examined the ability of certain people who have expanded their memory span. One subject who has been studied had a memory span for about 80 numbers. Researchers found that he had devised strategies for remembering the numbers such as turning one string of numbers into the time for an athletics world record (Ericsson and Delaney 1998).

The investigative interviewer wanting to maximise the activities that took place in working memory will wish to consider the following:

- How many things was the witness trying to remember?
- Was the witness able to "chunk" together the information into something meaningful, bearing in mind that without chunking there may be a limit of between four and nine items that can be stored in memory?
- What was the first thing the witness noticed?
- What was the last thing the witness noticed?
- Were short or long words used?
- What acoustic or semantic confusions could have arisen in what was remembered?
- Is the witness providing an account of what they have observed or of their memory of what they have been told?
- Did the witness have any mnemonic strategies for remembering important information such as relating it to some other fact that they knew?
- Did the witness rehearse the information and could this rehearsal have led to acoustic or semantic confusions?
- How much effort did the witness put into organising the information to be remembered and did they have an organising strategy?

1. Long-term Memory

Long-term memory may not be distinct from working memory. Long-term memory has attracted a considerable amount of research and one system divides it into episodic memory, semantic memory and procedural memory (Tulving, 2002). Episodic memory retains memories of events which you have experienced and it allows us to travel back and re-experience these events or episodes whether they were recent or a long time ago. Our semantic memory describes how our knowledge of the world is organised, including knowledge about words and factual information. Procedural memory describes the information that enables us to do things like walk or ride a bicycle or drive a car.

One influential theory of encoding suggests that it can vary according to the depth at which it was processed. This approach was developed by Craik and Lockhart and argues that deep, meaningful information processing will lead to more permanent retention than shallow sensory kinds of processing (Craik and Lockhart, 1972). People are three times more likely to recall a word if they had originally answered questions about its meaning rather than if they had answered questions about the word's physical appearance. Numerous reviews of deep processing research studies have shown that it generally produces better recall than shallow processing (Lockhart, 2001). Deeper processing occurs if one item to be recalled is different from other memory traces. Another factor is the amount of elaboration which requires rich processing of the stimuli in order to establish meaning and interconnected concepts. A third factor that has been studied has been called self-referencing which is where we remember more information if we can relate it to ourselves in some meaningful way. Subjects are asked to remember items in terms of either the word's visual characteristics, sound characteristics, meaning or how the word could be applied to themselves. Recall was poor for the items that involved shallow sensory processing of visual or acoustic properties but better when processed in terms of its meaning, and by far the best recall was when it could be self-referenced. The self-referencing system appears to handle positive information better than negative information. The self-referencing effect observed in over 129 studies appears to be very robust (Symons and Johnson, 1997). Shallow processing of faces like shallow processing of words leads to poor recall (Sporer, 1991). Deeper processing leads to encoding a greater number of features and so to superior recall.

In one experiment subjects were asked to imagine words spoken by a familiar person. Some subjects had to remember words spoken by a female and the other to remember words spoken by a male. Recall was later tested by having either a male or female speaker say each word and respondents had to indicate whether it was old or new. Some subjects had a match between the gender of the speaker and their imagined voice and for others it was a mismatch. Recognition was substantially more likely when the contexts were congruent (Geiselman and Glenny, 1977). Encoding specificity is strong in real life, including long delay situations where we can recall experiences that we had many years previously (Roediger and Guynn, 1996). It is also possible that physical context reinstatement may not be as important as mental context and may depend on how similar the environments feel rather than on how similar they look (Eich, 1995). Moscovitch and Craik found that people recall more if the retrieval conditions match the encoding conditions (Moscovitich and Craik, 1976). Therefore, it is possible that the encoding specificity may override the effect of levels of processing. We also recall more if our mood during encoding matches our mood during retrieval. Some studies have also shown mood congruence – that subjects in a pleasant mood remember pleasant material better than unpleasant material, and a person in an unpleasant mood should remember unpleasant material better (Fiedler, 2001; Schwatrz, 2001). Mood dependent memory studies have examined where the mood during encoding matches the mood during recall. It appears to be a weaker phenomenon than mood-congruence but may be stronger where the stimulus material relates to real life events (Urcos, 1989). The more we organise the material we encode the easier it is to retrieve. It is easier to retrieve a fact or episode if you are in the same context when you encoded it. We tend to rehearse emotionally charged events which can improve retrieval from long-term memory. But a caveat needs to be added since repeating the story over and over can give rise to elaboration of the account (Bartlett, 1932). Retrieval can also be affected by anxiety. When people experience a frightening situation giving rise to signs of panic it is very difficult to retrieve even very familiar information. Researchers have also studied people who have expertise in a particular area and there appears to be a strong correlation between knowledge about an area and memory performance in that area, although people who are expert in one area do not demonstrate outstanding general memory skills or have high scores on tests of intelligence (Matlin op cit: 149).

Eliciting information held in long-term memory will be helped if the investigative interviewer considers:

- How deeply did the witness think about the event to be remembered?
- Was the witness able to make sense of the event?
- Could the event be related to themselves in a meaningful way?
- Was the information positive or negative?
- Was the context of the event congruent or incongruent?

- Does the context help the witness to recall the experience?
- Can the witness recall how the context felt at the time? If the encoding and retrieval contexts match, the witness may be able to remember more.
- What was the witness's mood at the time and can this be recreated?

2. Remembering and Forgetting

Forgetting occurs because items decay over time or are replaced with new items. It is often difficult to know whether forgetting from long-term memory is due to a loss of storage (it is no longer there) or a failure in retrieval (it still exists but we cannot retrieve it). Retrieval can be affected by interference, which occurs when we try to use a cue to retrieve one item, and other items become active and interfere with our recovery of the target item. Forgetting is a function of time. A lot is forgotten within the first few hours, but after that the rate of forgetting slows down (Ebbinghaus, 1885; Bahrick and Phelphs, 1987). Research studies have involved two types of memory tasks: explicit, where a recall test requires the participants to reproduce items learned earlier, and an implicit memory task, where the stimuli are presented but subjects are then instructed to complete a cognitive task that does not directly ask them to recall or recognise the stimulus material. When subjects are asked to remember meaningless shapes a month afterwards, they can do so when measured using an implicit memory task even though they are unable to do so on explicit memory tasks. The stimuli presented earlier help them to perform better and demonstrate that the effects of our previous experience creep into our ongoing behaviour, even when we are not making a conscious effort to recall the past (Roediger, Marsh and Lee, 2002).

Another area that has been studied is autobiographical memory, which is memory for events related to ourselves. These studies have been particularly interested in the accuracy of the information recalled. Our memories for events are constructed at the time of retrieval and memories can be shaped to become more consistent with our current hypothesis. "Flashbulb" memories, a term which has been used to describe memory for events, such as a political assassination, that are very surprising and emotionally arousing, appear to be rich in content with people reporting clear memories of the event. Although people claim that their memory for the event is very vivid and they are very confident in the accuracy of their memory, the accuracy is far from perfect. In one study subjects were asked to report specific details of how they had learned about the terrorist attacks of September 11, 2001. They were also asked for information regarding an ordinary event that happened at the same time. Subjects were then tested either one week later, 6 weeks later or 32 weeks later. When the number of consistent and inconsistent details was counted it showed that the number of consistent details declines over time and that the number of inconsistent details rises for both types of memory, ordinary event and so-called flashbulb memory of the terrorist attacks. The subjects however reported that they were highly confident in their recall being accurate (Talarico and Rubin, 2003). The fact that these memories seem particularly vivid can be explained in part by frequent rehearsal and elaboration and so are not different kinds of memory. One way in which these memories can be shaped is through schemas which consist of our general knowledge or expectation of a particular event, which is distilled from our past experiences and provides a framework for summarizing important characteristics of the event. People sometimes experience what has been called a "feeling of knowing" when they have tried to recall a particular piece of information. There is a sense that it is lying in consciousness, we may even have a sense of the size of the word and know that we would recognise the word if we were supplied with it. We are likely to have a strong sense of feeling of knowing if we can retrieve a large amount of partial information (Schwarts and Perfect, 2002).

Various interviewing methodologies have been developed to help access information that is thought to lie buried in memory (see Fisher and Geiselman, 1992). In particular, investigators often believe that this information can be accessed using hypnosis, a technique that is used by some investigative interviewers.

3. Hypnosis

One immediate problem is that the public perception of what hypnosis is, perpetuated in the media, of a sleep-like trance in which people can transcend their normal waking capacities, either physical or mental, is just wrong. Hypnosis has been studied by psychologists for generations and has been at the centre of long-standing disputes which turned on whether hypnosis was actually a condition in which there were profound alterations to the subject's state, or whether the notion of hypnosis as an altered state of consciousness can be rejected since the so-called "hypnotic" phenomena are explicable by reference to ordinary psychological processes. An example of the state approach is "dissociation" theory – that as a result of entering into a hypnotic state the subject surrenders some of the normal control they have over their experiences, and in response to suggestion, phenomena such as movements of limbs are experienced as involuntary; pain is reduced; and memory and perception are distorted so that hallucinations become perceived as real.

Non-state theorists believe that people participating in hypnosis may be relaxed but there is no special state of "hypnosis." There is less of a gap between these two approaches as those who have adopted a dissociationist perspective now place less emphasis on a hypnotic state (Kirsch and Lynn, 1995). To test the state versus non-state hypotheses, researchers have compared the performance of two groups across a range of tasks, those who had been through hypnotic induction procedures and control groups that did not participate in the hypnotic procedures but that have been encouraged to relax, try harder or imagine. These studies have shown that hypnotic subjects are active and not passive, helpless automatons possessing abnormal powers. Instead, they have demonstrated that the non-hypnotic control groups can equal or surpass the hypnotic groups in feats of strength and tolerance of pain. There is now much less debate on hypnosis as some kind of transcendental state (Wagstaff 1996a, 1999).

Nevertheless the idea that hypnosis could provide additional information to assist in an investigation is an enduring one, and one to which forensic hypnosis experts subscribe (Haward, 1988). Others have argued strongly that any attempt to improve the memory of a witness through hypnosis should render that witness incompetent to testify. This ban has been introduced in several states in the United States (Laurence and Perry, 1988). Studies have been conducted on age regression, where through hypnosis subjects are able to recall events from childhood, apparently with amazing accuracy. This was tested by directing some subjects to fake hypnosis which found that their performance was indistinguishable from the hypnotic subjects. The phenomenon of age regression, including regression to past lives says more about the subject's imagination than powers of memory (O'Connell, Shor and Orne, 1970). There is now an overwhelming body of experimental evidence to show that hypnotic procedures do not improve the accuracy of memory to a level above that which is achievable in motivated non-hypnotic conditions. Although there may be an increase in recall for correct items by those that have gone through hypnotic induction processes, there is also an increase in incorrect responses. It may be that hypnosis encourages subjects to incorporate misleading information into their reports. Because there is a general belief that hypnosis improves memory, some subjects may report vague details that otherwise they may not have had the confidence to report (Wagstaff, 1999; Erdelyi, 1994).

It was this tendency to increase inaccurate reporting that resulted in a number of States banning witnesses and victims who had been interviewed with hypnosis from giving evidence in court by its failure to meet the Frye Rule, which requires that evidence derived from scientific tests are inadmissible unless generally recognised as reliable for the purpose by the appropriate scientific community. Hypnosis was not generally recognised as a reliable means of retrieving information, and interest in this technique began to dissipate (Gudjonsson, 1992). In England and Wales where the Frye rule does not apply, guidance on the use of hypnosis is contained in Home Office circular 66/1988, that includes a requirement that the interview should be videotaped. There does appear to be a demand for hypnotic interviews coming from the law enforcement community (McConkey and Sheehan, 1995). Gudjonsson and Haward describe a phase in which investigative hypnosis became popular. Haward had been using hypnosis in clinical practice as a means of anxiety reduction for impending witnesses who were not to be given anxiolytic medication. Haward explains that at its peak of popularity with U.K. police forces around 1980, he had conducted 17 investigative hypnosis interviews. In Australia there was a sharp increase in this methodology between 1981 and 1987. The drop in demand coincided with the development of new interview techniques such as the Cognitive Interview, and it appears that the putative benefits from investigative hypnosis can be explained in terms of the ordinary processes from mainstream psychology (Fisher and Geiselman, 1992).

There are a number of techniques that are used in a hypnotic interview and these may encourage a subject to do better than in a standard police interview. First the hypnotist establishes a rapport with the witness and explains what will happen in a way that will alleviate fears and make the witness feel comfortable. The witness is then asked to concentrate, for example, by staring at a target fixed on the wall. Next they are encouraged to relax; the hypnotist may tell the subject that "your eyelids are becoming heavy," and start to count telling the subject that they will go into a deeper and deeper state of hypnosis. The subject is asked to imagine that they are in a very relaxed situation such as lying on a sunny beach. Two techniques that are used are "age regression," where the subject is asked to go back and relive the experience in every detail, and the "television technique," where the subject is asked to imagine that they are watching the events on a television screen or video player where the subject can describe the events they are seeing and focus in on them or go forward or replay them. Witnesses are also instructed at the end of the session that their memory will improve in time and over future sessions. The subject is then woken up by the hypnotist counting while suggesting that the witness is becoming more awake. What is remarkable in this account of a typical hypnotic investigative interview (Wagstaff, 1999:169) is how similar these phases in the interview closely resemble what has been developed in other investigative interviewing procedures which began to be promulgated from the late 1980s onwards (Williamson, 2006). The difference between a hypnotic interview in the 1980s and a standard police interview was vast. The gap has begun to narrow with some of the more modern investigative interviewing methods. In a standard police interview police behaviour may impair the performance of a potential witness. The officer may begin abruptly, and there may not be an initial introductory phase where the officer tries to establish rapport and explain what is going to happen. They may not allow the subject an opportunity for free recall in which to provide the fullest account they can of the event they have witnessed, instead officers' frequently interrupt and rely heavily on the use of closed questions (who, what, why, where, when and how) rather than open-ended ones (Can you describe the clothing?). Closed questions reduce the amount of information that is elicited. Control of the interview lies with the interviewer which may prevent the active involvement of the witness, which is necessary for them to retrieve difficult to access information stored in long-term memory. Police officers can be brusque or tactless in what they say to witnesses, whereas someone trained in hypnosis may well have a clinical background and be more skilled in handling the psychological needs and fears of the witnesses.

Another reason why hypnotic interviews may appear to elicit new information is that they can be seen as an elaborate performance which provides the interviewee with an opportunity to volunteer information which they were too embarrassed to provide previously, or in the case of a witness who has lied previously, it creates a safe face-saving opportunity to recover the correct information ostensibly under the power of hypnosis. Wagstaff neatly sums up the differences between standard police interviews and hypnosis by saying that the hypnotic interview, "is more compatible with optimal recall; the interviewer automatically adopts a softer, less aggressive and authoritarian tone, encouraging the witness to relax, concentrate and report fully and openly, without interruption." He concludes that hypnotic interviews may indeed achieve genuine improvements in memory, but that they are the result of ordinary psychological processes and not some transcendental, or automaton-like, state (Wagstaff, 1999:170). In a direct comparison between the cognitive interview and hypnosis, there were no differences observed between the two techniques (Geiselman et al., 1985). The use of the cognitive interview also gets around the problem that a hypnotic interview may not be acceptable to the court purely because hypnosis has been employed. Wagstaff argues that rather than dismiss hypnotic interviews, it might be better to ask a series of questions about what the witness provided in a particular hypnotic session, and if the interview was conducted without any of the factors that contribute to distorting effects, there may be no reason to dismiss the testimony. Although distortion is not inevitable, the best advice may be "don't bother; use a cognitive interview instead" (Wagstaff, 1999:172-173).

CONCLUSION

It will be seen that memory is both a constructive and reconstructive process. The brain does not work like a video recorder. *The memory for an event can and does depart from the objective reality that gave rise to it, both at the time it is formed* (via constructive processes) *and then later over time* (via reconstructive memory). Given that testimony is a process of construction, investigators would be well advised to pay attention to the conditions that applied at the time of the event and to the subsequent activities that could have affected the cognitive processing of what was received from the senses. Particularly in serious cases, investigators could develop systems, analogous to those for the preservation of physical forensic evidence, which would reduce the risk of contamination. A better understanding of the cognitive process involved when a person is providing an account to an investigator will lead to the elicitation of more accurate information, more effective investigations and safer justice.

REFERENCES

Anastasia, A. and Urbina, S, (1997). *Psychological Testing, 7/e,* New York. Prentice-Hall.

Atkinson R.C. and Shiffrin, R.M. (1971b). "Human Memory: A proposed system and its control processes" in K.W. Spence (Ed), *The psychology of learning and motivation: Advances in research and theory.(pp89-195).* New York: Academic Press.

Baars, B.J. (1997). "In the theatre of consciousness: global workspace theory, a rigourous scientific theory of consciousness" *Journal of Consciousness Studies,* 4, 292-309.

Bargh, J. and Ferguson, M.J. (2000). "Beyond behaviourism: on the automaticity of higher mental processes" *Psychological Bulletin.* 126, 925-945.

Baddeley, A.D. (1986). *Working Memory*, Oxford, Clarendon.

Baddeley, A.D. (1990). *Human Memory: theory and Practice.* Boston: Allyn and Bacon.

Baddeley, A.D. (1999). *Essentials of human memory,* East Sussex: Psychological Press

Baddeley, A.D. (2000b). "The magic number and the episodic buffer" *Behavioral and Brain Sciences,* 24, 117-118.

Baddeley, A.D. (2000c). "Short-term and working memory" in E. Tulving and F.I.M. Craik (Eds.) *The Oxford handbook of memory* (77-92) New York: Oxford University Press.

Baddeley, A.D. (2001b). "Levels of working memory" in M. Naveh-Benjamin, M. Moscovitch, and H.L. Roediger, III, (Eds) *Perspectives on human memory and cognitive aging (111*-123, New York: Psychology Press.

Baddeley, A.D. and Hitch G.J. (1974). "Working Memory" in G. Bower (Ed) *Recent Advances in learning and memory* (Vol. 8, 47-90) New York: Academic Press.

Bahrick, H.P. and Phelphs, E. (1987). "Retention of Spanish vocabulary over eight years" *Journal of Experimental Psychology: Learning, Memory and Cognition,* 13, 344-349.

Baltes, P.B. and Lindenberger, U. (1997). Emergence of a powerful connection between sensory and cognitive functions across the adult life span: A new window to the study of cognitive aging? *Psychology and Aging,* 12, 12-21.

Block, N. (1995). "On a confusion about a function of consciousness" *Behavioral and Brain Science,* 18, 227-287.

Bower, G.H. (2000). "A brief history of memory research" in M.A. Conway, SE.E. Gathercole and C. Cornoldi (Eds.) *Theories of memory* (Vol. 2, 25-60) Hove, England: Psychology Press.

Bruce, C., Desimone, R., and Gross, C.G. (1981). "Visual properties of neurons in a polysensory area in superior temporal sulcus of the macaque" *Journal of Neurophysiology,* 46, 369-384.

Cansino, S., Williamson, S.J., and Karron, D. (1994). "Tonotopic organization of human auditory association cortex" *Brain Research,* 663, 38-50.

Cherry, E.C. (1953). "Some experiments on the recognition of speech with one and two ears" *Journal of the Acoustical Society,* 23, 975-979.

Coren, S. and Russell, J.A. (1992). "The relative dominance of different facial expressions of emotion under conditions of perceptual ambiguity" *Cognition and Emotion,* 6, 339-356.

Coren, S., Ward, L.M., and J. T. Enns, J.T. (2004). *Sensation and Perception* 6th Edition. Chichester: Wiley.

Cory, P., The Honourable Justice, (2006). "Foreword" in Williamson, T,M. (2006) (Ed) *Investigative Interviewing. Developments in Rights, Research and Regulation.* Cullompton, Devon. Willan.

Cowan, N. (2001). "The magical number 4 in short-term memory: A reconsideration of mental storage capacity" *Behavioural and Brain Sciences,* 24, 97-183.

Craik, F.I.M. and Lockhart, R.S. (1972). "Levels of processing: A framework for memory research" *Journal of Verbal Learning and Verbal behaviour,* 11, 671-684.

Ebbinghaus, H. (1885). *Uber das gedachthis*, Leipzig: Dunckes and Humbolt.

Eich, E. (1995a). "Mood as a mediator of place dependent memory" *Journal of Experimental Psychology: General,* 124, 293-308.

Erdelyi, M.W. (1994). "The empty set of hypermnesia" *Interrnational Journal of Clinical and Experimental Hypnosis,* Vol. 42, 379-390.

Ericsson, K.A. and Delaney, P.F. (1999). "Long-term working memory as an alternative to capacity models of working memory in everyday skilled performance" in A. Miyake and P. Shah, (Eds.) *Models of working memory: Mechanisms of active maintenance and executive control* (257-297) Cambridge, England: Cambridge University Press.

Fecteau, J.H., Chua, R., Franks, I., and Enns, J.T. (2001). "Visual awareness and the on-line modification of action" *Canadian Journal of Experimental Psychology,* 55, 106-112.

Feidler, K. (2001). "Affective states trigger processes of assimilation and accommodation. In L.I. Martin and G.L. Clore" (Eds.) *Theories of mood and cognition,* (85-98) Mahwah, NJ: Erlbaum.

Fisher, R.P. and Geiselman, R.E. (1992). *Memory Enhancing Techniques for Investigative Interviewing: The Cognitive Interview*, Springfield, Ill: Charles C. Thomas.

Geiselman, R.E. and Glenny, J. (1977). "Effects of imagining speakers' voices on retention of words presented visually" *Memory and Cognition*, 5, 4f99-504.

Geiselman, R.E., Fisher, R.P., MacKinnon, D.P., and Holland, H.L. (1985). "Eyewitness memory enhancement in the police interview: cognitive retrieval mnemonics versus hypnosis" *Journal of Applied Psychology,* vol. 70, 410-412.

Groome, D. (1999). *An introduction to cognitive psychology. Process and disorder.* East Sussex, England: Psychology Press.

Gudjonsson, G.H. and Haward, L.R.C. (1998). "Forensic Psychology. A Guide to Practice" London, Routledge.

Gudjonsson, Gisli (1992). *The Psychology of Interrogations, Confessions and Testimony.* Chichester, Wiley.

Hoffman, D.D. (1998). *Visual Intelligence: How We Create What We See.* New York: W.W.Norton and Company.

Hubel, D.H. and Wiesel, T.N. (1962). "Receptive fields, binocular interaction and functional architecture in the cat's visual cortex" *Journal of Physiology* (London) 160, 106-154.

Hudspeth, A.J. (1985). "The cellular basis of hearing: The biophysics of hair cells" *Science,* 230, 745-751.

James, W. (1890). *The Principles of Psychology*, New York: Jolt.

Kirsch, I. and Lynn, S.J. (1995). "Altered state of hypnosis: changes in the theoretical landscape" *American Psychologist,* Vol 50, 846-858.

Lamme, V.A.F. (2003). "Why visual attention and awareness are different" *Trends in cognitive Sciences,* 7, 12-18.

Laurence, J.R. and Perry, C.W. (1988). *Hypnosis, Will and Memory: a Psycho-legal* History, New York: Guilford.

Liberman, M.C. (1982). "Single-neuron labelling in the cat auditory nerve" *Science, 216,* 1239-1241.

Lockhart, R.S. (2001). "Commentary: Levels of processing and memory theory" in E. Tulving and F.I.M. Craik (Eds.) *The Oxford handbook of memory* (77-92) New York: Oxford University Press.

Loftus, E. F. and Palmer, J.C. (1974). "Reconstruction of automobile destruction" *Journal of Verbal Learning and Verbal Behaviour,* 13, 585-589.

Loftus, E., F., Loftus, G.R., and Messo, J. (1987). "Some facts about 'weapon focus'" *Law and Human Behaviour* 11, 55-62.

Logothetis, N.K., Leopold, D.A. and Scheinberg, D.L. (1996). "What is rivalling during binocular rivalry?" *Perception and Psychophysics,* 39, 427-436.

McConkey, K.M., and Sheehan, P.W. (1995). *Hypnosis, Memory, and Behaviour in Criminal Investigation*, London: The Guilford Press.

Maas, A. and Kohnken, G. (1989). "Eyewitness identification: Simulating the 'weapon effect'" *Law and Human Behaviour,* 13, 397-408.

Mack, A., and Rock, I. (1998). *Inattentional Blindness: Perception without Attention*, Cambridge, MA: The MIT Press.

Marshal, D.A., Blumer, L., and Moulton, D.G. (1981). "Odor detection curves for n-pentanic acid in dogs and humans" *Chemical Senses,* 6, 445-453.

Melon, A.W. (1963). "Implications of Short-Term Memory for a General Theory of Memory" *Journal of Verbal Learning and Verbal Behaviour*, 2:1-21.

Miller, G.A. (1956). "The magical number seven, plus or minus two: Some limits on our capacity for processing information" *Psychological Review,* 63, 81-97.

Moscovich, M., and Craik, F.I.M. (1976). "Depth of processing, retrieval cues, and uniqueness of encoding as factors in recall" *Journal of Verbal Learning and Verbal Behaviour*, 15, 447-458.

Naveh-Benjamin, M. and Ayres, T.J. (1986). "Digit span, reading rate, and linguistic relativity" *Quarterly Journal of Experimental Psychology,* 38, 739-751.

O'Connell, C.N., Shor, R.E., and Orne, M.T. (1970). "Hypnotic age regression: an empirical and methodological analysis" *Journal of Abnormal and Social Psychology,* monograph supplement, Vol 76, 1-32.

Palmer, S.E. (1999). *Vision science: Photons to phenomenology*, Cambridge, MA: MIT Press.

Polonsky, A., Blake, R., Braun, J., and Heger, D.J. (2000). "Neuronal activity in human primary visual cortex correlates with percepetion during binocular rivalry" *Nature Neuroscience,* 3, 153-159.

Rauschecker, J.P., and Tian, B. (2000). "Mechanisms and streams for processing, 'what' and 'where' in auditory cortex" *Proceedings of the National Academy of Science (USA)*, 97, 11800-11806.

Remmington, R. (1980). "Attention and saccadic eye movements" *Journal of Experimental Psychology: Human Perception and Performance*, 6, 726-744.

Rensink, R.A. (2002). "Change detection" *Annual Review of Psychology*, 53, 245-277.

Roediger, H.L., III, Marsh, E.J., and Lee, S.C. (2002). "Kinds of memory" in D. Medin (Ed.), *Stevens' handbook of experimental psychology*. (3rd ed., 1-41) New York: Wiley.

Rolls, E.T. (2000). "Hippocampo cortical and cortico cortical back-projections" *Hippocampus*, 10, 380-388.

Rosen, V.M. and Engle, R.W. (1997). "The role of working memory capacity in retrieval" *Journal of Experimental Psychology: General*, 126, 211-227.

Scharf, B., Quigley, S., Aoki, C., Peachey, N., and Reeves, A. (1987). "Focussed auditory attention and frequency selectivity" *Perception and Psychophysics*, 42, 215-223.

Scheinberg, D.L. and Logothetis, H.K. (1997). "The role of temporal cortical areas in perceptual organization" *Proceedings of the National Academy of Science, USA*, 94, 3408-3413.

Schwartz, B.L. (2001). "The relation of tip-of-the-tongue states and retrieval time" *Memory and Cognition*, 29, 117-126.

Schwartz, B.L. and Perfect, T.J.(2002). "Introduction: Toward an applied metacognition" in T.J. Perfect and B.L. Schwartz (Eds.) *Applied metacognition* (1-11) Cambridge, England: Cambridge University Press.

Shamma, S. (2001). "On the role of space and time in auditory processing" *Trends in cognitive Sciences*, 5, 340-348.

Shannon, C.E. and Weaver, W. (1949). *The Mathematical Theory of Communication*, Urbana: University of Illinois Press.

Simon, D.J. and Chabris, C.F. (1999). "Gorillas in our midst: Sustained inattentional blindness for dynamic events" *Perception*, 28, 1059-1074.

Spence, C.JJ. and Driver, J. (1997). "Audiovisual links in exogenous covert spatial orienting" *Perception and Psychophysics*, 59, 1-22.

Stevens, S.S. (1975). *Psychophysics: Introduction to Its Perceptual, Neural, and Social Prospects*, New York: Wiley.

Sporer, S.L., Penrod, S.D., Read, D. and Cutler, B.L. "Choosing, confidence, and accuracy. A meta-analysis of the confidence-accuracy relation in eyewitness identification studies" *Psychological Bulletin*, 118, 315-327.

Symons, C.S., and Johnson, B.T. (1997). "The self-reference effect in memory: A meta-analysios" *Psychological Bulletin*, 121, 371-394.

Talarico, J.M., and Rubin, D.C. (2003). "Confidence, not consistency, characterizes flashbulb memories" *Psychological Science*, 14, 455-461.

Taylor, J.G. (2002). "Paying attention to consciousness" *Trends in Cognitive Sciences*, 6, 206-210.

Tong, F., and Engel, S.A. (2001). "Interocular rivalry revealed in the human cortical blindspot representation" *Nature*, 411, 195 199.

Tulving, E. (2002). "Episodic memory: From mind to brain" *Annual Review of Psychology*, 53, 1-25.

Ucros, C.G. (1989). "Mood state-dependent memory: A meta-analysis" *Cognition and Emotion*, 3, 139-167.

Wagstaff, G.F.(1988). "A response to the comments of Gibson, Haward, and Orne"*British Journal of Experimental and clinical Hypnosis*, 5 (1), 45-49.

Wagstaff, G.F.(1999). "Hypnotically induced testimony" in Heaton-Armstrong, Anthony, Shepherd, Eric and Wolchover, David (1999) (Eds) *Analysing Witness Testimony: A Guide for Legal Practitioners and Other* Professionals, London, Blackstone Press.

Weiskrantz, L. (1986). *Blindsight: A Case Study and* Implications, Oxford: Oxford University Press.

Weiskrantz, L. (1997). *Consciousness Lost and Found: A neuropsychological* Exploration, Oxford: Oxford University Press.

Wells, G.L. (1995). "Scientific Study of witness memory: Implications for public and legal policy" *Psychology, Public Policy, and Law*, 1, 726-731.

Wells, G.L., Small, L., Penrod, S., Malpass, R.S., Fulero, S,M. and Brimacombe, C.A.E. (1998). "Eyewitness identification procedures: Recommendations for lineups and photospreads" *Law and Human Behaviour*, 22, 603-647.

Wickens, D.D., Dalezman, R.F., and Eggemeir, F.T. (1976). "Multiple coding of word attributes in memory" *Memory and Cognition*, 4, 307-310.

Williamson, T,M. (2006) (Ed). *Investigative Interviewing: Developments in Rights, Research and Regulation*, Cullompton, Devon. Willan.

Wood, N.L. and Cowan, N. (1995b). "The cocktail party phenomenon revisited: How frequent are attention shifts to one's name in an irrelevant auditory channel?" *Journal of Experimental Psychology: Learning, Memory, and Cognition,* 21, 255-260.

Yerkes-R.M., and Dodson, J.D. (1908). "The relation of strength of stimulus to rapidity of habit formation" *Journal of Comparative Neurology and Psychology,* 18, 393-482.

CHAPTER 4

Human Information Processing:

Social Influences that Shape the Construction and Elicitation of Testimony

Tom Williamson

The brain processes social information in much the same way as sensory information. The "truth" that results is constructed reflecting the choices that the brain has made in the interpretation of sensory and social information. Separate systems for dealing with attention, emotion and social knowledge have been identified that will influence how an event is interpreted. There are also separate systems for dealing with processing perception of faces compared to that of objects. It should not come as a surprise that humans, as social animals, should have neural circuitry that imbues our sensory processes with social and emotional information with all the inherent biases involved in social categorisations. The activity of parts of the brain may seem an unlikely focus for investigators but it is important because investigators will be better able to interpret and evaluate the information obtained from interviews if they have an understanding of the social influences that shape the construction of testimony. We will consider the evidence for how the brain processes social information and then examine the manner in which these social processes will influence the account that is provided to investigators.

A. THE SOCIAL BRAIN: NEURAL PROCESSING OF SOCIAL INFORMATION

Is the following a fair analogy? "You don't have to understand the internal combustion engine in order to be able to drive a car." The statement is true, you can learn the skill of driving a car without understanding the engine, but it is also true that an understanding of the way the engine works will inform driver behaviour, including how to make the engine work better, or more efficiently and avoid things that might go wrong such as keeping the oil topped up. Investigators may have learned the skill of interviewing, but are missing an understanding of the processes that would help them work more effectively and avoid things that might go wrong. What lies behind the generation of an account obtained during an interview is much more complicated than may appear when getting someone to explain what happened. We should understand that although under normal circumstances our cognitive processes are remarkably efficient and accurate, they are the result of an active process of construction and decision-making. This is necessary because our human information processing capacities are woefully inadequate to deal with all the information we need to successfully navigate around our world. The sensory load from the physical environment is minor in comparison to the quantity and complexity of social information that we are continuously processing. This is not objective but is rife with self-interest and self-protective processes (Cacioppo and Bernston, 2004). Since there is more information than can possibly be processed, information processing is biased, e.g., people tend to search for and attend to evidence that confirms what they expected and already believe to be true (Synder and Swann, 1978). Events that unfold unexpectedly are not reasoned as much as they are rationalised and the act of remembering is far more of a biased reconstruction than an accurate record of actual events (Roediger, Buckner, and McDermott, 1999). These biases in social cognition are automatic, spontaneous, requiring no cognitive effort and are ubiquitous in that they represent normal processing. To continue with our metaphor and understand why this is the case we need to consider the engine behind these processes, the brain.

The nervous system consists of billions of separate cells called neurons that communicate with each other through electrical and chemical pathways. A distinction is made between the central nervous system consisting of the brain, brain stem and spinal cord and the peripheral nervous system that includes all other nervous system fibres that conduct information to the brain. The highway to the brain is the spinal cord, a column of nerve fibres running through the middle of the body and protected by a bony structure which links the brain and the peripheral nervous system transmitting information between the brain and the body. There are three parts to the brain. As the spinal cord enters the skull it widens to form the brain stem and this includes structures that oversee basic bodily functions such as breathing, heartbeat, and digestion. It also contains a network of fibres that governs sleep and wakefulness. The limbic system is the next part which surrounds this core and is intimately related to our emotional lives. Finally, the cerebral cortex is the porridge-like substance that surrounds all other structures and is the seat of our highest mental powers, providing meaning to what we have experienced.

The limbic system, associated with emotion, appears to provide the combination of insight and foresight that is required for promoting both our own welfare and the welfare of others (Maclean, 1970:130-135). This is an important function because the frontal and temporal lobes of the human brain which process this information constitute 32 and 23% of the cerebral cortex respectively. This puts into minority status the sensorimotor cortices that dominate most mammalian brains. The frontal regions of the human brain are largely responsible for reasoning, planning and mental simulation and are engaged in remembering and working together. The temporal regions (those nearest the temples at the side of the head) are involved in social perception and communication. Using electrophysiological images of brain activity, it is possible to provide moment-by-moment information about how social cognition is unfolding in the brain, and to assign sets of neural structures to various stages of processing social information through making distinctions between different kinds of information; by categorization and generalization; and in the incorporation of past experience, thereby contributing to our social knowledge (Adolphs, 2003). Reappraisal and self-regulation provide feedback modulation whereby evaluation and emotional response to social stimuli can be volitionally influenced.

Brain damaged patients provide an example of these processes revealing how the brain interprets social information. Although by the 2nd century A.D. Galen was arguing that the faculties of reason lay within the brain, it was not until the 19th century that well-publicized clinical cases drew attention to the role of the brain, particularly the frontal and temporal regions, in social cognition, affective response and behaviour. The psychological study of how the brain determines social behaviour often commences with reference to the story of Phineas Gage. On September 13, 1848, Phineas P. Gage, a 25-year-old construction foreman for the Rutland and Burlington railroad in New England was in charge of detonations for laying the track for a new railroad. This involved drilling holes in the stone, partially filling the holes with explosive powder, covering the powder with sand and using a fuse and a tamping iron to trigger an explosion into the rock. Gage inadvertently tamped directly over the powder before his assistant had covered it with sand. A powerful explosion hurled the tamping iron through the face, skull, and brain of Gage and then into the sky. Although momentarily stunned Gage was fully conscious immediately afterwards and was able to talk and walk with the help of his men. He survived the accident but took on a new personality. Prior to the accident Gage had a reputation for being a highly responsible and socially well-adapted individual.

Gage recovered from the accident and remained able-bodied and appeared to be as intelligent as before the accident. New learning was intact with no loss of memory or intelligence, but his social skills were irrevocably changed. This gentle and polite man became coarse, irreverent and capricious with no respect for social conventions, and his abundant profanity caused offence. He was no longer reliable and could not be trusted to honour his commitments so his employers dismissed him. He died 12 years later in San Francisco in the custody of his family. John Harlow, the physician who treated him, contacted the family 20 years after the accident and obtained permission to exhume Gage's body. He recovered his intact skull together with the tamping iron alongside which Gage had been buried and these are now housed in the Medical Museum at Harvard University. Recent research has reconstructed images of Gage's skull and a trajectory for the tamping iron connecting the entry and exit points. As a result it was possible to identify which parts of the brain may have been affected by the accident.

The impairment to Gage's social and moral behaviour has also been observed in two adult patients who experienced frontal cortex lesions occurring before they were 16 months. Despite having normal basic cognitive abilities, both had suffered from severely impaired social behaviour. Tests showed that they were insensitive to future consequences of decisions, had defective autonomic responses to punishment and failed to respond to behavioural interventions. The acquisition of complex social conventions and moral rules had been impaired and their early-onset prefrontal damage resulted in a syndrome resembling psychopathy (Anderson et al., 1999). What this demonstrates is that what is a socially appropriate response to an event is determined and assigned in the brain.

The brain also determines the type of emotional response to an event. Early research often involved using higher primates with lesions to certain structures of their brain. Research in monkeys showed that parts of the brain are not just related to specific motor behaviours but go beyond that to provide meaning (Ruby and Decety, 2001). One part of the brain that appears to be involved in producing social cognition is in the limbic system. In one study, free-roaming monkeys were given a lesion before returning them to their social groups. It was found that these monkeys invariably were ostracized and most perished without the support of their troop (Dicks, Myers and Kling, 1969). This part of the brain also appears to be involved in evaluation of potential threats. In normal monkeys there is a hesitation in retrieving a food reward when it is placed with a fear inducing object (rubber snake) but lesioned monkeys show no such hesitation (Amaral et. al., 2003).

Brain imaging studies have also demonstrated that there are separate systems for attention, emotion and social knowledge (Yamasaki, LaBar and McCarthy, 2002). Another study demonstrated that different parts of the brain are involved in processing semantic knowledge about objects to that for processing semantic knowledge about individuals. Subjects were given brain scans while participating in making semantic judgments about either people or objects. These scans revealed that the processing of person judgments involved the brain areas that have previously been implicated in other aspects of social cognitive functioning. Humans routinely judge the social behaviour of others, and these judgments can be made on the basis of moral beliefs or an interpretation of an actor's intention and the several possible outcomes of that intention. These moral judgments rely on neural circuits concerned with complex cognitive and emotional processes (Mitchel, Heatherington and Macrae, 2002).

This is especially the case when subjects were presented with emotionally charged information compared to non-moral social judgments indicating that there are brain networks dedicated to processing stimuli endowed with social and emotional significance. Moll et al. gave subjects a visual sentence verification task of either an emotional or a moral statement. One part of the brain was specifically activated by moral judgments whereas other parts of the brain were involved in emotionally evocative judgments indicating that the cortex has dedicated sub-regions specialized in processing specific forms of social behaviour (Moll et al., 2002). What these studies enable us to conclude is that humans are not only endowed with capacities for processing attention, emotion and social perception but that there are areas dedicated to moral reasoning and interpretation of events that infuses these processes with a sense of their fairness and justice (Cacioppo and Berntson, 2005). Judgments about guilt may be formed at a very early stage in this interpretive process.

Brain imaging studies have also demonstrated that there are separate systems for face and object processing. Using a technique called magnetoencephalography which enables the researcher to investigate stages of processing in face perception in humans and to tease apart processing stages that may occur within tens of milliseconds of each other, Liu et al. mapped the stages of face processing in humans. This showed responses occurring only 100 milliseconds after stimulus onset and that this was correlated with successful categorization of stimuli from faces, but not with successful recognition of individual faces. This would indicate that facial processing proceeds through two stages. The first is an initial stage of face categorization, and a later stage at which the identity of the individual face is extracted. The neural response at 100 milliseconds was particularly sensitive to parts of the face whereas the neural response at 170 milliseconds was especially responsive to the configuration of a face and appears to be engaged in more holistic and fine grained information processing (Liu 2002).

B. EXTRACTING MEANING BY MIRRORING BEHAVIOUR

One suggestion as to how social factors influence our perceptual processes is that perceptual information is processed and then imitated in the brain which then enables the brain to assign an emotional categorization to the observed behaviour. Recent studies have demonstrated that there is a system of neurons that sub-serve an individual's capacity to recognize actions made by others, and in so doing, to mirror the observed actions. This may happen without conscious awareness or control by the individuals involved. These imitative reactions are faster than simple visual reaction times. Buccino *et al.* concluded that when individuals observe an action, an internal replica of that action is automatically generated in their cortex (Buccino et al., 2001).

Establishing rapport is an important skill in effective investigative interviewing, and the mirroring activity in the brain may play an important part in how this is achieved. The parts of the brain involved in mirroring are distinct from the areas of the brain that are important in emotion. What this may mean is that by unconsciously mimicking an observed action, individuals are in a better position to know themselves what the other person is feeling. How do we empathize with others? Empathy plays a fundamental social role, allowing the sharing of experiences, needs, and goals across individuals. However its functional and neural mechanisms are poorly understood (Carr et al., 2003). Brain imaging studies show that empathic individuals exhibit non-conscious mimicry of the postures, mannerisms, and facial expressions of others to a greater extent than non-empathic individuals (Chartrand and Bargh, 1999).[1] Carr et al. used brain imaging while subjects were either imitating or simply observing emotional facial expressions. Subjects were presented with a stimulus containing randomly ordered depictions of six emotions (happy, sad, angry, surprise, disgust and afraid). Of three stimulus sets, one contained only whole faces, the other two sets contained only eyes or only mouths cropped from the same set of whole faces. Each stimulus was presented for four seconds, and subjects were asked to imitate and internally generate the target emotion displayed on the

---

1 Conscious mirroring as taught on some interview training courses is not empathy. It is manipulation.

computer screen or alternatively to simply observe. Imitation and observation of emotions activated a similar network of brain areas but there was greater activity during imitation compared with observation of emotions. This could suggest that we understand what others feel by a mechanism of action representation that allows empathy and modulates our emotional content. Different emotions, such as fear and disgust, seem related to different neural systems (Carr et al., 2003). These studies have important implications for managing social interactions, particularly when someone is interviewed. Empathy has been shown to be a key ingredient in effective interviewing eliciting more disclosure (St-Yves et al., 2006; Williamson, 2006). Cognitive mirroring will happen sub-consciously and very quickly, but it points to the importance of managing emotions as part of functioning successfully in social situations.

Deficits in emotional signalling are considered to lead to poor judgment in decision-making in a social context. The concept of emotional intelligence has been used to study the use of emotions to guide human behaviour (Bechara et al., 2000a). This is closely related to social intelligence, a concept defined by the psychologist Thorndike in 1920, as the ability to perceive one's own and others' internal states, motives and behaviours, and to act toward them optimally on the basis of that information (Thorndike, 1920). One of the major differences between cognitive intelligence and emotional intelligence is that the former is thought to relate primarily to higher order mental processes like reasoning while the latter focuses more on perceiving, immediate processing and applying emotional and social content. Social or emotional intelligence may be more linked to the limbic system and by nature tactical, informing immediate behaviour suited to survival and adaptation, although this is not yet supported by empirical findings (Bar-On, 1997a). A study of 12 patients with lesions to the cortices involved in processing emotion were tested on the Emotional Quotient Inventory (EQ-I), a standardized psychometric measure of various aspects of emotional and social intelligence. The patients were also tested with other decision-making and social functioning tasks. The findings suggest that emotional and social intelligence is different from cognitive intelligence and involves different neural circuitry. It is argued that emotional and social intelligence has neural roots in the limbic areas of the brain and that impairment of these mechanisms may have a negative effect of one's ability to effectively cope with daily demands. Such impairment may include a decrease in one's ability to:

- be aware of and express oneself;
- function interpersonally;

- manage and control emotions;
- generate positive effect required in achieving personal goals;
- cope flexibly with the immediate situation, make decisions and solve problems of a personal and interpersonal nature.

Conversely, to perform well and be successful in one's professional and personal life requires the ability to make emotionally and socially intelligent decisions, more than just having a high IQ (Bar-On, 2003). It should not come as a surprise that humans, as social animals, should have hard-wired circuitry that imbues our cognitive processing with social and emotional information with all the inherent biases involved in processing social categorisations about other people. Successful investigative interviewing is highly dependant on managing emotions and making emotionally and socially sensitive decisions. This is an aspect of interviewing that is often very crudely conducted during police questioning.

1. Theory of Mind

We are constantly processing social information to develop a theory of what is in the mind of those we are interacting with. We accept that they have knowledge, beliefs and motives that lie behind their behaviours that we are allowed to see, and so we develop a theory of what is in their mind in order to predict their actions. We were not born with this faculty and most children do not develop a theory of mind until about age five. There is a long history in social psychology, of people, when asked to observe animations of geometric shapes, developing elaborate stories to explain the movements (Cacioppo and Berntson, 2005). The fact that people construct stories and even assign emotions to inanimate objects may seem most peculiar, but it reflects the tendency of the brain to construct a coherent narrative to explain what is being observed. In some brain imaging studies people are invited to attribute mental states to animated shapes in computer-presented animations. Four main areas of the brain appear to be involved that have previously been found to be associated with the perception of biological motion which may mean that the ability to make inferences about other people's mental states evolved from the ability to make inferences about other creatures' actions (Castelli et al., 2000; Cacioppo and Berntson, 2005). These studies indicate that humans powerfully interpret the behaviour of other people based on an understanding of what is in their minds, and that there are areas of the brain given over to processing socially relevant information such as assessing whether what we are being told is true or false (Saxe and Kanwisher, 2003). It is true of course that all parties engaged in any social interaction will be involved in this kind of mind game, monitoring the impression that others' are making.

2. Impression Formation

People think about other people and make judgments about them all the time. Social cognition examines people's subjective interpretations of their social experiences, as well as their modes of thinking about the social world. The two types of human information processing, one automatic and outside of conscious awareness, and the other a more deliberate activity of which we are fully aware, also applies to the way we process social information influencing our social behaviour and reactions to other people (Chaiken and Trope, 1999; Chen and Chaiken, 1999).

3. First Impressions of Others

How are our first impressions of another person formed? What is the contribution that visible ethnicity, age, gender and shape make to our first impressions? People are good at piecing together clues about others' characteristics, but the impressions are often inaccurate because of the many biases and fallacies that occur in the process of forming impressions of others. Studies have shown that we make judgments of others' personality on the basis of their physical attractiveness. Desirable personality characteristics are ascribed to those who are good looking who are seen as more sociable, friendly, poised, warm and well adjusted than those who are less attractive (Wheeler and Kim, 1997), even though there is little correlation between attractiveness and personality traits (Feingold, 1988b,1992). People tend to view good-looking individuals as more competent than less attractive individuals. Those individuals tend to secure better jobs with higher salaries (Langlois et al., 2000). However, it is argued that attractiveness has relatively little impact on perceptions of honesty and integrity (Eagly et al., 1991). Furthermore, people who have baby-faced features such as large eyes, smooth skin, and a rounded chin are seen as more honest and trustworthy, yet there is no association between baby-faced features and these traits (Zebrowitz, Collins and Dutta, 1998).

This shows that people tend to categorize one another, and these categories influence our impressions of others (Macrae and Bodenhausen, 2000). We store in our minds "schemas" which are organized beliefs and knowledge about people, objects, events, and situations. Schemas help in searching our memories for something that is consistent with the incoming information. This permits us to organize and process a great deal of information efficiently as we categorize experiences and remember only their most prominent features. Schemas for classes or subtypes of people are called "stereotypes" which are widely held beliefs that people have certain characteristics because of their membership in a particular group, such as gender, age, ethnicity and occupational groups as well as many other categories. Psychologists are interested in how stereotypes operate in order that we may be better prepared to limit their adverse effects and enable us to treat people more fairly. With repeated exposure to the influence of stereotypes about people, impressions can become automatic and habitual, operating outside of conscious awareness. Studies using priming techniques have demonstrated how stereotyping processes operate automatically. When subjects are presented with a list of words and asked to make up a sentence, those subjects with words which support a stereotype (the elderly) will actually demonstrate elderly stereotypical behaviour, whereas subjects who were not exposed to stereotypical words did not manifest this behaviour. As the subjects in this study thought they were taking part in a test of language ability, it appears that the stereotyping effect occurs at a non-conscious level (Bargh, Chen and Burrows, 1996). Our perceptions of stereotypes are constantly being reinforced through the media. Similar studies have used television advertisements to prime the stereotype of women as sex objects in one group of men while a separate group of men watched non-sexist advertisements. All the men were later asked to interview a woman for a job. Those primed to think of women in more stereotypical terms used more sexist questions and behaved in a more sexualised manner towards her (Rudman and Borgida, 1995). Stereotyping is the ghost in the interviewing room before either the investigator or interviewee arrives. Both will already have a stereotype in their mind of who they are going to meet, and it is important to realise that this may be operating at a sub-conscious level.

Non-conscious priming of pictures of snakes and spiders presented for less than 30 milliseconds can produce aversive feelings in phobics, even though the phobics could not report having seen anything frightening. Similarly when people who were not African American were shown photographs of young, male faces for less than 30 milliseconds then given a tedious computer task to undertake which was then disrupted, and then were told to do the entire task again, those who had been primed with African American faces reacted with more hostility. It is argued that priming an African American stereotype including the idea that African Americans are hostile, automatically generated hostile behaviour in participants without them being aware of it, and this applied whether they scored high or low on measures of racist attitudes (Fazio, Jackson, Dunton and Williams, 1995). Fazio and his colleagues also subliminally presented faces from different ethnic groups within a word evaluation task. The subjects were presented with a list of adjectives and asked to make a judgment as to whether a given adjective was good or bad and to respond as quickly as possible. The response times showed that European American participants viewing African American faces increased the speed of response to negative words and the opposite was true for African American participants who viewed European faces and who responded more quickly to negative words. It is argued that we use stereotypes to categorise people into in-groups and out-groups and that we automatically assign negative associations to out-groups, which facilitates negative responses. People tend to recognise biased social perceptions in others much more readily than in themselves (Pronin, Lin and Ross, 2002), and to immediately classify people as members of an in-group that one belongs to or identifies with, or an out-group that one does not identify with. This may activate two quite different brain circuits (Krebs and Denton, 1997).

Stereotypes and schemas may help us process information. Hamilton found that if people are explicitly instructed to remember as much information as they can about a person, they actually remember less than if they are simply told to try to form an impression (Hamilton, 1979). Stereotypes do help us to cope with processing an enormous amount of social information, and without them we would be very slow to form an impression of others. The price we pay for the efficiency that stereotypes bring are biases in our perceptions and our memories of the information given and in the inferences we make.

The first impression we receive has the greater impact on our overall impressions. We then make a judgment about the person on the basis of a stereotype. Further information is then assimilated in line with the initial judgment and we dismiss discrepant information as not representative. Our subsequent perceptions become increasingly schema-driven and relatively impervious to new data. These stereotypes encourage us to make judgments that go beyond the information given. We filter incoming information through our pre-existing stereotypes and actively construct our perceptions, memories and inferences. The effects of stereotypes on our perception, thinking and behaviour often remain invisible to us, and instead we often take our perceptions to be direct and unbiased representations of reality.

This needs to be taken seriously by investigators because once they are activated, stereotypes can set in motion a chain of behavioural processes that serve to draw out from others behaviour that confirms the initial stereotype, a kind of self-fulfilling prophecy. In one study to test this, interviewers were trained to reproduce both less friendly and more friendly interviewing styles for interviewing job applicants. The applicants were all European Americans and they were videotaped while being interviewed by an interviewer using one of these two interviewing styles. Judges who viewed the videotapes rated applicants who had been interviewed in a less friendly manner much lower on their interview performance compared with those who had been interviewed in a friendlier manner, confirming the hypothesis that people who hold stereotypes can interact in ways that actually evoke the stereotyped behaviours that sustain biased beliefs (Word, Zanna and Cooper, 1974). A suspect interviewed in an aggressive style may produce the kind of behaviour that reinforces the view that they are guilty. The reaction to the interviewing style becomes conflated with the stereotype of a guilty suspect. Research of this kind has led to the formulation of the concept of "stereotype threat" which suggests that the mere threat of being identified with a stereotype can raise an individual's anxiety level, which in turn degrades his or her performance (Steele, 1997). The cognitive and behavioural effects of stereotypes noted above that appear to be so automatic and far reaching in their consequences do raise the question of whether it is ever possible to be free from the pernicious effects of stereotypes.

Social psychologists have studied a process called "individuation" in which an individual's personal qualities are assessed on a person-by-person basis and not on the basis of a stereotype. Accurate impression formation requires much more controlled cognitive effort. Friske et al. have studied and charted the process of impression formation through from stereotypes to individuation (Friske et al., 1999). When we have ample information about someone, and when we are so motivated and are able to pay close attention to that information, we can eventually judge people on the basis of their character and not on the basis of our initial stereotypical judgment. It may also be the case that no matter how well motivated we are to make more thoughtful, accurate and individuated impressions of other people, we may never actually break free from stereotyping and categorization. A number of factors do help to break down stereotypical judgments. In one experiment participants met another student who was identified as a former mental patient. Having obtained verification that they were viewing the student in stereotypes of a former mental patient, they were then randomly assigned to either cooperate with this new acquaintance to jointly learn new material or to simply study that material independently but in the same room as the new acquaintance. Those who did cooperate moved away from their initial stereotyped impression and judged the new acquaintance more positively. They then extended their favourable impressions of their learning partner to former mental patients in general (Desforges et al. 1991). Successful interviewers are able to move beyond reacting to the interviewee in ways that can be interpreted as stereotypical. Although some psychologists argue about how often it is possible to control for stereotypical behaviour in every day life, there is some evidence to suggest that the biasing effects of stereotypes can be controlled if:

- we are aware of the negative effects of stereotypes;
- we are motivated to reduce prejudice on the basis of stereotypical judgments of others;
- we have sufficient attentional resources to engage in controlled and deliberate thinking about the judgments we are making.

Recent studies show that people who are highly identified with the goal of being non-prejudiced can overcome the harmful effects of stereotyping even in brief encounters, and also prevent the automatic activation of stereotypes (Devine et al., 2002).

4. Attributional Bias

Attributions function rather like stereotypes and are a second major factor in impression formation that has been studied by psychologists. Attribution refers to the intuitive attempts we make to infer the causes of events, others' behaviour and our own behaviour. Attribution theory was developed by Heider who asserted that people tend to locate the cause of behaviour either within a person – attributing it to personal factors, or outside a person – attributing it to environmental factors (Heider, 1958). Research has confirmed Heider's theory that we tend to make two kinds of attribution. The first is called "dispositional attribution" where we make an inference that something about the person is primarily responsible for the behaviour. The alternative is "situational attribution" where we make an inference that something in the situational context is primarily responsible for the observed behaviour. Impressions are formed of others from our attempts at understanding the causes of their behaviour. In addition to the internal-external dimension Weiner has shown that people also focus on the stability of the causes underlying behaviour (Weiner, 1994).

Attributions are inferences. They ultimately represent guesswork about the causes of events. We constantly make intuitive attempts to infer the causes of behaviour (Trope and Gaunt, 1999). We may infer that something about that person is responsible for their behaviour, that there is something about the person's beliefs, attitudes and personality characteristics that dispose them to behave in this way, e.g., they are hostile, untrustworthy, caring or reliable, in which case we infer that their behaviour is driven by internal dispositions. Sometimes we may infer that some situational cause is primarily responsible for their behaviour, e.g., the pressure they were under at the time, following instructions from their boss or that they did not have enough time to prepare properly. The *fundamental attribution error* is quite common and occurs when we underestimate the situational influences on behaviour and assume that some personal characteristic of the individual is responsible (Ross, 1977). One explanation for this may be that it is relatively simple to infer other's behaviour to their disposition and more difficult to explain people's behaviour in terms of their situation. We often may not possess all the information about their situation.

If we see someone behaving aggressively we assume that they have an aggressive personality rather than that the situation would have provoked similar aggression in most people. Research studies that have examined this bias have involved selecting subjects to read a speech which either supported or attacked a particular position, e.g., by Cuban leader Fidel Castro. Subjects were randomly assigned to debate one side of the issue or the other. The debater had no choice as to which side to argue. Despite this knowledge of the situational constraint, when people were asked to estimate the debater's actual attitude, they constantly inferred a position close to the one argued in the debate. In other words, they were making a dispositional attribution even though the situation was sufficient to fully account for the behaviour (Jones and Harris, 1967). In another study participants were asked to rate contestants taking part in a quiz game where the questioner was required to make up 10 difficult questions to which he or she knew the answer. When the contestant was unable to answer a question, the questioner gave the answer. The questioner was rated as superior by both the contestant and observers even though the situation gave the questioner an overwhelming advantage. Both questioner and contestants gave too much weight to dispositional causes and too little to situational causes, illustrating yet again the tendency to make the fundamental attribution error (Ross, Amabile and Steinmetz, 1977).

These causal attributions have been found to be governed by two different modes of thinking, one automatic and unintentional, and the other more controlled and deliberate. Causal attribution can be divided into two parts, the dispositional inference is the first, and the second is a situational correction, ascertaining what situational constraints might have caused the action. The first step of dispositional inference is more automatic than the second step of situational correction (Gilbert and Malone, 1995). The fundamental attribution error may occur because it is an overlearned, automatic process, and that it is only when we have the cognitive resources to think deliberately that we can correct the initial dispositional attributions with reference to situational causes. Because we are often carrying a heavy cognitive load forming impressions of others and managing the impression that others form of us, there is a tendency not to correct for the fundamental attribution error.

It should be noted that these processes of social cognition that have been studied in Western psychology may not be universal. Western cultures have tended to explain and classify other people's behaviour in terms of dispositional attributes, oriental cultures have preferred to explain similar behaviour in terms of situational attributions (Norensayan and Nisbett, 2000; Masuda and Nisbett, 2001). Asians tend to engage in more holistic thinking whereas westerners engage in more analytic thinking. "Holistic thinking" is an orientation toward the entire context or field and assigning causality to it, making relatively little use of categories and formal logic, relying instead on dialectical reasoning, which involves recognizing and transcending apparent contradictions. In contrast, "analytical thinking" is an orientation towards objects, detached from their contexts, with much use of categories and formal logic and the avoidance of contradiction. Oriental collectivist tendencies which can be traced back to the ancient Chinese focus on social harmony and collective agency, whereas individualist tendencies in the West can be traced back to the ancient Greek focus on personal agency. This illustrates that our thinking styles are malleable, shaped by those who came thousands of years before us and reinforced by contemporary social practices.

5. Interpersonal Attraction

The quality and quantity of information obtained during an interview may be influenced by whether the interviewee liked or disliked their questioner. A considerable amount of research has been devoted to the factors that are involved in interpersonal attraction. Many factors influence whether we will be attracted to a particular individual. The most important factors have been found to be physical attractiveness, proximity, similarity and what has been described as transference.

Physical attractiveness appears to be an important factor. Although surveys conducted over many decades have demonstrated that people do not rank physical attractiveness as very important in their liking or disliking other people, research on actual behaviour shows quite the opposite. Physical attractiveness appears to influence liking the other person, whereas measures of intelligence, social skills, or personality was not related to how much the other person was liked (Brehm, 1992). Married couples tend to be very similar in level of physical attractiveness (Feingold, 1988b).

The best single predictor of whether two people are friends is proximity; how far apart they live. Neighbours are likely to form a friendship simply because of proximity. One of the reasons that proximity has such an effect is that familiarity itself increases liking. When people were asked to rate photographs of unknown faces according to how much they thought they would like the person, the lowest ratings were made by those who had never seen the photograph before; the highest ratings of liking were made by those who had seen the photograph most often. This finding has been replicated and the results are the same where individuals are exposed to one another in real life (Zajonc, 1968).

A technique used in some investigative interviewing training courses is how to establish that you have something in common with the person about to be interviewed. In addition to proximity and familiarity, a third factor involved in whether we like someone or not is similarity and whether we have anything in common. Surveys of married couples and dating couples show that they are very similar in sociological characteristics such as age, race, religion, education and socio-economic class, and that they share similar psychological characteristics such as intelligence and physical characteristics such as height and physical attractiveness (Kalmijin, 1998). Those who were most similar in background at the beginning of the study were most likely to be together a year later. Couples who were most similar reported less marital conflict and greater closeness, friendliness and marital satisfaction than less similar spouses (Caspi and Herbener, 1990). One reason that similarity produces liking is that people value their own opinions and preferences and enjoy being with others who validate their choices, boosting their self-esteem in the process.

Recent research has demonstrated that when we encounter someone new who reminds us of someone who has been important to us in our past, that sense of recognition influences our perceptions and liking of the new person Simply being reminded of someone who has been significant to us in the past automatically activates schemas about the new person. We then process information about the new person in ways that are consistent with the schema. How much participants like a new acquaintance may depend on whether that new person shared characteristics with the participants' significant others and whether they held positive or negative attitudes about those significant others. Interviewees are likely to compare the interviewer with their significant others. As schemas can be activated automatically and, once activated, influence various aspects of information processing, including memory and inferences, schemas of significant others when triggered by new acquaintances who in some way resemble them, can produce the cognitive and behavioural effects that are expected (Chen and Andersen, 1999). These are all factors that are involved in establishing a relationship. When couples were asked to describe the relationship they had in terms of including the other in the self, it was found that the degree to which people include the other in their perception of themselves predicts how long a relationship will last (Aron, Aron and Smollen, 1992).

6. Attitudes and Persuasive Communication

Our attitudes are our likes and dislikes. "Attitudes" are favourable or unfavourable evaluations of and reactions to objects, people, situations, or other aspects of the world. Psychologists have traditionally conceived of attitudes being comprised of three components, a cognitive component, an affective component and a behavioural component. There have been decades of social psychological research on attitudes. A great deal of sophistication now exists in obtaining data about people's attitudes, with marketing and scientific polls producing assessments of public opinion. There is a key underlying assumption that people's attitudes predict their behaviour, and a corollary is that if we wish to change people's behaviours we need to start by changing their attitudes. Attitudes vary in terms of their strength, accessibility and ambivalence. Strong attitudes are ones that are firmly held, durable over time and that have a powerful effect on behaviour. How often we think about a particular attitude and how quickly it comes to our mind reflects the accessibility of an attitude. Some attitudes come quickly and are readily available. Attitude strength and accessibility tend to be highly correlated. We have ambivalent attitudes when we have a mixture of both positive and negative feelings about an object. When ambivalence is low, an attitude tends to be more predictive of behaviour and less susceptible to persuasion (Armitage and Conner, 2000). The more knowledge and information one has about an object the stronger one's attitude towards it tends to be, and thinking carefully about an attitude object can increase the strength of the attitude. A vested interest in an attitude tends to make it stronger. Whether a guilty suspect will confess is likely to be associated with the strength of their attitude towards making a confession. If they strongly believe that they should not confess, they are likely to be more resistant than someone who is more ambivalent about whether they should confess or not. Conversely, a suspect may start off ambivalent but the interviewer's behaviour may strengthen their attitude not to confess.

Particular interest has been shown by psychologists in persuasive communication. Few general principles emerged from early research on attitudes, which generally failed to find strong relationships between attitude and behaviour. This was partly solved through the realisation that normative influences on people's behaviour could go some way to explaining the puzzling failure of attitudes to predict behaviour. Fishbein and Ajzen argued that a person's beliefs, attitudes, intentions and behaviour were linked (Fishbein and Ajzen, 1975). In the 1980s, attention started to focus on new theories of persuasion that looked at two modes of cognitive processing, one more automatic and effortless, and the other more controlled and effortful (Chen and Chaiken, 1999). The elaboration likelihood model is an example of a dual process theory of persuasion (Petty and Wegener, 1999). Such models aim to predict where strength of argument and credibility of the source will count and when they won't. It is assumed that there is a continuum of likelihood elaboration so that sometimes we are motivated and able to pay attention, think and elaborate on the persuasive message, and at other times we cannot. If we are able and willing to think deeply, persuasion is said to follow a central route, relying on controlled and effortful thinking. At other times persuasion is said to follow a peripheral route relying on automatic and effortless thinking.

In one study participants read a communication about a controversial issue and wrote a one-sentence reaction to each argument. A week later participants were given an unexpected memory test asking them to recall both the arguments in the communication and their written reactions to those arguments. Opinions were assessed before receiving the communication and again at the time of the memory test. The results showed that the amount of opinion change produced by the communication was significantly correlated with both the supportiveness of participants' reactions to the communication and with their later recall of those reactions, but it was not significantly related to their recall of the actual arguments (Love and Greenwald, 1978). This is important because it demonstrates that opinion change is often unrelated to an individual's memory of the arguments that produced the change. The central route can be considered self-persuasion produced by the thoughts that the person generates while reading, listening to, or even just anticipating the communication.

Persuasion is said to follow the peripheral route when the individual responds not to the content of the intended persuasive communication, such as the argument presented, but responds instead to factors such as the sheer number of arguments or the context of the communication. Advertisers often use this method when they pair their product with images of beautiful scenery or rich and attractive people as a means of using the peripheral route to producing positive attitudes toward their product.

If an intended persuasive communication addresses an issue that the individual has a personal interest in, it is more likely that they will use the central route and draw upon the rich store of information they already possess about the subject to help inform their assessment of the communication. On the other hand, if it relates to an issue of no personal relevance, they are likely to use peripheral processing routes, including the use of heuristics, or rules of thumb.

In one study, participants were split into two groups, one which had high involvement in a discussion to change university policy which would affect them directly, and another group who were told the changes were not due to take effect for 10 years. The results tend to support the hypothesis that high personal involvement results in the information being processed through the central route whereas low involvement involves judgments based on peripheral route processing (Petty and Cacioppo 1984).

The process of persuasion consists of who (the source) communicates what (the message) by what means (the channel) to whom (the receiver). Persuasion tends to be more successful when the source has high credibility which can come from a person's expertise or the trustworthiness. People tend to accept messages from trustworthy sources uncritically (Priester and Petty, 1995). Trustworthiness is undermined when the source appears to have something to gain, and is enhanced when people seem to argue against their own interests. The same factors that are at work in attraction operate here too, so likeability increases the effectiveness of a persuasive source. This includes response to physical attractiveness and to sources that share similarity with them in ways that are relevant to the issue at hand (Mackie, Worth and Asuncion, 1990). Persuasive communicators will appear to combine trustworthiness, expertise and likeability.

As well as factors associated with the communicator there are factors associated with the message that will affect how persuasive it is likely to be. Raw repetition of a message does seem to be an effective strategy. Simply repeating a message, such as telling a suspect to confess, does not cause it to be perceived as more valid or true. Persuasive messages frequently attempt to engage your emotions, such as arousing fear. Fear appeals only appear to work if the recipient of the message actually experiences fear. They are most likely to work when the listeners consider the consequences described in the fear inducing message as exceedingly unpleasant, fairly probable and avoidable if they respond to the message (Witte et al., 1998). Case law often proscribes precisely this line of persuasion in the questioning of suspects. Interestingly, researchers have not found any personality traits that are reliably associated with susceptibility to persuasive communication (Petty and Wegener, 1998), although people vary in the degree to which they are suggestible (Gudjonsson, 1995). Forewarning also increases resistance to persuasion (Jain, Buchanan and Maheswaran, 2000). People who have knowledge related to the issue of the persuasive communication scrutinize the arguments more carefully and are more resistant to persuasion, and arguments that are in conflict with one's prior attitudes are scrutinized longer and more sceptically than those that are consistent with one's prior beliefs. It will be seen that attempting to change people's attitudes or behaviour through persuasive communication involves a complex range of factors. The fact that a suspect has received legal advice not to confess is likely to increase the strength of their attitude and their resistance to persuasive communication from the interviewer. However, attitude does not always predict behaviour.

7. Attitude and Behaviour

The notion that a person's attitudes will equate with their behaviour was challenged in a classical experiment conducted in the 1930s. A white professor travelled across the United States with a young Chinese couple. At that time there was strong prejudice against minority ethnic groups such as the Chinese. The three travellers stopped at more than 200 hotels, motels and restaurants and were served in all the restaurants and all but one of the hotels and motels without a problem. Later, a letter was sent to all of the restaurants and hotels asking them whether they would accept a Chinese couple as guests. Of the 128 replies received, 92% said that they would not, indicating that the expressed attitudes were more prejudiced than the actual behaviour (LaPiere, 1934).

Attitudes have been found in subsequent research to predict behaviour when they are strong and consistent, specifically related to the behaviour predicted, based on the person's direct experience and when the individual is aware of his or her attitudes. When affective and cognitive components of an attitude are not consistent, for example, when we like something that we know is bad for us, it is often difficult to predict behaviour (Norman, 1975). In one study specific attitudes toward nuclear war, nuclear weapons, and nuclear power plants were much better predictors of activist behaviours than more general attitudes (Newcomb, Rabow and Hernandez, 1992). Attitudes based on direct experience predict behaviour better than attitudes formed by reading or hearing about an issue. Students' attitudes towards a housing shortage at university, and their willingness to participate in signing and distributing petitions and joining committees, varied according to whether they had experience of the problem or had no direct experience (Fazio, 1990). People who are more aware of their attitudes are more likely to behave in ways that are consistent with those attitudes, and this is true whether they are people who are more focussed on their thoughts and feelings as part of their personalities or whether they are placed in situations designed to make them aware, such as in front of a mirror or video camera (Hutton and Baumeister, 1992). It is surprising how often we are not aware of our attitude being revealed in our behaviour, such as when we are angry but have not consciously registered it. The presence of a mirror in an interview room can assist the interviewer to better monitor their attitude and behaviour towards the interviewee.

It will be seen that there are many factors that can affect the resistance of a suspect with a strong attitude not to confess. In investigative interviewing research, the most persuasive communication appears to be the perception of the strength of the evidence that is in the possession of the interviewer (St Yves et al., 2006; Williamson, 1990).

CONCLUSION

This chapter has demonstrated that there are many social factors that influence the account that interviewees will provide to an investigator. The "truth" that they construct will be affected by the way the brain processes the information in order to categorize it and assign meaning. There are two processes involved, one working at a sub-conscious level and the other at a more conscious level. Social categories will often be assigned on the basis of stereotypes which are very difficult to override. We construct our interpretation of events drawing on schemas of what we would normally expect to happen in the circumstances. Social categorization is also involved in our attitudes to other people. The quality of the information obtained from an interviewee may be related to the impression that he or she forms of the interviewer. Persuasive communicators will appear to combine trustworthiness, expertise and likeability. How persuasive the interviewers' message is, will be affected by the strength of the interviewee's attitude towards the target behaviour. Forewarning, such as in receiving legal advice not to confess, is likely to increase resistance to a persuasive communication.

Attitude does not always predict behaviour. Persuasion is most likely to work when the listeners consider the consequences described in a fear-inducing message as exceedingly unpleasant, fairly probable and avoidable if they respond to the message. This form of persuasive questioning is specifically proscribed in most jurisdictions. The most persuasive factor appears to be the strength of the evidence that is in the possession of the interviewer (Williamson 1990). Cognitive and social processes are involved in the construction and elicitation of testimony. They are at work in the interaction between parties in an interview. Knowing about these processes may help an investigative interviewer to minimise their negative influence and to make better use of factors that positively influence disclosure of information.

REFERENCES

Adolphs, R. (2003). "Cognitive neuroscience of human social behaviour" *Neuroscience Reviews,* 4, 165-178.

Amaral, D.G., Capitanio, J.P., Jourdain, M., Mason, W.A., Mondoza, S.P., and Prather, M. (2003). "The amygdala: Is it an essential component of the neural network for social cognition?" *Neuropsychologica,* 41, 235-240.

Anderson, A.K., Christoff, K., Panitz, D., De Rosa, E. and Gabrieli, J.D.E. (2001). "Neural Correlates of the Automatic Processing of Threat Facial Signals" *The Journal of Neuroscience,* 23, 5627-5633.

Anderson, S.W., Bechara, A., Damasio, H., Tranel, D. and Damasio, A.R. (1999). "Impairment of Social and Moral Behaviour Related to Early Damage in Human Prefrontal Cortex" *Nature Neuroscience,* 2,(11), 1032-1037.

Armitage, C.J. and Conner, M. (2000). "Attitudinal ambivalence: a test of three key hypotheses" *Personality and Social Psychology Bulletin*, 26, 1421-1432.

Aron, A., Aron, E.N., and Smollan, D. (1992). "Inclusion of other in the self scale and the structure of interpersonal closeness" *Journal of Personality and Social Psychology*, 63, 596-612.

Bargh, J.A., Chen, M. and Burrows, L. (1996). "Automaticity of social behavior: Direct effects of trait construct and stereotype activation on action" *Journal of Personality and Social Psychology*, 71, 230-244.

Bar-On, R. (1997a). *The Bar-on Emotional Quotient Inventory (EQ-I): a test of emotional intelligence*, Toronto: MultiHealth Systems.

Bar-On, R., Tranel, D., Denburg, N.L., and Bechara, A. (2003). "Exploring the Neurological Substrate of Emotional and Social Intelligence" *Brain,* 126, 1790-1800.

Bechara, A., Tranel, D, Damasio A.R. (1996). "Poor judgment in spite of high intellect: neurological evidence for emotional intelligence" in Bar-On, R., Parker, J.D.A. (Eds) *The handbook of emotional intelligence*, San Francisco: Jossey-Bass.

Brehm, S.S. (1992). *Intimate relationships* (2nd ed.) New York: McGraw-Hill.

Buccino, G., Binkofski, F., Fink, G.R., Fadiga, L., Fogassi, V., Gallese, R.J., Seitz, K., Zilles, G., Rizzolatti, G. and Freund, H.J.(2001). "Action Observation Activates Premotor and Parietal Areas in a Somatopic Manner: An fMRI Study" *European Journal of Neuroscience,* 13 (2), 400-404.

Cacioppo, J.T. and Berntson, G.G. (2005) (Eds). *Social Neuroscience: Key Readings in Social Psychology*, Hove, England. Psychology Press.

Cacioppo, J.T. and Berntson, G.G. (2004). "Social Neuroscience" in M. Gazzaniga (Ed.) *The new cognitive neuroscience* (3rd edition) Cambridge, MA:MIT Press.

Carr, L., Icaboni,M., Dubeau, M., Mazziotta, J.C. and Lenzi, G.L. (2003). "Neural Mechanisms of Empathy in Humans: A Relay from Neural Systems for Imitation to Limbic Areas" *Proceddings of the National Academy of Sciences,* 100 (9), 5497-5502.

Caspi, A., and Moffit, T.E. (1991). "Continuity and change: Assortative marriage and the consistency of personality in adulthood" *Journal of Personality and Social Psychology,* 58, 250-258.

Chaiken, S, and Trope, Y (1999). *Dual-process theories in social psychology*, New York: Guilford.

Chartrand, T.L. and Bargh, J.A. (1999). *J. Pers.Soc. Psychol,* 76, 893-910.

Chen, S. and Chaiken, S. (1999). "The heuristic-systematic model in its broader context" in S. Chaiken and Y. Trope (Eds.) *Dual-process theories in social psychology* (73-96) New York:Guildford.

Desforges, D.M., Lord, C.G., Ramsey, S.L., Mason, J.A., Van Leeuwen, M.D., West, S.C. and Lepper, M.R. (1991). "Effects of structured cooperative contact on changing negative attitudes towards stigmatised social groups" *Journal of Personality and Social Psychology,* 60, 531-544.

Devine, P.G., Plant, E.A., Amodio, D.M., Harmon-Jones, E., and Vance, S.L. (2002). "The regulation of explicit and implicit race bias: The role of motivations to respond without prejudice" *Journal of Personality and Social Psychology* 82, 835-848.

Dicks, D., Myers, R.E. and Kling, A. (1969). "Uncus and amydalalesions: effects on social behaviour in the free ranging rhesus monkey" *Science,* 165. 69-71.

Eagly, A.H., Ashmore, R.D., Makhijani, M.G., and Longo, L.C. (1991). "What is beautiful is good but..:A meta-analytic review of research on the physical attractiveness stereotype" *Psychological Bulletin*, 110, 109-128.

Ekman, P. (1992). *An argument for basic emotions: Cognition and Emotion* 6:169-200.

Fazio, R.H. (1990). "Multiple processes by which attitudes guide behaviour: The MODE model as an integrative framework" In M.P. Zanna (Ed.) *Advances in experimental social psychology* (Vol. 23). San Diego: Academic Press.

Fazio, R.H., Jackson, J.R., Dunton, B.C., and Williamson, C.J. (1995). "Variability in automatic activation as an unobtrusive measure of racial attitudes: A bona fide pipeline?" *Journal of Personality and Social Psychology,* 69, 1013-1027.

Feingold, A. (1988b). "Gender differences in effects of physical attractiveness in romantic partners and same-sex friends: A meta-analysis and theoretical critique" *Psychological Bulletin*, 104, 226-235.

Feingold, A. (1992). "Good-looking people are not what we think" *Psychological Bulletin*, 111, 304-341.

Fishbein, M. and Ajzen, I. (1975). *Belief, attitude, intention and* behaviour, Reading, MA: Addison-Wesley.

Gilbert, D.T. and Malone, P.S. (1995). "The correspondence bias" *Psychological Bulletin,* 117, 21-38.

Grossman, E.D. and Blake, R., "Brain areas Active During Visual Perception of Biological Motion" *Neuron,* 35, 1167-1175.

Gudjonsson, G.H. (1995). "Interrogative suggestibility: does the setting where the subjects are tested make a difference to the scores on the

GSS12 and GSS2?" *Personality and Individual Differences*, 18, 441-442.

Hamilton. D.L. (1979). "A cognitive-attributional analysis of stereotyping" in L. Berkowitz (Ed.) *Advances in experimental social psychology* (Vol 12) New York: Academic Press.

Haxby, J.V. Gobbini, M.I., Furey, M.L., Ishai, A., Schouten, J.L. and Pietrini, P. "Distributed and Overlapping Representations of Faces and Objects in Ventral Temporal Cortex" *Science,* 239, 2425-2430.

Heider, F. (1958). *The psychology of interpersonal relations*, New York: Wiley.

Hutton, D.C. and Baumeister, R.F. (1992). "Self-awareness and attitude change: seeing oneself on the central route to persuasion" *Personality and Social Psychology Bulletin,* 18, 68-75.

Jain, S.P., Buchanan, B., and Maheswaran, D. (2000). "Comparative versus noncomparative advertising" *Journal of Consumer Psychology*, 9, 201-211. Jones, E.E. and Harris, V.A. (1967). "The attribution of attitudes" *Journal of Experimental Social Psychology,* 3, 1-24.

Kalmijin, M.J. (1998). "Intermarriage and homogamy: Causes, patterns, trends" *Annual Review of Sociology* 24, 395-421.

Krebs, D.L. and Denton, K. (1997). "Social illusions and self-deception: The evolution of biases in person perception" in J.A. Simpson and D.T. Kenrick (Eds.) *Evolutionary social psychology*, Mahwah, N.J.:Erlbaum.

Langlois, J.H., Kalakanis, L., Rubenstein, A.J., Larson, A., Hallam, M. and Smoot, M. (2000). "Maxims or myths of beauty? A meta-analytic and theoretical review" *Psychological Bulletin*, 126, 390-423.

Lapiere, R. (1934). "Attitudes versus actions" *Social Forces*, 13, 230-237.

Liu, J., Harris, A., and Kanwisher, N. (2002). "Stages in Processing in Face Perception: An MEG Study" *Nature Neuroscience*, 6 (9), 910-916.

Love, R.E. and Greenwald, A.C. (1978). "Cognitive responses to persuasion as mediators of opinion change" *Journal of Social Psychology,* 104, 231-241.

Mackie, D.M., Worth, L.T. and Asuncion, A.G. (1990). "Processing of persasive in-group messages" *Journal of Personality and Social Psychology*, 58, 812-822.

MacLean, P.D. (1970). "The Limbic Brain in Relation to the Psychoses" in P. Black *Physiological Correlates of Emotion*, New York: Academic Press.

Macrae, C.N. and Bodenhausen, G.V. (2000). "Social cognition: Thinking categorically about others" *Annual Review of Psychology*, 51, 93-120.

Masuda, T. and Nisbett, R.E. (2001). "Attending holistically versus analytically; Comparing the context sensitivity of Japanese and Americans" *Journal of Personality and Social Psychology*, 81, 922-934.

Mitchell, J.P., Heatherton, T.F., and Macrae, C.N. (2002). "Distinct Neural Systems Subserve Person and Object Knowledge" *Proceedings of the National Academy of Sciences*, 99 (23), 15238-1543.

Moll, J., De Oliveira-Souza, R., Bramati, I.E. and Grafman, J. (2002). "Functional Networks in Emotional Moral and Nonmoral Social Judgments" *NeuroImage* 16 (3-1) 696-703.

Newcombe, M.D., Rabow, J., and Hernandez, A.C.R. (1992). "A cross-national study of nuclear attitudes, normative support, and activist behavior: Additive and interactive effects" *Journal of Applied Social Psychology*, 22, 780-200.

Norensayan, A. and Nisbett, R.E. (2000). "Culture and causal cognition" *Current Directions in Psychological Science*, 9, 132-135.

Norman, R. (1975). "Affective-cognitive consistency, attitudes, conformity, and behaviour" *Journal of Personality and Social Psychology*, 32, 83-91.

Petty, R.E. and Cacioppo, J.T. (1984). "The effect of involvement on responses to arguments quantity and quality: Central and peripheral routes to persuasion" *Journal of Personality and Social Psychology*, 46, 69-81.

Petty, R.E. and Wegener, D.T. (1998). "Attitude change: Multiple roles for persuasion variables" in D.T. Gilbert, S.T.Fiske, and G. Lindzey (Eds) *The Handbook of social psychology*, New York: McGraw-Hill.

Petty, R.E. and Wegener, D.T. (1999). "The elaboration likelihood model: current status and controversies" in S. Chaiken and Y. Trope (Eds.) *Dual-process theories in social psychology* (73-96) New York:Guildford.

Preister, J.R. and Petty, R.E. (1995). "Source attributions and persuasion; Perceived honesty as a determinant of message scrutiny" *Personality and Social Psychology Bulletin*, 21, 637-654.

Pronin, E., Lin, D.Y. and Ross. L. (2002). "The bias blind spot: Perceptions of bias in self versus others" *Personality and Social Psychology Bulletin*, 28, 369-381.

Roediger, H.L., Buckner, R.L. and McDermott, K.B. (1999). "Components of processing" in J.K. Foster and M. Jelicic (Eds.) *Memory: systems, process, or function?* (31-65) New York: Oxford University Press.

Ross, L. (1977). "The intuitive psychologist and his shortcomings: Distortions in the attribution process" in L. Berkowitz (ed.) *Advances in experimental social psychology* Vol 10. New York: Academic Press.

Ross, L., Amabile, T.M. and Steinmetz, J.L. (1977). "Social roles, social control, and biases in social-perception processes" *Journal of Personality and Social Psychology,* 35, 485-494.

Ruby, P. and Decety, J. (2001). "Effect of subjective perspective taking during simulation of action: A PET investigation of agency" *Nature Neuroscience,* 4, 546-550.

Rudman, L.A. and Borgida, E. (1995). "The afterglow of construct accessibility: The behavioural consequences of priming men to view women as sexual objects" *Journal of Experimental Social Psychology,* 31, 493-517.

Sanfey, A.G., Rilling, J.A., Aronson, L.E., and Cohen, J.D. "The Neural Basis of Economic Decision-making in the Ultimatum game" *Science,* 300, 1755-1758.

Saxe, R. and Kanwisher, N. (2003). "People Thinking about Thinking People: The Role of the Temporo-Parietal Junction in 'Theory of Mind'" *NeuroImage,* 19 (4), 1835-1842.

Snyder, M. and Swann, W.B., Jr. (1978). "Hypothesis-testing processes in social interaction" *Journal of Personality and Social Psychology,* 35, 656-666.

St-Yves *et al.* (2006). Paper presented at 2nd International Investigative Interviewing conference, Portsmouth England 5/7 July 2006.

Steele, C.M. (1997). "A threat in the air: How stereotypes shape intellectual identity and performance" *American Psychologist,* 52, 613-629.

Thorndike, E.L. (1920). "Intelligence and its uses" *Harper's Magazine:* 140 227-235.

Trope, T., and Gaunt, R. (1999). "A dual-process model of overconfident attributional inferences" in S. Chaiken and Y. Trope (Eds) *Dual-process theories in social psychology* (161-178) New York: Guilford.

Weiner, B. (1994). *An attributional theory of motivation and emotion,* New York: Springer-Verlag.

Wheeler, L and Kim, Y. (1997). "What is beautiful is culturally good: The physical attractiveness stereotype has different content in collectivist cultures" *Personality and Social Psychology Bulletin,* 23, 795-800.

Williamson, T.M. (1990). "Strategic changes in police interrogation: an examination of police and suspect behaviour in the Metropolitan Police in order to determine the effects of new legislation, technology and organisational policies." Unpublished Ph.D. thesis, University of Kent at Canterbury.

Williamson, T.M. (2006) (Ed). *Investigative Interviewing: Developments in Rights, Research and Regulation,* Cullompton, Devon. Willan Publishing.

Witte, K., Berkowitz, J.M., Cameron, K.A. and McKeon, J.K. (1998). "Preventing the spread of genital warts: Using fear appeals to promote self-protective behaviours" *Health Education and Behaviour,* 25, 571-585.

Word, C.O., Zanna, M.P. and Cooper, J. (1974). "The nonverbal mediation of self-fulfilling prophecies in interracial interaction" *Journal of Experimental Social Psychology,* 10. 109-120.

Yamasaki, H., LaBar, K.S. and McCarthy, G. "Dissociable Prefrontal Brain systems for Attention and emotion" *Proceedings of the National Academy of Sciences,* 99 (17), 11447-11451.

Zajonc, R.B. (1968). "Attitudinal effects of mere exposure" *Journal of Personality and Social Psychology, Monograph supplement*, 9, 1-29.

Zebrowitz, L.A., Collins, M.A. and Dutta, R. (1998). "The relationship between appearance and personality across the life span" *Personality and Social Psychology.*

CHAPTER 5

Psychology of Non-verbal Communication:

Tools for Investigative Interviewing

Joe Navarro

If his lips are silent, he chatters with his fingertips

Freud

For millions of years, our early ancestors ambled on this planet, effectively navigating a very dangerous world. They did so by communicating effectively with each other their needs, observations and desires. Impressively, they achieved this through the use of non-verbal communications. Through chemical scent (musk glands we still possess), physiological changes (flushed face), gestures (pointing hand), facial reactions (quizzical look), symbols (drawings of animals), personal markers (tattoos), even vocal noises (shrieks and grunts are not verbal communication) they succeeded in a complex environment (Givens, 1998-2005). So much of this remains with us as part of our DNA and paleo (ancient) circuitry within our brains, that we still primarily communicate non-verbally, not verbally (Knapp and Hall, 1997, 400-437).

Our limbs, our faces, our eyes, even our hearts are controlled, at all times, by our brain. We do nothing without our brain and when it comes to non-verbal communications, there is interaction between the mind and the corporal self. Because non-verbal communications are intimately intertwined with our psyche (what is inside the brain) we can use our corporal behaviour (nonververbals) to decipher what is going on in our heads (Ratey, 2001, 174).

When we explore non-verbal communications we must do so from the perspective that all communication is also governed by the brain and that the study of the brain, literally psychology, must be done in its widest context; that is, from the study of the brain as a complex organic entity:

physiologically, emotionally, cognitively, spiritually and intra-psychically. It is from this perspective that we begin our analysis of the relationship between psychology and non-verbal behaviour (Jackiewicz, 2005). As we look at the psychology of non-verbal communications, it is useful to invoke images of a neonate and its immediate needs, in order to realize just how psychology and non-verbal behaviour (communication) are interwoven.

A child is born into this world shivering and crying, which prompts the mother to swathe the child in warm clothing to relieve the child from the cold. The child is thus immediately satisfied of its need for warmth; innately, it has communicated its first message non-verbally (shivering, crying) quite effectively. From this initial need for warmth, we have a window into all future communication and interaction between the brain and the body, each elegantly choreographing and building a repertoire to insure survival through effective communication (Ratey, 2001, 181; Knapp and Hall, 1997, 51).

Crying and shivering are soon followed by thumb sucking, a behaviour the child learns while still in the womb. This is a self serving behaviour on the part of the brain eager to be tranquil and pacified. The brain, for reasons yet unknown, will engage the physical body (in this case the thumb) in its quest for tranquility, which the body will be more than willing to accommodate in order to maintain homeostasis. This action (thumb sucking), will take place thousands of times in the future to release pleasure inducing endorphins (opiate-like substances) in the brain (Panksepp, 1998, 26, 252, 272). At the same time the child communicates to the observant mother that it is pleasantly occupied in oral bliss. As the child grows, it will develop other adaptive behaviours to pacify himself during stressful situations. Some will be obvious (e.g., gum chewing, pencil biting, lip touching) others not so obvious (e.g., playing with the hair, facial stroking, neck rubbing). And yet, they satisfy the same requirement of the brain; that is, for the body to do something which will stimulate nerves (releasing endorphins) so that the brain can be soothed (Panksepp, 1998, 272).

Progressively, the newborn will try to find the mother's nipple by awkwardly moving its head in the direction of the milk glands which it can accurately sense through very sensitive olfactory nerves in its nose. As the child begins to feed, rhythmically sucking the milk from the breast, the hands of the child instinctively press and massage the breast to assist in the process of lactation as well as generating a sense of comfort and well-being on the part of the mother.

This also begins the process of bonding between mother and child, which is often referred to as proto-socialization (the beginning of social harmony). It is both a physical (corporal) process and a psychological process (Givens, 2005, 121). Both parent and child receive great reward from the intimacy of breast-feeding, for as the child is fed, the mother begins to be rewarded for her efforts: milk is released, relieving pressure which builds within the mammary gland and powerful endorphins are once more discharged, soothing the mother as well as the child.

Thus, the child begins to communicate its pleasure in being comforted by the mother, while at the same time, the mother begins to observe and decode every nuance of the child's behaviour. This time spent close together will help the mother and child to understand each other and to communicate more effectively. The mother soon learns the various cries (non-verbal communication) of the child expressing hunger, cold, disgust, sickness, or sadness, essential for the child's survival and well being. Likewise, the child (within as little as 72 hours) begins to follow and observe its mother, mimicking facial behaviours, useful for developing facial muscles, but more importantly for communicating needs and sentiments (Ratey, 2001, 330). Within days, if not hours of birth, we begin the process of communicating (crying, sighing, smiling) our needs and sentiments. Eventually the child will be able to communicate more complex observations of the world around him.

As both parent and child decode and reinforce one another's behaviour they learn to communicate more precisely with each other. Eventually, the child will respond to spoken words, even other languages. And yet, how words are spoken and delivered (tone, loudness, speed, sentiment, eye contact, posture) are even more significant than the words themselves (Knapp and Hall, 1997, 400-425; Givens, 2005, 85). The non-verbal component of speech, in essence, the psychology of the message, will remain consciously and subconsciously significant to us for the rest of our lives. From how words are delivered we will derive comfort, discomfort, or indifference.

From the warm intimacy of interacting with its mother, the child will also develop communication tools for socializing with others. The child, without benefit of a guidebook or directions comes equipped to communicate non-verbally its likes and dislikes. Sensing something it dislikes, the brain, without conscious thought (subconsciously) immediately constricts the pupils and turns the body away from that which is perceived as negative (Garoutte, 1987, 106). These are very subtle behaviours which are part of our survival mechanism (limbic system). Thus, the brain, through the use of the body, transmits very precisely, its negative feelings and sentiments which family and friends will soon recognize (Knapp and Hall, 1997, 51). For example, when the child's torso stiffens away from the dinner table and the feet turn towards the nearest exit, the mother will have no problem precisely identifying the culprit (child's dislike for a particular food) and the message (I won't eat it). These key discomfort displays reflect what is in the head without having to say one word.

Conversely, when the brain likes something, it will again subconsciously compel the child to communicate those sentiments. Thus, when the mother enters the child's room in the early morning and looks in, the child's eyes will open wide, the pupils dilate, facial muscles will relax (permitting a full smile), and the head will tilt, exposing the vulnerable neck (Givens, 2005, 63, 128). These "comfort" behaviours will be useful in the decades to come in developing and maintaining friends as well as in facillitating courtship, ensuring a new generation to propagate the species.

It is in many ways wonderful that our brain requires us to act physically on its behalf to express sentiments. Anger, sadness, fear, surprise, happiness, and disgust manifested non-verbally, are universally recognized and are essential so that we may be attended to even when we can't speak. Our brains are so resourceful that children who have been born deaf and grow up together in the absence of adult instruction, will develop their own "sign" language in order to communicate complex thoughts with each other (Ratey, 2001, 262).

This interconnectedness between what is in the head and our non-verbal transmission of those sentiments is not unique to us. All animals do this, principally to insure survival of the species. But our brains transmit a lot more information non-verbally than just emotions. For example, when the brain is healthy and emotions are in check, the brain makes sure that we look well, healthy, and contented. When unhealthy emotions or illness affect the brain (picture a homeless schizophrenic), our bodies and that of all animals reflect the malady through lack of grooming, poor posture, troubled countenance, or erratic and shunted behaviour (Jackiewicz, 2005). All is reflected non-verbally, demonstrative of this wonderful interconnectedness between our psychology and non-verbal communication.

A. FREEZE, FLIGHT, OR FIGHT—WHAT TO DO?

To really understand the psychology of non-verbal behaviour, we have to understand in general terms how the brain has developed and is subdivided. There are three distinct structures within the cranial vault which evolved as we did. At the top of our brain stem is our very ancient reptilian brain (Panksepp, 1998, 43). The upper parts of the brain stem along with the medulla and the cerebellum handle internal body functions such as muscle movement, respiration, balance and cardiac activity. This part of the brain has no conscience, sense of self, or memory relative to the outside world (Myers, 1993, 35-39). It is reactive to the environment and is self adjusting to maintain homeostasis through the sympathetic system. This ancient part of the brain can, when other brain activity is damaged, keep us alive in a "constant vegetative state." This is important because understanding what we see on the part of someone else's behaviour requires an understanding of what part of the brain is controlling that behaviour. Unfortunately most people think of our brain as one brain, when in fact it is three brains. For example, when you see someone who is obviously intoxicated and losing their balance, it is because alcohol, a Central Nervous System (CNS) depressant acts directly on the cerebellum.

Because we have no control over our medulla and cerebellum, those behaviours controlled by these parts of the brain tend to be very honest. In other words, we can place greater reliability on those behaviours because we cannot cognitively regulate them. We can fake a smile but we can't fake being sober. If the medulla, in concert with the cerebellum, decides to speed up the heart as a result of a stimulus, or the hands tremble as a result of a highly stressful situation, we can take great comfort in knowing that this is a behaviour we can count on, unlike words.

An example of this occurred in December 1999, when an alert Customs Officer thwarted what came to be known as the "millennial bomber." Noting the nervousness and excessive sweating of Ahmed Reesam as he entered the United States from Canada, officer Diana Dean, asked Reesam to step out of his car for further questioning. At that point Reesam ran but was soon captured. In the car, officers found explosives and timing devices. Reesam was eventually convicted of attempting to bomb the Los Angeles Airport. What officer Dean observed, the nervousness and sweating, were regulated in part by the brain stem and the cerebellum as a result of immense stress. Because these behaviours are genuine, officer Dean relied on her accurate and precise observation and pursued this individual based on that reliability. This reflects the connectedness between the psychology of what is going on in the brain and how it manifests itself non-verbally. In this case, a would be bomber, who was obviously scared of being detected, gave away non-verbally what he was ideating.

1. Limbic Brain

In the evolutionary process, our early reptilian ancestors developed modules in front of the cerebellum which differentiated us as a species so that we could function more effectively on land. This became our early emotional memory and response system in the form of a thalamus, amygdala, hypothalamus, and hippocampus, which along with other structures forms what is called the "limbic brain." This is often referred to as our mammalian brain. It is the mammalian brain which evolved to deal with a terrestrial world which was far more complex and daunting than our previous aquatic life. It is the limbic brain which is most associated with keeping us alive insuring our survival (Navarro, 2008, 21-51). By reacting to external stimuli, it records and maintains a record of events (burned finger on stove, threatening gestures, an assault, or even painful words) as well as positive emotional events (Ledoux, 1996, 184-189). This is the emotive/reactive part of the brain which has allowed us to react to a dangerous often unforgiving world (Goleman, 1995, 10-21).

The beauty and downright elegance of the limbic system is that it reacts to the outside world immediately without having to conduct a lot of thinking and evaluation. For example, once the limbic system registers a dangerous animal through sight, this becomes imbedded in our emotional memory (a combination of the amygdala and the hippocampus) so that the next time we see that animal we will react instantly. If we run into the class bully 20 years later, negative feelings long ago felt will percolate once more, thanks to our limbic brain. This is why it is often difficult to forget when someone has hurt us, because it registers in the more primitive limbic system which was designed not to reason but to react.

Conversely, the limbic system also works efficiently to register positive emotions. A friendly or familiar face will also cause the limbic system to let down its guard psychologically, permitting friendly reactions much as we reacted to a loving mother. That initial reaction we have upon seeing someone from our youth is governed by the limbic brain. Immediately recognizing the face, the limbic system instantly permits muscles to relax, our posture to be more pliant, facial muscles to relax and our pupils to dilate (Givens, 2005, 63, 128). Those feelings of euphoria we feel for an old friend are in fact governed by the limbic system.

For investigators and observers of the world, the limbic brain psychologically is really where it's at. Why? Because it is the limbic brain, the reactive brain, that deals honestly with the world around us. Concerned only with our survival, it reacts to the world in real time, effortlessly and quickly (Panksepp, 1998, 33). We really could not ask for more as investigators. Our limbic brain does not take breaks; it is always "on," uniquely responsible for our survival. It sends signals to various other parts of the brain which in turn manifest as behaviours. These can be observed and decoded as they manifest physically in our feet, torso, arms, hands and faces. And unlike words, they are genuine.

We have all heard of the "fight or flight" reaction, and many people assume that this statement is in fact correct. It is not. It is only partially accurate and even then it is imprecise in the order in which the limbic brain reacts (Panksepp 1998, 206-222). The easiest way to understand the limbic brain is to think about predators and our reaction to them.

2. Freeze Response

A million years ago, as early hominids traversed the African savannah, there were predators all around. They were bigger, more powerful and quicker. For early man to succeed, the limbic brain, which had evolved from our amphibian antecedents, developed strategies to compensate for man's smaller stature and considerable powerlessness in comparison to predators. That strategy, or first response of the limbic system, is to "freeze" in the presence of a predator or a threat. Movement attracts attention. By holding still immediately upon seeing a threat, the limbic brain learned to react in the most effective fashion possible to ensure our survival. Most animals, certainly most predators, react to and are attracted by movement. This ability to freeze in the face of danger makes sense. Many predators will actually chase after other animals that move so that they can exercise the "chase, trip, bite" mechanism exhibited by felines, the primary predators of our ancestors.

Not only did we learn to freeze in the face of danger perceived or observed, others around us, who perhaps did not see the same threat, learned to react to the limbic behaviour (responses) of those around them. When one froze, the group also froze. This mimicry or isopraxism (same-movement) was key to social survival as well as social harmony.

We can see this in other animals, from bears to monkeys, to ducks. When the mother bear stops and freezes, so do the cubs; they hold still even as she does. Ducklings will do the same. When the mother spots trouble she hunkers down quietly and the ducklings follow suit without a peep. The same goes for the monkeys who will become immobile or will clutch on to their mothers. This clutching behaviour is part of the limbic freeze mechanism which is easily seen among primates and even young children. As we get older, we no longer clutch our parents, but we do clutch ourselves in the presence of a threat. For example, recently, a young girl who had been kidnapped was observed on CCTV entering a convenience store in the presence of her abductor. We can clearly see this young scared child, clutching herself, her arms wrapped around her body, indicative of the high threat in which she found herself.

This freezing action is often associated with the "deer in the headlights" effect. When we are suddenly caught doing something we should not, we immediately freeze before taking action. This often gives us the opportunity to think before we act impulsively. Imagine a marauding lion or a wolf walking into the very room you find yourself reading this book. Your most likely reaction will be to freeze. How comforting to know that we developed this automatic reaction as our first line of defence and first tool of survival. In day-to-day life, this manifests itself innocently when a person walking down the street stops suddenly, hitting himself on the forehead with the palm of his hand, before turning around and heading back to his apartment to turn off the stove. That momentary stop is enough for the brain to do some quick assessing, whether the threat comes from the outside in the form of a predator or a thought remembered, either way, the psyche must deal with a potentially dangerous situation.

Remarkably, we not only freeze when confronted by physical and visual threats, we also freeze when we hear things that threaten us. When being chastised most people hold very still. We see the same thing in the theatre of the interview. I have personally had dozens of cases where the interviewee would just freeze in the chair, flash frozen, like a pilot in an ejector seat, as I asked questions. Every time I have seen this behaviour, the interviewee was culpable. Because my questions and inquiry present a threat, the limbic brain freezes action during the interview just as we froze a million years ago when confronted by deadly lions.

A similar manifestation of the limbic freeze occurs during interviews when people hold their breath, or their breathing becomes very shallow. Again, this is a very ancient response to a threat. It is not noticed by the interviewee and yet it is quite observable. I have often had to tell them to relax and breathe deep. Polygraphers comment that when people come in for a polygraph exam this is the most common response to the stress of taking the test, and they have to be told not to hold their breath.

Consistent with the need to freeze when confronted by a threat, people will often fix their feet in a position of security (interlocked behind the chair legs) and hold that position for an inordinate period of time. When I see this, it tells me something is wrong; this is a limbic response which needs to be explored. The person may or may not be lying, I don't know, but I can be assured from their behaviour that something is stressing them and I will pursue it. Psychologically they are stressed by the interviewer, the interview process or location, the specific questions, or they fear apprehension or detection. It is up to the investigator to discern what is at issue and why.

Another way our limbic brain tries to protect us is by diminishing our exposure. During surveillance of shoplifters one of the things that stands out is how often they try to reduce their appearance or hold very still as if trying to be invisible. Of course it does not work. In fact it makes them stand out even further as most people walk around with their arms quite active and their posture upright rather than stooped. Psychologically they are trying to master their environment by trying to "hide" in the open.

One of the false myths about liars is that they tend to use their hands more and act more animated. This is far from the truth. In fact, one of the observed features of liars is that liars tend to gesture less, touch less, and move their arms and legs less than truthful people (Vrij, 2003, 65). This is consistent with limbic responses that in the face of a threat (e.g., having a lie detected) we move less so as not to attract attention. This lack of activity during interviews is often quite observable as the person's arms become very restrained while telling a lie and otherwise animated when telling the truth. It is useful to look for these changes as they are controlled by the limbic system and, thus, are more reliable indicating what is really in the head of the individual.

3. Limbic Hijacking

Limbic responses can, however, backfire. If the threat is considerable, the limbic brain can hijack cortical activity rendering the person incapable of remembering or unable to even complete a sentence. This is an often observed stress response. After a shootout, a person may not remember exactly what happened. In response to a threat, the limbic system hijacks cortical activity (high-level thinking) for survival purposes. Short-term and long-term memory may be severely affected as a result of the limbic system's response to this overwhelming situation. There is even speculation that by blocking out the event, the person is spared having to relive the horrible event, at least for the time being (Jackiewicz, 2005). Once more our limbic system rises to protect us at some cost; lasting memories.

Similarly, an investigator's question such as, "did you fire the gun?" can so threaten a person that they stumble with their words and are unable to speak normally. Guilty knowledge, in these cases, causes the stress, which the limbic system attempts to deal with at the expense of the thinking brain which may utter something totally unintelligible.

4. Flight Response

The second response of the limbic brain is to attempt "flight" from a threat. This is usually seen as an attempt by the individual to distance himself from any threat or unsavoury situation by leaning away, blocking it out, or simply running. Running, of course, is useful when it is practical, and as a survival mechanism our brain employed this tactic judiciously over millennia to escape from danger.

In the modern world, where we live in cities not in the wild, it is difficult to escape and run from threats. Walls, fences, busy crowded streets, even surveillance cameras inhibit such behaviour. During an interview, the interviewee is not going to be able to sprint out of the room; that alone looks suspicious. So the limbic brain has developed other unique techniques to deal with threats short of flight. Because movement is restricted during an interview, the limbic brain engages in other more subtle behaviours to either block or distance itself from the inquisitor's questions.

Just as the child turned away from the food at the table, the guilty may turn away from the investigator during questions that threaten. Blocking behaviours may be manifest with the closing of the eyes, rubbing of the eyes, or placing the hands in front of the face. The person may distance himself from the interviewer by leaning away, placing objects (backpack) on his lap, or turning the feet towards the nearest exit. All behaviours controlled by the limbic brain, indicate that the questions posed are a threat to the interviewee. Once more, these are not indicators of deception, they are, however, accurate indicators of stress due to the questions asked (Vrij, 2003, 22-23).

Because our limbic brain controls emotion, it also controls our commitment to what we think, feel and say. One observation familiar to investigators is that liars tend to make declarative statements which lack emphasis. Emphasis requires emotional commitment. Liars lack that commitment which is derived in part from the emotional commitment of the limbic brain (Navarro 2003). When the limbic system does not support something being said by the less reliable neo cortex (thinking brain) the statements sound shallow, non-emphatic and even mellow. This will manifest itself in the person saying "I didn't do it" softly rather than shouting it out and banging the fist on the table while saying "I didn't do it!" After more than 13,000 interviews over a 25-year career, I have never observed a liar dramatically emphasize his innocence. For investigators, emphasis is commensurate with validity. Where it is absent, further inquiry is necessitated.

5. Fight Response

The last response familiar to us is the "fight" response. Obviously when we are threatened and there is no escape, and holding still has not helped, we are left with no choice but to fight. As a species we developed, as other mammals did, the ability to turn fear into rage in order to fight off threats (Panksepp, 1998, 208). Rage, like running, in the modern world is not practical and may not be the wisest action to deal with a potential threat. Consequently, the limbic brain has developed other strategies beyond the more primitive fight response. One form of fighting, in the modern context, is to argue or make counter-allegations. By arguing, the subject of the matter is avoided and the interview is derailed. Controlled rage can be very effective. From merely being "passive aggressive" (handling aggression passively) to its more palpable form, arguing, we have evolved the capacity to do what other mammals are incapable of doing, arguing to save ourselves. It is a wonderful technique that is often not recognized for what it is since the "fight" (argument) may be won by the more vocal, hysterical, manipulative, clever, or versatile interviewee. By arguing with an investigator, the brain does not have to deal with the guilty knowledge it harbours or the facts, and instead puts the investigator on the defensive, much the same way as a counterattack serves in war (Panksepp, 1998, 54). Arguing serves to relieve the pressure and anxiety experienced aurally by the limbic brain.

Another way of fighting is to lie. Lying, as we said earlier, is a tool of social survival. By supplying the investigator with a lie, especially an effective lie (believable or plausible), anxiety is relieved as the investigator receives information which may cause him to back off or readily accept

(Inbau, Reid, and Buckley, 1986, 77). Unfortunately, investigators often equate production (interviewee speaking) with veracity.

Both of these techniques (arguing, lying) should be interpreted as a more sophisticated way for the brain to deal with threats by fighting, using verbal rather than pugilistic skills. In either case, it is a verbal course of action which also reflects the psychology of the person and his intentions. Resistance and obfuscation rather than cooperation.

6. Neo Cortex

The final part of the brain we must consider is the cortex which includes the neo (new) cortex. This is that part of the brain which controls high-order cognition and memory. This is the "thinking" brain that got us to the moon with its ability to remember, compute, analyze, dissect and intuit as no other brain on the planet. This newest part of our overall brain sets us apart from all other creatures and our more primitive ancestors which lacked our voluminous brain development (Myers, 1993, 33-39).

To an investigator dealing with the guilty, this is the least reliable of the three major brain components because this is the brain that can lie. While the limbic system may compel a person to squint (subconsciously) as an unsavoury person walks by, the cortex is quite capable of lying about true sentiments. The cortex which governs Brocca's area (our speaking region) after assessing the totality of the situation may decide to say to this very same person, "hello, so very nice to see you," even if it is not meant. It certainly is capable of saying very believably, "I did not have sexual relations with that woman." Or worse, it can say to a homicide investigator, in a very convincing voice, "I did not kill her." It is the thinking brain which in fact can lie, sometimes very effectively. This is the part of the brain which is least reliable when it comes to veracity and must be acknowledged as such.

Because the neo cortex is very capable and adept at lying, all information gained from a suspect or someone in question must be corroborated. Leading questions should always be avoided so that information is delivered and not derived by the interviewee. Recognizing that our higher brains are capable of avoiding, lying or obfuscating, questioning should always be intended to induce the person to bring information forward on their own, delivered rather than derived, from the interviewer's questions and comments. Poor interviewers often give away much more than they receive from the suspect, thus tainting the interview and contributing to false confessions.

Because lying is psychologically a "tool for social survival," we have to always be on notice of that potential. Unfortunately, most people reading this book, including law enforcement officers, will be no better than a coin toss (50/50) at detecting deception (Ekman and O'Sullivan, 1991, 913-920 ; Vrij, 2003, 74-75). So in order to help us decipher truthful statements, it is important to understand how the brain works and how each of the three major regions affect non-verbal behaviour. After all, what is in our brain is often reflected in our non-verbal or corporal behaviour. And the most reliable parts of our brain are those controlled by the ancient regions such as the limbic system.

B. WHO ARE YOU AND WHAT DO YOU INTEND?

1. Hierarchy

In order to insure social harmony, once our brain has assessed for danger, it then begins the process of assessing for hierarchy. When we enter a room full of people or are introduced to another person, our brain once more goes to work. The brain will immediately seek clues as to where to place itself in relation to others present. This subconscious hierarchical assessment contributes to social harmony, so that in essence, everyone has and knows their place in society (Morris, 1969, 52).

In the kinds of societies we lived in for tens of thousands of years, there was no question as to who was in charge (chief, village elders, etc.). Whether patriarchal, matrilineal, or bilineal, all societies enjoyed social harmony by establishing rules of hierarchy. Higher status individuals enjoyed privileges granted by subordinates usually in the form of non-verbal displays. Higher status individuals got to dress better, sit higher, were entitled to greater space and were contented with less physical contact with their subordinates (Morris, 1969, 40). It was no-less-so than the Queen of England receives today. When the conquistadores arrived in the new world, they had no problem whatsoever determining who the native kings were (Diaz, 1988). They were afforded the same courtesies as European royalty. The chiefs and the subordinates behaved in the same way they did back home in Spain. It is as if our paleo circuits have a permanent blueprint for social harmony through hierarchical displays and adjustments. Psychologically it makes sense.

In our modern society, far more complex and transitional, establishing hierarchy is much more difficult in that we grant high status to so many different people (judges, doctors, athletes, film actors, the rich, the beautiful) not just our leaders. Think about how we treat actors who walk down the "red carpet" and how people queue up to see them or follow their lives in the tabloids. Every organization has its own hierarchy (from CEO to mail-room clerk) as does every family and social unit. When the hierarchical schema is in disarray, that social component, be it a family or a military unit will suffer.

And so our brains are constantly assessing for hierarchical indicators such as profession, clothing, grooming, possessions, education, title, work or social associations to guide us. How these are manifest will subconsciously affect how individuals will interact with each other. Even such subtle things as beauty, height, weight, color of attire, and education will affect perceptions and how individuals are treated or accorded deference (Etcoff, 1999, 169-170).

For example, India, the world's largest democracy, is still hobbled by remnants of its old hierarchical caste system and the scourge of being a *dalits* or "untouchable." If you are born into one of the lower castes, people still treat you differently even though it is constitutionally illegal. Matrimonial "help pages" in India are dedicated to evincing the true status of individuals to determine if they are worthy of each other. Many societies, including ours, assess for hierarchy using any number of criteria, from family background, to race, to ethnicity, to education. It is inherent in all of us and shows up in all sorts of social and work situations.

During an interview, both the interviewer and the interviewee will be assessing each other hierarchically. The person with the higher status will dominate the interview; it is innate in all of us. If the interviewee looks down upon the interviewer and sees this person as hierarchically lower than himself, it will not be an effective interview (Cialdini, 1993, 222-229). We have a saying: "Adults don't confess to children." Psychologically this is what happens when there is hierarchical disparity between one individual and another. This often shows up during investigations when police officers who may not have a college education and who are paid relatively low wages, must interview the rich, the famous, or the highly educated. No matter that they have a badge and authority, too often they acquiesce to eminence.

Over the years, FBI Special Agents have had to interview the President of the United States, and in those cases they have come away commenting that they felt awkward conducting the interview even when they had full authority to do so. This too affects military investigators of lower rank who must interview higher-rank officers. Even though the higher-ranked person may be cooperative, the higher status of the officer, at a subconscious level, will affect the interview. It is extremely difficult for a lower-status individual to effectively interview a higher-status individual. The psychology behind this is so profound, it affects communication so significantly, that it has derailed many important investigations.

There are ways to improve status and once more they consist primarily of non-verbal cues. Improving posture, grooming, attire, and manners will actually elevate an individual's status and hierarchy. You can change how people treat you and respond to you by mimicking high-status displays (Morris 1968, 56-57).

And while status and hierarchy are part of our psychological makeup, it can also act against us. When we see annoying hierarchical displays of arrogance, haughtiness, superiority or indifference, we are left with bad feelings and resentment. When someone acts superior to us and they have not earned that right or been granted that privilege, we tend to isolate those individuals socially through distancing.

2. Psychological Intentions

One of the fascinating features of our elaborate brains is their capacity to communicate our intentions, and once more we do this non-verbally. As the psyche decides what action to take, our bodies begin to reflect these thoughts. Take for instance two people talking together face to face. As the time draws near for one of the two to go, his posture will change, one of the legs will point away from the other person towards the direction of intended exit and may even tilt in that direction. Or the person may begin to look at his watch with increasing concern. These are corporal manifestations of what is going on in the head.

Likewise, a person straining to get a better look at something may have his feet fixed on the cement, but the head clearly demonstrates that his interest is elsewhere (Givens, 2005, 60). We are all familiar with these behaviours including many courtship behaviours such as preening which usually precede someone walking over and starting a conversation. These intention behaviours have assisted us socially to communicate for tens of thousands of years. Those of us who recognize and adapt to them are far better equipped to deal with the world according Daniel Goleman in *Emotional Intelligence* (Goleman, 1995, 78-95).

Then there are those behaviours indicative of intentions that are most familiar to law enforcement officers as they reflect intentions to commit crimes. From years of study we know that all criminal acts have two constituent parts which are always constant. All criminal acts are first ideated, and once ideation begins, communication begins to take place both physiologically and non-verbally as the criminal draws nearer to committing the crime. This is the premise of the Universal Principles of Criminal Behaviour (UPCB) (Navarro and Schafer, 2003, 22-24). In other words, when crime is being thought about (ideated), planned, and executed, we humans tend to transmit out intentions through our non-verbal behaviour. Observant people around us will pick up these tell tale clues such as hyper activity, extra vigilance, changes in work and sleep habits, etc.

Consider this famous case. In 1963, a 39-year veteran detective of the Cleveland, Ohio Police Department watched two men walk back and forth in front of a store window. They took turns peeking into the shop and then walked away. After multiple passes (24 in all), the two men huddled at the end of the street looking over their shoulders as they spoke to yet a third person. Concerned that the men were "casing" the business and intending to rob the store, the detective moved in, patted down one of the men and found a concealed handgun. The detective arrested the three men thus thwarting a robbery and averting the potential loss of life. Officer McFadden's detailed observations became the basis for the landmark U.S. Supreme Court decision. Since 1968, this ruling has allowed police officers to stop and frisk individuals without a warrant where their behaviours telegraph their intentions to commit a crime (*Terry v. Ohio*, 1968. 392 U.S. 1). With this decision, the Supreme Court acknowledged that non-verbal behaviours presage criminality if behaviours are properly observed and decoded. Once again we see a demonstration of the relationship between our thoughts, intentions, and non-verbal behaviour.

CONCLUSION

From birth to death, our bodies form an important communication link with the brain. Not only for dealing with the immediate needs to maintain life, but also to communicate with the outside world. And while we have developed the unique ability to communicate verbally with extraordinary precision as a result of our abundantly large brain, we still, after millions of years, communicate primarily non-verbally. Hardly anything transpires in our minds or psychology that is not reflected in our non-verbal communications. From emotions, to bodily needs, to dislikes, to illness, to status displays, to intentions, our bodies are exquisitely equipped to communicate on multiple levels. By carefully studying non-verbal behaviour we gain great insight into that hidden dimension of our mind's psychology.

REFERENCES

Cialdini, Robert B. (1993) *Influence: the psychology of persuasion*, New York: William Morrow and Company, Inc.

Diaz, Bernal (1988) *The conquest of new Spain*, New York: Penguin Books.

Ekman, Paul and Maureen O'Sullivan (1991) "Who can catch a liar?" *American Psychologist,* 46, 913-920.

Etcoff, Nancy (1999) *Survival of the Prettiest: The Science of Beauty*, New York: Anchor Books.

Givens, David G. (2004) *The Non-verbal Dictionary of Gestures, Signs and Body Language Cues*. Spokane: Center for Non-verbal Studies, http://members.aol.com/non-verbal2/diction1.htm.

Givens, David (2005) *Love signals: a practical field guide to the body language of courtship*, New York: St. Martin's Press.

Goleman, Daniel (1995) *Emotional intelligence*, New York: Bantam Books.

Inbau, F. E., Reid, J. E., and Buckley, J. P. (1986) *Criminal interrogation and confessions* (3rd Ed.) Baltimore: Williams and Wilkins.

Jackiewicz, Joyce (2005) Interview by Joe Navarro, November 23, Washington, D.C.

Knapp, Mark L. and Judith A. Hall (1997) *Non-verbal communication in human interaction,* (3rd. Ed.) New York: Harcourt Brace Jovanovich.

Ledoux, Joseph (1996) *The emotional brain: the mysterious underpinnings of emotional life,* New York: Touchstone.

Morris, Desmond (1985) *Body watching*, New York: Crown Publishers.

Morris, Desmond (1969) *The human zoo*, New York: Dell Publishers.

Myers, David G. (1993) *Exploring psychology* (2nd ed.) New York: Worth Publishers.

Navarro, Joe (2008) *What Every Body Is Saying: An ex-FBI Agent's guide to speed reading people* (New York: Harper Collins, 21-51).

Navarro, Joe (2003) "A four-domain model of detecting deception: an alternative paradigm for interviewing" *FBI Law Enforcement Bulletin* (June) 19-24.

Navarro, Joe and John R. Schafer (2003) "Universal principles of criminal behaviour: a tool for analyzing criminal intent" *FBI Law Enforcement Bulletin* (January) 22-24.

Panksepp, Jaak (1998) *Affective neuroscience: the foundations of human and animal emotions*, New York: Oxford University Press, Inc.

Ratey, John J. (2001) *A user's guide to the brain: perception, attention, and the four theaters of the brain*, New York: Pantheon Books.

Vrij, Aldert (2003) *Detecting lies and deceit: the psychology of lying and the implications for professional practice,* New York: John Wiley and Sons, Ltd.

CHAPTER 6

The Psychology of Extreme Beliefs

Micheline Milot

Man does not always think when he acts [...], but he always acts on a thought.
The form in which such thought acts is the certainty.

E. Weil

In the search for truth, beliefs often present an enigma, particularly during a criminal investigation. Some murderers, disinterested from a material or financial point of view, justify their acts on religious grounds, raising the dilemma of how to deal with a criminal who seems to have lost all sense of rationality. Consider certain events that have stirred the popular imagination since the 1970s: the group suicide in Jonestown organized by Jim Jones, who foresaw the end of the capitalist era (1978); the Sarin gas attack by the Aum Shinri Kyo sect in the Tokyo subway (1995); the series of group suicides and murders among the Order of the Solar Temple (1994, 1995, 1997); the assassination of Israeli Prime Minister Yitzhak Rabin by a young Jewish university student (1995); and the numerous attacks perpetrated in the name of Allah by Islamic terrorists since 1992.

It is understandable that the expression "God's fools" has gained currency. At first glance, beliefs that impel such actions, so opposed to what society generally finds morally acceptable, seem completely irrational. We quickly identify those who act in these ways as mentally ill. Common sense tells us spontaneously that "if it's a matter of belief, it isn't actually true." Then again, for the believer, beliefs often acquire the status of truth; believers don't believe they *believe*, they believe they *know*. Two categories of truth clash in the investigator and the person investigated: the rationality that governs reasonable thought in the former, and the religious belief that justifies the behaviour of the latter.

If someone believes the future is written in the lines of their hand (to paraphrase the anthropologist Marcel Mauss), we must take account of that when attempting to understand that person's behaviour, no matter how apparently irrational. I propose, therefore, to discuss the intrinsic rationality of certain religious beliefs that explains reprehensible conduct as well as the mental state of the person who commits the acts. The goal is not to render acceptable what is not, but to come to grips with the psychological and sociological logic behind these extreme beliefs. It is a matter of decoding and interpreting a strange language (to borrow an analogy) so as to make the investigative process easier.

To begin with, I will discuss how psychology and sociology approach belief, how beliefs affect believers, and how beliefs are expressed in social interactions. Although both religious and non-religious beliefs will be presented, I will focus on the former. On the basis of that discussion, I will explore how the unusual rationality of fanatical beliefs can lead an individual to endanger the lives and security of others.

A. THE LOGIC OF BELIEFS

1. The Universality of Belief

Beliefs permeate individual and collective life. They, in fact, govern a large part of our daily existence, as prominent sociologists such as Durkheim, Weber, Pareto, and Boudon have abundantly demonstrated. Even if they are realized imperfectly, collective beliefs (concerning equality, democracy, liberty, justice, etc.) are the cement of societal life. This explains why E. Weil (1967), cited in the epigraph to this chapter, has said that certainty is what defines human life. In fact, our social behaviour depends largely on beliefs — political, religious, moral. For example, we prefer to vote for a particular party because we "believe" it is in a position to govern according to our interests, even though we realize that the objective probability of electing a good government is not absolute but quite relative. Similarly, most of us adhere, to differing degrees, to diverse beliefs concerning what the weather will be tomorrow, the chances of winning the lottery with the ticket purchased this morning, the existence of God, and the possibility of living to be 100 years old. These beliefs are probabilistic and generally have little effect on our social behaviour, but they nevertheless occupy a portion of our mental universe.

That said, positing that beliefs are a given in modern life seems to run counter to the widespread view that scientific and technological progress has eradicated belief founded in fantasy and irrationality. Numerous authors have adopted this pejorative conception, which originated in the Enlightenment and sets reason against creed: "Our best hope for the future is that the intellect — the scientific spirit, reason — may in time establish a dictatorship in the mental life of man," Freud declared in one of his lectures on psychoanalysis (1981, p. 226). This evolutionary perspective assumes human beings have experienced a period of infantile credulity before attaining the Age of Reason, a view that derived support for a time from scientific advances contradicting beliefs grounded in insufficient knowledge. For example, no one still believes the earth is flat.

We cannot always reduce belief to a lack of information. Indeed, new beliefs have grown from the development of scientific knowledge. For example, scientific research on galaxies and the conditions necessary for the emergence of life have made the existence of extraterrestrials conceivable (Bronner, 2003, p. 7), even if the degree of belief differs from person to person. The discovery of a method for the cloning of living cells has opened a whole new field of beliefs, from the idea that this might cure mortal or debilitating illness to the fantasy that it will permit the creation of perfect humans. We don't believe any less than we did in the past, but our certainties are directed toward different ends.

2. The Rationality of Belief

What do we mean by "rationality?" In the social sciences, the term has several meanings, but characteristically it denotes the use of means that seem best adapted to attaining the end sought. In choosing the most effective means, one must foresee, to the best of one's abilities, likely traps, obstacles, etc. The reasoning necessary to employ this or that means distinguishes rational from irrational actions. Rationality applies as much to actions as it does to the explanatory utterances which permit us to comprehend our conception of things. Of course, the means can prove ineffective and the explanations might not be shared by the majority, but such "failings" do not make the means irrational. There is no such thing as pure reason, or the perfect means that would, with incontrovertible success and without contradiction, bring an end to all debate, in the absolute sense.

Max Weber (1971) defined a type of rationality of particular interest here — "value-oriented" rationality. In this type of rationality, action is meant to pursue objectives *and* values. Broadly speaking, Weber demonstrated the extent to which value-oriented rationality exists at the heart of individual and social action. Heroic sacrifice, risking one's life to save others, or the decision to devote more time to family at the expense of one's work all correspond to value-oriented rationality: the actor clearly conceives the value inherent in the objective pursued and adjusts the means to that end. They are conscious of the human and material cost, but consider them secondary to the value endorsed.

Criminals who act in the name of God are not necessarily all rational; psychopaths of all sorts believe they hear divine voices commanding them to kill someone. I will not consider here these delirious states, as they are a matter of mental illness. However, some who commit acts of religious fanaticism do not exhibit the typical signs of mental illness. Some activists accused of religious terrorism no doubt suffer mental problems; some psychologically weak individuals are attracted to extreme ideas, and adherence to those ideas confers them with status, a role, an identity "by proxy," so to speak. However, the majority of such activists are "normal people, socially well adapted, but taking part in a particular community characterized by an extreme worldview" (Juergensmeyer, 2003, p. 14).

3. Resisting the Contradiction of Reality

While certain populations see ritual dance as a way of curing illness, westerners are more prone to believe medicine is most effective for this purpose, even if, quite often, it is of limited power and does not deliver the anticipated result. In the political and medical spheres, as in other spheres, belief often does not let the facts get in the way.

Adherence to a belief does not depend on the belief's empirical value, or on whether the believer has actually experienced its reality. The believer need not even see the object of the belief as an immediate possibility or as attainable by themselves. For example, many people believe the dead can communicate with the living, but these believers don't conceive of themselves experiencing such a phenomenon (Milot, 1992, p. 119). Numerous Islamists consider it plausible that Allah has commanded believers to wage jihad against Christians and Jews, and while they do not disapprove of those who volunteer for that war, they do not volunteer for this task.

Belief, like the emotion with which it is associated, is a mental state. It is a matter of degree and implies a course of action. For instance, my attitude toward a loved one will differ greatly according to whether I am certain of that person's love for me or whether I doubt it, no matter what that person actually feels for me. As this example makes clear, what makes this belief enigmatic, and lies at the core of the act of believing, is its double aspect, subjective and objective. Belief resides in taking as given something that cannot be proven empirically and even defies attempts to do so.

Belief is subjective insofar as adherents experience different degrees of certainty. Some individuals are absolutely convinced of God's existence, others suppose it is possible, and still others doubt it. The objectivity of belief is a matter of the degree to which the object of the belief is grounded in reality: God's existence is likely, probable, or simply possible. Belief is enigmatic insofar as it often gives rise to collusion, approaching confusion, between its subjective and objective aspects. Paul Ricoeur rightly emphasizes that "the believer does not distinguish degrees of certainty from degrees of truth, but ... takes the former for the latter" (1976, p. 172). This is why belief, generally, is indestructible (Fontaine, 2003, p. 147). It cannot be easily contradicted by argument that relies on the weakness or implausibility of the evidence.

4. Believing ... as Others Believe

Another characteristic of value-oriented rational beliefs is that they are shared by others. They play out in a system of social interaction (Boudon and Bourricaud, p. 133), that is, with others who invest the same certainty in them. The difference between such people and those with mental problems is that the latter find themselves isolated in their religious delirium. To believe that God commands you alone to act offensively borders on insanity. But *shared* belief in a sacred text that provides a belief code, and in a radical interpretation of this code by authority figures, can, under certain circumstances, generate an implacable logic that attracts indefectible adherents.

Individuals who share certainties concerning the state of the world constitute a subculture of their host society. They could not exist, as I have pointed out, without a belief system like that underlying all societies. This is what C. Castoriadis (1975) has called "the imaginary institution of society" — a structure that, in certain contexts and for certain groups, can take on radical and violent forms while remaining rationally intelligible.

Summary

The noteworthy fundamental characteristics of beliefs are:

- Belief is a universal state of mind.

- The degree of subjective certainty and objective reality vary from individual to individual.
- Belief is rational, value-oriented, and subjet to reasoning that adapts means to desired ends.
- Belief is unprovable.
- Belief is resistant to the contradictions of reality.
- Belief is shared by others, thereby assuring its credibility and legitimating conduct based on it.

B. ABSOLUTE AND EXCESSIVE BELIEFS THAT IMPEL VIOLENCE

Fanatical — that is, absolute and excessive — beliefs complicate the administration of justice. The absolute nature of beliefs means they are absolute and non-probabilistic and lack nuance; believers harbour no doubt. In itself, absolute belief is not necessarily fanatical. A woman who enters a convent with the aim of devoting her life to the adoration of God operates under absolute belief, but one that is inoffensive to others. On the other hand, belief that is absolute *and* extreme can go beyond what is socially acceptable and result in troublesome actions. It leads to actions "the object of which is defined by an imperative beyond what is immediately at stake" (Juergensmeyer, 2003, p. 121). This imperative "is a non-negotiable" value.

The examples given at the beginning of this chapter are all fanatical belief. While they follow the same logic described above, the confusion between the degrees of certainty and reality is absolute. They leave no room for doubt or for the probability that things could be differently conceived. The belief system becomes locked into a value or an ideal, and conduct is strictly governed by that idea (value-oriented rationality). I say "belief system" so as to convey that this type of belief never exists by itself. It is part of a series of beliefs comprising a series of beliefs that, like so many dominoes, leads inexorably to an entirely revamped worldview.

Concerning the subjective mechanics of these radical forms of certainty, three factors are of particular interest in the context of the investigative interview: unquestioning belief; the firmness of the belief; and psychological and physiological changes in adherents. One finds these factors expressed in various sorts of religious fanatics in different ways: in Yitzhak Rabin's assassin, Ygal Amir, and his ilk; in certain dangerous sects such as the Order of the Solar Temple; and in fundamentalist networks that advocate holy war.

1. Unquestioning Adherence to Belief

(a) The end justifies every means

One of the greatest determinants of the subjective mechanics of extreme beliefs is the unquestioned adherence to a value that no longer accords with other fundamental values in the social order. For example, "normal people" are against social injustice and political corruption, vexations which enrage terrorists, as well. The difference is that terrorists are prepared to murder for the ideal of re-establishing justice. In so doing, they contradict another value that normal people would take into consideration: respect for human life. But the terrorist ideal is an unquestioned end that justifies all means, including the sacrifice of other values. The same can be said of totalitarian communism, the belief that human equality is unconditionally important to the point that it should trump another important value, liberty. Political regimes of this type therefore were obliged to employ very repressive measures to suppress any attempt at liberty that might compromise the egalitarian ideal.

The imperative of attaining the ideal engages the collective absolutely; otherwise, the despair and shame over having been wrong could cause the group to implode. (One thinks in this sense of Jonestown and the Order of the Solar Temple.)

(b) Different types of extreme goals

The absolute primacy accorded a value thus justifies recourse to violent means. In a criminal investigation, it is useful to classify dangerous believers on the basis of the aims that motivate them. These aims will furnish benchmarks for interviews. "Eschatological" believers are those who want to bring about the end of the world (the Aum sect in Japan, the Order of the Solar Temple, and, in the non-religious sphere, the Oklahoma City bombers). "Ideological" believers want to impose an idea or order which they imbue with absolute value (Al Qaeda, neo-Nazis). "Nationalist" believers seek absolute equivalence of national and political agendas (the Amir case in Israel, the IRA in the clash between Irish Catholics and Protestants, the FLQ in Quebec in 1970). To these groups one could add "ecological radicals" who elevate "nature" to an ultimate value and seek to protect it against human interference. In each case, outside the context of their absolute values, the believers will appear to be loyal friends, loving parents, and model students, and will eschew murder. In other words, those who commit terrorist acts are complex beings.

"Closed sects" comprise another sort of belief group, in that they recreate an (ideal) universe *intra muros*, sheltered from societal corruption. They are distinct from the four types discussed above, by virtue of the fact that violence remains within the group (incest, humiliation, seizure of assets, etc.). Cut off from the world, such sects are difficult to locate, so that it is often family members or former adherents who sound the alarm about them.

(c) The social function of confession

Fanatics who commit terrorist acts without regard to their own lives are not interested in excusing their behaviour and will feel no guilt over it. Ideological, nationalist, and ecological beliefs can foster attitudes so unconventional that they are often diagnosed as psychopathic, the assumption being that no one would act in such a way consciously or, above all, rationally. When suspects admit their crimes freely, the presumption of mental pathology gains credence.

The interviewer's problem is not in getting a confession. "Religious" criminals pride themselves on their behaviour, considering themselves champions of justice. Indeed, for them confession serves a social function and completes the crime, making widely manifest, public, and visible the cause behind it. The investigator's real challenge is to try to prevent further similar acts by understanding the criminal's logic and that of their associates. An interview based solely on conventional rationality is clearly a waste of time. Generally, the interviewer will elicit more information, at least about the interviewee's motives and the possibility that his associates will commit similar crimes, if they try to understand the interviewee's rationale. This helps investigators appraise whether the act in question was one step toward attaining a goal or an end in itself. As well, it helps the interviewer to understand the goal and thereby evaluate the types of actions adherents could take to attain it.

(d) Stereotypical responses

Yet another investigative danger is saturation with stereotyped answers that are rationally derived from the logic of a belief system. Ideological, nationalist, and eschatological certainties derive from a *credo* that is usually written (sacred texts, group charters, etc.) and strictly interpreted by a leader who enjoys the believers' full confidence. In this context, "changing one belief would require changing a whole system of beliefs" (Frijda and Mesquita, 2000, p. 63). It is often futile during an interview, then, to try to deconstruct the system's elements.

Members of closed sects tend to respond differently to interrogation. Even if they live apart from society at large, they know that it will reject their religious justifications for incest or paedophilia, in contrast to appeals for social justice or nationalist goals. It is therefore more difficult for them to maintain that the end justifies the means. Although these individuals initially attempt to defend themselves with stereotypical answers, they are more readily shaken by fear of punishment (such as imprisonment) given their moral self-image.

2. Firmness of Belief

For a certainty to remain unquestioned, the firmness of belief must be (quasi-) unshakeable. Several factors combine to maintain such certainty, notably: an authority recognized as legitimate, a closed system of thought, and the continued existence of the deplored world.

(a) The role of authority recognized as legitimate

Religious belief entails "the acceptance of pre-existing authority" (Geertz, 1972, p. 45) that transforms the individual's singular experience. If the ultimate authority is divine, the believer must interpret the divinity's will. Unlike the mentally deranged, such individuals do not believe that God "speaks" directly to them. They accept the sovereignty of an authority who *knows.* Certainty takes on form and firmness in the framework of a collective interpretation of the divine will. A great deal of sociological and psychological research has studied the powers of persuasion that authority figures wield over those who accord them such authority. Insofar as certainty is not subject to evidentiary demonstration, believers must *trust*, that is, have faith in someone who gives the belief credence. With this power, the leader — whom believers obey blindly, whatever the price, often represents a "father-figure par excellence" (Luca, 2004). The leader may even come to incarnate the ideal sought.

The unquestioning believer internalizes the world view dictated by the leader, making it their own. Then again, the leader's authority is very much nourished and substantiated by the group — one believes *with* others. Interaction of group members is generally direct but, more and more, can be "virtual," particularly among Islamist radicals. An internal centripetal force operates on the individual who breaks ties with friends or family who do not endorse the unquestioned values they now hold sacred. This can make it difficult for investigators to invoke the effects of the believer's conduct on loved ones as an interrogation tool. In fact, while obtaining a confession related to a "glorious" crime might be easy, it is very difficult to get information about a leader: the worst sin is to snitch on one's master, earthly condemnation being nothing compared to the eternal damnation of a traitor or infidel.

(b) Thought and language closure

Single-mindedness — the control of thought and language (Luca, 2000) — is a powerful factor in solidifying belief, as with Nazi or communist ideology. In this model, rational explanation, becomes independent of the content of belief and operates as a system of seduction and fascination. This seduction can be accomplished through a linguistic system whose jargon has special meaning for the group. Language encloses thought, such that "any contradiction by reality threatens ideological thought, which is intolerant of external suggestion or of internal questioning that is not reducible to the established 'group-think'" (Kaës, 1980, p. 119).

According to Frijda and Mesquita (2000, p. 63), anticipatory emotion (as opposed to emotion experienced in response to present circumstances) also solidifies belief: "The thoughts are probably not much less powerful when there are no shivers but only glimpses of an unacceptable future state, offensive to one's values ... that can give beliefs their enormous power when challenged." External pressure will not engender doubt; rather, it can serve to deadbolt the closed mind.

Festinger (1968), among others, has pioneered our understanding of cognitive dissonance and the denial it engenders. Several studies have considered, for instance, contradictions of apocalyptic beliefs presuming the imminent end of the world. In each case the adherents reinterpret events to adjust them to their belief system. Denial repudiates what reality contradicts, comprising "the origin of all belief that survives contradictory experience" (Mannoni, 1969, p. 12). It is therefore difficult for an interviewer to rely on contradictions (that generally are numerous) to the believer's unquestioned ideal. On the other hand, the questioner can challenge the believer in the realm of their own logic, which, however rational, cannot resist every contradictory eventuality that might cause emotional defensiveness. This defensiveness becomes a valuable indicator of weaknesses in the interviewee's belief system.

(c) The persistence of the world

Individuals resort to terrorism when experience has engendered in them a specific understanding of the world and their place in it. Religious ideology often springs from genuine socio-political concerns.

Unlike the circumstances confronting apocalyptic sects, concerns that feed extreme ideological, nationalist, and ecological beliefs persist and can help sustain the beliefs. To the extent that the problem is not fully redressed (a utopian ideal, in any event), it sustains the belief, rooted generally in social and political protest (against social injustice, the occupation of land, political despotism, environmental depredation, etc.). In this way, belief remains strongly tied to the necessity for action: "participation in political violence or ... support [for] violent movements ... is facilitated by the firmness of one's beliefs regarding the states of the world motivating those actions, and that such firmness of belief is fed by the emotions connected to those states of the world" (Frijda, Manstead and Bem, 2000, p. 4).

Attacks against others arise out of a rational strategy founded in the conviction that violence is necessary in the service of political or ideological ends, and that it will prove effective and morally justifiable. A good number of such attacks are symbolic acts toward realizing a long-term vision of a world order. They accord with the belief-group's internal logic and possess a ritual value that sustains that logic.

3. Psychological and Physiological Change

Beliefs redefine one's vision of the world and dispose one to action. But in some people they alter psychological and even physiological states. Psychosocial studies of the gravely ill have demonstrated that belief improves the sick person's chances of recovery (Bateson and Ventis, 1982). More recently, physicians and psychologists have endorsed the link, despite the difficulties of establishing direct proof. However, factors such as the peace instilled by prayer and meditation, or the certainty that a supreme being watches over our destiny can affect neuro-transmitters and play a role in reducing suffering or stress during the recovery process. The psychological traits of "fanatical" believers also suggest the possibilities of such transformations. At play is a redefined conception of good and evil, a strong elitist sense, and an elevated degree of self-importance, all of which can trump respect for life.

(a) The shifting frontier of good and evil

Belief affects judgment (Channouf, 2004). Believers do not experience absolute and excessive belief as an evil. Indeed, their conception of good and evil has an altogether unconventional logic. According to P.L. Berger (1971, p. 66), religion is one of the most powerful forces validating institutions, values and actions. In acting on their beliefs, believers seek to inscribe their actions in the order God desires for the world. This psychological terrain lends itself to scrambled ethics and a shifting of the frontier between good and evil, because normative benchmarks are side-stepped.

While religion is meant to promote good over evil, history demonstrates the extent to which it in fact has justified the worst atrocities and injustice. Extreme belief does not depend for its morality on what the larger society considers morally acceptable. Rather, the absolutist ideal takes root in a world considered unjust, depraved, and corrupt. Profound convictions, especially religious convictions, generally instill a good conscience, a peaceful certainty that can relieve believers of responsibility and of their critical faculties. The more fanatical believers are prepared to use violence, the more they are convinced that their convictions are well-founded. Their sense of legitimacy grows with the violence employed, and is supported by the idea that their worldview is morally superior to the rest of society's. From this arises the second characteristic trait of extreme beliefs, elitism.

(b) The psychology of "superiority"

All extreme beliefs proceed from elitism — the idea the group ardently cultivates that it and its leader are superior. The logic of this elitism follows from: (1) unquestioning adherence to a supreme value; (2) denial of any contradiction founded in reality; (3) the division of the world into those who perceive what is "good" and those who do not; (4) the group's certainty that its own vision of the world (which avoids all contradictions) is necessarily correct. The group's sense of superiority, subscribed to by the individual believer, is powerful motivation. It leads to the disregard of individuals perceived as obstacles to the pursuit of the group ideal, and by extension, to attack "infidels" in the name of good and righteousness. "Considering others as superiors, as inferiors, or as equals dictates how to behave, how to distribute your time, how to set priorities" (Frijda and Mesquita, 2000, p. 63).

The sense of superiority is founded on a dualist and Manichean logic. To begin with, it distinguishes radically between inside (believers) and outside (danger, attack), between *us* and *them*. This logic also marks out a strict division between absolute good, as the group defines it, and the evil that permeates the rest of the world. Mistrust and dehumanization of others are important variables for investigative interviewers, given that interviewers themselves belong to the world of evil and infidels.

The idea, real or presumed, that "the other" will not understand, and threats of punishment or reprisal, can reinforce this logic, which itself often leads to a defensive, if not frankly paranoiac, ideology according to which everyone who doesn't share the group's worldview is a threat. Paranoia is most likely to arise when the belief system begins to crumble (for example, when reality poses overwhelming contradictions) or when the leader loses credibility (for example, as a result of behaviour at odds with that demanded of followers). The collapse of the Order of the Solar Temple and the fate of David Koresh's sect illustrate how this type of situation can degenerate into murderous paranoia.

(c) An elevated degree of self-assurance

Feeling superior, that one possesses *the* truth or belongs to an elite group enlightened (presumptively) by an infallible leader, confers on the believer a high level of psychological, and even physiological, self-assurance. This is evident in the apparent calm determination displayed in videos of Islamists preparing to commit terrorist acts. The terrorists seem convinced of the righteousness of their objective and the cause they serve. Indeed, this self-assurance grows in parallel with the level of responsibility and danger. It would not be inaccurate to speak of a psychological desensitization to violence and to risks such as arrest or even death (the latter being generally preferred by terrorists to capture and prosecution).

This self-assurance is not displayed in the same way in other criminal groups. That the biological principle of self-preservation can break down is disconcerting, as it assumes a conviction that overwhelms the fear of one's own annihilation. More common in cultures that value self-sacrifice for community good, such a conviction can, however, be nourished by individual interactions within the group. Systems of self-control are themselves anchored in the "collective I," a solidarity focused on continuously justifying each believer's determination to act violently, and assuring mutual control over individual fears until the last instant.

The training and conditioning of Islamists, for example, to endorse extreme violence in the name of their religion, do not in themselves suffice to ensure unflinching determination to that last moment. A whole arsenal of ritual is inculcated in them as a form of self-control against fear, stress, doubt, and anything else that could obstruct the progress of the terrorist action. Terrorists are surrounded by other Islamists only. An Al-Qaeda text reveals that conditioning for prayer assures clear thinking in moments of weakness. A set of spiritual advisories and rituals run parallel, step by step, with the intended action. Everything is justified by highly debatable interpretations of *suras* (chapters) in the Koran: "Adjust your clothing, as generations of the pious have done since the time of the Prophet. They adjusted their clothing before battle." "Forget completely this so-called world and life in it. The time for play-acting is over. It is time for serious action" (Marret, 2002, p. XII et XIII). In addition to praying, the terrorists ritually bless and sanctify sundry tools of their murderous task (pistols, procedural manuals, explosives, etc.) as well as everyday objects such as passports and identity cards. Indeed, the gun used to assassinate Egyptian president Anwar Sadat in 1981 was engraved with the words, "In the name of Allah, the avenger" (*Allah al-Mountaqim*).

Adherence to unquestioned belief contains fear to the point of inhibiting physiological signs of anxiety and malaise in the face of accusation. During a criminal investigation, such inhibition can no doubt mask the usual indicators, such as nervousness and sweating, that help determine the sincerity of a confession.

4. Ygal Amir as Prototype: the Logic of Fanaticism

On November 4, 1995, Yitzhak Rabin, the Israeli prime minister, was assassinated by Ygal Amir, a young Jewish university student who examining psychologists found to be mentally healthy. Amir was inspired by the writings of Theodore Herzl, who organized the First Zionist Congress in 1897 and is known as the Father of Zionism. Amir had a copy of the biography of B. Goldstein, who attacked Arabs at the Tomb of the Patriarchs in 1994 and admired the Israeli Eyal splinter group (the Warriors of Israel), fundamentalists who base their beliefs on a literal interpretation of certain sacred texts. In a statement published across the world, this group swore to "to execute whoever cedes the Promised Land of Judea and Samaria (the West Bank of the Jordan River) to Arabs." Astonishingly calm during his trial, Amir congratulated himself on his conduct, and claimed to have acted on divine command. Amir was not a serial killer, and he certainly would not accept the assassination of a fellow inmate he had befriended. However, he saw himself as justified in murdering Rabin.

Amir harboured the religious certainty that his act was in keeping logically with a long politico-religious history based on sacred received wisdom and saw the land of Israel as having been divinely bestowed upon the Hebrews. And that land included territories conquered during the 1967 war, with the consequent tensions this generated between Palestinians and Israelis. Young Amir's case fits rationally into this framework, which impels many Jews to interpret the geopolitical problem as a matter of theology.

Ygal Amir was educated as a Zionist, and was a member of the elite army unit stationed in the Golan Heights. He studied sacred texts, notably *Joshua* and *Deuteronomy*, according to which God gave the land of Israel to the Hebrews after they had violently conquered other nations.

A literal interpretation of these gives legitimacy to the political-religious belief that the land of Israel belongs exclusively to the Jews. Some public figures endorse this radical concept. General Moshe Dayan stated: "If we have the Bible, and if we consider ourselves the People of the Book, then we should take all the Land of the Bible" (quoted in the *Jerusalem Post*, August 10, 1967). Moshe Levinger, a rabbi who was instrumental in the establishment of settlements in the conquered Palestinian territories, welcomed the murder of Arab students at a West Bank high school, saying, "Whoever committed this act publicly honoured God." The 1994 attack against Muslims praying at the Tomb of the Patriarchs took place during the Jewish festival of Purim, which commemorates the deliverance of the Jews from the Persian king's vizier, who sought to exterminate them. Juergensmeyer remarks that "Goldstein had not killed faithful innocents at the Tomb of the Patriarchs, but Haman, Hitler, and Arafat, sanctifying the name of God with an act of vengeance. In slaughtering Muslims on this particular date, Goldstein sent a sort of message to Jews, entreating them to return to their traditions, avenge themselves against past humiliations, and give themselves the political means to live by the ideals they held dear... Goldstein had wanted to honour the Jewish tradition but also humiliate Islam" (Juergensmeyer, 2003, p. 132).

Prime Minister Rabin had worked ardently on the Oslo accords to have Israel share land with the Palestinians and withdraw from territory considered biblical land. In so doing, he acted, in the minds of the most extreme Zionists, contrary to God's will. The sacred texts say these extremist ancestors were inspired by God to occupy Israel by massacring the inhabitants. For modern extremists, this renders such action legitimate today.

This then becomes a rationale for murder, acceptable to the perpetrator and his supporters, although certainly not to all Jews. Amir believed that the sacred texts clearly express God's will, especially with regard to the endowment of the land of Israel to his Chosen People, and must be followed. It is therefore lawful to take it from anyone standing in destiny's way, just as it was lawful long ago. This value-oriented rationality displaces the dividing line between good and evil: Even though divine commandment forbids killing, respect for the land God has given Israel justifies recourse to the means to retake it. Thus, Amir felt absolutely no guilt over what he had done.

CONCLUSION

Extreme beliefs are grounded in values that arise in specific contexts and sub-groups, and are structured and legitimated by rational systems. As Bronner notes, "belief, no matter how extravagant, can be fully understood only as illuminating subjectively the rational mechanics which have led certain social beings to subscribe to it" (Bronner, 2003, p. 9).

These religious fanatics are different from criminals who act for personal gain or under some psychopathy. They require a different investigative approach. It is important to consider that the stranger a system seems to us, the more we discredit it as irrational and try to reconstruct it as an entity we subjectively consider more rational. A believer is superstitious in the eyes of those who do not hold the same beliefs. Conversely, to the believer the non-believer lives in an impenetrable ignorance. When an observer evaluates the behaviour of another as irrational, they project the characteristic givens of their own situation onto the individual observed (Boudon and Bourricaud, 2000, p. 485-486).

It is more productive to enter in some way into the rationality of the belief, which makes it easier to establish terms for a "relationship" with the believer and find the weak points in a belief system that appears impenetrable. All the same, and as detailed above, certain characteristics of the fanatical believer pose particular challenges for the interviewer:

- A sense of moral superiority over the interviewer, which instils mistrust. Negation of the other dehumanizes, making personal rapport impossible and the individual literally "elsewhere."
- *A priori*, disputing the correctness or reasonableness of the belief will only create distance between the interviewer and interviewee.
- Pressure or blackmail reinforces the perception of the interviewer as an enemy or aggressor. In any event, there is no willing dialogue with the "ungodly" or "infidels."
- Profound conviction enhances the sense of psychological security. Those who undertake dangerous missions have learned to face down fear.
- The fanatical believer has no physical or material interest in cooperating in the interrogation. Their certainty of reward in the hereafter, and of having acted according to divine will (as they interpret it), prevent them from fearing reprisal.
- Denunciation is much rarer among those in closed, fiercely loyal fringe groups, particularly if members are very motivated and show little interest in the material world. They have, to put it succinctly, nothing to lose. When you are prepared to make your body a weapon and death is an attractive option, ordinary external pressures are less effective.

It is certainly possible to prod the believer's confusion between their convictions and reality: How can they be absolutely certain that God endorses their attacks on others? Don't their beliefs really serve their own narcissistic interests? Instilling doubt in someone who had none is perhaps a promising avenue of securing a confession.

REFERENCES

Batson, C.D. and W.L. Ventis, W. Larry (1982). *The Religious Experience: A Social-Psychological Perspective*, New York, Oxford University Press.

Berger, P.L. (1971). *La religion dans la conscience moderne*, Paris, Centurion, [*The Sacred Canopy*, New York, Doubleday and Company, 1967].

Boudon, R. and F. Bourricaud (2000). "Croyances", *Dictionnaire critique de la sociologie*, Paris, Quadrige, p. 133-141.

Boudon, R. and F. Bourricaud (2000). "Rationalité", *Dictionnaire critique de la sociologie*, Paris, Quadrige, p. 479-487.

Boudon, R. (1995). *Le juste et le vrai*, Paris, Fayard.

Bronner, G. (2003). *L'empire des croyances*, Paris, PUF, coll. Sociologies.

Castoriadis, C. (1975). *L'institution imaginaire de la société*, Paris, Seuil.

Channouf, A. (2004). *Les influences inconscientes. De l'effet des émotions et des croyances sur le jugement*, Paris, Armand Colin.

Festinger, L. (1968). *A Theory of Cognitive Dissonance*, Stanford, Stanford University Press (reprint of the Evanston edition, 1957).

Fontaine, P. (2003). *La croyance*, Paris, Ellipses, coll. Philo.

Freud, S. (1981). *Nouvelles conférences sur la psychanalyse*, Paris, Gallimard.

Frijda, N. and B. Mesquita (2000). "Beliefs through Emotions", *Emotions and Beliefs. How Feelings Influence Thoughts,* Frijda, N. H., A. Manstead, S. Bem (eds.), Cambridge University Press.

Frijda, N., B. Mesquita and S. Bem (2000). "The Influence of Emotions on Beliefs", *Emotions and Beliefs. How Feelings Influence Thoughts,* Frijda, N. H., A. Manstead, S. Bem (eds.), Cambridge University Press.

Giguère, N. (Director) (1997). *Aller simple pour Syrius* (témoignages de-proches et d'ex-membres de l'Ordre du Temple Solaire), Verseau International.

Juergensmeyer, M. (2003). *Au nom de Dieu, ils tuent ! Chrétiens, juifs, musulmans, ils revendiquent la violence* (translation, *Terror in the mind of God*), Paris, Autrement.

Kaës, R. (1980). *L'idéologie. Études psychanalytiques*, Paris, Dunod.

Laborit, H. (1976). *Éloge de la fuite*, Paris, Robert Laffont.

Mannoni, O. (1969). "Je sais bien mais quand même", *Clefs pour l'Imaginaire, ou l'Autre scène*, Paris, Seuil, coll. Points.

Marret, J.-L. (2002). *Techniques du terrorisme*, Paris, PUF.

Milot, M. (1992). "Typologie des systèmes de croyances", *Les croyances des Québécois. Esquisses pour une approche empirique*, R. Lemieux and M. Milot (eds.), Sainte-Foy, Les Cahiers de recherche en sciences de la religion, vol. 11, p. 115-133.

Ricoeur, P. (1976). "Croyance", *Encyclopaedia Universalis*, vol. V, Paris.

Weber, M. (1971). *Économie et société*, I, Paris, Plon.

Weil, E. (1967). "Certitude", *Logique de la philosophie*, chap. IV, Paris, Vrin.

PART II

FALSE ALLEGATIONS

CHAPTER 7

False Rape Allegations:

When Victim Becomes Offender

Michel St-Yves

Nothing is closer to the true than the false.

Albert Einstein

False allegations of sexual assault by adults is a delicate subject, little documented and little understood. However, even Greek mythology and biblical stories refer to the phenomenon. Frustrated because Jacob's son Joseph refused to sleep with her, Potiphar's wife avenged herself by complaining to her husband that Jacob, Potiphar's majordomo, had tried to rape her. Potiphar seized Joseph and imprisoned him in a fortress as a prisoner of the king. Only several years later was Joseph's name cleared (Genesis 39: 6-20).

The fact that silence surrounds false allegations of rape does not mean they are rare. It is difficult to evaluate the extent of the phenomenon, and statistics – often from police sources – provoke controversy. This is understandable, given that certain authors claim that allegations of sexual assault are just as often false as well-founded (Kanin, 1994). Given more than 10,000[1] such assaults reported by adults each year in Canada alone, this is a major concern.

The goal of this chapter is to explore from a police perspective the phenomenon of false rape allegations by adults. What is the extent of the problem? What motive do women have for making these false statements

---

1 In 2004, there were 73.7 sexual assaults per 100,000 inhabitants in Canada (Statistics Canada, 2004), amounting to nearly 24,000 "official" attacks of that nature. In 2000, adult women aged 18 and over represented 45% of female victims (*Condition féminine Canada*, www.swc-cfc.gc.ca, updated November 9, 2005).

(it is most often women who do so)? How can false allegations be detected early to avoid costly investigations that can create true victims?

False allegations of sexual assault

A false allegation can be defined as a lie deliberately told by an alleged victim accusing a man of a rape[2] that never occurred. It can also be an imaginary claim that the complainant believes to be true (Katz and Mazur, 1979: 207). Thus there are false allegations that can be said to be willful, made knowingly with the aim of misleading, and false allegations made unwillfully, usually because the complainant believes or is convinced that she was the victim of a crime. Although in both cases the allegations are unfounded, there is an important distinction between "deliberate lying" and "honest mistake" (Burgess and Hazelwood, 2001: 180). Then, too, allegations can be partly false, as where there are exaggerations or omissions. In such cases it can be very difficult to evaluate whether a statement is true or false (Aiken, 1993).

The three principal criteria that classify a complaint as unfounded are:

1. *Confession.* The complainant admits that the allegations are false and that she has given an untrue statement (written or recorded).

2. *Evidence.* Scientific evidence, a medical examination, or an independent witness contradicts the "victim's" allegations.

3. *Victim credibility.* Evidence that the "victim" suffers from mental illness or has made allegations for a specific and inappropriate reason (Williamson, 1996), or instances where the complainant fails a polygraph test (Kanin, 1994) can raise doubts about the basis for the accusation.

The frequency of unfounded allegations

The occurrence of false sexual-assault allegations in adults varies greatly according to the definitions and criteria employed, as well as according to the person evaluating them (Katz and Mazur, 1979). Most of those who work with organizations focused on female victims believe the

---

2 In this essay, the words "rape" and "sexual assault" are used synonymously to describe sexual aggression against an adult.

occurrence rate is minimal, representing no more than 2% of sexual assaults (Chappell and Singer, 1977; London Rape Crisis Centre, 1984). Some go so far as to deny the existence of false rape, claiming the phenomenon reflects police mistrust of victims (Russell, 1984).

According to studies and criteria used to classify complaints as being founded or otherwise, the rate of false allegations varies from less than 1% (Krasner et al., 1976; O'Reilly, 1984) to more than 50% (Kanin, 1984; Comment, 1968). The highest rates occur in studies performed in the law enforcement milieu. Peters and his colleagues (1976) have observed that social workers report far fewer false accusations than do police officers (2% versus 18.2%). MacDonald (1971) notes that the Denver police eventually classified 25% of rapes as unfounded, and an additional 20% as doubtful. McDowell and Hibler (1987), as well as Buckley (1992) who use a total sample of 1824 sexual assaults, observed similar rates. Kanin (1994) examined all rapes reported between 1978 and 1987 in a small town in the midwestern United States, finding that out of the 109 reports, 45 (41%) were officially declared unfounded. These rates are comparable to those investigated by specialized sexual assault squads such as those of the Toronto Police Service.[3] These high rates in the law-enforcement sector are perhaps attributable, partly, to more sophisticated investigative methods. Yet they are not widely known in the general public because most false allegations are not reported anywhere, and the complainants are rarely accused of public mischief.

Some studies reveal that false allegations of sexual assault are more frequent than are false allegations of other types of serious crime. "In 1990, in Denver (Colorado), there were 472 reported rapes and 80 (that is, 16.9%) were unfounded. The same year, there were 965 thefts reported and 135 (14%) were unfounded. In most cities, there were reported more unfounded rapes than other unfounded major crimes" (MacDonald, 1995: 87). According to *Crime Index Offences*, out of all crimes reported to police across the United States, on average 4% are unfounded.

---

3 Analysis of serious sexual crime, in which the victims claimed they did not know the aggressors, showed that allegations in 60 of 232 files (30%) were unfounded (Carnell, B., "False Rape Claims – The Evidence from Canada," January 14, 2002: www.equityfeminism.com/archives/years/2002/000010.html).

A. THEORIES AND MOTIVATIONS

Psychoanalysts have long associated false allegations of rape with an unconscious masochistic desire to be raped (Deutsch, 1944 ; Freud, 1933) – a repressed erotic wish converted into a belief (MacDonald, 1973). For some, it signifies a neurotic personality converting fantasy into belief, occasionally going so far as to falsify memory (Bessmer, 1984). Others see it simply as an impulsive and desperate act masking distress (Kanin, 1994). Having been unsuccessful at meeting a need in an acceptable way, the complainant feels a need for attention and sympathy, and assumes the role of victim (Feldman and Escalona, 1991). Such persons choose rape, a form of violence which incites great emotion in general, as well as fear among medical and legal authorities of wrongly doubting the allegation (Feldman, Ford and Stone, 1994).

Reasons for making false allegations of rape vary from resentment to psychosis (MacDonald, 1973). McDowell and Hibler (1987) explain the phenomenon by way of an adaptational continuum extending from mild distortion to altogether false allegations. In extreme cases, statements can include bizarre scenarios supported by wounds and self-mutilation (Aiken, Burgess and Hazelwood, 1999).

Concerning adults, Kanin (1994) identifies three main motivations for making false rape allegations:

1. Providing an Alibi and Saving Face

Kanin (1994) has observed that the majority of complainants (56%) who make false statements do so to extricate themselves from an embarrassing situation and save face. An assailant is identified in approximately one half of these cases. The reasons motivating such allegations include: a way of explaining an extramarital affair; fear of being pregnant or having contracted a sexually-transmitted disease; and fear of reprimand by parents for having disobeyed them (Hayman et al., 1968; MacDonald, 1971; 1973; Schiff, 1969). In some cases, the reasons are more banal, such as the loss of money or valuable objects, an automobile accident, or the need to explain an absence. Then there is the case of the panicked young woman lost in the woods who, hoping for quick rescue, told the 911 operator that she had been raped.

2. Revenge

Kanin (1994) has observed that slightly more than one woman in four (27%) has falsely alleged rape out of hatred, frustration, or vengeance, often following rejection (real or imagined). When false allegations are made for vindictive reasons, the complainant always identifies the alleged aggressor.

In 1999, in a small municipality west of Montreal, a woman in her 30s contacted police to complain of a savage attack she had suffered three days earlier. In her statement she claimed that her neighbour, whom she formally identified, showed up at her home in broad daylight and assaulted her physically and sexually. Injuries to her arms and thighs were still visible. The medical report indicated that the wounds were compatible with the complainant's story.

The next day, police arrested the presumed attacker and interrogated him for three hours. Though the investigator confronted the man with the complainant's videotaped statement, he persistently denied having attacked her. He repeated that it wasn't him as he had been at work at the relevant time. Turning his face to the wall, the investigator confronted the suspect one last time after having again showed him the full taped statement:

Investigator: *How do you explain her injuries?*

Suspect: *She caused them herself.*

Investigator: *Why would she say things like this?*

Suspect: *Because she was in love with me and I didn't want to go on with the relationship* [the suspect had already had an affair with this neighbour].

After four days of detention, the suspect was freed until his court appearance. The investigation finally verified his alibi and did not corroborate the complainant's allegations. She had lied seeking revenge.

3. Need for Attention and Sympathy

Kanin (1994) has identified the need for attention and sympathy as the principal motivation among 18% of women making false sexual-assault claims. Often such complainants make quite a production of their allegations, hoping to enhance their credibility, sometimes going so far as fabricating evidence and doing themselves serious injury.

In June, 2001, the Sûreté du Québec received a call for help concerning a murder and multiple sexual assaults. The complainant said several people had mistreated and sexually assaulted her throughout her childhood, sometimes while she was on drugs, and that during this period she witnessed the murder of a little girl. At the time of the woman's call to police, she claimed that one of these attackers still had her under his control and continued to sexually assault her, though she was now 33 years old. The complainant disclosed these facts, initially during psychotherapy, in a 13-page manuscript that included drawings (Figures 1 to 4). Below is an excerpt:

> The only way I could see to free myself, to end the suffering and the nightmares, to stop seeing and hearing it happening, was to die. Sometimes I thought I felt their hands and mouths on my body, or their belts and their syringes. Now I'm afraid of everything, even of myself ... Filthy, disgusting, repugnant, sickening, ashamed, suffering horrible endless pain. I had to swallow sperm and then drink a bottle of my own pee. It never ended, every week for years. I hate the past, the present, the future, and life. I have no strength, no energy. Going on would be a waste of time for everyone around me. [translation]

The investigation revealed that no child reported missing at the relevant time met the description the complainant gave police. Claiming that her "attacker" had arranged a rendezvous with her to sexually assault her, she proposed that the police set up a sting. It turned out the "rendezvous" had been orchestrated by the complainant herself. Confronted with the complete lack of foundation for everything she had told police, the complainant admitted she had invented the whole story.

In some cases, the pseudo-victim's need for attention is pathological to the point that she injures or mutilates herself gravely. Asher (1951) has described this as the Münchausen Syndrome.

Münchausen Syndrome

Asher called this syndrome "Münchausen" in reference to Baron von Münchausen (1720-1797), a retired German cavalry officer and a notorious teller of tall tales. The symptoms reveal themselves as a feigned disorder, the main goal of which is to attract attention or sympathy from medical personnel or family and friends (Asher, 1951; Carney and Brown, 1983;

Roth, 1962). Sometimes the sufferer seeks secondary gain such as escaping the law, obtaining free lodging (Asher, 1951), avoiding an intolerable situation at home or among family (Hopkins, 1973; Forbes et al., 1974), or in response to financial problems (Snowden, Solomons and Druce, 1978). Some patients harbour more than one motivation simultaneously or successively (Carney and Brown, 1983). Asher first described Münchausen Syndrome, otherwise called *pseudologia fantastica*, in 1951, and reports from all over the world subsequently confirmed it (Ford, 1973).

The syndrome is often diagnosed as a form of borderline personality disorder (Carney and Brown, 1983; Spiro, 1968; Carney, 1980; Nadelson, 1979). The symptoms include mood instability, with impulsiveness and a tendency to self-mutilation. Some authors contend that such patients also exhibit signs of hysteria (Cramer, Gershberg and Stern, 1971). They are often manipulative, seductive, and attention-seekers.

B. OTHER MOTIVATIONS

1. Money

Money can also incite people to make false allegations of sexual assault (Bronson, 1918; Hall and Hall, 2001; MacDonald, 1995) – as with blackmail and demands for compensation from victims' aid centres. MacDonald (1995: 96) cites the example of a woman whose boyfriend dropped her off far from her home. She told authorities she was kidnapped and raped before being abandoned in a neighbouring town. Police drove her home, and the woman later admitted she had lied to avoid paying for a taxi. Some authors say financial gain is a more frequent motivating factor than attention seeking (MacDonald, 1995).

2. Alcohol and Drug Abuse

Alcohol or drug abuse can cause momentary loss of consciousness or hallucinations that lead a person to believe she has been sexually assaulted. Memory of the event is often vague and described as a dreamlike experience.

3. Psychosis and Delusional Disorder

False rape allegations are not unusual among paranoid psychotic women (MacDonald, 1973: 190). Generally "psychosis" denotes a loss of contact with reality. According to the DSM-IV, "psychotic" refers to delusional ideas, pronounced hallucinations (usually auditory or visual), disorganized speech, or disorganized or catatonic behaviour (American Psychiatric Association, 1996: 321). When psychotics or other delusional persons falsely allege rape, the three components of the allegation – the criminal act, the perpetrator, the scene of the crime – are invented (Aiken, Burgess and Hazelwood, 1999) and the allegations can be repetitive (Aiken, Burgess and Hazelwood, 1999; MacDonald, 1973).

In a 12-page statement, a woman complained that some persons had stolen her identity so as to use her credit card, cell phone, and e-mail address. Not until the fifth page did she say she had been sexually assaulted between 2001 and 2002. The allegations lacked coherence and seemed fabricated, filled as they were with the distortions and exaggerations associated with delusions of persecution. The delusional thinking became more pronounced page by page, and the narrative became less and less coherent and believable (more "made-up"). She wrote: "I was suffering so much, I was hearing voices during that time." She then described what amounted to symptoms of schizophrenia and ended her statement: "By the way, I'm proud to tell you that I no longer take any neuroleptic, sleeping, or tranquilizer pills" (neuroleptics being used to treat symptoms of psychosis). This seemed to confirm that the complainant suffered from schizophrenia. It was likely because she had stopped taking her medication that she disintegrated into psychotic behaviour.

4. False Recollections

Recent years have seen the publication of several studies on the phenomenon of "recovered memory" among persons claiming to have been sexually assaulted when they were children (see Davies and Dalgleish, 2001; Gudjonsson, 1997; Ost, 2006; Pendergrast, 1996; Pope and Brown, 1996). When these "mnesic" recoveries turn out to be false, they are associated with "false-memory syndrome," also called "false recollection." (See the work of Elizabeth Loftus.) The usual hypothesis is that psychotherapists provoke, or at least facilitate, this phenomenon by suggesting that the events happened (Leo, 1997; Ofshe and Watters, 1994). Traumatic recollections of sexual abuse, generally from childhood, recur many years later. However, these supposed recollections turn out to be baseless. In Quebec, a study of patients treated by 220 psychiatrists and psychologists has shown that, during therapy, one patient in 25 invents a recollection of childhood sexual abuse. This pseudo-abuse that "resurfaces" is usually particularly odious.[4] A simple remark by the therapist such as "listening to you, I get the impression that you were sexually abused during your childhood" is enough to unleash a feverish search in the recesses of memory with the single-minded objective of discovering who perpetrated this abuse.

Suggestion is the first step in creating a false recollection. Some psychotherapists believe that absence of childhood memories always suggests the possibility of incest. Others say, "if you have the least doubt, or if you display the pertinent symptoms, it is because you suffered such abuse." In the result, convinced that they have found the cause of their emotional suffering, patients falsely accuse others, often their parents, of having sexually abused them.

It has been clearly shown that encouragement to imagine a fictional event augments the probability of invented recollection. As well, Loftus and Ketcham (1991; 1994) have shown that suggestion and/or false information can implant "false recollections." Imagination can also play a role in producing false belief and false memory. When observers showed subjects sham advertising describing a visit to Disneyland, nearly a third recalled they had met Bugs Bunny. Several recalled having shaken his paw, others his ears or tail. Some even said they had hugged him (Braun, Ellis and Loftus, 2002; Loftus, 2003). However, given that Bugs Bunny is an animated character owned by Warner Brothers – which organization would not risk appropriating Disney property – the scenario described in the ad was complete invention (Braun, Ellis and Loftus, 2002).

The researchers drew two lessons from this:

1) Suggestion can generate false recollections;

2) Even if the recollection is reported with certainty, details and sensory elements, this does not necessarily signify that the events really occurred (McNally, 2003).

Hypnosis expert Spanos associates false-memory events with other phenomena such as multiple-personality disorder (dissociative disturbance), demonic possession, past-life beliefs and claims of having been kidnapped aboard UFOs (Spanos, 1994; 1996; Spanos et al. 1991; 1993). In 1995, one

---

4 *Le Journal de Montréal*, Sunday, November 2, 1997.

million Americans were convinced that extra-terrestrials had abducted them (Fredrickson, 1992).

The vast majority (92%) of "victims" of false-recovered memory syndrome are women; 74% of victims are between 31 and 50 years old and almost a third (31%) have post-secondary education. More than half (60%) claim to recall being sexually abused before the age of four. Most often they accuse their father (62%), while 30% accused both their mother and father of the abuse. A not insignificant percentage (18%) alleges sexual abuse during satanic rituals (University of Washington, 2001).

C. DETECTING FALSE ALLEGATIONS OF SEXUAL ASSAULT

Doubting a victim's story is always a matter of delicacy. Falsely accusing a victim of having lied can intensify her trauma and destroy the rapport established between her and the investigator (McDowell and Hibler, 1987). There is a myth that, following a rape, victims are hysterical and reduced to tears. Burgess and Holmstrom (1974) have observed the contrary. Victims display a variety of emotions in the hours following a sexual assault. The physical and emotional impact can be so intense that some victims enter a state of shock and don't believe what has happened to them. Burgess and Holmstrom (1974) distinguish two types of emotions expressed by victims: 1) expressive; and 2) controlled:

1) With the expressive type, the victim is agitated during the interview, becomes tense at certain questions, cries when she describes specific acts committed by her attacker, and occasionally laughs nervously.

2) The "controlled" victim masks or hides her feelings, appearing calm or even self-controlled (Burgess and Holmstrom, 1974: 38).

Investigators often suspect a complainant is making false allegations when she frequently changes her story. But they must be cautious in this, since mnesic recall could be at play (Burgess and Hazelwood, 2001: 179-180). Police officers are also inclined to accept that a rape has occurred if there is evidence of violence (Peters, 1973) and physical injury (Hayman et al., 1968; *University of Pennsylvania Law Review*, 1968): "If a woman walks into a police station and complains of rape with no such signs of violence, she must be closely interrogated" (Alan Firth, 1975: 1507).

Then again, police more often believe the victim if the aggressor is a stranger to them, the circumstances suggest there was more than one aggressor, the victim screamed and showed signs of resisting, and she seems upset (Peters, 1973). As well, police find the allegations more credible if the woman reports the crime quickly, a weapon was used, and the victim has a good reputation (*University of Pennsylvania Law Review*, 1968; MacDonald, 1971). In her study of the myths surrounding rape, Martha R. Burt (1980) has observed that more than half of people interviewed agree with statements such as: "A woman who goes to the home or apartment of a man on their first date implies she is willing to have sex"; "[I]n the majority of rapes, the victim is promiscuous or has a bad reputation" (Burt, 1980: 223).

Whether the victim is believed can also depend on her age and race. Hayman and his colleagues (1968) assert that children are accorded more credibility than adults. However, children more often make false allegations than adults do (Hursch and Selkin, 1974), and Caucasian adults are more often believed than non-whites (Hayman et al., 1968).

Kanin has sketched out the typical profile of those who make false complaints: a young white woman aged 22, only modestly educated, with a socio-economic background inferior to the population's average – in other words, the same profile as that for genuine victims of sexual assault (Kanin, 1994: 84).

Profile or none, those who have considered the matter have identified certain behaviours and characteristics often associated with unfounded complaints. One can group these indicators into six categories (see Table 1):

1) Reporting the assault;

2) The description of the perpetrator and his behaviour;

3) The nature of the sexual acts alleged;

4) The evidence and recollection of details;

5) Injuries;

6) The complainant's psychological profile.

No single indicator is conclusive. Sometimes called "red flags," the indicators serve as a warning (Aiken, Burgess and Hazelwood, 1999: 234), indicating to investigators that they must seek clarification. The more red flags, the greater the chance that the sexual assault complaint is untrue – all the more so if neither the complainant nor the investigation can provide answers to the questions the indicators raise.

1. Reporting the Crime

Not uncommonly, when a complainant, without explanation, delays reporting a crime to police, the allegation is false (McDowell and Hibler, 1987). The delay can be a matter of hours, but also months or even years, making investigation that much more difficult. As well, the complainant often speaks first to those close to her (family, friends, work colleagues) or to medical personnel (during a pregnancy test, for example, or an examination for a sexually transmitted disease) who then inform police or insist that the victim do so (McDowell and Hibler, 1987). It can be difficult to contact some supposed victims after they have complained, as they are unresponsive to telephone calls, move house without notice, or simply do not want to complain to the police (Ledray, 1994).

2. The Description of the Aggressor and his Behaviour

The description of the aggressor is essential to identifying the suspect and the creation of a police sketch for investigative use. With false sexual-assault allegations, the aggressor's description is sometimes vague or absent ("Joe Blow"), particularly compared to the detail provided in the rest of the statement (McDowell and Hibler, 1987; Ledray, 1994). Sometimes it is stereotyped: "He was dressed in black, a black jacket and gloves." To add credibility to her story, the complainant sometimes adds pre- or post-crime details. Some pseudo-victims claim they were threatened (in writing or by telephone) before or after the attack (McDowell and Hibler, 1987). Others describe being followed or harassed by the perpetrator (Ledray, 1994).

In comparing fabricated sexual assaults[5] (n = 30) to authentic assaults (n = 142), Alison and Marshall (2006) have observed that where the rapes were simulated there was no demand described for valuables or money (compared to 22.5% in the authentic category), no theft (26.8%), and many fewer prying questions on the assailant's part (6.7% versus 23.2%). The authors note that in the simulated category the assailants made significantly

5 Each participant recounted in writing that she had been the victim of a sexual assault by a stranger. Researchers instructed the participants to imagine a rape scenario of sufficient credibility that it would fool police.

fewer comments about themselves (3.3% versus 38.7%) and used a weapon to control the victim much less frequently (13.3% versus 50.7%). They also remark that false complaints of rape contain significantly more allegations of violent behaviour (including multiple acts of gratuitous violence), vulgar language (blasphemy, insults), and violent removal of clothing. One must interpret these results with care, given that they arise from simulated rapes, and the conditions and motives of the pseudo-victims do not mirror what one finds with false allegations in actual practice.

3. The Nature of the Sexual Acts

Not uncommonly, the complainant cannot describe the details and sequence in a sexual assault. She might say only, "he raped me." Sometimes there is nothing to show lack of consent or even that anything sexual occurred. Other times the sexual descriptions are plentiful and inappropriate, suggesting sexual fantasy. Often there is no description of collateral sexual acts (oral sex, sodomy), but only of vaginal penetration and touching of the genitals and breasts, at least where the collateral behaviour is not part of the complainant's sexual experience (McDowell and Hibler, 1987). In a sample of 45 pseudo-victims, Kanin (1994) found not a single report of forced oral or anal sex, whereas about one in four women complain of such acts in genuine sexual assaults. In comparing simulated and genuine sexual assaults, Alison and Marshall (2006) also found that statements regarding simulated attacks contained significantly fewer descriptions of collateral sexual acts such as non-violent sexual propositions, fellatio, cunnilingus and kissing.

4. The Evidence and the Alleged Facts

After crime-scene evidence, recollection of facts by witnesses is the most useful information in a criminal investigation. Where an allegation is false, the "victim" is faced with a dilemma: be believed and helped, but at the same time do everything to make sure the crime is not solved; unless, that is, the complainant is motivated by vengeance, mental problems or false memories. This is why the pseudo-victim often claims her eyes were closed or she was blindfolded, she lost consciousness, she was drugged, or she no longer remembers where the crime occurred (Aiken, Burgess and Hazelwood, 1999). That is, because there is no concrete evidence, the investigation goes nowhere (Jay, 1991). There is no evidence because there was no crime.

Occasionally the presumed victim gives very precise details about the crime scene or her assailant, but the peripheral details, although real and verifiable, are nothing more than red herrings. The pseudo-victim might describe perfectly the little street where she was led by force, the bench on which she was undressed and sexually assaulted, even the precise appearance of a residence. In some cases, she might even have convinced a witness that he saw or heard something corroborative. The complainant has the single-minded goal of enhancing the credibility of her accusations, a trap which is sometimes difficult for investigators to avoid. Then again, these details are nothing but illusion and will not corroborate the alleged facts. They are, as Mohandie, Hatcher and Raymond (1998) put it, pseudo-corroboration.

5. Injuries

The majority of rapists use force aimed not at wounding but at controlling the victim (Green, 1987; Weekley, 1986). Most often, sexual-assault victims resist only mildly, calculating that this improves their chances of survival (Corbett, Larcombe and Real Rape Law Coalition, 1993; McDowell and Hibler, 1987). When the allegation is false, it is not unusual for the complainant to claim to have struggled energetically but in vain (McDowell and Hibler, 1987). However, in these latter cases, generally there are no serious wounds, and particularly not to sensitive parts of the body such as the eyes, breasts, lips, or genitals. Nor, generally, are there lost teeth or broken bones (McDowell and Hibler, 1987). Superficial cuts and scratches are common (Ledray, 1994). Sometimes the pseudo-victims display scratches in the apparent form of letters or words, often on the abdomen or groin.

Self-inflicted wounds often appear in unusual places, easily accessible to the complainant. They are often caused by fingernails or a cutting instrument such as a razor blade or knife (Figures 5 to 8). If the complainant is right-handed, the cuts are most likely to appear on the inside of the left upper arm or left thigh, at an angle compatible with self-inflicted injury (Ledray, 1994). Frequently the complainant will be indifferent to such apparent wounds, and sometimes damage to clothing is incompatible with the nature of the wounds (McDowell and Hibler, 1987).

Table 1

25 indicators to help screen for adults who could be falsely alleging sexual assault

-I- Reporting the crime

1.	Unjustified or unexplained delay between the event and complaint made to police:	☐
2.	Complaint initially made to someone other than a police officer:	☐
3.	Someone other than the complainant contacts police:	☐
4.	Someone insists that the victim contact police:	☐
5.	The victim is reticent to report the incident/is difficult to contact after she complains:	☐

-II- The description of the perpetrator and his behaviour

6.	No description of the perpetrator:	☐
7.	Vague or stereotyped description:	☐
8.	Strange events arising before or after the attack:	☐

-III- The nature of the purported sexual acts

9.	Complainant unable to provide details or the sequence of events in the sexual assault:	☐
10.	Abundant or inappropriate discussion of sexual matters:	☐
11.	No collateral sexual acts:	☐

-IV- The evidence and fact recollection

12.	Victim saw nothing (e.g., was blindfolded)/was drugged/lost consciousness:	☐
13.	Victim can't remember where the crime took place:	☐
14.	Only peripheral details reported (signs of pseudo-corroboration):	☐
15.	Story is contradictory/implausible:	☐
16.	Nothing in victim's story can be corroborated:	☐

-V- Injuries

17.	Victim struggled energetically but has no serious injuries:	☐
18.	Unusual superficial cuts/scratches; superficial wounds in unusual places on body:	☐
19.	Indifference to apparent injuries:	☐
20.	Damage to clothing incompatible with wounds:	☐

-VI- Psychological profile of the complainant

21.	Personal/professional/marital/family problems:	☐
22.	Suspected psychological/psychiatric problems:	☐
23.	Regular/abusive consumption of alcohol/drugs/medication:	☐
24.	Earlier victimization in the same or similar crimes:	☐
25.	Allegations made following publicity regarding a crime of the same nature:	☐

6. The Complainant's Psychological Profile

Most people who make false allegations have problematic personal lives (Jay, 1991) – marital or professional problems, for instance, or psychological difficulties. Often they have unstable inter-personal relationships (McDowell and Hibler, 1987), with few close friends and few social resources (Ledray, 1994).

Commonly they have a history of making one or more previous false accusations (Hall and Hall, 2001; McDowell and Hibler, 1987) – complaints about crimes never clearly explained. Such allegations can also follow on reports of similar crimes (McDowell and Hibler, 1987). This is precisely what happened at a U.S. university campus where, one after the other, three students with no link between them reported to police that they had been sexually assaulted by an unknown person. Investigation into "the University Heights rapist" showed that none of the allegations was founded (Jay, 1991).

Some pseudo-victims display mental problems, (often documented in earlier psychiatric reports), or a hystrionic or borderline personality disorder (Hall and Hall, 2001; MacDonald, 1971; 1973; McDowell and Hibler, 1987). According to the American Psychiatric Association (1996), the essential characteristic of the histrionic personality is the overwhelming desire for attention. The hystrionic's demeanour is animated and theatrical, with a tendency to dramatize or exaggerate emotions. Their statements to police frequently contain superlatives ("horrible," "terrible," "terrorized," "unbelievable," "awful," etc.) and exclamation marks which sometimes betray the novelistic nature of their stories. They may act out scenes or invent stories. They may have a reputation for lying (mythomania) or for chronic exaggeration (Ledray, 1994). Their interaction with others often has an inappropriate seductive or provocative quality. Those with borderline personalities are unstable in various respects, including interpersonal relations (where they can vacillate between extreme idealization and utter denigration), identity and mood. Fear of abandonment, impulsivity, and self-mutilation are commonly present. Those suffering from Münchausen Syndrome can have a significant history of "strange" medical complaints or self-mutilation (McDowell and Hibler, 1987).

Fig. 1

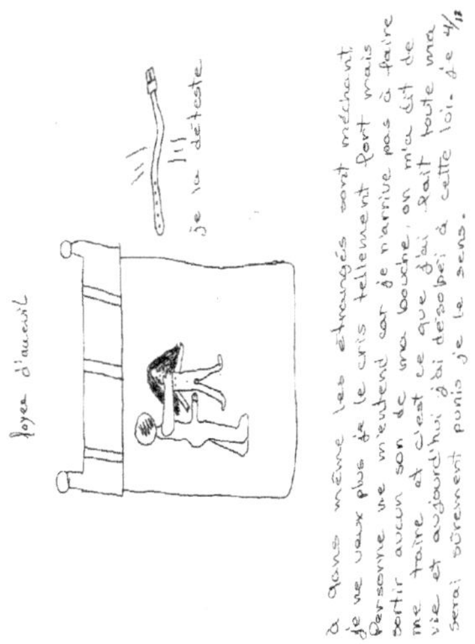

Fig. 2

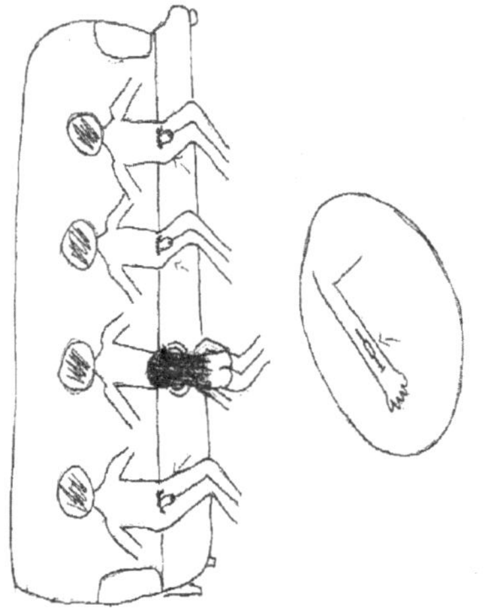

Fig. 3

Fig. 4

Fig. 5

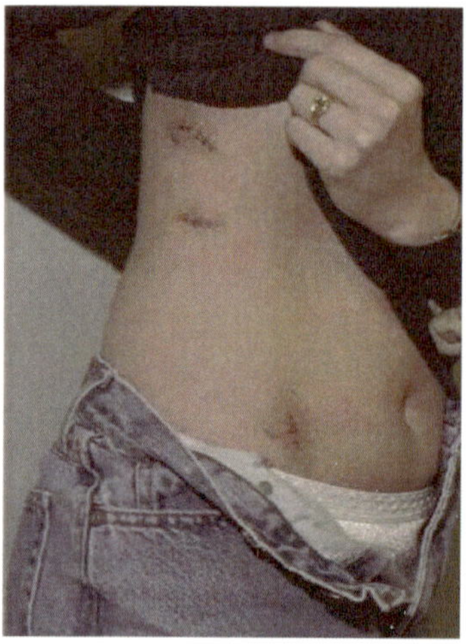

Fig. 6

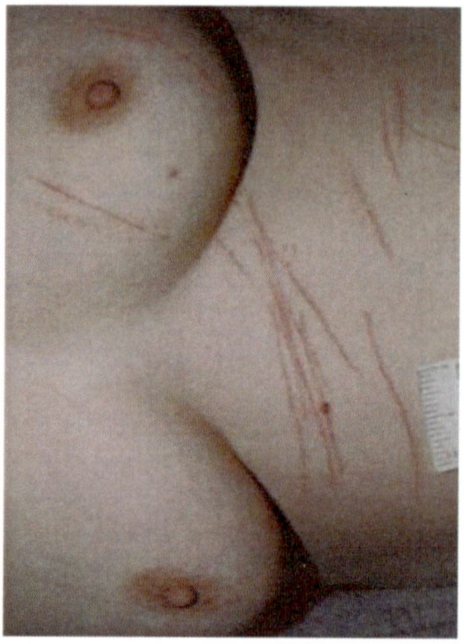

Photos Cornwall Community Police Service

Fig. 7

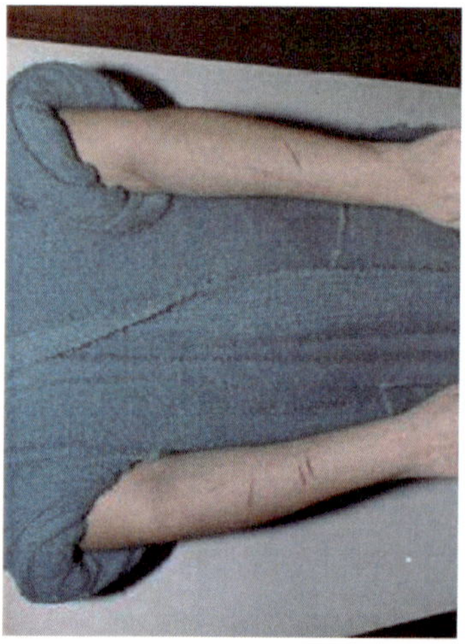

Fig. 8

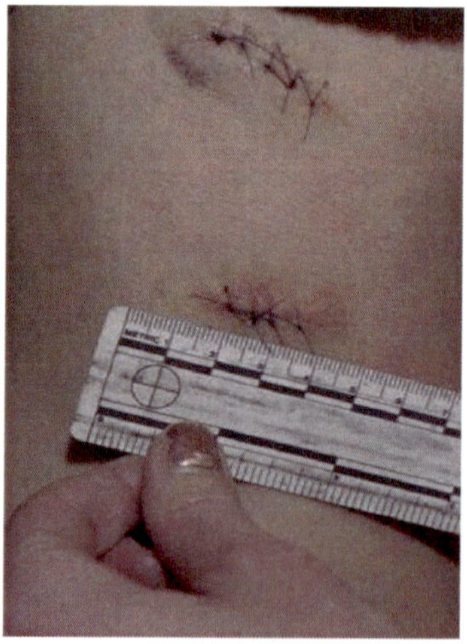

Photos Ontario Provincial Police

D. DEALING WITH FALSE ALLEGATIONS

It is a mistake to think something is false simply because you do not understand it. [translation]

Ghandi

It is always a delicate matter to confront a "victim," all the more so because accusing that person of lying can intensify trauma and destroy investigator-complainant rapport (McDowell and Hibler, 1987). It is less damaging for the victim, and more productive for the investigation, to presume initially that the allegations are genuine. With that approach, the complainant will cooperate openly and confidently whether the allegations are founded or not (National Center for Women and Policing, 2001). As Latts and Geiselman (1991:8) note:

> If the police do not believe the victim, they may directly or indirectly make this known to her, perhaps by excessive questioning that focuses on an absence of obvious injury or some delay in reporting the incident. The victim, in turn, may become upset and withdraw her cooperation. Though the woman may have been an actual survivor of rape, her lack of cooperation is itself considered grounds for marking a case as unfounded in most jurisdictions.

It is therefore important that investigators take the time to establish a rapport with the complainant, providing her with support and taking care that she doesn't feel judged. Carney (1980) has observed that the best approach is to establish a relationship aimed at discovering the underlying problems.

Pseudo-victims tend to direct the investigation so as to evoke sympathy or turn the focus toward subjects less risky for themselves – tactics altogether compatible with their motivations. When an interviewer asks them for collaboration, they often become indignant (McDowell and Hibler, 1987). It is important to recall that the complaint is often brought to police by someone other than the "victim." The victim finds herself imprisoned, if not victimized, by her own lie, with no idea how to free herself. The bigger the lie, the harder it is to confess it.

If the investigation has been thorough and reasonable doubt has been raised, investigators must confront the complainant with how her story does not accord with known fact. However, the confrontation must not be condemnatory (Nadelson, 1979). Cooperation is more likely where investigators progressively present the evidence so as to show the complainant, gently and indirectly, that they know her allegations are false. Lyell (1972) recommends this approach in cases where there is no criminal intent. Investigators should set out the evidence without ambiguity, if possible offering help. They must allow the pseudo-victim to provide her own explanation, one that permits her to save face. People often make false allegations as a way of protecting their self-esteem. Any attack bolsters defence mechanisms. It is important that investigators help the complainant maintain or regain her dignity.

In extreme cases, such as where Münchausen Syndrome is involved, complainants are not inclined to admit their mischief. On the contrary, they tend to become upset at suggestions that their problem is psychological (Nadelson, 1979; Pankratz, 1981). In a study by Carney and Brown (1983), four people admitted their lie, eight partly confessed, and 30 not at all. That is, fewer than 10% admitted lying, even if the simulated evidence overwhelmingly betrayed them (Carney and Brown, 1983). Several people afflicted with Münchausen Syndrome by Proxy persisted in denial even when caught bald-faced on video (Hanon, 1991).

CONCLUSION

There is no agreement on how often adults make false reports of sexual assault. Some researchers say the phenomenon is very marginal. Others see a plague. Then again, most studies show the phenomenon is common and of concern.

The reasons for such false accusations are numerous. They can be made in good faith, the complainant sincerely believing that she was sexually assaulted (as with false memory or some serious mental disorders), or intentionally and deliberately, as is usually the case. The three main reasons people knowingly make false allegations are:

1) To create an alibi and save face;

2) Revenge;

3) Need for attention and sympathy. In extreme cases, "victims" can badly mutilate themselves in the hope of making their rape stories more credible.

As there is rarely tangible evidence, detecting false allegations is difficult. While some indicators exist, most are essentially empirical and therefore must be used with caution, to deepen the investigation or in preparation for further interviews with the presumed victim. Such interviews are delicate, as their end is to confront (and sometimes warn) the complainant – who might indeed be a genuine victim – without inhibiting her co-operation.

Only rarely do the courts consider unfounded allegations of sexual assault. This makes it difficult to catalogue and evaluate instances of it precisely. One must not trivialize unfounded complaints, given that, if undetected, they can lead to wrongful accusations or even convictions (McDonald, 1971). Rarely punished, the pseudo-victims almost always achieve their goals, particularly where they seek revenge or attention.

Despite the scale of this phenomenon, investigators must avoid tunnel vision by keeping an open mind and interpreting the evidence cautiously (Jay, 1991). If there is any doubt, it is always preferable to seek a second opinion. A faulty diagnosis, from one side or the other, can be disastrous.

* * *

Midmorning on September 30, 2002, a 20-year-old female student appeared practically nude on a balcony. A man who said he was a bailiff had appeared at her door, she said, handcuffed her, threatened her with a knife and raped her. Then he tried to strangle her to death and set fire to her apartment.

Investigation revealed that normally on that morning the young woman would have been in class but had forgotten something in her apartment and had returned home. A polite man wearing a suit and tie met her there on the pretext that he was looking for a letter for the courts. The woman said she was unaware of any such letter, and the man asked to use her telephone. Then he asked to use her toilet. Once in the bathroom, he claimed he was having trouble with the toilet. The woman went to help, at which point the man brandished a knife and sexually assaulted her. According to the woman's statement, the man did not ejaculate. The rest was confusion. She started to suffocate and panicked. She remembered being handcuffed, strangled, verbally abused and threatened, at which point the man took her to her bedroom. Because she was frightened, she kept her eyes closed, but she heard the man crumple some paper then leave the room and return. He tried to strangle her again, then left, closing the door to her room. The smoke alarm went off, causing her to rise from her bed to discover three fires – in her closet, in a close hamper and on her mattress. She tried to extinguish the fires, first with a coat and then with pails of water. Experiencing difficulty breathing, she went out on the balcony and was seen there by passersby, who immediately called the fire department and police.

At first blush, investigators could not rule out the possibility of a false allegation. A young woman with an anxiety disorder stays home when normally she would have been in class. She claims a man in a suit and tie has raped her at knifepoint in the bathroom, then handcuffed her and strangled her repeatedly to the point that she lost consciousness. Then she had awoken in her bed to find three fires eating away at the perimeter of her apartment. She was saved in the nick of time by her smoke alarm. The suit-and-tie rapist had stolen nothing and apparently left no trace of his visit to the apartment.

Three days later, police arrested a man for other sexual crimes. His description corresponded with the composite sketch created with the young woman's help. The man made incriminating statements to a fellow detainee. The investigation progressed rapidly, and the suspect's DNA, found on the victim's clothing, confirmed he had indeed attacked her. The suit-and-tie rapist, as the media called him, was named Angelo Colalillo, and he was one of the worst sexual predators and serial killers that Quebec has known. He killed himself two days before he was to go to trial.

REFERENCES

Aiken, M.M. (1993). False allegation: A concept in the context of rape. *Journal of Psychosocial Nursing*, 31, 15-20.

Aiken, M.M., Burgess, A.W. and Hazelwood, R.R. (1999). False rape allegations. In R.R. Hazelwood and A.W. Burgess (dir.), *Practical Aspects of Investigation : A multidisciplinary Approach*, Second edition, CRC Press, 219-240.

Alison, L.J. and Marshall, B.C. (2006). Structural Behavioural Analysis as a Basis for Discriminating between Genuine and Simulated Rape Allegations. *Journal of Investigative Psychology and Offender Profiling*, 3 : 21-34.

American Psychiatric Association (1996). *DSM-IV : Manuel diagnostique et statistique des troubles mentaux*, 4e éd. (version internationale, Washington DC, 1995), traduction française par J.-D. Guelfi *et al.*, Paris, Masson.

Asher, R. (1951). Münchausen syndrome, *Lancet*.

Barker, J.C. (1962). The syndrome of hospital addiction (Münchausen Syndrome). A report on the investigation of seven cases. *Journal of Mental Science*, 108, 167-182.

Bessmer, S. (1984). *The Laws of Rape*, Praeger, New York.

Braun, K.A., Ellis, R., and Loftus, E.F. (2002). Make my memory : How advertising can change our memories of the past. *Psychology and Marketing*, 19, 1-23.

Bronson, F.R. (1918). False accusations of rape. *Am. J. Urol. Sex.* 14 : 509-510.

Buckley, S. (1992). Unfounded reports of rape confound area police investigators. *Washington Post*, June 27, 1992.

Burgess, A.W. and Hazelwood, R.R. (2001). False Rape Allegations. In Hazelwood, R.R., Burgess, A.W. (2001). *Practical aspects of rape investigation : A multidisciplinary approach*, third edition. CRC Press, 177-197.

Burgess, A.W. and Holmstrom, L.L. (1974). Sex stress situation, in *Rape : Victims of Crisis*, 23, 196-202, Bowie, MD : Brady Co.

Bursten, B. (1965). On Münchausen's syndrome. *Archives of General Psychiatry*, 13, 261-268.

Burt, M.R. (1980). Cultural Myths and Supports for Rape. *Journal of Personality and Social Psychology*. Vol. 38, No. 2, 217-230.

Carney, M.W. (1980). Artefactual Illness to Attract Medical Attention. *British Journal of Psychiatry*, 136, 542-547.

Carney, M.W. and Brown, J.P. (1983). Clinical features and motives among 42 artifactual illness patients. *British Journal of Medical Psychology*, 56, 57-66.

Carney, M.W.P. and Brozowic, M. (1978). Self-induced bleeding and bruising, *Lancet*, I, 924-925.

Chappell, D. and Singer, S. (1977). Rape in New York City. In Chappell and Singer (eds.), *Forcible Rape*, New York, Columbia University Press.

Corbett, L., Larcombe, W. and Real Rape Law Coalition (1993). Lunar Landscapes : The dark side of sexual assault and the law. In P.W. Easteal and S. McKillop (eds.), *Women and the Law : Proceedings of a conference held 24-26 September 1991*. Australian Institute of Criminology, Canberra.

Cramer, B., Gershberg, M.R. and Stern, M. (1971). Münchausen's syndrome : its relationship to malingering, hysteria and the physician-patient relationship. *Arch. Gen. Psychiatry*, 24, 573.

Davies, G.M. and Dalgleish, T. (2001). *Recovered Memories : Seeking the Middle Ground*. John Wiley and Sons Ltd.

Deutsch, H. (1944). *The Psychology of Women*, Vol. 1, Grune and Stratton, New York.

Federal Bureau of Investigation, Clarence M. Kelley, Director. *Crime in the United States*, Uniform Crime Reports, 1975. Washington, D.C. : U.S. Government Printing Office, Aug. 25, 1976.

Feldman, M.D. and Escalona, R. (1991). The longing for nurturance : a case of factitious cancer. *Psychosomatics*, 32 : 226-228.

Feldman, M.D., Ford, C.V. and Stone, T. (1994). Deceiving Others/ Deceiving Oneself : Four Cases of Factitious Rape. *Southern Medical Journal*, Vol. 87, No. 7, July 1994, 736-738.

Firth, A. (1975). Interrogation. *Police Review*, 28, November : 1507-1509.

Forbes, C.D., Prentice, C.R.M. and Sclare, A.B. (1974). Surreptitious ingestion of warfarin. *British Journal of Psychiatry*, 125, 245-247.

Ford, C.V. (1973). The Münchausen Syndrome : A Report of Four New Cases and a Review of Psychodynamic Considerations. *Psychiatry in Medicine*, Vol. 4, No. 1, 31-45.

Fredrickson, R. (1992). *Repressed memories : A journey to recovery from sexual abuse.* NY : Simon and Schuster.

Freud, S. (1933). *New Introductory Lectures on Psychoanalysis*, Norton, New York.

Green, L. (1987). South Australian research on common perceptions about rape. *Legal Service Bulletin*, vol. 12, April, 77-78.

Gudjonsson, G.H. (1997). Accusations by adults of childhood sexual abuse : A survey of the members of the British False Memory (BFMS). *Applied Cognitive Psychology*, 11, 3-18.

Hall, R.C.W. and Hall, R.C.W. (2001). False Allegations : The Role of the Forensic Psychiatrist. *Journal of Psychiatric Practice*, September, 343-346.

Hanon, K.A. (1991). Child Abuse : Münchausen's Syndrome by Proxy. *FBI Law Enforcement Bulletin*. December.

Hawkings, J.R., Jones, K.S., Sim, M. and Tibbetts, R.W. (1956). Deliberate disability. *British Medical Journal*, Feb. 18 (4963) : 361-367.

Hayman, C.R., Steward, W.F., Lewis, F.R. and Grant, M. (1968). Sexual Assault on Women and Children in the District of Columbia. *Public Health Reports*, 83 (12), 1021-1028, Dec.

Hazelwood, R.R and Burgess, A.W. (2001). *Practical aspects of rape investigation : A multidisciplinary approach*, third edition. CRC Press.

Hopkins, A. (1973). Pretending to be unconscious. *Lancet*, ii, 312-314.

Hursch, C.J. and Selkin, J. (1974). *Rape Prevention Research Project.* Mimeographed Annual Report of the Violence Research Unit, Division of Psychiatric Service, Department of Health and Hospitals, Denver. In Katz and Masur (1979).

Jay, D.R. (1991). Victimization on the College Campus : A Look at Three High-Profile Cases. *Campus Law Enforcement Journal*, 21(1), 35-37.

Kanin, E.J. (1982). Female Rape Fantasies : A Victimization Study. *Victimology : An International Journal*, Vol. 7, No. 1-4, 114-121.

Kanin, E.J. (1994). False rape allegations, *Archives of Sexual Behavior*, 2(1), 81-92.

Katz, S. and Mazur, M. (1979). *Understanding the rape victim*, John Wiley and Sons, New York.

Krasner, W., Meyer, L. and Carroll, N. (1976). *Victims of Rape*. U.S. Government Printing Office : Washington, DC.

Latts, M.G. and Geiselman, R.E. (1991). Interviewing survivors of rape. *Journal of Police and Criminal Psychology*, 7(1), 8-16.

Ledray, L.E. (1994). Rape or self-injury ? *Journal of Emergency Nursing*, 20(2), 88-90.

Leo, R.A. (1997). The social and legal construction of repressed memory. *Law and Social Inquiry*, 22(5), 653-693.

Loftus, E.F. (2003). Our changeable memories : legal and practical implications. *Nature*, 4, 231-234.

Loftus, E.F. and Ketcham, K. (1994). *The myth of repressed memory*. New York : St. Martin's Press.

Loftus, E.F. and Ketcham, K. (1991). *Witness for the defense*. New York : St. Martin's Press.

London Rape Crisis Centre (1984). *Sexual Violence : The reality for women.* The women's Press, London.

Lyell, A. (1972). Dermatitis artefacta and self-inflicted disease. *Scottish Medical Journal*, 17, 187-196.

MacDonald, J.M. (1995). *Rape : Controversial Issues.* Criminal Profiles, Date Rape, False Reports and False Memories. Charles C. Thomas Publisher.

MacDonald, J.M. (1973). False Accusations of Rape. *Medical Aspects of Human Sexuality*, May 1973, 173-194.

MacDonald, J.M. (1971). *Rape : Offenders and their Victims.* Springfield, IL : Charles C. Thomas.

McDowell, C.P. and Hibler, N.S. (1987). False allegations (Chapter 11, p. 275-299). In R.R. Hazelwood and A.W. Burgess (eds.), *Practical Aspects of Rape Investigation : A Multidisciplinary Approach.* Elsevier : New York.

McNally, R.J. (2003). *Remembering trauma.* Cambridge, MA : Harvard University Press.

Mohandie, K., Hatcher, C. and Raymond, D. (1998). False Victimization Syndromes in Stalking, in Meloy, J. Reid (1998). *The Psychology of Stalking. Clinical and Forensic Perspectives.* Academic Press. California, 225-256.

Nadelson, T. (1979). The Münchausen spectrum : borderline character features, *Gen. Hosp. Psychiatry*, 1(1), 11.

Ofshe, R. and Watters, E. (1994). *Making Monsters : False Memories, Psychotherapy, and Sexual Hysteria.* New York : Scribner.

O'Reilly, H.J. (1984). Crisis intervention with victims of forcible rape : A police perspective. In J. Hopkins (dir.), *Perspectives on Rape and Sexual Assault.* Harper and Row : London (89-103).

Ost, J. (2006). Recovered memories. In T. Williamson (Ed.), *Investigative Interviewing. Rights, research, regulation*, Willan Publishing, 259-291.

Pankratz, L. (1981). A review of the Münchausen syndrome, *Clin. Psychol. Rev.*, 1, 65.

Pendergrast, M. (1996). *Victims of Memory : Incest Accusations and Shattered Lives* (second edition). Hinesburg, VT : Upper Access, Inc.

Peters, J.J. (1973). *The Philadelphia Rape Victim Study.* A report presented at the First International Symposium on Victimology, Jerusalem, Israel. Sept. 1973. Mimeographed copy from The Center for Rape Concern, Philadelphia General Hospital. In Katz et Mazur (1979).

Peters, J.J., Meyer, L.C. and Carroll, N.E. (1976). *The Philadelphia Assault Victim Study.* Final Report from the National Institute of Mental Health. ROIMH 21304, June 30. In Katz and Masur (1979).

Pope, K.S. and Brown, L.S. (1996). *Recovered memories of abuse : Assessment, therapy, forensics.* Washington, DC : American Psychological Association.

Roth, M. (1962). The desire to be ill. *University of Durham Medical Gazette*, 57, 1-18.

Russell, D.E.H. (1984). *Sexual exploitation.* Beverly Hills : Sage.

Sapir, A. (1996). *The L.S.I. Scan Workshop Guidebook : Scientific Content Analysis (SCAN).* Laboratory for Scientific Interrogation.

Schiff, A.F. (1969). Statistical Features of Rape. *Journal of Forensic Sciences*, 14(1), 102-111, Jan.

Simpson, M.A. (1976). Self-mutilation. *British Journal of Hospital Medicine*, 16, 430-438.

Smith, N. (2001). *Reading between the lines : An evaluation of the Scientific Content Analysis technique (SCAN).* Police Research Series. Paper 135. Home Office. United Kingdom.

Snowden, J., Solomons, R. and Druce, H. (1978). Feigned bereavement : Twelve cases. *British Journal of Psychiatry*, 133, 15-19.

Spanos, N.P. (1996). *Multiple Identities and False Memories : A Sociocognitive Perspective.* New York, NY : American Psychological Association.

Spanos, N.P. (1994). Multiple identity enactments and multiple personality disorder : A sociocognitive perspective. *Psychological Bulletin*, 116, 143-165.

Spanos, N.P., Cross, P.A., Dickson, K. and DuBreuil, S.C. (1993). Close encounters : an examination of UFO experiences, *Journal of Abnormal Psychology*, 95, 21-23.

Spanos, N.P. Menary, E., Gabora, N.J., DuBreuil, S.C. and Dewhirst, B. (1991). Secondary identity enactments during hypnotic past-life regression : a sociocognitive perspective, *Journal of Personality and Social Psychology*, 61 : 308-320.

Spiro, H.R. (1968). Chronic factitious illness : Münchausen's syndrome. *Archives of General Psychiatry*, 18, 569-579.

St-Yves, M., Pilon, M. and Landry, J. (2004). La détection du mensonge. In M. St-Yves and J. Landry (eds.), *Psychologie des entrevues d'enquête : de la recherche à la pratique*. Cowansville : Éditions Yvon Blais, 257-288.

The National Center for Women and Policing (2001). *Successfully Investigating Acquaintance Sexual Assault : A National Manual for Law Enforcement*. Mai 2001. www.womenandpolicing. org/. See June 12, 2006.

University of Washington, (2001) http://www.washington.edu/). http://www.sciencedaily.com/releases/2001/06/010612065657.htm.

University of Pennsylvania Law Review (1968). *Police Discretion and the Judgement That a Crime Has Been Committed – Rape in Philadelphia*. 117, 277-322.

Weekley, K.J.C. (1986). *Rape : A 4 Year Policy Study of Victims*, South Australian Police Department, South Australia.

Williamson, T. (1996). Police Investigations – separating the false and genuine. *Med. Sci. Law*, Vol. 36, No. 2.

CHAPTER 8

Assessing False Allegations of Child Sexual Abuse

Mireille Cyr and Guy Bruneau

Sexual abuse against children is overwhelmingly a crime of silence, and when that silence is broken it is often a matter of the child's word against an adult's. To determine the truth, though, one must negotiate diametrically opposed views – one holding that children are so vulnerable they must always be believed, the other positing that children are so susceptible to suggestion that one must regard their allegations with great scepticism.

The stakes are high: failing to believe an abused child or believing a child who has not been abused has heavy consequences for the child, the alleged offender, the non-offender parent and family – and also for the social workers, police officers and judicial authorities concerned. If only the investigator could find an infallible method of separating the truth from manipulation and fantasy.

In keeping with our goal of enhancing the vigilance of socio-legal authorities, we felt it was important to approach this chapter impartially, laying out the current thinking on what influences the veracity, suggestibility, and credibility of children's allegations. More exactly, after defining the construct of false allegations and considering its significance, we explore factors that foster the phenomenon, particularly lying, memory, questioning and suggestibility, divorce situations, rumour, as well as other indicators. We also briefly consider the use of validity checklists in evaluating disclosures. In concluding, we underscore the attitudes that should be adopted preferentially in the course of investigations.

A. DEFINITION

The literature provides no consensus on what is meant by "false allegations." According to Poole and Lamb (1998), the term should be reserved for cases in which children explicitly make an allegation that is untrue. However, the term often encompasses cases where parents or neighbours harbour suspicions that turn out to be unsubstantiated upon investigation or are based on a misinterpretation of what a child has said, whether sexual abuse has been alleged or not (Poole and Lamb, 1998). For Ceci and Bruck (1995), the term should also cover allegations produced by "coaching," deliberate or not, the misinterpretation of events, or allegations that arise from inadequate interview techniques. Obviously, prevalence of the phenomenon will vary as a function of the definition applied.

In addition, the definition should also extend to cases in which a child has been abused but lies about it. As Van Gijseghem (1991) has pointed out, the rate of false allegations is probably lower than the rate of false denials, that is, children who seek to minimize the intensity and frequency of abuse (Berliner and Barbieri, 1984).

B. PREVALENCE

As there exists no generally accepted scientific method for determining when claims of sexual abuse are true or not, it is difficult to establish the prevalence of false allegations with any sort of accuracy (Poole and Lindsay, 1998). The problem in part is that rarely are there confirmatory external facts, such as a confession from the offender, medical evidence, or pornographic photos of the child. According to articles published in the 1980s and the *American Professional Society on the Abuse of Children* (APSAC, 1993), 5% to 8% of sexual-abuse allegations are false. In court, the rate frequently cited by experts is 6% (Ceci and Bruck, 1995). In truth, however, the problem has been the focus of scant research.

Among the few studies that have sought to document the phenomenon, Jones and McGraw (1987) examined 576 cases of sexual abuse investigated in a single year. Authorities had deemed 53% of these to be substantiated, 23% to be unsubstantiated, and the remaining 24% to lack sufficient information to permit a clear appraisal. Of the unsubstantiated cases, 6 of the 23 percentage points represented false claims deliberately or maliciously made, while allegations made in good faith but proven false upon investigation accounted for the other 17 points. For their part, Anthony and Watkeys (1991) analyzed 410 sexual-abuse complaints referred to police or social workers in England. In 350 of these, authorities employed a multi-disciplinary approach (police, social, medical) and deemed 197 (56.3%) to be substantiated. Among the 153 unsubstantiated cases (43.7%), 63 (18% of all cases) arose from false allegations, of which half were considered untruthful and malicious. The others stemmed from investigations undertaken either because another child of the family had been abused or because situations had been reported by professionals or non-professionals on the basis of concern or suspicion. The researchers concluded that the problem of false allegations was of low importance.

In another study, Oates, Jones, Denson, Sirotnak, Gary and Krugman (2000) looked at a sample of 551 cases referred to Australian child-protection services and observed that 34% had been deemed unsubstantiated. Of these false allegations, those made by children accounted for 2.5 percentage points, and these were most likely to have been advanced by older girls. More recently, using data concerning the Canadian experience (CIS-98), Trocmé and Bala (2005) examined a representative sample of 7672 cases of abuse investigated by child-protection authorities. They found that, of the unsubstantiated cases, only 4 of 35 percentage points were the product of intentional fabrication. This rate was slightly higher in cases of sexual abuse (6%) compared with cases of physical abuse (4%), neglect (4%), and emotional maltreatment (2%). However, none of the false allegations of sexual abuse had come from the children themselves.

On the other hand, Ceci and Bruck (1995) believe these rates to be artificially low, given that only intentionally false allegations are generally considered. When other factors are taken into account, such as misunderstanding what the child says or problems arising with presumed indicators of abuse following suggestive interviews, the rate of false allegations rises considerably, reaching 6% to 23% (Jones and McGraw, 1987) and even upwards of 35% (Faller, 1991) in divorce situations.

This evidence of more frequent false allegations in the context of divorce and disputes over child custody (Ehrenberg and Elterman, 1995) raises a particularly thorny question that has received some research attention. In a study covering six months, Thoennes and Tjaden (1990) examined court motions to review custody and visitation rights. They observed that approximately 2% of 9000 cases involved sexual abuse, which translated into a disclosure rate six times as high as in the general population. The authors also demonstrated that allegations concerning a family member under these circumstances were no more likely to be false than were similar allegations in the general population. Anthony and Watkeys (1991) observed that 6% of false or malicious sexual-abuse allegations were made by adults in the context of custody rights.

In 1991, Faller analyzed 136 cases in which children of divorced parents had been referred to a university-based clinic conducting a study of abuse and neglect. She concluded that sexual abuse occurred in 65% of the cases, and that there was no abuse in the remaining 35%. Faller divided this percentage into three subgroups: possible cases of false allegations but with inconclusive evidence to this effect (8.8 percentage points); cases reflecting the dynamics of divorce (11 points); and cases of false allegations arising from the acrimonious climate of the divorce (14 points). For Ceci and Bruck (1995), however, all cases in the Faller study where sexual abuse was unsubstantiated should be counted as false allegations (35% and not merely 14%). Following up on the above study, Faller and DeVoe (1995) examined 215 allegations of sexual violence within families going through divorce. They concluded that 14.4% of the allegations were unfounded. Of these 45 cases, 34 (15.8% of all cases) were classified as a misinterpretation by adults, 10 (4.7% of all cases) as knowingly false allegations, and 1 as uncertain. In a Canadian study by Trocmé and Bala (2005), false allegations occurred more frequently in families in which there were custody disputes than in other settings (12% vs. 3%). It must be emphasized that in this particular study, allegations of neglect occurred much more frequently than allegations of sexual abuse.

In sum, there is no consensus on the prevalence of false allegations and the definition of a false allegation bears upon the rates observed.

C. FACTORS FAVOURING FALSE ALLEGATIONS

In this section we discuss various factors that can favour false allegations. Some of these are related to the child's personal traits, others with the child's environment, and others still with the socio-legal context.

1. Secrets and Lies

One cannot completely understand the phenomenon of false allegations without considering the role of secrets and lies. According to the Oxford English Dictionary, a lie is "an intentionally false statement." From a certain point of view, secrets and lies go hand in hand and cannot be dissociated: Lies make it possible to keep something secret; to keep a secret safe a child will tend to lie.

Children learn very young that certain lies are permitted or even advisable. Indeed, children constantly interact with adults, and those closest to them can make poor role models by lying more often than they imagine – for example, where someone says to a child, "Don't tell Mum we're having a party for her tomorrow; it's our secret" or when we ask a child to tell callers we are not home or to lie about their age at a restaurant so as to get a discounted meal. This makes it easier for an offender to manipulate a child and press them to lie and keep a secret.

Studies that have investigated lying in children (Ceci and Bruck, 1995) seem to indicate that, like adults, children are sensitive to context and can lie or withhold information for different reasons. Even very young children lie to avoid punishment or embarrassment, to keep a promise, to conform to the rules of a game, or to gain a personal advantage such as a reward. Also, Haesevoets (2000) has indicated that lies can also be aggressive in nature or motivated by the desire to hurt, as where vengeance is the goal.

2. Children's Memory

Among the factors that can cause children to make false allegations, one of the most frequently studied is the stage of development characterized by their capacity to remember events. Indeed, our knowledge of memory development in children has progressed at lightning speed over the last 20 years. Laboratory studies have been conducted and their findings applied in real investigative situations, the majority of the research having concentrated on very young children (aged two to four) or school-aged children. Rather than attempt an exhaustive review of memory development in children, we will discuss various aspects of relevance to sexual abuse.

We can understand memory as consisting of three processes: encoding (registering events), storage (retaining and storing information), and retrieval (recall) of events (Melton, 1963; Ornstein, 1995). Children's ability to perform these processes is dependent on their personal development, and their memory can be affected by problems involving any one of them (Cyr and Dion, 2006). In the following paragraphs, we detail what is known about the capacity of children to remember important autobiographical events.

In their literature review, Pipe, Lamb, Orbach and Esplin (2004) reported that even three-year-olds were able to provide reports that were coherent and organized temporally. Although they might tend to give briefer accounts than older children or adults do, younger children's accounts can accurately reflect the facts. As well, children can remember events experienced several months or years earlier (Fivush, Peterson, and Schwarzmueller, 2002). For example, children eight years of age can recall events that they experienced five years earlier (Fivush and Schwarzmueller, 1998).

However, children, like adults, forget over time, and this more often leads to errors of omission than of commission (Steward, 1993). Moreover, younger children are more likely than older ones to forget (Brainerd and Ornstein, 1991). Hence, age is clearly an determinant of the quality of memory in children, although even the very young can provide information useful in prosecutions (Pipe et al., 2004; Poole and Lamb, 1998; Poole and Lindsay, 1998). Children also tend to remember their own personal experiences more than events they merely witnessed (Sas, 2002). It is also important to emphasize that no gender-related differences have been observed with respect to memory, be it for the encoding or the recall of events.

Pipe et al. (2004) also point out that, according to certain studies, children retain the memory of negative experiences longer than they do that of everyday events. Also, talking with others about an event has been found to influence the memory of it. However, retrospective studies with adults suggest that, during childhood, young victims rarely discuss with others the abuse they suffer. Consequently, this silence could affect how much detail children retain or remember.

A child's understanding of the subject committed to memory can also affect that memory (Pipe et al., 2004; Saywitz and Lyon, 2002). Recent studies have shown that children who understand events they experience — such as painful or distressing medical procedures, accidental injury and its treatment, or natural disasters — report more detail about the events than do children who understand less about the matter (Greenhoot, 2000; Sutherland, Pipe, Schick, Murray, and Gobbo, 2003). Children recall traumatic experiences such as natural disasters in greater detail and more accurately when they understand the events or someone explains to them what has happened. Therefore, in the context of sexual abuse, where a child is subjected to acts about which they are ignorant or have a poor understanding, certain experiences are likely to be committed to memory less well than others. As well, as Saywitz (1995) remarked, young children do not take some information into memory until they have learned certain concepts or gained a better understanding of them. These include tables of measurement (time, distance, age, and height), parts of the body, ordinal positions (first and last), family relationships and ties (first cousin, aunt), and frequency of occurrence (real numbers).

More research is needed to better understand how emotional factors influence memory of trauma. Sas (2002) pointed out that although some studies have suggested that distress could inhibit registering an event's secondary details, by creating a fragmented mnesic trace, it could also facilitate registering central details, which would then occupy an exaggerated place in memory. Moreover, Pipe et al. (2004) indicated that shame, a sense of personal responsibility, embarrassment, or guilt could also affect how abusive or traumatic experiences are registered and recalled.

Particularly in cases of intrafamilial abuse, a significant percentage of children are victimized repeatedly for months or years. In this regard, research (see Pipe et al., 2004) has shown a clear difference between memory of repeated events and that of one-time occurrences. The former is often referred to as "script memory" given that one has better recall of elements common to repeated experiences than of the unique aspects of individual occurrences. Script memory is more resistant to suggestion and misinformation, which suggests stronger memory representations of events. On the downside, however, these accounts tend to be sketchy, providing the common components and basic outline of the repeated abuse but none of the details that could vary from one episode to the next. In this connection, similar studies (Roberts, 2002; Roberts and Powell, 2001) found that while children may remember exactly what they experienced, they tend to confuse one episode with another and cannot recall precisely to which specific episode certain details belong.

Moreover, the longer the time lapse between events and recall, especially when legal action is undertaken months or years after the fact, the greater the tendency to rely on scripts and to confuse details among different episodes. To help a child provide as many particulars as possible about repeated abuse, it is important to refer to specific episodes (Cyr and Dion, 2006) in the knowledge that, although it must be borne in mind that while the details given will be true and accurate, they might not necessary belong to the episode to which the child ascribes them. Consequently, delays in judicial proceedings, which can often stretch over years, carry the risk that accounts given by the child grow sketchier over time.

The last factor that can influence a child's memory is source monitoring, which is particularly problematic in younger children (Parker, 1995). According to Poole and Lindsay (1998), children have trouble distinguishing between events actually witnessed and those recounted to them, through storybooks or otherwise. This is why it is advisable to question the child as little as possible and, above all, to consider very carefully the types of questions to be used (Van Gijseghem, 1992). Indeed, specific questions (e.g. "Did he touch your bottom?") and repeated suggestions (e.g. "Daddy touched you, didn't he?") can induce errors in information storage, such that the child will not be able to determine the information's source.

In sum, young children have relatively accurate long-term memory of events experienced and can provide a report of these memories under favourable conditions. The factors that can influence a child's memory and foster false or inaccurate allegations include: the child's capacity to source monitor memories; the time lapse between events and their recall (the longer the lapse, the less detailed the account); the child's lack of knowledge of sexual abuse (which will affect how information is stored in memory); and the child's age (which bears on the amount of detail that can be retained and recalled).

3. Questioning and Children's Suggestibility

Alongside the abundant research into children's memory, there is an impressive body of work concerned with children-interviewing techniques and the suggestibility of children during questioning. On the strength of numerous studies, various authors (Fivush et al., 2002; Hershkowitz, 2001; Poole and Lamb, 1998; Poole and Lindsay, 1998; Saywitz and Lyon, 2002) have pointed to inappropriate questioning as the central cause of false allegations. Indeed, such questioning often begins upon the child's disclosure, when a teacher, parent, family member or other person close to the child is likely to ask many questions before reporting the incident to the proper authorities. Sometimes questioning begins in the absence of any disclosure by the child, as when, in cases of recent separation or divorce, the misinterpretation of certain reactions or attitudes in the child leads one parent to suspect the other of abuse (Ehrenberg and Elterman, 1995; Faller, 1991).

Research has also shown that even when investigators receive training in the most effective interview techniques, they often have difficulty employing those methods when questioning children (Aldridge, 1992; Aldridge and Cameron, 1999; Cederborg, Orbach, Sternberg, and Lamb, 2000; Cyr, Bruneau, Perron, and Vignola, 2007; Davey and Hill, 1999; Faller, 1996; Lamb et al., 1996; Orbach, Hershkowitz, Lamb, Esplin, and Horowitz, 2000; Sternberg, Lamb, Esplin, Orbach, and Hershkowitz, 2002; Sternberg, Lamb, Hershkowitz, Esplin, Redlich, and Sunshine, 1996; Warren, Woodall, Hunt, and Perry, 1996). In the following paragraphs we explore how investigative interviews can lead a child to provide misinformation or to make false allegations.

In their review of the literature on the factors influencing children's testimony, Pipe et al. (2004) indicate that stress can affect different types of memory in different ways, both at the encoding stage and at recall. In other words, the context in which the child provides information — regardless of whether the interview is with social workers, police officers, prosecutors, or judges — can be stressful, independently of the stress linked to the abuse itself. Although researchers have yet to study the effect of stress at the moment of recall, certain studies that examined how social support and supportive practices by interviewers might lower stress provide reasonable evidence that stress at time of recall can indeed affect a child's recall capacity.

Subtle differences in style among interviewers can also affect suggestibility in children. Little research has been carried out into the matter, but results so far have been mixed. On the one hand, some studies (Carter, Bottoms, and Levine, 1996; Davis and Bottoms, 2002; Goodman, Bottoms, Schwartz-Kenney, and Rudy, 1991) show that children are more influenced by leading questions when these are asked by neutral, "kind," or supportive interviewers. On the other hand, it has been reported that children are more likely to accept suggestions made in an accusatory environment. In short, then, if interviewers are overly supportive or intimidating, children are likely to go along with leading questions (e.g. "He touched you, didn't he?") either out of the desire to please, in the case of a "nice" interviewer, or out of fear, in the case of an intimidating interviewer (Bruck, Ceci, and Hembrooke, 2002; Saywitz and Lyon, 2002).

Another source of suggestibility in children is their ignorance of the interviewer's goals or intentions during questioning. Poole and Lindsay (1998) remarked that children seem to consider the interview as an invitation to prove or demonstrate their knowledge, regardless of the source of the information. This can lead children to describe things they might have seen or heard in other contexts as against what they actually experienced. At play is the source monitoring of memory interacting with the desire to please and to come across as knowledgeable.

Poole and Lindsay (1995) have also noted that false reports occur even in the absence of coercive or highly suggestive questioning. In this regard, they showed that children whose parents read them stories about events they did not actually experience were likely to commit free-recall errors. Research has clearly established that the probability of misinformation increases steadily as interviewers move from free recall questions (e.g. "You say he took off his shirt; what was his shirt like?"), to directive questions (e.g. "What colour was his shirt?"; Goodman et al., 1991), to leading (Walker, Lunning, and Eilts, 1996) or suggestive questions (e.g. "You do remember that his shirt was blue, don't you?"; Ceci, Huffman,

Smith, and Loftus, 1994; Goodman et al., 1991; Poole and Lindsay, 1995, 1998). The explanation for this phenomenon is that information elicited via free-recall prompts (e.g. "Tell me what happened") is more likely to be accurate than is information derived from recognition memory.

Put otherwise, although information the child retrieves freely from recall memory can be incomplete, it is likely to be more accurate than specific information elicited from the child through questioning. According to Pipe et al. (2004), questions relying on recognition memory are more likely to draw false answers on account of a response bias, that is, the tendency to say "yes" or "no" without reflection (Peterson and Grant, 2001), or the false recognition of details the child picked up in previous interviews. Moreover, suggestive or leading questions are more likely to influence responses where memory is not rich or recent, or when its substance is imagined instead of experienced.

Poole and Lindsay (1998) concluded that research clearly shows children are quite accurate without suggestion from adults, but that a significant portion of children are susceptible to suggestive procedures. Children generally are less precise under direct questioning, and younger children (principally three- and four-year-olds) are more likely to acquiesce to questions about touching they have not actually experienced. Moreover, it has been demonstrated that when children are asked repeatedly to think about events that have not actually occurred, their resistance to suggestion is reduced and the likelihood of false reports increases (Ceci et al., 1994). Suggestibility increases as well with the introduction of anatomically correct dolls in concert with related specific questions (Stewart and Stewart, 1996). According to Hershkowitz (2001), when children do not understand certain questions, believe the interviewer expects a particular response, or are unclear about the information sought, their answers tend to incorporate information suggested by the questions. As well, errors increase when one asks children to try to imagine what could have happened (Pipe et al., 2004).

Investigative interviewers can take comfort in the fact that, generally speaking, it is more difficult to get children, no matter their age, to recount false violent or negative scenarios than it is false positive ones (Eisen, Goodman, Qin, and Davis, 1998). When children have not been injured, they resist suggestions to the contrary rather well. It also seems that suggestibility, especially regarding central details, diminishes with age, which perhaps has more to do with increasing developmental capacity than memory performance per se (Hershkowitz, 2001).

Suggestibility involves not just communicative and memory processes, but complex social processes as well. Children sometimes answer inaccurately because: they believe the interviewer prefers a particular response (Ceci and Bruck, 1993); the interviewer reinforces or encourages certain types of response; they want to cooperate but do not understand the questions; or they are responding to stereotypical depictions of the target individual. One sees the phenomenon as well where the child views the interviewer as an authority figure or a person of status; in these situations, the child feels obliged to go along with the interviewer's construction of the events. This is what Ceci and Bruck (1997) have referred to as "interviewer bias." Such skewed interviews are not the doing of professionals exclusively; parents, teachers, and other persons with an agenda, too, can produce the same effect when questioning children.

In sum, questioning a child about sexual abuse is a complex task involving several factors related to suggestibility, including multiple social, communicative, and memory processes. Though research results have been mixed and contradictory at times, numerous consistencies have emerged as well. First, children are more susceptible than adults to influence, and young children are more susceptible than older ones. Second, interview-related factors such as interrogation style (open, direct, leading, suggestive), emotional attitude of the interviewer (intimidating, judgmental, supportive), and the child's understanding of the task at hand can all influence the answers provided by children about events they have experienced. Third, as source monitoring of information is poorly developed in young children, any discussion of, or questioning about, sexual abuse before an official investigative interview can etch itself in their memory. The same holds true of any other questioning that occurs outside the official investigative process, whether during or after. This phenomenon, commonly referred to as memory contamination, is difficult to prevent, evaluate, and measure.

These results urge us to exercise greater caution when interviewing children and choose questions carefully, in order to minimize suggestibility. On the basis of the research outlined above, it is clear that the interviewer, not the child, must assume responsibility for suggestibility. Unless children are asked the right type of question and are allowed to recount their experiences freely, we risk doing more harm than good. There of course exist guidelines for appropriate interview techniques (Bruneau and Lemay, 2004; Cronch, Viljoen, and Hansen, 2006; Poole and Lamb, 1998; Quas, Goodman, Ghetti, and Redlich, 2000). Their adoption should be encouraged, as we know that when interviewers employ them children can furnish accurate accounts of events that have happened in their lives. Against this background, the use of a structured interview protocol, such as that developed by Lamb, Orbach, Sternberg and colleagues (Orbach et al., 2000; see also Cyr and Dion, 2006; Cyr et al., 2007), would prove highly beneficial.

4. Divorce Cases

We have already pointed out that divorce or disputes over child custody can lead to allegations of sexual abuse – some substantiated, others false. There are several reasons such allegations arise in these contexts.

On the one hand, the discovery of genuine sexual abuse against a child creates a climate of familial tension that can lead to marital breakdown (Bala, Lee, and McNamara, 2001). On the other, a couple's separation can provide opportunities for sexual abuse of a child, opportunities that do not exist in intact families (Bala et al., 2001). Where divorce precipitates abuse, clinicians and researchers have noted, stress related to the divorce and loss of the family structure can bring about behaviour that was not present before (Faller, 1991). Alleged offenders can be overcome by loneliness and can exhibit regressive behaviour in several spheres of their lives. It is therefore important to investigate whether a sexual attraction to children had been observed prior to the divorce. According to Faller (1991), these pre-divorce indicators include inappropriate touching and caressing, tongue-kissing, sleeping with a child, and erections upon contact with the child's body.

As well, there are several reasons a child is more likely to disclose sexual abuse committed by a parent after separation. First, the child might feel more secure in reporting long-term abuse once the offender no longer lives under the same roof (Faller, 1991). In such cases it also is more difficult for the offender to prevent the child from talking (Fahn, 1991; Thoennes and Tjaden, 1990). Often the non-offender parent is also more disposed to listen to and believe the child (Faller, 1991). In addition, the child might have kept the abuse secret because they were told that disclosure would destroy the family.

Faller (1991) believes that calculated and deliberate allegations are relatively rare in divorce cases. More typically, these allegations, though implausible, are based in part on reality (Faller, 1991; Green, 1991). For example, anxious parents can misinterpret borderline symptoms (e.g. skin abrasions, anxiety in the child in the father's presence) and jump to inappropriate conclusions, generally believing the worst. Faller notes that, contrary to the dynamics of intrafamilial sexual abuse, where the mother finds it difficult to believe that her partner is sexually abusing their child, the opposite can occur in divorce. Amid the disappointment and disenchantment of marital breakup, divorced parents can convince themselves that their former partners are capable of almost anything, including sexual abuse. The risk of allegations by the custodial parent increases when the child presents regressive symptoms — such as crying, nightmares and bed-wetting — or signs of depression, anger, opposition and aggressiveness following a visit to the non-custodial parent (Ehrenberg and Elterman, 1995; Faller, 1991; Green, 1991).

Green (1991) adds that the custodial parent can reach an erroneous conclusion about the care the non-custodial parent gives the child or about normal sexual behaviour in children. Similarly, the custodial parent may misinterpret as sexual any increased physical contact — such as kissing, holding the child, and caresses — between the child and the other parent. These physical displays of affection can develop because of unusual and long absences caused by the divorce. Moreover, once the non-custodial parent has moved out of the home, it is typical for children of divorced families to fear that the custodial parent will abandon them (Ehrenberg and Elterman, 1995). These children are more dependent and more susceptible to parental influence. In these cases of implausible allegations, often termed "parental alienation," children use sexual or very specific terminology that seems adult. Nevertheless, it is important to consider that the children could have learned to talk in these adult terms during frequent and inappropriate discussions with the alleged offender-parent.

In evaluating cases related to divorce and custody disputes, Ehrenberg and Elterman (1995) remarked, it should be borne in mind that implausible allegations are generally more often made by parents than by children. As these cases are complex and often involve repeated interviews and evaluations, reviewing the transcripts of the earliest interviews with the child can help determine whether any pressure was exerted over the course of the other interviews. Also of importance is that the alleged offender-parent or the custodial parent might have a history of unresolved sexual abuse of their own.

Another indicator of false allegations, according to Ehrenberg and Elterman (1995), is related to the fact that when a child is indeed sexually abused, parents can feel ashamed or stigmatized about coming forth and might blame themselves for failing to protect the child. Where the allegations are unlikely to be genuine, instead, parents who make the allegations are less likely to experience these feelings and will speak with relative ease about sexual matters concerning the child.

In sum, several factors are likely to promote sexual-abuse allegations in situations of divorce or child-custody disputes. Pearson and Thoennes (1990) concluded that these cases attract the most attention because they are more complex and, therefore, more frustrating for professionals in the legal community. They are thus among the most time-consuming to investigate, even though they do not occur appreciably more often than cases within intact families.

5. The Influence of Rumour on the Testimony of Young Children

In the course of a judicial investigation it sometimes happens that children incorporate in their statements rumour spread by their peers or adults. This is likely to occur in cases of sexual abuse that arise in contexts where numerous children intermingle, as in day-care centres, schools, and sports teams. Principe, Kanaya, Ceci and Singh (2006) studied this phenomenon among 175 pre-schoolers aged three to five years and found that these children could integrate false rumour into their memory, whether it was propagated by adults or children. According to the researchers, the children tended to report as eye-witnessed what had actually only ever been hearsay. In this context, interview style seemed to have no effect on the rumour. Indeed, when children freely recalled events, elements grounded in rumour were more present than when interviewers used specific questions or suggestions. In other words, the effect of rumour was more significant than the type of question used. For the authors, this demonstrated the power of rumour to confuse young children as to the source of the information registered in their memories. This study shows that rumour (propagated by adults or peers) can not only engender false recall of a fictional event, it can also impact how children believe they experienced the event. When a rumour becomes integrated into memory, children tend to adorn it with added fictional detail.

Although these results can be explained in part by the fragility and spottiness of children's memory, particularly as regards source monitoring of information, this does not in the least diminish the influence of rumour on older children and adults. According to Rosnow (1991), rumour serves to explain an otherwise unexplained event, and thus arises from general uncertainty. Moreover, rumour takes root in situations that are important or preoccupy people. When associated with feelings of personal anxiety over a situation, rumour spreads more rapidly, insofar as it legitimates the anxiety. Finally, rumour circulates as a function of its credibility, that is, the extent to which it seems plausible or reliable.

These factors can apply equally to children and adults. Until more extensive research can be conducted regarding the potential impact of rumour on the development of false allegations, it would be wise to consider this possible impact in cases of sexual abuse involving numerous witnesses who are regularly in contact with one another.

6. Tunnel Vision

As we have seen, suggestive questions constitute the most insidious pitfall in the investigative process. According to Van Gijseghem (1999), investigators who approach a file with preconceived notions have a tendency to ask suggestive questions and to focus their attention on elements that confirm their beliefs, to the point of turning a deaf ear to information that disproves them. This phenomenon has been referred to by Ceci and Bruck (1995) as interviewer bias. Where it exists, this bias causes interviewers to structure the interview so that it conforms to their *a priori* notions. Aside from seeking only confirmatory elements in support of their hypotheses, they avoid exploring avenues that might yield contradictory information.

The problem of tunnel vision and the serious consequences it can bring are such that the Heads of Prosecutions Committee of Canada's Department of Justice devoted an entire chapter to the matter in their 2004 report on the prevention of miscarriages of justice. The committee presented the following definition: Tunnel vision is "the single minded and overly narrow focus on an investigation or prosecutorial theory so as to unreasonably colour the evaluation of information received and one's conduct in response to the information." Clearly, to avoid falling into this trap, professionals (police officers, social workers, prosecutors) must endeavour to obtain information from multiple sources and to analyze all of it in the light of multiple hypotheses.

7. Allegations by Parents

There is some consensus in the scientific literature that parental allegations made in the absence of disclosure by the child are more likely to be false. In the most exhaustive study of the phenomenon, out of 576 reported cases of sexual abuse, Jones and McGraw (1987) found that 6% were fictitious. Of these, allegations by adults accounted for 5 percentage points and those by children for only 1. Anthony and Watkeys (1991) observed that, of the 8.5% of allegations they deemed false and intentionally fabricated, those made by adults accounted for 6 percentage points and those by children for only 2.5. These results are in line with those of Trocmé and Bala (2005), who observed that none of the false allegations of sexual abuse in their study emanated from children. With other types of maltreatment, rates varied from 1% to 5%. These results do not prove that all allegations of sexual abuse made by parents are likely to be false, but they do show that investigators must examine multiple hypotheses.

8. Parent Does not Believe Child

Parental attitudes and beliefs are another variable that can influence abuse disclosure. Elliott and Briere (1994) found a higher disclosure rate among children whose mother accepted the possibility of abuse, compared with those whose mother refuted the possibility despite third-party confirmation. When this is the case, children who initially disclose are more likely to retract in the course of the investigative process (Sorenson and Snow, 1991).

9. Child's Age

As few studies have considered what role the child's age plays in false allegations, it is difficult to draw definitive conclusions regarding this variable. The available data seems to suggest that adolescents are more likely than children to deliberately formulate false allegations. In their study, Anthony and Watkeys (1991) noted that nine false allegations of intrafamilial abuse — 2.6% of the sample studied — were made by adolescents who wanted the alleged offender out of the family home. These adolescents lived in unsatisfactory conditions and received little or no support from their mothers. For their part, Everson and Boat (1989) sought to document false allegations by analyzing assessments performed by social workers in child-protection facilities. These authors observed that the workers reported a higher rate of false allegations among adolescents than among children (8% vs. 2 %). The rates covered only allegations that were intentionally false.

10. Child's Attitude During the Investigative Interview

According to Poole and Lindsay (1998), observing children during interviews is a problematic method for determining whether they are telling the truth. In terms of how children present emotionally, Haskett, Wayland, Hutcheson and Tavana (1995) indicate that some disclose sexual abuse simply as a matter of fact, whereas others are more hesitant or embarrassed. These authors conclude that, given the wide range of affective and behavioural responses exhibited by abused children (Kendall-Tackett, Williams, and Finkelhor, 1993) and the difficulty of separating out the child's reactions to the alleged abuse from their reactions to the interview process, validating allegations on the basis of observation is an extremely questionable approach. Indeed, analyzing 55 videotaped interviews of sexual abuse cases, Wood, Orsak, Murphy and Cross (1996) noted that most of the children were attentive, focused on the task, relaxed and, therefore, not very emotional.

D. VALIDITY CHECKLISTS AND CHILD'S STATEMENTS

Once a child discloses and testifies to sexual abuse, professionals who work in the field must determine whether the facts reported are true. To help in this delicate task, a number of instruments have been developed, but the one that has drawn the most attention and that is the most widely used in the world (Vrij, Kneller, and Mann, 2000) is without contention the *Criterion-Based Content Analysis* (CBCA; Raskin and Esplin, 1991; Steller and Kohnken, 1989; Yuille, 1988). The CBCA is one of the three components of the *Statement Validity Analysis* (SVA). This analytical checklist comprises a high-quality investigative interview, an analysis of the interview using the CBCA, and an overview, facilitated by the *Validity Checklist,* of all the investigative material. The SVA grew out of the work of Undeutsch (1989), who devoted his career as a forensic psychologist to the study of German court cases concerning sexual-abuse allegations by children. Undeutsch championed the hypothesis that statements based on memories of real events differ in content and quality from fantasy-based statements or statements made under the influence of external factors. Steller and Kohnken (1989) formalized 19 criteria — adopted by Raskin and Esplin (1991) — for quantifying a child's statements and systematically evaluating the credibility of the report. These criteria are related to general characteristics (e.g. narrative coherence, spontaneous verbalization), specific contents (e.g. unexpected complications, descriptions of interactions), peculiarities of content (e.g. peripheral or unusual detail), contents related to motivation (e.g. acknowledgment of a lapse of memory, disapproval of one's participation), and characteristics specific to the offence (Haesevoets, 2000; see St-Yves, Pilon, and Landry, 2004, for a detailed description of the criteria).

The early studies by Boychuk (1991) and of Raskin and Esplin (1991) showed the CBCA to be a promising technique for discriminating between reports of events experienced and those of events that never occurred. However, these studies have faced criticism given that the researchers collected the data from their own case studies, or from those of colleagues.

Since then, the CBCA has been the focus of a large number of studies (see Vrij, 2005, for a review). These have shown the CBCA to be reliable for several criteria, although not all (Horowitz, Lamb, Esplin, Boychuk, Krispin, and Reiter-Lavery, 1997). Some controversy exists over the exclusion of criteria deemed inadequate (see, for example, Craig, Scheibe, Raskin, Kircher, and Dodd, 1999; Hershkowitz, 1999; Horowitz et al., 1997), and Vrij et al. (2000) have suggested the inclusion of additional criteria.

Criticism of the CBCA's validity has focused on its capacity to discriminate true allegations from false ones. For example, it has been noted that the CBCA is biased towards false positives, tending to recognize wrongful allegations as credible (Steller, 1989; Yuille, 1988). In addition, it has also been found that familiarity with the event can influence CBCA scores (Blandon-Gitlin, Pezdek, Rogers, and Brodie, 2005; Pezdek, et al., 2004): the greater the familiarity with the event reported, the higher the CBCA score. Several studies also have shown that the number of criteria met increases with age: younger children verbalize less than older children and thus divulge fewer details that satisfy the CBCA criteria (Anson, Golding, and Gully, 1993; Buck, Warren, Betman, and Brigham, 2002; Craig et al., 1999; Davies, Westcott, and Horan, 2000, Horowitz et al., 1997; Lamb et al., 1997; Lamers-Winkelman and Buffing, 1996; Pezdek et al., 2004).

Two recent studies (Hershkowitz, 1999; Lamb et al., 1997) have attempted to examine the capacity of the CBCA to discriminate plausible from implausible cases – a strategy employed given the difficulty of finding interviews where one can confirm that the child has lied about sexual abuse or was not sexually abused. This sort of case is rather rare, which contributes to render research in the area laborious.

Thus, Lamb et al. (1997) rated 98 out of 1187 sexual abuse interviews on the basis of the plausibility of the allegations. Using information such as the results of medical examinations, witness testimony, alleged-offender confession and physical evidence, the researchers determined improbability independently of the interview. While the cases judged plausible met more of the CBCA criteria than did the implausible cases, the difference was small, and several of the criteria were not significantly more prevalent in the plausible cases. In fact, only 5 of the 14 criteria used — unstructured production, abundant detail, contextual embedding (e.g. reference to time or place), description of interactions, and reproduction of conversations — distinguished plausible from implausible reports. These marked the implausible reports less often than they did the plausible ones.

In a 1999 study, Hershkowitz analyzed interviews of 24 children aged 4 to 13 — split evenly between plausible and implausible allegations – selected from the 98 included in the Lamb et al. (1997) study. The results indicate that: the two groups of children provide answers of comparable length and richness; the interviewers asked the two groups the same types of questions; and the number of CBCA criteria met was similar for the two groups.

On the basis of these and other research results concerning the CBCA, Lamb et al. (1997), Poole and Lamb (1998), Pezdek et al. (2004) and Vrij (2005) concluded that the CBCA still lacked sufficient accuracy to be designated a valid and reliable instrument for court use. The statistically significant relationship between CBCA results and an event's plausibility should not obscure the fact that weak results can be attributed to a variety of factors, such as the poor quality of an interview or reticence on the part of the child, independent of the veracity of the testimony. The strategies used in questioning children are important in that more open approaches would result in a greater number of CBCA criteria being met, thereby making it easier to distinguish true from false reports.

Vrij et al. (2002, 2004) examined the effect of various individual variables, including social anxiety, social skill, and self-monitoring, which can influence the way persons present both themselves and their report. Their studies suggest that children and adults who are socially capable, who are well-mannered, and who show little social anxiety obtain higher scores on the CBCA, and that this relationship is stronger among liars who are less anxious and more socially skilled.

For these reasons, Vrij et al. (2004) recommend that evaluators who use the SVA consider social skills when assessing CBCA results. As well, Lamb et al. (1997) suggest that those who use the SVA always follow the three steps, particularly the validity checklist. However, this checklist has never been the subject of any systematic empirical study. Moreover, certain items on the list have not been formulated with the precision necessary to ensure adequate inter-rater reliability. In its present form, the validity checklist constitutes an interesting tool for reminding investigators of numerous factors that can affect a child's credibility as much as a child's ability to be deemed competent (Vrij, 2005). For the instrument to become credible and robust, its items must be formulated more objectively and unambiguously, its inter-rater reliability must be examined, and the checklist itself must be validated.

CONCLUSION

The question of false allegations is a complex one for which we have only partial answers. Although the research to date suggests that false allegations are rarely made intentionally and are more often made by adolescents and adults than by children, the scale of the phenomenon remains difficult to gauge with precision. A larger number of studies, instead, have focused on cases of alleged sexual abuse reported in good faith but ultimately proven groundless. Should these cases, which often arise from a misinterpretation of certain events or realities in a child's life, also be counted as "false" allegations? The question remains open. In the absence of a reliable method of lie detection, then, investigators must take all the necessary precautions to avoid errors of judgment and work toward resolving any doubts. This entails both individual and institutional responsibilities, as such a process can be implemented fairly and correctly only if the requisite rigour and expertise can be guaranteed.

Family context (e.g. abuse, neglect, divorce), the child's developmental stage, the child's mnemonic and relational capacities, and the source of disclosure are key variables that can favour false allegations. These must not be overlooked. For the purposes of investigative interviews, be they with the alleged victim or other witnesses, interviewers would be well advised to take a supportive attitude and ask open questions appropriate to the person's stage of development. Validity checklists such as the SVA and CBCA can be useful but are merely one toll among the many that should be employed to explore multiple hypotheses. Because of the uncertainty surrounding sexual-abuse allegations, therefore, only a rigorous and painstaking investigation, based on an array of hypotheses and information sources, is likely to reconcile the quest for truth with absolute respect for the child.

REFERENCES

Aldridge, J. (1992). The further training of professionals dealing with child witnesses. In H. Dent and R. Flin (eds.), *Children as witnesses* (pp. 231-244). Oxford: John Wiley and Sons.

Aldridge, J., and Cameron, S. (1999). Interviewing child witnesses: Questioning techniques and the role of training. *Applied Developmental Science, 3*, 136-147.

American Professional Society on the Abuse of Children (1993). Press release. *APSAC Advisor, 6*, 23-24.

Anson, D.A., Golding S.L., and Gully, K.J. (1993). Child sexual abuse allegations: Reliability of criteria-based content analysis. *Law and Human Behavior, 17*, 331-341.

Anthony, G., and Watkeys, J. (1991). False allegations in child sexual abuse: The pattern of referral in an area where reporting is not mandatory. *Children and Society, 5*, 111-122.

Bala, N., Lee, J., and McNamara, E. (2001). Children as witnesses: Understanding their capacities, needs, and experiences. *Journal of Social Distress and the Homeless, 10*, 41-68.

Berliner, L., and Barbieri, M. (1984). The testimony of the child victim of sexual abuse. *Journal of Social Issues, 40*, 125-137.

Blandon-Gitlin, I., Pezdek, K., Rogers, M., and Brodie, L. (2005). Detecting deception in children: An experimental study of the effect of event familiarity on CBCA ratings. *Law and Human Behavior, 29*, 187-197.

Boychuk, T.D. (1991). Criteria-based content analysis of children's statements about sexual abuse: A field-based validation study. *Dissertation Abstracts International, 52*, 2272.

Brainerd, C., and Ornstein, P.A. (1991). Children's memory for witnessed events: The developmental backdrop. In J. Doris (ed.), *The suggestibility of children's recollections* (pp. 10-20). Washington, DC: American Psychological Association.

Bruck, M., Ceci, S.J., and Hembrooke, H. (2002). The nature of children's true and false narratives. *Developmental Review, 22*, 520-554.

Buck, J.A., Warren, A.R., Betman, S.I., and Brigham, J.C. (2002). Age differences in criteria-based content analysis scores in typical child sexual abuse interviews. *Journal of Applied Developmental Psychology, 23*, 267-283.

Bruneau, G., and Lemay, L. (2004). L'entrevue policière de l'enfant victime ou témoin. In M. St-Yves and J. Landry (eds.), *Psychologie d'enquête de la recherche à la pratique* (pp. 193-220). Cowansville, Québec: Éditions Yvon Blais.

Carter, C.A., Bottoms, B.L., and Levine, M. (1996). Linguistic and socioemotional influences on the accuracy of children's reports. *Law and Human Behavior, 20*, 335-358.

Ceci, S.J., and Bruck, M. (1993). Suggestibility of the child witness: A historical review and synthesis. *Psychological Bulletin, 113*, 403-439.

Ceci, S.J., Huffman, M.L.C., Smith, E., and Loftus, E.F. (1994). Repeatedly thinking about a non-event: Source misattributions among preschoolers. *Consciousness and Cognition: An International Journal, 3*, 388-407.

Ceci, S.J., and Bruck, M. (1995). *Jeopardy in the Courtroom: A Scientific Analysis of Children's Testimony*. Washington, DC: American Psychological Association.

Cederborg, A.-C., Orbach, Y., Sternberg, K.J., and Lamb, M.E. (2000). Child witnesses in Sweden. *Child Abuse and Neglect, 24*, 1355-1361.

Craig, R.A., Scheibe, R., Raskin, D.C., Kircher, J.C., and Dodd, D.H. (1999). Interviewer questions and content analysis of children's statements of sexual abuse. *Applied Developmental Science, 3*, 77-85.

Cronch, L.E., Viljoen, J.L., and Hansen, D.J. (2006). Forensic interviewing in child sexual abuse cases: Current techniques and future directions. *Aggression and Violent Behavior, 11*, 195-207.

Cyr, M., and Dion, J. (2006). Quand des guides d'entrevue servent à protéger la mémoire des enfants : l'exemple du protocole NICHD. *Revue québécoise de psychologie, 27,* 157-175.

Cyr, M., Bruneau, G., Perron, A., and Vignola, V. (2007). Application d'un guide d'entrevue d'investigation auprès de jeunes victimes d'agression sexuelle: résultats d'une expérience québécoise. In M. Tardif, (ed.), *L'agression sexuelle : Coopérer au-delà des frontières* (pp. 493-506). Digital work of the CIFAS. http://www.cifas.ca/pages/LivreCifas.html

Davey, R.I., and Hill J. (1999). The variability of practice in interviews used by professionals to investigate child sexual abuse. *Child Abuse and Neglect*, *23*, 571-578.

Davies, G.M., Westcott, H.L., and Horan, N. (2000). The impact of questioning style on the content of investigative interviews with suspected child sexual abuse victims. *Psychology, Crime and Law*, *6*, 81-97.

Davis, S.L., and Bottoms, B.L. (2002). The effects of social support on the accuracy of children's reports: Implications for the forensic interview. In M.L. Eisen, J.A. Quas and G.S. Goodman (eds.), *Memory and suggestibility in the forensic interview* (pp. 437-457). Mahwah, NJ: Lawrence Erlbaum Associates.

Department of Justice Canada (2004). FPT Heads of Prosecutions Committee Report of the Working Group on the Prevention of Miscarriages of Justice. http://canada.justice.gc.ca/en/dept/pub/hop/toc.html

Ehrenberg, M.F., and Elterman, M.F. (1995). Evaluating allegations of sexual abuse in the context of divorce, child custody, and access disputes. In T. Ney (ed.), *True and false allegations of child sexual abuse: Assessment and case management* (pp. 209-230). Philadelphia, PA: Brunner/Mazel.

Eisen, M.L., Goodman, G.S., Qin, J., and Davis, S.L. (1998). Memory and suggestibility in maltreated children: New research relevant to evaluating allegations of abuse. In S.J. Lynn and K.M. McConkey (eds.), *Truth in memory* (pp. 163-189). New York: Guilford Press.

Elliot, M., and Briere J. (1994). Forensic sexual abuse evaluations in older children: Disclosure and symptomatology. *Behavioral Sciences and the Law*, *12*, 261-277.

Everson, M.D., and Boat, B.W. (1989). False allegations of sexual abuse by children and adolescents. *Journal of the American Academy of Child and Adolescent Psychiatry*, *28*, 230-235.

Fahn, M.S. (1991). Allegations of child sexual abuse in custody disputes: Getting to the truth of the matter. *Family Law Quarterly, 25*, 193-216.

Faller, K.C. (1991). Possible explanations for child sexual abuse allegations in divorce. *American Journal of Orthopsychiatry, 61*, 86-91.

Faller, K.C. (1996). Interviewing children who may have been abused: A historical perspective and overview of controversies. *Child Maltreatment, 1*, 83-95.

Faller, K.C., and DeVoe, E. (1995). Allegations of sexual abuse in divorce, *Journal of Child Sexual Abuse, 4*, 1-25.

Fivush, R., and Schwarzmueller, A. (1998). Children remember childhood: Implications for childhood amnesia. *Applied Cognitive Psychology, 12*, 455-473.

Fivush, R., Peterson, C., and Schwarzmueller, A. (2002). Questions and answers: The credibility of child witnesses in the context of specific questioning techniques. In M.L. Eisen, J.A. Quas and G.S. Goodman (eds.), *Memory and suggestibility in the forensic interview* (pp. 331-354). Mahwah, NJ: Lawrence Erlbaum Associates.

Friedrich, W.N., Grambisch, P., Damon, L., Hewitt, S., Koverola, C., Lang, R. et al. (1992). The child sexual behaviour inventory: Normative and clinical findings. *Psychological Assessment, 4*, 303-311.

Goodman, G.S., Bottoms, B.L., Schwartz-Kenney, B.M., and Rudy, L. (1991). Children's testimony about a stressful event: Improving children's reports. *Journal of Narrative and Life History, 1*, 69-99.

Green, A.H. (1991). Factors contributing to false allegations of child sexual abuse in custody disputes. *Child and Youth Services, 15*, 177-189.

Greenhoot, A.F. (2000). Remembering and understanding: The effects of changes in underlying knowledge on children's recollections. *Child Development, 71*, 1309-1328.

Haesevoets, Y.-H. (2000). *L'enfant en questions. De la parole à l'épreuve du doute dans les allégations d'abus sexuels*. Paris-Bruxelles: Université De Boeck.

Haskett, M.E, Wayland, K., Hutcheson, J.S., and Tavana, T. (1995). Substantiation of sexual abuse allegations: Factors involved in the decision-making process. *Journal of Child Sexual Abuse*, *4*, 19-47.

Hershkowitz, I. (1999). The dynamics of interviews involving plausible and implausible allegations of child sexual abuse. *Applied Developmental Science*, *3*, 86-91

Hershkowitz, I. (2001). A case study of child sexual false allegation. *Child Abuse and Neglect*, *25*, 1397-1411.

Horowitz, S.W., Lamb, M.E., Esplin, P.W., Boychuk, T.D., Krispin, O., and Reiter-Lavery, L. (1997). Reliability of criteria-based content analysis of child witness statements. *Legal and Criminological Psychology*, *2* (Part 1), 11-21.

Jones, D., and McGraw, E.M. (1987). Reliable and fictitious accounts of sexual abuse to children. *Journal of Interpersonal Violence*, *2*, 27-46.

Kendall-Tackett, K.A., Williams, L.M., and Finkelhor, D. (1993). Impact of sexual abuse on children: A review and synthesis of recent empirical studies. *Psychological Bulletin*, *113*, 164-180.

Melton, A.W. (1963). Implications of short-term memory for a general theory of memory. *Journal of Verbal Learning and Verbal Behavior*, *2*, 1-21.

Michael, E.L., Hershkowitz, I., Sternberg, K.J., Esplin, P.W., Hovav, M., Manor, T. et al. (1996). Effects of investigative utterance types on Israeli children's responses. *International Journal of Behavioral Development*, *19*, 627-637.

Lamb, M.E., Hershkowitz, I., Sternberg, K.J., Boat, B., and Everson, M.D. (1996a). Investigative interviews of alleged sexual abuse victims with and without anatomical dolls. *Child Abuse and Neglect*, *20*, 1251-1259.

Lamb, M.E., Orbach, Y., Sternberg, K.J., Hershkowitz, I., and Horowitz, D. (2000). Accuracy of investigators' verbatim notes of their forensic interviews with alleged child abuse victims. *Law and Human Behavior*, *24*, 699-708.

Lamb, M.E., Sternberg, K.J., Esplin P.W., Hershkowitz, I., Orbach Y., and Hovav, M. (1997). Criterion-based content analysis: A field validation study. *Child Abuse and Neglect, 21*, 255-264.

Lamers-Winkelman, F., and Buffing, F. (1996). Children's testimony in the Netherlands: A study of statement validity analysis. In B.L. Bottoms and G.S. Goodman (eds.), *International perspectives on child abuse and children's testimony: Psychological research and law* (pp. 45-61). Thousand Oaks, CA: Sage Publications, Inc.

Landry, K.L., and Brigham, J.C. (1992). The effect of training in criteria-based content analysis on the ability to detect deception in adults. *Law and Human Behavior, 16*, 663-676.

Oates, R.K., Jones, D.P.H., Denson, D., Sirotnak, A., Gary, N., and Krugman, R.D. (2000). Erroneous concerns about child sexual abuse. *Child Abuse and Neglect, 24*, 149-157.

Orbach, Y., Hershkowitz, I., Lamb, M.E., Esplin, P.W., and Horowitz, D. (2000). Assessing the value of structured protocols for forensic interviews of alleged child abuse victims. *Child Abuse and Neglect, 24*, 733-752.

Ornstein, P.A. (1995). Children's long-term retention of salient personal experiences. *Journal of Traumatic Stress, 8*, 581-605.

Parker, J.F. (1995). Age differences in source monitoring of performed and imagined actions on immediate and delayed tests. *Journal of Experimental Child Psychology, 60*, 84-101.

Pearson, J., and Thoennes, N. (1990). Custody after divorce: Demographic and attitudinal patterns. *American Journal of Orthopsychiatry, 60*, 233-249.

Peterson, C., and Grant, M. (2001). Forced-choice: Are forensic interviewers asking the right questions? *Canadian Journal of Behavioural Science, 33*, 118-127.

Pezdek, K., Morrow, A. Blandon-Gitlin, I., Goodman, G.S., Quas, J.A., Saywitz, K.J. et al. (2004). Detecting deception in children: Event familiarity affects criterion-based content analysis ratings. *Journal of Applied Psychology, 89*, 119-126.

Pipe, M.-E., Lamb, M.E., Orbach, Y., and Esplin, P.W. (2004). Recent research on children's testimony about experienced and witnessed events. *Developmental Review, 24*, 440-468.

Poole, D.A., and Lamb, M.E. (1998). *Investigative interviews of children: A guide for helping professionals.* Washington (DC): American Psychological Association.

Poole, D.A., and Lindsay D. (1998). Assessing the accuracy of young children's reports: Lessons from the investigation of child sexual abuse. *Applied and Preventive Psychology, 7*, 1-26.

Poole, D.A., and Lindsay, D.S. (1995). Interviewing preschoolers: Effects of nonsuggestive techniques, parental coaching, and leading questions on reports of nonexperienced events. *Journal of Experimental Child Psychology, 60*(1), 129-154.

Principe, G.F., Kanaya, T., Ceci, S.J., and Singh, M. (2006). Believing is seeing: How rumors can engender false memories in preschoolers. *Psychological Science, 17*, 243-248.

Quas, J.A., Goodman, G.S., Ghetti, S., and Redlich, A.D. (2000). Questioning the child witness: What can we conclude from the research thus far? *Trauma, Violence, and Abuse, 1*, 223-249.

Raskin, D.C., and Esplin, P.W. (1991). Statement validity assessment: Interview procedures and content analysis of children's statements of sexual abuse. *Behavioral Assessment, 13*, 265-291.

Roberts, K.P. (2002). Children's ability to distinguish between memories from multiple sources: Implications for the quality and accuracy of eyewitness statements. *Developmental Review, 22*, 403-435.

Roberts, K.P., and Powell, M.B. (2001). Describing individual incidents of sexual abuse: A review of research on the effects of multiple sources of information on children's reports. *Child Abuse and Neglect, 25*, 1643-1659.

Rosnow, R.L. (1991). Inside rumor: A personal journey. *American Psychologist, 46*(5), 484-496.

Sas, G.A. (2002).The internal interlocutor. *Journal of Clinical Psychoanalysis, 11*, 191-208.

Saywitz, K.J. (1995). Improving children's testimony: The question, the answer, and the environment. In M.S. Zaragoza, J.R. Graham, G.C.N. Hall, R. Hirschman and Y.S. Ben-Porath (eds.), *Memory and testimony in the child witness* (pp. 113-140). Thousand Oaks, CA: Sage Publications, Inc.

Saywitz, K.J., and Lyon, T.D. (2002). Coming to grips with children's suggestibility. In M.L. Eisen, J.A. Quas and G.S. Goodman (eds.), *Memory and suggestibility in the forensic interview* (pp. 85-113). Mahwah, NJ: Lawrence Erlbaum Associates.

Sorenson, T., and Snow, B. (1991). How children tell: The process of disclosure in child sexual abuse. *Child Welfare, LXX*, 3-15.

Steller, M. (1989). Recent developments in statement analysis. In J.C. Yuille (ed.), *Credibility assessment* (pp. 135-154). New York, NY, US: Kluwer Academic/Plenum.

Steller, M., and Kohnken, G. (1989). Statement analysis: Credibility assessment of children's testimonies in sexual abuse cases. In D. C. Raskin (ed.), *Psychological methods in criminal investigations and evidence* (pp. 217-245). New York: Springer.

Sternberg, K.J., Lamb, M.E., Hershkowitz, I., Esplin, P.W., Redlich, A., and Sunshine, N. (1996). The relation between investigative utterance types and the informativeness of child witnesses. *Journal of Applied Developmental Psychology, 17*(3), 439-451.

Sternberg, K.J., Lamb, M.E., Esplin, P.W., Orbach, Y., and Hershkowitz, I. (2002). Using a structured interview protocol to improve the quality of investigative interviews. In M.L. Eisen, J.A. Quas and G.S. Goodman (eds.), *Memory and suggestibility in the forensic interview* (pp. 409-436). Mahwah, NJ: Lawrence Erlbaum Associates.

Steward, M.S. (1993). Understanding children's memories of medical procedures: "He didn't touch me and it didn't hurt!" In C.A. Nelson (ed.), *Memory and affect in development* (pp. 171-225). Hillsdale, NJ: Lawrence Erlbaum.

Stewart, M.S., and Stewart, D.S. (1996). Interviewing young children about body touch and handling. Monograph of the Society for Research in Child Development, *61*(4-5, Serial No. 248).

St-Yves, M., Pilon, M., and Landry, J. (2004). La détection du mensonge. In M. St-Yves and J. Landry (eds.), *Psychologie d'enquête : de la recherche à la pratique* (pp. 257-288). Cowansville, Québec: Éditions Yvon Blais.

Sutherland, R., Pipe, M.E., Schick, K., Murray, J., and Gobbo, C. (2003). Knowing in advance: The impact of prior event information on memory and event knowledge. *Journal of Experimental Child Psychology, 84*, 244-263.

Thoennes, N., and Tjaden, P.G. (1990). The extent, nature, and validity of sexual abuse allegations in custody/visitation disputes. *Child Abuse and Neglect, 4*, 151-163.

Trocmé, N., and Bala, N. (2005). False allegations of abuse and neglect when parents separate. *Child Abuse and Neglect, 29*, 1333-1345.

Undeutsch, U. (1989). The development of statement reality analysis. In J.C. Yuille (ed.), *Credibility assessment* (pp. 101-119). New York: Kluwer Academic/Plenum Publishers.

Van Gijseghem, H. (ed.). (1999). *Us et Abus. De la mise en mots en matière d'abus sexuel.* Montréal, Québec, Canada: Éditions du Méridien.

Van Gijseghem, H. (ed.). (1992). *L'enfant mis à nu. L'allégation d'abus sexuel : la recherche de la vérité*. Montréal, Québec, Canada: Éditions du Méridien.

Van Gijseghem, H. (1991). Les fausses allégations d'abus sexuel dans les causes de divorce, de garde d'enfants, de droits de visite. *Revue canadienne de psycho-éducation, 20*, 75-91.

Vrij, A. (2005). Criteria-based content analysis: A qualitative review of the first 37 studies. *Psychology, Public Policy, and Law, 11*, 3-41.

Vrij, A., Kneller, W., and Mann, S. (2000). The effect of informing liars about criteria-based content analysis on their ability to deceive CBCA raters. *Legal and Criminological Psychology, 5*, 57-70.

Vrij, A., Akehurst, L., Soukara S., and Bull, R. (2004). Let me inform you how to tell a convincing story: CBCA and reality monitoring scores as a function of age, coaching, and deception. *Canadian Journal of Behavioural Science, 36*, 113-124.

Vrij, A., Akehurst, L., Soukara, S., and Bull, R. (2002). Will the truth come out?: The effect of deception, age, status, coaching, and social skills on CBCA scores. *Law and Human Behavior*, *26*, 261-284.

Walker, N.E., Lunning, S.M., and Eilts, J.L. (1996). *Do children respond accurately to forced choice questions?: Yes or no.* Paper presented at Recollections of Trauma: Scientific Research and Clinical Practice, NATO Advanced Study Institute, Port de Bougenay, France.

Warren, A.R., Woodall, C.E., Hunt J.S., and Perry N.W. (1996). "It sounds good in theory, but...": Do investigative interviewers follow guidelines based on memory research? *Child Maltreatment*, *1*, 231-245.

Wood, B., Orsak, C., Murphy, M., and Cross, H.J. (1996). Semistructured child sexual abuse interviews: Interview and child characteristics related to credibility of disclosure. *Child Abuse and Neglect*, *20*, 81-92.

Yuille, J.C. (1988). The systematic assessment of children's testimony. *Canadian Psychology*, *29*, 247-262.

Yuille, J.C., and Cutshall, J. (1989). Analysis of the statements of victims, witnesses and suspects. In J.C. Yuille (ed.), *Credibility Assessment* (pp. 175-191). New York: Kluwer Academic/Plenum.

CHAPTER 9

911 Emergency Calls: Towards a Characterization of the Spurious Caller

Marty Laforest, Dominique Blais and Michel St-Yves[1]

Words once spoken can never be recalled.

Horace

Many police investigations begin with a call to the 911 emergency service: "My baby stopped breathing! Please send help right away!" In almost all cases, the caller is completely sincere. But investigation reveals a small number of individuals who misrepresent the facts they report in one way or another so as to conceal or minimize their own role in the events. Sometimes the allegations are altogether false. Although these spurious callers or complainants are generally found out, they complicate investigators' work and cause them to waste precious time.

The task of the operator who receives the 911 call consists of quickly obtaining the information that allows for the most efficient intervention. One could say that operators must focus all their attention on the content of the caller's words, and that this attention is directed and selective: above all, the operator must understand the caller's needs and identify where emergency service is required. One therefore focuses on certain elements rather than others, and these elements are actively sought in the caller's words. The remainder of call content is virtually ignored. However, we believe that if the call can furnish information revealing the spurious nature of a caller, then such information is to be found in the way the caller delivers the information. Spurious callers exercise control over their speech, since they want to control the listener's understanding of events. Compared with sincere callers, who dial 911 without thinking about the message, spurious callers, we believe, prepare their speech before calling — i.e. create a script — hoping to make their stories as credible as possible. Our hypothesis is

---

1 This research was supported by the Social Sciences and Humanities Research Council of Canada. We would like to thank Diane Vincent and Martina Drescher for their comments on a preliminary version of the text.

that spurious callers speak less spontaneously — because they speak from a prepared script — than do sincere callers, and that they betray this control of information in their speech.

The objective of the preliminary research whose initial results are presented here was to verify whether 911 calls contain indicators of caller manipulation.

A. THEORETICAL FRAMEWORK

Our research, in essence, concerns the caller's speech, although it also considers certain prosodic indicators provided by his voice — for example, the variation in intensity when a person begins to weep or whisper. The caller's speech can be analyzed from two perspectives: 1) the content of the speech; 2) the manner in which the caller articulates and delivers this content in response to the operator. As in a game of chess, each utterance restricts the other speaker's room for manoeuvre, since each response must take into account what has come before.

Most social sciences use what individuals say — their words and opinions expressed in surveys, investigations, life narratives, or more or less directed interviews — as evidence of their thoughts. Although methodologies and orientations vary, researchers are usually concerned only with speech content. Discourse analysts generally criticize these procedures for treating language as totally "transparent," as a vehicle for ideas, a tool that is of no particular interest in itself. For them, language *is* information, on the same level as the ideas it serves to encode; accordingly, language is material that must be analyzed. In the police world, Sapir (1996) arrived at a similar conclusion, although by another route: He bases his SCAN method of evaluating the truth of witness statements on the analysis of discursive structures that witnesses or suspects employ in freely-written statements.

Considering, then, the materiality of language in itself, we must also consider the importance of interaction. To speak means to address someone with a particular goal in mind and at a particular time, a speech context we cannot ignore. Indeed, during the last part of the 20th century numerous researchers showed that to speak is to act upon others (Austin, [1962] 1970) and that language plays a role in the construction of the social order (among others, Garfinkel, 1967; Sacks, [1964-1972] 1992; Garfinkel and Sacks, 1970; Atkinson and Heritage, 1984). From this perspective, the most banal talk-in-interaction becomes interesting insofar as it manifests and maintains social roles, attitudes, norms of behaviour, and certain assumptions that each speaker harbours about what others know, for to speak is to continually anticipate how others will interpret our words (Flahaut, 1978). The manner of expression adopted by a speaker, who knows that the party he or she is addressing in communication situation X occupies social standing Y and plays role Z in this particular interaction, cannot be neglected; if it is, essential information on the meaning of the speech acts is lost.

The discourse of 911 calls will therefore be conceptualized as a linguistic "doing," a collective and progressive construction of all parties involved in the interaction, during which meaning emerges and is a matter of negotiation. Thus, meaning for us is not a given, prior to the interaction, that words merely convey. Such a conception of discourse presupposes a very close observation of the linguistic forms deployed during the interaction. This is why the verbal exchanges that are the subject of our analysis were transcribed — transcription providing a peerless vehicle of interpretation in that it requires multiple listenings — employing a protocol that aims for as little "denaturing" as possible. This procedure allows for the very precise observation of not only the words, as pronounced (even those apparently devoid of sense, such as "mm-hmm"), but also hesitation, voice changes, multiple repetitions or reformulations, talking over other speakers, etc. This always imperfect, never completed transcription is our main work tool.

B. DATA AND METHODOLOGY

The *Service de l'analyse du comportement* [behavioural analysis service] of the Sûreté du Québec[2] provided the recordings that form the corpus of this study. Our research compared calls from sincere complainants ("spontaneous" calls) to calls from false complainants ("premeditated" calls), matched for type of crime. This allowed us to highlight the differences in the way a sincere caller presents information as contrasted with a spurious caller, and the different ways in which the operator reacts. In each case the investigation had been completed, which made it possible to determine spurious calls from the outset. As pre-meditated calls were much less frequent, we began by collecting the greatest possible number of these, and then searched out various spontaneous calls, matching them by type of crime. The resulting corpus comprised 19 calls: 10 spontaneous and 9 pre-

2 We would like to thank the Sûreté du Québec, which authorized this research, as well as all the police-force operators who selected calls likely to be useful for analysis. We gratefully acknowledge their assistance.

meditated. The calls concerned either theft, material damages, or assaults (sexual or otherwise) phoned in by the victim or a witness (see Table 1).

Table 1: Distribution of Calls Analyzed

Type of Crime	Spontaneous Calls	Premeditated Calls
Theft or material damages break and enter (caller = victim)	5	4
Assault (caller = victim)	3	2
Assault (caller = witness)	2	3
Total	10	9

Due to the limited size of the corpus, we consider our study exploratory. We hope that the differentiation characteristics revealed by our preliminary analyses will provide us with the means to pursue further research in data sets large enough to allow us to confirm our conclusions.

C. 911 CALL AS AN INTERACTIONAL GENRE

We have focused our attention on 1) the structure of the caller's main intervention, which we term the "heart" of the call, and 2) the appropriateness of the caller's responses to the operator's questions. But before addressing these two points, we must review some considerations about the call itself as a particular interactional genre.

The 911 call constitutes an asymmetrical interaction, in the sense that the two participants are not peers. Their status differs, each has a specific, non-interchangeable role to play, and this differential status plays itself out in their dialogue. The caller solicits help, while the operator must respond to this request and contact those likely to provide assistance. The speech acts expected of the participants differs in that the caller's interactional role is to relate his or her problem with sufficient clarity so that the operator can react adequately to the request for help, whereas that of the operator is to collect the information necessary to evaluate the appropriate help needed.

In the dialogue, actions to perform are organized into a structural template that is the same, in essence, for all 911 calls (Table 2).

Table 2: Structure of the 911 Call

Speaker	Action required	Speech device
Caller	Explanation of the problem	Mini-narrative
Operator	Seek details needed to determine / organize assistance	Question (where, who, etc.) x times

D. THE "HEART" OF THE CALL

As with all interactions, the 911 call includes at least three parts: the opening sequence, the body of the interaction (its substance, which can, during a long interaction, be subdivided into blocks or sequences identifiable by their thematic unity) and the closing sequence. Whatever genre of interaction is in question, the opening and closing sequences are fairly stereotypical, in the sense that their content can be largely predicted (Schegloff, [1968] 1972; Schegloff and Sacks, 1973). The opening sequence serves to establish contact between the speakers. Generally, it consists of greetings, but it can also include making sure the channels of communication are open and verifying or presenting the identity of the speaker or the institution he or she represents (see Example 1). The closing sequence breaks off contact and generally also includes greetings and thank-you's or wishes (see Example 2). These sequences can be very brief, or even absent, in emergency situations.

Example 1

1[3]	Operator:	Sûreté du Québec hello
2	Caller:	Hello [...]

Example 2

46	Operator:	Okay thanks leave your cell phone on
47	Caller:	Okay thanks.
48	Operator:	Okay goodbye.

---

3 In all examples this number indicates the "round" or turn taken by the speaker. Here, therefore, it indicates the first words spoken, the very beginning of the call.

The development of the body of the interaction is clearly more random, in the sense that the number and form of possible speech "turns" are much more extensive, although the degree of unpredictability varies with the situation. In 911 calls, operators follow a set procedure and the subject matter is of limited scope, which reduces the randomness. Certain specific items of information must be obtained, and specific "standard" questions are systematically asked if the caller fails to provide these. In addition, questions particular to the situation may also arise, in reaction to the caller's interventions.

The body of the 911 call is generally initiated by the caller, immediately following the opening sequence, and follows the canonical structure below (the material in brackets is optional):

Turn 1 (operator):	Identification of the service [greeting]	*Opening sequence begins*
Turn 2 (caller):	[Return greeting] Heart of the call	*Opening sequence ends* *Body of the interaction begins*

We use "the heart of the call" to describe the first caller's intervention that is part of the body of the interaction, in other words, the first intervention that states, however minimally, the reason for the call to 911. The heart of the call can vary in length and include the following elements:

1. Shifter: This element does not provide content but serves to launch the conversation, through, for example, "Urn, well."

2. Caller identification.

3. An explicit request or a statement of intention that can be paraphrased "I want/Could you." For example: "Could you please send an ambulance?" "I want to file a complaint."

4. The reason for the call. For example: "I've just been robbed."

5. Narrative elements, that is, an explanation of the context of events. For example: "I was on my way to get change from the bank on Pine Street in St. Oscar, then I stopped at the supermarket." / "One of the bags had change in it."

6. Mention of the caller's location.

Although none of these elements is absolutely necessary, the heart of the call should include mention of the reason for the call, which is the basic information required to send help.

The heart of the call is interesting in that its structure is not limited by questions from the operator. The structure depends entirely on the caller and reflects what he or she believes is expected of him or her in this communicative situation, at this stage of the interaction. It is the only point at which the caller more or less directs the dialogue, subsequent exchanges being more often initiated by the operator, who orients the course of the interaction with a series of questions. From this point of view, the heart, however briefly, is that part of the call that comes closest to the "pure statement" on which the SCAN method is founded (Sapir, 1996).

Two elements in particular emerge from our first observations of the body of the calls: the time required to begin the heart of the call, and the clarity of the reason for the call. Differences in these two elements allow one to distinguish between spontaneous and pre-meditated calls.

1. Time Required to Begin the Heart of the Call

Given the nature of 911 calls, in most cases the substance of the call is quickly ascertained, since the opening sequence is reduced to its simplest expression. Following the first turn, in which the operator identifies the institution or service he or she represents (his or her response to the ringing of the telephone: Schegloff, [1968] 1972) and sometimes briefly greets the caller, the latter begins talking. This second turn generally constitutes the heart of the call, although its first part may mark the end of the opening sequence. In this respect, Example 3 is quite typical:

1	Operator	Sûreté du Québec hello	*Opening sequence begins*
2	Caller	Hello	*Opening sequence ends*
		uh: my name is Marie Tremblay[4] < yes> I'm calling 'cause: whew I have to' someone just stole my car, it ain't in the lot where I parked it.[5]	*Heart*

4 To preserve the anonymity of the people involved, we have changed all names, streets, and telephone numbers.

All spontaneous calls follow this pattern: the heart is in the second turn, immediately following the end of the opening sequence. In pre-meditated calls, however, the opening sequence is often prolonged, and the heart's position is more variable and does not always begin with the caller's first turn. Thus, in Example 4, the heart is not seen until turn 8. The heart of the call is delayed because of operator confusion in the face of the caller's apparent assumption (in turn 2) that there are different emergency services for each region. Several turns are necessary to work out the misunderstanding. In other cases, the heart of the call can be delayed by the caller's greetings and his or her wait for a greeting in response. This may all be a matter of chance, but in fact none of the spontaneous calls studied featured this prolonged opening sequence.[6] With spurious complaints, on the other hand, one senses what may be an unwillingness to get to the heart of the matter.[7]

Example 4

1	Operator	Sûreté du Québec hello	*Opening sequence begins*
1	Operator:	Sûreté du Québec	*Beginning of opening sequence begins*
2	Caller:	Yes, hello hmm: Region of St.-Oscar please	
3	Operator:	Pardon me? Sorry	
4	Caller:	Region of St.-Oscar	
5	Operator:	Yes?	
6	Caller:	This is the right number?	
7	Operator:	Uh: we take calls for them, yes	
8	Caller:	Okay:	*End of opening sequence ends*
		What it's about, me, my wife went to work this morning but [...]	*Heart of the call begins*

5 See the appendix for the transcription conventions used in this chapter.

6 We have taken into consideration the relative urgency of the calls. The two examples regarding the time at which the "heart" appears belong to the "less urgent" category, where one expects to more frequently find some delay than with very urgent calls.

7 We do not mean to suggest that this is a conscious manoeuvre, as we have no way of verifying that hypothesis. But whether it is conscious or not, the effect on the discourse is the same.

2. Clarity of Reason for Call

The second point of differentiation we observed is related to the clarity and precision of the reason for the call — the central point of any call. Of course, there is a middle ground between total clarity and total confusion. Our evaluation of clarity is based first and foremost on the operators' reactions. When the reason for the call is clear to the operator, that person can proceed with questions about the service requested — where aid is needed (if the caller does not spontaneously provide this information in the heart of the call) or the safety of those involved in the event reported. When the reason is vague or altogether absent from the heart of the call, the operators' questions clearly indicate their incomprehension and call for clarification. Motive can be obscure in both spontaneous and pre-meditated calls, but spurious callers much more frequently experience difficulty in clearly expressing why they have called for help. In this light, one can compare Example 5 (clear motive) to Example 6 (vague motive), each dealing with armed robbery.

Example 5

2	Caller:	Uh, yes, I'm the victim of an armed robbery	*Reason for the call*
3	Operator:	Where?	

Example 6

2	Caller:	Uh, good evening, there were two *[sobbing, difficulty speaking]* then: to take every-thing'	*Reason for the call*
3	Operator:	Everything?	*Request for an explanation of the reason for the call*
	Caller:	The money, everything.	*Details of the reason*

E. APPROPRIATENESS OF CALLER'S ANSWERS TO OPERATOR'S QUESTIONS

Once the heart of the call has begun, the operator takes control of the interaction, rapidly posing a series of questions, which can be open or closed. The answers are brief, but the callers still have room to manoeuvre and provide answers of variable length that illustrate their understanding of what is expected of them. We therefore studied the difference in the way spontaneous and pre-meditated callers respond to questions.

Our analyses show a difference in the degree of question-answer coherence – coherence being the semantic link uniting one statement to another. When this link is strong and easy to establish, the words seem to flow together naturally. With a weak link, discourse seems more or less disjointed. Speakers are in some ways programmed to "make sense" of what they hear, and a good part of the interpretive work they must do to understand what they hear consists of establishing links between statements, as a function of the communicative situation and knowledge more or less shared with their interlocutor. Generally, the link between statements is automatic and rapid. When one asks (or wonders) why speaker X says a certain thing following something else, it is because the cognitive effort necessary to establish a link is significant enough to have become conscious. We evaluated the coherence and scope of the answer relative to the question by classifying the answers into three categories:

1. Perfect appropriateness, where the caller provides the exact information requested and no more (see Example 7).

Example 7

11	Operator:	Were you present at this accident, sir?	*Question*
12	Caller:	Yes.	*Information requested*

2. Poor appropriateness, where it is difficult to establish a link between the question posed and the information supplied, generally resulting in a reformulation of the question or the posing of a new question on the same subject[8] (see Example 8).

---

8 Truly incoherent narratives are very rare, and our data included no such instances. In almost every case, one can make out how this or that response is

Example 8

27	Caller:	I was out cold a good while	
28	Operator:	Were/Are you sleeping in the ditch there?	*Question*
29	Caller:	See I went uh, I went to do some work, an estimate for some electrical work at, uh: Pine Boulevard for a guy, then I left there it must've been 11:30- midnight, then now you're sayin' it's three o'clock, so:	*Information difficult to reconcile with the question*
30	Operator:	You mean you were unconscious, sir?	*New question on same subject*

3. Appropriateness with added information, where the caller adds unrequested information (see Example 9).

Example 9

52	Operator:	You don't have a description of the vehicle, that's it?	*Question*
53	Caller:	No.	*Information requested*
		Cause I didn't see them coming, then my, there, it was running down my arm *[the caller is bleeding]* [...] I was trying to find a way to stop it, that's why.	*Surplus information*

---

pertinent. Responses classed in this category are those whose relevance is not immediately apparent.

We looked at the total number of questions raised in each group of calls.[9] In both spontaneous and pre-meditated calls, the vast majority of answers are brief and correspond coherently to the questions asked, and the caller gives no additional information. This brevity, remarkable compared to other interactional genres based on alternating questions and answers, derives from the emergency setting. The element of differentiation lies in answers of poor appropriateness. This happens rarely, but in all cases except one it occurs in pre-meditated calls.

The same is true of our results concerning "surplus" answers — appropriateness with added information. The nature of the added (unrequested) information varies, and can include justification for an unexpected negative answer[10] (on this subject, see Pomerantz, 1984) (see Example 9, turn 53) — the caller answering a question he or she anticipates — and the addition of a detail or clarification to information in response to a question (see Example 10). But whatever the nature of the surplus information, the semantic link connecting it with the original information given may, again, be more or less easily established. Thus, in Example 10, since the operator is unsure of the location of the IGA supermarket, it is easy to understand why the caller provides an extra detail about the situation there after having responded positively to the operator's question. But in some cases it is difficult to understand what links the two parts of the response, as shown in Example 11.

Example 10

13	Operator:	The IGA on Pine *[Street]?*	*Question*
14	Caller:	Yes	*Information requested*
		There's a drugstore on the corner	*Surplus information*

9 The number of questions varies from one call to another, but on average it is somewhat higher in premeditated calls (19 questions per call) than in spontaneous calls (15 questions per call).

10 In this context, negative responses are unexpected, and are generally accompanied by some justification, in contrast to expected responses, for which justification is unnecessary — see Pomerantz, 1984.

Example 11

21	Operator:	At what number can we reach you?	*Question*
22	Caller:	Uh: 555-55-55.	*Information requested*
		So I don't dare get undressed anymore and leave anything lying around, but...	*Surplus information*

Instances like this, where the new information is an inappropriate extension of the information preceding it, are infrequent; again, however, they were much more evident in the pre-meditated than in the spontaneous calls examined. The spurious caller thus appears more inclined than others to introduce digressions (as in Example 11) or to provide information beyond the range of expected answers to a particular question, as if his or her speech reflected a kind of hesitancy about conforming to the mould imposed by the emergency situation and the operator's questions.

CONCLUSION

Audio and video technologies are recording interactions between complainants and police more and more systematically. We have probably not yet measured all that this archive might contribute to police investigations. As Veyrat (2004: 368) has remarked, audio-visual observation techniques expand with our ability to replay and re-listen to each interaction as many times as necessary and in that way focus our attention on what we inevitably miss in the heat of the moment. In this regard, discourse analysis seems just as pertinent, investigatively, as techniques for observing bodies and gestures. Such analysis engages all aspects of vocal-verbal behaviour and can certainly refine our comprehension of what is at play in dialogue, as certain applications in the police world have begun to demonstrate (among others, Zimmerman, 1997 and 1998; Tracy, 1997; Shuy, 1998).

Our research on 911 calls is situated within this context and this chapter provides a glimpse of the possibilities in this field. These calls, which have been recorded for several years, have not yet been the object of analyses likely to interest police investigators. Is it possible to find signs of spurious complaints in them right from the start — in the first words, even — that can help direct the investigation? We cannot answer this question with certainty for now, but we hope we have succeeded in demonstrating, at least, that 911 calls may be systematically studied for clues to crimes that might otherwise go unnoticed.

Our preliminary analyses make it clear that "premeditated" calls differ from "spontaneous" calls. Spurious callers take more time than sincere callers to begin explaining the reason for the call, tend to formulate their reasons less clearly, and provide more "digressive" and indirect information in response to operators' questions. Spurious callers create drama, constructing narratives they imagine a sincere caller would provide when overwhelmed by events. But their interpretation of this role has no objective reality, since few individuals have the opportunity to observe the behaviour of sincere 911 callers. Spurious callers, therefore, can only imagine the nature of such behaviour, and we believe that analyzing their discourse will make it possible to evaluate the gap between reality and their representation of reality.

Appendix
Transcription Symbols

Symbol	**Interpretation**	
'	Sound stretch	
:	Vowel stretching or vocalized pause.	Ending, low falling, intonation
.	Falling tone with clear pause	
,	Brief pause	
(x sec.)	Longer pause of x seconds	Indication of a longer pause
?	Clearly interrogative?	Interrogative intonation
<x>	Back-channel signal (indicates the operator is listening)	
(xxx)	Words are unclear	
[*xxx*]	Analyst's comment	

REFERENCES

Atkinson, J.M. and J. Heritage (eds.) (1984). *Structures of Social Actions. Studies in Conversational Analysis,* Cambridge: Cambridge University Press.

Austin, J. (1962). *How to do things with words,* Oxford: Oxford University Press.

Bakhtine, M. ([1929] 1977). *Le marxisme et la philosophie du langage,* Paris : Ed. de Minuit.

Flahaut, F. (1978). *La parole intermediaire,* Paris : Ed. du Seuil.

Garfinkel, H. (1967). *Studies in Ethnomethodology,* Englewood Cliffs (NJ): Prentice Hall.

Garfinkel, H. and H. Sacks (1970). "On formal structures of practical actions", in J. C. McKinney and E. Tiryakian (eds.), *Theoretical Sociology,* New York: Appleton Century Crofts, 338-366.

Pomerantz, A. (1984). "Agreeing and disagreeing with assessments: some features of preferred/dispreferred turn shapes," in J.M. Atkinson and J. Heritage (eds.). *Structures of Social Actions. Studies in Conversational Analysis,* Cambridge: Cambridge University Press, 57-101.

Sacks, H. ([1964-1972] 1995). *Lectures on Conversation,* Oxford: Blackwell.

Sapir, A. (1996). *The L.S.I. Scan Workshop Guidebook: Scientific Content Analysis (SCAN).* Laboratory for Scientific Interrogation.

Schegloff, E.A. ([1968] 1972). "Sequencing in conversational openings", in J.J. Gumperz and D. Hymes (eds.), *Directions in Sociolinguistics. The Ethnography of Communication,* Oxford: Blackwell, 346-380.

Schegloff, E.A. and H. Sacks (1973). "Openings up closings", *Semiotica,* 7, 4, 289-327.

Shuy, R.W. (1998). *The Language of Confession, Interrogation, and Deception,* Thousand Oaks: Sage.

Tracy, K. (1997). "Interactional trouble in emergency service requests: A problem of frame", *Research on Language and Social Interaction, 30,* 4, 315-343.

Veyrat, J.-P. (2004). "L'analyse morphogestuelle comme aide d'observation aux entrevues d'enquête", in M. St-Yves and J. Landry (eds.), *Psychologie des entrevues d'enquête. De la recherche à la pratique.* Cowansville: Éditions Yvon Blais, 329-370.

Zimmennan, D.H. (1998). "Observations on the display and management of emotion in naturally occurring activities: The case of 'histeria' in calls to 911, *Social Psychology Quarterly,* 61, 2,141-159.

Zimmennan, D.H. (1997). "Sequential and institutional context in calls for help", *Social Psychology Quarterly,* 50, 2,172-185.

CHAPTER 10

Analyzing Written Statements

Michel St-Yves and Michel Tanguay

Whatever is well conceived is clearly said,
and the words to say it flow with ease.

Nicolas Boileau

On receiving a crime call, one of the first things police do is take a written statement from witnesses.[1] This testimony often contains the key to resolving the investigation. But the information collected must be accurate, and investigators must ask themselves whether police questioning has influenced the narrative. Have investigators reported faithfully what the witnesses said (is the report a verbatim account?) or have they summarized it, using their own words? Is the narrative a true account of what happened, or has the witness twisted it, voluntarily or not? Did the reported event really happen?

The vast majority of statements made to police are well-founded but inaccurate. They very often contain errors and omissions. According to Sapir, at least 90% of those who give statements to police do so "honestly." The others generally do not lie directly. They hedge, "omit" to relay certain crucial facts, pretend to forget, or feign ignorance. They act in this way because they are uncomfortable with their lies (Lesce, 1990).

In this chapter our objective is not to describe the different indicators of whether a statement is well-founded, true, or deceitful. This type of approach would be non-probative and risky, given that most of the research shows such methods do not detect lies efficiently (see Mann et al., 2004; Vrij, 2000). Moreover, a baseless statement can be made in good faith. In this chapter, we first explain the main factors influencing witness accounts, and then discuss methods for taking a written statement that most faithfully reflects what has occurred. We also consider the principal criteria police apply to the analysis of written statements, and how these can help prepare for further interviews with witnesses.

---

1 In this chapter, a "witness" is either a witness or a victim.

A. COLLECTING WITNESS STATEMENTS

1. Quality of Recall

Memory permits us to capture, encode, store, and reproduce information we perceive. While humans have an enormous capacity for memory storage, memory capture is not a perfect process, like some sort of perfect tape recorder: it is susceptible to lapses, distortions, and errors. Beliefs, expectations, cognitive development, acquired knowledge, and the context of events can all influence perception and encoding (Laurence, 2004).

It is rare for the police to get to a witness or victim of a crime immediately after it has occurred. Generally victims or witnesses have already contacted the 911 emergency service and spoken with someone close to them, or a neighbour, emergency response personnel, etc. All of these exchanges can alter their memories —a process known as contamination. The passage of time may also alter memories. Typically, our brains eliminate any useless encumbrances to their functioning. "The vaguer the memory the easier it is to modify" (Laurence, 2004: 225).

Suggestion can also influence recall. If we ask a witness, "did he have a moustache?" we oblige them to consider a detail to which they perhaps paid no attention and, consequently, risk adding this detail to their recollection. Such a question can also create doubt in the witness. It is therefore better to say, "describe his face in detail." Loftus and Palmer (1974) have observed that, simply replacing the verb "hit" — as in "what speed were the vehicles travelling when they *hit* each other?" — with words such as "came into contact," "bumped into," "collided with," or "smashed" causes mnesic representation of motor vehicle accidents to vary considerably. The verb "smash" produced the highest speed (40.8 mph) and the phrase "came into contact" produced the slowest (31.8 mph) — a difference of nearly 15 km/hr. Moreover, 32% of subjects who were asked a question using the verb "smashed" reported that windows were broken, compared to 14% of those asked a question using the verb "hit." These results show that leading questions and word choice can considerably influence witness statements.

The fact that a memory is reported with conviction, complete with sensory and other details, does not mean that the events recalled actually occurred. Reconstructed memory possesses all the subjective attributes of accurate memory. Emotions linked to the memory and the confidence with which it is recounted do not guarantee historical veracity (Laurence, 2004:

224). Witnesses may be uncertain but accurate, just as they may be certain but inaccurate (Demarchi and Py, in press).

2. Taking the Written Statement

Context can also influence a statement's quality. Taking a statement in the corner of an office, in a motor vehicle in plain view of passers-by, or in a noisy and distracting setting is likely to compromise a witness's concentration and influence the content of their statement; the time of day the statement is taken may play a similar role. The investigator's attitude can also be an important factor (see St-Yves, Tanguay and Crépault, 2004), as can the time elapsed since the event in question. Time alters the quality of mnesic recall, such that the sooner one gives a statement after the event, the more likely it is to be accurate.

As memory is fragile and subject to lapses, investigators must collect testimony in the same way they investigate crime scenes. Just as one protects a crime scene, investigators must use every means to avoid contaminating witnesses' memories, ensuring that their version of the facts faithfully reflects what has happened (St-Yves and Landry, 2004: 1). Every question — even the choice of words —is likely to influence witnesses' recall. For this reason, open-ended questions ("tell me everything you know about this event") are more reliable. They allow investigators to collect much more, and better, information.

B. STATEMENT ANALYSIS

Analyzing written statements entails the application of analytic techniques to written discourse. It does not denote graphological analysis; rather, it concerns analysis of the content and structure of statements given by witnesses, victims, and suspects (St-Yves, Pilon and Landry, 2004: 270-271). In North America, one of the tools used most often in this regard is the SCAN (Scientific Content Analysis)[2] method, which is based on the principle that each person has their own linguistic code, and that a liar expresses his or herself differently than does an honest person, particularly with regard to narrative content and structure (Sapir, 1996). It considers the statement's structure, narrative chronology, word choice, pronouns and verbs used, and emotions expressed, among other characteristics. To a great extent, the purity of the statement determines the quality of the analysis.

---

2 SCAN is the statement-analysis technique developed by Avinoam Sapir. For more information, see www.1siscan.com.

Any contamination of the declarant, by questions or other means, risks denaturing the story recounted and, consequently, diminishing the reliability of the analysis. A spontaneous narrative, given as soon as possible after the event in question, ensures greater purity (St-Yves, Pilon and Landry, 2004: 271).

The success of SCAN rests on a very few empirical studies (Porter and Yuille, 1996; Ruby and Brigham, 1997). A Home Office (United Kingdom) study by Smith (2001) reported that SCAN-trained investigators discriminated between truthful and untruthful declarants 80% of the time, while other investigators were only able to do so 58% of the time. Used as a complement to other investigative techniques, SCAN can help identify certain points that investigators need to clarify in subsequent interviews (Adams, 1996).

The SCAN method entails two principal steps: 1) taking of the statement; and 2) analysis of the written statement.

1. Taking the Statement

The statement must be as pure as possible, which is to say free of external "contamination." As mentioned earlier, contamination can arise before or during the statement's drafting. Thus, the written statement should not contain words suggested by the investigator, nor even a proposed structure. Neither should the investigator give instructions as to the length of the statement or the time to be taken in its composition. It is therefore preferable to allow the witness to write out their own statement, along the lines of "Describe your day from the time you woke up until the police arrived."

2. Analyzing the Written Statement

The SCAN method evaluates the accuracy of pure statements on the basis of various criteria. It classifies these criteria into two categories: 1) *Form,* including, principally, the structure and chronology of the statement; and 2) *The content,* which is to say, pronouns, verb tense, emotions, changes in language, superfluous information, etc.

An investigator need not have met a witness to analyze their statement; the words become more important than who has written them: "The person is dead. The statement is alive" (Avinoam Sapir, quoted in Lesce, 1990). Once the investigator has taken the statement, they must scrutinize the details word for word, line by line, and extract from it everything that might help shed light on the relevant occurrence. There is no set number of criteria that must be met to establish credibility, although the meeting of only one will not suffice. What follows is a summary description — an outline — of the principal criteria used to evaluate the accuracy of a written statement.

3. Criteria Based on Form

a) The statement's structure

Normally a narrative comprises three parts: 1) *The introduction*, which describes what happened before the event that is the subject-matter of the written declaration; 2) *The development,* which contains the description of the crime (the heart of the statement) which the author has witnessed or endured as victim; 3) *The conclusion,* which includes the event's end and the witness's actions after the event (for example, calling the police). A normally constructed narrative contains a short introduction (about 20% of the statement), a full development (about 50% of the statement), and a brief conclusion (about 30% of the statement) (Sapir, 1987; Driscoll, 1994; Smith, 2001). There is some debate about the definition of a normally constructed statement. Some contend that each part of the statement should be the same length — one third per section (Adams, 1996), while others state simply that the introduction should not be too long (Adams and Jarvis, 2004). In determining whether a written statement is well-founded, police rely most strongly on how the parts balance out (Smith, 2001).

b) The narrative's chronology

Narrative chronology — "I got up at 6:40 [...] I arrived at work at 8:00" — can often be of interest in statement analysis, providing reference points for the narrative and informing investigators about the time spent on each of the activities described. It can also permit investigators to corroborate facts with other witnesses. Driscoll (1994) and Smith (2001) remark that the number of lines written should be proportional to the length and (subjective) importance of the events reported. For example, if a witness uses five lines to describe 15 minutes of real time, then describes in two lines events that extended over several hours, it may be that the statement's author is omitting (voluntarily or otherwise) certain relevant facts.

4. Content-based Criteria

a) Pronouns

The absence or inappropriate use of pronouns can indicate that the witness has little investment, or has difficulty assuming or sharing responsibility for their acts (Driscoll, 1994; Adams, 1996; Sapir, 1987; Smith, 2001). For instance, a man who speaks of his child as "*the* baby" may be distant or detached from the child. Pronouns can also inform us about the responsibility witnesses assume for their statements; for example, "*we* tried to [...] then *we* called the police."

b) The social introduction

"Social introduction" refers to the manner in which the actors in the narrative are presented. It instructs us as to the nature of the relationship between the declarant and those mentioned in the statement. The absence of a social introduction, regarding one or several persons mentioned in the statement, can indicate tension between the declarant and that person, or a need to protect that person's identity by keeping their identity and role vague; for example, "*we* [no mention of whom] were with *a friend* [no mention of whom].

c) Verbs

Sapir (1987) notes that all changes in verb tense can indicate untruthfulness. In most cases, declarants write their narratives in the simple past tense. Passages in the present tense can show that the person is imagining or creating as they write and is not recounting events from memory (Driscoll, 1994; Adams, 1996; Smith, 2001). For example, "I *arrived* at work at about 8:00. Suddenly two men *appear* at the door, *come* toward me and *hit* me in the face. They *take* the contents of cash register. After I *regained* consciousness, I *called* the police."

Verb choice can be revealing as well. A person who reports the theft of his car by writing "my vehicle disappeared" might be demonstrating that he or she is not at ease with the word "stolen." Again, in a narrative about sexual assault, questions about consent can arise where the complainant says the aggressor "*caressed* my breasts" or "*made love.*"

d) Connectors

Connectors are adverbs such as "then," "after," "because" ("as") and "later." Sapir (1987) notes that a connector positioned close to the recitation of the heart of the event can be revealing. For example, an "after" in the narrative core can suggest that the author is trying to mislead by omitting certain facts (after what?), or a "because" can hide an excessive need to justify what one says.

e) Emotions

According to some authors, emotion in a statement can indicate whether the narrative is well-founded. Sapir (1987) is particularly insistent about the significance of the location of emotional passages in the statement. Theoretically, emotions described in the introduction or at the event's core signal lies. Sapir contends that emotions are often re-experienced, or at least mentioned, by witnesses in the conclusion. Describing them during the incident therefore suggests that the person is inventing and logically situates emotions at the action's core. As well, absence of emotion from a narrative, particularly one regarding a violent crime, can indicate that it is unfounded.

f) Changes in written language

According to Sapir (1987), "a change of language reflects a change in reality" (Smith, 2001). While some authors believe such shifts to be strong indications of lying (Driscoll, 1994; Adams, 1996), Smith (2001) suggests that reliance upon them is a matter, above all, of the intuition of investigating officers.

As well, a narrative containing spontaneous corrections and deletions often raises suspicion, while the absence of such changes frequently is perceived as indicating veracity (Driscoll, 1994). Sapir (1987) only takes into account corrections that seem to reflect hesitancy.

g) Generalizations and "gaps" in memory

Some witnesses deliberately avoid mentioning details they believe might damage them (Adams, 1996; Smith, 2001). Such omissions can take different forms: "as usual" suggests the author is avoiding going into detail; "we talked" omits stating the subject of the discussion; hesitations and gaps in memory ("I can't remember," "I believe," "it was something like that") suggest the witness is reticent to furnish details.

h) Superfluous information and embellishments

In trying to construct a plausible narrative, some who are lying will give more detail than necessary (Adams, 1996). For instance, it can seem excessive to say "I slipped into my underwear and socks, and then I put on my black trousers" especially when the author is otherwise miserly with details about the event they supposedly witnessed. Driscoll (1994) and Smith (2001) describe this criterion as legitimate but rarely mentioned in statement analyses.

Embellishment concerning certain facts or people can also betray an author's attempt to convince the reader; for example, the father of a shaken baby may claim that the child was happy, smiled all the time, and never cried. The best example of embellishment is undoubtedly that of the witness who ends his statement with "It's the truth, the whole truth, and nothing but the truth."

C. LIMITATIONS IN THE ANALYSIS OF WRITTEN STATEMENTS

There are two principal limitations to the analysis of written statements. First, the statement's quality: rarely does one find a pure statement taken immediately after the relevant event. Second, the subjective, or even stereotypical, character of several of the criteria regarding truth and lies. Studies on statement analysis are few in number and of doubtful rigor.

There is also a bias specific to police forces. When investigators send statements for analysis it is because, for the most part, they are already suspect or problematic. This prejudice can be transmitted to those performing the analysis, making them vulnerable to losing their objectivity. This is particularly true where the questioner informs analysts of certain facts or impressions before the analysts begin their work.

CONCLUSION

There are many factors that can influence the quality of witness statements, beginning with the way in which the information is stored in memory and with the witness's interactions with others after the event. This makes it important to interview witnesses as soon as possible after the event, in the best conditions possible, using open questions so that they may speak freely, in their own words (ideally), about everything they did on the relevant day. Only they know, and there are no second chances for a first statement. Only this so-called "pure statement" is amenable to truly objective content analysis.

Analyzing written statements is not a science. Subjective interpretation, voluntary or unconscious, frequently occurs and can greatly alter the investigation's direction. It can also prejudice innocent people. But while such analysis does not seem effective in discriminating between truth and lies, it can prove a useful tool for raising questions such as: Why did this person choose to relate his story in this way? Why this word and not another? As noted, omissions are often of greater interest than what was actually said, and analysis of written statements can demonstrate the witness's state of mind during their writing. Some mental disorders — notably psychotic or delusional disorders — sometimes become evident, permitting the investigator to understand the witness's psychological motivation for saying what they do. This post-mortem of the statement can serve, as well, to help investigators prepare for a new interview, if necessary. In any event, all that needs to be said has not necessarily been said even when the written statement is (or seems) complete. Fundamentally, it is not the analysis of the statement that is important, but rather the taking of it.

REFERENCES

Adams, S. (1996). Statement analysis: what do suspects' words really reveal? *FBI Law Enforcement Bulletin,* vol. 65, no.10.

Adams, S. and Jarvis, J. (2004). Are you telling me the truth?: Indicators of veracity in written statements. *FBI Law Enforcement Bulletin,* vol. 73, no. 10, 7-12.

Demarchi, S. and Py, J. (in press). L'entretien cognitif: son efficacité, son application et ses spécificité. *Revue québécoise de psychologie.*

Driscoll, L. (1994). A validity assessment of written statements from suspects in criminal investigations using the SCAN technique. *Police studies,* vol. XVII, no. 4, 77-88.

Laurence, J.R. (2004). Hypnose et mémoire: un bref survol de la littérature scientifique. In M. St- Yves et J. Landry (eds.), *Psychologie des entrevues d'enquête: de la recherche à la pratique,* Cowansville: Éditions Yvon Blais, Canada, 221-243.

Lesce, T. (1990). SCAN: Deception Detection by Scientific Content Analysis. *Law and Order,* vol. 38, no. 8, August, 3-4.

Loftus, E.F. and Palmer, J.C. (1974). Reconstruction of Automobile Destruction: An Example of the Interaction Between Language and Memory. *Journal of Verbal Learning Behavior,* 13,585-589.

Mann, S., Vrij, A. and Bull, R. (2004). Detecting true lies: Police officers' ability to detect suspects' lies. *Journal of applied psychology,* vol. 89, no. 1, 137-149.

Porter, S. and Yuille, J. (1996). The language of deceit: an investigation of the verbal clues to deception in the interrogation context. *Law and human behavior,* vol. 20, no. 4, 443-458.

Ruby, C.L., and Brigham, J.C. (1997). The usefulness of the criteria-based content analysis technique in distinguishing between truthful and fabricated allegations. *Psychology, Public Policy, and Law,* 3, 705-737.

Sapir, A. (1996). *The L.S.I. Scan Workshop Guidebook: Scientific Content Analysis (SCAN).* Laboratory for Scientific Interrogation.

Sapir, A. (1987). *Scientific content analysis (SCAN),* Participant's paper. Phoenix, Arizona, USA: Laboratory for scientific interrogation (L.S.I.).

Smith, N. (2001). *Reading between the lines: An evaluation of the Scientific Content Analysis technique (SCAN).* Home office, Police research series, no. 135.

St-Yves, M. and Landry, J. (2004). La pratique de l'interrogatoire de police. In St-Yves, M. and Landry, J. (eds.) *Psychologie des entrevues d' enquête: de la recherche à la pratique,* Cowansville: Éditions Yvon Blais, Canada, 546 pages.

St-Yves, M., Pilon, M. and Landry J. (2004). La détection du mensonge. In M. St-Yves and J. Landry (eds.), Psychologie des entrevues d'enquête: *de la recherche à la pratique,* Cowansville: Éditions Yvon Blais, Canada, 257-288.

St-Yves, M., Tanguay, M. and Crépault, D. (2004). La psychologie de la relation: cinq règles de base. In M. St-Yves and J. Landry (eds.), *Psychologie des entrevues d'enquête: de la recherche à la pratique,* Cowansville: Éditions Yvon Blais, Canada, 135-153.

Vrij, A. (2000). *Detecting Lies and Deceit. The Psychology of Lying and the Implications for Professional Practice.* John Wiley and Sons, Ltd. Chichester, United Kingdom.

PART III

RISK AND THREAT ASSESSMENT

CHAPTER 11

Psychology of Criminal Harassment

Peter I. Collins, Peter Smerick and Michel St-Yves

Every breath you take, every move you make, every bond you break, every step you take, I'll be watching you...

The Police

It was only in August 1993 that the long awaited provisions of the *Criminal Code* of Canada on criminal harassment came into effect. The impetus for the legislation was a number of well-publicized fatal attacks against women by their estranged partners. Prior to the murders, these women had been harassed and stalked. Although the intent of the legislation was to better protect members of society from being harassed and stalked, there was also the recognition that the law would be useful in dealing with the harassment of individuals by members of ideologically or politically motivated causes, and in other situations unrelated to personal matters.

Stalking is a social, legal and psychiatric problem. As a social construct, reflected in media accounts, it has evolved from being labeled, in the period between 1980 and 1989, as "psychological rape" and "obsessive following" to stalking and "star stalking" reflecting the high profile cases of movie stars and television personalities stalked, and in the famous case of Rebecca Shaffer, killed by her emotionally disturbed pursuer (Lowney and Best, 1995). Stalking evolved, according to Lowney and Best (1995), into a women's issue.

From a behavioural perspective there are different definitions of stalking. Meloy and Gothard (1995) prefer the aforementioned label of "obsessional following" considering it to be a clinical corollary to stalking, defined as "an abnormal or long-term pattern of threat or harassment toward a specific individual" (p.259). Pathe and Mullen (1997, p.12) define stalking as a "constellation of behaviours in which one individual inflicts on another repeated unwanted intrusions and communications."

The most current Statistics Canada police and court data relating to criminal harassment reveal the following facts for 2002 (Justice Canada, 2006):

- In total, 9,080 criminal harassment incidents were reported to a sample of 123 police forces in Canada in 2002. This number accounts for slightly over 4% of all violent incidents reported to those police forces that year.
- Of those 9,080 incidents, 4 in 10 (45%) were cleared of the charge, and the complainant declined to lay charges in 1 in 6 (16%).
- Of the victims, 3 in 4 were female (76%).
- Female victims tended to be younger than male victims. Of the female victims, 4 in 10 (42%) were under 30 years of age, compared to 27% of male victims.
- Of the accused, 8 out of 10 were male (84%).
- Of the female victims, 1 in 3 (31%) was criminally harassed by a current or former intimate partner; slightly fewer female victims were harassed by an acquaintance or a friend (23% each).
- Of the male victims, 4 in 10 (39%) were criminally harassed by a casual acquaintance, while only 13% were stalked by a current or former intimate partner.
- Two thirds (66%) of all criminal harassment incidents occurred at the victim's home.
- Although victims almost always suffered emotional harm, physical injury was recorded by the police in less than 2% of all cases.

Stalking is not a psychiatric diagnosis, and no single psychological profile exists for stalkers. Individuals who harass and stalk can have one or more of a variety of psychological difficulties ranging from personality disorders to major illness. Some of these conditions are described in the American Psychiatric Association's *Diagnostic and Statistical Manual of Mental Disorders – Fourth Edition – Text Revision* - DSM-IV TR (1999). The DSM –IV TR is the standard classification used by clinicians in North America, describing inclusion and exclusion criteria for a wide variety of emotionally disturbed behaviour. It does not classify distinct categories for harassing behaviour or stalking.

Stalking and harassing behaviour can take many forms. Some of the behaviour would be considered socially appropriate in a different context (*e.g.*, sending cards or gifts), but at the end of the behavioural spectrum there can be acts of violence. Stalking is often a building block crime, a series of small events with the potential to escalate to violent behaviour. The actions of the stalker, or intrusions as described by Pathé and Mullen (1997), may include repeated telephone calls, letters, electronic mail, loitering nearby, surveillance, graffiti, vandalism, killing pets and physical violence. Stalking can be a series of events that compound one another.

Stalking appears to be more common than was once believed. According to the United States Department of Justice the lifetime prevalence rate is estimated at 8% of all women and 4% of all men when the definition requires the victim to feel a high level of fear. If a less-stringent definition is used – one requiring victims to feel only somewhat frightened – the stalking rate increases dramatically to 12% of women but remains 4% for men. (Tjaden and Thoennes, 1998).

The purpose of this chapter is to examine the typologies that have been introduced over the past decade and a half and discuss what is presently being utilized in clinical settings and in threat assessment. We will also discuss certain intervention strategies affecting stalkers and their victims. We will conclude with a study of a phenomenon that is rare but that cannot be dismissed in a criminal investigation, false victimization stalking.

A. TYPOLOGIES OF PATHOLOGICAL HARASSMENT

Since the introduction of the first anti-stalking law in the United States in 1990, there have been a number of attempts to create typologies from both psychiatric and law enforcement perspectives. There have been no fewer then 12 published efforts to categorize patterns of stalking behaviour. According to Mohandie *et al.* (2006) the more commonly cited typologies infer motivations based on psychiatric diagnoses and use mental health labels; rely on the inferred or discerned motives of the subject; highlight the degree of previous intimate relationship; attempt to categorize the level of risk or underscore the extent to which the victim is a private citizen or public figure. Some of these typologies overlap and combine dimensions (Boon and Sheridan, 2001; Mullen *et al.*, 1999; Wright *et al.*, 1996).

1. The Los Angeles Police Department Typology

The typology developed by the Los Angeles Police Department Threat Management Unit is one of the best-known and most referenced typologies in the literature. Despite some limitations, it is the typology used by both the Behavioural Sciences Section of the Ontario Provincial Police and the Behavioural Sciences Branch of the Royal Canadian Mounted Police.

In reviewing the first 74 cases the Threat Management Unit handled they combined aspects of the stalker's mental health with their motivation and their relationship with the victim. This three-part typology is based on the nature of the stalkers obsession with the victim (Zona, Sharma and Lane, 1993). A follow-up study looked at 341 stalkers (Zona, Palarea and Lane, 1998).

(a) The erotomanic stalker

Only seven of the 74 cases (9.5%) described by Zona, Sharma and Lane (1993) involved individuals who would meet the criteria for erotomania. This is not surprising, for although it is a clinical presentation well described in the literature, it is a relatively uncommon condition despite recent media attention. Erotomanic fans have figured prominently in the mental state of many "celebrity stalkers" and "obsessed fans." The fact that it has been the theme in a number of movies has fuelled the myth that this type of stalker is the most common. Teresa Saldana, of the television show *The Commish*, was one of the first to gain widespread international attention after Arthur Richard Jackson stabbed her outside her apartment on March 12, 1982. Well known celebrities have been victimized by erotomanic stalkers including Michael J. Fox, Anne Murray and Shania Twain, to name a few. The author (PC) has been consulted on cases that have involved nationally known television newsreaders, a host of an ethnic cable television program, internationally known singers, a major league baseball player and a player in the National Basketball League. All their pursuers were erotomanic, and the media was only aware of one case.

Despite this public and media perception, in the majority of cases involving erotomanic stalkers, the victim is not a public figure. One of the more notable legal cases involving erotomania was the murder of Tatiana Tarasoff by a male acquaintance, Prosenjit Poddar. Poddar misinterpreted a New Year's kiss from Tarasoff as a sign that she loved him. After repeated attempts to gain her attention and affection, Poddar planned to create a dangerous situation in which he would rescue Tarasoff. He believed his heroic act would reveal to Tarasoff the depth for her feelings for him. His plan went terribly awry and he fatally stabbed Tarasoff. The civil suit resulting from her death has had far-reaching effects in changing the parameters of privilege in doctor-patient relationships and the concept of duty to warn.

Although such behaviour has been reported since ancient times (Segal, 1989), the salient features of erotomania were first described by the French psychiatrist Gatien de Clérambault in his 1921 study of five cases of "psychose passionale" and the condition is often still referred to as de Clérambault syndrome. The DSM-IV equivalent of de Clérambault syndrome is delusional disorder – erotomanic type. Individuals with delusional disorders present as essentially normal with the exception that they have a reasonably well-circumscribed delusion, which is non-bizarre in quality. Non-bizarre delusions involve situations, which can conceivably occur in real life (*e.g.*, being loved at a distance, followed, poisoned, infected or deceived by one's spouse or partner).

The central theme, in the erotomanic subtype, is that the subject has a delusion that another person is in love with them. It often concerns idealized love and "spirtual union" rather than sexual attraction according to the *Diagnostic and Statistical Manual of Mental Disorders – Fourth Edition – Text Revision* - DSM-IV TR (1999). The person is convinced that the object of their attention, usually of the opposite sex, fervently loves him or her and would return the affection if it were not for some external influence. The person about whom this conviction is held is usually of a higher status than the subject but, as noted above, is often not a celebrity. It could be a supervisor at work, a paediatrician, the church minister, or the police officer who stopped them for a traffic violation but did not charge them. Sometimes it is a complete stranger. Efforts to contact the object of their delusion through telephone calls, electronic mail, letters, gifts, visits, surveillance and stalking are common, but occasionally the person keeps the delusion secret.

A common cognitive feature operating in the minds of erotomanics is that of ideas of reference. They will misinterpret events, the actions of others, or otherwise usual occurrences as having specific meaning for them. These ideas of reference serve to reinforce their delusional thinking and they will reject evidence to the contrary, which is the hallmark of delusional thought. To further complicate matters, it has been observed that many of these individuals lead an isolated and solitary existence with few social contacts or supports (Seeman, 1978).

As an illustration, in one of the original cases described by de Clérambault, a 53-year-old French woman was absolutely convinced that King George V of England was in love with her. She was certain that English sailors and tourists were messengers sent by the King. In several trips she took to England, starting in 1918, she patiently waited outside Buckingham Palace. On one occasion she saw a curtain moving in a window and interpreted this as a signal from the King (Segal, 1989).

Clinically, it was initially felt that the erotic delusional disorder was a condition that only affected females. In the past couple of decades, however, there has been more of a realization that men can also be erotomanic and that erotomanic males can pose a greater risk for acting out violently (Goldstein, 1987). Other common diagnostic features comprising de Clérambault syndrome are: the patient believes that the object of the delusion was first to fall in love; the patient believes that the object of the delusion was the first to make advances; the amorous delusion always remains unchanged; the delusion can become chronic; and hallucinations are absent (Ellis and Mellsop, 1985).

Case 1: The erotomanic stalker

S. A. is a 40-year-old man of Iranian birth. After serving as a non-comissioned oficer in the Iran-Iraq war, he immigrated to Canada. He settled in a southern Ontario community, becoming a co-owner of a variety store. A frequent visitor to the store was Ms. E., 44-year-old real estate agent who worked in a group agency around the corner from the variety store. One evening, while she was alone in the office, Mr. A. appeared and asked her out on a date. Some mild amorous overtures were attempted by Mr. A. which were easily rebuffed by Ms. E. She explained that she was engaged to get married and was transferring to an office in another community. Over the next few weeks, S. A. frequently called Ms. E, left notes, flowers and sent her gifts declaring his love for her. She came into the variety store to purchase cigarettes and to repeat the statement that she could not marry him. S.A. knew that this could not be true because she was wearing a blue dress, which meant that she had romantic thoughts about him.

Ms. E. moved to another community, married and assumed her husband's last name. S. A. sold his share of the store and moved to the city where Ms. E. resettled in an attempt to locate her. He did not know where she lived or was employed but knew where her brother worked.

He was charged with assaulting the brother when the brother did not reveal his sister's whereabouts.

S.A. refuses psychiatric treatment. He maintains the delusional belief that Ms. E. is in love with him but their love cannot be realized because of her family – he is Iranian and she is a Canadian-born white Anglo-Saxon protestant. He believes it is her family who are objecting to the relationship.

This case is a good illustration of how preoccupation with the love object can be all consuming and may ultimately lead to the injury or death of another party. Spouses, the children of the victim, friends and even co-workers can be at risk from the erotomanic stalker if he or she perceives them as being in the way of his or her desire. A related example is John Hinkley's attempted assassination of President Ronald Reagan to impress Jodie Foster, whom he stalked.

The erotomanic stalker is the rarest category of stalker and constitutes less then 10% of the cases referred to the Behavioural Sciences Section of the Ontario Provincial Police. In Zona, Sharma and Lane's (1993) original examination of the cases referred to the Los Angeles Police Department Threat Management Unit the erotomanic type constituted only 7% of the cases.

(b) Love obsessional stalker

These cases are characterized by the absence of an existing relationship between the stalker and the victim. Often the victims are only known through the media. They may be radio, television or motion picture celebrities. It is rare for a victim of a love obsessional stalker to be an "ordinary" individual. More commonly, this type of stalker focuses on a celebrity or public figure (Zona, Palarea, and Lane, 1998).

Many of these stalkers are diagnosed as suffering from a major mental illness such as schizophrenia or bipolar mood disorder. (Meloy, 1996). Regardless of the specific disorder, they share the common delusional precept that if only provided with the opportunity, they could win over the love of the victim or target. In addition to their underlying illness, many are socially naïve and have rarely been involved in an intimate relationship. In some cases, this may be related to the early onset of their illness. Typically schizophrenia develops in adolescence. These individuals may retreat to a life of fantasy relationships with individuals they hardly know. They believe that they can make the object of their affection love them, and desperately want to establish a personal relationship with their victim. When the victim refuses to respond to the stalker as desired, then the stalker may attempt to force the victim to comply through threats or intimidation.

In general, stalkers who have a major mental illness generally pose less of a risk when compared to stalkers who are personality disordered.

Case 2: The love obsessional stalker

Mr. R. B., aged 32, was a long-standing patient of a psychiatric hospital in a large urban area. He had first been diagnosed as suffering from bipolar illness at age 18. He had many hospitalizations to a number of psychiatric facilities in the city but the majority of his inpatient and outpatient care was where a nurse, Ms. Y., was employed as a case-worker. Mr. B. began to feel that he could have a relationship with this particular nurse. By coincidence, Ms. Y. was having a "break-up" of her marriage. It was never determined whether the patient had knowledge of that fact. He began to follow Ms. Y. and found out where she lived. The ensuing number of notes, letters and visits to her place of residence naturally caused the victim great concern. The proclamations of love eventually developed into paranoid anger with eventual threats of harm. Despite the fact that the patient was banned from the hospital, Ms. Y. sought employment elsewhere.

Case 3: The female love obsessional stalker

L.C. was a 21-year-old university student. Over a period of a year her marks began to deteriorate and she isolated herself from friends and family. Her parents were divorced and she lived with her father and brother who did not notice the change in her behaviour. She had been a basketball fan since high school and with money from a summer job she bought a single season ticket to the professional basketball team that played in her community. Ms. C. became enamoured with a particular player and claims to have met him at a bar and subsequently had sex with him back at his residence. She tried to establish a relationship, with that particular player, but was rebuffed. A few months later she then began to send gifts and letters to another player. The content of the letters went beyond normal fan mail in her suggestion that he father her child. As well as describing her physical appearance she also sent nude pictures of herself. The team contacted Ms. C. requesting that she cease with the sending of gifts and letters.

By coincidence the player was traded to another team. The letters continued and were sent to his parent's residence in the state of California. Ms. C. traveled to where the player was now based, bought a single ticket but left the game before the national anthem because of the movements of the cheerleaders and the speed of the stadium clock which she interpreted as negative. She went back to her hotel room, believing that the player would join her after the game. Ms. C. was eventually assessed and has now been diagnosed as a schizophrenic. The patient and family have been educated about the illness and she responded well to medication. Ten years after the above episode, the author (Collins) learned that she has developed the delusional belief that she would marry a psychiatrist in the hospital where she is being treated.

In some instances, there is a foundation of fact upon which a delusional structure of fantasy is constructed. In the case of Ms. C., both the assessing psychiatrist and the security personnel of the National Basketball League believed her account of the sexual encounter with another player she met in the bar, who later thwarted her romantic overtures.

c) *Simple obsessive stalker*

The third category described by Zona, Sharma and Lane (1993) is the simple obsessive group. Although the simple obsessive stalking category only made up 47% of the stalkers they examined, a later review of the subject confirms what we have known clinically – that this is the most common form of stalking and potentially the most dangerous (Zona, Palaera and Lane, 1998). The majority of these stalkers have been in some form of relationship with the victim. The contact may have been minimal such as a blind date or more commonly, a prolonged dating relationship, common-law union or marriage. This corresponds with Spitzberg's (2002) meta-analytic finding that 49% of stalking cases involve prior sexual intimacies.

The perpetrator refuses to recognize that the relationship with another person is over and has the prevailing attitude of "if I can't have her (or him) then no one else will." A campaign of harassment, intimidation and psychological terror is mounted. The motivation for the harassment and stalking varies from revenge to the belief that they can convince or coerce the victim back into the relationship.

This form of stalking is almost always, but not exclusively, a male activity. In a Justice Canada working document, the accused in the cases examined were men (91%) and the majority of the victims (88%) were women. An analysis by accused-victim relationship showed a large proportion of female victims were stalked by an ex-husband or ex-boyfriend (Gill and Brockman, 1996). In contrast, for male victims the relationship of the accused was quite different. Few were stalked by an ex-spouse (9%) or ex-girlfriend (4%), yet almost half (46%) were stalked by a casual acquaintance, usually male (Kong, 1996).

In essence, intimate partner stalking is an extension of domestic violence. Domestic violence is conceptualized as an abuser's attempt to use physical, sexual and/or psychological force to take away a woman's power and control over her life (Walker and Meloy, 1998). The attempt to gain power and control, over the victim, is continued and can even escalate if the woman leaves or tries to leave the relationship. A cycle of domestic violence is often described in three hypothetical phases - *the tension building phase,* in which there is a gradual escalation of tension and minor but increasing incidents of abuse; *the acute battering phase,* in which the violence erupts and *the loving contrition (or honeymoon) phase,* during which the abuser apologizes and begs for forgiveness, stating remorse and promising change (Walker, 1979).

Stalking can mirror this cycle of violence, but as with domestic violence, not all victims will experience each of these phases. In stalking there can be a *tension building phase* where the behaviour consists of repeated phone calls, hang-up calls, odd gifts and then actual threats, surveillance of the victim, contacting friends and family of the victim, following and gradually more serious attempts to control and terrorize. In the *explosive phase* minor acts of violence can become major attacks involving abduction, physical or sexual assault, violence towards the victim's family and, in some cases, murder or murder/suicide. A third phase can sometimes separate these two phases - the *"hearts and flowers"* phase (Shaum and Parish, 1995). The stalker will either ask forgiveness or switch techniques. Sometimes there will be a period of quiescence leaving the victim feeling temporarily safe only to have the campaign of harassment begin anew.

In a U.S. study, a total of 141 undergraduate women completed a questionnaire designed to assess the occurrence of threatening or violent behaviours in former heterosexual romantic relationships (Coleman, 1997). Based on their responses to questions modeled on Florida's anti-stalking law, the subjects were placed in a control, harassed, or stalked group. A scale was used to gauge the presence of domestic violence during the relationship, and the Stalking Behaviour Checklist was completed to measure the occurrence of stalking behaviours after the relationship was terminated. The results of the study showed that males who were verbally or physically abusive during relationships are more likely to pursue their partners in a harassing or violent manner after the relationships end.

Some practitioners in the field of threat assessment have complained that the term "simple" in the simple obsessional category can be misunderstood by victims. The term simple can imply, to some, that the situation is not serious. The contrary is true. The simple obsessive stalker is more likely be the perpetrator of violence and less likely to have a major mental illness. Many will have antisocial, narcissistic, paranoid or dependent personality disorders or traits of these disorders.

Ackley (2006) of the Federal Bureau of Investigation National Center for the Analysis of Violent Crime has identified factors that increase the risk of homicide in cases of domestic violence. These include stalking, prior abuse in the relationship, perception of threat on the part of the victim, threatening to leave the abusive relationship, "dramatic moments" (e.g. court decisions), prior general criminal behaviour, substance abuse, access and/or fascination with weapons, threats, stressors, violation of protection order, externalizing blame, pervasive jealously, a sense of entitlement, perception of a loss of control and depression. The key to risk assessment, in intimate partner violence, is not only to understand the most prevalent risk factors but the relationship between those factors and the offender's personality, especially regarding response to rejection and infidelity (imagined, anticipated or real).

Higher rates of domestic violence, during a relationship, are associated with greater risk of stalking with violence and homicide during and after separation, and the rates remain elevated, on average, for two years after separation. Up to 90% of women murdered by ex-partners were stalked prior to the homicide (Ackley, 2006).

Case 4: The simple obsessive stalker

Mr. D.P. and Ms. M.M. dated only six months before they got married. He was 26 and she was 22 years of age. Ms. M.M. witnessed a couple of verbal confrontations between D.P. and his father and was told of past fisticuffs with his brother, but otherwise D.P. seemed to be an ideal partner.

Over the first year of marriage, D.P. became more controlling. He would tell her what to wear. He was displeased if M.M. went out after work with girlfriends. He demeaned her, cruelly commenting on her weight gain and calling her a dumb cow if she made what he perceived to be stupid mistakes. He would tell her what to wear. After an argument over finances, he forcibly confined her to the bedroom, and she was late for work by a few hours.

With the help of her family, she moved out. In the first month after she left D.P. called her at work over 200 times. He would beg her to return, but later on he became more menacing and derogatory. He left a bouquet of flowers on the hood of her car prior to slashing the tires. During their relationship, and with M.M.'s consent and knowledge, D.P. had video taped them having sex. After the break-up, he began to send copies of the videotapes, initially to members of her family, and later to individuals at her workplace.

He was arrested, charged and later convicted of criminal harassment. He received a sentence of eight months including time served. It was suspected, but there was never enough evidence to prove, that he was responsible for the arson at M.M.'s parent's cottage.

2. Alternative Typologies

A consultant criminologist with the Federal Bureau of Investigation has developed what he regards as a preliminary typology of stalkers. It resolves some of the deficiencies of the above-noted LAPD typology but has not been subjected to the same empirical examination. It is intended to be developmental and heuristic, in the recognition that the danger of typologies lies primarily in the likelihood that they may be viewed as an absolute classification schema (Mahaffy-Sapp and Sapp, 1998).

This preliminary typology proposes seven types of stalkers: the random target stalker; celebrity stalker; single-issue stalker; casual acquaintance stalker; co-worker stalker; intimate partner stalker; and domestic violence stalker. The intimate partner and domestic violence stalkers are the most similar to the simple obsessional stalker.

a) The paraphilic stalker

Another recognized but not well-studied group of stalkers stalk as a component of their paraphilic (sexually deviant) focus. Some rapists, paedophiles and other paraphilic men have stalked because stalking is incorporated into their sexually deviant fantasies and offending behaviour (Collins, 1999). Mullen, Pathé and Purcell (2000) refer to these men as predatory stalkers. The stalking behaviours are intended as preparatory to an assault, usually sexual, and are a combination of information gathering, rehearsal, intrusion through surreptitious observation, and the exercise of power. The stalker's intent in most cases is not to disturb or alert the victim prior to the fantasized or planned attack. Mullen, Pathé and Purcell (2000) also note that the stalker can demonstrate deficiencies in self-efficacy and social relations.

Paul Bernardo was a stalker. After stalking and raping young women in the community of Scarborough, Ontario between 1988 and 1990, he moved to St. Catherines, Ontario where he continued to stalk women. The stalking escalated to murder. He went as far as video taping unsuspecting victims in their own residences, some of whom will always remain blissfully ignorant that they were being followed by the man who was subsequently found to be a dangerous offender after being found guilty of the murder of Lesley Mahaffey and Kristen French. In his review of the Bernardo investigation, Mr. Justice Archie Campbell stated that stalking was the "hallmark" of Bernardo and that the police regretfully did not take his stalking seriously since their was no investigative follow-up (Campbell, 1996).

b) Internet stalking

Criminal harassment can be conducted through the use of a computer system, including the Internet. Although this type of conduct is described in various ways, not all such conduct falls within Canada's definition of criminal harassment. For example, "cyber-stalking" or "online harassment" is often used to refer to (1) direct communication through e-mail; (2) Internet harassment, where the offender publishes offensive or threatening information about the victim on the Internet; and (3) unauthorized use, control or sabotage of the victim's computer. In some cyber-stalking situations, criminal harassment charges may be appropriate; however, depending on the activity involved, charges under sections 342.1 (unauthorized use of a computer), 342.2 (possession of device to obtain computer service) and subsection 430(1.1) (mischief in relation to data) should also be considered (Justice Canada, 2006). Activities that can be considered cyber-stalking can include delivering threatening or harassing messages through one or more of the following:

- e-mail;
- chat rooms;
- message boards;
- newsgroups; and
- forums.

Other variations of cyber-stalking include the following:

- sending inappropriate electronic greeting cards;
- posting personal advertisements in the victim's name;
- creating Web sites that contain threatening or harassing messages or that contain provocative or pornographic photographs, most of which have been altered;
- sending viruses to the victim's computer;
- using spy-ware to track Web site visits or record keystrokes the victim makes; and
- sending harassing messages to the victim's employers, co-workers, students, teachers, customers, friends, families or churches, or sending harassing messages forged in the victim's name to others (Hitchcock, 2003).

Some 20% of the cases referred to the Threat Management Unit of the LAPD involve stalking through electronic mail. One out of four of the 600 cases referred to the Sex Crimes Unit of the NYPD in a recent study involved cyber-stalking (Nair, 2003).

B. STRATEGIES FOR DEALING WITH STALKERS

Stalking has been described as the act of following, viewing, communicating with, or moving threateningly or menacingly toward another person. The purpose of stalking resides in the mind of the stalkers who are compulsive individuals with a mis-perceived fixation. Stalking is the result of an underlying emotional conflict that propels the offender to stalk and/or harass a target. The majority of stalking victims are women and the majority of stalkers are men.

Developing strategies for dealing with stalkers is a task the law enforcement community has not routinely been trained to perform. Law enforcement officers are reactive in nature, i.e., a crime is committed, an investigation is conducted where physical evidence is collected, interviews occur and a suspect may be identified, arrested, tried, convicted and incarcerated. The crime of "stalking," however, is not a solitary act. It is a pattern of conduct which may feature a cluster of behaviors occurring over an extended period of time. Stalker tactics may include using the telephone, sending letters, e-mail messages or gifts, graffiti, vandalism, surveillance or physical altercations. Taken individually, these harassing acts may be considered a "nuisance" type of crime and not taken seriously by investigators. Collectively, this pattern of behavior may be more serious. Investigators must be able to analyze the situation correctly, which may prevent the crime of stalking from escalating into the crime of kidnaping, rape or homicide. Obtaining a restraining order or arresting the offender may inflame the situation and may not always be a course of action that would ensure (as much as possible) the safety of the victim.

The investigation of the crime of stalking, therefore, requires a more pro-active approach by investigators and an understanding of the mind of the offender by assessing the stalker's behaviour. Stalking victims will frequently ask investigators for advice on how to deal with the problem and whether the threats should be taken seriously. The advice provided by the investigating officer can have life and death consequences. At no time should an investigator "guarantee" the victim's safety, because no one can predict with absolute certainty when and if a person will commit an act of violence. There is one factor worth considering:

"Past behavior is frequently an indicator of future behavior."

If the stalker has a history of using violence in the past to resolve issues, the potential for violence being directed towards the victim escalates.

Frequently, the victim's strategy for dealing with a stalker initially consists of trying to ignore the harassing behavior. When that fails, the victim may ask, plead, or demand that the offender stop harassing her. In some instances, the victim may even have a third party intervene on her behalf. It is only after the harassment has continued unabated or increased that the victim contacts law enforcement officials. Stalking is one of the few criminal offenses where the victim has the responsibility for gathering and preserving the physical and behavioural evidence required for successful prosecution. Unfortunately, many times the victim has destroyed the cards, letters, e-mails, and gifts sent by the offender prior to her contacting law enforcement.

Consequently, there is no hard evidence the investigator can produce for the prosecuting attorney and no proof that a crime has occurred. It is the victim's word against the offender's.

During the initial interview of the victim, the investigator must maintain an "open mind" regarding the victim's recitation of the stalking events and not form a preliminary opinion as to the truthfulness of the complainant's allegations based upon the complainant's physical and verbal demeanor. As with rape victims, investigators occasionally have a pre-conceived idea on how a rape (or stalking) victim should behave. A crime victim can display a range of emotions from hysterical anger on one end to apparent indifference on the other. Initially, the investigator should just listen to the victim's story and then ask specific questions.

At some point, the investigator should ask the following questions about the stalker:

- Does he have a history of violence?
- Has he threatened to commit acts of violence?
- Is he easily frustrated?
- Does he have a temper?
- Does he perceive himself to be misunderstood?
- Is he obsessed with her?
- Does he have violent beliefs?
- Does he use/abuse alcohol and/or drugs?
- Does he have access to weapons?
- Does he suffer from any mental illness or personality disorders?

A positive answer to many of these questions would suggest the stalker shares traits and characteristics of many violent individuals and poses a greater risk to the safety of the complainant.

Stalking (like many crimes), is a crime of "power and control." From the very outset, one of the investigator's objectives is to restore some semblance of control back into the victim's life.

During the preliminary interview, if the investigator believes that the stalker's described behavioural patterns demonstrate a potential for violence, he can offer the following suggestions:

1. She should save and photograph every gift or letter sent to her. These items should be handled minimally to preserve fingerprint evidence. Letters and envelopes should be preserved in manilla type envelopes. Do not place photocopied documents in plastic envelopes as the toner may adhere to the plastic. DNA, hairs and fibers may also be present on the envelope's glue.

2. E-mail communications should be retained and any telephone calls should be recorded. Don't disconnect your old number. Place that phone in another room with a recorder and use a cell phone for normal communications.

3. A daily journal or diary should be maintained by the victim documenting all events to include verbal and written communications sent by the offender. Notations should also be made regarding any suspicious vehicles observed (to include license plate numbers). In addition, loitering, surveillance, acts of vandalism, etc., should be noted. The time, date, and place of these occurrences should be explained in the journal. Avoid using profanity or derogatory remarks regarding the offender when composing the diary, since the diary may be introduced during court proceedings.

4. A camera should be carried at all times to photograph the offender or his vehicle, especially if he is violating a restraining order. At home, the victim should ensure that there is a peephole in her front door and sturdy door and window locks. If affordable, a home security system should be considered. If the exterior of the victim's home is being vandalized, consider installing a time lapse camera to record activity outside her residence. Outdoor motion activated lights may be effective but not in areas where there is extensive wildlife.

5. Establish a pattern of calling or being called by a friend and establish a "password" which will communicate the need for them to call law enforcement, should the offender be in close proximity to the victim so that she fears for her safety.

6. Vary her schedule and points of travel, and know the location of police and fire stations.

7. If confronted by the "Stalker," attempt to maintain your composure. Avoid any topics which historically have "set him off." Change the subject.

One of the most dangerous times for a woman in our society is when she has been involved with a very jealous, possessive, and potentially violent man. Whether the victim is a wife or girlfriend, frequently she is the victim of psychological and/or physical domestic violence. Ironically, the potential for physical harm toward the victim may increase *not* while she is still actively involved in the relationship, but when she ended it or is in the process of ending it. The motivation of these "domestic stalkers" is to continue or re-establish a previous relationship. In these situations, stalking may be the precursor of more violent behavior as the offender adapts the attitude of: "If I can't have you, no one can have you."

If the investigator believes that the stalker poses a potentially dangerous risk to the victim's well-being, a strategy has to be developed (with the victim's cooperation and input) as to what would be her verbal and non-verbal response should the offender confront her.

This exercise is not designed to increase the victim's sense of paranoia, but to prepare for the worst case scenario. In other words, can the victim think of any words or themes that she could express to the offender which would pull him back from the abyss and deter him from harming her? There can be multiple themes developed based upon the nature of the possible confrontation. The victim's response to the crisis could differ if she is alone as opposed to having her children or a new boyfriend with her. The victim should not memorize these themes, but rehearsing them in front of a mirror may be of value.

Once again, the stalking victim should be advised that her actions cannot guarantee her safety but may defuse the situation enough so that the offender calms down and perhaps can be reasoned with. If the offender is under the influence of alcohol, drugs, or is delusional, no themes may be effective.

This strategy of "theme development" was utilized in the following situation:

Case 5 : The story of John and Lisa

Lisa was a 19-year-old, white female living in her grandmother's single family home. Upon graduating from high school, she received training to become a paralegal and was employed at a small law firm. She had a pleasant, non-aggressive personality and enjoyed going to night clubs with her friends where she drank alcohol in moderation.

John was a 26-year-old, white male living in a two-bedroom apartment in the same community. He attended two years of college and was employed as an insurance company automobile claims representative. He displayed superficial charm but was also very demanding and manipulative and considered himself to be a "man's man."

John and Lisa met at a nightclub and hit it off immediately. Within several months, she left her grandmother's home and moved into John's apartment. For a few months, their relationship appeared to blossom, and John would proclaim to Lisa that he was her "guardian angel." In time, however, John became more possessive of Lisa, insisting she spend more time with him and not her friends, and dress according to his standards. The final straw, however, was when John attempted to convince Lisa to participate in an insurance scam, where automobile accidents (with fake injuries) would be staged.

Lisa left John and moved back into her grandmother's home. Shortly thereafter, John began stalking Lisa via the telephone, through e-mails, and by following her to and from work. When she began seeing her male and female friends again, John became outraged at her perceived "betrayal" and his stalking behavior (especially surveillance), intensified.

His communications to her became more threatening and frequent.

Lisa chose to ignore his behavior, hoping that in time John would get on with his life. For several months, this pattern of stalking conduct continued and then abruptly ended and Lisa felt a sense of relief. This relief was short lived, however. One morning, as Lisa was exiting her vehicle at her place of employment, a white van pulled up alongside her. Her former boyfriend and an unknown male jumped out of the van and kidnapped her.

Once inside the van, duct tape was used to bind and gag Lisa and her former boyfriend announced that soon he and his friend would rape, torture, and kill her. Lisa was terrified, but was able to regain her composure and contemplated if there was any way out of her dire predicament.

John and his accomplice drove for several hours and eventually stopped at a hunting cabin in another state that was closed for the season. They broke into the cabin and brought Lisa into the house. When they removed the duct tape from her mouth, Lisa knew that if she cried, screamed, or pleaded with John, her efforts would be futile.

Instead, during her two hours of captivity, Lisa mentally conducted an indirect personality assessment of John to include his strengths and weaknesses, likes and dislikes, traits and characteristics, and remembered that he had frequently described himself to her as her "guardian angel."

When the duct tape was removed from her mouth, instead of becoming hysterical, Lisa told John that she had done a lot of thinking during her journey about their relationship, and finally came to the conclusion that she had been a fool. She had failed to understand how deeply he loved her and that he was only trying to protect her from her controlling, immature friends, and not run her life. She apologized to John for her past behavior, and admitted she had never been with a man before who loved her so much that he was willing to spirit her away like a "knight in shining armor" to save her from herself.

She said he had every right to hate her, but asked him for one more chance because she had "a lot of growing up to do," and with his guidance, hopefully she could become a woman worthy of his love and devotion.

Initially, John was taken aback by her unexpected response, but continued to talk with her. Eventually, Lisa was able to convince John that she was sincerely interested in making their relationship work and suggested they (without his friend) continue their journey as a couple. John agreed, and took his kidnapping accomplice to a bus station and gave him a sum of money for his assistance.

By this time, the FBI was working this case as a kidnapping matter and the FBI's Behavioral Science Unit had conducted an indirect personality assessment of both the victim and the offender. Their assessment of the situation suggested that, if the victim was able to talk her way out of her predicament, John would allow her to call her grandmother and explain that there had been a huge misunderstanding and that she and John had eloped.

Lisa's grandmother was coached by the FBI's Behavioral Science Unit on how to verbally and emotionally respond should Lisa call her, with the knowledge that John would be monitoring the call. Several days after the kidnapping, Lisa did call her grandmother and her grandmother feigned happiness for the couple and advised she would notify the police to call off their search for Lisa.

John and Lisa continued on their journey and eventually arrived at a ski resort. Lisa, in order to "prove" her love for John, insisted on paying for everything during their trip, using her credit cards. These credit card transactions were monitored by the FBI. By the time the couple reached the ski resort, John was convinced of Lisa's love and left her alone in a motel room while he went to purchase some sandwiches. Lisa did not attempt to flee (for fear John was waiting outside the motel room), but managed to make a quick telephone call to her grandmother regarding her location. Within an hour, John was arrested and Lisa was rescued. John was subsequently tried and convicted for the kidnapping, rape and imprisonment of his former girlfriend Lisa.

This case represents an example of a stalking victim who was able to think her way through a life threatening situation and survive. The key to Lisa's survival was her ability to analyze the personality and behavioural traits of her former boyfriend and make (as it turned out) the right decision on how to approach him. This strategy worked in this case, but should not be interpreted as a template to be used by stalking victims facing a similar death potential scenario. The personality of the stalker and the victim must be evaluated in every case.

Stalking victims and investigators should be concerned if the stalking behaviour ends for *no apparent reason*. Investigators should attempt to discreetly ascertain what has changed in the offender's life, environment, or career, which would compel him to suddenly stop harassing his target. The unexpected cessation of stalking may be a precursor of more violent behaviour.

Fortunately, the overwhelming number of stalking cases do not culminate with the victim being killed. However, targets of stalkers often feel trapped in an environment filled with anxiety, stress, and fear, which often results in their having to make drastic adjustments in how they live their lives. In extreme cases, targets of stalkers have joined the military, quit their jobs, changed their names, and moved to other parts of the country.

There is no one "strategy" that can be utilized in all stalking cases. Each case presents unique problems and requires a customized solution. In some instances, the intervention of a friend, a restraining order, a visit by a uniformed police officer, or the arrest of the offender on stalking charges can be an effective way of ending the problem. In other cases, the best strategy may be to endure the harassment until the offender focuses his attention on someone else. One "rule of thumb" that most experts on stalking appear to agree on, however, is that the victim should cease all contact with the offender (if possible), for any contact whatsoever will be misconstrued by the stalker as the target showing an interest in him. A problem arises, however, when the offender had a relationship with the victim and child visitation rights are involved; or the victim and the offender work at the same place. Supervisors can certainly separate the victim and the stalker at the workplace, but that would not prevent the stalker from pursuing his target elsewhere.

In every stalking case, however, there is one constant. Before any of the above mentioned strategies is implemented, an *indirect personality assessment* must be conducted regarding the offender. A series of behaviourally oriented questions should be posed to trusted individuals who are acquainted with the subject. These individuals must be chosen carefully, however, for it is imperative that the stalker not be made aware that an assessment of him is being conducted. Information from multiple individuals is desired because there are many facets to a person's personality and there are public, private and secret sides to everyone of us. Co-workers may have a different opinion of the subject than his neighbours, his church congregation or his hunting buddies.

The accuracy of any indirect personality assessment is dependent upon the quantity and quality of the information gathered. Even after the necessary intelligence about the offender is obtained, there will be situations where an obvious solution to the problem is not apparent.

Questions asked of individuals familiar with the subject should focus on the following areas:

- family history
- physical characteristics and appearance
- health
- employment
- marriage (traditional or common law)
- hobbies and leisure activities
- behaviour and personality
- personality characteristics

When the stalking victim is questioned about the subject, she should be instructed to provide an unbiased, objective evaluation of the strengths and weaknesses of the offender, and include a timeline of activities regarding her personal, social, and/or professional relationship with him. It is important to understand how the subject behaved and reacted in the beginning, middle and toward the end of their time together.

There will be times when direct intervention by a law enforcement officer may not be the recommended course of action to resolve a stalking situation, as illustrated by the following case:

Case 6: The story of Mary and Sam[1]

Mary was a 21-year-old, single, white female who recently graduated from college with a degree in Business Administration. She was fortunate to land an entry level job at a hotel whose busy season coincided with the ski season in a resort community. Mary was a very outgoing, friendly, naïve woman who got along well with others.

Sam was a 45-year-old, single, white male who had been employed as a part-time marketing expert for the same hotel for 12 years during the ski season (November through March). For the rest of the year, he lived and worked on his parent's farm in another state. Sam was basically a

---

1 It should be pointed out that this case occurred in the United States where the investigation of harassment is somewhat different than it is in Canada.

loner and also very narcissistic. Management tolerated his behavioural quirks and demands because he was effective in his position.

Sam befriended Mary and took her "under his wing" to train her. Frequently, they would have lunch together, and in time, Sam misconstrued Mary's friendliness as Mary showing a romantic interest in him. Sam began asking Mary out on dates, and Mary politely refused his offers, but continued to have lunch with him. Sam had a very difficult time accepting "no" for an answer.

He continued to ask her out, began telephoning her at home, sent flowers and cards to her residence, and even showed up unexpectedly when Mary was on an outing with her Girl Scout Troop.

Mary continued to politely tell Sam that she was not romantically interested in him, but she did not notify her supervisors about his stalking behaviour. By early March, Mary was becoming concerned about Sam's persistence and thought that, if she began dating other men at the weather station, Sam would get the message and lose interest in her.

Instead, Sam arrived at work one morning and walked over to the cubicle of the two male employees who had recently been dating Mary. Sam was carrying a briefcase and initially engaged the two men in business related conversation. Sam then opened the briefcase and brandished a .40 caliber Glock semi-automatic pistol. (A loaded magazine for the weapon was in the briefcase.) He told the astonished men that he purchased the weapon for his own safety and then added that, for their information, he and Mary were an "item" and "were going" together, and he would appreciate it if they would stop asking Mary out. Sam then placed the weapon into his briefcase and walked back to his office.

The men quickly reported the incident to their supervisors, who in turn, interviewed Mary. They quickly learned they had a potentially very serious stalking incident occurring. To management's chagrin, they soon learned that the company did not have a sexual harassment policy or a policy regarding weapons in the workplace.

When dealing with a stalking situation such as the one described above, there are many forms of intervention that can be considered. Since Mary had not been documenting Sam's stalking behavior, and Sam had not directly threatened to harm the two male employees who had been dating Mary, arresting Sam for stalking or assault was not a viable law enforcement option.

Law enforcement officers could be called in to "just talk" with Sam about his behavior, and they could give him a stern warning to leave Mary alone and refrain from bringing a firearm to the weather station or there could be consequences.

Managers could counsel Sam about harassing Mary and advise him that carrying weapons into the workplace would not be tolerated. They could also advise him that, if his inappropriate behaviour continues, he could be dismissed from his position.

When an indirect personality assessment was conducted of Sam, it was determined that he could be classified as an "acquaintance stalker," i.e., an actual relationship never existed and that Sam misinterpreted the depth of his interaction with Mary. The motivation behind Sam's behavior was a need to control or dominate his love interest. When stalking occurs in the workplace, there is frequently a knee jerk reaction from management: Fire the offender. While this action may remove the offender from the workplace, it may not end the stalking of the victim. In this case, as a result of many discreet interviews, it was determined that Sam was passionate about his career with this establishment and would be very bitter about being terminated, especially if he perceived his termination was the result of Mary accusing him of stalking her or because of the gun incident.

Consequently, the following strategy was devised: Since Sam had only three weeks remaining on his current contract, he would be allowed to remain in the workplace. He would not be counseled regarding his stalking of Mary or his intimidation of two male co-workers who had dated Mary. Mary would make excuses as to why she couldn't have lunch with Sam, but remain polite and professional. She would ignore (but record and document) his telephone calls she received at home. The men who had dated Mary would not ask her out again and limit their contact with her in the office. Sam would believe that his two competitors for Mary's affection had "gotten his message" so there would be no further need for Sam to approach them.

Sam was obliged to work on the family farm and would not be in a position to remain in the community where he could continue to obsess over Mary. Once Sam left the hotel, management would reorganize the office and eliminate Sam's position. Six months later, when Sam re-applied for his old job, he would be told that, because of the downturn in the economy, unnamed figures in upper management had decided to cut costs by eliminating certain jobs.

Sam returned home and initially telephoned Mary frequently, and sent her cards and gifts, which Mary retained and documented. Mary never responded to Sam's efforts to maintain contact with her, and local law enforcement agencies were made aware of the situation.

Six months later, when Sam reapplied for his job, he was advised that the company would not be in a position to renew his contract. As to be expected, Sam was outraged that a 12-year veteran, such as he, was let go. Sam visited the hotel and demanded his old job back. Management stood firm, however, and Sam left angry and dejected. Sam returned home and periodically sent letters to his former supervisors, attempting to get them to intervene on his behalf, all to no avail.

Sam's attention was refocused, away from Mary and her two male co-workers, which was the desired objective. Sam eventually got on with his life, and the letters and telephone calls to Mary ended.

As previously indicated, every stalking situation demands a careful evaluation of the victim, offender, and stalking environment. Before any intervention strategy can be developed, an indirect personality assessment of the offender must be conducted. While the tactics of most stalkers are the same, dealing with their behaviour requires a very careful analysis, and there can never be a guarantee that the stalking will end.

C. FALSE ALLEGATIONS OF STALKING

Interest in false allegations of stalking is very recent. This can be explained in part because the phenomenon is rare — approximately 2% of all reported cases (Mohandie, Hatcher and Raymond, 1998; Zona, Lane and Moore, 1996). Given that no charges are brought in most cases, the actual rate is probably higher (Mohandie, Hatcher and Raymond, 1998). However, these false claims often cost a great deal of time and money, and can implicate or even convict innocent people.

1. Types of False Allegations

Mohandie, Hatcher and Raymond (1998) identify three types of false victimization syndrome: *Type* 1 concerns only victims who report physical symptoms of an unknown cause, notably Münchausen syndrome and Münchausen syndrome by proxy (see Asher, 1951; Meadow, 1982). In the other types, the "victim" reports a crime or series of crimes for which the assailant is known *(Type* 2) or unknown *(Type* 3). There can be a single offence, such as rape, assault or a hate crime, or serial offences, such as stalking. In the latter case, the victim is followed, harassed, and sometimes assaulted.

Case 7: Example of a Type 3 false allegation (serial crime)

A letter threatening a woman with death is faxed to reporters and the police. Police interview the woman. The anonymous letter is concise and direct. In coarse language, the author says he intends to kill the woman on the very day he has sent the letter. Given the apparent imminent danger, the police offer the woman protection and even provide her with a bullet-proof vest. In the ensuing two months, the woman receives several threatening letters. She also claims someone is watching her. The stalker seems to know all about her: her telephone and fax numbers, how she spends her time, her personal life. Analysis of the threatening letters and of the "victim's" statements raises serious doubts that the threats are real. The evidence suggests that there is no motive for them. According to files that were never closed, the complainant was a victim of three similar incidents in the past, involving death threats and an attempt on her life. The complainant never admitted any misdeeds, and a few days after police confronted her with the fact that the evidence pointed at her, she received further threats. This time the letter was less direct about imminent death and the author showed signs of resignation. Then, the threats stopped, leaving a lingering doubt in the minds of those who did not believe her. . .

2. Detecting False Allegations of Harassment

Most of those who suffer harassing behaviour do not immediately conclude they are victims. Often they are in denial, manifesting a desire not to believe it is happening. When the allegations are false, the victim does not express this denial or manifest resistance to recognizing their victimization. Rather, they conclude directly, "I'm a stalking victim" (Mohandie, Hatcher and Raymond, 1998). The true victim is usually reluctant to file a complaint, and often only does so under pressure from those close to her ("You have to do something about all this!"). She is also reticent and ambivalent, fearing that she will aggravate the situation or bring vengeance down on herself, whereas the false victim expresses neither fear nor feelings of vulnerability. She gloats and displays confidence, and tends to participate enthusiastically in the investigation (Mohandie, Hatcher and Raymond, 1998).

While the genuine victim is often embarrassed and prefers to attract the least attention possible, the false victim generally looks for secondary gains, seeking especially to attract attention — particularly if she alleges crimes at school or the workplace (Mohandie, Hatcher and Raymond, 1998). Such claims can even result in special arrangements for the complainant, as was the case with an employer who was notified of racist death threats aimed at a black employee. The employer gave the woman paid leave, only to discover that she had been sending the threats herself.

Often the false victim describes the suspect in Hollywood terms or in ways reminiscent of sensationalist newspapers. Examining medical experts generally find no particular injuries. When there are wounds, they are often compatible with self-mutilation. Sometimes there is so-called pseudo-corroboration, as where the "victim" receives a non-harassing telephone call but complains to a friend who heard the phone ring that a harasser had been on the line. There are also phantom suspects — "It just happened," "You just missed it" (Mohandie, Hatcher and Raymond, 1998). This always occurs within a small window of opportunity, without any corroboration. Some pseudo-victims are very imaginative, as in the following example.

Case 8: Manon's false allegations

Manon (not her real name) complains to the police that her former partner has stalked her and threatened her with death. She shows police officers letters and e-mails, sometimes anonymous, sometimes signed. An investigation indicates that all the documents were written by the same person, and handwriting analysis shows Manon is not their author. However, the threats seem cartoonish, even Hollywoodesque. As well, the complainant has a long history of false allegations (involving graffiti on her residence, anonymous calls, anonymous threatening letters, vandalism, etc.). At last, further investigation shows that she is, in fact, the author of the documents in question but had asked an acquaintance to write down her (the complainant's) words and send the letters for her.

False harassment claims closely resemble false allegations of sexual assault. The choice of crime (harassment) is perhaps related to the fact that this type of offence can seem less serious and intimate than a sexual assault. In that respect, it could be easier to manage as a matter of self-esteem. In addition, medical examination is not required, as it is in cases of alleged sexual assault (Mohandie, Hatcher and Raymond, 1998). The principal motivation is to attract attention and sympathy, although the complaint can also be motivated by revenge or the desire to maintain a relationship of dependency.

Victimological analysis generally provides the key to solving the case. Once investigators have thoroughly examined those close to the complainant, usually there remains only one investigative route, leading to the complainant: *Who are they?* Many false victims suffer from histrionic or borderline personality disorder. Symptoms characteristic of these personality disorders include manipulation, fear of abandonment, impulsiveness, self-mutilation, theatricality and a need for attention (American Psychiatric Association, 1996) — the same profile one finds with many false-sexual-assault complainants (Hall and Hall, 2001; MacDonald, 1971; McDowell and Hibler, 1987). In the weeks before the complaint, situational stressors such as abandonment, loss, rejection, and other relational problems can unleash or incite the filing of false harassment claims, which is, in fact, an inappropriate coping mechanism. The idea for the claim may be inspired from publicity surrounding a similar crime. Does the victim report having experienced similar events under mysterious circumstances? Do they have a history of false claims or excessive medical consultations? What is their relationship, if any, with the alleged harasser? Are they attracted to the alleged harasser, or have they been rejected? How do those close to them view them? Do they have a reputation for lying (mythomania) or exaggeration?

3. Dealing with False Allegations of Harassment

In dealing with false allegations, one must first gather all the evidence (medical reports, handwriting analysis, surveillance reports, statements, etc.) indicating that the allegation is untrue. Consulting mental-health experts can help investigators understand what motivates the person to fabricate stories in this way. Mohandie, Hatcher and Raymond (1998) remark that one can trap the false victim by telling them what "normally" would have happened — for instance: "Normally, this type of harasser would begin by calling you at night." Then one waits to see what follows, taking care to verify all calls.

Once there is sufficient information to suspect the harassment claim is false, a well-constructed interview can shed light on the case. The investigator must review the investigation from A to Z, with the alleged victim to show them that nothing has been neglected and that everything has been investigated except the possible culpability of the victim herself. Mohandie, Hatcher and Raymond (1998) suggest that investigators confront the pseudo-victim by stating: "The events did not occur in the way you've told us." Then they can provide them with a morally acceptable reason — a cry for help, for example — i.e., an option for helping them preserve their self-esteem and save face. An empathic, non-judgmental approach is most effective (Mohandie, Hatcher and Raymond, 1998). McDowell and Hibler (1987) suggest that, to allow the officer in charge of the file to maintain rapport with the pseudo-victim, a different investigator should conduct this later interview. The importance of preserving rapport is twofold — confessions are rare and recidivism is frequent.

CONCLUSION

Stalking is defined as the act of following another person, observing them, accosting them, or communicating with them in a disturbing or threatening way. Its purpose resides in the mind of the stalker, a compulsive individual with a poorly understood fixation. Stalking results from underlying emotional conflict that impels the offender to follow or harass their target.

Stalking is an insidious offence that can appear benign and inoffensive when each of its components is considered in isolation. The stalker progressively inserts themselves into the victim's personal life, invading their privacy, sometimes going so far as to physically attack them. Even though stalkers rarely become violent, they can inflict significant psychological harm. Over time, stalking overwhelms its victims, who suffer a prolonged and intense sense of intimidation, and psychological and emotional turmoil. Generally, victims fear that the stalker's behaviour will become more frequent and intense, a fear accompanied by the victim's sense that they have lost control of their life.

Typical traumatic reactions to stalking include:

- remorse
- the tendency to minimize the effects of the harassment

- interpreting the stalking as a private problem
- a sense of betrayal and shame
- anxiety and fear, because of the unpredictability of the stalker's behaviour
- a sense of powerlessness and of a loss of control over one's life
- mistrust of police, which impedes victims from reporting the crime
- inaction due to ignorance of the criminal nature of harassment
- denial or embarrassment

A significant proportion of stalking victims of both sexes suffer from depression or anxiety necessitating psychotherapeutic and pharmacological treatment.

The level of risk that a given pathological stalker poses to their victim will dictate how to deal with that individual. Sometimes a simple interview and warning are sufficient. In the case of recidivists or the potentially violent, legal proceedings, from peace bonds to imprisonment, can prove more effective and safe. Sometimes it is preferable to endure the harassing behaviour until it exhausts itself or the stalker changes targets.

Victimological analysis is no doubt the key to successfully resolving investigations into stalking. Focusing on the victim can help investigators understand why they, in particular, are the target of so much time and effort on the stalker's part. Sometimes one discovers neither the motive nor the perpetrator. The investigation stalls or goes in circles, coming back again and again to the victim. Once more, by turning attention to her, investigators might discover that the allegations have been fabricated out of revenge, a desire for attention or emotional distress. In such instances, investigators realize that, sometimes after several months of work, the true victim in the case is themselves.

REFERENCES

Ackley, C. (2006). Personal communication with Supervisory Special Agent Ackley in New Orleans, LA, August 2006 and Quantico, VA, September 2006.

American Psychiatric Association (1999). *Diagnostic and Statistical Manual of Mental Disorders,* Fourth Edition - Text Revision. Washington, D.C. : American Psychiatric Association Press.

American Psychiatric Association (1996). DSM-IV: manuel diagnostique et statistique des troubles mentaux. 4e ed. Paris, Edition Masson.

Asher, R (1951). Munchausen syndrome, *Lancet.*

Boon, J.C. et Sheridan, L. (2001). Stalker typologies: a law enforcement perspective. *Journal of Threat Assessment,* 1, 75-97.

Campbell, A. (1996). Bernardo Investigation Review. Government of Ontario.

Coleman, F.L (1997). Stalking behavior and the cycle of domestic violence. *Journal of Interpersonal Violence,* 12,420-432.

Collins, P.I. (1999). Psychiatric aspects of stalking. In Cornish, J., Murray, K. and Collins, P.I., *The Criminal Lawyers' Guide to the Law of Criminal Harassment and Stalking.* Aurora, ON : Canada Law Book, 1-16.

de Clerembault, G. (1942). Les psychoses passionnelles. In *Oeuvres Psychiatriques.* Paris: Presses Universitaires de France, 323-443.

Ellis, P. and Mellsop, G. (1985). De Clerembault syndrome - A nosological entity? *British Journal of Psychiatry,* 153, 90-95.

Gill, R and Brockman, J. (1996). A Review of Section 264 (Criminal Harassment) of the Criminal Code of Canada - Working Document 1996 - 7th.

Goldstein, RL. (1987). More forensic romances: de Clerembault's syndrome in men. *Bulletin of the American Academy of Psychiatry and the Law,* 15,267-274.

Hall, RC.W. and Hall, RC.W. (2001). False Allegations: The Role of the Forensic Psychiatrist. *Journal of Psychiatric Practice,* September, 343-346.

Hitchcock, J.A. (2003). Cyberstalking and Law Enforcement. *Police Chief,* 12, 16-27.

Justice Canada (2006). *Criminal Harassment: a guide for police and prosecutors.* http://www.justice.gc.ca/en/ps/fm/pub/harassment/partl.html.

Kong, R (1996). *Criminal Harassment-* Canadian Centre for Justice Studies Juristat Statistics Canada Catalogue #85-002-XPE, 16, No.12.

Lowney, K.S. and Best, J. (1995). Stalking strangers and lovers: changing media typifications of a new crime problem. Dans J. Best (dir.), *Images of Issues: Typifying Contemporary Social Problems.* New York: Aldine De Gruyter, 35-37.

MacDonald, J.M. (1971). *Rape: Offenders and their Victims.* Springfield, IL : Charles C Thomas.

Mahaffey-Sapp, C. and Sapp, A. (1998). *An analysis and preliminary typology of stalkers.* [unpublished] at 1-34. Personal communication with Dr. Alan Sapp at FBI Academy, Quantico, Virginia, March 1998 and at Ontario Provincial Police General Headquarters, Orillia, Ontario, September 1998.

McDowell, C.P. and Hibler, N.S. (1987). False allegations. Dans RR Hazelwood and A.W. Burgess (eds.), *Practical Aspects of Rape Investigation: A Multidisciplinary Approach,* Elsevier: New York, 275-299.

Meadow, R (1982). Munchausen syndrome by proxy. *Archives of Disease in Childhood,* Feb., 57(2) : 92-8.

Meloy, J.R. (1996). Stalking (obsessional following) : A review of some preliminary studies. *Aggression and Violent Behaviour,* 1, 147-162.

Meloy, J.R. and Gothard, S. (1995). A demographic and clinical comparison of obsessional followers and offenders with mental disorders. *American Journal of Psychiatry,* 152, 258-263.

Mohandie, K., Hatcher, C., and Raymond, D. (1998) False Victimization Syndromes in Stalking. Dans J. Reid Meloy (eds.) *The Psychology of Stalking: Clinical and Forensic Perspectives.* San Diego: Academic Press, 225-256.

Mohandie, K., Meloy, J.R., McGowan, M.G. and Williams, J. (2006). The RECON typology of stalking: reliability and validity based upon a large sample of North American stalkers. *Journal of Forensic Sciences,* 51 (1) 147-155.

Mullen, P.E., Pathe, M and Purcell, R. (2000). *Stalkers and their victims.* New York: Cambridge University Press.

Mullen, P.E., Pathe, M., Purcell, R. and Stuart, G.W. (1999). A Study of Stalkers. *American Journal of Psychiatry,* 156, 1244-1249.

Nair, M. (2003). Stalking. In R. Rosner (ed.) *Principles and Practice of Forensic Psychiatry,* 2nd ed. London: Holder.

Pathe, M. and Mullen, P.E. (1997). The impact of stalkers on their victims. *British Journal of Psychiatry,* 170, 12-17.

Seeman, M.V. (1978). Delusional loving. *Archives of General Psychiatry,* 35,1265-1267.

Segal, J.H. (1989). Erotomania Revisited: From Kraeplin to DSM-III-R. *American Journal of Psychiatry* 146,1261-1266.

Shaum, M. and Parish, K. (1995). *Stalked - Breaking the silence in the crime of stalking in America.* Toronto: Pocket Books.

Spitzerg, B. (2002). The tactical topography of stalking victimization and management. *Trauma Violence Abuse* 3, 261-288.

Tjaden, P. and Thoennes, N. (1998). *Stalking in America: Findings from the National Violence against Women Study.* Washington, D.C.: National Institute of Justice and Centers for Disease Control and Prevention.

Walker, L. (1979). *The Battered Woman.* New York: Harper and Row.

Walker, L. and Meloy, J.R. (1998). Stalking and domestic violence. In J. Reid Meloy (eds.) *The Psychology of Stalking : Clinical and Forensic Perspectives.* San Diego: Academic Press, 139-161.

Wright, J.A, Burgess, AG., Burgess, AW., Laszlo, AT., McCrary, G.O. and Douglas, J .E. (1996). A typology of interpersonal stalking. *Journal of Interpersonal Violence.* 11, 1487-502.

Zona, M.A., Lane, J. and Moore, M. (1996). *The psychology and behavior of stalkers.* Paper presented at the American Academy of Forensic Sciences Annual Meeting, Nashvill, Tennessee.

Zona, M.A., Palarea, R.E. and Lane, J. (1998). Psychiatric diagnosis and the offender-victim typology of stalking. In J. Reid Meloy (ed.) *The Psychology of Stalking: Clinical and Forensic Perspectives.* San Diego: Academic Press, 70-84.

Zona, M.A., Sharma, K.K. and Lane, J. (1993). A comparative study of erotomanic and obsessional subjects in a forensic sample. *Journal of Forensic Sciences,* 38(4), 894-903.

CHAPTER 12

The Psychology of Crisis Negotiation

Michel St-Yves and Michel Tanguay

Man accepts change only out of necessity,
and he sees necessity only
in the midst of crisis.

Jean Monnet

Crisis intervention by police is often synonymous with dramatic events, such as: the deaths at Columbine High School in Colorado; the long and tragic hostage-taking in Beslan, Russia, which ended with more than 300 deaths, half of which were of children; and the massacre at the Polytechnique de Montréal, in which 14 young women were shot dead by a madman seeking to attack feminism. However, most crisis interventions do not make headlines, and involve desperate men (95% are male) barricaded alone in their homes with a gun, threatening to kill themselves if anyone tries to get in[1] (Michaud and St-Yves, 2006). Their main demand is to end their suffering or die.

On average each year, the Sûreté du Québec[2] responds to about 30 situations requiring the deployment of its crisis-intervention team.[3] The vast majority of these calls (86.6%) involve mentally agitated persons, especially

---

1 Three out of four (77%) barricade themselves in their residences, alone (87%) or with their (ex-) spouses and/or children (62% of hostages), while in possession of a firearm (73%), usually a hunting weapon (Michaud and St-Yves, 2006).

2 The mission of the Sûreté du Québec, the provincial police force, is to maintain peace and public order throughout Quebec, protect Quebecers' lives, security, and fundamental rights, and safeguard Quebecers' property. The Sûreté du Québec also coordinates large-scale police operations, contributes to the integrity of government institutions and ensures the safety of the transportation networks under Quebec jurisdiction (Statement of Services to the public, Sûreté du Québec, 2007, www.surete.qc.ca).

3 In addition to the commander, the principal members of the crisis intervention team are sub-commanders, police negotiators, investigators, a tactical intervention team, an electronic surveillance team (providing technical support), and a behaviour analysis service (forensic psychologist).

persons barricaded alone or threatening to jump from a high structure. Close to half of these individuals (47%) have a history of psychiatric problems, generally mood disorders (91.9%) (Michaud and St-Yves, 2006). Amendola, Learning and Martin (1996) define a barricade situation as an incident in which one or several armed or possibly armed persons barricade themselves in a space (building, residence, vehicle, bridge), with or without hostages, and refuse to surrender to police. Hostage-taking is rare (13.4% of cases), and when it occurs it is more often a matter of simple confinement than of true hostage-taking [4] (St-Yves, Tanguay and St-Pierre, 2001). These statistics are comparable to those from the FBI's Hostage Barricade System database (HOBAS).[5]

During the last few years, and more particularly during the new millennium, the number of crises necessitating police-negotiator intervention has decreased considerably in Quebec. From an average of about 50 interventions[6] per year during the 1990s (St-Yves, Tanguay, and St-Pierre, 2001), we now see about 20 (Michaud and St-Yves, 2006). This marked decrease, which seems common among police forces responding to these events, is attributable to several factors, such as the greater accessibility of help for individuals in crisis, but particularly to more judicious evaluations of crisis situations — which do not always require the immediate deployment of crisis intervention teams — as well as more appropriate intervention by first responders.

This chapter describes the police-intervention process in crisis situations, which special attention to the role of police negotiators, as well as the main types of crisis situations. In addition, the genesis of crises and the techniques for intervening in different types of crises will be discussed. Finally, the SINCRO model,[7] the crisis-intervention model developed by the Sûreté du Québec (Quebec provincial police) and taught at l'École nationale de police du Quebec (Quebec police college), will be presented.

---

4 The FBI classifies these situations as "non-hostage situations", as the individual in crisis has no precise or realistic demands, although they attack another person with the intention of harming or killing them. The object of the attack is thus more a victim than a hostage (Noesner, 1999).

5 Statistical report based on 3000 crisis situations (see Noesner, 1999).

6 Number of crisis situations only in the territory served by the Sûreté du Québec.

7 **S**trategy of **I**ntervention and **N**egotiation by **C**olours according to **R**hythm **O**bserved (in French, **S**tratégie d'**I**ntervention et de **N**égociation par **C**ouleurs selon le **R**ythme **O**bservé: St-Yves, Tanguay and St-Pierre, 2001).

The Role of the First Responders

Police intervention usually begins with a call to the 911 emergency service by a witness or individual in crisis. The report is transmitted to officers on patrol, who proceed to the scene to assess the situation. As this is the riskiest phase of the crisis (see Dolan and Fuselier, 1989; Noesner and Dolan, 1992) — the point at which the risks of suicide and homicide are highest (Feldmann, 2001) — the priority for first responders is to secure the scene. Whenever possible, the first responders try to establish contact with the individual in crisis, and to maintain that contact by using techniques of active listening. This helps reduce the intensity of the individual in crisis' emotions and stress level. The first responders also collect as much information as possible (on the individual and the motives for his actions) until negotiators are ready to take over (Slatkin, 2005: 12).

Types of Crisis Situations

Crisis situations are usually classified on the basis of their authors' motivation (see Goldaber, 1979; Hacker, 1976). There exist three principal motivations (see Table 1):

1. *Psychological.* Typical of individuals who are suicidal, vindictive, or mentally disturbed.

2. *Criminal.* Typical of individuals apprehended in the midst of a criminal act, prisoners (rioters), and kidnappers for ransom.

3. *Political/cult.* Typical of protesters, ideological activists, and terrorists.

The FBI divides critical incidents into two categories, according to whether they are "hostage situations" (involving "rational individuals") or "non-hostage" (involving mentally-disturbed individuals) (see McMains and Mullins, 2001; Noesner, 1999).

"Rational" individuals act with a precise goal and reasons justifying their behaviour. Hostages, when taken, serve as bargaining chips for substantial demands such as money, escape and exchanges. Therefore, it is not in these individuals' interests to harm their hostages, who are bargaining chips. The FBI's recommended approach in such cases is to launch a high-visibility intervention, attempt to gain time (so as to reduce the hostage-taker's expectations) (Klein, 2003), demonstrate the benefits of surrendering over resisting, use negotiation techniques (techniques of persuasion and influence), and allow the hostage-taker to surrender without losing face.

"Mentally-disturbed" individuals are often self-destructive, lack precise goals, and are motivated by anger, frustration, or depression. Generally they do not have precise or realistic demands. Those who do make demands (one in four) ask to speak to a person in particular (63%), request special treatment (24%), or merely ask for cigarettes (19%) (Michaud and St-Yves, 2006). If they confine any individuals, they attack them with the intention of injuring or killing them; in this sense, the confined individuals are not "hostages" in the usual sense of the word. Because mentally disturbed people can become very anxious and react inappropriately, particularly if they are paranoid, the FBI recommends that tactical intervention units be deployed with discretion in such cases. In contrast to the case when dealing with "rational" individuals, the unit's approach should be patient, non-threatening, non-judgemental, and non-confrontational. Such cases sometimes require making concessions without expecting anything in return. These crises are best defused through active listening and therapeutic communication, in order to reduce the emotional intensity and establish a relationship of trust with the individual in crisis. Hostages and victims are less likely to be harmed while such interventions are going on. Individuals in crisis should also be offered a non-violent and reassuring solution that allows them an honourable exit strategy.

Therapeutic Communication and Active Listening

Therapeutic communication is a technique used by mental-health professionals to resolve conflicts involving mentally disturbed persons. This technique differs greatly from ordinary conversation: it is calculated and deliberate, and each action has a precise objective (Slatkin, 1996).

Active listening is a communication technique developed by the psychologist Carl Rogers (1902-1987). It aims to stimulate expression without interrupting the speaker. Its principal ingredients are:

- ***Encouragement***, which consists of signalling, without interrupting the speaker, that one is truly listening to what they are saying. The signals can be visual (facial expressions, nodding of the head, posture, etc.) or verbal ("Okay", "I see", "Mm-hmm"). Encouragement can increase the amount of information transmitted by three to four times (Wainwright, 1993), while lack of it can block expression by suggesting lack of interest or attention.

- ***Paraphrasing***, which may take many forms, including reformulation (reformulating in one's own words what the speaker has said) and reflection, commonly called "echoing" (repeating the person's last words or ideas). Paraphrasing reassures the speaker that they are being listened to and understood, which stimulates exchange and facilitates the building of rapport.

- ***Identifying emotions***, which consists of putting the person's emotions into words, to indicate empathy. This facilitates awareness or "insight." Bolton (1984) contends that negotiators can improve communication by developing an ear for identifying the intensity of words (emotions) used by individuals in crisis.

- ***Open questions***, i.e. avoiding closed questions that require only "yes" or "no" answers. Open questions invite richer answers and favour the expression of emotion.

- ***Tolerating silences***. It is better so say nothing than to try to stimulate or reassure the person through awkward improvisation. Silence often has its place and generally can be beneficial. Silences allow interviewers to take a break and to reflect.

A. HOW CRISES ARE BORN

The word "crisis" derives from the Greek *krisis*, itself a derivative of *krino*, meaning "to separate." Crises are, therefore, ruptures, opportunities for change and improvement. But this is only if they are perceived and accepted in this way" [translation] (Combalbert, 2005: 129). Caplan (1961) defines a "crisis" as a state arising when a person faces an obstacle to important life goals — an obstacle that is, for a time, insurmountable by the use of customary methods of problem solving. This triggers a period of disorganization and of upsets during which many abortive attempts at solution are made. Eventually, the person succeeds in adapting to the situation, although this may not be in the best interests of the individual or those close to them.

The most-often noted triggering events are marital problems (42.6%) and other problems related to family life (14.9%) (Michaud and St-Yves, 2006). The most common mental disorders encountered in crisis situations are mood disorders, such as depression and bipolar disorder, and paranoid schizophrenia (Soskis and VanZandt, 1986; Michaud and St-Yves, 2006). During crisis intervention, three out of four individuals express suicidal intentions (Michaud and St-Yves, 2006).

Table 1

Table 1

TYPES OF CRISIS SITUATIONS									
Motivation	**PSYCHOLOGICAL**			**CRIMINAL**			**POLITICAL/CULT**		
	Suicidal	**Vindictive**	**Disturbed**	**Red-Handed**	**Prisoner**	**Kidnapper**	**Protestor**	**Ideological**	**Terrorist**
General profile	Unstable, hopeless, depressed	Angry, seeking vengeance	In crisis or chronically unbalanced	In theory, any criminal	Frustrated, desperate leader who can organize other inmates	Cold, professional criminal	Idealistic, educated, young	Fanatic, indoctrinated cult member	Willing to sacrifice themselves to further their political convictions
Mental and personality disorders	Depression / bipolar disorder Intoxication All personality disorders		Psychotic Delusional Herostratic	Antisocial Narcissistic			Narcissistic		
		Paranoid delusional		Borderline Paranoid Intoxicated				Paranoid	
Distinguishing characteristics	Unafraid of dying	Irrational motivation	Lack of judgment, poor contact with reality	Caught in the act with no backup plan	Familiar with the prison setting and authorities, and their victims	Knowledgeable about and respectful of police power	Exuberant participant in a mass demonstration	Willing to sacrifice themselves for their beliefs	Has realistic assessment of impact of their act
Location of crisis	Wherever they are when their defenses fail	Wherever gives them maximum satisfaction	In any setting	Wherever they are when they are trapped	In their own environment	At a location of their choosing	At a demonstration or high-visibility location	Anywhere	Where victim is unprotected
Point at which hostages are taken	When they have decompensated	After meticulous planning	When they perceive this as a solution to their problem	In desperation, when victims are available	After planning, or when pushed beyond endurance	As part of a carefully prepared plot	When they feel they need to eliminate a social injustice	After they have sustained a wrong	When there is a possibility of publicity
Motivation for taking hostages	To cause someone else to fulfill their death wish	To gain revenge	To solve their problem	To effect escape or request / negotiate something	To improve their conditions or obtain freedom	To obtain money	To effect social change or attain social justice	To redress a grievance	To attain political change
Characteristics of actions against hostages	Irrational complaints	Public or covert	Improvised, illogical	With a weapon, well thought out	Planning, domination, force	With a weapon, calculated	In a massed group or blockade	Robot-like, with or without violence	Emotional, violent, cunning plot
Common Intervention Strategies									
Intervention	Discrete deployment of tactical unit			High-visibility deployment of tactical unit					
	Crisis intervention (active listening)			Negotiation / Tactical unit intervention					
		Tactical unit intervention							

Inspired by Goldaber's (1979) classification, with the addition of two dimensions: 1) Mental and personality disorders usually present in these individuals; 2) Common intervention strategies.

1. Suicide

In Canada, a man commits suicide every three hours.[8] The highest suicide rate is to be found in Quebec (about 20 per 100,000 inhabitants), with second place going to Alberta (Boyer et al., 2000; Langlois and Morrison, 2002). The Quebec rate has increased in recent years, while the rate in other provinces has been stable or decreased (Association québécoise de prévention du suicide, 1996). According to the World Health Organization, for every successful suicide there are 20 attempts.

In Quebec, three out of four men who commit suicide are younger than 50. Men commit suicide four times more often than women, and choose more dependably lethal methods, such as firearms. Women tend to poison themselves (drug and medication overdoses) or employ methods of suffocation (hanging, strangulation) (Langlois and Morisson, 2002).

a) The suicidal process

There are many reasons people kill themselves: these include loss (the breakdown of a relationship, death, bankruptcy, job loss, etc.), psychological distress, rebelliousness or a sense of injustice, symptoms of depression, impulsivity exacerbated by drugs or alcohol, chronic suicidal ideation, acute identity crisis in youth, and existential depression marked by feelings of loneliness and uselessness.

The tendency to keep one's life in balance, known as homeostasis, is universal. In a crisis, the mechanisms of homeostasis prove ineffective, which engenders stress and significant disorganization of thought. The individual in crisis tries to find new solutions and adaptive strategies. But the repeated failure of these solutions and strategies leads to a state of acute anxiety that cannot be tolerated for long. To diminish or escape the suffering, the person may somatize (become physically ill), consume psychoactive substances to numb the pain, or resort to other methods likely to temporarily calm the pain. Should the pain be intolerable, suicide will come to appear to be a solution (Association québécoise de prévention du suicide, 1996).

During the suicidal process, suicidal ideation grows until suicide becomes the only solution (Figure 1). It is not death that is sought, but rather the end of suffering. But because suicidal individuals remain ambivalent,

---

8 *Le Droit*, Canadian Press, Peterborough, Ontario, April 15, 1996.

their suicidal process can be thwarted by the presence of another person, active listening, the prospect of alternative solutions, and hope. "By building on this ambivalence and hope we can help and support the individual in crisis, and prevent their suicide" (Association québécoise de prévention du suicide, 1996).

Figure 1

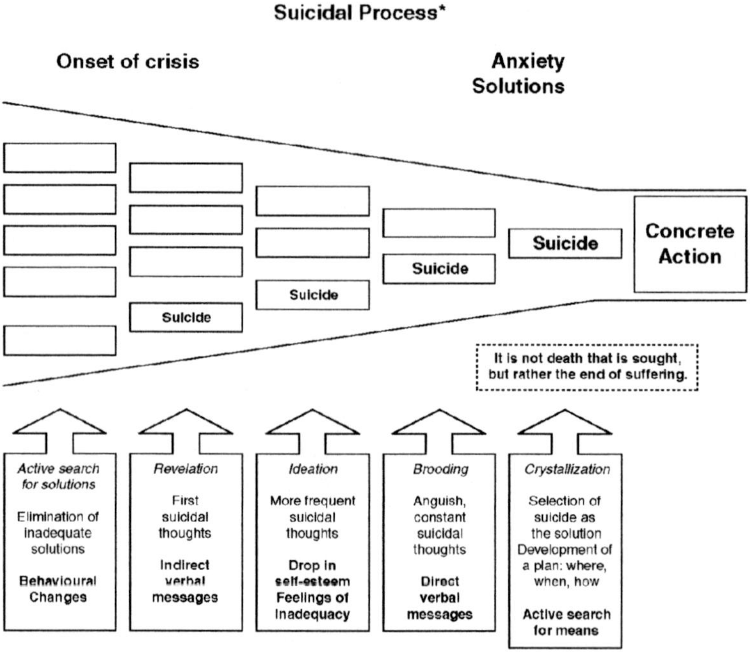

As Figure 1 shows, during the suicidal process, suicidal ideation grows until suicide becomes the only solution. The suicide does not seek death but the end of suffering. Ambivalence is present throughout the process, which is why the presence of another person, listening, and the possibility of renewed hope can interrupt the process. "By taking advantage of this ambivalence and hope we can help, supporting the person in crisis and preventing his suicide" (Association québécoise de prévention du suicide, 1996).

* Source: Phaneuf, J. and M. Séguin. Adapted by Association québécoise de prévention du suicide (1996).

b) Intervention with suicidal persons

Intervention must centre upon preventing the suicide and managing the crisis. Usually, the attenuation of suicidal ideas leads to surrender. The following guidelines for interventions with suicidal persons are based on the recommendations of McMains and Mullins (2001) and the Association québécoise de prévention du suicide (1996):

1) Establish a rapport with the individual in crisis:

    a. Introduce yourself and ask them how you can help.

    b. Don't be afraid to discuss suicide. Doing so shows the individual in crisis that you take their threats seriously. It also opens the door to them expressing their suffering.

    c. Listen attentively and communicate empathetically. Proceed slowly. Depressed people often have cognitive deficits. Give them time. Ask open questions and be prepared for long pauses. Be ready to ask direct questions should the person fail to respond to open ones.

    d. Be empathic. Give voice to the person's emotions, without comment or judgment.

    e. Give the person the time to trust you, to realize your sincerity.

    f. Offer the person food, drink, etc. (but not alcohol).

2) Secure the environment ("Could you please put down your gun for now?").

3) Assess the suicide risk (intentions, plan, means, motivation).

4) Try to elicit information regarding their problems.

5) Support the part of the person that wants to live: "I know that you're suffering, but something in you is still looking for hope."

6) Focus on one problem at a time, starting with the main one.

7) Discuss the alternatives the person has already tried, and suggest others.

8) Try to establish a no-suicide pact.

9) Develop a concrete post-crisis plan that includes an agreement with friends and family, and immediate referral to a physician, clinic, or hospital.

10) Create hope. The individual in crisis sees only two options: living in (intolerable) pain or dying (putting an end to the suffering). The negotiator must build hope, while remaining realistic, and identify sources of situational support and new coping mechanisms. This entails convincing the individual threatening suicide to change two of their ideas: 1) Their pain will never leave; 2) Their loss is all there is (McMains and Mullins, 2001). To inspire hope, the negotiator must convince the individual in crisis that their pain is not eternal and that they can find a way to come to terms with their loss (Seligman, 1991).

c) Intervention in cases involving high structures

The number of suicides resulting from falls from high structures varies from one region to another, and reflects the presence or absence of sites liable to attract suicidal individuals. For example, in Hong Kong and Singapore, voluntary jumps from high structures account for 44% and 60% of suicides, respectively, while in the United States the figure is 5% (World Health Organization). Until very recently, the Jacques-Cartier bridge — which links the island of Montreal with the city of Longueuil — posted the second-highest suicide rate in the world for bridges, behind only San Francisco's Golden Gate bridge. Between 1986 and 1991, suicide deaths at the Jacques-Cartier bridge were eight to ten times more frequent than deaths in traffic accidents (Brown et al., 1985). Prior to 2004, according to data from the Sûreté du Québec's operational statistics division,[9] there was an average

9 In 2004, dissuasive barriers were installed on the bridge, in accordance with the recommendations of the Groupe de travail sur les suicides au pont Jacques-Cartier ([working group concerning suicides on the Jacques-Cartier bridge] *Le pont Jacques-Cartier, un pont sécuritaire pour tous*, submitted to Coroner Paul Dionne, Montreal, 2002).

of one suicide per month[10] and approximately one dissuasive intervention per week (Prévost, Julien and Brown, 1995).

d) Motivation and profile of individuals who commit suicide by jumping from high structures

Suicidal individuals who choose a high public structure such as the Empire State Building, the Eiffel Tower, or the Jacques-Cartier Bridge usually do so for one of the following reasons:

1) They are already on the verge of actually committing suicide.
2) Because the structures are very visible, their suicide attempt is more likely to result in a rescue attempt.
3) The structures assure them a public.
4) The site is symbolic.

The majority of those who choose this method of suicide are male (80-85%), younger than 40 (mean: 33), suffering from a mental disorder (35-54%) — most commonly depression or psychosis — and intoxicated at the moment of their suicide attempt (Michaud and St-Yves, 2006; Romano, 2003). According to Romano (2003), three out of four persons who jump are intoxicated. Most rescue interventions are brief: normally, after a few minutes of conversation, police succeed in persuading the person not to jump and to come away with them. Romano (2003) recommends that interveners first persuade the individual in crisis to move to a safe place, and to announce their movements before making them. He identifies four main indicators of an improving situation:

1) The person makes visual contact with the negotiator.
2) The person allows the negotiator to approach them.
3) The person tells the negotiator that they are afraid.
4) The person tells the negotiator what they really want.

---

10 Generally, these were spontaneous suicides. By the time police were alerted, the person had jumped.

2. Mood Disorders: Depression and Bipolar Disorder

Mood disturbances provoke symptoms of depression and/or manic episodes. According to the American Psychiatric Association (1996), the typical symptoms of depression are:

- dysphoria (sadness)
- loss of interest or absence of pleasure in most of the individual's usual activities
- loss of appetite
- change in weight
- sleep disorders and motor system stimulation or depression
- reduced energy level
- difficulty concentrating
- suicidal ideation, attempted suicide

Depressed individuals usually describe themselves as depressed, sad, discouraged, without hope, and at the end of their rope.

In bipolar disorders such as manic-depression, the symptoms of a manic episode are:

- euphoria, cheerfulness, expansiveness, irritability
- hyperactivity
- logorrhea (rapid and extensive speech)
- distractibility
- inflated self-esteem
- decreased need for sleep
- excessive or dangerous behaviour (e.g. extravagant purchases, promiscuity, rash investments, dangerous driving)

In addition, psychotic episodes (manic-depressive psychosis [MDP]) are sometimes present.

As with suicidal individuals, interventions must be centered on suicide prevention and crisis management. Depression often masks suffering and anger, and getting an individual in crisis to express these emotions will result in their being more rational, more guided by their head than by their "guts," and, consequently, more reasonable. Interveners can encourage individuals in crisis by pointing out that 90% of depressions recede in six to eight weeks (McMains and Mullins, 2001: 260); this helps them see that their situation is only temporary.

3. Psychotic and Delusional Disorders

Psychosis is usually defined as a loss of contact with reality. According to the DSM-IV, the term "psychotic" denotes the presence of delusional ideas, pronounced hallucinations, disorganized speech, or disorganized or catatonic behaviour (American Psychiatric Association, 1996: 321). This disorder can be chronic, or can be triggered by major stress or an overwhelming event (brief psychotic disorder). The most common psychotic disorder is schizophrenia.

a) Schizophrenia

Schizophrenics often have bizarre delusional ideas or delusions of persecution. In paranoid schizophrenia, individuals believe that others spy on them, spread false rumours about them, or plan to do them harm. Such individuals may think that a television host is making fun of them, that others hear their thoughts or are trying to steal them, or that outside thoughts are entering their mind. In some cases, the delusional ideas have somatic, megalomaniacal, or religious themes (American Psychiatric Association, 1996). The person often reports that they have a mission to accomplish (Fuselier, 1981).

The hallucinations are usually auditory or visual. Often, schizophrenics hear voices that make insolent remarks or order them to act; this may incite them to act dangerously toward themselves or others. Affect is often blunted, even absent; for example, speech may be in a monotone, facial expression may be frozen. In other cases, affect may be inappropriate, that is, incongruent with speech: an individual may, for example, burst out laughing while speaking of their father's death. Brusque changes in affect may also occur.

Intervention with schizophrenic individuals

The most problematic individuals are paranoid schizophrenics, as they may be a danger to themselves and others (Strentz, 1986). Intervention in such cases is therefore a delicate matter. The best approach is to accept the delusions as true and real for the person experiencing them (Fuselier, 1986). Above all, one must not try to convince the schizophrenic that their beliefs are unfounded, and not feed their delusions. One simply says, "I can't hear the voices you mention but I understand what this means for you."

b) Paranoia

Paranoia characteristically involves persistent delusional ideas of persecution or jealousy. Such individuals believe themselves to be tricked, spied upon, poisoned or drugged, harassed, or thwarted in the pursuit of their goals. In cases of delusional jealousy, individuals sometimes are convinced that their partner has been unfaithful and searches for corroborating evidence. It is not unusual for such individuals to write letters complaining of sundry injustices, and to launch legal actions. Usually only social (or marital) functioning is seriously disturbed. In cases of grandiose delusion, individuals may believe that they have a special link with a well-known person, or with God. Cult leaders often believe they have a special mission to accomplish.

Intervention with paranoid individuals

Because paranoid individuals harbour irrational distrust, it can be very difficult to build a rapport with them. McMains and Mullins (2001) propose the following approach to interventions with paranoid individuals:

1) Make contact logically, non-emotionally, factually. Maintain a calm voice, ask the person their view of the situation.

2) Reformulate what they tell you, without comment or judgment.

3) Expect rejection and anger. Ask for clarification, by either reformulating what they said or reassuring them that you, as a specialized intervener (or negotiator), are different than the others, and

that you want to see everyone get out of the situation unharmed (Bradstreet, 1992).

4) Allow them to express their emotions. This will reduce their anger and fear. If this does not work, distract them by changing the subject.

5) Show them that you respect and are interested in them.

6) Do not dwell on the delusions (Fuselier, 1986).

7) Build a sense of safety, by reassuring them that your intention is to help, and gradually modify your language by using "we" rather than "you."

4. Intoxicated Individuals

Of the 509 crisis situations involving the Sûreté du Québec between 1990 and 2004, two thirds (66.7%) involved individuals who were intoxicated. Alcohol (80.4%), drugs (17.4%), and medication (23.1%) were the most common intoxicants. In more than half (52.6%) the cases, the intoxication was considered extreme (Michaud and St-Yves, 2006). Slatkin (2000a) has also observed that alcohol is often involved in hostage-taking or barricade situations. In a study involving 2,078 subjects in the FBI's Hostage Barricade System database (HOBAS), 44% of subjects had a history of alcohol abuse and 62% were intoxicated at the time of the crisis incident (McMains and Mullins, 2001: 287).

Alcohol abuse can precipitate an incident and incite anger and aggressiveness. As well, it is very difficult to accurately diagnose someone who is intoxicated by alcohol. Alcohol acts as a central nervous system depressant, and can induce a depressive mood or accentuate existing depression. It is, therefore, strongly recommended that the individual in crisis be encouraged to stop or reduce their alcohol consumption; it should be pointed out to them that they could accidentally endanger their own life or that of others, particularly if they lose control of the situation. In rare cases, highly irritable individuals, particularly chronic alcoholics, may be calmed or rendered less anxious by alcohol (Slatkin 2000b). Those close to the individual in crisis can provide information on their consumption habits and behaviour when intoxicated. Intoxicated individuals usually have difficulty negotiating, as they lack sufficient concentration and judgment, and have diminished problem-solving ability (Slatkin, 2000a).

Some psychotropic drugs, such as cocaine and hallucinogens, can induce a temporary mental disturbance resembling bipolar disorder (rapid alternation between euphoric and depressive moods), paranoia, and psychosis. Phencyclidine (PCP), for example, sometimes induces a psychotic state accompanied by extremely violent behaviour (Crowley, 2003).

Intervention with intoxicated individuals

Negotiators confronted with a person who has consumed alcohol and/or drugs must be patient and play for time. They must also adapt what they say to their audience: slower speech, repetition of words, simple and concise constructions, avoidance of abstractions, side comments, and judgments about the consumption of alcohol and drugs. Intoxicated individuals can be very impulsive until the effects of the intoxicant dissipate. Negotiators should therefore be prudent and weigh their words.

5. The Herostratus Syndrome

In 356 B.C., Herostratus set fire to Artemis's temple in Ephesus, a monument venerated throughout Greece for its beauty. His act was intended to assure that history would remember him, but the authorities executed him and forbade the mention of his name. But their order was not respected by everyone, as his name has come down through the ages to us. Ultimately, then, his wish was fulfilled (Carlier, 1995).

Many people dream of being rich and famous, of being surrounded by admirers, pretty girls, handsome boys. Some people will do anything for fame, a few minutes of glory, the front page — even kill.[11] Typically, these people have mental health issues, and are unsuccessful and eternally frustrated. They thirst to associate their hitherto unknown names, with that of an eminent person or unforgettable event. One has only to think of individuals such as Marc Lepine,[12] Richard Durn[13] and Mark David Chapman[14] to realize that this strategy can, unfortunately, be successful. Such people avoid their fate of passing unknown, unappreciated, ignored. Their act guarantees them wide publicity, fleeting fame, and — perhaps — a place in history.

---

11 Christophe Ferré, Paradis Turquoise, Flammarion, 2005.

12 Killed 14 female engineering students at the École Polytechnique de Montréal.

13 Responsible for the Nanterre slaughter on March 26-27, 2002.

14 Assassinated John Lennon in New York on December 8, 1980.

Despair, an intolerable sense of humiliation, and the ardent desire to become spontaneously famous — at the risk of their own life — are generally more decisive than the political and ideological motives these people invoke to justify their actions. The choice of victim is often arbitrary. These types of individuals often suffer from a mental disorder such as paranoia or paranoid schizophrenia. They are usually solitary and unstable, and have experienced numerous setbacks in both their emotional and occupational lives. They perceive themselves as "losers," as failures. Their siege becomes a way of proving to those close to them that they can succeed at something: "I'll show them that I'm capable of doing something" (Fuselier, 1981). The crisis incident attracts the attention of authority figures and the media, and may be the high point of the individual's life (Fuselier, 1981; Strentz, 1983).

Intervention with herostratic individuals

Unfortunately, by the time police are called to deal with this type of crisis, the harm has usually been done. Under these circumstances, contact with individuals in crisis must be focussed on making them aware — often through the media — that they have attained their goal, and that their message (if one exists) has been heard. Interveners should also attempt to stoke the individual's sense of self-worth, since this is precisely the core issue underlying the crisis.

6. Criminals

Criminals caught red-handed in the midst of perpetrating a crime will sometimes barricade themselves against capture, with or without hostages. The criminals have no reason to injure or kill the hostages, who represent their bargaining chips. Unlike terrorists, barricaded criminals seek to extricate themselves from the situation as cleanly as possible. They must, however, be convinced that their surrender will occur safely and without complications, should they release their hostages (Fuselier, 1981). Parolees know that their precarious status means that they will be immediately reincarcerated and, most likely, obliged to serve a longer sentence. There are many possible demands when hostages are involved; these include: a vehicle or money to assist flight; a reduction of charges or consultation with a lawyer; incarceration in a specified institution; communication with a spouse or with family prior to arrest; negotiation of conditions of surrender.

a) Prison riots

In riot situations, the climate is tense. The rioters fear police intervention and violence among themselves. Some take advantage of the situation to settle accounts or savagely attack those formerly in protective custody. Group pressure is very strong on the leader or spokesperson, who must negotiate even with fellow detainees. Prisoners serving life sentences often feel that nothing they do can worsen their situation; if they are the leaders, the situation can become very dangerous.

As the rioters' goal usually is to inform the public about their conditions in detention, they may demand to negotiate with the prison director or with another person who has decision-making power — a government representative, for example.

b) Intervention with antisocial individuals

The antisocial personality is characterized by disrespect for and flouting of the rights of others (American Psychiatric Association, 1996: 739). The defining characteristic of antisocial individuals is the inability to conform to the social norms underlying law-abiding conduct. Concrete manifestations of this inability include: repeated behaviour that can result in arrest; chronic lying; impulsivity or the inability to plan in advance; persistent irresponsibility; irritability and aggression, expressed in frequent brawling; the absence of remorse for their behaviour. Antisocial individuals commit all manner of crimes, with simple theft, aggravated theft, breaking and entering, drug crimes, misdemeanours, and assaults being particularly common. Often, the seriousness of the crimes escalates over time (St-Yves, 2004: 79).

Antisocial individuals need constant stimulation (Fuselier, 1981), and negotiators must, therefore, maintain ongoing contact with them. Selfish by nature, antisocial individuals will attempt to obtain what they want at little cost. They do not bond with negotiators or hostages; accordingly, the Stockholm syndrome is rarely observed with these individuals (McMains and Mullins, 1996). If the individual in crisis is manipulative, negotiators must identify the individual's tactics, avoid falling into their traps, and be clear about the rules of negotiation (Dry, 1991). Criminals who belong to well-established organizations know the rules of the game and are less likely to resist arrest. On the other hand, impulsive criminals are unpredictable: they have nothing to lose, want to avoid returning to prison, may be intoxicated by alcohol or drugs, and may be mentally disturbed and prone to violence.

In some cases, what they are seeking is suicide by proxy, commonly called "suicide by cop" (Geberth, 1993).

B. NEGOTIATION

Four types of intervention are available in critical incidents (Schlossberg, 1979; Strentz, 1979): 1) assault; 2) sniper, 3) chemical agents; 4) negotiation.

1) *Assault.* This option provides a quick ending to the incident. However, the risk is very high. The majority of hostages who die (78%) during critical incidents are killed during police assaults (Schlossberg, 1979; Strentz, 1979).

2) *Sniper.* This option brings the incident to an end, and saves the lives of seriously threatened hostages.

3) *Chemical agents.* These are often used together with assault. The risk to the hostages' health is sometimes elevated, as was evident in the October 2002 Moscow theatre attack by terrorists.[15]

4) *Negotiation.* This option saves lives and is more positively viewed by the public. Whereas the three other types of intervention are confrontational and increase the likelihood of violence, negotiation is the safest approach for all concerned.

According to the Oxford English Dictionary, negotiation is "discussion aimed at reaching an agreement." Compromise is therefore always a component of negotiation. However, with mentally disturbed individuals, there is nothing to negotiate: one must simply manage the crisis, with intervention an exercise in "first aid."

The role of communication

Communication is a relatively simple process: there is a transmitter and a receiver. The former translates (encodes) their thoughts into words and uses a method (a channel) — here, words — to transmit their message. The latter receives the message and understands (decodes) it (see the dia-

---

15 More than a hundred persons succumbed to the effects of a mysterious gas used by the Russian special forces to neutralize Chechen commandos.

gram below.) Because individuals in crisis can distort or misinterpret messages (due to poor decoding), and consequently over-react or respond inappropriately, negotiators must encode their messages with great care.

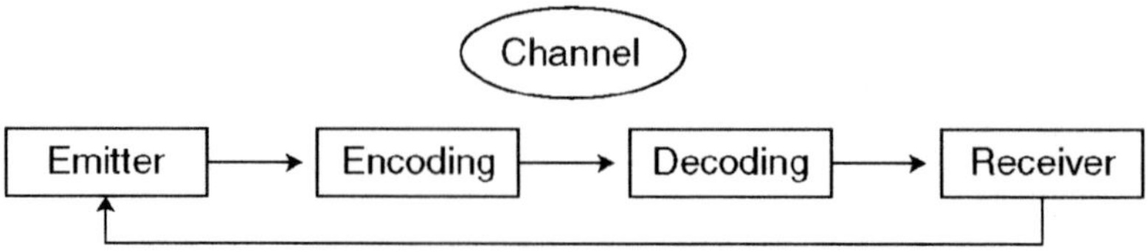

The communication process (Shannon, 1952)

The ability to listen plays a key role in the communication techniques in critical incidents. Negotiators must analyze the individual in crisis' choice of words, decode their message, and determine whether problems are real or imagined (Wargo, 1990). Words' role in negotiation extends far beyond their literal meaning. Voice inflection, tone, and rhythm also are significant in communication (Divasto, 1996, Wargo, 1990). For example, the word "problem" should be avoided, and be replaced by "difficulty." Similarly, the name of a hostage or victim should be used in place of "hostage."

The final fundamental principle of effective and sincere communication is the imperative to listen. Listening allows negotiators to observe and analyze, respond appropriately, and take into account the point of view of the individual in crisis and build a rapport with them. "Fundamentally it is the quality of the relationship that determines the quality of the communication" (Abric, 2003: 155).

C. SINCRO : THE RHYTHM OF THE CRISIS

The intervention philosophy of the Sûreté du Québec is *Pax per conloquium* "resolution through dialogue" (St-Yves, Tanguay and St-Pierre, 2001: 4). Between 1990 and 2004, negotiation resulted in the peaceful resolution of 86% of the 358 crisis situations the Sûreté du Québec was involved in (Michaud and St-Yves, 2006). The remaining cases ended in either tactical-squad intervention or suicide of the individual in crisis.[16] According to Leviton and Greenstone (2002), tactical interventions, includ-

16 Between 1990 and 2004, there were 20 deaths, all suicides, when the crisis intervention group was deployed. Three of the deaths were "suicide by cop" incidents (Michaud and St-Yves, 2006).

ing the use of chemical agents, are responsible for relatively high injury and mortality rates, compared to negotiation (rates of less than 1%).

Since almost all crisis intervention involves mentally-disturbed persons, achieving peaceful surrender demands crisis management. Such interventions are more a matter of "*psychotiation*" rather than of negotiation *per se* (St-Yves, Tanguay and St-Pierre, 2001: 4). Essentially, crisis intervention is a question of managing the immediate crisis rather than resolving problems (Greenstone, 1995). The negotiator's primary role is to offer hope, not necessarily solutions (Strandberg, 1999).

The SINCRO model

The classic crisis situation comprises three phases (see Slatkin, 2000b; Butler, Leitenberg and Fuselier, 1993): the crisis, problem resolution, and surrender. Frequently pressed to defuse the crisis and obtain surrender, negotiators too often find themselves in resolution mode, while the individual in crisis is in crisis mode. The classic scenario, using the terminology of the SINCRO model (see Table 2), is as follows: the negotiator works at the rational, "problem-resolution" level (yellow) while the individual in crisis is at the emotional level (red). This not only brings the situation to a standstill, but also increases the risk of the situation degenerating (St-Yves, Tanguay and St-Pierre, 2001: 4).

Inspired by the work of Butler, Leitenberg and Fuselier (1993), we have developed the SINCRO model, an intervention model primarily based on the individual in crisis' process (St-Yves, Tanguay and St-Pierre, 2001).[17] While the model does describe the objectives and features of the three classic intervention phases, it innovates by guiding negotiators through each step of the crisis, helping them not get ahead of the individual in crisis, and identifying (by transition phases that bridge the major steps) markers of the individual in crisis' receptivity to progressing to the next step.

---

17 **S**tratégie d'**I**ntervention et de **N**égociation par **C**ouleurs selon le **R**ythme **Ob**servé (colour-coded intervention and negotiation strategy based on observed rhythm).

Phase 1: The crisis (red)

The first phase is the crisis phase. It is during this critical phase that the risk is highest (Dolan and Fuselier, 1989; Noester and Dolan, 1992). At this point, the negotiator's first concern is establishing and maintaining contact with the individual in crisis. In most cases, this contact is made by telephone (three out of four) or with the help of a bullhorn (Michaud and St-Yves, 2006). If the individual in crisis is not armed or in a dangerous position (e.g. on a high structure), negotiation can proceed *viva voce*. The negotiator must listen carefully and promote free exchange by asking open questions, in order to allow the individual in crisis to verbalize and express their emotions. Any information obtained in this way facilitates the diagnosis of the individual's mental and physical condition and the identification of the factors (often irrational) that brought on the crisis. Active listening remains the best tool for intervening at this stage of the crisis (Noesner and Webster, 1997).

Buying time

Over time, a rapport will develop between the individual in crisis and the negotiator and, secondarily, between the individual and the hostages (Fuselier, 1981). Time is always on the negotiator's side. Sometimes, doing nothing is better than doing something (Schlossberg, 1979: 1). Time permits the negotiator to establish a rapport with the individual in crisis, reduces the individual in crisis' anxiety, and, by extension, induce the individual in crisis to act more rationally. As well, by allowing time for further information gathering, a period of reflection, analysis of the individual in crisis' changes in behaviour, determination of the types of questions to pose, and consultation with experts, it also helps investigators to improve their negotiation and intervention strategies. Finally, time can allow negotiators to extricate themselves from difficulty, or simply to rest.

Transition A (orange)

Once the emotion/tension has been sufficiently alleviated for the individual in crisis to listen and understand — in other words, once they are less self-centred, less upset, and less aggressive — the negotiator can move on to Phase Two (yellow): problem resolution. However, the transition from red to yellow is not direct. There is a transition zone that bridges the crisis and resolution phases. From this point on, the negotiator must be very attentive to the indicators, sometimes subtle, that the individual is ready to transition to the next phase.

During Transition Phase A, individuals in crisis frequently regress to an emotional state, before being ready for the next step. This is often because they have not sufficiently expressed their emotions or have not found a sympathetic ear. Negotiators must therefore respect the individual's process, maintaining Phase One (red) until the individual is ready to move on.

Phase 2: Problem resolution (yellow)

Once Phase Two (yellow) has entered, the risk involved can be considered moderate: the individual in crisis is now capable of reflecting about the consequences of their acts and is more receptive to solutions the negotiator proposes. Now negotiators must be more voluble and creative, master techniques for defusing crisis situations, and find a satisfactory solution for the individual in crisis. They may use various techniques of persuasion (see Cialdini et al., 1975; Gouldner, 1960; Dry, 1991). The negotiators' principal objective here is to create hope.

Transition B (lime green)

Once Phase Two is well advanced and the individual in crisis is receptive to solutions, negotiators must be attentive to any indication that transition to Phase Three (surrender) is possible. At this point, the individual in crisis shows signs of resignation and is preoccupied with what will happen to them (the consequences of their acts). If they have forcibly confined someone (kidnapping or hostage taking), they are no longer threatening toward them and no longer oppose freeing them.

The Stockholm Syndrome

On August, 23, 1973, Jen Erik Olsson, a prison escapee, attempted to rob the Stockholm Kreditbanken. When police intervened, he remained in the bank, taking four employees hostage. He won the release of his cellmate, Clark Olofsson, who came immediately to join him. Surprising statements by the hostages were reported by the media: "We completely trust these two bandits"; "The robbers are protecting us from the police" (Crocq, 1989; 1998). "Six days of negotiation led, at last, to the liberation of the hostages, during which the latter placed themselves between their kidnappers and the police forces. They refused to testify at the hostage-takers' trial, contributed to their defence, and visited them in prison. One victim fell in love with Jan Erik Olsson, and ended up marrying him." (Torres and Grenier-Boley, 2000).

This paradoxical conduct was christened "the Stockholm Syndrome" by Frank Ochberg, the American psychiatrist who first described it in 1978. Ochberg established three diagnostic criteria for the syndrome:

1) Feelings of trust, even sympathy, between the hostages and their kidnapper.

2) Reciprocal positive feelings between the kidnapper and the hostages.

3) Hostility by the hostages toward the police.

Three conditions are necessary for the development of this syndrome (Skurnik, 1987): 1) The criminal must be able to convince their victims of the ideological justification of their acts; 2) The criminal must feel no ethnic antagonism, racism, or hate towards the hostages; 3) The potential victims must have no prior knowledge of the existence of this syndrome.

The positive feelings arise independently of any mental manipulation (Joule and Beauvois, 1998). Crocq (1989) speaks of the victim's "subjugation" by the kidnapper, emphasizing the word's double meaning: "under the yoke *(jugum)*" and "seduce."

Some authors explain the phenomenon as a regression to childhood and a state of dependency, and a need for security (Ochberg, 1980; Strentz, 1979). Symonds (1983), on the other hand, sees it as a form of pathological transference. The syndrome is most common among the young, women, and those sympathetic to the kidnapper's cause. It requires a siege of some duration for the syndrome to develop (see McMains and Mullins, 2001; Torres and Grenier-Boley, 2000). Its effects fade with time, but it can be weeks or even months before the hostages return to their normal selves. Post-trauma debriefing can help reduce the recovery time (McMains and Mullins, 2001: 172).

Table 2

The SINCRO Model

St-Yves, Tanguay & St-Pierre (2001)

PHASE 1: CRISIS

In this phase, the mood is often quite tense. The individual in crisis experiences — and manifests — intense emotion. Negotiators should listen carefully and stimulate exchanges that allow the individual to verbalize and vent.

Objectives	HOW?
• **Establish contact with the individual and reassure them**	• **Introduce yourself, inform the individual of your mandate and role, confirm their identity**
• **Collect information on the individual (mental disorders, intoxication, danger) and on the nature of the problem** • **Assess the risks of suicide and homicide** • **Build a rapport**	• **Ask open questions to learn what is happening:** – Ask the individual to tell you the events that preceded the incidents (the preceding 24 hours) – Ask them what emotional impact these events had on them – Ask them if the events began a few days ago or if the onset of the crisis was sudden – Find out what the triggering event was, and what factors are affecting their problem-resolution skills – Find out their perception of the triggering event – Find out the situational support mechanisms on which they depend – Find out what they usually do when confronted with a problem – Find out whether they are intoxicated; if so, find out what they consumed., how much they consumed, and when they consumed it – Ask them whether they have taken any action against the victims – Ask them if they have any weapons – Find out what their state of mental and physical health is, and their intentions
• **Help the individual vent, in order to disarm the crisis**	• **Assess the risk of suicide, then identify the risk factors for homicide or suicide by cop**
• **Identify the individual's demands**	• **Use active listening techniques, to allow the individual to vent** • **Play for time, in order to favour more rational behaviour from the individual**

Transition A: Crisis ➡ Problem Resolution

This is a critical phase that allows negotiators to determine whether the individual is ready to proceed to problem resolution. During this phase, the individual talks less emotionally and less aggressively, and is no longer completely self-centred.

Objectives	WHEN?
• **Ensure that you are ready to initiate the problem resolution phase with the individual in crisis**	• **Be attentive to clues that the individual has vented enough (has become less emotional) and is less self-centred. For example, they ask questions, exhibit interest in you or others, pay attention to their basic needs.**

Table 2 (cont'd)

PHASE 2: PROBLEM RESOLUTION

At this point, the individual should not backslide or become too emotional. Everything possible should be done to keep them as rational as possible and lead them through the resolution of the problem.

Objectives	HOW?
• **Help the individual in crisis correct their false or distorted impressions** • **Identify with them appropriate situational support mechanisms** • **Identify a coping strategy for (temporarily) facing their problem** • **Create hope** • **Get them to take responsibility**	• **Use crisis-intervention and negotiation techniques suited to the profile of the individual and their problem.** • **Ask the individual if they have experienced a similar situation in the past. If they have, ask them what they did to get over it. If they have not, suggest alternatives and/or available resources (even if they are only temporary solutions), in order to create hope.** • **Use personal examples with which the individual can identify. Use positive reinforcement and analogies and clichés such as "one day at a time", and "small temps".** • **Make them part of the solution.** • **To get them to take responsibility, show them that while they are the only ones who can decide what happens next, they do have to make a choice.**

Transition B: Problem Resolution ➡ Surrender

At this point, negotiations are sufficiently advanced that surrender is a possibility. The individual in crisis appears preoccupied by what will happen to them ("What'll happen to me?") or worried about those close to them ("Who'll take care of my dog?").

Objective	WHEN?
• **Lead the individual in crisis to establish a plan for surrender** • **Recover the victims safely**	• **The individual in crisis is more rational (serious tone of voice) and shows signs of resignation. They listen to the negotiators' instructions and ask questions about what will happen to them.** • **They are no longer threatening to their victims or hostages (if any) and do not oppose freeing them.**

PHASE 3: SURRENDER

The final phase. May be very short. The individual in crisis is ready to surrender to the police and face the consequences of their acts. Prior to the actual surrender, the risk of a last-minute reversal (e.g. suicide by cop) should be assessed.

Objectives	HOW?
• **Allow the individual in crisis to save face** • **Obtain a non-violent surrender**	• **Praise the individual in crisis (congratulate them on their courage) for their decision to surrender to the police. Allow them to retain some dignity.** • **Inform the individual how the exit strategy will unwind and make sure that they have completely understood their instructions.**

Phase 3: Surrender (green)

To preserve the individual in crisis' dignity and facilitate their surrender, the negotiator must reinforce their decision to give themselves up to police. Before the actual surrender occurs, the negotiator must be certain that the individual is receptive to instructions and agrees to give themselves up of their own free will and in a safe manner. During this phase, the individual often defies authority one last time, by either briefly ignoring the pre-agreed deadline or asking for time to smoke yet one more "last" cigarette before coming out . . . anything to be able to claim victory, however small, and restore their dignity. This is the so-called "final cha-cha." To avoid panic that would frustrate all the effort to this point, it is important that negotiators prepare the individual in crisis for what awaits them outside. Although the individual in theory no longer represents a risk to themselves or others, sudden about-faces do occur. Poor interpretation of the risk factors by the negotiators or a sudden change in attitude by the individual in crisis usually explains such unexpected reversals. The crisis situation is never over until the individual in crisis is in the physical custody of the police.

D. THE POST-TRAUMA DEBRIEFING

All the actors involved in a crisis situation, including the crisis intervention team, can be affected by the incident, particularly if a siege lasts a long time or ends tragically. Every person's coping mechanisms are different, and the shock can be immediate or deferred; symptoms may appear right away, days, or even weeks after the event. Bohl (1992) identified two sources of stress among negotiators:

1) **External pressure:** If crisis management drags on and doesn't seem to be going anywhere, the intervention team may pressure the negotiators to end negotiations and allow them to intervene, even if the negotiators believe that there is still a chance of obtaining a negotiated surrender.

2) **Internal pressure:** This is principally due to the fear that the situation will take a turn for the worse. It is a form of performance anxiety, and may be compounded by the reactions and attitudes of the individual in crisis.

The debriefing session

Ideally, the post-trauma debriefing session should take place 24-48 hours after the incident. Debriefing sessions are not therapy. During a debriefing session, those involved in the incident are asked to describe their perception and experience of the event (see Bohl, 1992). Additionally, they are made aware of the principal symptoms that can accompany intense or prolonged stress, namely:

1) *Physical symptoms*, including gastrointestinal problems, headaches, and fatigue.

2) *Cognitive, emotional, and psychological symptoms*, such as difficulty concentrating, poor attention span, recurring thoughts or dreams, troubling doubt ("if only I had. . ."), guilt, anger, and loss of self-confidence.

3) *Behavioural symptoms*, such as social withdrawal, aggression, insomnia, changes in appetite, increased alcohol consumption, etc.

Counselling is also given to those involved, with further resources made available to those who require it. The meeting ends with a summary, moving around the table one last time and coming full circle. Some will experience no further difficulty, perceiving the experience as positive and enriching, while others will be more seriously affected. If these latter individuals are not vigilant about their level of stress, their symptoms can persist and degenerate into more serious problems such as depression. And we have seen where that can lead. . .

CONCLUSION

The majority of crisis situations involve mentally-disturbed individuals, typically men who are depressed, barricaded, and alone and in distress, and who threaten to kill themselves. The primary objective is to end their suffering — through death, if necessary. Hostage-taking is rare and, when present, usually takes the form of the confinement of family members involved in domestic violence disputes, rather than hostage-taking *per se*. Negotiation is the most effective and safest means of resolving the crisis. To defuse the situation, negotiators must create a rapport with the individual in crisis, listening so that the latter can vent and reduce the intensity of their emotions, and ultimately become more rational. Investigators must collect as much information as possible about the individual in crisis and constantly assess the risks. They should walk the individual in crisis through the various stages of the intervention model, letting the individual work through their own process, up to surrender — voluntarily, if possible. In the final act, negotiators must do everything to permit the individual in crisis to retain or regain his dignity. In the individual in crisis' eyes, that could be all they have left.

REFERENCES

Abric, J.C. (2003). *Psychologie de la communication: Théories et méthodes.* Éditions Colin, Paris.

Amendola, K., Learning, M. and Martin, J. (1996). *Analyzing characteristics of Police-Citizen Encounters in High Risk Search Warrant Issuances, Domestic Disturbances, Hostage and Barricaded Persons Incidents, and Encounters with Fleeing Felony Suspects.* (Grant 92-IJ-CX-KOI9). Washington D.C.: Police Foundation.

American Psychiatric Association (1996). *DSM-IV: Manuel diagnostique et statistique des troubles mentaux,* 4e édition (version internationale, Washington DC, 1995), French translation by J.-D. Guelfi et al., Paris, Masson.

Association québécoise de prévention du suicide (1996). Le suicide : comprendre et intervenir. http://www.aqps.info (visited June 7, 2006).

Bohl, N. (1992). Hostage Negotiator Stress. *FBI Law Enforcement Bulletin,* v. 61(8), Aug. 1992, 23-26.

Bolton, R (1984). *People Skills.* Englewood Cliffs, NJ: Prentice Hall.

Boyer, R, St-Laurent, D., Preville, M., Legare, G., Masse, R and Poulin, C. (2000). *Idées suicidaires et parasuicides.* Enquête Sociale et de Santé 1998, Sainte-Foy, Les Publications du Québec, 355-368.

Bradstreet, R (1992). *Communications: Getting on the Right Wavelength.* Presented at SAPD Basic Hostage Negotiations School. San Antonio, TX: September.

Brown, B., Salami, RL., Lecours, S. and Battista, RN. (1985). Motor vehicle related injury on the bridges between Montreal and South Shore of the St-Lawrence River, 1978-82. *Am. J. Public Health.*

Butler, W.H., Leitenberg, H. and Fuselier, G.D. (1993). The Use of Mental Health Professional Consultants to Hostage Negotiation Teams. *Behavioral Science and Law,* 1, 213-221.

Caplan, G. (1961). *An approach to community mental health.* New York, Grune and Stratton.

Carlier, P. (1995). *Le IVe siècle grec jusqu'à la mort d'Alexandre.* Paris. Points-Seuil.

Cialdini, RB., Vincent, J.E., Lewis, S.K., Catalan, J., Wheeler, D. and Darby, B.L. (1975). Reciprocal Concessions Procedure for Inducing Compliance: The Door-in-the-Face Technique. *Journal of Personality and Social Psychology,* vol. 31, no. 2, 206-215.

Combalbert, L. (2005). *Le Management des situations de crise. Anticiper les risques et gérer les crises.* Collection Formation Permanente, ESF Éditeur.

Crocq, L. (1989). Pour une nouvelle définition du syndrome de Stockholm — *Études Épidémiologiques,* **1,** 165-179.

Crocq, L. (1998). *Les otages et la violence.* Document de formation du CISCP, Paris.

Divasto, P.V. (1996). Negotiating with Foreign Language-Speaking Subjects. *FBI Law Enforcement Bulletin.* June 1992, 11-15.

Dolan, J.T. and Fuselier, G.D. (1989). A Guide for First Responders to Hostage Situations. *FBI Law Enforcement Bulletin.* April 1989, 9-13.

Feldmann, T.B. (2001). Characteristics of hostage and barricade incidents: implications for negotiation strategies and training. *Journal of Police Crisis Negotiations: an international journal,* vol. 1 (1), 3-34.

Fuselier, G.W. (1986). A Practical Overview of Hostage Negotiations. *FBI Law Enforcement Bulletin.* June/July 1981, Revised, 1986, 1-11.

Fuselier, G.W. (1981). A Practical Overview of Hostage Negotiations (Part I). *FBI Law Enforcement Bulletin.* June 1981. 2-6.

Geberth, V. (1993). Suicide-By-Cop: Inviting death from the hands of a police officer. *Law and Order.* July 1993, 105-109.

Goldaber, I. (1979). A Typology of Hostage-Takers. *The Police Chief, 46* (2), 1979, 21-22.

Gouldner, A.W. (1960). The norm of reciprocity: A preliminary statement. *American Sociological Review* 25, 161-178.

Greenstone, J.L. (1995). Crisis Intervention Skills: Training for Police Negotiators. *Police Chief,* vol. 62 (8), August 1995, 30-34.

Hacker, F.J. (1976). *Crusaders, criminals, crazies: terror and terrorism in our time.* New York: W.W. Norton and Company, 355 p.

Joule, R.V. and Beauvois, J.L. (1998). *La soumission librement consentie* Presses Universitaires de France, 214 pages.

Klein, G.C. (2003). Thinking SWAT: twenty-two lessons to be learned from a hostage role play. *Journal of Police Crisis Negotiations: an international journal,* vol. 3 (1), 59-84.

Lanceley, F.J. (1999). *On-Scene Guide for Crisis Negotiators.* CRC Press, 213 p.

Langlois and Morrison. (2002). Suicides et tentatives de suicide. Rapports sur la santé, vol. 13, no 2, janvier. Statistique Canada, no 82-003 au catalogue.

Leviton, S.C. and Greenstone, J.L. (2002). The hostage and crisis negotiator's training laboratory. *Journal of Police Crisis Negotiations, 21-34.*

McMains, M.J. and Mullins, W.C. (1996). *Crisis Negotiations: Managing Critical Incidents and Hostage Situations in Law Enforcement and Corrections.* Anderson Publishing Co./Cincinnati, OR, Elisabeth Roszmann Ebben, editor.

McMains, M.J. and Mullins, W.C. (2001). *Crisis Negotiations: Managing Critical Incidents and Hostage Situations in Law Enforcement and Corrections.* Anderson Publishing Co./Cincinnati, OR.

Michaud, P. and St-Yves, M. (2006). *Analyse des situations de crise survenues entre 1990 et 2004 sur le territoire desservi par la Sûreté du Québec.* Unpublished.

Noesner, G.W. (1999). Negotiation Concepts for Commanders. *FBI Law Enforcement Bulletin.* Jan. 1999, 6-14.

Noesner, G.W. and Dolan, J.T. (1992). First Responder Negotiation Training. *FBI Law Enforcement Bulletin.* Aug. 1992, 1-4.

Noesner, G.W. and Webster, M. (1997). Crisis Intervention: Using Active Listening Skills in Negotiations. *FBI Law Enforcement Bulletin.* Aug. 1997, 13-17.

Ochberg, F.M. (1980). Victims of terrorism. *Journal of Clinical Psychiatry,* 41: 73-74.

Prévost, C., Julien, M., Brown, B. (1995). *Suicides associés au pont Jacques-Cartier de 1988 à 1993 : analyse descriptive et proposition d'intervention.* Direction de la Sante publique de la Montéregie, Régie régionale de la santé et des services sociaux, août 1995.

Romano, S. (2003). *Jumpers: An ongoing HOBAS Study.* FBI Academy, Quantico, VA Paper presented at the ninth annual Calgary Crisis Negotiation Seminar, October 19-21, Calgary, Canada.

Schlossberg, H. (1979). Police Response to Hostage Situations. In J.T. O'Brien and M. Marcus (ed.), *Crime and Justice in America — Critical Issues for the Future.* Elmsford, NY: Pergamon Press.

Seligman, M.E.P. (1991). *Learned Optimism.* New York, NY: Alfred A Knopf.

Shannon, C.P. (1952). *The Mathematical Theory of Communication.* University of Illinois Press, Urbana.

Skurnik, N. (1987). Le syndrome de Stockholm, essai et étude de ses critères — Société médico-psychologique. *Ann. Méd. Psy.,* vol. 146, nos 1 et 2, octobre 1987, 174-181.

Slatkin, AA (2005). Communication in Crisis and Hostage Negotiations. Charles C Thomas Publisher, Ltd. Springfield, Illinois.

Slatkin, AA (2000a). Negotiating Skills: Dealing With an Alcohol-Impaired Hostage Taker or Barricaded Subject. *Law and Order.* vol. 48 (4), April 2000, 123-126.

Slatkin, AA (2000b). The Role of the Mental Health Consultant in Hostage Negotiations: Questions to Ask During the Incident Phase. *The Police Chief* July 2000, 64-66.

Slatkin, AA (1996). Enhancing Negotiator Training Therapeutic Communication. *FBI Law Enforcement Bulletin.* May 1996, 1-6.

Soskis, D. and VanZandt, C.R. (1986). Hostage negotiation: Law enforcement's most effective non-lethal weapon. *Management Quarterly,* 6(4), 1-10.

Strandberg, K.W. (1999). Hostage Negotiations. *Law Enforcement Technology.* vol. 26 (1), January 1999, 64-70.

Strentz, T. (1986). Negotiating with the Hostage-Taker Exhibiting Paranoid Schizophrenic Symptoms. *Journal of Police Science and Administration,* 14, 1986, 12-16.

Strentz, T. (1983). The Inadequate Personality as a Hostage Taker. *Journal of Police Science and Administration,* 11, 1983, 363-368.

Strentz, T. (1979). Law Enforcement Policy and Ego Defenses of the Hostage. *FBI Law Enforcement Bulletin* 48:4, 2-12.

St-Yves, M. (2004). La psychologie du suspect. In M. St-Yves and J. Landry (eds.). *Psychologie des entrevues d'enquête: de la recherche à la pratique.* Cowansville: Éditions Yvon Blais, p. 73-84.

St-Yves, M., Tanguay, M. and St-Pierre, J. (2001). Le rythme de la crise/ Following the rhythm of a crisis. *Revue Internationale de Police Criminelle/International Criminal Police Review.* Interpol, No. 491, 4-9.

Symonds, M. (1983). Victimization and Rehabilitative Treatment. In B. Eichelman, D.A. Soskis and W. Reid (eds.). *Terrorism: Interdisciplinary Perspectives.* Washington, DC: American Psychiatric Association, 69-82.

Torres, E. and Grenier-Boley, V. (2000). Syndrome de Stockholm: pourquoi ce paradoxe ? *Le Generaliste,* no 1996, janvier 2000.

Ury, W. (1991). *Getting Past No: Negotiating with Difficult People.* New York, NY : Bantam Books.

Wainwright, G.R. (1993). *Teach yourself body language.* London: Hodder Headlines Plc.

Wargo, M.G. (1990). Communication Skills for Hostage Negociators. *Police Marksman.* March/April 1990, 52.

World Health Organization. *Prevention of Suicidal Behaviours: A Task for All,* http://www.who.int/mentaLhealth/topicsuicide4.htm. consulted March 2, 2001.

CHAPTER 13

Risk Assessment in Crisis Situations

Michel St-Yves, Patrick Michaud and Michel Tanguay

Foresee the unforeseeable to prevent the irreversible.

CCNE[1]

On November 29, 1995, in a little town in eastern Quebec, a depressed man contacts police and says that he is at the end of his rope and is about to kill himself. After three hours of discussion, he decides to come outside. He keeps his word and kills himself. On September 11, 1995, in Quebec's Saguenay region, a man, very high on phencyclidine (PCP), barricades himself in his home with a firearm and refuses to negotiate. Eventually he comes out, and fires at the police, who kill him. Every time such a situation occurs, it raises the same questions: Could it have been prevented? Predicted?

Risk assessment is the very first course of action in a crisis situation. It involves assessing the risk to others, including hostages if there are any, and to anyone at the scene or nearby, including police. Finally, one assesses the risk of auto-aggressive behaviour, particularly suicide, by the person in crisis.

This chapter examines the main factors associated with hetero- and auto-aggressive behaviours in crisis situations, and particularly the risks of homicide and suicide. We will see that risk assessment is a complex task that is itself subject to some risks, such as the risk of being mistaken. Experts clearly tend to overestimate the danger. At best, one prediction in three is correct (Monahan, 1981). Even though it is not always possible to predict the level of risk, even though some tragedies cannot be avoided, a better understanding of risk factors can help orient risk assessment and decision making that minimize harm and save lives.

---

1 Comité consultatif National d'Éthique (National Consultation Committee on Ethics) (1987), *Recherche biomédicale et respect de la personne humaine,* Paris, French documentation.

A. RISK ASSESSMENT

Agnew's "strain theory" (1992) sets out a general explanation for the recourse to violence in crisis situations. Following significant stress they consider unjust, some individuals may experience intense negative reactions, such as anger, resentment, anxiety, and depression, that trigger a disorganized state (a crisis) ripe for violence. This tension can arise from feelings of betrayal or abandonment (past events), disturbances arising from a difficult situation (present events), or anxiety about failure (future events). If such "distressed" individuals have deficient or ineffective coping strategies, they may become overwhelmed with emotion and be driven to violent offending in an attempt to overcome the pain associated with their negative affects. Violence against others and suicide are two inappropriate coping strategies for putting an end to suffering that are commonly encountered (see Brezina, 1996; Durkheim, 1897).

There are two approaches to risk assessment:

1. Assessment based on *clinical data*, i.e. on interviews, observations, and case studies (Monahan, 1981).
2. Assessment based on probability-based *actuarial instruments*, such as those used by insurance companies.

The actuarial instruments most often used in assessing the risk of violence are the Hare Psychopathy Checklist (PCL-R), which uses 20 criteria to diagnose criminal psychopathy (Hare, 1991), the Violence Risk Assessment Guide (VRAG) (Quinsey et al., 1998), and the HCR-20 (Historical, Clinical and Risk Management Scales) (Webster et al., 1997), which assesses the risk of violent recidivism on the basis of criteria that include Hare's psychopathy checklist. Although actuarial methods are usually more accurate than clinical methods (Quinsey et al., 1998), they are far from perfect and cannot be used to assess the possibility of imminent violence—precisely what one wants to know in a crisis situation.

B. PREDICTORS OF VIOLENCE

Generally, the first 45 minutes of a crisis situation are the most critical (Dolan and Fuselier, 1989; Noesner and Dolan, 1992). During that time, the person in crisis is intensely emotional and often angry. Their judgment is often altered, either by emotions or intoxicants, which considerably increase the risk of heteroaggressive behaviour, particularly towards hostages (a sevenfold increase in risk) and police (a twofold increase in risk) (Michaud and St-Yves, 2006). Certain psychotropic drugs, such as cocaine and hallucinogens, can lead to transitory mental disorders which resemble bipolar illness, paranoia, and psychosis. Phencyclidine (PCP) sometimes induces a disorganized psychotic state associated with extremely violent behaviour (Crowley, 2003). Serious mental disorders such as paranoid delusions can increase the risk to others, particularly where psychotic decompensation is rapid (Link, Andrews and Cullen, 1992; Link and Stueve, 1994). Mohandie and Duffy (1999) have observed that violent behaviour is five times more likely among schizophrenics, especially those who experience hallucinations or delusions, than among those free of mental disorder. In addition, individuals with psychiatric problems are three times more likely to engage in auto-aggressive behaviour in crisis situations (Michaud and St-Yves, 2006).

It is often said that the past predicts the future, and this seems particularly true when it comes to predicting violence. Indeed, a history of violence is certainly one of the best predictors of future violence, and most studies of risk assessment and criminal dangerousness support this. Michaud and St-Yves (2006) have noted that barricaded individuals with a record of violent crime engage in violence towards others, especially hostages and police, more often than do those with no such history. Furthermore, the presence of weapons increases the risk of violence. According to "Danger Assessment," developed during the 1980s by Jacquelyn C. Campbell (see Campbell et al., 2003), women are 20 times more likely to die if their spouses threaten them or attack them with a weapon, 15 times more likely to die if their spouse has previously threatened them with death or injury, 10 times more likely to die if their spouse has previously attempted to strangle them, and 9 times more likely to die if their spouse has a violent temper or is chronically jealous. In cases of domestic violence, the risk of homicide is six times greater when there is a firearm in the house. In crisis situations, the more weapons the barricaded person has, the greater the risk of violence against police. As well, there is a much greater risk of violence against hostages if there has been random, non-lethal gunfire before the police arrive (Michaud and St-Yves, 2006).

The context of the crisis situation can also be a predictor of the outcome of the crisis: Is the venue a workplace from which the individual was fired? Is the individual a desperate man who is holding his ex-spouse captive and threatening to commit a murder-suicide to stop her from leaving him? The potential for violence is higher when the person in crisis is in their own home—in a state Flood and Dalphonso (2005) call "bunker" or "king of the castle" mentality—or has chosen the site deliberately to attack its occupants or settle accounts (see Michaud and St-Yves, 2006; Strentz, 2006).

There are several elements that can help orient risk assessment during negotiations (see Strentz, 1991). It is usually a bad sign if the person in crisis makes no clear or realistic demands after several hours of negotiation. When the person in crisis insists that a particular person be present (his ex-spouse, for example), he may be seeking an audience for his planned activities. If the person in crisis resists attempts by negotiators to build a rapport, the chances for success are also lower (Strentz, 1991). It is very difficult to create contact with angry adolescents, who often feel resentment toward authority figures and sometimes imagine themselves immortal. Young hostage-takers are more impulsive and violent than adults (Strentz, 2006). Also, there is a higher risk of violence if the hostages were taken by a group rather than an individual, and very long sieges, such as the 1993 Waco, Texas, incident, often end in tragedy (see Michaud and St-Yves, 2006; Strentz, 2006).

Types of Threats

The word "threat" denotes an expression of anger intended to instil a fear of harm. In crisis situations, threats are always synonymous with danger. There are three principal types:

1. *Unconditional,* or direct threats made without conditions, against which police have almost no power—for example, "I'm going to kill that son-of-a..." This is the most dangerous type of threat (Strentz, 2006).

2. *Offensive,* which confront in order to obtain a response to a precise demand—for example, "If I don't get what I'm asking for in 30 minutes, I'll kill the hostage." Ultimatums, commonly called "deadlines," always create tension and insecurity, given their association with imminent, potentially fatal, behaviour. The person in crisis makes such threats to put pressure on the police. Ultimatums are rare, occurring in about 5% of crisis situations, and range from threats of property damage to threats of suicide or homicide. Only one in four persons actually acts on such threats, and their acts usually result in property damage without injury to others (Michaud and St-Yves, 2006).

3. *Defensive:* This type of threat is the most frequent (Strentz, 2006), and is meant to protect or defend without attacking; for example,

"If someone comes in here, I'll kill him." Such threats compel police to keep their distance and respect the subject's comfort zone. The formulation of defensive threats is a good predictor of surrender. Defensive threats generally provide persons in crisis with time to get their message across, and indicate that they are seeking an honourable solution that will allow them to save face (Strentz, 2006).

Although threats often indicate risk, their absence does not mean the situation is risk-free (Flood and Dalphonso, 2005).

C. THE RISK OF SUICIDE

Suicidal individuals almost always show signs of their suffering. These precursors can be obvious or very subtle, and can take various forms (see Table 1).

To effectively assess the potential for suicide, negotiators must consider several factors (Divasto, Lanceley and Gruys, 1992): What recent events in the person's life might have disturbed them? The greater the number of stressors (stressful events in a short timeframe) and the greater their intensity (death of someone close, marital breakdown, loss of work), the greater the amount of adaptive energy required to establish emotional equilibrium (Holmes and Rahe, 1967). If an individual thinks he lacks the necessary adaptive energy, they may see suicide as a way to end their suffering. Is the individual depressed? Distressed? Depression and distress are closely associated with suicide (Evans and Farberow, 1988; Reynolds and Farberow, 1976). Does the individual express hostility? Unexpressed anger towards others can motivate someone to suicide, as the individual turns the anger inwards on themselves. Is the individual intoxicated, or have they consumed alcohol or drugs? (Alcohol depresses the central nervous system, and studies have demonstrated a strong association between alcoholism and suicide (Frances, Franklin and Flavin, 1987). Have they chosen a method or mapped out a plan to take their own life? If the individual has advanced to this stage, they are at the end of the suicide process: their decision is made and suicide is imminent.

The potential for suicide is a product of two distinct variables: 1) suicidal risk; 2) suicidal urgency (Association québécoise de prévention du suicide, 2004). Suicidal risk is the probability that a person will commit suicide within the next two years, while suicidal urgency is the probability that a person will commit suicide within the next 48 hours. The two

Table 1

Signs of Suicide			
Verbal messages		**Other types of messages**	
Direct	**Indirect**	**Behavioural**	**Emotional**
I'm going to kill myself. . .	Soon you'll have peace. . .	Sudden gifts of property	Disinterest; loss of pleasure, desire
I want to die. . .	Sometimes I'd rather be dead. . .	Drop in performance at school or work	Tears, sadness, apathy, discouragement
I don't want to live anymore. . .	Don't worry, I'll soon be gone. . .	Withdrawal, isolation	Incoherence, confusion in language
I have everything I need to do it. . .		Putting affairs in order, resolving conflicts	
		Changes in eating habits and/or hygiene	Rapid changes in mood, aggression
		Purchase of a firearm or rope, accumulation of medication	Contradictory, shifting emotions (e.g., laughter followed by tears)
		Unaccustomed consumption of drugs, alcohol, medication	
Adapted from Association québécoise de prévention du suicide (2004).			

types of risk (long-term and very short-term, if not in fact imminent) call for different evaluative criteria.

Assessment of the mid- to long-term suicidal risk requires knowledge of a variety of aspects of the person's history. Persons in crisis often have suffered several losses and/or failures. Assessment of suicidal emergencies is a matter of crisis response. As there is a risk of imminent death, responders must make the assessment in the first minutes of contact with the person, asking: Where? When? How? With what? Why today? They must ask these questions directly. The clearer and more precise the questions, the clearer and more precise the answers (Association québécoise de prévention du suicide, 2004). If the person in distress verbalizes their intentions clearly, has a precise plan (showing premeditation) and has chosen the moment of their death (e.g. a symbolic date), there is a greater risk of them carry out the suicide (Association québécoise de prévention du suicide, 2004 ; Strentz, 1991).

1. Indicators of Imminent Suicide

Perrou (2004) identifies three indicators of imminent suicide: 1) *Hyper-vigilance:* the person sweeps his glance from left to right (from one shoulder to the other), indicating that they are in distress and fatalistic. 2) *Change in breathing rhythm:* The person takes deep breaths, apparently out of uncontrollable fear (possibly of death or suffering). 3) *The count-down*—the last act before death. Individuals who leap from high structures often "count down" before "the big jump." This is the equivalent of "1,2,3, GO!" or "On your marks, get set. . ." Perrou suggests intervening immediately with "STOP! I hear [see] you and I know what you're about to do. I'm telling you to stop now. STOP! Talk to me. Don't do it." [translation] (Perrou, 2004: 235). This can help gain precious seconds of life and interrupt the final act.

2. "Suicide by Cop"

Annually, the police are responsible for 300 deaths in the United States (Uniform Crime Reports for the United States, 2001), about 10 deaths in Canada, 5 deaths in Australia, and even fewer in New Zealand and the United Kingdom (Parent, 2004). Some studies contend that 10-30% of such deaths are attributable to suicide by proxy, commonly known as "suicide by cop" (Lord, 2004; Mohandie and Meloy, 2000; Perrou, 2004). This latter expression was recently coined by Geberth to describe "incidents in which individuals, bent on self-destruction, engage in life-threatening and criminal behavior to force the police to kill them" (Geberth, 1993: 105).

According to Kennedy, Homant, and Hupp (1998), suicide by cop is part of the "hidden suicide" family, along with certain "accidents" and "natural deaths." Most of the time, individuals who want to die in this way do something that assures police response—provoking a police chase, engaging in domestic violence, shooting at passers-by, threatening neighbours, etc. They might even advise police themselves that they are about to commit a crime. Such individuals will do everything possible to get a police response (Paynter, 2000). Once police arrive, they try to raise the level of tension, by deliberately acting provocatively. They may move toward police, refuse to drop their weapons, point a firearm at others, or threaten hostages. Sometimes such individuals insist on negotiating face-to-face with police—this is an unusual tactic, and could betray an inclination toward suicide by cop (Strentz, 1991). Some perceive their behaviour as an act of courage. While they do not want to die, their pride drives them to confront the police rather than surrender.

3. Recognizing a "Suicide by Cop" Situation

Hutson et al. (1998) established four criteria for diagnosing suicide by cop:

1. The individual expresses a desire to die and asks police to kill them.
2. The individual leaves a suicide message (written or verbal) for a friend or member of the family.
3. The individual possesses an apparently or actually lethal weapon.
4. The individual deliberately escalates the tension or is provocative to incite the police to kill them.

When suicide by cop is imminent, the individual usually gives a signal (a "go") to show they have reached the final stage. Their actions are usually very violent and are intended to procure self-annihilation, not simple wounding. Very aggressive or depressive people are more likely to kill themselves in this way (Hal Brown, in Paynter, 2000). Sometimes, the would-be victim consumes drugs to bolster their courage (Mohandie and Meloy, 2000). While Scoville (1998) observed that the weapons brandished are more commonly real and loaded, rather than fake, Geberth and Van Zandt (in Burke and Rigsby, 1999) reported a contradictory finding, namely that these individuals' firearms are usually unloaded or non-functional.

4. Possible Interventions

Responders must identify a possible suicide by proxy as quickly as possible. When they suspect it, they must directly confront the person and ask why they want the police to kill them. Their goal is to make the person realize the seriousness of his or her actions (Lindsay and Dickson, 2004). Above all, responders should not challenge the individual or react to his or her provocations. Would-be suicides are likely seeking a pretext or propitious moment to put their plan into action. To avoid violence, they must sometimes momentarily be given the power they seek. One must be careful not to fall into their traps, as they may take others along with them when they die. Active listening is the recommended approach, as it allows individuals to express their emotions, which in turn diminishes their aggressiveness.

If the individual is intoxicated, responders must take into consideration the type and quantity of intoxicant ingested. Some psychotropic drugs increase irritability and aggression, and if they have been consumed, responders must wait for the effects to dissipate so that negotiation can proceed on a rational basis. Responders must never lose sight of the fact that this is a suicide. The only difference is the choice of weapon. Normally, the suicide's choice of weapon is a firearm, a knife, or medication. With suicide by cop, the weapon is the police (Lindsay and Dickson, 2004:154).

5. Death by Indifference

Statistics on suicide by cop sometimes include the phenomenon Williams and Praet (see Williams, 2003) have recently described, in Law and Order, as "death by indifference." Unlike suicide by cop, there is no clear indicator in this case that the subject intends suicide—no suicide note, no hints of suicide to those close to him. Often, persons in this group have no criminal record or a record of minor infractions only. But like those who commit suicide by cop they are usually intoxicated, suffering from a mental disorder, confronted by an emotionally charged situation (marital dispute, police chase, extreme anger), and in possession of a weapon.

In their intoxicated and/or disturbed state, the thought of being killed no longer matters to them, at least not in the moment. Even though firearms are pointed at them, they will advance threateningly toward police until the officers fire on them. Such individuals are not suicidal; rather, they are indifferent to the consequences of their actions—which appear suicidal under the circumstances (Williams, 2003).

CONCLUSION

Risk assessment is a complex and sometimes arbitrary task. "Crucial predictors of occasionally or permanently dangerous conditions give way to the unpredictability of human activity and circumstance [. . .] The multiplicity of hazards in which all individual existence evolves, and the impossibility of gathering the totality of prognostic information, dictates that certain events are independent of the person and his psychology, and cannot be readily anticipated" (Bénézech, 2004: 15).

One can predict a hurricane like Katrina, which devastated New Orleans in August 2005, but one cannot avoid its damaging effects. All the same, predicting such a catastrophe makes emergency planning possible, so that we can reduce harm and save lives. The same is true of crisis situations. Risk assessment can help prevent tragedy, albeit not all the time. A tragic end is not always synonymous with a bad prognosis. Often, it is a matter of the person in crisis making a bad choice.

REFERENCES

Agnew, R. (1992). Foundation for a general strain theory of crime and delinquency. *Criminology,* 30, 475-500.

Association québécoise de prévention du suicide (2004). *Le suicide : comprendre et intervenir.* http://www.aqps.info (consulted September 28, 2006).

Bénézech, M. (2004). Introduction à l'étude de la dangerosité. In C. de Beaurepaire, M. Bénézech and C. Kottler (eds.). *Les dangerosités.* Éditions John Libbey Eurotext. Paris, 7-23.

Brezina, T. (1996). Adapting to strain: An examination of delinquant coping responses. *Criminology,* 34, p. 39-60.

Burke, T. and Rigsby, R. (1999). Suicide by Cop Revisited. *Law and Order,* v. 47(6), June 1999, 97-102.

Campbell, J. C., Webster, D., Koziol-McLain, J., Block C.R., Campbell, D., Curry, M.A., Gary, F., Sachs, C. Sharps, P.W., Wilt, S., Manganello, J., Xu, X. (2003). Risk factors for femicide in abusive relationships: Results from a multi-site case control study. *American Journal of Public Health,* 93, 1089-1097.

Crowley, B. (2003). The assessment of danger in everyday practice. *Psychiatric Times,* 20(6), 1-6.

Divasto, P., Lanceley, F.J. and Gruys, A. (1992). Critical Issues in Suicide Intervention. *FBI Law Enforcement Bulletin.* Aug. 1992, 13-16.

Dolan, J.T. and Fuselier, G.D. (1989). A Guide for First Responders to Hostage Situations. *FBI Law Enforcement Bulletin.* April 1989, 9-13.

Durkheim, E. (1897). *Le suicide : Étude de sociologie.* Paris: Les Presses universitaires de France, 2e édition, 1967, 462 pages.

Evans, G. and Farberow, N. (1988). *The Encyclopedia of Suicide.* New York, New York: Facts on File, 153-154.

Flood, J. and Dalphonso, V. (2005). *Critical Incident.* 11th Crisis Negotiation Seminar. Calgary. October 16th to 18th.

Frances, R, Franklin, J. and Flavin, D. (1987). Suicide and Alcoholism. *American Journal of Drug and Alcohol Abuse.* 13 (3) 327-341.

Geberth, V.J. (1993). Suicide by cop. *Law and Order.* July, 105-108.

Hare, R.D. (1991). *The Hare Psychopathy Check-list Revised.* Toronto: Multi-Health Systems.

Holmes, T. and Rahe, R. (1967). The social readjustment rating scale. *Journal of Psychosomatic Research.* 11, 213-218.

Hutson, H.R, Anglin, D., Yarbrough, J., Hardaway, K., Russell, M., Strote, J., Canter, M. and Blum, B. (1998). Suicide-by-cop. *Annals of Emergency Medicine.* 32(6),665-669.

Kennedy, D., Homant, R. and Hupp, T. (1998). Suicide by Cop. The *FBI Law Enforcement Bulletin.* 67, 30-48.

Lindsay, M.S. and Dickson, D. (2004). Negotiating with the Suicide by Cop Subject. In Lord, V. (2004). *Suicide by Cop: Inducing Officers to Shoot.* New York Loose Leaf Law Publications, 153-162.

Link, B., Andrews, H. and Cullen, F. (1992). The violent and illegal behavior of mental patients reconsidered. *American Sociological Review.* 57, 275-292.

Link, B. and Stueve, A. (1994). Psychotic symptoms and the violent/illegal behavior of mental patients compared to community controls. *Violence and Mental disorder.* Monahan J. and Steadman H. (eds.). The University of Chicago Press. 137-159.

Lord, V. (2004). *Suicide by Cop: Inducing Officers to Shoot.* New York Loose Leaf Law Publications, 304 pages.

Michaud, P. and St-Yves, M. (2006). *Analyse des situations de crise survenues entre 1990 et 2004 sur le territoire desservi par la Sûreté du Québec.* Unpublished.

Mohandie, K. and Duffy, J. (1999). Understanding subjects with paranoid schizophrenia. *FBI Law Enforcement Bulletin,* December 1999, 8-16.

Mohandie K. and Meloy J. (2000). Clinical and forensic indicators of "suicide by cop". *Journal of Forensic Sciences.* 45(2) : 384-389.

Monahan, J. (1981). *Predicting violent behavior. An assessment of clinical techniques.* London, Sage.

Noesner, G.W. and Dolan, J.T. (1992). First Responder Negotiation Training. *FBI Law Enforcement Bulletin.* Aug. 1992, 1-4.

Parent, R.B. (2004). Police Use of Deadly Force in the Pacific Northwest Victim-Precipitated Homicide. In Lord, V. (2004). *Suicide by Cop: Inducing Officers to Shoot.* New York Loose Leaf Law Publications, 31-56.

Paynter, R. (2000). Suicide by cop. *Law Enforcement Technology.* 27 (6), 40-44.

Perrou, B. (2004). Antecedent (Pre-Death) Behaviors as Indicators of Imminent Violence. In Lord, V. (2004). *Suicide by Cop: Inducing Officers to Shoot.* New York Loose Leaf Law Publications, 231-237.

Quinsey, L., Harris, G.T., Rice, M.E. and Cormier, C.A. (1998). *Violent Offenders: Appraising and Managing the Risk.* Washington D.C.: American Psychological Association.

Reynolds, D. and Farberow, N. (1976). *Suicide: inside and out.* University of California Press. 226 pages.

Scoville, D. (1998). Getting you to pull the trigger. *Police: The Law Enforcement Magazine,* 22 (11), 36-44.

Strentz, T. (2006). *Psychological Aspects of Crisis Negotiation.* CRC Press. 272 pages.

Strentz, T. (1991). Thirteen Indicators of Volatile Negotiations. *Law and Order.* vol. 39 (9), September 1991, 135-139.

Uniform Crime Reports for the United States (2001). Federal Bureau of Investigation. U.S. Department of Justice. Washington D.C.

Webster, C.D., Douglas, K.S. Eaves, D. and Hart, S.D. (1997). *HCR-20 Assessing Risk for Violence, version* 2. Mental Health, Law, and Policy Institute, British Columbia, Canada: Simon Fraser University.

Williams, G.T. (2003). Death by Indifference: A new understanding of suspect actions leading to deadly force. *Law and Order.* December, 2003.

CHAPTER 14

Threat Assessment Involving Anonymous Correspondence

Mario J. Scalora, Gary L. Plank and Katherine A. Schoeneman

Law enforcement and security professionals often deal with a range of threatening and hoax activity from initially unidentified sources. The purpose of this chapter is to describe the implementation of threat assessment methodology to anonymous correspondence sent to a range of potential targets of concern, particularly public officials.

Threatening contacts may reach targets and come to the attention of law enforcement or security professionals in a variety of ways. In some instances, the subject makes direct contact with the target (e.g., through written letters, telephone calls, faxes, e-mails, sending packages, or showing up in the target's workplace). In other cases, the subject may become known as a result of statements made or actions taken in public. Such activities do not involve direct contact, but still reference a target. These statements or actions might be observed by a third party who decides to report the individual to law enforcement (e.g., making disturbing comments or engaging in disturbing actions in the presence of a co-worker, on a television station, or through Internet websites/blogs), or they might be observed by law enforcement themselves.

While the majority of threatening or harassing contacts toward public officials are not necessarily presented from anonymous sources (Scalora, M.J., Baumgartner, J. V., Callaway, D., Zimmerman, W., Hatch-Maillette, M. A., Covell, C. N., Palarea, R. E., Krebs, J. A., and Washington, D. O., 2002), such anonymous threats do cause a disproportionate amount of concern and need to be taken seriously as any threatening communication. In addition, certain types of threatening communications such as bomb threats, product tampering threats and related hoax activity often present as anonymous threats (see Logan, 1993: Tunkel, 2002 for reviews). In order to develop effective threat assessment and management strategies to deal with anonymous threatening correspondence, a review of the various motivations underlying such communications is warranted.

A. MOTIVATIONS UNDERLYING THE ANONYMOUS THREAT

The motivations for anonymous threatening and harassing communication are as diverse as those with identified authors. A range of motivations are present throughout such communications, which include attempts at harassment, help-seeking, raising awareness for domestic or international political issues, desires to initiate relationships, threat and intimidation, as well as delusion-related themes. In the case of communications involving anonymous threats, however, additional motivational factors such as inducing fear (e.g., stalking behavior) and hoax activity to generate a protective response which will incovenience the targets and first responders.

In many incidents of targeted violence such as stalking or workplace violence, the perpetrator may be an individual otherwise known by the target who chooses to remain anonymous in order to avoid consequences for the threatening behavior (see e.g., Scalora, Washington, Casady, and Newel, 2003). In other words, anonymous threats may suggest an aggressor known to the target who may have prolonged contact with the potential victim. Such individuals may need to exercise caution and distance themselves from threatening acts by concealing their identity, whereas aggressors who are less likely to have subsequent contact with the victim may be less concerned about concealing identity (Borden, 1975; Richardson, Bernstein, and Taylor 1979). Regardless of motivation, an awareness of empirically supported threat assessment risk factors predictive of problematic approach behavior is critical to ascertain the level of concern posed by a particular communication (and related pattern of communications when applicable) as well as determine the appropriate threat management strategy.

B. THREAT ASSESSMENT METHODOLOGY AND CORRESPONDENCE

Written correspondence has always been a prevalent method of contacting public officials. For decades, the primary method of contact with public officials has been through letters and phone contact. However, technological and security considerations have shifted the manner by which persons contact public figures and governmental institutions. Shortly after the terrorist attacks of September 11, 2001, the United States witnessed an unexpected form of letter threat with the appearance of anthrax in envelopes shipped via the United States Postal Service. Because of this new biochemical threat, the government increasingly encouraged constituents to contact their elected public officials, including legislators, via e-mail. With an increase in e-mail correspondence emerged an increase in the number of threats received electronically. In addition to e-mail, increased comment regarding a range of public topics has also involved posting on Internet websites and blogs. The Congressional Management Foundation found that "Congress received four times more communications in 2004 than 1995—all of the increase from Internet-based communications" (Fitch and Goldschmidt, 2005, p. 4). They went on to specify that Congress received 18,335,594 letters by post and 182,053,399 communications via the Internet during 2004, compared to 53,000,000 postal letters and no e-mails were received in 1995. Fitzgerald (2003) has made comparisons of the amount of effort needed to send a threatening letter versus a threatening e-mail. He points out that it takes far fewer steps to send an e-mail than to send a letter, as e-mails can be typed in minutes and received instantaneously, while letters can take hours to write and days to be received. Ultimately, this suggests that the computer and Internet have simplified the process of sending inappropriate or threatening correspondence. Fitzgerald (2003) has concluded that "with less than half the required steps, and a fraction of the time, the computer based threat maker has many fewer actions to perform. Thus, he has much less time to think, or 'decompress', about halting a potentially illegal activity before completing it" (p. 5).

Early research showed that electronic communications (e.g., via e-mail or Internet postings) contained a higher level of aggressive language as indicated through name-calling, swearing, insults, and hostile comments, than communications that take place in face-to-face exchanges (e.g., Kiesler and Sproull, 1992). Research has also found that anonymity (whether actual or perceived) contributes to increased hostile or aggressive language as a result of lowered inhibition (e.g., Siegel, Dubrovsky, Kiesler, and McGuire, 1986). In addition, increased physical distance and ease of quick-replying may contribute to more hostile language (Wallace, 1999). It has also been the experience of the authors that hostile subjects can quickly develop and send their e-mails at any time of the day when compared to hostile letter writers.

While investigative issues such as determining authorial attribution may be necessary for law enforcement and security professionals, the goal of threat assessment is not to determine the presence of a crime, but ascertain how the communication may fit within a pattern of contacts that may pose a threat to the target.

Regardless of the modality of contact, the authors have researched harassing and threatening contacts toward state and federal officials spanning several thousand cases (Baumgartner, Scalora, and Plank, 2001; Scalora, Baumgartner, and Plank, 2003; Scalora, Baumgartner, Zimmerman, et al., 2002; Scalora, Baumgartner, Zimmerman, et al., 2003). The research resulted in identifying empirically validated risk factors for problematic approach that were also operationally relevant for law enforcement personnel investigating such contacts. As detailed below in Figure 1, the research suggests a model for the interaction of a range of contextual, subject-related (when available), motivational, target, protective and contact-related factors to guide the assessment of threatened targeted violence and intimidation. The factors inherent within this model, to be described below, are as applicable for problematic contacts from both anonymous and known subjects. Table 1 details questions covering each domain that may assist with the threat assessment process.

Figure 1: Threat Assessment Approach Factors

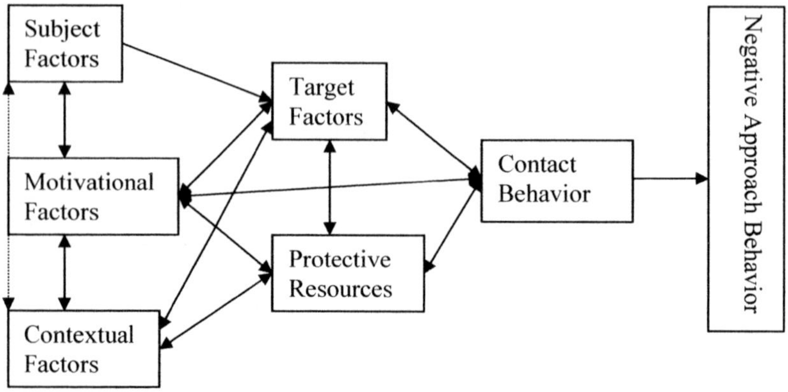

Contextual factors, though not powerful predictors of problematic approach behavior by themselves, do suggest the likelihood of increased contacts (Scalora, Baumgartner, Zimmerman, et al., 2002). Contextual factors that potentially increase problematic communications include recent negative attention or concern regarding the target (e.g., negative press, recent scandal) as well as a recent act of targeted violence that has garnered attention. In addition, recent media or political attention to a controversial issue also raises the likelihood of threatening contacts toward political targets (Scalora, Baumgartner, Zimmerman, et al., 2002). Given the copycat nature of hoax events, it is not surprising that recent threatening, tampering or hoax events often result in clusters of problematic threatening and hoax activity that demand substantial attention. Further, it is the experience of the authors that a significant anniversary to the subject (e.g., recent death of loved one, date of discharge from job or military) or to the target (e.g., terrorist act) also suggest the increased likelihood of problematic contacts.

Subject factors predictive of problematic approach are a challenge to ascertain in cases involving anonymous contacts. However, especially with cases involving multiple contacts or single contacts with extensive detail, some subject-related factors may be inferred from the contact. For example, incoherent or information suggesting conspiratorial or other delusional activity, may suggest the presence of serious mental illness. For example, in the case of one individual who left the following message within a government building attached to a lengthy and disorganized treatise covering a range of disparate topics, one might assume mental health difficulties are present:

> "Unless this is a training area- I don't trust any kind of one-way mine communications without any type of aware confirmation. So anyway, I have been leaving reports every couple of days and hope you are pleased with the data."

Subjects who display mental illness symptoms tied to the target or to a personal motive demonstrate a heightened risk of problematic approach behavior (Baumgartner, Scalora, and Plank, 2001; Scalora, Baumgartner, and Plank, 2003; Scalora, Baumgartner, Zimmerman, et al., 2003). While some research has been inconsistent in this regard, the prevalence of certain mental illness symptoms, namely threat-control override symptoms, has been found by the authors as predictive of problematic approach within contacts by mentally ill persons toward public officials (Scalora, Baumgartner, and Plank, 2003). Threat-control override symptoms suggest the presence of immediate harm to the individual (e.g., paranoia) as well as challenges to the ability to control one's thoughts or behavior (e.g., insertion or removal of thoughts from one's mind, control of thoughts from an outside entity such as satellites) Regardless of mental status, subjects who contact multiple targets (particularly other agencies) with their grievance were also more likely to engage in problematic approach behavior (Scalora, Baumgartner, and Plank, 2003; Scalora, Baumgartner, Zimmerman, et al., 2003). Within anonymous contacts, threat assessment professionals should also attempt to note whether subjects are portraying recent life stressors that may either exacerbate or challenge coping mechanisms (e.g., recent financial or relationship difficulties). Though not discernible in cases involving anonymous subjects, subjects with prior arrest records particularly involving harassment or threat-related charges (such as violation of protection order, terrorist threat or harassment by phone) are at heightened risk for problematic approach.

Motivational factors are discernible through assessing thematic information inherent within the verbal or written communication. The likelihood of problematic approach is significantly heightened with the perceived level of personal relevance of issue presented by the subject, especially if help-seeking requests or other demands are made (Baumgartner, Scalora, and Plank, 2001; Calhoun, 1998; Scalora, Baumgartner, and Plank, 2003; Scalora, Baumgartner, Zimmerman, et al., 2002; Scalora, Baumgartner, Zimmerman, et al., 2003). In a similar vein, the relationship of the expressed motives or desires to the target also relate to the likelihood of approach. For example, if the target is viewed (rationally or otherwise) as able to assist with a child custody dispute, or if the target were somehow tied into harm to the subject noted within his delusional thoughts, problematic approach is likely to occur. Content themes indicative of venting regarding domestic or foreign policy by themselves were not generally related to problematic approach.

While *target* and *protective* factors are sometimes difficult to ascertain, it is clear that high-profile and media-involved targets are more likely to be subjected to problematic approach and related precursor contacts (Scalora, Baumgartner, Zimmerman, et al., 2002). While public figures tend to encourage public contact, those who are more accessible tend to also receive more problematic contacts. In a related vein concerning protective factors, it is not surprising that targeted public figures with heightened physical or personal security tend to receive fewer problematic approaches. Contacts that make references to the nature of the target's security (or lack thereof) also raise significant concern. Correspondence addressed or packaged a manner designed to avoid security screening also raises the level of concern posed by the subject.

Concerning risk factors indicated within *contact* behavior, subjects who made multiple contacts through multiple modalities (e.g., phone, written, electronic) were more likely to engage in problematic approach behavior. Therefore it is critical that any anonymous contacts be evaluated within the context of how the communication in hand fits within a pattern of related communications (Chang, Scalora, Schoeneman, Zimmerman, and Garner, 2005; Scalora, Baumgartner, Zimmerman, et al., 2002; Scalora, Baumgartner, Zimmerman, et al., 2003). Regarding other contact behaviors, the presence of personal, racial, or sexually insulting language in themselves are not predictive of problematic approach. Further, substantial research has suggested that subjects who make direct threats are less likely to engage in problematic approach behavior (Calhoun, 1998; Dietz, Matthews, Martell, et al. 1991; Scalora, Baumgartner, Zimmerman, et al., 2002; Scalora, Baumgartner, Zimmerman, et al., 2003). However, if the threats emerged as part of an escalating pattern of problematic contacts, problematic approach was likely to occur (Scalora, Baumgartner, and Plank, 2003; Scalora, Baumgartner, Zimmerman, et al., 2003). Further, the same research indicated that while persons with mental illness were less likely to make threatening statements, those who made threats were also more likely to engage in approach behavior. Such a finding is not surprising given that persons with mental illness were aware of the likelihood of being placed in protective custody or other legal ramifications of threatening actions. It appears that these impaired subjects were either "at the end of their rope" or "decompensated" in their functioning enough to be unconcerned about the outcomes of their actions.

Given the recent increases in e-mail contacts toward political officials described earlier within this chapter, recent research comparing threatening/harassing letters with similar e-mail contacts have found some differences, though noteworthy similarities. In an initial study comparing problematic e-mail with letter correspondence, Schoeneman and colleagues found that e-mailers were more likely than letter writers to focus their correspondence on government concerns, use obscene language, display disorganized writing, and write shorter communications (Schoeneman, Scalora, Chang, Zimmerman, and Garner, 2006). In a follow-up study, Schoeneman, Scalora, Chang, Zimmerman, and McGaffin (2006) found that the risk factors for approach found in letter-writing and e-mailing subjects are consistent with the previous literature that identified risk factors for approach without segregating cases by method of contact. Both letter writers and e-mailers who approached their targets were more likely than their counterparts to exhibit indicators of serious mental illness and threat-control override symptoms, to engage in prior contact with the target, and to use multiple methods of contact. The authors also found that both letter-writing and e-mailing "approachers" were also more likely to emphasize personal themes (e.g., help-seeking, entitlement claims, etc.) in their writing and to have made significantly more contacts toward their targets overall.

The various threat assessment factors reviewed above indicate that no set profile for the anonymous author who engages in problematic approach exists. As the following cases indicate, investigators and threat assessment professionals should evaluate not only the content of the communication, but how the communication fits within a pattern of related communications and other contextual factors. To maintain the privacy of the victims and the integrity of the case files, the names, addresses and other identifying information used in the case studies will be changed. All quotations from the anonymous written communications (except for identifying information) will be exactly as the subjects communicated them. This will include their use (or lack thereof) of capitalization, punctuation, grammar, and spelling.

Table 1
Threat Assessment Factors Relevant to Anonymous Communication Analysis

Contextual Factors:
Increased attention or concern regarding target or recent violent incident, topic area?
Heightened concern re: specific target or issue?
Other recent threatening, tampering or hoax events?
Anniversary of significant event to subject or target?
Subject Factors
Mental illness symptoms tied to target or personal motive
Prior arrest record (particularly with prior harassment/threat-related charges)
History of contacts with other agencies
Access to protectee/target?
Recent life stressors implied/described ?
Specific mental illness symptoms (including threat-control override symptoms) indicated?
Motivational Factors
Issue at hand personally relevant to subject?
Relationship of motive to target?
Issue related to delusional activity of personal relevance to subject?
Protective factors
Was correspondence addressed or packaged a manner designed to avoid security screening?
Were references made to police or security involvement?
References made to target's security?
Contact behavior
Multiple prior contacts/multiple methods of contact?
Nature of threatening language?
Surveillance or stalking-like behavior present indicated or suspected?
Contact across multiple settings?
Any demands made?
Have other suspicious activities taken place?
Contact part of a pattern of other suspicious or threatening behavior?
Escalation in rhetoric or threatening language?
Target Factors
Intensity of focus—subjects were focused on particular target or issue–but contacted multiple targets?
Target Dispersion: What other contacts have taken place? With whom?
Intensity of relationship of rhetoric to target?
Risk appraisal by target re: reporting etc.?
Potential symbolic/instrumental objectives of target?
Accessibility of target?

Case 1: The Joan Wright affair

Joan Wright, a public figure, began to receive phone calls at her home and office. The caller's voice was electronically altered to prevent identification of the caller. Joan also received hang-up calls at home and work at all hours of the day and night. When Joan was at home, the caller would often make the call shortly after Joan's husband had left their home and the caller would begin the conversation by stating, "I know you are alone." The caller told Joan things such as "you are the most beautiful woman that I've ever seen," "I want to make love to you," "how can I get you interested," and "what do I have to do to get you to make love to me." A short time after the calls began, Joan started to receive e-mail messages at work and home. The e-mail messages were from "mystery man" and the e-mail address was "amaninlove50@. . ." (The e-mail was addressed to the victim and in the subject line of the e-mail was the victim's first name.) The following is the body of one of those messages:

> " joan,
>
> if you know who this is, please don't tell anyone about my feelings about you. joan, i think you're the most amazing and prettiest woman that i have ever known. please joan, i need to know what you think of this! i am head over heels for you, please joan reply back to me. if you know who this is please don't tell anyone. if you don't know who this is i'll start giving you clues on who this might be!
>
> from,
>
> ???"

The messages continued to be received at Joan's home and office and were quite disturbing to Joan.

Joan notified the local police department as well as her employer regarding the communications she had been receiving. The next step in the process was to provide Joan with a victim briefing. Joan was advised that these situations can sometimes be long-term. Joan was requested to maintain records of all communications which would include saving and printing all e-mail messages, recording all telephone and voice-mail messages, as well as attempting to trace all telephone communications.

These communications appear to have been authored by an individual in his midlife. This belief was based on the phrases used in the communications, for example, "i am head over heels for you." The individual also had basic computer knowledge as well as an understanding of some basic technologies (the electronic voice altering device).

The lengths to which the individual went in order to conceal his identity indicated that the subject was known to the victim. The subject was believed to be a work associate or acquaintance of the victim. Several months later the offender was identified as a fellow employee at the victim's workplace. Shortly after the victim began to work at the site, the offender made a pass at her which she quickly turned down.

Case 2: State agency harassing e-mails

A state agency received an e-mail message through their public website. The message was from the e-mail address funeforniadmv666@yahoo.com (address changed to prevent identification). The name connected to the e-mail address was listed as "toWADMVlegalscamartist" (name changed to prevent identification). The message was as follows:

> "You all think your smart but I finally have enough information and proof on you that is going to make you remember this message. Your $$$$ hustling days are over and this is only to inform you messed with the wrong person. You will hear from me again State [name changed to prevent identification] DMV Seaseme Street cracked out inbreed thunder cunts."

This message was apparently sent by an individual who was upset about the amount of taxes and fees paid to license a vehicle. This person was upset with the cost of government services and was venting their anger through the website. The use of the website and the disguised e-mail address indicates that the person did not want to be known to this government entity. The message also did not enumerate any particular threat besides "You will hear from me again. . ." Most of the communication is used to call the agency derogatory terms. This individual was most likely just needing to vent feelings of anger and frustration with the government agency. By venting in this manner the person may have felt that some level of satisfaction already. In research done by Baumgartner, Scalora and Plank (2001), it was determined that individuals who contact government agencies and use themes related to sarcastic/insulting language, legal/political concerns, or revenge motives are less likely to engage in approach behaviors. This communication was believed to be a way for the subject to "extract his pound of flesh" so to speak. It was believed that this individual was at low risk to act out violently toward any employee in this agency at the time. The subject did not engage in any subsequent problematic contacts toward the agency.

CONCLUSION

While no set profile for the anonymous threat maker exists, consideration of the range of contextual, contact, motivational, target and subject factors that can be inferred from the communication can inform the level of concern posed by the specific contact. Threatening communications from anonymous sources reflect a diverse range of motivations and must be taken as seriously as threats from known sources. Despite the challenges sometimes inherent with ascertaining subject motives within anonymous communications, threat assessment professionals are still capable of considering a range of assessment factors while determining whether the communication may relate to other problematic contacts toward the victim or related targets. While some operationally relevant threat assessment research exists, the field will still continue to benefit from continued scholarship and empirical inquiry.

REFERENCES

Baumgartner, J. V., Scalora, M. J., and Plank, G. L. (2001). Case characteristics of threats toward state officials investigated by a midwestern state. *Journal of Threat Assessment, 1(3), 41-60.*

Borden, R. J., (1975). Witnessed aggression: Influence of an observer's sex and values on aggressive responding. *Journal of Personality and Social Psychology, 31, 567-573.*

Calhoun, F. S. (1998). *Hunters and howlers: Threats and violence against federal judicial officials in the United States, 1789-1993.* (USMS Publication No. 80). Washington, DC: U. S. Department of Justice.

Dietz, P. E., Matthews, D. B., Van Duyne, C., Martell, D. A., Parry, C. D. H., Stewart, T. M., Warren, J., and Crowder, J. D. (1991). Threatening and otherwise inappropriate letters to Hollywood celebrities. *Journal of Forensic Sciences, 36, 185-209.*

Fitch, B., and Goldschmidt, K. (2005). *Communicating with Congress: How Capitol Hill is coping with the surge in citizen advocacy.* Washington, DC: Congressional Management Foundation.

Fitzgerald, J. (2003). *Communicated threats: Undertaking assessments within a behavioral and forensic linguistic framework.* Unpublished manuscript, Federal Bureau of Investigations.

Kiesler, S., and Sproull, L. S. (1986). Response effects in the electronic survey. *Public Opinion Quarterly, 50, 402-413.*

Logan, B. (1993). Product tampering crime: A review. *Journal of Forensic Sciences, 38, 918-927.*

Richardson, D. R., Bernstein, S., and Taylor, S. P. (1979). The effect of situational contingencies on female retaliative behavior. *Journal of Personality and Social Psychology, 37, 2044-2048.*

Scalora, M. J., Baumgartner, J. V., and Plank, G. L. (2003). The relationship of mental illness to targeted contact behavior toward state government agencies and officials. *Behavioral Sciences and the Law, 21, 239-249.*

Scalora, M. J., Baumgartner, J. V., Zimmerman, W., Callaway, D., Hatch Maillette, M. A., Covell, C. N., Palarea, R. E., Krebs, J. A., and Washington, D. O. (2002). An epidemiological assessment of problematic contacts to members of congress. *Journal of Forensic Sciences, 47, 1360-1364.*

Scalora, M. J., Baumgartner, J. V., Zimmerman, W., Callaway, D., Hatch Maillette, M. A., Covell, C. N., Palarea, R. E., Krebs, J. A., and Washington, D. O. (2003). Risk factors for approach behavior toward the U.S. Congress. *Journal of Threat Assessment, 2 (2), 35-55.*

Scalora, M. J., Washington, D. O., Casady, T., and Newell, S. P. (2002). Non-Fatal Workplace Violence: Risk Factors: Data From a Police Contact Sample. *Journal of Interpersonal Violence, 18, 310-327.*

Schoeneman, K. A., Scalora, M. J., Chang, G. H., Zimmerman, W. J., and Garner, Y. (2006). *A comparison of e-mail versus letter threat contacts toward members of the United States Congress.* Manuscript submitted for publication.

Schoeneman, K. A., Scalora, M. J., Chang, G. H., Zimmerman, W. J., and McGaffin, C. M. (2006, March). *Differential risk factors for problematic approach behavior toward Legislators: Are letter writers or e-mailers more dangerous?* Poster session presented at the annual meeting of the American Psychology–Law Society, St. Petersburg, FL.

Siegel, J., Dubrovsky, V., Kiesler, S., and McGuire, T. (1986). Group processes in computer-mediated communications. *Organizational Behavior and Human Decision Processes, 37, 157-187.*

Tunkel, R. F. (2002). Bomb threat assessments. *FBI Law Enforcement Bulletin, 71, 6-7.*

Wallace, P. (1999). *The psychology of the internet.* New York: Cambridge University Press.

CHAPTER 15

Criminal Psychopathy: An Introduction for Police[1]

Matt Logan and Robert D. Hare

Psychopathy been described as the single most important *clinical* construct in the criminal justice system (Hare, 1996) and, more recently, as "what may be the most important *forensic* concept of the early 21st century" (Monahan, 2006). The term refers to a personality disorder that includes a cluster of interpersonal, affective, lifestyle, and antisocial traits and behaviours, including deception, manipulation, irresponsibility, impulsivity, stimulation-seeking, poor behavioural controls, shallow affect, a lack of empathy, guilt or remorse, sexual promiscuity, a callous disregard for the rights of others, and a range of unethical and antisocial behaviours. In this chapter we provide brief descriptions of psychopathy, its measurement with the *Hare Psychopathy Checklist-Revised* (PCL-R), its implications for criminal justice, and the application of theory and research on psychopathy to law enforcement. Detailed discussions of the extensive literature on these and related topics are available elsewhere (Babiak and Hare, 2006; Felthous and Sass, 2007; Hare, 1999; Hervé and Yuille, 2007; Meloy, 1988, 2000; O'Toole, 2007; Patrick, 2006; Ramsland, 2005).

A. WHY IS PSYCHOPATHY IMPORTANT TO POLICE?

Patrol officers and police investigators encounter all sorts of individuals in the course of a day, some of whom will be psychopaths. In the investigation of serious and violent crime, many of the suspects and offenders will be psychopaths. It is critical that those in law enforcement should understand as much as possible about the nature and manifestations of psychopathy. Armed with knowledge about how psychopaths think and behave might be a key element in resolving a difficult street situation or solving a case. It might also save an officer's life. A 1992 FBI Report on

---

1 This chapter draws on several more extensive discussions of the topics contained herein (Book, Clark, Forth, & Hare, 2006; Hare 2002, 2003, 2006; Hare & Neumann, 2005, 2006; Logan, Hare, & O'Toole, 2004).

cop killers is noteworthy and chilling. Almost half of those who killed officers on duty were referred to in the FBI report as having antisocial and psychopathic traits, including a sense of entitlement, lack of remorse, were unconcerned about others, blameful of others, manipulative and conning, affectively cold, irresponsible, and with poor understanding of, and adherence to, social norms. These killers were not simply persistently antisocial individuals, such as those who meet the criteria for antisocial personality disorder (APD) in the *Diagnostic and Statistical Manual of Mental Disorders* (DSM-IV; American Psychiatric Association, 1994). Rather, they were psychopaths – remorseless predators who use charm, intimidation and, if necessary, impulsive and cold-blooded violence to attain their ends.

Of course not all killers are psychopaths, nor are all psychopaths killers or even routinely violent. However, many of the attitudes and behaviours of psychopaths are predatory in nature. These individuals apparently see others as little more than a source of emotional, physical and financial gratification, and feel justified in their belief that the world is made up of givers and takers. They are skilled at camouflage (deception and manipulation), stalking and locating feeding grounds and watering holes. The reactions of psychopaths to the damage they have inflicted are more likely to be cool indifference and a sense of power, pleasure or smug satisfaction than regret or concern for what they have done. The ease with which psychopaths engage in violence has very real significance for society in general and for law enforcement personnel in particular (Hare, 1999; Logan, Hare and O'Toole, 2005; Woodworth and Porter, 2002).

Although not all psychopaths come into formal contact with the criminal justice system (Babiak and Hare, 2006; Hare, 1999), their defining features clearly place them at high risk for crime and violence. Many of the characteristics important for inhibiting antisocial and violent behaviour – empathy, close emotional bonds, fear of punishment, guilt – are lacking or seriously deficient in psychopaths. Moreover, their egocentricity, grandiosity, sense of entitlement, impulsivity, general lack of behavioural inhibitions, and need for power and control, constitute what might be described as the perfect prescription for asocial, antisocial, and criminal acts. As Silver, Mulvey, and Monahan (1999) put it, "Psychopathy's defining characteristics... make the conceptual link between violence and psychopathy straightforward" (p. 244). This would help to explain why psychopaths make up only about 1% of the general population but as much as a quarter of our prison populations. It also would explain why they find it so easy to victimize the vulnerable and to use intimidation and violence as tools to achieve power and control over others. Their violence is more gratuitous and sadistic than that of other offenders, and frequently is instrumental, callous and predatory in nature (Woodworth and Porter, 2002). These factors are significant for crime scene investigators (see O'Toole, 2007).

In a "camouflage society," a society in which some psychopathic traits- egocentricity, lack of concern for others, superficiality, style over substance, being "cool," manipulating others for personal gain are increasingly tolerated and even valued, it is easy to see how both psychopaths and those with APD could blend in readily with groups holding antisocial or criminal values (Hare, 1999). It is more difficult to envisage how these individuals could hide out among more prosocial segments of society. Yet psychopaths have little difficulty infiltrating the domains of business, politics, law enforcement, government, academia and other social structures (Babiak, 1995; Babiak and Hare, 2006). It is the egocentric, cold-blooded and remorseless psychopaths who blend into all aspects of society and have such devastating impacts on people around them that send chills down the spines of law enforcement officers. Consider, for example, the following rough estimates of the prevalence of psychopathy, as measured by the PCL-R: General population, 1%; Child molesters/pedophiles, 10%; Forensic psychiatric patients, 15%; Female offenders, 10%; Male offenders, 15-20%; Persistent spouse assaulters, 20%; Rapists, 35%; Killers of police, 45%; Hostage takers, 50%; Rapists who also molest children, 65%; Violent recidivists, 70%; Serial killers, 90%. These estimates are based on the use of a cut score of 30 for psychopathy (see section on Assessment of Psychopathy).

B. WHERE DO THEY COME FROM?

There is little doubt that a large proportion of criminals come from seriously dysfunctional and disruptive family backgrounds. Many might be described as *sociopathic* (Lykken, 1995), a term that has been applied to individuals whose antisocial attitudes and behaviours largely are molded by their early experiences, role models, and peer groups. Unlike psychopaths, who cannot be understood solely in terms of adverse social forces, they may have a capacity for empathy, remorse, and loyalty to their own group.

Although it is clear that adult psychopathy has to come from *somewhere*, the idea of looking for its biological roots in childhood is disturbing to those who believe that all behavioural problems result from early adverse social and environmental forces. For example, early child abuse often has been posited as a contributor to the development of psychopathy (Weiler and Widom 1996). But any association between child abuse and psychopathy is weak at best, not necessarily causal in nature, and more related to an impulsive and irresponsible lifestyle than to the capacity for empathy, guilt, or remorse (Poythress, Skeem, and Lilienfeld, 2006). Moreover, it is clear from recent research that genetic and biological factors and dispositions contribute significantly to the formation of the personality traits and temperament considered essential to the disorder (Blonigen, Hicks, Kreuger, Patrick, and Iacono, 2005; Larsson, Andershed, and Lichstenstien, 2006; Waldman and Rhee, 2006; Viding, Blair, Moffitt, and Plomin, 2005). Certainly, the traits and behaviours that define adult psychopathy begin to manifest themselves early in childhood (Frick and Marsee, 2006; Lynam, 1996). For example, Frick and Marsee (2006) have shown that callous-unemotional (CU) traits can be observed at a very early age and that these traits have considerable explanatory and predictive value. Lynam (2004) concluded that juvenile psychopathy can be measured at an early age, that it provides predictive utility, is quite stable from adolescence into early adulthood, and that it is unlikely that developmentally normative change will masquerade as psychopathy. The findings from behavioural genetics research are broadly consistent with the evolutionary psychology view that psychopathy is less a result of a neurobiological defect than a heritable, adaptive life-strategy (Harris and Rice, 2006. In this view, the early emergence of antisocial behaviour, including aggressive sexuality, is central to psychopathy. This is not to say that early experiences are unimportant in helping us to understand psychopathy. The lifelong *expression* of the disorder is certainly a product of complex interactions between biological/temperamental predispositions and social forces (MacDonald and Iacono, 2006).

There are several neurobiological and information-processing models of psychopathy. Blair and his colleagues (Blair, 2005; Blair, Blair, Mitchell, and Peschardt, 2005) have provided an extensive discussion of current models of psychopathy based on cognitive/affective neuroscience. Kiehl (2006; also see Kiehl, Bates, Laurens, Hare, and Liddle, 2006; Kiehl et al., 2004) has described a model in which "the relevant functional neuroanatomy of psychopathy includes limbic and paralimbic structures, which may be collectively termed the paralimbic system." Newman and his colleagues (e.g., Newman, Brinkley, Lorenz, Hiatt, and MacCoon, 2006) have conducted an extensive program of research involving cognitive/emotional processing deficits in psychopathy. Their model suggests that psychopaths fail to pay appropriate attention to the cues that others use to guide and control their behaviour. Models based on evolutionary psychology view psychopathy as less a disorder than an evolved "cheater" strategy for passing on one's gene pool (Harris and Rice, 2006). Some investigators consider psychopathy to be a pathological variant of normal personality (Hicklin and Widiger, 2006), while others describe and account for psychopathy in terms of psychodynamic mechanisms and processes (see Kernberg, 1984; Meloy, 1988).

For law enforcement, perhaps the most useful model is one that views psychopathy as a failure to appreciate the emotional significance of events (Hare, 1998a). Recent neuroimaging research indicates that normal people, but not psychopaths, make extensive use of structures in the limbic system (the "emotional brain") to process emotional material (Kiehl et al., 2001, 2004; Kiehl, Bates, Laurens, Hare, and Liddle, 2006). What is an emotional event or experience for most of us is more or less neutral for psychopaths. Like Spock on Star Trek, they find what should be an emotional event to be more "interesting" or "fascinating" than arousing, distressing, or pleasurable. For example, psychopaths respond to emotional words and pictures as if they were neutral in connotation (Hare, 1998a; Williamson, Harpur, and Hare, 1991; Kiehl et al., 2001). An important implication of this model is that we should not assume that a suspect necessarily thinks, feels, perceives the world, or uses language as we do. *Psychopathic* suspects do not think or feel as we do, do not fear what we fear, and do not spend very much time or effort in thinking about the consequences of their actions. With respect to language, an apt phrase is, "they know the words but not the music." Words such as "I love you," or "I'm really sorry I hurt you," often reflect only dictionary meaning, with little or no emotional connotation.

C. ASSESSMENT OF PSYCHOPATHY

The international standard for the assessment of psychopathy is the *Hare Psychopathy Checklist-Revised* (PCL-R; Hare, 1991; 2003). The extensive evidence for the reliability and validity of the PCL-R led the Buros 12th Mental Measurements Yearbook to describe it as "state of the art. . .both clinically and in research use" (Fulero, 1995). Following publication of the 2nd edition of the PCL-R (Hare, 2003), the 16th Mental Measurements Yearbook referred to it as "the gold standard for the assessment of psychopathy" (Acheson, 2005). The instrument has helped to fill a diagnostic and assessment void by providing researchers and clinicians with a common metric in an array of populations and contexts. Although the PCL-R was designed to measure the construct of psychopathy for research purposes, it is widely used as a key factor in assessing treatment options and risk for recidivism and violence. It also is used in American proceedings for civil commitment of sexually violent predators (SVPs), Canadian applications to have an offender declared a dangerous offender (DO) or long-term offender (LTO), and in U.K. designations of dangerous and severe personality disorder DSPD). The past decade has seen a sharp rise in its use by forensic clinicians (Archer, Buffingtom-Vollum, Stredny, and Handel, 2006; Lally, 2003) and in its acceptance by the courts (Walsh and Walsh, 2006). There have also been concerns (some overstated; e.g., Edens, 2006) about its potential for misuse (Hare, 1998a).

To ensure accurate diagnosis the PCL-R uses expert observer (i.e., clinical) ratings, based on a semi-structured interview, a review of case history materials such as criminal or psychiatric records, interviews with family members and employers, and supplemented with behavioural observations whenever possible. Specific scoring criteria are used to rate each of 20 items on a 3-point scale (0, 1, 2) according to the extent to which it applies to a given individual. Total scores can range from 0 to 40 and reflect the degree to which the individual matches the prototypical psychopath. The mean score is about 22-24 in offender populations, about 18-20 in forensic psychiatric populations, and less than 5 in the general population. A score of 30 typically is used as a convenient (though not absolute) cut score for psychopathy, although some investigators adopt less stringent cut scores for certain populations. In any event, scores in the 20+ range reflect a relatively heavy "dose" of psychopathic features. PCL-R assessments are highly reliable and valid when made by qualified clinicians and researchers. Statistical analyses indicate that 18 of the 20 PCL-R items cluster into four groups or factors (Table 1). Two items, *Promiscuous sexual behaviour* (Item 11), and *Many short-term marital relationships* (Item 17), contribute to the Total PCL-R score but do not fall into any of the clusters.

Table 1

Items and Factors in the Hare PCL-R	
Interpersonal	**Affective**
1. Glibness/superficial charm	6. Lack of remorse
2. Grandiose self-worth	7. Shallow affect
4. Pathological lying	8. Lack of empathy
5. Conning/manipulative	16. Will not accept responsibility
Lifestyle	**Antisocial**
3. Need for stimulation	10. Poor behavioural controls
9. Parasitic lifestyle	12. Early behavioural problems
13. Lack of goals	18. Juvenile delinquency
14. Impulsivity	19. Revocation conditional release
15. Irresponsibility	20. Criminal versatility

Note: The items are from Hare (1991, 2003). Copyright 1991 R.D. Hare and Multi-Health Systems, 3770 Victoria Park Avenue, Toronto, Ontario, M2H 3M6. All rights reserved. Reprinted by permission. Note that the item titles cannot be scored without reference to the formal criteria contained in the PCL-R Manual. Two items, *Promiscuous sexual behaviour* (Item 11), and *Many short-term marital relationships* (Item 17), contribute to the Total PCL-R score but do not load on any factors.

There are two direct derivatives of the PCL-R, the *Psychopathy Checklist: Screening Version* (PCL: SV; Hart, Cox, and Hare, 1995), and the *Psychopathy Checklist: Youth Version* (PCL: YV; Forth, Kosson, and Hare, 2003). The PCL: SV is a 12-item scale (see Table 2) that is frequently used as a screening tool or with non-forensic populations. The items are described in non-technical terms, with many examples, in *Without Conscience* (Hare, 1999). Scores can range from 0 to 24, with 18 often used as a cut score for psychopathy. The PCL: YV is a 20-item scale used with adolescents. Note that although the PCL: YV has the same descriptive and predictive properties as the PCL-R and PCL: SV, *it is not used to diagnose individuals as psychopathic*.

Table 2

Items and Factors in the Hare PCL: SV	
Interpersonal	**Affective**
1. Superficial	7. Impulsive
2. Grandiose	9. Lacking goals
3. Disloyal	10. Irresponsibility
Lifestyle	**Antisocial**
4. Feels no remorse	8. Poor behavioural controls
5. Lacks empathy	11. Antisocial behaviour as an adolescent
6. Does accept responsibility for his or her actions	12. Antisocial behaviour as an adult
Note: The items are from Hat, Cox and Hare (1995). © 1995 R.D. Hare and Multi-Health Systems, 3770 Victoria Park Avenue, Toronto, Ontario, M2H 3M6. All rights reserved. Reprinted by permission. Note that the item titles cannot be scored without reference to the formal criteria contained in the PCL: SV Manual.	

The PCL-R and APD

In some respects, the attributes measured by the PCL-R are similar to the criteria for antisocial personality disorder (APD) contained in DSM-IV. An important difference is that APD places heavy emphasis on delinquent and antisocial behaviour, whereas the PCL-R includes the personality traits traditionally used to describe psychopathy (Hare, 2003; Rogers, Salekin, Sewell, and Cruise, 2000; Widiger et al., 1996). In forensic populations the prevalence of APD is much higher (> 50%) than the prevalence of psychopathy (< 30%), resulting in an asymmetric association between the PCL-R and APD. In this respect, it is noteworthy that APD is strongly associated with the PCL-R lifestyle and antisocial factors, but only weakly associated with the PCL-R interpersonal and affective factors. Most psychopaths meet the criteria for APD, but most of the offenders with APD are not psychopaths. Rogers et al., (2000) had this to say about the situation: "DSM-IV does considerable disservice to diagnostic clarity in its equating of APD to psychopathy" (pp. 236-237). Or, as Lykken (2006, p. 4) put it, "Identifying someone as 'having' APD is about as nonspecific and scientifically unhelpful as diagnosing a sick patient as having a fever or an infectious or a neurological disorder." (p. 211-212). The PCL-R and its derivatives do *not* measure the same construct as does APD.

D. PSYCHOPATHY CRIME[2]

In the past few years there has been a dramatic change in the perceived and actual role played by psychopathy in the criminal justice system. Formerly, a prevailing view was that clinical diagnoses such as psychopathy were of little value in understanding and predicting criminal behaviours. As indicated earlier, however, the features that describe psychopathy constitute the perfect prescription for asocial, antisocial, and criminal acts (Hare, 2003; Porter and Porter, 2007). This would help to explain why psychopaths make up only about 1% of the general population but as much as a quarter of our prison populations. It also would explain why they find it so easy to victimize the vulnerable and to use intimidation and violence as tools to achieve power and control over others.

1. Assessment of Risk

Extensive discussions of the theories and methodologies of risk assessment are provided elsewhere (e.g., see Monahan and Steadman, 1994; Monahan et al., 2001; Quinsey, Harris, Rice, and Cormier, 1998). The latest generation of risk assessment instruments has largely dispelled the belief that useful predictions cannot be made about criminal behaviour. Much of the recent debate is concerned with the relative effectiveness of actuarial instruments and structured clinical assessments. The former are empirically-derived sets of static (primarily criminal history, demographic) risk factors, and include the *Violent Risk Appraisal Guide* (VRAG; Quinsey et al., 1998), and the *Sex Offender Risk Appraisal Guide* (SORAG; Quinsey et al., 1998), instruments that improve considerably on unstructured clinical judgments or impressions. However, procedures that include *structured* clinical decisions based on specific criteria are proving to be at least as good as purely actuarial scales. For example, the *HCR-20: Assessing risk for violence* (Webster, Douglas, Eaves, and Hart, 1997) assesses 10 historical (H) variables, 5 clinical (C) variables, and 5 risk management (R) variables. Because of the importance of psychopathy in the assessment of risk, the PCL-R or the PCL: SV is one of the variables (often the most predictive) included in the VRAG, SORAG, and HCR-20. In many cases, the PCL-R or PCL: SV

---

2 Much of this section is based on Hare (2006a).

have the same predictive power on their own as the larger risk battery in which they are embedded.

Validated risk tools are important for helping to determine "the likelihood a sexual offender will be unable to control his sexual impulses and cause more injury, pain, or other evil" (test set out by s. 753(1) (b) CCC). The Nova Scotia Court of Appeal urged judges to give more weight to these instruments than to clinical observation in determining a dangerous offender designation (The Lawyers Weekly, Nov. 29, 2002).

2. Recidivism and Violence

A detailed account of psychopathy as a risk for recidivism and violence is beyond the scope of this article. However, its significance as a robust risk factor for institutional problems, for recidivism in general, and for violence in particular, is now well established (see meta-analyses and reviews by Dolan and Doyle, 2000; Douglas, Vincent, and Edens, 2006; Gendreau, Goggin, and Smith, 2002; Hemphill, 2007; Hemphill and Hare, 2004; Porter and Woodworth, 2006; Salekin, Rogers, and Sewell, 1996). The predictive value of psychopathy applies not only to adult male offenders but to adult female offenders (e.g., Verona and Vitale, 2006), adolescent offenders (e.g., Edens, Campbell, and Weir, 2007; Forth, et al. 2003; Gretton, Hare, and Catchpole, 2004; Stafford and Cornell, 2003), forensic psychiatric patients, including those with Axis I disorders (e.g., Doyle, Dolan, and McGovern, 2002; Hill, Rogers, and Bickford, 1996; Heilbrun et al., 1998; Rice and Harris, 1992; Tengström, Grann, Långström, and Kullgren, 2000), and civil psychiatric patients (Douglas, Ogloff, and Nicholls, 1997; Steadman et al., 1999).

The study by Steadman et al. (1999) is of particular interest. It was a report of the MacArthur Foundation's findings on risk for violence in civil psychiatric patients. The most extensive and thorough study of its sort ever conducted, it evaluated 134 potential predictors of violence in 939 patients following discharge from a civil psychiatric facility. In presenting their results, the authors used a "classification tree" approach in which a hierarchy of decisions is made about the risk posed by a given patient. The single best predictor was the PCL: SV, developed for use in the study. In this scheme, the first decision is whether or not the patient has a PCL: SV score of 13 or more. Silver et al., (1999) used a sub-sample of these patients to investigate the impact that neighbourhood factors have on individual risk factors for violence in discharged patients. Again, the single best predictor of violence was the PCL: SV. Although patients discharged into neighbourhoods with "concentrated poverty" generally were at higher risk for violence than were those discharged into neighbourhoods with less poverty, this did not apply to patients with high PCL: SV scores. That is, their risk of the latter patients was independent of the neighbourhood into which they were discharged.

In a recent reanalysis of the MacArthur data, Vitacco, Neumann, and Jackson (2005) found that the two of the four PCL: SV factors (affective, antisocial) were strongly correlated with violence at 20 weeks. Harris, Rice, and Camilleri (2004) applied a modified 10-item version of the VRAG to the MacArthur data and reported that its predictive validity was almost as high as that of the classification tree approach used by Steadman et al. (1999). Of the items in this version of the VRAG, the PCL: SV was by far the best predictor. Harris et al. commented that even if the base rate of psychopathy or psychopathic features in a population is relatively low, "... the personality traits associated with psychopathy are among the most important causes of aggression" (p. 1070). Further, they stated that the fact that "psychopathy is such a robust predictor of violence across populations suggests that personality traits associated with psychopathy must be among its most important causes" (p. 1072).

3. Sexual Violence

The last few years have seen a sharp increase in public and professional attention paid to sex offenders, particularly those who commit a new offense following release from a treatment program or prison. It has long been recognized that psychopathic sex offenders present special problems for therapists and the criminal justice system. Quinsey, Rice, and Harris (1995) concluded from their research that psychopathy functions as a general predictor of sexual and violent recidivism. Not only are the offences of psychopathic sex offenders likely to be more violent than those of other sex offenders, they tend to be more sadistic (Hare, 2003; Harris, Rice, Quinsey, Lalumière, and Boer, 2003). In extreme cases, for example, among serial killers, comorbidity of psychopathy and sadistic personality is very high (Hare, Cooke, and Hart, 1999; Stone, 1998). In their PCL-R study of murderers, Porter, Woodworth, Earle, Drugge, and Boer (2003) concluded that "not only are psychopathic offenders disproportionately more likely to engage in sexual homicide (than are other murderers), but, when they do, they use significantly more gratuitous and sadistic violence" (p. 467).

One of the most potent combinations to emerge from the recent research on sex offenders is psychopathy coupled with evidence of deviant sexual arousal. Rice and Harris (1997) reported that sexual recidivism was strongly predicted by a combination of a high PCL-R score and deviant sexual arousal, defined by phallometric evidence of a preference for deviant stimuli, such as children, rape cues or nonsexual violence cues. Several studies indicate that psychopathy and behavioural or structured clinical evidence of deviant sexual arousal is also a strong predictor of sexual violence (Harris and Hanson, 1998; Hildebrand, de Ruiter, and de Vogel, 2004; Serin, Mailloux, and Malcolm, 2001). Gretton, McBride, O'Shaughnessy, Kumka, and Hare (2001) found that this combination was highly predictive of general and violent re-offending in adolescent sex offenders. Recently, Harris et al. (2003) reported that in a large-sample study involving four sites, the psychopathy-sexual deviance combination was predictive of violent recidivism in general, both sexual and nonsexual. The authors commented, "[b]ecause of the robustness of this (psychopathy and sexual deviance) interaction and its prognostic significance, its inclusion in the next generation of actuarial instruments for sex offenders should increase predictive accuracy" of general violent recidivism.

4. Treatment

Unlike most other offenders, psychopaths suffer little personal distress, see little wrong with their attitudes and behaviour, and seek treatment only when it is in their best interests to do so, such as when seeking probation or parole. Not surprisingly, they derive little benefit from traditional prison programs, particularly those aimed at the development of empathy, conscience, and interpersonal skills (Harris and Rice, 2006; Richards, Casey, and Lucente, 2003; Wong and Hare, 2005). Indeed, there have been reports that some programs designed to modify the behaviour of psychopathic offenders resulted in an *increase* in post-release criminal behaviour (Hare, Clark, Grann, and Thornton, 2000; Rice, Harris, and Cormier, 1992). These were group therapy and insight-oriented programs that presumably help psychopaths to develop better ways of manipulating, deceiving, and using people, but do little to help them to understand themselves. Programs that do not take into account the nature of psychopathic offenders are unlikely to be effective. Hobson, Shine, and Roberts (2000) found that offenders with high PCL-R scores obtained on admission to a well-developed prison therapeutic community program engaged in a variety of counter-productive behaviours during later therapy sessions. These behaviours included manipulation of the system to satisfy a personal need for power, control, and prestige, playing "head games" with other inmates and staff, continually testing the boundaries, exploitation of other patients, and a lack of genuine interest in changing their own attitudes and behaviours. Nevertheless, they managed to manipulate and fool some staff into thinking their efforts were sincere and that they were making good progress. Presumably, psychopathic suspects will use similar manipulative tactics with law enforcement officers.

E. PSYCHOPATHY AND THE LIFE COURSE PERSISTENT OFFENDER

Although psychopathy is closely associated with antisocial and criminal behaviour, psychopaths are qualitatively different from others who routinely engage in criminal behaviour, including those whose criminal conduct is extremely serious and persistent. The typical criminal career is relatively short, but there are individuals who devote most of their adolescent and adult life to delinquent and criminal activities. Among these persistent offenders are psychopaths, who begin their antisocial and criminal activities at a relatively early age, and continue to engage in these activities throughout much their lives. Their behavioural patterns may include biting and hitting at age 4, shoplifting at age 10, selling drugs and stealing cars at age 15, rape and robbery at age 20, and fraud and domestic assault at age 30. The patterns are cross-situational and may include cheating at school, lying at home, stealing at work, fighting in bars, drunk driving, spouse abuse, erratic work histories, unpaid debts, multiple unstable relationships, child abuse, and serious criminal acts (Tremblay, 2000).

As continuity is the hallmark of the life-course-persistent antisocial individual, discontinuity is the hallmark for the adolescence-limited antisocial type, whose antisocial behaviours decrease dramatically with the approach of adulthood. Adolescence-limited antisocial behaviour largely involves mimicry of successful, antisocial models, a strategy that may be abandoned when prosocial behaviours are more valuable or rewarding (Moffitt, 1993).

Exposure to peer models in puberty is an important determinant of adolescence-onset cases of delinquency. From an adult perspective, we might wonder why normal children would want to hang around with those we consider to be losers. However, many adolescents covet the freedom and autonomy of their life-course-persistent and potentially psychopathic peers. Healthy adolescents may notice that the style of the life-course-persistent individuals resembles adulthood and maturity in which they make their own decisions and rules relatively free of family restraints. Life-course-persistent youths have opportunity and possessions obtained by theft or vice that otherwise are inaccessible to teens. They are more experienced sexually and live on the fast track, taking risks and doing dangerous things that appeal to those who wish to break away from parental restraint. Moffitt

(1993) describes the life-course-persistent youths as magnets for novice delinquents during adolescence; they serve as models and trainers for recruits within deviant peer networks. Social mimicry of delinquency can range from an active education of recruits to motivated learners observing antisocial models from a distance.

Many adolescence-limited youths fall into the snares that entangle life-course-persistent persons (i.e., drug addiction, incarceration, teen pregnancy), making it difficult for them to desist from antisocial behaviours. The adolescence-limited youths are relatively free from personality disorder and cognitive deficits and in general have adequate social skills, academic achievement, and intelligence, and are better able to form close relationships than their life-course-persistent counterparts. At the crossroads of young adulthood, adolescence-limited and life-course persistent delinquents go different ways. This happens because the developmental histories and personal traits of adolescence-limiteds allow them the option of exploring new life pathways. The histories and traits of the life-course-persistents have foreclosed their options, entrenching them in the antisocial path (Moffitt, 1993, p. 691).

The research on the life-course-persistent offender highlights or "spotlights" a small group of individuals (5% of the population) who demand our attention, not only because they are models for the formation of deviant peer groups but because they commit over 50% of serious and violent crime in our society. Dealing with these individuals requires early detection and intervention, using a multi-disciplinary approach that involves educators, social workers, mental health professionals, police, corrections, prosecutors and judges (Logan, 1995).

F. POLICING: IMPLICATIONS AND APPLICATIONS

Psychopathic criminals are high-risk, high-density offenders, responsible for a disproportionate amount of serious crime. Understanding their personality and behavioural traits allows us to develop appropriate investigative and management strategies for dealing with them effectively. Although psychopathy should be diagnosed by a mental health professional with specialized training, the traits specified in the PCL-R and the PCL: SV are often detectable by skilled and experienced law enforcement personnel. To facilitate their efforts, we are presently working on an "I-Scan" to be used by police investigators to detect psychopathy. This will be a computer-based tool with which a suspect or target can be scored using a simple rating scheme. Immediate feedback will be provided to the investigator, along with recommended strategies for communication, interviewing, negotiations, and undercover work (see abbreviated examples in Appendix A and B). Behavioural Science Units within the FBI and RCMP can be reached for clarification and for assistance with crime scene analysis, crime cycle analysis, indirect personality assessment, and direct personality assessment.

G. INTERVIEWING AND NEGOTIATING WITH THE PSYCHOPATHIC OFFENDER

It is paramount that a police interviewer or negotiator should learn as much as possible about a "target" prior to initial contact. In particular, police officers should use whatever sources are available to them to provide in-depth information about individuals known to be "high risk offenders." Perhaps the best source of this knowledge comes through our partners in Corrections. In Canada, the Correctional Service of Canada (CSC) and their provincial counterparts are pleased to work with us in active investigation of an offender. Both National Law and Policy allow them to interact with us freely, providing us with all reports pertaining to the particular offender being investigated. The ability to have information about psychological and psychiatric assessments, including actuarial and PCL-R or PCL: SV ratings, can provide a basis for developing effective interview or negotiation strategies. Such information may allow the police officer to speculate about whether or not the target or person of interest (POI) is likely to have the capacity for empathy or for an emotional connection to someone else. If there is no indication that the POI is psychopathic, then the investigator can look for emotional hooks that could be used with, for example, a barricaded individual, an apparently suicidal person, or in an interview. Those emotional hooks are often people who are precious to the individual (i.e., children). If the officer believes that the POI may be psychopathic it is unlikely that the usual emotional hooks will be effective. Police can, however, learn other techniques with a suspected psychopathic individual, including appeals to the individual's sense of importance and self-interest.

Appendix A discusses strategies for using psychopathic traits to establish truthful and fruitful lines of communication in the face of a barrier, whether physical (as in hostage negotiations) or psychological (as in attempting to obtain a confession). The following factors can help in developing a strategy for dealing with someone suspected of being psychopathic.

1. **Ego dominant.** Psychopaths have a grossly inflated sense of self and are often opinionated and cocky in their presentation. They are quick to extol their attributes and accomplishments. The interviewer/negoti-

ator strokes the ego in an effort to build rapport and bridge the communication gap.

2. **Charismatic**. Psychopaths may exude charm and appear completely at ease in what should be a stressful situation. There are several reasons for this ease of interaction, including a general lack of social anxiety, and enjoyment at having the "edge" or in "playing head games" with others. Their interactions may appear pseudo-intellectual or "too clever," and will often reflect a "duping delight" when they feel they are superior to others or that they hold the best hand.

3. **Impulsive**. Although psychopaths often use violence that is instrumental (planned and goal directed) in nature, they also can act in an impulsive manner. Understanding the psychopath's impulsivity allows us to understand and use their "it seemed like the right thing to do at the time" mentality.

4. **Proneness to boredom**. The psychopath's need for stimulation and proneness to boredom means that time may be on our side in a hostage/barricade situation or in a lengthy interview.

5. **Grandiose**. The need to feel respected by someone who is respected allows the arresting officers or the undercover team to build up the interviewer as "the top dog" or "the boss." This can set up a desire for the psychopath to want to relate to that individual.

6. **Strives for recognition**. A narcissistic and grandiose individual wants to be seen as a "solid guy." The co-construction of a strategy that allows him or her to feel important and to have a degree of control should be the goal.

7. **Manipulative**. One of the keys to understanding psychopaths is understanding that it's all about them. Their need to gratify themselves and their lack of empathy is a brutal combination. They use insincere charm and manipulation to get what they want. If that doesn't work they will use other tactics in their behavioural repertoire, including intimidation and violence.

8. **Abrasive and derogatory**. The charm that is often seen can vanish quickly if the psychopath perceives that it's not working. It can be replaced by an aggressive and abrasive personality that worked for

them in the past. Staying professional and business-like will let investigators deflect the barrage and show the POI that they cannot be bullied.

9. **Little fear**. Clinical and neuroimaging research indicates that psychopaths do not experience the same depth of emotions (including fear) that we do. A heavy handed, threatening strategy is unlikely to be successful with these individuals.

10. **Consequences not a factor**. The possibility that their actions may result in going to jail or back to jail may have little impact on the decisions psychopaths make. They may be quick to remind the investigator that "having three squares a day" and not having to put up with "straight johns" is not a bad deal. In negotiations or in media releases involving an individual suspected of being psychopathic, it may be useful to remind the individual that only he has the power to choose not to create any more victims through his own actions.

11. **Blames others.** Psychopaths are quick to blame, rationalize, minimize, and deny. This is an opportunity for the interviewer/negotiator to do some "joining." We want to "join" the POI in any way we can, and as cops we can blame with the best! If the psychopathic individual wants to blame the "system" or "the old lady" the strategy is to join them and even use some self disclosure to reveal that "we think the same way." Joining is one of the precursors of rapport building.

12. **Underestimates problems**. Unable to accept blame, psychopaths are quick to minimize their involvement in something that reflects negatively on them. They also do not want to take on responsibility for their actions and deny that any real problems exist. The investigator gets a "foot in the door" by minimizing the problem or the extent of the damage or injury caused by the psychopath. This may facilitate disclosure by the suspect of at least some of the details of the offence.

13. **Exaggerates and lies**. "You know the psychopath is lying when you see his lips move" may be an overstatement, but the investigator should keep in mind that psychopaths "throw out a lot of shit" in the belief that some of it will stick. Their lies may be self-serving, a cover-up for the truth, or simply a means to impress others. An investigator may think that the suspect is lying and can use this to advantage later in the interview. Directly challenging the lies as they emerge may be counterproductive early in the interview and may be detrimental at any stage in negotiations with a psychopath.

14. **No Loyalty.** One of the things that differentiates the antisocial personality disordered (APD) individual from the psychopath is that the former can and often does have loyalty to a gang or deviant peer group. Psychopaths may fervently profess to having intense and everlasting loyalty to a group or code, but when it becomes a choice between this loyalty and their own self-interest, there is no contest. For this reason psychopaths often make great informants. Caution must be exercised, however, as the psychopath's charm and manipulation can turn a rookie cop or an unsuspecting veteran inside out, with the result that he "works" the investigator. Another caution is to negotiators in the use by psychopaths of third-party intermediaries. Having no true loyalty to another person, they may wish to speak to or for the intermediary for an ulterior motive. Parenthetically, psychopaths very seldom commit suicide, but if they do so it will be on their terms, perhaps with third-party intermediaries as an audience or as unwitting accomplices. It is likely that some "death by cop" scenarios are staged by psychopaths who want to go out in a blaze of glory, "exit stage left," cameras rolling.

15. **Sense of Entitlement.** If you think that teenagers believe the world owes them a living, introduce yourself to a psychopath. "What's mine is mine and what's yours should be mine" sums up their sense of entitlement. The male psychopath sees a woman in a relationship as "my woman" and often uses her as he would any other property. The psychopath may stalk and murder his "property," feeling justified because she didn't comply with his demands.

16. **Competitive.** Psychopaths see themselves as superior to others, and their stance during negotiations or an interview may be condescending or competitive (e.g., "I can take you"). They may also experience delight and satisfaction in being able to play the investigator. The result may be that the investigator's competitive spirit and desire to win may induce him to attempt to play the same game, with potentially negative consequences for the investigation. It is important to have a second negotiator or interviewer who can observe and influence what is happening.

H. INVESTIGATION AND THE PSYCHOPATHIC OFFENDER

A crime is like a play. We don't understand everything that is going on until we see all of the scenes. The denouement is the synergistic effect of the characters, their roles, the plots, theatrical techniques, even the reaction of the audience. So it is in a violent crime; as events evolve we learn more and more about the offender and his interaction with the victim(s). As things unfold, the dynamics change, and our perceptions of the victim-offender behaviours reflect these changes. In the end, the final scene or scenes reflect, behaviourally and forensically, the victim-offender interaction and the reasons the crime occurred, and we are provided with a much better look into the offender's psyche (O'Toole, 2006).

Our colleague, Special Supervisory Agent Mary Ellen O'Toole, Ph.D., is working on psychopathy as a behaviour classification system for violent and serial crime scenes. She is a "profiler" in the Federal Bureau of Investigation's (FBI) Behavioural Analysis Unit (BAU), part of the National Center for the Analysis of Violent Crime (NCAVC), located at the FBI Academy in Quantico, Virginia. She makes particular use of four traits from the psychopathic construct (impulsivity; sensation seeking; glib and superficial charm; and conning and manipulation) to better identify and interpret what appear to be psychopathic behaviours manifested at a violent crime scene. The selection of these traits (items in the Hare PCL-R) is based on the extensive research literature on psychopathy. The goal of her efforts is to apply what we know about psychopathy to crime-scene analysis in order to generate hypotheses about the nature of the perpetrator. The work is a reflection of collaboration among the FBI BSU in Virginia, the RCMP Behavioural Science Group (BSG) in British Columbia, and the authors of this chapter (for more details see Hare, 2006b).

The BSG in British Columbia conducts criminal investigative analysis and crime scene analysis related to the *unknown* offender. The BSG is also involved in work with the *known* offender, with special attention to the high risk offender, many of whom are psychopathic. As part of the latter work, the BSG develops intelligence networks that capture any and all information available for high risk offenders. It begins with the creation of a template for the most salient factors that research has indicated tend to be associated with the particular crime type. The template constructed for the *Integrated Sexual Predator Intelligence Network* (I-SPIN) captures actuarial and other risk factors identified in the research literature on crime. A similar template for *Threat to Criminal Justice Official* (TCJO) is under construction.

Once the I-Spin template is constructed for a given crime type, the files of individuals deemed to be at highest risk are collected, analyzed, given a score and placed in the network. All information available from police, corrections, and the courts is gathered and placed in electronic folders. A comprehensive reporting form is then constructed. This form contains information relating to description, level of dangerousness, victim target group, known residences, associates, vehicles, psychological profile, crime cycle, release conditions, and recommendations to investigators for interview, negotiation, and undercover strategies. This report accompanies any report to Crown counsel (prosecutor) on future charges or breaches, and is submitted to the courts by the Crown. In many cases a letter of opinion from the criminal/investigative psychologist in the BSG is also submitted to the courts.

Once the network is set up, every known sex offender is mapped. In British Columbia there currently are some 1400 such offenders in I-SPIN (about 30% being considered a high risk offender). All of the known locations frequented by each offender are plotted on the electronic mapping system. Locations are color-coded to reflect the template score given to each offender. The relevance of this system is obvious; should there be a sexual assault or kidnapping in a particular location, the mapping system will identify the most likely suspects. The goal of the programs is to allow police to proactively provide safer homes and communities.

1. Partnerships

Law enforcement agencies work alongside corrections officials, who provide file information on high-risk offenders, including actuarial risk and psychopathy assessments. The police work with their correctional partners to monitor high-risk offenders, paying close attention to observations or information indicating movement into a crime cycle.

Collaboration with other police agencies is also crucial. For instance, RCMP and municipal police officers in British Columbia work together on *Integrated Sexual Predator Observation Teams* (ISPOTS) to follow high-risk offenders who have been released on parole or probation, with conditions imposed by the court. If a team has behavioural evidence that a given high risk offender is returning to his crime cycle, it can select and implement an appropriate intervention strategy.

Police in behavioural sciences also work closely with Crown prosecutors and judges to provide information on high risk offenders, psychopathy, crime cycle progression, and breaches of conditional release.

2. Assessment and Selection

Police use a ten-point scale to assess high-risk offenders on the I-SPIN Template. Five points are based on scores from actuarial risk instruments. The other five points are based on factors that research has shown to be highly predictive of violent recidivism. These factors include psychopathy, deviant sexual arousal, low impulse control, previous violence, sadistic elements, and the offender's immediate environment. Once assessed, police can determine which individuals are likely the most dangerous to the public and the most likely to re-offend.

3. Training

To solidify the partnership between corrections and policing, training is offered to help all stakeholders develop skills and knowledge in detecting crime cycle progression. They receive training in how to identify paraphilia (an individual's sexual arousal to unusual or socially unacceptable objects or acts) deviant fantasy, crime cycle and predatory behaviour, all of which are high-risk indicators.

4. Enforcement Goals

The goals of law enforcement officers are to reduce sexual violence and sexual exploitation by focusing on those offenders deemed to be at high risk for sexual re-offending. By conducting short-term surveillance on high-risk offenders living in the community under court-imposed conditions, they can ascertain the level of non-compliance with those conditions. Non-compliance with conditions is the most evident form of a return to a crime cycle. A high risk offender being unlawfully at large is a clear indication of a crime cycle and a concerted effort must be made to apprehend this individual. Police can then arrest and take before the court high-risk sexual predators that have entered a crime cycle and are breaching their conditional release orders.

Perhaps the most integral part of the enforcement initiative with the sexual predator is the use of the ISPOTs. These teams, ideally full-time units of 10 police officers, are trained in surveillance techniques as well as in understanding sexual offenders and their specific crime cycles.

5. Crime Cycle

A crime cycle can be determined for each sexual offender with previous sexual offences. It illustrates an offender's behavioural progression to another victim. Often these crime cycles have been written down by the offender while in a prison therapy program. It is very helpful if this written account can be obtained. Otherwise, the investigator must piece together the elements that constitute the offender's crime cycle and that move him to the next victim.

> Feelings of rejection and abandonment → frustration with inability to do something → feeling like a loser → masturbate → find woman to masturbate in front of → vengeful → rejected → get wasted → bored → steal car or bike → stalk victim → masturbate in bathroom stall or park.

This is an abbreviated form of a crime cycle given by a psychopathic offender who was known as an exhibitionist. Within 24 hours of being released from prison he was back into his crime cycle. After consuming alcohol and stealing a bike he went to a park and began to masturbate in front of a two-year-old girl. The girl's grandmother saw him and tried to chase him away. The offender took his knife and repeatedly stabbed the grandmother leaving his knife in the woman's eye socket.

A crime cycle is the progression of thought, emotion, and behaviour that leads to sexual re-offending (i.e., stress, leading to violent sexual fantasy, moving to drug/alcohol consumption, initiating hunting or predatory behaviour which culminates in impulsive or instrumental acts of violence). By developing a clear understanding of high-risk traits and factors, and identifying the progression of a crime cycle, police can play a critical role in keeping the most dangerous offenders from repeating their cycle of violence.

I. INTRODUCING PSYCHOPATHY TO THE COURTS

In 2004 the authors spoke at the Crown Counsel Spring Conference in Harrison Hot Springs. BC. They introduced the research on psychopathy and its implications for policing. On May 6, 2005, they addressed the Judges Spring Conference in Penticton, B.C., on the topics of psychopathy, sexual predators, and I-SPIN. Since then, several workshops and presentations have been provided to the criminal justice community, including the National Parole Board. Perhaps the greatest impact of the education has been in the recent sentencing of high-risk sexual offenders. In 2005 the courts handed down sentences of 15 months or two years on breaches of condition and have noted the work of the authors and the BSG in their reasons for sentencing. Letters of opinion and risk assessments for police [Appendix B] are written by the criminal/investigative psychologist and are often referred to by the courts in reasons for judgment. The following was written by a B.C. court judge in sentencing a psychopathic, high-risk sex offender to a maximum and consecutive sentence, plus a period of supervision:

> Also filed in regards to these proceedings is a risk assessment, authored by Sergeant Matt Logan, who is a doctor of psychology. This report was prepared in March 2004, which it will be noted was prior to any of the breaches of Mr. X's recognizance. In words that seem prophetic, given that they were written prior to the problems surfacing in the summer of this year, Dr. Logan concluded his report with this:
>
> While I support a healthy relationship for X, I am also concerned about two things: First that he is looking at this relationship as the silver bullet to have all of his problems laid to rest. I am concerned that the relationship centres on sex, and in particular, bondage and S and M. While this may be consensual within this relationship, what happens when the distance relationship becomes too stressful or if it ends suddenly? I trust that the new regime of therapy will continue to address core issues. Secondly, I am concerned about the presence of Ms. Y's daughter, who is right in the target range of Mr X's fantasy regarding promiscuous teenagers. X and I discussed this concern and he had already considered the fact that this girl is "13 going on 21," and has a group of promiscuous friends she is hanging around with these days. X agreed this would not be a good environment for him, but then later talked about going down to visit Ms. Y and her daughter. Finally, this is an individual who is obsessed with sex and was open enough to acknowledge that when alone in waking hours he seldom stops masturbating. At the present time he seems to be absorbed in a sexual world with a woman and much of his time is spent online with her. This seems to be a mitigating factor to sexual re-offending, but may be temporary. X acknowledges that his fantasies give him an adrenalin rush, and that they are progressive. He noted that, "they don't give me the same rush after the third time, so I have to add to it."

1. Threat to Criminal Justice Officials—A Post Mayerthorpe Initiative

On March 3, 2005 in Mayerthorpe, Alberta four RCMP officers were killed in the line of duty. They were ambushed and shot to death in cold blood by a known criminal described by members of the community as dangerous and reclusive. This massacre might have been prevented had the police been thoroughly briefed on the risk posed by the killer. The Mayerthorpe killings contributed to initiatives designed to coordinate information about high-risk offenders and to protect not only the public but law enforcement personnel.

2. Threat to Criminal Justice Officials (TCJO)

The TCJO initiative focuses on the risk posed by individuals who are identified as dangerous to police or other criminal justice officials, including police officers, Crown lawyers (provincial or federal, criminal and civil), judiciary and jury members, sheriffs, and corrections officials. The risk evaluation requires examination of available case materials and background information regarding the subject and potential victims. *Risk enhancing* and *risk reducing* factors, which are often dynamic and responsive to changing circumstances, are identified and articulated in a written report. These factors are derived from statistical information based on research conducted by experts in various fields, including psychiatry, psychology, law enforcement, and threat assessment. They are used, along with a review of the subject's current circumstances, to estimate the level of risk involved in the situation: *no risk*, *low risk*, *moderate risk*, *high risk,* or *imminent* risk. An operational plan, based on the identified risk factors and a realistic appraisal of the capabilities of the agency or agencies responsible for intervening and managing the risk, is recommended.

In every policing jurisdiction in Canada, the police are aware of individuals who pose an elevated risk to police officers due to mental illness, psychopathy, personality disorders or being career criminals. However, most if not all agencies, do not have a strategy to deal with these individuals and therefore lack specific tactical response plans. Mayerthorpe is an example of a worst case scenario, but police officers often find themselves in potentially life-threatening situations without sufficient information about the risks they face.

The determination that an individual is dangerous to police involves the gathering of as much relevant information as possible about his or her interests, the acquisition of intelligence, an analysis of the reasons for the anti-police attitude, an assessment of the risks in various circumstances (chance encounter, vehicle stop, arrest away from the residence, entry onto property or into residence, and hostage/barricaded situations). This evaluation and the recommendations would then be used by the agency of jurisdiction to develop a tactical response plan(s) for dealing with the individual.

The RCMP Behavioural Sciences Group in E Division, Major Crime, uses an empirical approach to assess threat and risk for violence. The Threat Evaluation and Management (TEAM) Unit and the criminal/investigative psychologist provide risk assessments of persons dangerous to police. The criminal/Investigative psychologist also constructs templates based on research and related experiences that can help identify the individuals most dangerous to criminal justice officials. Targets are identified by police agencies and integrated teams formed to apply a research template, gather information, extract and analyze the key information, and finally, to develop plans for tactical communication and tactical operations. There will always be potential assailants who fly under the radar, but the judicious use of trained threat evaluation units can reduce the threat they pose to those responsible for criminal justice.

REFERENCES

Acheson, S. K. (2005). Review of the Hare Psychopathy Checklist-Revised, 2nd Edition. In R. A. Spies and B. S. Plake (Eds.), *The sixteenth mental measurements yearbook* (pp. 429-431). Lincoln, NE: Buros Institute of Mental Measurements.

Archer, R. P., Buffington-Vollum, J. K., Stredney, R. V., and Handel, R. W. (2006). A survey of psychological test use patterns among forensic psychologists. *Journal of Personality Assessment, 87*, 84-94.

American Psychiatric Association. (1994). *Diagnostic and Statistical Manual of Mental Disorders* (4th ed.). Washington: Author.

Babiak, P. (1995). When psychopaths go to work. *International Journal of Applied Psychology, 44,* 171-188.

Babiak, P., and Hare, R. D. (2006). *Snakes in suits: When psychopaths go to work.* New York: Harper/Collins.

Blair, R. J. R. (2005). Applying a cognitive neuroscience perspective to the disorder of psychopathy. *Development and Psychopathology, 17*, 865-891.

Blair, J. Blair, K., Mitchell, D. and Peschardt, K. (2005). *The psychopath: Emotion and the brain.* Malden MA: Blackwell.

Blonigen, D. M., Hicks, B. R., Kreuger, R. F., Patrick, C. J. and Iacono, W. G. (2005). Psychopathic personality traits: Heritability and genetic overlap with internalizing and externalizing psychopathology. *Psychological Medicine, 35*, 637-648.

Book, A. S., Clark, H. J., Forth, A. E., and Hare, R. D. (2006). The PCL-R and PCL: YV: Forensic applications and limitations In R. P. Archer (Ed.), *Clinical assessment instruments in forensic settings: Uses and Limitations* (pp. 147-179). Mahwah, NJ: Lawrence Erlbaum and Associates.

Dolan, M., and Doyle, M. (2000). Violence risk prediction: Clinical and actuarial measures and the role of the Psychopathy Checklist. *British Journal of Psychiatry, 177*, 303-311.

Douglas, K. S., Ogloff, J. R. P., and Nicholls, T. L. (1997, June). *Personality disorders and violence in civil psychiatric patients*. Paper presented at the 5th International Congress on the Disorders of Personality, Vancouver, British Columbia.

Douglas, K. S., Vincent, G. M., and Edens, J. F. (2006). Risk for criminal recidivism: The role of psychopathy. In C. J. Patrick (Ed.), *Handbook of Psychopathy* (pp. 533-554). New York: Guilford Press.

Doyle, M., Dolan, M., and McGovern, J. (2002). The validity of North American risk assessment tools in predicting in-patient violent behaviour in England. *Legal and Criminological Psychology, 7*, 141-154.

Edens, J. F. (2006). Unresolved controversies concerning psychopathy: Implications for clinical and forensic decision making. *Professional Psychology: Research and Practice, 37*, 59-65.

Edens, J. F., Campbell, J. S., and Weir, J. M. (2007). Youth psychopathy and criminal recidivism: A meta-analysis of the Psychopathy Checklist Measures. *Law and Human Behaviour*, 31, 53-75

Felthous, A., and Sass, H. (Eds.). (2007). *International handbook of psychopathic disorders and the law.* Vol. 1. New York: Wiley.

Forth, A. E., Kosson, D., and Hare, R. D. (2003). *The Hare Psychopathy Checklist: Youth Version.* Toronto, ON: Multi-Health Systems. (www.mhs.com).

Frick, P. J., and Marsee, M. A. (2006). Psychopathy and developmental pathways to antisocial behaviour in youth. In C. J. Patrick (Ed.), *Handbook of psychopathy* (pp. 353-374). New York: Guilford Press.

Fulero, S. M. (1995). Review of the Hare Psychopathy Checklist-Revised. In J. C. Conoley and J. C. Impara (Eds.), *The twelfth mental measurements yearbook* (pp. 453-454). Lincoln, NE: Buros Institute of Mental Measurements.

Gendreau, P., Goggin, C., and Smith, P. (2002). Is the PCL-R really the "unparalleled" measure of offender risk? A lesson in knowledge cumulation. *Criminal Justice and Behaviour, 29*, 397-426.

Gretton, H. M., Hare, R. D., and Catchpole, R. (2004). Psychopathy and recidivism in adolescent offenders: A ten year follow up. *Journal of Clinical and Consulting Psychology, 72*, 636-645.

Gretton, H. M., McBride, M., O'Shaughnessy, R., Kumka, G. and Hare, R. D. (2001). Psychopathy and recidivism in adolescent sex offenders. *Criminal Justice and Behaviour, 28*, 427-449.

Hare, R. D. (1991). *The Hare Psychopathy Checklist—Revised.* Toronto, ON: Multi-Health Systems. (www.mhs.com).

Hare, R. D. (1996). Psychopathy: A construct whose time has come. *Criminal Justice and Behaviour, 23*, 25-54.

Hare, R. D. (1998a). Psychopathy, affect, and behaviour. In D. J. Cooke, A. E. Forth, and R. D. Hare (Eds.), *Psychopathy: Theory, research, and implications for society* (pp. 105-137). Dordrecht, The Netherlands: Kluwer.

Hare, R.D. (1998b). The PCL-R assessment of psychopathy: Some issues and concerns. *Legal and Criminological Psychology,* 3, 101-122.

Hare, R. D. (1999). *Without conscience: The disturbing world of the psychopaths among us*. New York: Guilford Press.

Hare, R. D. (2002). Psychopathy and risk for recidivism and violence. In N. Gray, J. Laing, and L. Noaks (Eds.), *Criminal Justice, Mental Health, and the Politics of Risk* (pp. 27-47). London: Cavendish Publishing.

Hare, R. D. (2003). *The Hare Psychopathy Checklist-Revised.* 2nd Edition. Toronto, ON: Multi-Health Systems. (www.mhs.com).

Hare, R. D. (2006). Psychopathy: A clinical and forensic overview. *Psychiatric Clinics of North America, 29*, 709-724.

Hare, R. D., Clark, D., Grann, M., and Thornton, D. (2000). Psychopathy and the predictive validity of the PCL-R: An international perspective. *Behavioural Sciences and the Law, 18*, 623-645.

Hare, R. D., Cooke, D. J., and Hart, S. D. (1999). Psychopathy and sadistic personality disorder. In T. Millon, P. Blaney, and R. Davis (Eds.),

Oxford textbook of psychopathology (pp. 555-584). Oxford: Oxford University Press.

Hare, R. D., and Neumann, C. S. (2005). Structural models of psychopathy, *Current Psychiatry Reports, 7*, 57-64.

Hare, R. D., and Neumann, C. S. (2006). The PCL-R assessment of psychopathy: Development, structural properties, and new directions. In C. Patrick (Ed.), *Handbook of Psychopathy* (pp. 58-88). New York: Guilford Press.

Harris, A. J. R., and Hanson, R. K. (1998, October). *Supervising the psychopathic sex deviant in the community.* Paper presented at the 17th Annual Research and Treatment Conference, The Association for the Treatment of Sexual Abusers, Vancouver, Canada.

Harris, G. T., and Rice, M. E. (2006). The treatment of psychopaths. In C. Patrick (Ed.), *Handbook of psychopath* (pp. 555-572). New York: Guilford Press.

Harris, G. T., Rice, M. E., and Camilleri, J. A. (2004). Applying a forensic actuarial instrument (the Violence Risk Appraisal Guide) to nonforensic patients. *The Journal of Interpersonal Violence, 19*, 1063-1074.

Harris, G. T., Rice, M. E., Quinsey, V. L., Lalumière, M. L., and Boer, D. (2003). A multi-site comparison of actuarial risk instruments for sex offenders. *Psychological Assessment, 15*, 413-425.

Hart, S. D., Cox, D. N., and Hare, R. D. (1995). *The Hare Psychopathy Checklist: Screening Version.* Toronto, ON: Multi-Health Systems. (www.mhs.com).

Heilbrun, K., Hart, S. D., Hare, R. D., Gustafson, D., Nunez, C., and White, A. (1998). Inpatient and post-discharge aggression in mentally disordered offenders: The role of psychopathy. *Journal of Interpersonal Violence, 13,* 514-527.

Hemphill, J. F. (2007). The Hare Psychopathy Checklist and recidivism: Methodological issues and critical evaluation of empirical evidence. In H Hervé and J. Yuille (Eds.), *The psychopath: Theory, research, and practice* (pp. 141-170). Mahwah, NJ: Lawrence Erlbaum and Associates.

Hemphill, J. F., and Hare, R. D. (2004). Some misconceptions About the Hare PCL-R and Risk Assessment: A Reply to Gendreau, Goggin, and Smith. *Criminal Justice and Behaviour, 31*, 203-243.

Hervé, H., and Yuille, J. (Eds.) (2007). *The psychopath: Theory, research, and practice.* Mahwah, NJ: Lawrence Erlbaum and Associates.

Hicklin, J., and Widiger, T. A. (2005). Similarities and Differences Among Anti-social and Psychopathic Self-Report Inventories from the Perspective of General Personality. Functioning. *European Journal of Personality, 19*, 325-341.

Hildebrand, M., de Ruiter, C., and de Vogel, V. (2004). Psychopathy and sexual deviance in treated rapists: Association with (sexual) recidivism. *Sexual Abuse: A Journal of Research and Treatment, 16*, 1-24.

Hill, C. D., Rogers, R., and Bickford, M. E. (1996). Predicting aggressive and socially disruptive behaviour in a maximum security forensic psychiatric hospital. *Journal of Forensic Sciences, 41,* 56-59.

Hobson, J., Shine, J., and Roberts, R. (2000). How do psychopaths behave in a prison therapeutic community? *Psychology, Crime, and the Law, 6*, 139-154.

Kernberg, O. (1984). *Severe personality disorders.* New Haven: Yale University Press.

Kiehl, K. A. (2006). A cognitive neuroscience perspective on psychopathy: Evidence for paralimbic system dysfunction. *Psychiatry Research,* 142, 107-128.

Kiehl, K. A., Bates, A. T., Laurens, K. R., Hare, R. D., and Liddle, P. F. (2006). Brain potentials implicate temporal lobe abnormalities in criminal psychopaths. *Journal of Abnormal Psychology, 115*, 443-453.

Kiehl, K. A., Smith, A. M., Hare, R. D., Mendrek, A., Forster, B. B., Brink, J., and Liddle, P. F. (2001). Limbic abnormalities in affective processing by criminal psychopaths as revealed by functional magnetic resonance imaging. *Biological Psychiatry, 50*, 677-684.

Kiehl, K. A., Smith, A. M., Mendrek, A., Forster, B. B., Hare, R. D., and Liddle, P. F. (2004). Temporal lobe abnormalities in semantic processing by criminal psychopaths as revealed by functional magnetic resonance imaging. *Psychiatry Research: Neuroimaging, 130*, 27-42.

Lally, S. J. (2003). What tests are acceptable for use in forensic evaluations? A survey of experts. *Professional Psychology: Research and Practice, 34*, 491-498.

Larsson, H., Andershed, H., and Lichtenstein, P. (2006). A genetic factor explains most of the variation in the psychopathic personality. *Journal of Abnormal Psychology, 115*, 221-230.

Logan, M. H. (1995). *Deviant peer association.* Unpublished Paper.

Logan, M. H., Hare, R. D., O'Toole, M. E. (2005). The psychopathic offender. *The RCMP Gazette, 66*, 36-38.

Logan, M. H., and Pylypiak, S. (2005). *Integrated sexual predator intelligence network: A crime reduction strategy.* Unpublished Paper.

Lykken, D. T. (1995). *The antisocial personalities.* Hillsdale, NJ: Lawrence Erlbaum and Associates.

Lykken, D. T. (2006). Psychopathic personality: The scope of the problem. In C. Patrick (Ed.), *Handbook of Psychopathy* (pp. 3-13). New York: Guilford Press.

Lynam, D. R. (1996). Early identification of chronic offenders: Who is the fledgling psychopath? *Psychological Bulletin, 120,* 209-234.

Lynam, D. R. (2004). *Development and psychopathy.* Colloquium at the Department of Psychology, Northwestern University, Evanston, IL, November 4, 2004.

MacDonald, A. W., and Iacono, W. G. (2006). Toward an integrated perspective on the etiology on psychopathy. In C. J. Patrick (Ed.), *Handbook of psychopathy* (pp. 375-385). New York: Guilford Press.

Meloy, J. R. (1988). *The psychopathic mind: Origins, dynamics and treatment.* Northvale, NJ: Jason Aronson.

Meloy, J. R. (2000). *Violence risk and threat assessment.* San Diego, CA: Specialized Training Services.

Moffitt, T. E. (1993). Adolescent-limited and life-course persistent antisocial behaviour: A developmental taxonomy. *Psychological Review, 100*, 674-701.

Monahan, J. (2006). Comments on cover jacket of C. J. Patrick, Ed., *Handbook of psychopathy*. New York: Guilford Press.

Monahan, J., and Steadman, H. (1994). (Eds.). *Violence and mental disorder: Developments in risk assessment*. Chicago: University of Chicago Press.

Monahan, J. , Steadman, H. J., Silver, E., Appelbaum, P. S., Robins, P. C., Mulvey, E. P., Roth, L. R., Grisso, T., and Banks, S. (2001). *Rethinking risk assessment: The McArthur study of mental disorder and violence.* New York: Oxford University Press.

Newman, J. P., Brinkley, C. A., Lorenz, A. R., Hiatt, K. D., MacCoon, D. G. (2006). Psychopathy as psychopathology: Beyond the clinical utility of the Psychopathy Checklist–Revised. In H. Hervé and J. Yuille (Eds.), *The psychopath: Theory, research, and practice* (pp. 173-206). Mahwah, NJ: Lawrence Erlbaum and Associates.

O'Toole, M. E. (2007). Psychopathy as a Behaviour Classification System for Violent and Serial Crime Scenes. In H. Hervé and J. Yuille (Eds.), *The psychopath: Theory, research, and practice* (pp. 301-325). Mahwah, NJ: Lawrence Erlbaum and Associates.

Patrick, C. J. (Ed.) (2006). *Handbook of psychopathy*. New York: Guilford Press.

Porter, S., and Porter, S. (2007). Psychopathy and violent crime. In H. Hervé and J. Yuille (Eds.). *The psychopath: Theory, research, and practice* (pp. 287-300). Mahwah, NJ: Lawrence Erlbaum and Associates.

Porter, S., and Woodworth, M. (2006). Psychopathy and aggression. In C. J. Patrick (Ed.), *Handbook of psychopathy* (pp. 481-494). New York: Guilford Press.

Porter, S., Woodworth, M., Earle, J., Drugge, J., and Boer, D. (2003). Characteristics of sexual homicides committed by psychopathic and nonpsychopathic offenders. *Law and Human Behaviour, 27*, 459-470.

Poythress, N. G., Skeem, J. L., and Lilienfeld, S. O. (2006). Associations among early abuse, dissociation, and psychopathy in an offender sample. *Journal of Abnormal Psychology, 115*, 288-297.

Quinsey, V. L., Harris, G. E., Rice, M. E., and Cormier, C. (1998). *Violent and offenders: Appraising and managing risk.* Washington: American Psychological Association.

Quinsey, V. L., Rice, M. E., and Harris, G. T. (1995). Actuarial prediction of sexual recidivism. *Journal of Interpersonal Violence, 10,* 85-105.

Ramsland, K. (2005). *The human predator.* New York: Penguin Group.

Rice, M. E., and Harris, G. T. (1992). A comparison of criminal recidivism among schizophrenic and nonschizophrenic offenders. *International Journal of Law and Psychiatry, 15,* 397-408.

Rice, M. E., and Harris, G. T. (1997). Cross-validation and extension of the Violence Risk Appraisal Guide for child molesters and rapists. *Law and Human Behaviour, 21,* 231-241.

Rice, M. E., Harris, G. T., and Cormier, C. A. (1992). An evaluation of a maximum security therapeutic community for psychopaths and other mentally disordered offenders. *Law and Human Behaviour, 16,* 399-412.

Richards, H. J., Casey, J. O., and Lucente, S. W. (2003). Psychopathy And treatment response in incarcerated female substance abusers. *Criminal Justice and Behaviour, 30*, 251-276.

Rogers, R., Salekin, R. T., Sewell, K. W., and Cruise, K. R. (2000). Prototypical analysis of antisocial personality disorder: A study of inmate samples. *Criminal Justice and Behaviour, 27,* 234-255.

Salekin, R., Rogers, R., and Sewell, K. (1996). A review and meta-analysis of the Psychopathy Checklist and Psychopathy Checklist-Revised: Predictive validity of dangerousness. *Clinical Psychology: Science and Practice, 3,* 203-215.

Serin, R. C., Mailloux, D. L., and Malcolm, P. B. (2001). Psychopathy, sexual arousal, and recidivism. *Journal of Interpersonal Violence, 16,* 234-247.

Silver, E., Mulvey, E. P., and Monahan, J. (1999). Assessing violence risk among discharged psychiatric patients: Toward an ecological approach. *Law and Human Behaviour, 23,* 237-255.

Stafford, E., and Cornell, D. (2003). Psychopathy scores predict adolescent inpatient aggression. *Assessment, 10,* 102-112.

Steadman, H. J., Silver, E., Monahan, J., Appelbaum, P. S., Robbins, P. M., Mulvey, E. P., Grisso, T., Roth, L. H., and Banks, S. (1999). A classification tree approach to the development of actuarial violence risk assessment tools. *Law and Human Behaviour, 24,* 83-100.

Stone, M. H. (1998). The personalities of murderers: The importance of psychopathy and sadism. In A. E. Skodol (Ed.), *Psychopathology and violent crime* (pp. 29-52). Washington: American Psychiatric Association.

Tengström, A., Grann, M., Långström, N., and Kullgren, G. (2000). Psychopathy (PCL-R) as a predictor of violent recidivism among criminal offenders with schizophrenia. *Law and Human Behaviour, 24,* 45-58.

Tremblay, R. E. (2000). The development of aggressive behaviour during childhood: What have we learned in the past century? *International Journal of Behavioural Development*, 24, 129-141.

Verona, E., and Vitale, J. (2006). Psychopathy in women: Assessment, manifestations, and etiology. In C. Patrick (Ed.), *Handbook of psychopath* (pp. 415-436). New York: Guilford Press.

Viding, E., Blair, R. J. R., Moffitt, T. E., and Plomin, R. (2005). Evidence for substantial genetic risk for psychopathy in 7-year-olds. *Journal of Child Psychology and Psychiatry, 46*, 592-597.

Vitacco, M. J.., Neumann, C. S., and, Jackson, R. L. (2005). Testing a four-factor model of psychopathy and its association with ethnicity, gender, intelligence, and violence. *Journal of Consulting and Clinical Psychology, 73*, 466-476.

Waldman, I. D., and Rhee, S. H. (2006). Genetic and environmental influences on psychopathy and antisocial behaviour. In C. J. Patrick (Ed.), *Handbook of Psychopathy* (pp. 205-228). New York: Guilford Press.

Walsh, T., and Walsh, Z. (2006). The evidentiary introduction of Psychopathy Checklist-Revised assessed psychopathy in U.S. Courts: Extent and appropriateness. *Law and Human Behaviour, 30*, 493-507.

Webster, C., Douglas, K., Eaves, D., and Hart, S. (1997). *HCR-20 Assessing Risk for Violence: Version II.* Burnaby, BC: Mental Health, Law and Policy Institute, Simon Fraser University.

Weiler, B., and Widom, C. S. (1996). Psychopathy and violent behaviour in abused and neglected young adults. *Criminal Behaviour and Mental Health, 6,* 253-271.

Widiger, T. A., Cadoret, R., Hare, R. D., Robins, L., Rutherford, M., Zanarini, M., Alterman, A., Apple, M., Corbitt, E., Forth, A., Hart, S., Kulterman, J., and Woody, G. (1996). DSM-IV Anti-social Personality Disorder Field Trial. *Journal of Abnormal Psychology, 105,* 3-16.

Williamson, S. E., Harpur, T. J., and Hare, R. D. (1991). Abnormal processing of affective words by psychopaths. *Psychophysiology, 28*, 260-273.

Wong, S., and Hare, R. D. (2005). *Guidelines for a psychopathy treatment program.* Toronto, ON: Multi-Health Systems. (www.mhs.com).

Woodworth, M., and Porter, S. (2002). In cold blood: Characteristics of criminal homicides as a function of psychopathy. *Journal of Abnormal Psychology, 111*, 436-445.

APPENDIX A

Implications for Crisis (Hostage) Negotiators

Psychopathic Trait	Strategy
Ego Dominant	Feed to self-destruct
Charismatic	"Enlighten me"
Impulsive	Emotionless/cool
Prone to boredom	Time is on our side
Grandiose	Respect by respected
Strives for recognition	Co-construct "solid" option
Manipulative	Controlled choices
Abrasive/derogatory	Professional/business
Little fear	No threats/intimidation
Consequences not a factor	Face-saving out
Blames others	Use others' incompetence
Underestimates problem	Use minimization
Exaggerates/lies	Absorb and use later
No loyalty	Caution with TPI
Sense of entitlement	Stroke the ego
Competitive	Don't argue

APPENDIX B

Risk Assessments for Police (RAP) Program

Purpose:

To provide comprehensive reports, written for a police audience, where there is a clear appraisal of (a) the subject's risk to re-offend; (b) the subject's crime cycle; and (c) strategies for police intervention. These reports will be based on factual information and professional judgment. The subjects of these reports will be (a) high-risk offenders that are in the community or whose release is imminent; (b) suspects in a serious crime investigation; and (c) persons charged with a violent offence.

Access:

Police would have access on secure e-mail and InfoNet. Corrections, Crown counsel and judges could also gain access to the reports in determining sentencing and conditions for release.

Benefits:

Reports based on review of institutional files that summarizes psychological/psychiatric assessments, pre-sentence reports, assessments for decision, correctional plans (CSC), post-treatment reviews, crime autobiographies from treatment programs, reports to crown counsel, VICLAS reports, and any other available documentation.

Completion of Psychological Risk Assessment, if not available, that could include PCL-R, VRAG, HCR-20 and other instruments specific to the crime type. An interview of the subject can be attempted with proper informed consent procedure or within the condition of parole that stipulates "assessment as directed by parole officer."

This is a sample of the final page of a RAP (Risk Assessment for Police). It makes recommendations and proposes strategies for dealing with a suspect or target; in this case, a psychopathic individual:

Considerations/Implications for Police

This is a conning, manipulative, egocentric liar who is also callous with no remorse or empathy for his victims. He is a psychopath with a strong similarity in profile to the other person of interest in the C. murder. The strongest similarity is in the personality profile which indicates both suspects are psychopathic with strong antisocial, narcissistic, and sadistic traits. The next similarity is in their sexual preference with the predominate target group being young females. Another notable similarity is that both enjoy having an audience to their sexual exploits. These factors add credibility to the assumption that they were both actively involved in the sexual assault and murder of C.

A. will continue to prey on adolescent girls and will use a woman to recruit or legitimize his presence with young women. He is quite capable of disposing of victims after using them since he has already served federal time as a result of victim testimony. Since he has already been involved in at least three murders (disposing of victim), it will not be a difficult decision for him.

This is a psychopathic sex offender. Research indicates that 64% of these individuals are polymorphous or mixed molesters/rapists (Porter, 2000). This means that, although he has a preference for intercourse with 13-17 yr. old girls, he might also rape adult women or abuse children of either gender.

Psychopaths experience emotions and express emotion but it is "word deep." Expressed emotion (i.e., grief and sadness) may at times seem sincere but when dissected it is found to be self-pity and self-serving to the individual.

The "Mr. Big" scenario always works well with a psychopath but would be difficult with A. as he is aware of the tactic which was used in the recent past. A theme that may work with A. is to play on his desire to be validated for his intelligence. He was quite interested in joining the Mensa Society. A scenario could be set up where an operator could be introduced through an IQ testing site. This would play to the ego which is the predominate hook, and the relationship with the operator could migrate into the world of pornography. This would look totally different than the "criminal organization" scenario and may not ring the warning bells for A.

A. submitted to PPG (Penile Plethysmograph) testing which indicated a strong sexual arousal to a young female. Although not noted in the PPG report, it is likely that the arousal was to the depiction of an adult male having sex with this young female. It may be equally stimulating to have another male involved; not involved with him, but enjoying the young female with him.

Although there is no history of hostage taking, this is an individual who uses dramatic behaviour to draw attention and has attempted suicide a few times. None of these attempts have been serious. This individual may set himself up in a suicide by cop situation.

In an interview or interrogation he will attempt to control and manipulate. His weakness is his ego and he is prone to be boastful and overconfident. Play on the ego because he may incriminate himself. Pathological lying is a hallmark of the psychopath and often letting them lie will give the interviewer more ammunition. A seasoned interviewer is important for two reasons. First, he/she will not react to efforts of manipulation and will recognize the "cat and mouse" game used to elicit information from the interviewer. Secondly, there needs to be a perception of the interviewer being a powerful person. The psychopath relates to power and so the interviewer should be built up by the arrest team as a highly competent officer who commands respect. Preparation for the interview is paramount and facts should be presented and supported by logic and evidence.

LOGAN SCALE / PASTE ASSESSMENT TEMPLATE

SECTION 1 **ASSESSMENT DATE: 2006-02-11**

TOMBSTONE DATA	
Name (surname, given)	
Date of Birth	
FPS #	
Sentence Commencement	
Statutory Release Date	
Warrant Expiry Date	
Location (community or institution)	

PHYSICAL DESCRIPTORS	
Height	
Weight	
Race	
Hair Colour	
Eye Colour	
Scars	
Tattoos	
Other	

REMARKS
(Identifiers such as crime cycle, grooming techniques, forcible confinement, age and sex of targets, coercion, offence environment)

TOTAL CUMULATIVE SCORE	
ACTUARIAL SCORES / RISK ASSESSMENT	
OTHER FACTORS	
TOTAL	

SECTION 2

ACTUARIAL SCORES / RISK ASSESSMENT

PCL-R				
RISK LEVEL	RAW SCORE	PERCENTILE SCORE	RATING	
EXTREME	> 33	> 90.9%	5	
HIGH	28 to 33	67.3% - 90.9%	4	
MOD/HIGH	22 to 27	41.7% - 63.5%	3	
MODERATE	17 to 21	22.2% - 37.1%	2	
LOW/MOD	12 to 16	10.9% - 19.1%	1	
LOW	< 12	< 10	0	

VRAG or SORAG				
RISK LEVEL	7 YEARS	10 YEARS	RATING	
EXTREME	> 76%	> 82%	5	
HIGH	55% - 76%	64% - 82%	4	
MOD/HIGH	44%	58%	3	
MODERATE	35%	48%	2	
LOW/MOD	17%	31%	1	
LOW	8% - 12%	10% - 24%	0	

PSYCHOLOGICAL OR PSYCHIATRIC ASSESSMENT RATING OF RISK TO RE-OFFEND		
RISK LEVEL	RATING	
EXTREME	5	
HIGH	4	
MOD/HIGH	3	
MODERATE	2	
LOW/MOD	1	
LOW	0	

ACTUARIAL OR RISK ASSESSMENT SCORES	
PCL-R	
OTHER:	
OTHER:	
OTHER:	
TOTAL AVERAGED SCORE	

SECTION 3

OTHER FACTORS

DEVIANT SEXUAL BEHAVIOUR		
INDICATION OF PARAPHILIA (e.g. exhibitionism, fetishism, pedophilia, necrophilia, sexual sadism or masochism)	1.0	
ELEVATED AROUSAL TO NON-CONSENT (adult or child) or EVIDENCE OF PREDATORY NATURE, i.e., victim/stranger	0.5	
NONE OF THE ABOVE	0	

PREVIOUS VIOLENCE (Total number of acts of violence OR age at first violent act)				
ACTS OF VIOLENCE		AGE AT 1ST VIOLENT ACT	RATING	
> 2	OR	< 20 yrs	1.0	
1 or 2		20 - 39 yrs	0.5	
0		n/a	0	

TARGET ENVIRONMENT		
ENVIRONMENT	RATING	
ACCESS TO DESTABILIZERS (drugs or alcohol, target rich environment/access to target population)	0.5	
LACK OF SUPPORT	0.5	
SUPPORTIVE ENVIRONMENT without access to destabilizers	0	

MENTAL DISORDERS		
DISORDER TYPE	RATING	
MAJOR MENTAL ILLNESS (schizophrenia or manic depression/bi-polar)	0.5	
PERSONALITY DISORDERS (e.g. borderline, narcissistic, paranoid) including Conduct and Drug/Alcohol Disorders, excluding Anti-Social Personality Disorder	0.5	
NO DIAGNOSED DISORDER	0	

RATE OF OFFENDING *(Number of Victims Based on Charges and Convictions)*		
NUMBER OF VICTIMS	RATING	
> 4	1.0	
2 - 4	0.5	
0 - 1	0	

OTHER FACTORS	
TOTAL	

SEXUAL PREDATOR INTELLIGENCE REPORT

, DOB: FPS:

Last Updated: 2006-11-06

SUBJECT				THREAT/RISK ASSESSMENT /10
SURNAME				PHOTO
GIVEN 1		GIVEN 2		
GIVEN 3		GIVEN 4		
DOB		FPS		
HEIGHT	cm	WEIGHT	kg	
HAIR		EYES		
SKIN				
OTHER DESCRIPTORS & INFO.				
PROBATION / PAROLE OFFICER CONTACT INFORMATION				
NAME:				
PHONE/E-MAIL:				Photo Date:

VISIBLE CHARACTERISTICS - Tattoos w/ description, Piercings, Scars, Deformities, Amputations			
Type of mark/ description:		Body Location:	
Type of mark/ description:		Body Location:	
Type of mark/ description:		Body Location:	
Type of mark/ description:		Body Location:	

Remarks	Date	Source

Current Release Conditions (Bail, Probation, Parole, 810 etc.)
1.

Known Aliases		Source
1.		
2.		
3.		

Known Addresses					
	Address	City/Prov	Type	Date(s)	Source
1.					
2.					
3.					

Known Associates and Addresses					
	Name & Address	City/Prov	Type	Date(s)	Source
1.					
2.					
3.					
4.					
5.					
6.					

Known Employers				
	Name & Address / Offender's duties	City/Prov	Date(s)	Source
1.				
2.				
3.				
4.				
5.				
6.				

Known Vehicles								
	Make	Model	Colour	Year	License	Prov	Date	Source
1.								
2.								
3.								
4.								
5.								

Criminal Versatility (Subject's criminal history grouped by crime type, with number of incidents)				
	Crime Type	Number of Occurrences	Date(s)	Source
1.				
2.				
3.				

Known Actuarial Measures (e.g., PCL-R, VRAG, SORAG, SVR-20, HCR-20, Static-99)			Source
1.			
2.			
3.			
4.			
5.			
6.			

PREFERRED VICTIM TYPES	SOURCE

KNOWN BEHAVIOURAL PROGRESSION ("CRIME CYCLE")	SOURCE

KNOWN HUNTING STYLE	SOURCE

PSYCHOLOGICAL / PSYCHIATRIC FINDINGS	SOURCE

OTHER FINDINGS	SOURCE

HOBBIES / INTERESTS / RECREATIONAL ACTIVITIES	SOURCE

RECOMMENDED RELEASE CONDITIONS (Bail, Probation, Parole, 810 etc.)

*Please note that these are recommendations only. It is your responsibility to check CPIC for current Conditions this offender may be under.

1. Keep the peace and be of good behaviour.
2. Within 24 hours of your release from the (FACILITY NAME), you are directed to report in person to a Probation Officer at the (COURT OFFICE), located at (ADDRESS) (closest Court office location) and thereafter as and when directed by the Probation Officer.
3. Reside at a residence approved of by the Probation Officer and do not change that residence without prior written approval from the Probation Officer.
4. Report in person to (NAMED ENFORCEMENT OFFICIAL) or his/her replacement or delegate at the (RECEIVING ENFORCEMENT OFFICE) each and every (SPECIFY DAY) between the hours of 9:00 a.m. and 4:00 p.m. until the expiration of this order, or until further directed.
5. Report in person to an investigator (or a detective) or his/her designate in the High Risk Offender Unit at the Vancouver Police Department.
6. Remain within the Province of British Columbia unless prior written permission to go outside the Province is obtained from the Court or the Probation Officer.
7. Carry a copy of this Recognizance on your person at all times and produce it immediately upon being questioned by any Peace Officer.
8. Attend and participate in assessments, counselling or educational programming as may be directed by the Probation Officer.
9. Submit to having your picture taken upon demand of any Probation Officer throughout your term of supervision.

PART IV

SEX CRIMES AND CRIMINAL PROFILING

CHAPTER 16

Sexual Aggressors:

Motivation, Modus Operandi, and Lifestyle

Chantal Blanchette, Michel St-Yves and Jean Proulx

We first make our habits, and then our habits make us.

John Dryden

Sexual crimes always provoke public indignation. Each time a woman is found lifeless and half nude in the woods, or a child is sexually assaulted in a park, the public, like the police, asks the same questions: *Who* could do this? *Why?*

Police use several investigative techniques to find the answers to these questions. First, they minutely analyze the crime scene, hoping to come away with as many clues as possible. Then they try to collect as many witness statements as possible. With the help of criminal profilers or psychologists, they sketch out a profile of the perpetrator, their aim being to apprehend that person as soon as possible. The profile usually depends on crime-scene analysis (and classification of the scene as "organized" or "disorganized") and on the sexual offender's modus operandi (see Ressler, Burgess, and Douglas, 1988). This analysis generally allows investigators to infer the offender's motivation, behaviour, and personality, as well as characteristics such as age, race, place of residence, criminal record, intelligence or educational level, and type of job. The profile's objective is to narrow down the number of suspects for investigation, by prioritizing the investigation of those who correspond to it, and make it possible for those who know the aggressor to identify him.

One study of incarcerated sexual aggressors has stimulated our interest in lifestyle, a dimension that could prove very useful in creating profiles of unidentified criminals of this type. We have examined their daily lives in the community, and interviewed them about their home lives, their leisure and social activities, and the healthiness of their lifestyle. With this information, we have identified three lifestyles shared by rapists and paedophiles:

festive, orderly, and isolated. Offenders in these categories differ not only in lifestyle but also in modus operandi.

This chapter considers the different types, motivations, modus operandi, and lifestyles of rapists and paedophiles. We believe that adding a lifestyle dimension will prove useful in criminal profiling and assist in the identification of unknown suspects.

A. RAPISTS

In Canada, about 27,000 sexual offences—about 1% of criminal cases—are reported to police each year (Statistics Canada, 1999). Close to half the victims are 15 or older.[1] Most of them are single women, aged 14 to 24, who live in cities where going out at night is common. The sexual aggressors are men in their early thirties—in one out of three cases, a person unknown to the victim (Kong, Johnson, Beattie, and Cardillo, 2003).

Rape results from the interaction of several factors, such as: arousal by coercive sexual activity with a non-consenting woman; beliefs that justify rape; hostility towards women; and an antisocial personality (Hall and Hirschman, 1991; Marshall and Barbaree, 1990). Biological, neurological, and endocrinological factors (see Pinard, 1993), as well as transitory disinhibitors such as negative affect, alcohol and pornography (see Barbaree et. al., 1983; Malamuth and Check, 1983; Proulx, McKibben and Lusignan, 1996) can also help explain some rapes.

1. Motivating Factors

For Groth and Birnbaum (1979), all violent sexual assaults possess three components: power, anger, and sexuality. The type of sexual offender is determined by the component which is dominant. If the crime is motivated by *power*, sex becomes a way of dominating the victim by force, control, and authority (Groth and Birnbaum, 1979). Typically, this type of aggressor uses only the force necessary to commit his crime. He might employ threats or a weapon, but only as a method of intimidation—so-called "instrumental violence." The affect at the moment of the criminal act is often mixed and may include sexual arousal, anxiety, and fear. Some offenders entertain fantasies of sexual conquest: following the rape, they believe they seduced

---

1 Of the 5,247 sexual offences committed in Quebec in 2004, 47% of victims were aged 15 and older (Motard, 2006).

the victim, who succumbed to their charms. In fact, this type of aggressor often denies that he forced anything on the victim, contending, rather, that she wanted the contact and found it pleasurable. Such aggressors usually choose victims for their availability, accessibility, and vulnerability. The deviant sexual act is generally repetitive and compulsive, and the crime may be either premeditated or opportunistic. The opportunistic rapist is generally impulsive and seeks immediate satisfaction (Knight and Prentky, 1990). When this type of rapist kills his victim, his intention is usually to eliminate witnesses (see Beauregard, Proulx, and St-Yves, 2007).

If the motivation is *anger*, sex is the ultimate method for actualizing the rage. The angry aggressor acts impulsively, without premeditation, and generally does not report having had sexual fantasies before the assault. He is physically brutal and seeks to humiliate his victim. Gratification is associated with the expression of his rage rather than with sexual arousal (Groth and Birnbaum, 1979; Knight and Prentky, 1990; Proulx, St-Yves, Guay, and Ouimet, 1999). In exceptional cases, the anger is eroticized and the rape becomes sadistic. Sadistic predators generally use a weapon and have planned their crimes. They often choose victims who are previously unknown to them, and their pleasure is a function of the suffering they inflict on the victim (Groth and Birnbaum, 1979). Angry rapists and sadistic predators are the sexual offenders who most often kill their victims (for more on sexual murder, see Proulx, Beauregard, Cusson, and Nicole, 2007).

Polaschek, Hudson, Ward, and Siegert (2001) have developed a model that improves our understanding of what motivates someone to sexually assault an adult. Through interviews, they explored six behavioural, cognitive, and affective dimensions of such assailants: 1) their daily lives and the manner in which they cope with problems; 2) the goal of their aggression; 3) the manner in which they approach their victim; 4) their decision to engage in sexual acts; 5) the degree of coercion they use; and 6) their reaction to their crime. This study showed that there is a direct association between the type of aggression and the aggressor's profile for each of these dimensions.

2. Rapist Lifestyles

Our study of the lifestyles of rapists[2] has led us to identify three distinct lifestyles:[3] 1) the festive rapist; 2) the orderly rapist; and 3) the isolated rapist. The three types also exhibit different modus operandi (see tables 1 and 2).

a) The festive rapist

Of the three, the festive rapist's profile most resembles that of offenders in general: he is antisocial. Marshall and Barbaree (1990) have noted that characteristics of the antisocial personality are a direct, causal or facilitating, factor in coercive sexual behaviour toward women. The interpersonal relations of individuals with this personality disorder are usually marked by hostility, lack of empathy, and preoccupation with satisfying their own immediate desires. Moreover, such individuals are often more susceptible to cultural influences advocating domination (sexual or otherwise) of women by men. When this type of relational style manifests itself in the sexual sphere, it becomes a direct cause of coercive sexual behaviour.

The "festive" rapist is a sensation seeker. He constantly seeks pleasure and immediate gratification. He considers partying a central element in life and neglects other aspects, viewing them as lesser in importance (Cusson, 2005). The time he devotes to his amusement and criminal activities leaves him no time to invest in a romantic relationship or steady job. He regularly consumes alcohol and drugs, and is a habitué of bars, strip clubs, and nightclubs. More than half of these rapists spend more than seven hours a week in bars. They are nocturnal individuals who wander about with no particular goal. Only rarely do they own a motor vehicle, and they generally live in rented accommodation.

The festive rapist's crimes are rarely premeditated, and often committed while he is intoxicated. He often uses a weapon or physical force, which explains the high rate of injury among his victims. Indeed, this group is responsible for the greatest number of sexual murders. Their consumption of intoxicants in the hours preceding the crime, as well as their choice of

2 In this study we have used the generic term "rapist" when the victim is 15 or older.

3 Sub-types created with the help of taxonomic analysis. This type of statistical analysis creates clusters of subjects on the basis of selected characteristics (Blanchette, in preparation).

TABLE 1

Lifestyle Factors of Rapists, by Lifestyle Category[4]

	Festive N=23	Orderly N=8	Isolated N=6
Has regular contact with immediate family	87%	71.4%	66.7%
Has regular contact with extended family	43.5%	57.1%	33.3%
Has post-secondary schooling	39.1%	25%	33%
Frequently eats in restaurants	36.8%	33.3%	0%
Has a vehicle in excellent condition	50%	87.5%	75%
Has good personal hygiene	82.6%	100%	100%
Lives with another person	60.9%	87.5%	50%
Owns home**	13%	75%	0%
Regularly frequents bars*	56.5%	37.5%	0%
Regularly frequents nightclubs	34.8%	25%	16.7%
Regularly frequents strip clubs	21.7%	0%	16.7%
Goes for walks/rambles	60.9%	25%	33.3%
Owns motor vehicle*	34.8%	87.5%	66.7%
Usually goes to bed after midnight	26.1%	12.5%	16.7%
Is unmarried***	82.2%	0%	83.3%
Regularly consumes alcohol*	82.6%	50%	33.3%
Regularly consumes drugs*	65.2%	25%	16.7%
Has a job at the time of the offence	39.1%	37.5%	83.3%
Has at least one close friend[MS]	95.7%	62.5%	83.3%
Frequents bars > 7 hours/week	43.8%	33.3%	0%

*$p < 0.05$; **$p < 0.01$; ***$p < 0.001$; MS = marginally significant.

4 St-Yves, Proulx and McKibben, 1994.

TABLE 2

Modus Operandi of Rapists, by Lifestyle Category[5]

	Festive N=23	Orderly N=8	Isolated N=6
Consumption of drugs before the crime	63.6%	25%	33.3%
Consumption of alcohol before the crime[MS]	78.3%	37.5%	50%
Consumption of pornography before the crime	17.4%	0%	0%
Friendly or emotional relationship with victim	34.8%	62.5%	33.3%
Premeditation	73.9%	87.5%	83.3%
Pre-selection of victim	26.1%	37.5%	16.7%
Coitus with the victim	60.9%	71.4%	100%
Vaginal penetration[MS]	47.8%	62.5%	100%
Anal penetration	17.4%	0%	0%
Cunnilingus[MS]	30.4%	0%	50%
Fellatio demanded*	47.8%	12.5%	83.3%
Masturbation of the victim[MS]	0%	0%	16.7%
Coercive approach to the crime	87%	87.5%	100%
Use of force	43.5%	25%	33.3%
Use of a weapon	56.5%	50%	33.3%
Infliction of a wound on the victim	69.6%	50%	50%
Humiliation of victim	56.5%	62.5%	50%
Mutilation of victim	13%	0%	0%
Victim is physically handicapped	4.3%	25%	0%
Victim is prostitute/exotic dancer/escort	17.4%	25%	16.7%
Victim is poor/from dysfunctional milieu	40.9%	42.9%	0%
Deviant sexual fantasies in the 48 hours preceding the crime	26.1%	25%	0%
Selection of victim on the basis of particular characteristics	13%	25%	16.7%
Victim forced to perform sexual acts	52.2%	37.5%	83.3%
Touching of genitals	68.2%	62.5%	83.3%
Digital penetration of vagina	30.4%	25%	50%
Victim in bed at time of offence	13%	12.5%	33.3%

*$p < 0.05$; MS = marginally significant

5 St-Yves, Proulx and McKibben, 1994.

victims from marginal social milieus, suggest a certain continuity between their lifestyle and crimes.

b) The orderly rapist

Of the three types of rapists, the orderly rapist is most likely to be in a stable romantic relationship and to live with another person. He often owns his own home and automobile, the latter well cared for. He is organized, with good personal hygiene; he is usually in bed by midnight. Even if some rapists of this type frequent bars, their social activities generally are limited. Some regularly drink alcohol, but few use drugs. Despite his apparently conformist lifestyle, the orderly rapist is the least educated of the three types, and the least likely to be employed at the time of his crime.

Orderly rapists are the most likely to premeditate their crimes. In more than 50% of cases, they know the victim. Sometimes, they hunt vulnerable prey such as exotic dancers, prostitutes, handicapped women, or women from dysfunctional backgrounds. Orderly rapists are the types most likely to consume alcohol or drugs before committing their sexual assaults. They are less likely to use force, but in half the cases injure their victim. Orderly rapists also distinguish themselves from the other types by what they do *not* do: only rarely do they force their victims to touch them sexually, masturbate them, or perform fellatio. Rather, they seem to derive pleasure from their victim's humiliation, fear, and suffering. They employ a weapon and inflict injury in 50% of cases.

c) The isolated rapist

As the name indicates, the isolated rapist has an almost non-existent social life. He does not seek interaction with others, lives reclusively—often alone—and does not have romantic relationships. He rarely visits public places such as bars or restaurants, and does not consume alcohol or drugs. Generally, he is employed at the time of his crime.

Although his crimes generally are premeditated, they do not seem to be motivated by deviant sexual fantasies. He does not pre-select his victim but most often chooses someone unknown to him. The sexual acts associated with his assaults include vaginal penetration, fellatio, genital touching, digital penetration, cunnilingus, and masturbation. Only rarely does the isolated rapist use a weapon, but he begins the assault coercively.

B. PAEDOPHILES

Because the definition of "sexual assault" varies from study to study—particularly regarding the victim's age, the assailant's age, and the type of assailant-victim contact (physical or not, coercive or not) (Salter, 1992)—it is difficult to estimate the prevalence of sexual assaults of children. A Quebec study suggests that 53% of children younger than 15 have had unwanted sexual contact (Motard, 2006). In addition, 30% of all sexual crimes are committed against pre-pubescent children (children younger than 12), two girls being victimized for every boy. Crimes committed by hebephiles—assailants who prey on adolescents—accounted for 36% of the sexual crimes committed in Quebec in 2004. The assailant was known to the victim in 84% of these cases, and was a family member in 38% of the cases involving a known assailant (Motard, 2006).

Two principal diagnostic criteria distinguish the paedophile: 1) the presence, over a period of one to six months, of intense, recurrent sexually exciting fantasies, sexual impulses, or behaviours involving sexual activity with one or more prepubescent children (in general, no older than 13); 2) an aggressor who is at least 16 years old and at least six years older than the victimized child (American Psychiatric Association, 1994). When the victimized child is older than 13 (adolescent), the diagnostic category is usually hebephilia. Some paedophiles are exclusively sexually interested in girls, others only in boys, and yet others in both sexes. According to Marshall (1997), only 40% of extra-familial sexual assailants and 25% of intra-familial sexual assailants meet the American Psychiatric Association's diagnostic criteria for paedophilia (1996).

According to Finkelhor (1984), paedophilia can be explained by four factors:

1. *Emotional congruence.* Paedophiles feel inferior to other adults. (Finkelhor, 1984; Finkelhor and Araji, 1986). For this reason, they seek out the company of children, who, they feel, appreciate and do not judge them; this increases the paedophiles' self-esteem. With children (but not adults), they see themselves in positions of power and control (Proulx et al., 1999).

2. *Sexual arousal.* Paedophiles have a preferential genital response for children. The sexual interests of "primary" or "fixed" paedophiles are oriented solely towards children (Knight, Carter, and Prentky, 1989). "Situational" or "non-preferential" paedophiles en-

gage in isolated or non-preferential acts; this is typical of incestuous fathers.

3. *Poor social skills.* Paedophiles experience difficulty having relationships or sexual relations with consenting adult partners. According to Ward, Hudson, and Marshall (1996), 85% of those who sexually assault children display insecure attachment, compared to 35% of men who have no sexual interest in children. Individuals with secure attachment have a positive perception of themselves and others, which permits them to establish satisfying relationships with other adults. Men with insecure attachment tend to live in emotional solitude, and seek intimate, interpersonal, and sexual contact with children (Marshall, 1989, 1993).

4. *Disinhibitors.* Transitory disinhibitors such as alcohol, pro-paedophilic cognitive distortions, and negative affect can all lower inhibitions, and promote and help justify paedophilic behaviour.

Based on a sample group composed principally (83.7%) of paedophiles, Hudson, Ward, and McCormack (1999) have developed a model of the sequence of events of paedophilic crimes. During the various phases of the crimes (initiation, planning, execution), assailants engage in different decisional processes. The six phases comprise individual options: 1) the aggressor's affect can be positive or negative; 2) planning of the crime can be explicit, implicit, or absent; 3) sexual arousal and cognitive distortion in risky situations can be present or absent; 4) the goal of the crime can be to obtain pleasure for the offender, the victim, or both; 5) the offender can judge his act negatively or positively; and 6) the offender can intend to avoid or repeat the same type of crime.

Hudson et al. (1999) noted that nearly 75% of their sample chose three principal sequences out of eight. The first sequence, representing 32.5% of their sample, comprises a positive affect at the time of the offence, explicit planning, a positive affect leading to sexual arousal and cognitive distortion, a goal of mutual pleasure, a positive assessment of the experience, and a desire to repeat it. This type of paedophile claims to like his victim and to want to develop an intimate, long-term relationship with the child.

Paedophiles following the second sequence (16.3%) are depressed or lonely, plan the offence, harbour selfish pleasure as their goal, feel guilty about the offence and have no desire to repeat it. In these offenders, sexual assault is an inappropriate attempt to deal with negative emotions.

The third sequence resembles the second, but planning is absent. Paedophiles following this path (24.4%) claim that they do not act with premeditation, and will even deny they derive any sexual satisfaction from the experience.

1. Motivation

Most paedophiles use non-coercive methods such, as seduction and persuasion, to satisfy their sexual impulses (see Groth, 1977). They are manipulative, and claim to like the child, be concerned about the child's problems, and want to help and participate in the child's life (McKibben, 1993). When the motivation is interpersonal, the offence is often limited to caresses and masturbating the child, with the aggressor perceiving his actions as a mark of affection or love (Knight, Carter, and Prentky, 1989). Sexual assailants who use a manipulative approach are more likely to report having had deviant sexual fantasies in the hours preceding their offences (Leclerc, Carpentier, and Proulx, 2006).

According to Lacoste and Tremblay (2003), paedophiles can adapt to the situation and choose the strategy that best fits their goals. If manipulation does not work, they may resort to coercion (Christiansen and Blake, 1990). In some cases, the aggressor uses violent means to achieve his end. "The child becomes a receptacle for the aggressor's hostility or desire for domination, for submission to him." (McKibben, 1993: 70). As a consequence, the aggressor rarely maintains a relationship with the child, except where he is already someone close to the child or a person in authority. This type of aggressor is often impulsive, narcissistic, and egocentric. His behaviour is oriented totally toward the satisfaction of his sexual impulses, with no thought of the consequences for the victim (Knight, Carter, and Prentky, 1989). "Non-sadistic-aggressive" paedophiles brutalize their victims out of rage. Violence precedes or, usually, coincides with the sexual assault. "Sadistic" paedophiles engage in bizarre, ritualized behaviour such as shaving the victim, urinating on them, using statuettes or other cult objects, violently sodomizing the victim, or cutting, pinching, or mutilating their genitals (Knight, Carter, and Prentky, 1989).

2. Lifestyles

We have identified three paedophile lifestyles with characteristic modus operandi:[6] 1) festive; 2) orderly; 3) isolated (see tables 3 and 4).

a) The festive paedophile

Of the three, the festive paedophile's profile most resembles that of offenders in general: he is antisocial. His behaviour is guided by impulsiveness and the search for immediate satisfaction. The festive paedophile regularly consumes alcohol and drugs. He frequents bars and nightclubs, enjoys going out without any particular goal and, unlike other types of paedophiles, is a night-owl. Typically, at the time he commits his crimes, he is unemployed. Only rarely does he own his own residence or automobile.

More often than other paedophiles, the festive paedophile is intoxicated when he commits his crimes. He is not much given to premeditation, but tends to select a victim on the basis of precise characteristics—typically, intoxicated victims or victims from dysfunctional milieus. He often adopts a coercive approach, and his sexual acts consist mostly of forcing victims to perform fellatio on him, penetrating the victims vaginally, and performing cunnilingus on his victims.

b) The orderly paedophile

The orderly pedophile rarely lives alone: in more than half of cases, he is in a stable romantic relationship. He seems to lead an orderly life, rarely visiting bars, usually going to bed before midnight, owning his own residence, and possessing an automobile. He is often employed at the time he commits his crimes.

6 In this study we have used the generic term "paedophile" when the victim is under the age of 15.

TABLE 3

Lifestyle Factors of Paedophiles, by Lifestyle Category[7]

	Festive N=29	**Orderly N=17**	**Isolated N=22**
Has regular contact with immediate family	85.2%	88.2%	90.5%
Has regular contact with extended family	51.9%	41.2%	45%
Participates in sports	79.3%	70.6%	71.4%
Has post-secondary schooling	27.6%	29.4%	45.5%
Has a vehicle in good condition	36.8%	47.1%	46.7%
Has good personal hygiene	82.8%	76.5%	68.2%
Lives with another person***	75.9%	88.2%	31.8%
Owns home***	20.7%	100%	4.5%
Regularly frequents bars^{MS}	31%	17.6%	4.5%
Regularly frequents nightclubs	20.7%	5.9%	4.5%
Regularly frequents strip clubs	10.3%	5.9%	4.5%
Goes for walks/rambles**	48.3%	5.9%	45.5%
Owns motor vehicle*	65.5%	100%	68.2%
Usually goes to bed after midnight**	37.9%	5.9%	9.1%
Is unmarried**	72.4%	41.2%	90.9%
Regularly consumes alcohol***	86.2%	29.4%	4.5%
Regularly consumes drugs***	82.8%	5.9%	4.5%
Has a job at the time of the offence	44.8%	64.7%	63.6%

*$p < 0.05$; ** $p < 0.01$; ***$p < 0.001$; MS = marginally significant

7 St-Yves, Proulx and McKibben, 1994.

TABLE 4

Modus Operandi of Paedophiles, by Lifestyle Category[8]

	Festive N=29	Orderly N=17	Isolated N=22
Consumption of drugs before the crime**	42.6%	5.9%	9.1%
Consumption of alcohol before the crime*	46.4%	29.4%	13.6%
Consumption of medication before the crime*	21.4%	0%	0%
Consumption of pornography before the crime	14.3%	29.4%	9.5%
Intimate friendship between victim and aggressor[MS]	69%	76.5%	45.5%
Aggressor is family member[MS]	75.9%	88.2%	54.5%
Premeditation*	69%	94.1%	90.9%
Pre-selection of victim	13.8%	5.9%	13.6%
Selection of victim on the basis of particular characteristics	31%	17.6%	13.6%
Coitus with victim	69%	64.7%	45.5%
Vaginal penetration	37.9%	35.3%	13.6%
Digital penetration of vagina*	55.2%	58.8%	22.7%
Cunnilingus	44.8%	35.3%	18.2%
Fellatio by aggressor*	17.2%	5.9%	40.9%
Fellatio demanded	62.1%	41.2%	40.9%
Masturbation of the victim	27.6%	5.9%	31.8%
Coercive approach to the crime	20.7%	5.9%	4.5%
Victim in bed at time of offence	13.8%	23.5%	27.3%
Victim under the effects of drugs/ alcohol[MS]	17.2%	0%	4.5%
Victim is poor/from dysfunctional milieu	63.6%	30%	25%
Victim is male**	24.1%	17.6%	59.1%
Deviant sexual fantasies	31%	52.9%	22.7%

*$p < 0.05$; **$p < 0.01$; ***$p < 0.001$; MS = marginally significant

8 St-Yves, Proulx and McKibben, 1994.

The orderly paedophile's victim is often a family member or other intimate. His crimes are pre-meditated, but he does not specifically select his victims. While some consume alcohol before committing their crimes, few consume drugs. The orderly paedophile is more likely than the other types to consume pornography before the offence. His sexual acts are principally vaginal penetration (including digital penetration), fellatio, and cunnilingus.

c) The isolated paedophile

The isolated paedophile rarely frequents bars and does not consume alcohol or drugs. Few of this type maintain romantic relationships or cohabit with someone. Isolated paedophiles usually live in rented accommodation. They are the most educated of the three types of paedophiles, and often have post-secondary schooling. They are usually employed at the time of their offences.

Although isolated paedophiles premeditate their crimes, they are not coercive. Their victims are often male; the sexual acts are usually limited to fellatio (40.9%)—both by and on the victim—and masturbation of the victim (31.8%). Their modus operandi is similar to that of homosexual paedophiles (see Proulx, Perreault, and Ouimet, 1999). To manipulate the child, they attempt to inspire confidence. They are "obsessive" paedophiles, and hope to develop an intimate relationship with the victim.

CONCLUSION

Criminal profiling is based essentially on analysis of crime scenes, offenders' motivations, and offenders' modus operandi. We believe that adding the offenders' lifestyle factors to the profile complements existing classifications. Indeed, examining these factors can not only help identify suspects—how the suspect's neighbours, work colleagues, and those closest to him describe him (the *who*)—but also provide information on where to find suspects (the *where*) and the best time to apprehend them (the *when*).

By itself, criminal profiling can never put a face or name to the sexual aggressor; rather, it is an investigative tool than can help prioritize suspects and orient an investigation. The success of a criminal profile also depends on neighbours, colleagues, and intimates—the more precise the profile, the greater the chances that they will identify a suspect.

REFERENCES

American Psychiatric Association. (1994). *Diagnostic and Statistical Manual of Mental Disorders (DSM-IV),* Washington (DC). American Psychiatric Association.

Barbaree, H.E., Marshall, W.L., Yates, E., and Lightfoot, L.O. (1983). Alcohol intoxication and deviant sexual arousal in male social drinkers. *Behaviour Research and Therapy,* 21,365-373.

Beauregard, E., Proulx, J., and St-Yves, M. (2007). Angry or sadistic: Two types of sexual murderers. In J. Proulx, E. Beauregard, M. Cusson, and A. Nicole (eds.), Sexual murder: A Comparative analysis and perspectives (pp. 123-141). Winchester, U.K.: Wiley.

Christiansen, J.R, and Blake, RH. (1990). The grooming process in father-daughter incest. In A.L. Horton, B.L. Johnson, L.M. Roundy, and D. Williams (eds.). *The Incest Perpetrator: The Family Member No One Wants to Treat* (pp. 88-98). Newbury Park: Sage.

Cusson, M. (2005). *La délinquance, une vie choisie* : *Entre plaisir et crime.* Cahiers du Québec, Hurtubise HMH, Montreal.

Finkelhor, D. (1984). *Child sexual abuse: New theory and research.* New York: The Free Press.

Finkelhor, D. and Araji, S. (1986). Explanation of pedophilia: a four factor model. *The Journal of Sex Research,* 22,145-161.

Groth, A.N. (1979) *Men who rape: The psychology of the offender.* Harper and Row, New York.

Groth, A.N. and Birnbaum, H.J. (1979). *Men Who Rape: The Psychology of the Offender.* New York, Plenum Press.

Hall, G.C.N., and Hirchman, R (1991). Toward a theory of sexual aggression: A quadripartite model. *Journal of consulting and clinical psychology,* 59, 662-669.

Hudson S.M., Ward, T. and McCormack, J.C. (1999). Offence Pathways in Sexual Offenders. *Journal of Interpersonal Violence.* 14.8, August: 779-798.

Knight, R.A. Carter, D.L. and Prentky, RA (1989). A system for the classification of child molesters: Reliability and application. *Journal of Interpersonal Violence.* Vol. 4(1), 3-23.

Knigth, R.A. and Prentky, R.A. (1990). Classifying sexual offenders: The development and corroboration of taxonomic model. In Burgess, A. (ed.) *Rape and sexual assault: A Research Handbook.* New York: Garland, p. 23-52.

Kong, R., Johnson, H., Beattie, S. and Cardillo, A. (2003). *Sexual Offences in Canada.* Juristat, Statistics Canada catalogue number 85-002-XIE, Canadian Centre for Justice Statistics. Ottawa, Department of Industry, vol. 23, no 6.

Lacoste, J. and Tremblay, P. (2003). Crime and innovation: a procedural analysis of patterns in check forgery. In M.-J. Smith and D.-B. Cornish (eds.), *Theory for Practice in situational crime prevention.* Crime Prevention Studies (169-196) Monsey (NY): Criminal Justice Press.

Leclerc, B., Carpentier, J. and Proulx, J. (2006). Strategies adopted by sexual offenders to involve children in sexual activity. In R. Wortley and S. Smallbone (eds.), *Situational prevention of child sexual abuse (251*270). Crime Prevention Studies. Vol. 19. Monsey, N.Y.: Criminal Justice Press.

Malamuth, N., and Check, J. (1983). Sexual arousal to rape depictions: Individual differences. *Journal of Abnormal Psychology,* 92, 55-67.

Marshall, W.L. (1997). Pedophilia: Psychopathology and theory. In D. R. Laws and W. O'Donohue (eds.). *Sexual deviance: Theory, assessment and treatment.* New York: Guilford, 152-174.

Marshall, W.L. (1993). The role of attachment, intimacy and loneliness in the etiology and maintenance of sexual offending. *Sexual and Marital Therapy,* 8, 109-121.

Marshall, W.L. (1989). Intimacy, loneliness and sexual offenders. *Behaviour Research and Therapy,* 27, 491-503.

Marshall, W.L. and Barbaree, H.E. Marshall, William L., Laws, D.R., et al. (1990). Handbook of sexual assault: Issues, theories, and treatment of the offender. *Applied clinical psychology* (257-275). New York, NY: Plenum Press. xvii, p. 405.

McKibben, A. (1993). La classification des agresseurs sexuels. In Aubut, J. et al. *Les agresseurs sexuels : Théorie, évaluation et traitement.* Les Éditions de la Chenelière, Montreal, and Maloine, Paris, 58-77.

Motard, L. (2006). *Les agressions sexuelles au Québec.* Statistiques 2004. Sainte-Foy, Quebec, ministere de la Securite publique, p. 31.

Pinard, G.-F. (1993). Les théories biologiques. In Jocelyn Aubut et al., *Les agresseurs sexuels* : *Théorie, évaluation et traitement.* Les Éditions de la Chenelière, Montreal, p. 2-20.

Polaschek, D.L.L., Hudson, S.M., Ward, T., and Siegert, RJ. (2001). Rapists' offense processes: A preliminary descriptive model. *Journal of Interpersonal Violence,* 16, 523-544.

Proulx, J., Beauregard, E., Cusson, M., and Nicole, A (2007). Sexual Murderers: A Comparative Analysis and New Perspectives. Chichester, UK: Wiley.

Proulx, J., McKibben, A and Lusignan, R. (1996). Relationships Between Affective Components and Sexual Behaviors in Sexual Aggressors. *Sexual Abuse: A Journal of Research and Treatment,* 9, 279-289.

Proulx, J., Perreault, C. and Ouimet, M. (1999). Pathways in the offending process of extrafamilial sexual child molesters. *Sexual Abuse: Journal of Research and Treatment,* vol. 11(2),117-129.

Proulx, J., St-Yves, M., Guay, J.-P. and Ouimet, M. (1999). Les agresseurs sexuels de femmes: Scénarios délictuels et troubles de personnalité. In Proulx, J., Cusson, M. and Ouimet, M., *Les Violences criminelles,* Saint-Nicolas, Quebec, Presses de l'Université Laval, 157-185.

Ressler, R.K., Burgess, A.W., and Douglas, J.E. (1988). *Sexual homicide: Patterns and motives.* New York: The Free Press.

Salter, A. (1992). Epidemiology of child sexual abuse. In W. O'Donohue, and J. H. Geer, *The Sexual Abuse of Children: Theory and Research,* vol. 1, Hillsdale, N.J.: Lawrence Erlbaum Associates, 108-138.

Statistique Canada (1999). *Sex Offenders. Integration and Analysis Program.* Juristat, Statistics Canada catalogue number 85-002-XIF, Canadian Centre for Justice Statistics, Ottawa, Department of Industry, vol. 19, no 3.

St-Yves, M., Proulx, J. and McKibben, A (1994). *Questionnaire informatisé sur les délinquants sexuels.* Centre Régional de Réception, Correctional Service of Canada. Unpublished.

Ward, T., Hudson, S.M. and Marshall, W.L. (1996). Attachment style in sex offenders: a preliminary study. *The Journal of Sex Research, 33,* 17-26.

Ward, T., Louden, K., Hudson, S.M. and Marshall, W.L. (1995). A Descriptive Model of the Offense Chain for Child Molesters, *Journal of Interpersonal Violence,* 10 (4), p. 452-472.

CHAPTER 17

Cyberpaedophilia:

Profiling Consumers of Child Pornography

Francis Fortin and Julie Roy

The advent of the Internet has changed certain aspects of criminality across the planet. Lapointe (2000) identifies three types of problematic and criminal uses of the Internet: problematic but non-criminal use, traditional crimes that have shifted to the Internet, and new forms of crime. While the Internet has encouraged the growth of deviance (Lamb, 1998), the form that has attracted the most attention is child pornography, which in fact predates the Internet (Lapointe, 2000). Since the 1994 explosion in web usage, the Internet has been used for the viewing, exchange, and collection of child pornography. This chapter reviews the literature on consumers of child pornography, in contrast to earlier studies, which have focused on the consumption of pornography by sexual aggressors (Marshall, Barbaree and Christophe, 1986; Langevin et al. 1988; Proulx, Perreault and Ouimet, 1999; Rettinger, 2000).

A. THE PHENOMENON OF CHILD PORNOGRAPHY

COPINE (Combating Paedophile Information Networks in Europe) is one of the most important research projects on child pornography. It was initiated in 1997 at Ireland's University of Cork, by Max Taylor and his colleagues, its principal goals being to: demonstrate the vulnerability of children to new technologies; maintain a database on child pornography; assess the danger posed by paedophiles' collections of pornographic materials; and investigate the child sex trade in Europe and the nature and prevalence of sexual tourism affecting children (Taylor, Quayle and Holland, 2001).

As part of the COPINE project, Taylor et al. (2001) developed a classification system for images of child pornography on the Internet, relying on systematic downloading of material available on Usenet newsgroups.[1] The team analyzed more than 80,000 images and more than 400 videos (Taylor, Quayle and Holland, 2001). They were then able to create a classification system consisting of ten graded levels:

Level 1: *Indicative.* Material that is neither erotic nor sexual, taken from commercial sources such as catalogues and photo albums. The children are clothed in underwear or swim suits.

Level 2: *Nudity.* Images or videos showing partial or complete nudity in an appropriate setting.

Level 3: *Erotica.* Clandestine images of children who are in underclothing or nude.

Level 4: *Posing*. Photos of children in deliberately suggestive, sexual poses.

Level 5: *Erotic posing* Images or videos of a sexual or provocative nature.

Level 6: *Explicit erotic posing.* Images or videos of a sexual or provocative nature — like the preceding level — but focusing on the child's genitals.

Level 7: *Explicit sexual activity*. Images depicting children engaging in sexual activities — masturbation, oral sex, or sexual touching. At this level, the activity is between children only, with no direct adult participation.

Level 8: *Assault*. Images and videos of adults engaging in sexual activities with children.

Level 9: *Gross assault.* Depictions of sexual aggression involving penetration of a child by an adult.

Level 10: *Sadism/bestiality*. Images or videos involving bestiality, sadism, or the infliction of pain on the child.

The COPINE researchers add an important detail to this classification system: The images in the lower levels (1, 2, 3) can also have a sexual connotation, and provoke, favour, or maintain sexual fantasies. Content

1 All the newsgroup messages distributed daily over the network (OLF, 1998).

showing children in underwear can be sexually attractive and promote deviant sexual fantasies in consumers of child pornography. This typology well encapsulates the broad scope of material which pleases individuals who are sexually attracted to children (Taylor, Quayle and Holland, 2001).

Qualitative analyses of collections of child pornography have revealed that the victims are increasingly younger, and the abuse increasingly violent (Carr, 2004). The decrease in the age of victims can be explained by the fact that very young victims find it more difficult to reveal the assaults they experience than do older children (Taylor, Quayle and Holland, 2001). In 1999, COPINE calculated that an average of four new children were depicted in child pornography every month (Carr, 2004).

Quantitative analysis of the database revealed that more than half of the 80,000 images and 400 videos depicted young girls and were of at least Level 7 (explicit sexual activity). For boys, 26% of cases were of at least Level 7, and the images are recent. Among these, 41% depicted young girls and 56% boys. The children's ages ranged from 9 to 12. An estimated 300-350 of the children in more recent material had been victims of sexual violence (Level 7 and higher) (Taylor et al., 2001).

Most of what one finds on the Internet comes from industrialized countries, where the technology necessary for content creation is most accessible. However, a large part of the material seized in the Netherlands and Sweden in recent years has been produced by, and depicts, sexual tourists on trips to Asia. There is thus a direct link between child pornography and sexual tourism, the latter facilitating the production of the former (Fillieule and Montiel, 1997). Thailand, the Philippines, India, and South America seem to be gaining popularity as destinations for the production of child pornography (Taylor and Quayle, 2003; Carr, 2004).

Although the COPINE project constantly updates these statistics, the project team believes that their statistics underestimate the phenomenon and that certain clandestine material is inaccessible to researchers (Taylor, Quayle and Holland, 2001). There is anecdotal support for this view: a police officer has stated that it is common today for consumers of this material to possess more than 5,000 photographs and videos (Savary, 2005).[2] Research and projects such as COPINE have furthered our understanding

2 In 2005, following the discovery of more than 44,000 photographs and 106 films depicting child pornography in the possession of a suspect, a Sûreté du Québec investigator stated in court, "This is the average size of seizures in recent years."

of the nature of material exchanged through Internet newsgroups. It would be valuable to analyze the perspective of the consumers of this pornography, to understand what their collections mean to them.

B. CONSUMERS OF CHILD PORNOGRAPHY AND THEIR COLLECTIONS

Consumers of child pornography may have different interests in the material. As Tremblay (2002), Rettinger (2000), and Taylor and Quayle (2003) note, these consumers, as well as paedophiles, also consume non-pornographic material. A 2004 study by Roy reveals that, in a number of cases "consumption of child pornography began with consumption of regular pornography" (Roy, 2004). In fact, close to three quarters of those who sexually assault children admit to fantasizing over material not specifically conceived as pornography (Howitt, 1995). This licit material can be in magazines, children's films, television programs, and even family photo albums (Creighton, 2003).

Some consumers prefer images with non-sexual content (Taylor and Quayle, 2003), as they can indulge their fantasies in an apparently legal context. Be that as it may, this material allows the consumer to obtain some sexual satisfaction (Creighton, 2003). Consuming licit material also procures some protection against being apprehended. To some extent, consumers of child pornography fear being apprehended by the police. By obtaining licit material with non-sexual content, they can indulge their fantasies while remaining within the boundaries of the law. The material that attracts them is not necessarily sexually explicit (Tremblay, 2002).

In addition to consuming licit material, some consumers produce content. Several researchers have noted the ease with which content can be produced, stored and distributed thanks to new information technologies (Fortin, 2005; Stanley 2001). For some years now, Internet usage has become commonplace. The hardware (computer and modem) can now be had inexpensively (Foley, 2002; Stanley, 2001). The diversification of communication technologies has been accompanied by a growth of offences for the possession, distribution, and production of child pornography (Carr, 2004). The Internet provides a multitude of ways to transmit text, images, photographs, videos, and other audio-visual material in real time by webcam. One can even find sites with "homemade" images. Thanks to such equipment, several thousand images can be produced from a single instance of sexual abuse (Creighton, 2003). The risks in producing child pornography are thereby reduced: producers do not have to develop their photographs through third parties such as retailers, who could report their activity (ECPAT, 2002). Studies have shown that child pornography is produced on an individual basis, and generally exchanged or collected by private collectors (Rettinger, 2000; Badley, 1984; Howitt, 1995). Often, paedophiles produce it for their own use (Rettinger, 2000).

1. The Nature of Collections

Researchers have investigated these collections' composition, role in fantasy life, and place in daily life. According to the Oxford English Dictionary, a "collection" is "a group of accumulated items of a particular kind." Belk (1995) remarks that the very act of collecting reveals something about the objects to which the collector is attached. The processes of selecting, acquiring, and deciding are integral to the collector's passion. Muensterberger (1994) states that the central element of collecting resides in the constant acquisition of the prized object. This is what captivates collectors. Their efforts to overcome obstacles to acquiring a new item, the difficulty involved in its acquisition, is an important aspect of this (Taylor and Quayle, 2003). While collectors differ in what they collect, they have some points in common: First, the object of their collections must be accessible, and the items composing the collections must be capable of classification and organization. Moreover, the collection can be either public or private. Collectors devote a great deal of time and money to their collection, and often take pleasure in return (ECPAT, 2002). Taylor et al. (2001) believe that, despite the excuses and rationalizations proffered by collectors of child pornography, it is no accident that they collect material depicting children: they act deliberately, with the goal of requiring this material specifically.

2. Use of the Collection

How do collectors of child pornography use their collections? According to Lanning (1992), there are five ways in which individuals use collections of child pornography:

1. Sexual gratification. The individual employs the material as a prelude to a sexual assault on a child, the pornography feeding the aggressor's fantasies before or during the assault or masturbation. However, there is some debate about this point. Quayle et al. (2000) believe that individuals who use the Internet to collect child pornography do not employ the material as a prelude to assault. Very often, they simply view or share the material.

2. To lower children's inhibitions. In some cases, the collector shows the victim material in which children seem to enjoy the sexual activity depicted. In this way, the victim learns to unconsciously normalize this sort of sexual behaviour (Stanley, 2001; Feather, 1999). In some children, a lowering of inhibitions is paralleled by an increase in sexual curiosity, a process known as "grooming" (Berson and Tampa, 2003, Krone, 2004).

3. For blackmailing. For example, an aggressor may attempt to make a child believe they are partly responsible for the assault. Such blackmail prevents the child from divulging the sexual abuse.

4. As currency. Consumers of child pornography may use it in transactions with other collectors, selling or exchanging their own child pornography in return for material from private or commercial sources.

5. To preserve images of children. Through their collections, collectors can tirelessly review depictions of specific types of children (e.g. of a certain age, at a certain stage of development). These characteristics reflect the collector's sexual interests.

Research on the creation and acquisition of this material helps determine the utility of these collections as a currency of exchange.

3. Contents of the Collection

The quantity of child pornography is an important factor in establishing a profile of the collector (Taylor and Quayle, 2003). The act of collecting incites some individuals to continually increase the size of their collections (Lanning, 1984) and to acquire material whose content is more and more extreme. Acquisition of the material reinforces existing deviant sexual fantasies and incites the individual to act on them (Taylor and Quayle, 2002). Taylor and Quayle (2002) write of a subject who grew bored with acquiring "soft" child pornography and began collecting more extreme and explicit material.

> I was getting quite bored with the child pornography I could find on the Internet... That's when I became obsessed with pictures of children in bondage... or tortured.

Collectors are very meticulous about their collections, leaving nothing to chance. While collection processes vary from collector to collector, collections are invariably classified logically on the basis of multiple criteria (Mclaughlin, 2000): most collections are highly organized by age, sex, type of acts depicted, etc. (Taylor et al., 2001). For the collector, the series of objects constitutes an ongoing narrative. Sometimes, the pleasure arises from the difficulty and effort associated with finding a missing image in a series, even when the collector does not in fact find the material attractive or exciting (Taylor and Quayle, 2002). Collection development itself seems to be an important psychological process.

Collectors say material acquisition is like a ritual. The collector derives pleasure during the activity (Carr, 2004), and the collected articles acquire permanence through their conservation on diskettes, CD-ROMs, or hard-drives (Taylor and Quayle, 2002). For Carr (2004), the collection of child pornography is a process that snowballs. The material on suspects' computers can be not only constantly reviewed, but also redistributed to other consumers. New material is always an addition to a collection — existing material is rarely deleted (Carr, 2004). Archived material can be used for reference or as a bargaining chip for new material (Quayle and Taylor, 2002). In 1999, Taylor suggested that an understanding of the collectors of child pornography must be grounded in analysis of the collection from the collector's perspective, given that each collector has unique interests in what is depicted and how it is depicted. These differences suggest that collectors do not form a homogeneous group (Carr, 2004).

C. SOCIETY, THE VIRTUAL COMMUNITY AND THE CHILD PORNOGRAPHY CONSUMER

The collection of child pornography stimulates collectors to make contact with other collectors, which enlarges their social network. Through such virtual communities, collectors expand their collections (Creighton, 2003). Thanks to the Internet, collectors weave a network of worldwide contacts (Forde and Patterson, 1998), facilitating the development of subgroups (Durkin and Bryant, 1995; Forde and Patterson, 1998; Feather, 1999, O'Connell, 2001) whose social organization resembles that of "colleagues" (Taylor et al., 2000). Inside this organization collectors can behave according to their own norms and convictions. Among themselves, they approve what society disapproves. Over the Internet, marginalized individuals (such as paedophiles) can lose themselves in a larger virtual community (Quayle and Taylor, 2002).

Mayer (1985) notes that paedophiles are very skilled at minimizing and rationalizing their behaviour. They deploy a multitude of beliefs and explanations to justify their interest in children (Abel, Becker and Cunningham-Rathner, 1984). Communicating with like-minded individuals allows them to confirm their feelings and desires (Goldstein et al., 1973; Feather, 1999). Group affiliation thus alleviates feelings of guilt that may be present (Tremblay, 2002).

Clearly, this retreat into virtual communities is reinforced by popular pressure against consumers of abusive images. Society perceives adults who are sexually attracted to, or engage in, sexual activity with children as its most deviant members. In a poll regarding perceptions of paedophilia among the general public, none of the 2,753 respondents stated that it was "normal" to have sexual contact with children (Janus and Janus, 1993). These results confirm those reported almost 15 years earlier by Finkelhor (1979).

1. The Justifications Offered

In an attempt to better understand how paedophiles manage to flout public opinion, Durkin and Bryant (1999) studied the rationalizations paedophiles use to explain their deviance. Their sample comprised 41 paedophiles from the Internet discussion group *alt.support.boy-lovers.* The researchers studied 154 messages exchanged by participants during a one-month period. They found the explanation most frequently given by paedophiles (39%) was *denial of injury* (see Sykes and Matza, 1970). Individuals advancing this explanation contended that sexual relations between a child and an adult caused the child no physical, psychological, or emotional harm. The asserted that they did not believe that sexually assaulted children were upset by the assault, and that the sexual relations were consensual (Durkin and Bryant, 1999).

Condemnation of condemners was the second-most common explanation (31%). In this instance, paedophiles turned on those who condemn them — police, professional intervenors, teachers, and parents. They depicted themselves as part of an oppressed minority group, like homosexuals. Over time, society became more open, and more tolerant of homosexuals, and the paedophiles in this group believe that it is only a matter of time before a similar change occurs with regard to them.

The third explanation, comprising 14.6%, consists of what is known as *BIRGing*. Paedophiles in this category invoke the names of famous people through the ages who were interested in children, arguing that the paedophilia of such leading lights justifies and reinforces their own deviance.

Another type of explanation is *claim of benefit*. This explanation, advanced by 9% of participants, is an extension of the *denial of harm* explanation, and posits that sexual relations between adults and children is beneficial to the children — is, in fact, an enriching learning experience (Durkin and Bryant, 1999).

Finally, the least frequently used explanation (4.9%) is the *appeal of loyalties*. referring to children's rights. Paedophiles who subscribe to this view present themselves as militants for the sexual rights for minors or part of a more general children's rights movement. In Durkin and Bryant's (1999) study, more than half the paedophiles (24.4%) invoked an amalgam of different rationalizations (*polythematic account*).

These results show that the creation of virtual communities and subgroups can have an impact on beliefs, rationalizations, and justifications, and modify paedophiles' self-perception, allowing them to define themselves as adults with a "romantic interest" in children (Durkin and Bryant, 1999). These individuals redefine paedophilia as acceptable, and maintain and reinforce a positive self-image. They scorn society's image of them (Durkin and Bryant, 1999). Thus, as Collins points out (2006), websites nourish cognitive distortions that existed before the Internet and continue as deeply held, offence-facilitating beliefs.

The Wonderland network[3] (Taylor and Quayle, 2003) provides an eloquent example of the importance of groups and collections to consumers of child pornography. Wonderland was an Internet discussion group created to facilitate the exchange of child pornography. A police operation revealed that participants came from some 15 countries. The Wonderland group was highly structured and required its members to abide by a series of rules. The group comprised more than 200 members, each of whom paid US $100 per month for access to the network. Beyond the subscription fee, they were required to make at least 10,000 images of child pornography accessible to the network. In 2002, police inventoried more than 750,000 images of child pornography on the network. More than 1,200 children, aged 3 months to 10 years, appeared in these images (Creighton, 2003; Hunter, 2001; Taylor and Quayle, 2003).

---

3 According to Collins (2006), members named the group in honour of Lewis Caroll, known for his sexual interest in children.

In summary, the exchange, marketing, and sale of child pornography over the Internet contributes to the development of certain types of markets and new forms of socialization. On the one hand, there exists a very lucrative market for such material (Berberi et al., 2003), although there is very little empirical evidence concerning the individuals motivated by money. On the other hand, individuals engaged in such exchanges participate, at various levels, in communities based on the possession of, and search for, such material (Jenkins, 2001; Healy, 1996; Quayle and Taylor, 2002; Svedin and Back, 1996). Collection and distribution are the visible aspects of a series of more important interactions that consist of informational exchange and personal contact (O'Connell, 2001). In studying the relationship between collection and collector, researchers also seek to globally understand collectors of child pornography.

2. The Socio-demographic Profile of Collectors of Child Pornography

There have been few studies of the socio-demographic profile of consumers of child pornography. Based on subjects clearly identified as sexual aggressors, we studied the socio-demographics of a sample of 199 Quebec consumers of child pornography. The data on sex, age and occupation presented in Table 1 are taken from Quebec police reports and were collected between 1998 and 2004.

Thus, from a police perspective, it is almost always men who consume child pornography. Males represent 96.5% of those arrested in Quebec (Fortin and Roy, 2006). In only one case was a woman the sole consumer of child pornography, other cases involved women acting in conjunction with men. These results agree with those obtained by Seto and Eke (2005), who identified 205 individuals associated with cases of child pornography in Ontario. Only one woman figured in the cases, and the authors note that this women, in her forties, was co-accused with a male (Seto and Eke, 2005). A survey of various studies, notably from the United States and New Zealand, report similar results. There were only two women (both married) in Mclaughlin's (2000) study of 200 individuals. Fewer than 1% of the 429 participants in Wolak et. al.'s (2005) study were female. Similarly, in Carr's (2004) study, the vast majority (105 of 106) of the sample was male. It seems, then, that women do not consume child pornography, or at least very rarely do so on their own. Some authors go so far as to exclude females from their analyses, considering their usage a distinct phenomenon (Fortin and Roy, 2006).

The average age of Quebec consumers of pedopornography is 35.4. As Roy (2004) points out, the young are well represented in this figure, with 38.2% of subjects younger than 29. Wolak et al. (2005) observed that 3% of their subjects were younger than 18, 11% were 18 to 25, 41% were 26 to 39, and 45% were at least 40. Moreover, Eke and Seto (2005) have reported results, with the average age of 201 individuals arrested in Ontario for child pornography being 38. In McLaughlin's (2000) study, the average age was 35, with 10.5% of the sample younger than 18, 15% of the sample older than 50, and the percentage of the sample in their twenties, thirties, and forties between 23.5% and 26%. It would seem, then, that the percentage of individuals younger than 18 is quite variable, which is likely due to differences in the way minors and adults are treated in the courts. In addition, there is little significant variation in the age of suspects, the average hovering around 35. If one compares studies undertaken before and after the rise of the Internet, we can, however, suggest that the 18-to-39-year-old group is over-represented (Fortin and Roy, 2006). In Burgess's pre-Internet study (1984) of 55 offenders, the media age was 45 (range: 25-74); notably, 90% (46 of 51) were between 30 and 59 years old.

In our Quebec sample, occupations vary widely, although the largest number of participants were students (20%) or unemployed (16.8%); participants in the labourer/worker and construction worker/trucker/bus driver categories each represented 10.3% of the sample. In McLaughlin's (2000) study, the principal occupations were student (22%), labourer (22%), information-technology worker (13%) and white-collar worker (11%) and retired (11%). While Wolak et al. (2005) could reach no conclusions as to the social class of the suspects in their sample, Burgess (1984) determined that the majority of offenders in his study were at least middle class. Thus, the arrival of the Internet has democratized access to various material, to the point that consumers of child pornography today come from all economic backgrounds. While it is difficult to draw any conclusions about the occupations of the subjects in our study, it may be that increased free time to explore the Internet is an important factor.

Wolak et. al. (2005b) have created the best socio-demographic profile of child pornography consumers:

> These consumers of child pornography are quite diverse. They range in age from 15 to 70. Some were well educated, and some had not finished high school. They come from every social class. Some were active in their community, others were heads of companies. Some seemed isolated and obsessed with the Internet.

Table 1: Characteristics of the sample

	Number	Percentage
Sex		
F	7	3.5
M	192	96.5
Age		
10-18	27	13.6
19-29	49	24.6
30-40	53	26.6
41-51	38	19.1
52-62	24	12.1
63 +	8	4.0
Mean	35.4	
Occupation		
Students	31	20
Unemployed/welfare/workers' compensation	26	16.8
Construction/trucker/bus driver	16	10.3
Labourer/worker	16	10.3
Sales/service	14	9
Maintenance/restoration	13	8.4
Information technology	12	7.7
Professional/administration	12	7.7
Business	6	3.9
Security	5	3.2
Private income/retired	4	2.6
Unknown	44	

Fortin and Roy (2006)

3. Related and Previous Crimes

Often, an arrest for possession of child pornography is the first contact consumers of this material have with the criminal justice system. Fortin and Roy (2006) reported that close to 65% of their sample had no known criminal record at the time of their arrest. Because some authors suggest a link between child pornography and sexual assaults, a useful approach is to verify whether those involved in crimes involving child pornography have a record of sexual offences. Fortin and Roy (2006) found that 10.4% of their subjects had such a record; notably, 25.4% had records for non-sexual offences. In total, more than a third (35.4%) had a known criminal record. In Burgess' (1984) study, 38.2% of the sample had never committed a crime, and 41.8% had committed no sexual offence; sexual offenders accounted for 34.6% of all offenders. Carr (2004) reported that 18 of 106 individuals (16.9%) in their sample had criminal records: 11.3% had been convicted of sex crimes, and 1.8% had been convicted of each of theft, possession of child pornography, and possession of drugs. Roy (2004) obtained the same results, with 13.5% of the subjects she studied possessing at least one previous conviction. In Fortin and Roy's (2006) study, there were no repeat offenders for possession of child pornography, although 5.4% of the sample were repeat offenders for non-sexual crimes. Seto and Eke (2005) concluded that nearly three quarters of their sample (n = 201) had no record of sexual crime, although 56% had previous convictions (24% for sexual offences and 15% for offences related to child pornography). Moreover, the results suggest that individuals with convictions related to child pornography are more likely to re-offend if they already have a criminal record (Seto and Eke, 2005).

How should one interpret these results concerning the criminal record of offenders? Only a minority have a previous record of sexual crime, suggesting that the majority do not escalate from consumption to offending. However, the prevalence of a record of sexual offending is much higher than in the population generally. Overall, therefore, individuals accused of crimes involving child pornography are more prone to violent sexual behaviour than are members of the general population. Further, the low rate of reporting of these crimes (Russel, 1984), as well as a trend toward younger victims, (Taylor, Quayle and Holland, 2001) are especially worrisome.

Another approach is to analyze the crimes surrounding offences related to child pornography. Police reports occasionally mention that other types of crimes have led to the discovery of offences related to child pornography, and vice versa. Table 2 is based on Fortin and Roy's (2006) sample.

Table 2: Other crimes involved with child-pornography offences

Crime	Definition	Number
Sex crime	Immoral act, indecency, sexual assault, aggravated sexual assault, luring, other sex crimes	29
Threats	Threatening behaviour, stalking	4
Procuring	Prostitution of those younger than 18/procuring same, living off the avails of prostitution/procuring	5
Property crimes	Fraud, theft under $5,000, receiving stolen goods	5
Drug offences	All drug-related offences	16
Other	Mischief, criminal damage more than $5,000, possession of a weapon	3
Total		**81**

The many crimes observed in parallel with those involving child pornography are worthy of special attention. As Table 2 indicates, a total of 81 crimes were associated with arrests for child pornography. Sexual crimes (29), followed by drug-related offences (16) were the crimes most frequently observed in association with these arrests. It is important to note that despite the great improvement in the techniques for the investigation of Internet-related crime, the discovery of some crimes is still a matter of chance. From a policing perspective, these findings suggest that the investigation of child pornography facilitates the discovery of other offences, and vice versa.

The prevalence of a criminal record ranged widely in the studies reviewed above. This may be due to methodological differences, as there is some inconsistency in the way criminal records are reported.

4. Type of Content Encountered

Lanning (1992) has reviewed the types of material that paedophiles collect; this material includes books, magazines, newspaper articles, photographs, films, souvenirs, toys, and clothes. Although the specific articles collected differs from individual to individual, the clear point of commonality among these articles is that they are all related to children. In 2004, Roy conducted a study of Quebeckers arrested for the possession or distribution of Internet child pornography. The research had two principal aims: to determine whether those arrested for possession or distribution of child pornography material had a record of sexual crime, and to shed light on the characteristics of Quebeckers arrested for the possession or distribution of Internet child pornography, and the circumstances surrounding their arrest. Particular attention was paid to the quantity of child pornography found on suspects' computers. In three cases, no images were found. Nearly a third of the subjects (12) possessed fewer than 1,000 images, and 62% possessed fewer than 5,000. In two cases, there were more than 10,000 images or videos (13,000 and 20,700). These results contrast with those of Wolak et al. (2005), who reported that 48% of individuals arrested for possession of child pornography had more than 100 images on their computers and that 14% possessed more than 1,000. Moreover, 37% had fewer than 100 images on their computers. Wolak et al. state that the quantities reported may be inaccurate and should be treated as conservative. Given that several years separate the studies, one might ask whether the constant improvement of processing speeds and increased computer storage capacity are not partly responsible for the different figures.

In Roy's (2004) study, 16% of the images were of boys only, 32% were of girls only, and more than half (51%) were of children of both sexes. Wolak et al. (2005) observed different rates: 14% boys, 62% girls, and only 15% of both sexes.

5. Profiling of Child Pornography Consumers

Only recently has research been conducted on collectors of child pornography. However, Cooper et al. (1999) laid the foundation for a general theory that deserves special attention. According to these authors, there are three types of users, or, equivalently, three different ways of engaging in sexual activity online: 1) The *recreational* user, a person who can be seen as the "average" user, simply wants to satisfy his sexual curiosity with content available over the Internet. Generally speaking, his searches are not problematic and he prefers face-to-face relationships to online activity. 2)

The *sexual compulsive* user already engages in unconventional sexual behaviour — he consumes pornography, experiments in multi-partner sex, frequents prostitutes, etc. The authors point out that for this type of user, the Internet has a "normalizing" effect that facilitates the individual's acceptance of this behaviour. 3) Finally, there is the *user at risk,* someone who has no history of compulsive sexual behaviour but whose online habits have significant repercussions in his life. The authors contend that this group would not have sexual problems in the absence of the Internet. The *depressive* sub-type takes refuge on the Internet during depressive episodes, while the *stress-reactive* sub-type uses the Internet to escape the stress of everyday life. The latter is more proactive and more sophisticated in his online social ability than is the depressive.

This last study has the merit of being a general model of all paraphilias. Its goal is to suggest differential treatment for sexual compulsives. The studies presented below illustrate the points of view of consumers of child pornography and its place in their offences.

The developmental or stage approach

Before we consider the types of consumers of child pornography, a discussion of Taylor et al.'s 2001 study is essential. In that study, the authors attempted to establish a modus operandi for this type of consumer. Consumers are said to pass through a number of stages in their use of the Internet. Figure 1 illustrates the fact that consumption of regular pornography precedes consumption of child pornography. This begins a cycle in which the increasing amount of time spent online is inversely proportional to the consumer's participation in outside activities. Increased time online multiplies contacts with others, normalizes collection activities, and teaches the consumer how best to increase his collection. Following the creation of large collections, behaviours such as sorting, classifying, and categorizing material become increasingly important.

Figure 1: Operational stages of Taylor et al. (2001)

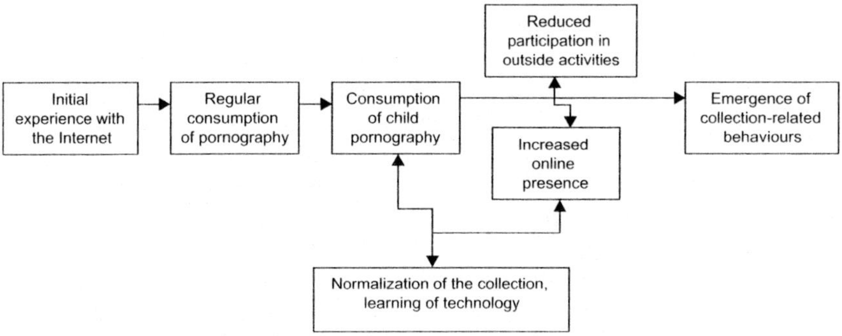

An offending-process-based typology of consumers of child pornography

The studies discussed in this section have attempted to develop, on the basis of the goals individuals pursue in their use of deviant material, typologies of consumers of child pornography. In 1984, Hartman et al. identified four types of collectors:

1. *Secret,* who surreptitiously collect child pornography from commercial sources. Apparently, this type of collector has no criminal record of sexual assaults on children.

2. *Isolated,* who sexually assault children. These collectors use their collections to both assuage their sexual needs and gain their victims' confidence. Their collections may also include articles related to their prior sexual assaults on children.

3. *Familial,* who collect and exchange material with others. They share their collections to validate their behaviour to others without fear of retribution.

4. *Commercial,* who consider their collections primarily a vehicle for profit. They may therefore exchange their material with other consumers as if it was a business. Hartman et al. also consider this type of collector a sexual aggressor of children.

As Internet use has become more widespread, the typologies of paedophiles operating online have become more precise. Thus Klain et al. (2001) have identified five types of Internet paedophiles, differing in their degree of organization. The first such type is the *closet collector*, who denies any sexual interest in children and conceals all his child pornography. He does not establish communication with other consumers and accesses pornographic material discreetly, on commercial websites. The images he collects are of nude children engaging in sexual and non-sexual acts. He is aware of the fact that children should not be sexually abused by adults.

On the other hand, *the trader* communicates with other pornography collectors, but does not sexually abuse others.

The *isolated collector* is not part of the paedophile community and is essentially a child abuser. This type of consumer of child pornography hides his activities so as to avoid detection by authorities. He obtains pornographic material from commercial sites or produces his own material as he sexually abuses children.

The *cottage collector* sexually abuses children and shares his child pornography collection with other collectors, but does not necessarily benefit financially from this exchange. He sexually abuses children within a group context, his goal being not financial gain but the establishment of relationships with other paedophiles. Cottage collectors occupy a position of confidence in their communities, and their Internet friendships provide external support for their sexual abuse of children. They succeed in exploiting children by convincing their victims that the latter are totally in their power and have much to lose by not yielding to the abuser's sexual desires.

Finally, the *commercial collector* commercially produces, copies, and distributes his own and others' child pornography.

Krone's (2004) inventory of offences related to online child pornography is presented in Table 3. Krone's typology comprises nine role-types, each with their own characteristics, risk of online exposure, level of security, and type of abuse. The innovative feature of this typology is the correlation of the offender's sexual interest in children and his interest in child pornography.

The *navigator* comes by his name honestly, as his exposure to child pornography is accidental (for example, through spam). However, he does choose to save the material to which he is exposed. In his case, the concepts of exposure risk and level of security are inapplicable. The abuse is indirect, as he does not interact with any child.

Table 3: Typology of online offences related to child pornography

Role type	Characteristics	Risk of exposure	Level of Security	Nature of abuse
Navigator	Accidentally discovers material. Saves the material	Zero	Zero	Indirect
Private fantasy	Deviant sexual fantasies. No sexual agression.	Zero	Zero	Indirect
Trawler	Searches for material accessibility	Low	Zero	Indirect
Unsecure collector	Child pornography peer-to-peer[4])	High	Zero	Indirect
Secure collector	Secure sites. Collects and exchanges material	High	Safe	Indirect
Groomer	Online relationship with child. Pornography facilitates sexual abuse	Depends on the online contact with individual child	Depends on the child	Direct
Physical abuser	Abuses children. Pornography facilitates sexual abuse	Depends on the physical contact with individual child	Depends on the child	Direct
Producer	Produces images of sexual abuse	Depends on whether producer becomes distributor	Depends on the child	Direct
Distributor	Distributes child pornography	Varies	Tends to be secure	Indirect

Krone (2004)

4 Technology that allows Internet users to exchange files directly without going through a central server (OLF, 2007).

In the second role-type, *private fantasy*, deviant sexual fantasies are present. Sometimes these fantasies do not go beyond thought, with the offender concretizing his fantasies in writing or digital images that he alone uses. There is no thought of proceeding to real-life action. In all other respects, this type is the same as the navigator.

Unlike the first two types, the *trawler* actively seeks out child pornography. He uses different computer servers without fear. The risk of exposure is low, there is no security, and the abuse is indirect.

As the name indicates, the *unsecure collector* also seeks out child pornography, preferably through peer-to-peer networks. He exchanges material with different sources and discussion groups on the Internet (Krone, 2004). His level of computer security is higher than that of trawlers, and he sometimes uses passwords and encryption.

The *secure collector* differs from the unsecure collector in that he searches secure networks. He is a collector, with a high risk of exposure and high level of security.

The *groomer* uses the Internet to initiate contact with a child. Once he gains the child's trust, he focuses on a single objective: having real or virtual sexual relations with the child. With these offenders, child pornography is a way of overcoming a child's inhibitions. The risk of exposure and level of security depend on the child. The abuse is direct — the offender intends to actually abuse a child.

As the name indicates, *physical abusers* sexually assault children they meet on the Internet. They maintain a personal collection of pornography but do not consider distributing it to other consumers. The risk of exposure, the level of security, and the nature of the abuse are the same as with groomers.

Producers differ from physical abusers by virtue of the fact that they produce images of the sexual abuse they or others practice on children.

Distributors profit from their child abuse. According to Krone (2004), not all distributors are sexually attracted to children. Their prime motivation is purely monetary, with no thought to the content of the material distributed. The nature of the abuse is indirect.

Alexy et al. (2005) used current events to paint a portrait of 225 individuals arrested for offences related to child pornography. They identified three types. The *trader* (n = 133) collects or exchanges images of child pornography. The *traveller* (n = 49) engages in online conversations to meet children and obtain sexual favours (n = 49). The *trader/traveller* (n = 43) combines the characteristics of these types. The study makes evident the formidable task of classifying criminals of this genre. The reliance on data from the popular media certainly did not make their task easier. In an attempt to address these difficulties, other authors have opted for approaches that combine individual characteristics and online activities.

One of the studies that best addresses the question of offending process is without question that of Seto et. al. (2006). The authors' starting point was the question: "Is an individual arrested for offences related to child pornography a paedophile?" They hypothesized that: 1) images of children elicit a greater phallometric response in child pornography offenders than do images of adults; 2) the phallometric response of child sex offenders is greater than that of individuals with a criminal record of sexual assault of adult women or of individuals undergoing counselling with a sexologist. The authors studied 685 patients at the Kurt Freund Laboratory of the Centre for Addiction and Mental Health in Ontario. They divided these men into nine subgroups:

- individuals arrested for child pornography crimes but who had not sexually assaulted any children
- individuals arrested for child pornography crimes who had sexually assaulted children
- sexual aggressors of children (one victim, two victims, three or more victims)
- sexual aggressors of women (one victim, two victims, three or more victims)
- patients in therapy with a sexologist

Individuals arrested for child pornography crimes — regardless of whether they had actually assaulted children — exhibited greater arousal when exposed to depictions of children (rather than adults) than did all other subgroups. These two subgroups (child pornography crimes with and without victims) are thus distinct from the others by virtue of their greater sexual arousal by children. Moreover, these subgroups exhibited much greater arousal than did the subgroups comprising sexual aggressors of children (one, two, or three or more victims). It therefore appears that the prevalence of paedophilia is higher among those arrested for offences related to child pornography than among sexual aggressors of women or individuals in therapy with a sexologist (Seto, Cantor and Blanchard, 2006).

A typology of consumers of child pornography based on individual characteristics and online activities

In Quebec, we have created a typology of men arrested for child pornography offences. Of all the variables related to socio-demographics and criminal history, only the following have proved significant: the offender's age at the time of the offence; the offender's criminal record; charges laid; and whether the offender was a student. Four types emerged from this analysis: the explorer, the solitary deviant, the organized deviant, and the polymorph.

The first and most important group is the *explorer*. Its members were relatively young (mean: 24.1) and had little or no criminal history (0.10 sexual assault charges and an average of one previous charge). Rarely was a member of this group involved in a sexual assault or crime involving child pornography. Notable as well is that all the students in our sample were explorers. François' (not his real name) story is typical:

> The German police reported to their Quebec counterparts that François, a Quebec resident, was exchanging child pornography over the Internet. Quebec authorities apprehended François shortly thereafter. At the time of his arrest, he was 21 years old, single, and a computer science student, and had no known criminal record. François very much enjoyed the IRC network. During a search of his residence, police seized two computers, from which they retrieved 800 images and videos of child pornography involving both boys and girls. Police also found pornography involving adults. The material was organized by category: young, interracial, teen, adults. François told police he knew what child pornography was and that it was forbidden to possess or exchange it. When an investigator asked him if he was sexually aroused by the images, François responded, "By some of them, yes, but in general, no." François attempted to justify his behaviour by stating, "I didn't personally take any of the photos and I don't make the photos available to others with the intention of hurting anyone. . ."

The explorer seems to be one of the types most oriented toward collecting on a large scale. The Internet provides users with an arsenal of techniques for such collecting. As well, it is possible to amass a collection simply by using software that manages exchanges of the material — what is called an F-serve (file server), which acts essentially like an FTP server.[5]

The *deviant* group comprised much older individuals, (mean age: 49.2). Its members had more previous convictions for sexual and non-sexual crimes, but many fewer than the third type. In a way, deviants are comparable to the "ordinary" man. Investigators have remarked something singular about the group, namely, its distinct pattern of online activity. While our data does not provide empirical evidence of this, there is a continuum in the level of involvement of consumers of child pornography in virtual communities. Analysis of police observations indicates the existence of two subtypes. The first, the *solitary deviant*, works alone, acquiring material from commercial sites or by responding spontaneously to online offers. He does not hesitate to use his credit card and provide personal information. Unlike the explorer, who presumably has fewer financial resources, given his youth and student status, the isolated deviant is able to pay for this sort of material, as the following example illustrates.

> Suspects Martin and Richard (not their real names) made contact through an electronic messaging service. They discussed different types of videos depicting child pornography as well as the system requirements for viewing them. Some weeks later, Richard ordered pedopornographic videos and made an electronic money transfer of $320 to Martin. In his statement to police, Richard confirmed, "I wanted it to satisfy my personal curiosity, but I have to admit that I'm aroused when I watch this kind of video. I play with myself."

Next there is the *organized deviant,* who has a strong virtual presence. He takes advantage of advice and techniques suggested by other members of the community, and, more importantly, exchanges material with them. Consider Serge's (not his real name) case:

> A Quebec resident laid a complaint with police about an individual searching the Internet for children with whom he could have sexual relations. Serge, a 39-year-old employed in the service industry, had a common-law relationship with his boyfriend. Serge used the IRC network, making explicit his interests there. While executing a search warrant, police seized an obsolete computer from his untidy residence.

5 File Transfer Protocol. A client-server file-transfer protocol that allows one to download a data file from another computer. The downloaded file may be of any type (text, images, sound). See www.olf.qc.ca.

Several years earlier, Serge had been convicted of sexual assault and gross indecency. In the interim, he had experienced other legal skirmishes involving breaking and entering, and breach of probation. From his computer, police recovered 1,500 images of young boys, but no pornography depicting adults. The type of sexual relations Serge was seeking was hardly surprising.

While the subjects of these two case histories belong to the same type, their involvement in the virtual community was very different. As Serge's case shows, and as investigators know to their frustration, it is very difficult to establish whether sexual abuse actually occurs. As one investigator has commented, only rarely can one clearly establish on the basis of computer-related evidence whether there has been abuse and whether the individual of interest is a group member.

The third group has few members (n = 8) and an average age of 42.8, and was markedly different from the others. On average, its members had more than 17 previous charges, including 3 charges of sexual assault. This group has the highest sexual assault: child pornography rate (0.50). Police are particularly interested in this group given the greater risk it poses to young potential victims.

Despite the group's small size, its members are responsible for a great number of crimes; it is therefore important to better understand them. Investigators say this type of suspect is fairly rare but more important, given that his crimes involve multiple victims. The use of child pornography does not appear to be the preferred criminal lifestyle. Individuals in this group combine sexual assault with several other types of crime.

McLaughlin (2000) has also studied the online behaviour of consumers of child pornography. The author has created a typology based on online activity and information from 200 police cases involving suspects in the U.S. and elsewhere. The typology comprises four types: 1) collectors (n = 143); 2) travellers (n = 48); 3) manufacturers (n = 8); and 4) chatters (n = 1).

With 143 members, the *collectors* are the largest group. While these individuals can be differentiated on the basis of age (13-65), several other observations about them merit attention. First, they are considered *entry-level offenders*. They appear to have no previous convictions and their child pornography offence does not appear to be part of a larger offending process. Their child pornography offence is their first criminal experience. They would not have committed any criminal act if the material had not been easily accessible and had it not been for the pervasive sense of impunity surrounding illicit online activity. These elements lower external inhibitions and facilitate offending. The Internet sharpens these individuals' sexual preferences. These people are also single and socially isolated. While they do not have criminal records, it seems that some of them harbour a "dangerous combination." In fact, 21% of the group were involved in child-related activities (social workers, teachers, summer-camp staff, etc.). Finally, the online activity of this group is oriented toward collection. Through chatrooms devoted to very specific content, and newsgroups, (see O'Connell, 2001) collectors can find, classify, and organize their collections according to their preferences (McLaughlin, 2000).

Travellers are also collectors of child pornography. Their average age is 35 and their main aim is to organize meetings rather than grow their collections. To this end, they use a series of subterfuges and strategies, greatly assisted by the Internet: false adolescent identities, sexual discussions, extraction of personal information, and the sending of pornographic images. More than half of them have sent photos of themselves, often nude. Their objectives clearly are to seduce victims and, eventually, organize an encounter. Some go so far as to send the victim money for this purpose.

Collectors could not survive without *manufacturers*. McLaughlin (2000) found the manufacturer/collector ratio to be about 1:18. In our study, there were 8 manufacturers (mean age: 41). Essentially, manufacturers provide content from several sources. While the majority of material derives from the 1970s and 1980s (Taylor and Quayle, 2003), the last decade has seen the appearance of new sources: live webcam shows, spy cameras, and even live recording of sexual assaults on children (McLaughlin, 2000, see Arnaldo, 2001).

It is also worth noting the extent to which the distribution of new products is a source of validation for manufacturers (Quayle and Taylor, 2003). Such new content can also include portrayals of sexual assaults of children practised by the manufacturers themselves: some manufacturers have a record of sexual crimes and distribute records of their assaults. Contrary to the dictates of common sense, it seems that only one manufacturer in our study created material for financial gain — estimated to be US $1,000. This finding runs counter to popular belief.

The last group is of little statistical importance (n = 1) but still merits attention. The *chatter* collects images of children in non-sexual contexts, such as in advertising or on nudist websites. This type stays just within legal boundaries, engaging in cybersex conversation, conducting online relationships, and presenting himself to children and adolescents as the only person they can trust —without ever asking to meet the children. They spend a great deal of time online, and tend to have most of their relationships there. They are very ritualistic, as they repeat approach techniques that have worked for them in the past. In summary, this type avoids official sanction because he stays within the limits of the law.

CONCLUSION

The arrival of the Internet provided pro-paedophile groups with a platform. While the cognitive distortions of paedophiles, consumers of child pornography, and "boy-lovers" might once have been known only to specialists working with these groups, the entire web is now their playground. Several studies have observed that individuals who experience doubt about this way of thinking can now obtain reassurance by sharing their thoughts with like-minded individuals. They no longer feel alone, and develop affiliations with those who share their worldview. Their community endorses its members' views and reinforces their cognitive distortions.

Research on the types of child-pornography consumers has taken many forms. Some authors have investigated the pathways of collectors, i.e. the context in which their interest in collecting child pornography developed. Their collecting began with the consumption of adult pornography online, and progressed to interest in child pornography. This in turn led to the devotion of time and effort to the search for content, as well as the establishment of online relationships.

Some studies have classified consumers of child pornography on the basis of the extent to which the material is distributed (Hartman, 1984), the level of organization (Klain et al., 2001), the level of risk and security (Krone, 2004), and the type of use (Alexy et al., 2005). The central question remains: Is the activity of the collector distinct from that of the collector-aggressor?

While one cannot ignore the role of the justice system, it does not seem the best route for obtaining answers. Studies on consumers of child pornography have shown that we know nothing about the pathways of the many collectors who have no sexual or general criminal record. Fernandez (2000a, 2000b) cites pre-sentence reports showing 46% of 54 subjects arrested for producing, distributing, and possessing child pornography had

had previous contact offences (Collins, 2006). After therapy, 79.6% of this group admitted having such contacts, signifying that 1,371 victims had not been detected by the justice system (Collins, 2006). As Seto et al. (2006) have shown, offences involving child pornography are an important variable in paedophilia.

The developmental approach — the study of the stages that lead to the consumption of child pornography and, ultimately, to sexual assault — seems the most promising. As Blundel et al. (2002) point out, the more fantasy is maintained and elaborated, the greater the chance that the individual will offend. Currently there are no longitudinal and empirical studies explaining the developmental patterns that lead individuals from the consumption of child pornography to the sexual assault of children. It is probably necessary to know somewhat more about consumers of child pornography, since, as McLaughlin (2000) puts it, "It is difficult to spot the aggressor in this ocean."

The consumer of child pornography is like a person who arrives at a train station. Most of the population does not go there, or actively avoids it, but he likes it and lingers. Some studies suggest that certain consumers arrive at the station on the sexual assault train, while others go to the station to get on that train. The number of consumers at the station is staggering, but we know nothing of their comings and goings. Some may even choose to stay at the station, without going anywhere — just train-watching, they say, is enough. In this respect, the station is a good place for watching and interacting with passengers both big and small.

REFERENCES

Alexy, E.M., Burgess, A.W., and Baker, T. (2005). Internet offenders: Traders, travelers, and combination trader/travelers. *Journal of Interpersonal Violence*, 20(5).

Badgley, R. (1984). *Infractions sexuelles à l'égard des enfants.* Ottawa: Centre d'édition du gouvernement du Canada.

Beauregard, E. (1999). T*ypologie de scénarios délictuels de meurtriers sexuels.* Montréal: Rapport de stage inédit, École de criminologie, Université de Montréal.

Belk, R.W. (1995). Collecting as Luxury Consumption: Effects on Individuals and Household. *Journal of Economic Psychology*, 16, 477-490.

Berberi, S. Boulanger, S., Fortin, F., Maleza, D., Ouellet, G., Paquin, J., Rodrigue, S. (2003). *La cybercriminalité au Québec.* Montréal: Sûreté du Québec, Service du renseignement criminel. Ministère de la Sécurité publique. Rapport d'analyse stratégique, 50-77.

Berson, I.R. and Tampa, F. (2003). Grooming Cybervictims: The Psychosocial Effects of Online Exploitation for Youth. *Journal of School Violence*, 2 (1), 5-18.

Carr, A. (2004). *Internet Traders of Child Pornography and Other Censorship Offenders in New Zealand.* Wellington: Department of Internal Affairs Te Tari Taiwhenua.

Carr, J. (2004). Child abuse, child pornography and Internet. Cusson, M. et Ouimet, M. (eds.), *Les violences criminelles* (157-185). Québec: Les Presses de l'Université Laval.

Costello, T. (2001). Gambling's great web of lies. *The Age*, 3 April, 15.

Creighton, S.J. (2003). *Child pornography: Images of the Abuse of Children.* London: NSPCC Research Department.

Durkin, N.F and Bryant, C.D. (1995). Log on to sex: Some notes on the carnal computer and erotic cyberspace as an emerging research frontier, *Deviant Behavior: An interdisciplinary journal*, 16, 179-200.

End Child Prostitution and Trafficking (ECPAT) (2002). *Child Pornography: Frequently asked questions about commercial sexual exploitation of children*. Consulted May 20, 2003. www.ecpat. net/eng/csec/faq.

Environics Research Group (2001). Les jeunes Canadiens dans un monde branché: la perspective des élèves. Consulté le 12 mai 2003. http://www.educationmedias.ca/francais/recherche/ JCMB/index.cfm.

Feather, M. (1999). *Internet and Child victimisation*. Paper presented at the Children and Crime: victims and offenders conference convened by the Australian Institute of Criminology, Brisbane, June 17-18, 1999.

Finkelhor, D. and Ormrod, R. (2004). Child pornography: patterns from NIBRS (*Child Justice Bulletin* NCJ 204911). Washington DC: U.S. Department of Justice, Office of Justice Programs, Office of Child and Delinquency Prevention.

Foley, T. (in press). *The Forensic Assessment of Internet Child Pornography Offenders*. Philadelphia, PA: Joseph J. Peters Institute.

Forde, P. and Patterson, A. (1998). Paedophiles Internet Activity. *Trends and Issues in Crime and Criminal justice*, 97, 1-6.

Fortin, F. (2005: May 26). *Criminalité informatique: un survol des tendances en évolution*. Conférence présentée au congrès de la Société de Criminologie du Québec de Montréal, Sainte-Adèle.

Fortin, F. and Lapointe, S. (2002: June 7). *Internet qu'est-ce que ça change ? Usages problématiques et criminels d'Internet*. Conférence présentée au congrès de l'Association des médecins psychiatres, Mont-Tremblant.

Goldstein, M.J., Kant, H.S. and Hartman, J.J. (1973). *Pornography and Sexual Deviance*. Los Angeles: University of California Press.

Healy, M.A. (1996). *Child Pornography: an international perspective*. Stockholm: World Congress against Commercial Sexual Exploitation of Children.

Howitt, D. (1995). *Paedophiles and Sexual Offences against Children*. Chichester, England: J. Wiley.

Hunter, M. (2001). How to beat the Net? *Community care*, February 22-28, p. 12.

Itzin, C. (1992). *Pornography: women, violence and civil liberties.* Oxford: Oxford University Press.

Jenkins, P. (2001). *Beyond Tolerance: Child Pornography Online.* New York: New York University Press.

Kelly, L. (1992). Pornography and Child Sexual Abuse. In C. Itzen (dir.), *Pornography; Women, Violence and Civil Liberties* (113-123). Oxford: Oxford University Press.

Klain, E.J., Davies, H.J., and Hicks, M.A. (2001). *Child pornography: The criminal-justice-system response* (Report No. NC81). Alexandria, VA: American Bar Association Center on Children and the Law.

Krone, T. (2005). *Does Thinking Make It So ? Defining Online Child Pornography Possession Offences.* Canberra: Australian High Tech Crime Center. Consulted December 16, 2005, http://www. aic.gov.au/ publications/tandi2/tandi299.pdf.

Lacroix, E. (2002). *Sondage NETendances 2002: Utilisation d'Internet au Québec.* Centre francophone d'informatisation des organisations (CEFRIO). Consulted July 3, 2004: https:// extranet.cefrio.qc.ca/ indexWeb.cfm ?type= produits.

Langevin, R., Lang, R.A., Wright, P., Handy, L., Frenzel, R.R. and Black, E.L. (1988). Pornography and Sexual Offences. *Annals of Sex Research*, 1, 335-362.

Lanning, K. (1992). *Child Molesters: A Behavioural Analysis.* Washington, DC: National Center for Missing and Exploited Children.

Lanning, K.V. (1984). Collectors. In A.W. Burgess. (ed.), *Child Pornography and Sex Rings* (83-109). Lexington, MA: Lexington Books.

Marshall, W.L., Barbaree, H.E. and Christophe, D. (1984). Sexual offenders against female children: Sexual preferences for age of victims and type of behaviour. *Revue canadienne des sciences du comportement*, 18, 424-439.

Mayer, A. (1985). *Sexual abuse: causes, consequences and treatment of incestuous and pedophilic act*. Holmes Beach, FL: Learning.

McLaughlin, J. F. (2000). *Cyber child sex offender typology*. Retrieved August 8, 2000, from www.ci.keene.nh.us/police/Typology.html.

Muensterberger, W. (1994). *Collecting: An Unruly Passion*. Princeton, NJ: Princeton University Press.

O'Connell, R. (2001). Paedophiles networking on the Internet. In C.A. Arnaldo (ed.). *Child abuse on the Internet: Ending the silence*. Berghahn Books and UNESCO, Paris, pp. 65-79.

Office de la langue française. (1998). Le grand dictionnaire terminologique. Consulted January 7, 2005 and March 19, 2007. http://www.granddictionnaire.com/btml/fra/r_motclef/index800_1.asp.

Oswell, D. (2004). (In press). *When images matter: internet child pornography, forms of observation and an ethics of the virtual*. Consulted January 7, 2005. http://www.xuk.biz/ UKLR/Landslide/library/13a/oswell_images_matter.pdf. Protectkids. Protecting children in cyberspace. http://www. protectkids.com/dangers/stats.htm. 27 août 2006.

Proulx, J., Perreault, C. and Ouimet, M. (1999a). Pathways in the Offending Process of Extra-familial Sexual Child Molester. *Sexual Abuse: A journal of Research and Treatment*, 11, 117-129.

Proulx, J., St-Yves, M., Guay, J.-P. and Ouimet, M. (1999b). Les agresseurs sexuels de femmes: Scénarios délictuels et troubles de la personnalité. In J. Proulx, M. Cusson and M. Ouimet (eds.). *Les violences criminelles* (187-216). Québec: Presses de l'Université Laval.

Proulx, J., Perreault, C., Ouimet, M. and Guay, J.P. (1999c). Les agresseurs sexuels d'enfants: scénarios délictuels et troubles de la personnalité. In J. Proulx, M. Cusson and M. Ouimet (eds.). *Les violences criminelles* (187-216). Québec: Presses de l'Université Laval.

Quayle, E., Holland, G., Linehan, C. and Taylor, M. (2000). The Internet and Offending Behaviour: a case study. *Journal of Sexual Agression*, 6 (1/2), 78-96.

Rettinger, L.J. (2000). *La relation entre la pornographie juvénile et les infractions sexuelles contre les enfants: Une analyse documentaire.* Ottawa: ministère de la Justice du Canada.

Roy, J. (2004). *Étude exploratoire des événements et des caractéristiques des individus mis en cause dans des cas de possession et de distribution de matériel pornographique juvénile sur Internet.* Montréal: Rapport de stage inédit, École de criminologie, Université de Montréal.

Russel, D. (1984). *Sexual exploitation, child sexual abuse, and workplace harassment.* Beverley Hills, California: Sage.

Savary, Claude (2005). *Le Nouvelliste* (Trois-Rivières) Actualités, samedi 23 avril 2005, p. 3. La Couronne réclame la prison ferme contre André Von Gunten. L'accusé a été trouvé en possession de 44 000 photos de pornographie juvénile.

Seto, M., and Eke, A. (2005). Criminal histories and later offending of child pornography offenders. *Sexual Abuse: A Journal of Research and Treatment*, 17, 201-210.

Stanley, J. (2001). *Child abuse and the Internet.* National child Protection Clearinghouse. Australian Institute of family studies, no 15.

Svedin, C.G. and Back, K.B. (1996). *Children who don't speak out: about children being used in child pornography.* Stockholm: Swedish save the Children.

Sykes G.M., Matza D. (1957). Techniques of neutralization: a theory of delinquency. *Am. J. Sociol.* 22: 664-70.

Taylor, M. (1999). *The Nature and Dimensions of Child Pornography on the Internet.* Combating child pornography on the Internet conference, Vienna. Consulted January 17, 2005, www.asem.org/Documents/aa-confvienna/pa_taylor.html.

Taylor, M. and Quayle, E. (2003). *Child Pornography an Internet Crime.* New York: Routledge.

Taylor, M. and Quayle, E. (2002). Child Pornography and the Internet: Perpetuating a cycle of abuse. *Deviant Behavior: An Interdisciplinary Journal*, 23, 331-361.

Taylor, M., Quayle, E. and Holland, G. (2001). La pornographie infantile, l'Internet et les comportements délinquants. *ISUMA*, 2 (2), 1-12.

Tremblay, P. (2002). Social Interactions among Paedophiles. *Cahiers de criminologie*, 36, (50). Montréal: Université de Montréal, Centre international de criminologie comparée.

Wellard, S. (2001). Cause and effect, *Community Care*, 15-21, March, 26-27.

Wolak, J., Finkelhor, D., and Mitchell, K.J. (2005b). *Child-Pornography Possessors Arrested in Internet-Related Crimes: Findings from the National Child Online Victimisation Studys*. Alexandria, VA: National Centre for Missing and Exploited Children.

Wyre, R. (1992). Pornography and Sexual Violence: Working with Sex Offenders. In C. Itzen (dir.), *Pornography: women, violence and civil liberties* (237-247). Oxford: Oxford University Press.

CHAPTER 18

Criminal Profiling

Éric Latour, Jim Van Allen, Marc Lépine and Pierre Nezan

When you have eliminated the impossible, whatever remains, however improbable, must be the truth.

Sir Arthur Conan Doyle

One cannot say precisely where and when criminal profiling first came to be. The earliest instance we have found in forensic annals is profiling by the British surgeon Thomas Bond, who performed the autopsy on Mary Kelly, Jack the Ripper's last victim. The doctor characterized the killer's surgical knowledge and suggested certain characteristics of the killer revealed by the crime scene: calm, apparently inoffensive, of average age, well-groomed, and not employed in the meat industry, given that he had no technical skill in dismemberment. Bond also demonstrated that this murder was related to three others (Sugden, 1995). While his profile was never confirmed (the crimes have yet to be solved), some consider Bond's report to be a precursor of criminal profiling, establishing links between several crimes and profiling the killer based on investigative fact.

Others nominate as pioneer the American psychiatrist James Brussel, who produced a criminal profile of rare accuracy as part of the "Mad Bomber" investigation[1] in New York in the 1950s. Having examined the investigative file and letters written by the bomber, Brussel deduced the suspect was a strong man, of average age, born outside the United States, Catholic, unmarried, and living with a sibling (Geberth, 1996). He added that this man was paranoid, hated his father, obsessively in love with his mother, and living in the state of Connecticut. Dr. Brussel even told police, "When you catch him, there's a good chance he'll be wearing a double-breasted jacket." The profile turned out to be astonishingly accurate — apparently even down to the double-breasted jacket's being buttoned.

1 Between 1940 and 1956, Georges Metesky ("the Mad Bomber") committed 30 bombings in New York.

Today, police services around the world benefit from criminal profiling as an investigative tool. However, their uses of the tool differ.

In the United Kingdom, the British psychologist David Canter popularized the technique after his successful profiling of the serial "Railway Rapist," John Duffy. Canter's approach was based on applied research more than on experience. He brought together concepts from criminology, social psychology, and forensic psychiatry to create empirical data permitting generalizations about violent crimes. His model rests on five principal bases: interpersonal coherence, spatial and temporal factors, offender characteristics, criminal career, and forensic evidence (see Canter, 1995; 2000; Wilson and Soothill, 1996).

Criminal profiling in Canada is inspired largely by the model developed at the Federal Bureau of Investigation (FBI). United States investigators have used criminal profiling for more than three decades, but its popularity in the policing community exploded at the beginning of the 1990s with the release of Thomas Harris's film, *The Silence of the Lambs.* Today, numerous books and TV series are devoted to criminal profiling. Unfortunately, what is depicted in film and literature does not always provide a true picture of criminal profiling or, especially, criminal analysts (profilers). This describes the nature, usefulness, and limits of criminal profiling, and provides an overview of the role of criminal analysts in crime-scene analysis.

A. CRIMINAL PROFILING AS AN INVESTIGATIVE TOOL

A crime scene presents a vast array of variables to the investigator. A template or checklist approach to crime scene analysis is, therefore, not possible. However, the procedures of criminal analysts can be helpful in providing additional insights, organizing investigative information, and understanding the behaviour, motivation, and personality characteristics of the offender. Essentially, the procedure used by criminal analysts is not unlike that used by experienced criminal investigators. They also rely heavily on their experience as criminal investigators, and have received specialized training in criminal and deviant sexual behaviour.

The goal of the criminal analyst or the investigator is to achieve the best possible understanding of the cause of the crime and the dynamics of the crime scene, on the basis of observable elements and evidence of offender-victim interaction. The analyst attempts to articulate this understanding for the consideration and benefit of the entire investigative team. They also endeavour to answer the following questions: Who would do this? Why this victim, at this time, at this location, in this manner? Answering any or all of these questions points the way toward determining the identity of the offender responsible for the crime.

In this process, the criminal analyst will integrate information gleaned from traditional types of evidence — such as fingerprints, DNA, weapon information, and items left by the offender — as well as behavioural information, such as modus operandi and expressions of offender desires or emotions.

Behavioural analysis is built on the premises that thinking directs behaviour, and that our personalities remain constant across all types of activities. It necessarily follows that core personality traits motivate and influence behaviour during the commission of a crime, just as how we conduct ourselves during our occupational or social activities says something about "who we are." Expressions of behaviour give outward shape to our personalities and thinking. Of course, other relevant factors such as alcohol and drugs may also influence behaviour (Alison, Bennell, Mokros and Ormerod, 2002).

While a criminal investigator may examine a knife for fingerprints, or attempt to trace its owner by its history of manufacture and sale, a criminal analyst asks the following questions: Why did the offender feel the need to arm themselves against this particular victim? How was the weapon used? How effectively was it used? Does the way the weapon was used tell us anything about the offender's competence, experience or empathy? It is not enough to know that the victim was stabbed. Consider an autopsy that reveals that the victim received 20 stab wounds, all but 3 of which were superficial, non-lethal, and inflicted on non-lethal areas of the body. This may suggest that the offender is inexperienced, and found great difficulty in overpowering the victim, who only eventually succumbed to their wounds and was possibly killed with final "coup de grace" wounds. This might also indicate an offender with no history of physical violence or an offender of small stature.

Does a vicious neck slashing suggest an offender who is bereft of empathy and would surely demonstrate a similar lack of empathy in other relationships? Does an abundance of lacerations to the victim's face suggest an explosive emotional venting or an intimate and highly personal relationship between the offender and the victim? Do superficial wounds to a sexual assault victim or wounds inflicted as torture suggest a sadistic intent? Does the pattern of post-mortem wounds suggest that the offender took pleasure simply in stabbing the victim after their death? The greater the number of violent crimes seen, the more extensive the repertoire of cases to which comparisons can be made, and the greater the probability of producing accurate analyses.

Behavioural observations based on crime-scene dynamics may enable the criminal analyst to infer the offender's intelligence, motivation, criminal competence and experience, likely criminal history, and other key characteristics (particularly motivation and intent). Crime scene behaviour —specifically, the time and effort devoted to eliminating evidence — may indicate the offender's sophistication. Evidence of planning and premeditation, mobility, or resources all say something about the offender.

The authors are frequently asked whether or not they feel the current popularity of crime-scene television programs enhance offenders' ability to commit a perfect crime. While an offender's knowledge of investigative techniques could well complicate evidence recovery, we feel that the overwhelming majority of offenders will still default to their core behaviours in the face of the high emotions commonly experienced during the commission of murder or sexual assault. These television shows provide good entertainment, but rarely, if ever, reflect the harsh and sobering realities of the most severe crimes of interpersonal violence. Nevertheless, a recent FBI report indicates that the percentage of unsolved rape cases in the United States is increasing, and that this may be due to offenders' increased use of bleach, condoms and gloves.[2]

Experience teaches us that no matter how an offender plans to commit a murder, the overwhelming number of murders are non-serial events. An offender's reaction to the realities of increased adrenalin, unexpected complications, an aggressively resisting victim fighting for their life, or other unforeseen contingencies will usually provide insight into their actual abilities, characteristics and traits and their response to extremely stressful events. Experienced criminal analysts know the typical characteristics of crimes, and recognize a crime scene staged on the basis of what an offender has read or seen in a movie.

After many years of personal experience in major crime investigation and involvement in hundreds of homicide investigations, we have come to the conclusion that investigations fail for many reasons, not all of which are

---

2 Audrey Dutton, "More rape cases go unsolved" (Washington Bureau, newsday.com, September, 19, 2006).

the fault of the investigators. However, we have witnessed investigators commit faults of logic, due, amongst other things, to inaccurate interpretation of the crime scene, pre-conceived notions, reliance on inaccurate forensic analysis, the imposition of their "expectations" on the offender, tunnel vision, and twisting crime-scene evidence to fit their theory rather than ensuring that the theory fits every aspect of the evidence. As long as humans investigate crimes, there will be human error. It's unavoidable. Police are as capable of making mistakes as any other group of professionals, including lawyers, judges, and doctors. And we humbly admit that experience has taught us that our analyses have not always been correct, either.

In practice, investigators can establish an essentially accurate investigative "lead" in the great majority of cases in they examine every facet of the available information and not rush to judgment in the absence of vital information, keep an open mind, use the combined assistance of the entire investigative team, including specialists, and apply common sense. The authors also recognize that exigent circumstances do sometimes require investigators to develop and pursue a theory without confirming all the facts by additional investigation, witness interviews, or forensic analyses.

Even the most experienced investigators may be taken aback by certain graphically violent or complex crime scenes. Other scenes may be outside the realm of experience of relatively inexperienced investigators. A small police force may have no history dealing with strange, unusual, or bizarre crimes. In these scenarios —as, in fact, with other cases — the investigative team will benefit from crime-scene analysis founded on a logical process.

The analysis of any violent crime has to begin with an assessment of the victim. North American crime statistics indicate that almost 84% of all murder victims are killed by someone known to them — family members, other relatives, friends, acquaintances of varying degrees, or sexual partners. This is a distinct advantage and an overwhelmingly significant and valuable indicator for crime investigators. But what of the 12% of homicides committed by strangers, or the 4% about which nothing is known? And what about crime scenes with multiple victims, or crimes that indicate possible offender focus in theft and murder, or sexual assault and murder? Did the offender enter the home to steal, but killed when confronted by an occupant? Did the offender enter a home to commit sexual assault but later felt the need to kill to protect their identity? Or was the victim targeted for murder, and the crime scene "staged" to disguise the manner of death or the true motive for the crime? These are the very real challenges and dilemmas faced by real-life investigators, in contrast to detectives on television.

Methodically examining the "big picture," and breaking it up into smaller pieces and labelling them is a better way to understand complex crimes and crime scenes. The criminal analyst's methodology for the examination of these complex puzzles facilitates the establishment of the significance of each piece and its relationship to the others.

The Crime Classification Manual (Douglas, Burgess, Burgess and Ressler, 1992) provides a system for classifying offences on the basis of motivation. Such classification systems provide investigators with possible motivations for a murder that can be retained or eliminated. Does a killing look conflict-based? Does the victim's recent financial, relationship, or business histories suggest a trigger for the murder? Does a deteriorating intimate relationship or marriage, or an extra-marital affair, suggest that the offender would personally gain from the victim's demise? Did the victim's lifestyle, circle of associates, participation in crimes, or substance use or other high-risk activities provide any valuable insight as to why someone would select them as a victim?

Considering the victim's risk level can be helpful in understanding why the offender chose them. High-risk victims such as habitual criminals or sex-trade workers regularly expose themselves to a violent segment of society. We expect them to be victimized at a greater rate, often by strangers or other criminals. Individuals with a low victimization risk, including the elderly and children, are also victimized. However, in our experience, low-risk victims who are violently murdered in their own home or while not engaged in an activity that elevates their victimization risk can reliably be assumed to have been targeted by the offender (Safarick, Jarvis and Nussbaum, 2002).

The experienced investigator should also consider and examine the possible significance of other possible motives, (profit, revenge, sex, political issues) (see Douglas, Burgess, Burgess and Ressler, 1992). To what extent did the offender focus on a specific victim or a specific activity? While no single interpretation can explain all human action, and no behavioural theory is absolute, there are general patterns of behaviour that tend to be reliable. The amount of time and money spent on activities tends to be an indication of their focus of a person's life. What holds true in the domain of normal human activity is also true of criminal behaviour. In cases of multiple homicide, the primary victim may be the one who received the brunt of the offender's attention. If more time was spent killing a victim than in stealing from them, it may be that the offender's intent was to kill a targeted victim, and that the theft was an opportunistic afterthought.

Is the time spent committing the crime out of balance with the offender's efforts to destroy or conceal evidence? Was significant time invested in preparing the crime scene of a murder, for example, by disabling phone lines or alarm systems, or reducing a victim's possibility of escape? Was time spent protecting personal or valuable possessions from damage, which suggests "ownership" of the protected property and, by extension, the possible identity of the offender?

Does the experienced investigator recognize that the offender's technique or modus operandi differs from that typical of a particular category of offender? Does the point of entry or method of forcible entry correspond to those typically used by burglars? Did the offender pay attention to the things offenders of their type typically do, or were they apparently oblivious to lights, alarms, animals that may have alerted someone to their presence, or obvious markers of human presence or activity, such as parked cars? Did the offender cut a screen far from a door lock, or unnecessarily cut a screen that they eventually removed? Was their choice of point of entry risky or foolhardy given the presence of more logical points of entry? Did the offender's choices suggest the absence of the preparation typical of most offenders prior to a break-in? None of these interpretations are insignificant in efforts to understand a crime scene. As Alan Brantley, an eminent criminal analyst, and former FBI Special Supervisory Agent, points out, atypical and unusual crime scene behaviour reflects atypical and unusual offender motivation. This succinct statement is a valuable adage investigators should bear in mind when their observations of offender behaviour don't seem to add up, or are inconsistent with typical offender behaviour.

The authors have seen sexual motivations go unrecognized or inaccurately assessed in some crimes. Investigators may fail to recognize evidence of sexually deviant interests which seem to them irrelevant. Similarly, sexual motivation may go unrecognized in cases of unsuccessful sexual offences.

Generally, sexual motivation should be carefully considered and assessed in every case in which a female is victimized with no clear or probable motive. The presence of a sexual motivation for the crime is suggested not only by the sex and age of the victim, but also by the victim's posture and position, the disorder of the crime scene, the partial or complete removal of the victim's clothing, evidence or suggestions of sexual activity, evidence of the offender's interest in a sexual area of the body, the presence of bodily fluids (including saliva), and the insertion of foreign objects into body cavities. The presence of sperm in the victim's body or actions involving urine or feces may likewise suggest deviant sexual interests. Ostensible evidence of sexual motivation that is not confirmed by forensic analysis may raise questions and suggest that the offender staged the crime scene.

One of the most reliable indications of the experience of the offender is how well the offender controlled the victim. Those who have acquired experience in coercive violence in previous assaults tend to exercise good control, while those who are on their "maiden voyage" into criminal violence may find that it is more difficult than they imagined to subdue a terrorized and resisting victim, and may be surprised to learn how difficult it is to kill somebody.

In the pre-crime planning phase of a crime, all options are available to a potential killer. They can shoot, stab, bomb, poison, strangle, bludgeon, or burn their adversary. They can kill the victim whether the latter is at home, at work, or driving somewhere. However, as the killer gets closer to the crime, key choices must be made, and these decisions "speak" about the offender. People generally select what they are familiar with, what they are good at, or what is available to them. A physically powerful male who is confident in his ability to overwhelm a victim may choose to forego a weapon. Typically, people — including the police and the military — arm themselves to gain an advantage over a superior opponent. The failure to plan and bring a weapon to a crime, and the use an object available at the crime scene, may suggest a low degree of planning and premeditation, or a spontaneous type of crime. We have always believed that offenders who arm themselves with a knife when setting out to commit violence against a woman (weaker, on average, than most males) possess a personality defect or a lack of self-confidence.

In our experience, when offenders who have a free choice of weapon choose a firearm, the calibre of the firearm is an indication of their self-confidence. Large-calibre firearms suggest a subtle need on the offender's part to "outgun" a victim who may be difficult to overpower. These questions may help investigators develop a theory as to the identity of the person who made those choices.

A similar approach is possible with regard to control. What, if any, restraints were used by the offender? Do the restraints indicate planning on the part of the offender — handcuffs, self-clinching wrap fasteners, adhesive tape, pre-cut lengths of rope? Did the offender demonstrate resourcefulness by using items that were available at the crime scene, such as extension cords or telephone wires? Is there adhesive apparent on the victim's wrists or ankles, indicating removal of the tape following a murder in order to deny police valuable evidence? Are there small puncture-like wounds along a victim's ribcage or along the back of an arm that suggest coercive knife-point prodding to gain control of the victim during an abduction?

Reconstructing the likely sequence of events during a crime may provide valuable insight into the dynamics of the crime, and refute inaccurate theories or defensive scenarios. Blood spatter, and the "layering" of fallen items may indicate the order in which events occurred. In one case, the placing of personal items belonging to a victim on top of a blood stain reliably indicated that the offender showed particular interest in the victim's personal information after the murder. This led to the conclusion that the killer was a former intimate partner and not, as he attempted to mislead investigators, a stranger. In another case, investigators noted a large drop of blood on top of a thin blood-transfer smear that was almost surely caused by the victim's final movements. From this, investigators concluded that the large drop was almost certainly shed by the offender as they moved around the crime scene following the murder. DNA testing of that particular sample provided valuable evidence against the offender.

The authors have learned through experience that most behaviour — including criminal behaviour — is purposeful. "Everything people do is for a reason." So, if investigators, thinking logically, are unable to determine the motive for a specific criminal act, it may be that the offender's thought process is different, if not indeed irrational. Bizarre or extremely unusual crime-scene behaviour may signal that the offender is mentally disordered, or perhaps even detached from reality due to a serious mental illness. Unnecessary explorative or symbolic cutting of a victim's body, as well as blood smearing and other unexplained and possibly ritualistic behaviour, may be symptoms of serious mental illness.

Most people, investigators included, are shocked and repulsed by any cutting or dismemberment of a body. While some react emotionally to unusual crime scenes of this type, and publicly describe the offender as a "monster," there is a comprehensible motive for such acts. The motivation for criminal mutilation falls into a number of categories (see Rajs, Lundstrom, Broberg, Lindberg and Lindquist, 1998). The dismembering of a body merely to facilitate disposal is referred to as "defensive" mutilation.

The offender feels an urgent need to dispose of the "evidence" of their crime, or protect their identity, so as to hinder identification of the victim. "Aggressive" mutilation generally involves the cutting of the victim's face, ears, or genitals, and is an extension of the rage the offender experienced when committing the murder. "Offensive" mutilation is sexualized violence involving the cutting or excision of sexual areas of the victim's body. "Necromanic" mutilation is post-mortem cutting, generally signifying the offender's interest in the victim's dead body and, usually, the offender's psychopathology.

In only a few rare crimes will there be such an absence of observable activity that in-depth crime-scene analysis is impossible. This process has enabled criminal analysts to recognize murders that were staged as accidents or accidental drownings, or appeared to be suicides. Crime-scene analysis has also helped identify murderers who were former intimate partners or current spouses, when the overall picture suggested otherwise.

Thorough crime-scene analysis helps establish the profile of the offender and select appropriate interview strategies and approaches; even more importantly, it helps identify approaches to avoid with specific offenders.

The valuable insights gained from painstaking, thoughtful, and thorough crime-scene analysis help establish an offender's motive and develop a profile of an unknown offender. Armed with this information, criminal analysts can suggest the investigative strategies best suited to a particular personality type and, even, the most appropriate interview strategies.

B. CRIME-SCENE ANALYSIS

Ressler et al. (Ressler, Burgess, and Douglas, 1988) created the first dichotomous classification of criminals, classifying them as "organized" or "disorganized" (Table 1). It is important to note that this dichotomy is not based on clinical entities and is intended to allow investigators to orient their investigation. Some authors associate the organized type with psychopaths and the disorganized type with psychotics (Geberth 1996; Schlesinger 2004). Others refer to "asocial disorganized" and "non-social organized" types (Holmes and Holmes 2002).

1. The "Organized" Crime Scene

A crime's level of organization is a function of, among other things, the level of control apparent at the crime scene, the victim's submissiveness, the use of restraints, the recourse to ante-mortem torture, the existence of multiple crime scenes, and the absence of evidence (see Photo 1). Generally, organized individuals have an average or above-average level of intelligence, and adequate social skills. They usually are employed and may have apparently normal marital and family lives. In brief, they fit in well with society. On the other hand, those around them may perceive them as self-centred, narcissistic, and having a violent temper. They are good talkers and manipulators, able to approach victims without making them feel threatened.

2. The "Disorganized" Crime Scene

Disorganized crime scenes (see Photo 2) are characterized by disorder and confusion; in addition, the victim's body has been left in plain sight, there are post-mortem acts — including sexual acts — against the victim, and the crime appears to have been spontaneous. In most cases, there was some relationship between the offender and the victim. Disorganized individuals are generally loners, unmarried, poorly educated, and socially inept. They have poor self-esteem and often suffer from mental disorders. Those around them sometimes describe them as strange or bizarre.

The organized/disorganized classification is not purely dichotomous but rather a continuum. A crime scene can display features of both types. Furthermore, a perpetrator can become more or less disorganized; in such cases, it may be that there were two criminals or a single criminal under the influence of alcohol or drugs at the time of the crime. The degree of organization reflected by a crime scene can also be seen in other aspects of the criminal's life; this relationship is the starting point for the construction of the criminal's behavioural profile.

Table I

	Organized	**Disorganized**
Operational Modes of Sexual Murderers	• murder planned • victim previously unknown to murderer • victim personalized • conversation controlled • crime scene reflects control • submission demanded of victim • restraints used • ante-mortem aggression (eroticization of murder) • body hidden • weapon / evidence absent • victim's body transported to another location	• murder spontaneous • victim or location previously unknown to murderer • victim depersonalized • conversation minimal • crime scene chaotic • attack sudden • minimal use of restraints • post-mortem mutilation, sexual acts • victim's body positioned • body left in plain sight • evidence / weapon usually present • body left at crime scene
Psychosocial Characteristics of Sexual Murderers	• good intelligence • socially competent • prefers work requiring manual skills • sexually competent • usually one of the oldest in the family • father with stable employment • inconsistent childhood discipline • controlled mood during crime • use of alcohol prior to or during crime • situational stress the trigger • has a romantic partner • is mobile, with car in good condition • follows the crime in media • may change jobs or leave town after crime	• average intelligence • socially immature • no work history • sexually incompetent • usually one of the youngest in the family • father with unstable employment • harsh discipline in childhood • anxious during crime • minimal use of alcohol prior to or during crime • minimal situational stress • lives alone • lives and works near crime scene • minimal interest in media coverage of the crime • minimal change in lifestyle

Adapted from Ressler, Burgess, and Douglas (1988).

3. Motivation

Crime-scene analysis and victimology can provide insight about the underlying motive of a crime. Once the motive has been identified, it is sometimes easier to focus the investigation on a specific suspect or group of suspects. Victimology — comprehensive investigation regarding the victim, including that person's daily routine and character traits — is an essential element of this analysis.

The Crime Classification Manual (Douglas, Burgess, Burgess and Ressler, 1992) sets out a comprehensive list of motives for violent acts. Sometimes the motive is evident — when, for instance, a debt-ridden man has bought life insurance on his spouse soon before her murder, or a murder victim has ties to a criminal organization. Other times, as the following case shows, only deeper analysis will reveal motive.

> A grandmother and her two grandchildren had been burned alive in the grandmother's home. Forensic analysis revealed the fire to be arson. The grandmother was alone with the children on the night of the tragedy. The children's parents were separated and engaged in a court battle over child custody. The father of the children had been accused of domestic violence, and was under court order to stay away from the grandmother's home. Police quickly focused their investigation on the father, given his conflict with his former spouse and the fact that he was near the scene of the tragedy when it occurred. Exhaustive crime-scene analysis and victimology revealed that the grandmother probably killed herself and her grandchildren. The coroner considered this to be the most likely scenario.

4. Crime-Scene Staging

Crime-scene staging occurs when an individual deliberately alters a scene before police arrive (Douglas, Burgess, Burgess and Ressler, 1992). The individual's prime motivation is to misdirect the police investigation and deflect suspicion from themselves. Usually, the offender will be someone related to or closely associated with the victim. In addition to altering the scene to create confusion, the suspect often cooperates with investigators and the victim's family, and pretends to be upset.

When a suspect attempts to mislead police with crime-scene staging, he usually attempts to convey the impression that the death was related to sexual assault, an accidental fire, or armed robbery, or was a suicide. In their attempt to make the staging credible to police and mask their motives, stagers draw on their own knowledge, often taken from movies. As a result, the staging often comprises errors, as can be seen from the following examples.

Case 1

A couple's son stabbed them more than 70 times (Photo 3). The son had staged the scene so that it looked as though a robbery had gone wrong (Photo 4). Three rooms had been ransacked but nothing had been stolen (Photo 5). Police found the victims in their bedroom, where they had apparently been surprised by their attacker. Five knives had been used, suggesting that there had been multiple criminals. A giant question mark had been drawn on the kitchen table in ketchup. Was this the work of a psychopath toying with the police? Two vehicles belonging to the residents had been parked in their designated places: nothing suggested that the home had been empty. The evidence was incompatible with the theory of an interrupted house-breaking. The son eventually pleaded guilty to two counts of second-degree murder.

Case 2

An individual contacted police, stating that he had found his spouse hanging in the garage of their home. Could this have been suicide? Investigation revealed multiple inconsistencies in the caller's version and that the couple had not been getting along. An autopsy and crime-scene analysis revealed strong evidence of scene staging (Photos 6-8). The spouse was convicted of second-degree murder.

There are several indicators of a staged crime scene; investigators must take care to consider them as a whole, rather than focus on any one. Was the suspect's point of entry logical, or were there other, easier, points of entry? Were valuable objects in plain sight not stolen? Did the suspect choose an obviously occupied home rather than a vacant one? Is there no evidence of sexual assault at autopsy? Is the version of witnesses inconsistent with the evidence, or improbable? These questions help establish whether the scene has been staged, and, if so, the reason for the staging.

"Organized" versus "disorganized" crime scene

Photo 1

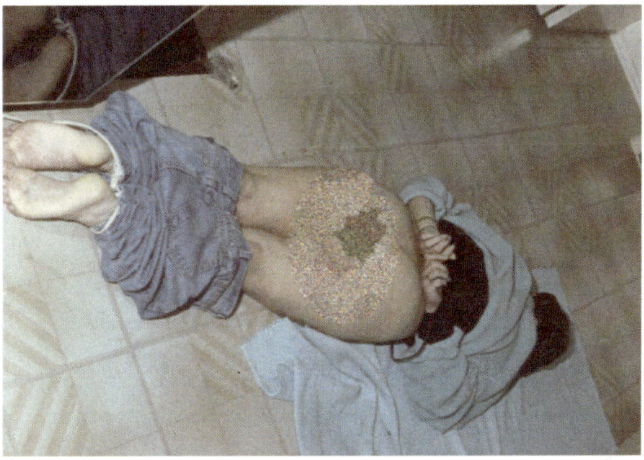

Photo Sûreté du Québec

Organized killer: The victim had been visited by a stranger interested in buying the victim's house. The victim had been bound and subjected to sadistic acts (insertion of an object in the anal cavity). Everything indicated that the murderer had been in complete control of the situation.

Photo 2

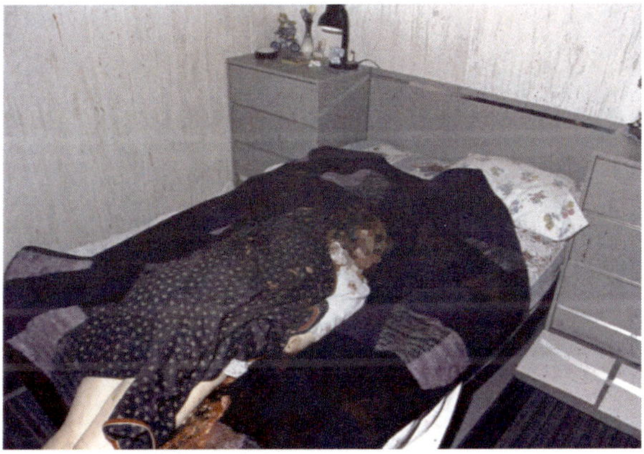

Photo Sûreté du Québec

Disorganized killer: Woman killed by an intimate friend who suffered from serious mental problems. The victim's skull had been caved in by a hammer. The scene exhibited many signs of disorganization (pieces of brain and skull scattered through the room; blood spatter on the walls).

Staged crime scenes

Photo 3

Photo Sûreté du Québec

The victims had received more than 70 knife wounds.

Photo 4

Photo Sûreté du Québec

The criminal made the room look as if it had been searched.

Photo 5

Photo Sûreté du Québec

Neither the wallet, nor valuable objects, nor some American money had been stolen.

Photo 6

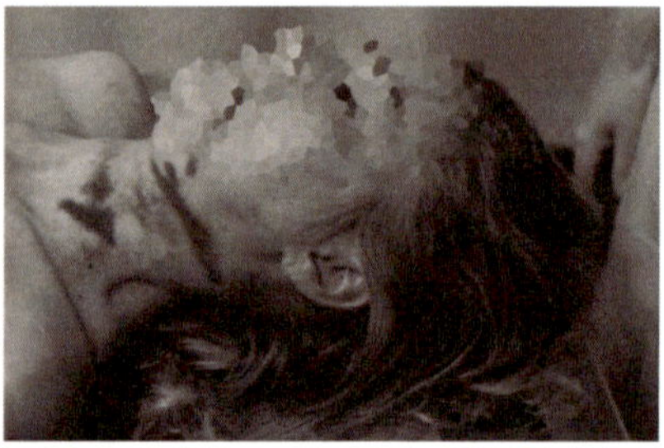

Photo Sûreté du Québec

The nature of the wounds to the neck was incompatible with the spouse's version of the events, namely that he had found the victim hanged.

Photo 7

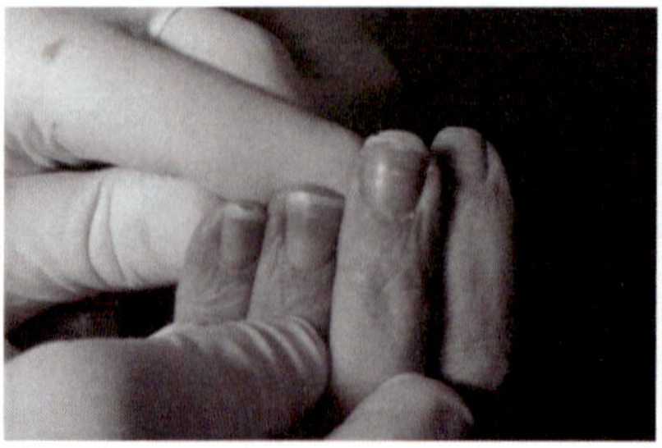

Photo Sûreté du Québec

Broken fingernails revealed that the victim had fought with her assailant.

Photo 8

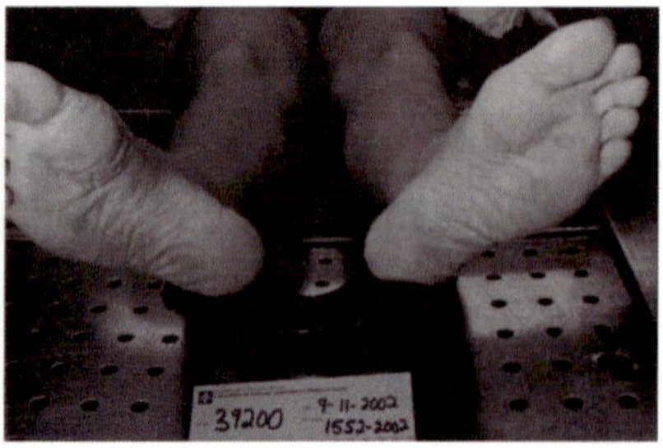

Photo Sûreté du Québec

The victim's feet were clean, but the garage floor was covered with dust and other dirt. She therefore could not have walked through it.

C. TRACKING DOWN SEXUAL PREDATORS[3]

Biological fluids, pubic hair and skin, and fibres retrieved from the victim's body or the crime scene can provide investigators with good leads. Information collected over the course of an investigation — such as the victim's description of the offender, witness statements, and information from police databases, surveillance tapes, and bank transactions — can also help investigators identify and charge a suspect. But what if there is no evidence?

To determine a sexual aggressor's motivation, it is necessary to take apart the crime step by step. This can help to determine whether the perpetrator was trying to concretize his sexual fantasies, whether he acted impulsively, and whether he was the type to engage in ritualized sexual behaviour. Investigators must obtain this information in detail, keeping in mind that the victim is the best source of information on the aggressor's verbal, physical, and sexual behaviour. In addition, victimology can help establish the victim's risk level.

1. The Victim's Risk Level

The victim's risk level varies from low to high. People, such as children or the elderly, whose personal, occupational, and social lives cause them little or no exposure to criminal victimization are considered to be at low risk. People who live or travel in high-crime areas or go to such areas late at night are considered to be at moderate or elevated risk. People whose lifestyle regularly exposes them to danger — persons with links to organized crime or who frequent criminalized venues, prostitutes, people who too easily trust strangers and accompany them to unfamiliar places — are at high or very high risk. When the victim has a high or very high risk level, the pool of suspects is usually very large.

2. The Aggressor's Strategy for Making Contact

To achieve their goals, sexual aggressors must make contact with their victims. Generally, they choose a strategy with which they feel most at ease. One finds three main strategies (Hazelwood and Burgess, 2001):

---

3 With the permission of Robert R. Hazelwood, this section is taken largely from the third edition of the book, *Practical Aspects of Rape Investigation*, by Hazelwood and Burgess (2001).

1. In the "con" strategy, the aggressor uses subterfuge to make contact with the victim. To gain trust, he might offer or ask for help: "Excuse me, could you tell me how to get to ..." He does this in a friendly way, and when he believes the victim will offer little or no resistance, he overpowers her. This strategy type suggests that the aggressor is confident in his ability to interact with women in general and that he is not intimidated by them.

2. With the "blitz" strategy, the victim has no time to react or negotiate with the aggressor. Force is immediately used, and results in injuries to the victim. Most of the time, the aggressor uses his fists, he may also render the victim unconscious by placing a cloth soaked in a chemical such as chloroform over her mouth and nose. In yet other cases, there is strangulation. The use of this strategy often denotes hatred for women, an attitude that is often observable in the aggressor's daily relations with women.

3. Examples of the "surprise" strategy including bursting in on the victim as she sleeps, hiding behind the front seat of the victim's car, or surprising the victim in an alley or path. The aggressor often uses verbal threats or a weapon to coerce the victim. This strategy suggests that the aggressor pre-selected his victim; the use of a weapon can reveal he is not confident enough to use the "con" strategy but is loath to use the extreme violence of the "blitz" strategy.

3. The Degree of Force Employed

Following initial contact with the victim, the aggressor must maintain control of her. He can do this simply by virtue of his physical presence, or through the use of intimidation, verbal threats, a weapon, or physical force. The use of force and the intensity of the force used are key elements in determining the motivation of a sexual aggressor.

Investigators generally encounter four levels of force: 1) minimal force (a slap, physical control), which causes no injuries; 2) moderate force (e.g. repeated blows); 3) excessive force, which may leave bruises and necessitate medical attention or hospitalization; 4) brutal force, which leaves significant injury, and may result in death.

4. Resistance by the Victim

The level of force used by the aggressor may be related to resistance by the victim. Victims may acquiesce to the aggressor or offer resistance. Resistance by the victim is defined with reference to the totality of actions by the victim to reduce the effects of the attack.

Passive resistance occurs when the victim refuses to obey but does not defend herself or cry out. Verbal resistance occurs when the victim calls out, begs the aggressor, or attempts to negotiate. Physical resistance occurs when the victim strikes the aggressor or tries to escape.

It is essential to observe the aggressor's reaction to all forms of resistance at this point in the assault. Some aggressors abandon their demands, compromise and negotiate, flee, threaten, or use force. These reactions may arise from the aggressor's natural fears of failure, being identified and arrested, being wounded, or being ridiculed.

5. The Aggressor's Sexual Behaviour

The victim may be too embarrassed to describe everything her assailant did to her or demanded that she do. But these details, essential to profiling the aggressor, can come only from the victim. The investigator must create a favourable climate for such cooperation, by being empathetic and explaining to the victim the importance of these details. What were the key points of the sequence of specifically sexual events? Why did the aggressor act in this way? Did he control the victim or was he obliged to improvise in the face of her resistance? What can one make of an aggressor who tries to embrace the victim "affectionately"? Who inserts an object into the victim's vagina or anus? The answers can shed light on the aggressor's personality traits and sexual fantasies.

6. The Aggressor's Verbal Behaviour

The verbal element is one of the features that sheds the most light on an aggressor's motivation. It is therefore important to establish exactly what he said to the victim and how he said it. What was his tone and attitude? Did he compliment her and concern himself with her comfort, or was he arrogant, degrading? Some aggressors can be very polite, going so far as to apologize for what they did. and sometimes attempt to act out their assault as part of an intimate, consensual relationship.

Occasionally the aggressor wants or forces the victim to say or repeat certain things to him, such as, "tell me I'm better than your boyfriend." This type of aggressor usually is motivated by power, and aggressors who force victims to degrade themselves seek domination and absolute power. In these cases, rage is usually the trigger for the assault.

7. Assessing the Aggressor's Criminal Experience

It is important to determine what experience the criminal demonstrates in committing the crime. This can be established by analyzing the actions he takes to assure the crime's success, protect his identity, and facilitate his escape. Measures he takes to protect his identity and the degree of sophistication he shows in committing the crime will reveal whether the offender is an experienced aggressor.

Inexperienced aggressors may wear a mask and gloves to avoid being identified, and may wear a condom during coitus, but may nevertheless force the victim to perform unprotected fellatio, with no thought to the traces of sperm he may leave behind. This may indicate that he knows little about forensic techniques.

Organized aggressors often prepare a "kit" containing binding equipment (nylon ties, ropes, handcuffs), condoms, surgical gloves and lubricant. If he touches or ejaculates on the victim's clothing, he takes it with him when he flees. He might also make the victim wash out her mouth, and wash her genitalia or other body part on which he might have left bodily fluids or fibres. Such behaviour can show that the aggressor is experienced and perhaps has a history of similar crimes. The theft from the victim of objects of little value (e.g. CDs, stereo equipment, DVD player) indicates an aggressor who is young. Older and more experienced aggressors, in contrast, tend to ignore such items and take money and jewellery.

Aggressors sometimes steal and keep objects — photographs of the victim, underclothes, identity cards, jewellery (regardless of its value), or any object that represents her — as a trophy or souvenir. These objects help the attacker recall what was to him a pleasant experience, or serve as a fetish object during masturbatory activity. Generally "gentlemanly" offenders keep such articles as souvenirs. Some aggressors return the stolen objects to their victims. This may be done to intimidate the victim, terrorize her, or attempt to have her think of him as a "good guy." However, physically violent aggressors keep the objects as a sign of victory — they are his trophies.

D. THE SEXUAL AGGRESSOR'S MOTIVATION

Determining what type of sexual aggressor an investigator faces requires a thorough analysis of many characteristics, including the offender's method of approach. How did he control, or fail to control, the victim? What level of force did he use to gain control? Did the victim react? If she did react, what was the aggressor's reaction? Does the aggressor suffer from sexual dysfunction? What sexual acts took place, and in what sequence? What, if anything, did the attacker say? Did his attitude change during the attack? If so, what preceded the change? Before leaving the victim, did he take any of her possessions? If so, what? The answers to these questions will help identify the sexual aggressor's motivation. Did he seek sexual satisfaction? Power? An outlet for his rage? Some combination of goals?

The FBI has developed a typology — based on the work of Groth (see Groth, Burgess and Holmstrom, 1977; Groth, 1979; Groth and Birnbaum, 1979) — of sexual aggressors' motivation. This typology identifies four principal motivations: 1) the need to confirm virility; 2) the desire to confirm power; 3) vengeance; 4) sexual sadism.

1. The Need to Confirm Virility

Sexual aggressors in this category use the assault to concretize a fantasy scenario in which he is the victim's lover. Although he acts out his sexual fantasies, he is not necessarily excited by the use of force to satisfy his sexual impulses. The complexity of these fantasies explains why he usually invests time and effort in attempting to realize them. Very often, this aggressor is also a predatory voyeur. He commits his assaults through overpowering and controlling his victim. Use of coercion, including physical force, reassures him of his own virility. Although his actions are degrading and may result in lifelong trauma for the victim, this type of aggressor is unaware of his crime's impacts (perhaps because he is too self-centred?) and does not wish them upon his victim. He prefers to avoid any confrontation that would lead to an escalation of the level of violence.

Aggressors who seek to confirm their virility generally use minimal to moderate force. They are polite and apologize for what they do. In general, however, this is false altruism. Their hunting range is usually limited to their comfort zone. They sometimes target several victims in the same area; if they fail in one assault attempt, they are likely to try again with another victim soon after. They usually attack late at night or early in the morning, using the surprise or con strategies. They sometimes pretend to have a weapon, or will carry one and show it to the victim to intimidate her. They choose victims around their own age and, often, force them to undress themselves. If the victim complies with their demands, they satisfy their sexual fantasies.

This type of aggressor can also demonstrate sexual paraphilia, such as fetishism and voyeurism. If the victim resists, they negotiate in order to obtain sexual satisfaction. They sometimes apologize and ask the victim to forget what has happened. Occasionally they take a personal object, such as underclothing or a photograph, from the victim as a souvenir. In some cases, they telephone or write to the victim to apologize.

2. The Desire to Confirm Power

This type of aggressor does not doubt his masculinity. He is "macho" in the real sense of that term. Sexual aggression allows him to express his virility and his dominance of women. He cares nothing for his victim and feels no remorse. He views women merely as objects to be used for his personal benefit. His choice of victims varies greatly and is opportunistic: he can attack total strangers, acquaintances, or even his own spouse. He generally uses a con strategy and moderate to excessive force. His victims are usually in his own age group.

His assaults can take place anywhere, so long as the location suits him and appears safe for his purposes. He does not hesitate to tear the victim's clothes, and repeatedly assaults his victims. If he is sexually dysfunctional, his dysfunction is very likely to be delayed ejaculation. He usually leaves the victim partly clothed or totally nude. He has a periodic pattern of sexual aggression.

3. Revenge

The assailant who acts out of vengeance is very impulsive and his actions toward the victim are characterized by excessive violence. Of the four types of aggressors, he is the least likely to harbour sexual fantasies. His motivations are rage and revenge: he hates women and uses sex as a weapon to hurt, punish, and degrade them. The force he uses is brutal and excessive.

This offender's crimes are not premeditated, and he therefore does not pre-select his victim, who may be simply walking down the street, waiting for a bus, or in a public restroom. He uses the blitz strategy and leaves her no chance of resisting. He violently pulls or tears off her clothing. The time, place, and frequency of attack are unpredictable, given that the victim is whoever crosses his path in the wrong place at the wrong time. The victim is usually older than the aggressor, and symbolizes another woman — or all women — whom he sees as the source of all his problems. He generally uses his fists and feet to inflict serious injury, but can also use anything available as a weapon, including the victim's belt, a piece of wood, a rock, a chair, etc. If the victim is not actually killed, she is often seriously injured and left for dead.

4. Sexual Sadism

According to the American Psychiatric Association (1996), sexual sadism consists of inflicting physical or psychological suffering on another person to obtain sexual arousal, regardless of whether the partner consents or not. This type of aggressor is sexually aroused by the victim's physical or psychological suffering. Ritual plays a major role in his sexual fantasies, which are rich in paraphilias, including voyeurism, bondage, fetishism, and sadism. Sadistic aggressors represent 1-5% of all sexual aggressors (see Beauregard, Proulx, and St-Yves, 2007; Hazelwood and Burgess, 2001; Proulx, St-Yves, Guay and Ouimet, 1999). The more experienced he is, the more methodical and planned his assaults will be. Everything he does will be thought out well in advance, and repeated if it is successful in procuring the arousal sought.

He uses brutal force, inflicting injuries that are often fatal. Most often, his victim is a stranger. He uses a con strategy to gain the victim's trust, confines her as soon as the opportunity presents itself, then takes her to an isolated location that he has already selected. Sometimes the sexual sadist will build a dungeon in which he confines his victims and repeatedly acts out his sexual fantasies over hours, or even days. A common component of the ritual torture practised by these aggressors is the insertion of objects into the victim's vagina or anus. He may use a variety of hand-made articles, and often photographs or records his sexual assaults. Some sadists may make drawings that depict their sexual fantasies.

E. THE EFFECTIVENESS OF CRIMINAL PROFILING

It is difficult to measure how effective criminal profiling is in solving crimes. Most of the time, an investigation's success rests on several factors.

Some studies have reported that profiles created by criminal analysts are relatively accurate (more than 70% of the information correct) and that sometimes assist in the identification and charging of suspects (Copson, 1995). The results of a comparative study by Kocsis, Irwin, Hayes and Nunn (2000) indicate that police officers who receive training as criminal analysts are better at identifying aggressors' cognitive processes, physical and social characteristics, lifestyle, and criminal behaviour than are other officers. Moreover, most studies of the usefulness of criminal profiling report it to be helpful and highly valued by investigators. Although profiling does not always lead to the solving of a crime, police officers state that it enhances their understanding of a case and helps them better understand the perpetrator's behaviour (see Beauregard and Proulx, 2001).

F. THE CRIMINAL ANALYST AS EXPERT WITNESS

In both the United States and Canada, criminal analysts are rarely afforded the status of expert witness. While some judgments in the United States accord analysts a certain status (*State v. Stevens),* others refuse to do so *(State* v. *Lowe)* or reverse judgments that have done so *(State v. Fortin).* In Canada, there have been few cases in which the courts have had to rule on the status of criminal analysts. In one case, however, the court accorded an analyst expert status and authorized her testimony concerning crime-scene reconstruction *(R. v. Clark* and *R. v. Ranger*). The current trend is to consider that testimony regarding the motivation behind a crime inadmissible as evidence *(R. v. Clark; R. v. Croteau).* As a matter of the law of evidence, the primary question is whether certain aspects of criminal profiling are scientifically reliable — which speaks to a need for more research in this area.

In a 2001 judgment from the State of Tennessee, the court concluded:

> Most of [Gregg] McCrary's proffered testimony dealt with conclusions he reached after analyzing the scene of the crime. For instance, he concluded that the manner in which various household items had been carefully moved, displayed, damaged or destroyed indicated that the perpetrator had staged, or altered, the scene in an effort to confuse the authorities. The court found this type of testimony to be sufficiently reliable to present to the jury. However, McCrary's testimony regarding the perpetrator's motivation, although based in part on physical evidence at the scene, appeared to be much more speculative (p. 12).

In light of this contemporary juridical view, it is important to recall that the analyst's role is essentially to help investigators identify and arrest criminals.

CONCLUSION

Criminal profiling is a methodical, logical, and analytic process of assessing information gathered at a crime scene. Criminal analysts assess and interpret the criminal's behaviour at the scene and render an opinion (the profile) on the type of individual who could have committed the crime. To do this, they use their experience and training, and empirical research. Contrary to popular belief, analysts do not solve crimes. They help and support investigators by proposing investigative strategies and helping to prioritize potential suspects. Their analyses can be useful in creating strategies or an interrogation plan. Quite often, they raise more questions than they answer. Their goal is to advance the investigation, not to solve the crime.

REFERENCES

Alison, L., Bennell, G., Mokros, A., and Ormerod, D. (2002). The personality paradox in offender profiling: A theoretical review of the processes involved in deriving background characteristics from crime scene actions. *Psychology, Public Policy and Law*, 8, 115-135.

American Psychiatric Association. (1996). *DSM-IV : manuel diagnostic et statistique des troubles mentaux.* 4e édition. Paris, Édition Masson.

Beauregard, E. and Proulx, J. (2001). Profilage criminel: Évolution et nouvelles perspectives dans l'établissement de modèles prédictifs. Interpol: *Revue Internationale de Police Criminelle*, 486, 20-28.

Beauregard, E., Proulx, J., and St-Yves, M. (2007). Angry or sadistic: Two types of sexual murderers. In J. Proulx, E. Beauregard, M. Cusson, and A. Nicole (eds.), Sexual murder: A comparative analysis and new perspectives (pp. 123-141). Winchester, UK: Wiley.

Canter, D. (1995). The Psychology of Offender Profiling. In R. Bull and D. Carson (eds.), *Handbook of psychology in legal contexts.* Chichester: Wiley.

Canter, D. (2000). Seven assumptions for an investigative environmental psychology. In S. Wapner, J. Dmick, T. Yamamoto and H. Minami (eds.), *Theoretical perspectives in environmental behaviour research: underlying assumptions, research problems and methodologies* (191-206). New York: Plenum Press.

Canter, D. (2004). Offending profiling and Investigative Psychology. *Journal of Investigative Psychology and Offender Profiling*, 1, 1-15.

Copson, G. (1995). *Coals to Newcastle ? A Study of Offender Profiling*, Part 1. (Special Interest Series: Paper 7). London: Police Research Group, Home Office Police Department.

Douglas, J.E, Burgess, A.W., Burgess, A.G. and Ressler, R.K. (1992). *Crime Classification manual. A standard System for Investigating and Classifying Violent Crimes.* Jossey-Bass, San Francisco (CA).

Geberth, V. J. (1996). *Practical Homicide Investigation: Tactics, Procedures and Forensic Techniques.* Boca Raton: CRC Press.

Groth, A.N., Burgess, A.W. and Holstrom, L.L. (1977). Rape: power, anger and sexuality, *American Journal of Psychiatry*, Vol. 134 : 1239-1243.

Groth, A.N. (1979). *Men who rape: The psychology of the offender.* Harper and Row, New York.

Groth, A. N. et Birnbaum, H. J. (1979). *Men Who Rape: The Psychology of the Offender*, New York, Plenum Press.

Hazelwood, R.R., and Burgess, A.W. (2001). *Practical aspects of rape investigation : A multidisciplinary approach*, third edition. CRC Press.

Holmes, R.M., and Holmes, S.T. (2002). *Profiling violent crimes* (3rd ed.). Thousand Oaks: Sage Publications.

Kocsis, R., Irwin, H.J., Hayes, A.F., and Nunn, R. (2000). Expertise in Psychological Profiling: A Comparative Assessment. *Journal of Interpersonal Violence*, 15 (3), 311-331.

Lowe v. State, 599 N.E. 2d 783 (Ohio App. 1991).

Proulx, J., St-Yves, M., Guay, J.-P. and Ouimet, M. (1999). Les agresseurs sexuels de femmes : Scénarios délictuels et troubles de personnalité. In J. Proulx, M. Cusson et M. Ouimet, Les Violences criminelles, Saint-Nicolas, Québec, Presses de l'Université Laval, p.157-185.

Rajs, J., Lundstrom, M., Broberg, M., Lidberg, L., and Lindquist, O. (1998). Criminal mutilation of the human body in Sweden – a thirty-year medico-legal and forensic psychiatric study. *Journal of Forensic Science*, 43(3): 563-580.

R. v. *Clark,* [2004] O.J. No. 195.

R. c. *Croteau*, C.S. 505-01-036531-024.

Ressler, R.K., Burgess, A.W., and Douglas, J.E. (1988). *Sexual homicides: Patterns and motives.* New York: Lexington Books.

Safarik, M.E., Jarvis, J.P., and Nussbaum, K.E. (2002). Sexual homicide of elderly females: Linking offender characteristics to victim and crime scene attributes. *Journal of Interpersonal Violence*, 17 (5), 500-525.

State v. *Fortin*, 724 A. 2d 818 (N.J. Super. 1999).

State v. *Stevens*, [2001] WL 579034, Tenn. Crim. App. 2001.

Sugden, P. (1995). *The Complete History of Jack the Ripper*. London: Robinson.

Wilson, P. and Soothill, K.L. (1996). Psychological profiling: red, green or amber ? *Police Journal*, 1: 12-20.

CHAPTER 19

An Analytical Protocol for the Assessment of Violent Crime

Michel Bénézech and the Groupe Analyse Comportementale of the *Gendarmerie Nationale Française*

If all criminals acted alike, it would be a simple matter to interrogate, charge, judge and convict them. As we will see, this is not necessarily the case. The most brutal homicide, sometimes apparently a lunatic act, can in fact be perpetrated by a relatively reasonable person. The converse is also true: a clearly disorganized psychotic sometimes commits the deliberate, planned homicide of an experienced hitman. Yet the fundamental principle of profiling is that the crime scene reflects the criminal's personality! In this chapter, we first consider the classification of violent homicides. We then present a new support tool for behavioural analysis, applicable to both crimes and crime scenes, based on qualitative and quantitative research on representative factors of the six variables inherent in six dimensions underlying the most serious antisocial acts (murders, sexual assaults, and kidnappings). We conclude with some general observations on the relationship between violent crime and its perpetrators.

A. VIOLENT CRIMES, MAD CRIMES

1. Definitions (Table 1)

The most serious physical attacks — which is to say the most violent — are homicides, serious sexual assaults, and arson. Our research work does not extend to arson, although we acknowledge that it can accompany murder, generally with the aim of destroying evidence. Every murder is inherently violent at some level, be it the circumstances, method used to cause death, nature of the wounds, or victim's fear and suffering. Death can be more or less instantaneous (bullet to the head or heart by a professional killer), quick (gunshot or knife wound to a vital body part such as the chest), slow, or very slow (prolonged agony, mistreatment, torture, confinement without fresh air or food).

Reading through the daily news we are exposed to, and learn about murders — sometimes committed by unexpected assailants, such as police officers, physicians, notaries, and clerics — that are particularly horrific, revolting, monstrous and incomprehensible, out of all proportion to their avowed cause, or indeed in some cases, without any motive at all, sometimes committed by unexpected assailants such as police officers, physicians, notaries and clerics. The general public labels these crimes "mad" and imagines that only those suffering from serious mental disorders could perpetrate such gratuitous brutality on innocent victims (particularly women and children). The 15 characteristics of murders that render them acts of apparent insanity considered "mad" are presented in Table 1. In fact, those who commit such atrocities are seldom found criminally insane. Insane crimes are not always committed by insane individuals (i.e. not synonymous with personal insanity, and a "mad" crime does not necessarily denote a criminal whose is mad in the conventional sense). Violent crime does not always involve unlimited, unbridled aggression. On the contrary, it can reflect a paradoxical obsession in those not psychologically ready to kill — a persistent internal struggle against homicidal ideation, that ends with the murderer inflicting violence on themselves in order to actually throw themselves into the brutal mindset necessary for the commission of a savage killing — the internal turmoil of those not psychologically ready to kill.

2. Personality Profiles of Aggressors (Tables 2 and 3)

As early as 1871, Isaac Ray noted an interesting parallel between the behaviour of "normal" murderers and insane killers. Guttmacher (1965) contends that the differences between non-pathological criminals and criminals who are seriously mentally ill (Table 2) are highly significant.

Table 1 – Mad or apparently mad murders

1.	Individual crime (single aggressor)
2.	No evident motive
3.	A single crime scene
4.	Victim is known or targeted in the geographical neighborhood
5.	Disorganized crime scene (abundant evidence)
6.	Weapon of opportunity (feet, hands, blunt object, knife, firearm)
7.	Face-to-face murder in close proximity, confrontation with victim (defensive wounds)
8.	Multiple wounds not targetting vital organs
9.	Strangling
10.	Overkill
11.	Depersonalization of victim
12.	Sexual assault, in some cases
13.	No evidence of crime-scene staging
14.	No evidence of multiple perpetrators
15.	Presence of the classic tragic unities of time, place and action (Classic tragedy with unity)

The FBI's typology of sexual murderers comprises two principal profiles: the organized killer and the disorganized killer (Ressler, Burgess and Douglas, 1993). For some time, one of authors of this chapter has employed a specific nosography to differentiate psychopathic from psychotic murderers (Bénézech, 1994). In their analysis of multiple assaults by the mentally ill, MacCulloch, Bailey and Robinson (1995) grouped individuals into two categories — those whose attacks were pre-meditated, and those whose attacks were not. Other researchers have studied the personality types, levels of extroversion, aggression control, impulsivity, emotivity (Jackson and Bekerian, 1997; Salfati and Canter, 1999; Santtila, Hakkanen, Canter and Elfgren, 2003; Toutin, 2000; Turvey, 1999). Despite disparities among the populations studied, these classifications reveal numerous similarities with overlaps observed between organized, extroverted, antisocial, psychopathic, narcissistic, sadistic, under-controlled operational types, on the one hand, and disorganized, introverted, schizoid, psychotic, dependent-avoidant, over-controlled, emotional types, on the other. It, therefore, seems possible that perpetrators of violent crime, both sexual and non-sexual, can be schematically classified into two personality profiles (see Table 3) (Bénézech, 1994; Bénézech, 1995).

3. Classification

Taking as our starting point the distinction between violent crime and criminal insanity (serious crimes against persons, whose circumstances, motives or actors are so irrational as to escape comprehension), we can distinguish six main categories of homicidal behaviour.

a) Crimes of passion

This type of violence results from emotional conflicts between spouses, romantic partners or those in more casual relationships. Such conflict usually arises when one person threatens to leave the other, a romantic relationship breaks down, or a couple's relationship disintegrates. These events, assisted by the consumption of alcohol or drugs, can lead to a murderous explosion. The victims can be the aggressor's partner (heterosexual or homosexual), a romantic rival, the couple's children, or even an outsider killed by mistake or in place of others (by a telescoping or identity confusion arising from a state of crisis). The murder of an occasional partner of the same sex sometimes results from a mechanism of denial of homosexuality at the time triggered by an attempted seduction. Perpetrators of crimes of passion often suffer from personality disorders such as dependency, passive-aggressiveness, narcissism, borderline personality disorder and antisociality, and are driven by feelings of depression, despair, jealousy, hatred and humiliation. This is why their attacks frequently involve overkill, even on a victim who is already dead.

Table 2 – Non-pathological vs. mentally disturbed murderers (Ray and Guttmacher)

"Normal" murderer	"Insane" murderer
– Has prior convictions (2/5 cases)	– Has history of mental disturbance or institutionalization (1/3 cases)
– Frequently consumes alcohol prior to crime (1/2 cases)	– Rarely consumes alcohol prior to crime (10%)
– May plan crime	– Does not plan crime
– Chooses a non-family victim (2/3 cases)	– Chooses an intimate as a victim (2/3 cases)
– Selects weapon beforehand	– Uses weapon of opportunity
– Does not indulge in gratuitous violence	– Commits extremely bloody crimes
– May have accomplices	– Does not have accomplices
– Attempts to avoid having witnesses if possible	– Commits crime before witnesses
– Usually remorseful, confesses under pressure	– Shows no remorse, confesses spontaneously
– Almost always has memory of crime (absent total inebriation)	– Frequently has no memory of crime (1/3 cases)
– Has an understandable motive	– Has a motive out of proportion to the crime

Table 3 – The two main personality profiles of violent aggressors

Profile 1	Profile 2
– Organized	– Disorganized
– Extroverted	– Introverted
– Antisocial	– Schizoid/borderline
– Psychopath/sociopath	– Psychotic
– Narcissistic	– Dependent-avoidant
– Sadistic	– Passive-aggressive
– Undercontrolled	– Overcontrolled
– Well socialized	– Socially isolated
– Socially competent	– Socially immature
– Rational	– Irrational
– Instrumental/cognitive	– Expressive – impulsive
– Operational	– Emotional

b) Sex crimes

According to the FBI, sexual homicides display one or more of the following indicators: 1) the victim's clothing is dishevelled; 2) the victim's genital organs are exposed; 3) the victim's body is left in a sexual position; 4) objects have been inserted into the victim's body cavities; 5) there is evidence of sexual relations (oral, anal, vaginal) with the victim; 6) there is evidence of substitutive sexual activity, sexualized acts or sadistic fantasies (characteristic mutilation or torture) on the victim's body, the victim's clothes or the crime scene (Ressler, Burgess and Douglas, 1993). Thus, the murderer may not have engaged in sexual acts with the victim. Sexual murders — both angry (emotional) and sadistic (non-emotional) — may be accompanied by kidnapping or confinement, physical restraint, torture, mutilation before or after death, and dismemberment. Such predatory, destructive behaviour is more common among sadistic killers who have an appetite for hardcore pornography, deviant erotic fantasy and multiple paraphilias. Asphyxiation (strangulation, suffocation) is most often the cause of death. Sexual criminals sometimes attack those of their own sex (homosexual assailants) and children (paedophiles). A crime that is apparently sexual in nature (e.g. sexual assault-murder) may be committed in a context that is not overtly sexual, as with vile murder, torture to make someone divulge where they have hidden money or jewellery, domestic homicides staged as sexual crimes, religious homicide as part of a sadistic cult, and homicidal swarming as a result of group agitation. In such false sexual homicides, the prime motives are property damage, the settling of family disputes (with staging to escape justice), extremist ideology, and arousal by pure violence. On the other hand, assaults on the victim's genitals specifically indicate sadistic crime.

We endorse the classification of sexual assault on the basis of motive: rage (anger), sadism, compensation (reassurance), and domination (power) (Jackson and Bekerian, 1997; Ressler, Douglas and Burgess, 1993; Turvey, 1999). We would add sexual assault due to antisocial behaviour, intrafamilial sexual assault, and psychotic sexual assault. The most physically and psychologically violent sexual assaults are typically committed when the motive is power, rage, or sadism.

c) Pathological crimes

Pathological crimes involve explosions of aggression toward others — most often parents or persons known to the aggressor — as a result of psychotic and/or manic-depressive processes frequently associated with abnormal personalities and addictive behaviours. The serious mental disorders responsible for homicide can be both acute and transitory (delirium, psychotic disorder linked to substance abuse, psychotic episodes, or recurrent short-lived depression), or longer lasting (paranoid schizophrenia, major depression, bipolar disorder, delusional paranoia). Homicides committed by schizophrenics may be accompanied by sexual violence, cannibalism, or self-mutilation (enucleation, castration). The behaviour of the criminally psychotic is generally disturbed before, during, and after the homicide, reflecting the murderer's disorganized thinking, and the presence of delusional and hallucinatory ideas grounded in persecution, religion, megalomania, jealousy, erotomania and somatization. Similar to this category of crimes are homicides, sudden and inexplicable violence of which ("stroke of madness") suggests a psychotic act, even though their authors exhibit no clinical sign of psychotic symptoms preceding or accompanying the homicide. Such criminals usually experience strong aggressive impulses and have weak and fragile egos. Under the impetus of conflict, disputes, stress or alcohol intoxication, they may experience episodic disinhibition, loss of contact with reality, persecutory ideation, or extremely fleeting depersonalization — all of which lead to disorganized offending. Today we classify such individuals as borderline personalities, although Guttmacher (1965) classified them as "temporarily psychotic."

d) Crimes motivated by conflict, vengeance or settling of accounts

Homicide due to "partying gone bad" among close relations (domestic crimes, conjugal violence and sexual assault), drinking companions, or strangers (circumstantial crime) is one of the most banal types of homicides. Murderous violence can also be set off by a drug, weapon or stolen-property transaction gone wrong, a theft (situational, violent murders), a personal conflict (family, neighbourhood, or occupational disputes), an unexpected encounter with a mortal enemy (who seizes the opportunity for vengeance), or a settling of accounts related to organized crime or narcotics (the victim being someone who has broken the criminal code or fights crime). In some cases, the homicide is an unpremeditated, spur-of-the-moment, face-to-face attack resulting from a chance encounter. The murder will often be especially violent if the attacker is particularly impulsive, prone to anger, or under the influence of psychoactive disinhibitors such as alcohol, cannabis or medication.

e) Multiple crimes

Multiple crimes inflame public opinion because of the number and nature (e.g. close relations, class of schoolchildren) of their victims. Among mass or spree killers, particularly notable are: 1) psychotics (schizophrenics), who most often massacre members of their own families; 2) individuals who take revenge for the loss of their job (authority-motivated murderers) by shooting former colleagues in the workplace (targeted victims) or strangers who are in the wrong public place at the wrong time (random victims). Alternatively, they may be a settling of accounts between rival criminal organizations (clans, cartels), or a robbery that becomes a bloodbath when witnesses or victims refuse to obey, or revolt. Finally, serial killers are not all sexual aggressors (either angry or sadistic) or drug addicts (responsible for multiple deadly brawling under the influence of alcohol or drugs). There are also serial killers who either have political or religious motivations (separatists, extremists, terrorists, members of satanic cults) or operational motivations (family poisonings, hired killers, isolated or organized robber-killers), or are avengers (organized crime, vendetta), egocentric altruists ("heroic" homicide, euthanasia, repeated infanticides by a mother), or chronically psychotic (schizophrenic and paranoid individuals with persecutory, mystical, or sadistic ideation).

f) Crimes that are unclassifiable or have no clear motive

This last category of violent or "mad" crimes comprises unmotivated ("gratuitous") lethal assaults resulting from: 1) uncontrollable anger (intermittent explosive disorder, amok); 2) clinically abnormal alcoholic addiction (excito-motor intoxication with blackout); 3) severe existential "malaise" in which moral and philosophical disturbance play an essential role, although other reactional psychiatric disorders (e.g. depression, sub-delusional ideation, alcoholism) may also be present. The existential crisis typically results from family (separation or divorce), work-related (loss of employment, failure to win promotion), or religious (faith-related problems) difficulties, but may also be the result of bereavement, serious illness, or ageing. The moral distress, rebellion, or questioning of social and personal values sparked by these life-altering events can trigger violent offending, which may be either impulsive and irrational, or, more rarely, pre-meditated and organized. These outbursts of violence (e.g. mass shootings) reflect not only suicidal bitterness, but also a need to go on — a need that can only be assuaged by the notoriety and the narcissistic and megalomaniacal gratification afforded by the publicity related to, and emotion elicited by, a spectacular mass crime.

B. THE SIX CONSTITUTENT VARIABLES

1. Presentation

In a study published in 2004, one author of the present chapter outlined an original protocol for the behavioural analysis of homicide and homicide crime scenes (Bénézech, 2004). It appears that the operational mode for homicidal and sexual assaults can be assessed in terms of six fundamental components, namely, violence, emotions, modus operandi, sexuality, relationships, and circumstances. All but the sexual component are present, to varying degrees, in all types of violent crime. The sexual component is present in sexual crimes and in crime scenes staged to disguise the real motive for the crime. The material elements (scene, corpse), modus operandi (contact with the victim, offending process) and psycho-criminal elements (motivation, pre-crime, crime, and post-crime affect) related to these components arise from information obtained from the crime scene and other sources (from expert testimony, depositions, victimological analysis, crime-scene reconstruction). Assuming they are in a state to be questioned, victims of unsuccessful murder attempts can provide valuable information about the identity, motive, and actions of their attackers.

2. Constituent Variables (Table 4)

a) Violence

An assailant may do violence to the victim's property as well as to their person. When the crime takes place in a closed space (residence, workplace, cultural space, vehicle), there may be signs of breaking-and-entering, vandalism and arson. Noteworthy signs of bodily harm include the number, nature (sexual/non-sexual), location (targeted/generalized) and seriousness of any wounds, and evidence of overkill, mutilation or dismemberment. Investigators must carefully examine the state of the victim's clothing, the objects used in committing the crime and any restraints. The level of violence is generally related to degree of emotionality and the number of aggressors present. Violence motivated by emotion is termed "affective," while violence primarily motivated by concrete benefit is termed "predatory." These two types are not mutually exclusive, however, and are frequently both present.

b) Emotions

The criminal's affective involvement at the time of the crime is a key determinant of the conditions and modalities of the offending process. Anger, hatred, jealousy, frustration, distress and despair are powerful sentiments that can impel uncontrolled violence. These factors are often compounded by personality disorders such as impulsivity; substance dependence (alcohol, drugs, medication); paraphilias; psychosis or depression. The murderer's emotional state is reflected by several behaviours. Attacks often occur in the midst of a dispute, sometimes of long standing; these arise suddenly, are disorganized and involve a weapon of opportunity— such as fists and feet, knives, guns and blunt objects — and restraints of opportunity.

To commit this confrontational murder — which may leave defensive wounds on the victim if the attack is face-to-face — the murderer may rely on a combination of improvised methods, such as manual or ligature strangulation, bludgeoning, and close-range knife and gun wounds. Highly emotional attacks are generally brief (lasting no more than a few minutes) and contextually simple, unfolding like a classic drama with unities of time, place, and action. The murderer uses an opportunistic weapon, which is usually left, like the victim's body, at the crime scene. The murderer is often incautious, and leaves numerous clues at the scene. In crimes of passion, the murder may commit acts of reparation (first aid, arrangement of the body, call for help). Very often, the murderer does not try very hard to escape, and may even turn themselves in. Where emotion makes little or no contribution, the modus operandi may be more elaborate, and best accounts for the characteristics of the crime.

c) Modus operandi

This variable comprises conduct and techniques instrumental to the success of the violent attack. The sophistication of the modus operandi reflects the killer's pre-meditation, self-control, and cognitive and rational behaviour. Here, the crime tends to be planned and organized, even complex. The murderer is well prepared, having pre-selected a crime scene, obtained restraints, weapons and the use of a vehicle, and assembled a rape kit. The killer uses a specific strategy (surprise, violent abduction, ruse) to approach the victim, who may be targeted on the spot, pre-selected, or simply a close acquaintance of the criminal. The crime may unfold over some time, in cases of kidnapping and forcible confinement, or, if the murder is part of a criminal enterprise, may be quite brief.

Generally the murderer tries to eradicate any evidence (e.g. cleaning the scene, removing the weapon) and conceal the victim's body (e.g. camouflage, removal, burial, submersion, burning). In addition, crime-scene staging is possible. The murderer will attempt to leave the area unseen. There may be one or more accomplices, and the violence may be accompanied by the theft of goods or valuables (civil documents, credit cards, money, cellular telephones, valuable objects).

In highly organized kidnappings, there are commonly several crime scenes: the abduction site, the vehicle used to transport the victim, the confinement site, the actual crime scene, and sites at which the body is found or stolen means of payment used. Spatiotemporal aspects of the modus operandi — the geographical context, distances, the time between first contact with the victim and the discovery of the corpse — are essential to the assessment and classification of violent offences.

d) Sexuality

As previously noted, the sexual component is found not only in sex crimes per se. In an attempt to escape justice, an offender may simulate a sexual assault. Domestic assaults, crimes of passion, and crimes of profit may be preceded by more or less consensual sex; this is also true of some brutal homicides or settlings of accounts in which anal or vaginal rape is meant as an additional punishment. Genuine sexual homicide occurs where the motivation is principally genital, whether or not the offender commits sexual acts on the victim's body. Under these circumstances, there are six non-exclusive causes of death: 1) accident (circumstantially); 2) the need to exert force in order to commit a sexual assault (operational); 3) the need to prevent the victim from testifying against the murderer (operational); 4) anger at victim resistance (emotional); 5) satisfaction of aggressive, deviant sexual impulses and fantasies (emotional and operational); 6) schizophrenic delusions (psychiatric/emotional) (Bénézech, 1997).

e) Relationships

The relationship between an unknown criminal and the deceased victim can be sketched out from victimological analysis, spatio-temporal factors, context, and other information collected by investigators. Obviously it is easier to determine the relationship if the victim or assailant is able to provide their version of events. The victim's age, sex, state of health, intelligence, personality, wariness, experience, education, personal and work habits, way of life, and potential high-risk behaviour provide valuable information about how they were approached, their possible reactions to the attack, and their ability to physically and psychologically resist the attack.

The verbal interaction between the actors in the offence can range from none to long conversations. A victim attacked from behind with no defensive wounds suggests a hyper-violent, sudden assault with no pre-assault dialogue, while a ruse approach necessitates verbal exchange to mislead and persuade. One can determine the murderer's behaviour from details of their modus operandi: Did they depersonalize (objectify) the victim, or did they treat the victim as an individual (personalized) human being they had carefully chosen?

Offender-victim interaction is emotional as well as verbal. Victims can react in various ways: They can play along so as to defuse the violence and attempt to escape the worst of it, weep, beg, fight back, or struggle desperately for their lives or honour, the marks on their bodies giving eloquent testimony to their struggle, the outcome of which is sometimes shaped by a fortuitous outside event. The assailant's reaction to resistance can profoundly change the sequence of events, leading, for example, to abandonment of the attack, anger, or unpremeditated murder.

f) Circumstances

Simple chance can intervene to mitigate the consequences of a criminal attack or aggravate it. The unexpected arrival of a third party can frustrate a criminal attempt or transform it into an incident with no police involvement. Simply being at the wrong place at the wrong time can make one a victim of totally foreign circumstances or of violent offenders (e.g. drug-addicted thief looking for money, agitated group, criminal who kills an accidental witness, or a terrorist using explosives or a firebomb). Unexpected events, opportunity, happenstance, coincidence, good (or bad) luck, the nature of the surroundings, weather, geography, and the intervention or simple presence of others are all capable of influencing the course of violent acts and changing the consequences for both aggressor and victim.

The principal characteristics of each constituent variable are presented in Table 4 (Bénézech, 2004). These form the basis of an original classification system for modus operandi and for the relationships between crime-scene characteristics, offender motives, and the offenders' psychological profiles. The system builds on the work of: MacCulloch, Bailey and Robinson (1995) concerning serious, spontaneous violence (both premeditated and unpremeditated) by the mentally ill; Salfati and Canter (1999) on the behavioural styles of unidentified murderers (expressive-impulsive, instrumental-opportunist, instrumental-cognitive crime scenes); Santtila, Hakkanen, Canter and Elfgren (2003), also concerning behavioural crime-scene themes. To further operationalize our method, we have adapted our analytical protocol based on the six constituent variables of violent crime to take into account police practice. To do so, we identified the principal components for each classic period of criminal activity — pre-offending phase, offending phase (the modus operandi *per se*), and post-offending phase. This has produced three separate tools with which to analyse and score the crime scene and the criminal process.

Table 4 – The six components of violent crime and their characteristics

1. Violence	2. Emotions	3. Modus Operandi	4. Sexuality	5. Relationships	6. Circumstances
Aggressivity	**Affectivity**	**Technicality**	**Genitality**	**Personality**	**Unpredictability**
1. Property damage	1. Impulsivity	1. Rationality	1. Sexualized anger	**Interactivity**	1. Chance
2. Arson	2. Anger, rage	2. Cognition instrumentality	2. Deviant fantasies	1. Verbal interaction	2. Opportunity
3. Injuries	3. Anguish	3. Self-control	3. Undressing	2. Emotional Interaction	3. Happenstance
4. Overkill	4. Depression	4. Organization	4. Sexual assault	3. Victim resistance	4. Coincidence
5. Mutilation	5. Delerium	5. Premeditation	5. Insertion of objects	**Personalization**	5. Witnesses
6. Dismemberment	6. Confrontation	6. Contact strategy	6. Sexual acts	4. Selection	6. Interventions
7. Aggressors X*	7. Disorganization	7. Variable duration	7. Masturbation	5. Contact strategy	7. Environments
	8. Spontaneity	8. Weapon pre-selected	8. Sexual positioning of body	6. Dialogue	
	9. Shortness	9. Restraints	9. Exposure of victim's genitals	7. Victim as subject	
	10. Weapon of opportunity	10. Clues rare	10. Obscene signs	**Depersonalization**	
	11. Clues X	11. Destruction of evidence	11. Genital wounds	8. Brutal attack	
	12. Abandonment of body	12. Hidden body	12. Torture	9. Absence of dialogue	
	13. Reparation	13. Crime scene staged	13. Sadism	10. Disfigurement	
	14. Single aggressor	14. Utilitarian theft		11. Victim as object	
	15. Victims X	15. Locations X			
		16. Aggressors X			

* multiple

3. The Pre-offending Phase (Table 5)

This stage, which precedes the actual offence by several moments to several days, can be reconstituted *a posteriori* if the aggressor is identified and arrested. However, analysis of the totality of the investigative file can often lead to reasonable hypotheses about the unknown criminal's or murderer-suicide's behaviour just before the commission of the crime. This is the case for certain domestic and sexual murders, crimes of passion, and murders motivated by revenge, disputes, authority or illicit trafficking.

In the pre-offending phase, the emotions underlying a criminal's motive culminate (e.g. motivation by chronic conflict or paraphilic fantasies), or materialize (e.g. motivation by occasional disputes). Such emotions include jealousy, passion, vengeance, anger, hatred, depression, delusion, sexual arousal and strong individual or group feeling. With other motives — contract killings, criminal settlings of accounts, murders for profit, hostage takings, murder by paramilitary extremists — the perpetrator coldly calculates the crime, without the pre-crime emotional storm. Alcohol and other psychoactive substances are involved in practically all types of murders, but are most probably less common in those associated with organized crime. The circumstances of the contact with the victim are high variable and range from chance to opportunism to active target-hunting to confrontation with a known victim. For offenders who are psychologically prepared for criminal activity and who adopt classic contact strategies, the murder is a crime of opportunity and is completely unpremeditated. Once the murderer has identified the crime scene and victim, they must see to the technical details — vehicle, weapon, restraints, gloves, disguises, housebreaking tools, rape kit, etc.

4. The Offending Phase (Table 6)

With the "blitz attack," the victim is killed, sexually assaulted or incapacitated immediately on contact with the victim. This is common in contract killings, settlings of accounts, psychotic assaults and rape as an expression of power. But most often it is after several verbal exchanges, threats, a dispute, or existing differences that direct or indirect confrontation becomes tragic; two contrasting scenarios are possible.

The first scenario is emotional: premeditation is absent and there is anger, arousal, the use of a weapon of opportunity and rapid escalation to action. Conversely, the second scenario involves psychological and material preparation by an offender who commits the crime with *sang froid*, in some cases taking some time between first contact with the victim and the murder. Of course, these two extremes are rare in practice, most instances of violent crime falling somewhere between the two. It should be noted that there is no statistical association between the degree of violence (Violent component) and the degree of organization (Emotions and Modus Operandi). A reactive murder during a burglary or a dispute can be limited to a blow from a knife, while a carefully planned murder can become a bloodbath — and vice versa. Moreover, the offender's emotional state can be influenced by several factors, chief among them verbal or physical resistance by the victim. With sexual murders, one must keep in mind that the victim's death is not necessarily intended *a priori* but can result from the murderer's angry reaction, an accident (e.g. a game that goes too far), or an attempt to keep the victim from crying out, or be intended to prevent the victim from reporting the crime (Bénézech, 1995; Bénézech, 1997).

Crimes involving several victims (double, triple, mass, spree murders) and/or several attackers (accomplices, gangs — structured or otherwise) pose complex problems related to the interpretation of clues, the chronology of deaths, and the determination of whether each offender was a passive or active participant. Again, the voluntary or involuntary intervention of one or more witnesses can change the criminal state of mind and, consequently, the crime script.

5. The Post-offending Phase (Table 7)

Once the victim is dead, the killer might stay at the scene, or engage in activities intended to a) cover up the crime and escape justice (hiding or destroying the corpse, eliminating traces and clues from the crime scene and themselves, staging a suicide or accident); b) prolong their aggressive or sexual impulses (post-mortem attacks, characteristic marking of the scene, theft, the taking of fetishist souvenirs; c) relieve feelings of guilt (covering the victim's face, calling for help, cleaning the body and making it dignified). Absent crime-scene staging by the offender or involuntary or voluntary modification of the crime scene by third parties, the crime scene generally reflects the aggressor's emotional state at the time of the crime. Again, there is a continuum of crime scenes, from improvised, disordered scenes that are rich in clues to pre-selected crime scenes reflecting an elaborate modus operandi. When a series of crimes involves a multiplicity of crime-related sites, the RIGEL geographical-profiling software package can prove useful; such cases include long-term spree killing, kidnapping, and confinement (during which the offender might use the victim's cellular phone or credit cards), as well as serial murders, sexual assaults, arson, assaults and aggravated robberies.

Table 5 – Pre-offending Phase

1. Violence	2. Emotions	3. Modus Operandi	4. Sexuality	5. Relationships	6. Circumstances
Aggressivity	**Affectivity**	**Technicality**	**Genitality**	**Personality**	**Unpredictability**
1. Crisis 2. Conflict and violence to crime 3. Intimidation 4. Harassment 5. Obscene calls 6. Death threats 7. High level of force during initial contact	1. Alcohol, drugs 2. Desire to kill 3. Extremist ideology 4. Anger, vengeance, jealousy, stress 5. Depressive state 6. Feelings of injustice 7. Romantic passion 8. Group excitation 9. Sexual arousal 10. Unexpressed aggressivity 11. Psycotic disorders 12. Direct confrontation 13. Absence of pre-meditation	1. Targeted victim (pre-selection, planning) 2. Contact strategy 3. Victim hunting 4. Drugging of victim 5. Already possesses weapon 6. Equipment prepared (gloves, mask, housebreaking tools, etc.) 7. Vehicle used 8. Pre-selected crime scene 9. Deserted or intimate crime scene 10. Settling of accounts 11. Accomplices 12. Preparation of crime	1. Deviant aggressive, sexual fantasies 2. Rage displaced onto victim 3. Victim is explicitly sexually solicited 4. Rape kit 5. Bondage equipment	1. Family, marital, work, socio-cultural, criminal context 2. Prior aggressor-victim relationship 3. Media surveillance of victim 4. Victim approach fraudulently, through a ruse or abuse of authority, etc. 5. Provocation by the victim	1. Favourable environment 2. Favourable timing 3. Chance encounter 4. Wrong place, wrong time 5. Terrorism 6. Group or gang activity 7. Witnesses 8. Sex, age, habits, lifestyle, behaviour of aggressor and victim 9. Victim's risk factors

Table 6 – Offending Phase

1. Violence	2. Emotions	3. Modus Operandi	4. Sexuality	5. Relationships	6. Circumstances
Aggressivity	**Affectivity**	**Technicality**	**Genitality**	**Personality**	**Unpredictability**
1. High level of force during attack 2. Site nature, gravity, number, cause of injuries 3. Asphyxia, burns, lacerations 4. Physical or mental torture 5. Evisceration 6. Overkill 7. Vandalism 8. Arson of scene 9. Several victims or aggressors 10. Blitz attack	1. Coldness or anger, rage, hatred, arousal, domination, anxiety, reassurance 2. Consumption of alcohol 3. Means of the attack found at the scene 4. Scene is random and disorganized 5. Crime is often brief 6. Emotional violence	1. Self-control 2. Highly organized 3. Surprise, violent abduction or ruse 4. Burglary, kidnapping, confinement 5. Various threats 6. Immobilisation 7. Restraints, blindfold, gag 8. Nature of the weapon 9. Objects stolen 10. Writing, drawings at scene 11. Planned scene 12. Crime is sometimes of long duration 13. Burglary, armed robbery 14. Organized violence 15. Instrumental violence	1. Undressing 2. Sexual bondage 3. Caressing, petting, kissing, sucking, licking, biting 4. Body shaving 5. Flagellation, humiliation, psychological terror 6. Penetration of an orifice by penis, finger or object 7. Masturbation, urination, defecation on body or at scene 8. Vaginal washing or douching 9. Sadistic mutilation 10. Fetishist behaviour and theft	1. Negotiation with victim 2. Questions-and-answer 3. Change of aggressor's attitude during contact with victim 4. Aggressor's reaction to victim's physical or verbal resistance 5. Execution of a mental scenario	1. Place, day, time of crime 2. Situation in which the victim was seen for the last time 3. Witnesses 4. Modification, interruption of crime script by a third party 5. Death is accidental or to eliminate witnesses

Table 7 – Post-offending Phase

1. Violence	2. Emotions	3. Modus Operandi	4. Sexuality	5. Relationships	6. Circumstances
Aggressivity	**Affectivity**	**Technicality**	**Genitality**	**Personality**	**Unpredictability**
1. Injuries, mutilation 2. Post-mortem disfiguration	1. Fear, relief, pleasure, guilt 2. Post-mortem covering of face 3. Attempts at reparation 4. Corpse left at scene 5. Many clues at scene	1. Removal of or destruction of forensic evidence 2. Removal of or destruction of bedding 3. Leaves with weapon 4. Moves corpse 5. Hides corpse 6. Corpse is dismembered, burned, incinerated, buried, submerged 7. Staging to fool investigators 8. Aggressor cleans scene and themselves	1. Post-mortem sexual acts 2. Sexual positioning of body 3. Obscene signs at scene	1. Oral or written contact with investigators or victim's family 2. Follows crime in the news	1. Aggressor attempts to escape justice 2. Aggressor surrenders to authorities 3. Aggressor lets self be caught easily 4. Witnesses

C. BEHAVIOURAL ANALYSIS

Tables 5, 6, and 7 above are intended to provide a global, theoretical outline of the violent behaviours of individuals and small groups, with the exception of arson and collective illegal violence such as urban violence, terrorism, riots, revolutions, and guerrilla warfare. It seems to us indispensable to adapt the general framework of behavioural analysis to the specific investigative techniques related to these crimes. Therefore, the Groupe Analyse Comportementale (GAC, behavioural analysis unit)[1] of the Gendarmerie Nationale Française has experimented with a new spreadsheet-based[2] crime and crime-scene assessment protocol.

It should be noted that behavioural analysis is a broader concept than profiling, initially intended to track down serial killers. It is a multi-disciplinary study of objective elements gleaned from the crime scene. Therefore, the GAC method is intended to help orient criminal investigations by highlighting the behavioural and personality characteristics of likely potential suspects.

1. Modifications to the Model

1.1 The Basics (Figures 1 to 3)

A table is produced from the objective data obtained from the crime scene (inductive analysis), and serves as the basis for a profile of the criminal (deductive analysis). The key element for the purposes of computerized analysis is the Acting Out table (figures 1, 4, 7-10; See also Paragraph 1.2.3.2). The goal here is to identify the maximum number of items relevant to actual practice, rather than describe the vast majority of violent criminal behaviours. To eliminate confusion on the part of analysts about the specific nature of the items, all items are clearly defined in a glossary (see Paragraph 2.1.3.1). For example, Item 8 in Column 6 of Figure 1, "Death precipitated by the assault," is defined as "Initially, the offender does not intend to kill the victim. The death is situational, occurring particularly where the victim resists, such that the violence escalates." The definitions eliminate interpretive errors.

---

1 The experimental and computerized protocol was developed by all the members of the Groupe Analyse Comportementale who participated in the study: Pascal Thys, Pierre Chaignon, Marie-Laure Brunel-Dupin, Elen Vuidard, and Stéphanie Le Maoût.

2 We would like to thank Sébastien Dupin, programmer-analyst, for his valuable contribution.

Tables 5 to 7, "Pre-Offending Phase," "Offending Phase" and "Post-Offending Phase," as modified by the GAC, serve as study aids. Used on their own, they cannot provide behavioural analysis. Rather, they serve as guidelines, to ensure that investigators neglect no particular element in a case. The integration of these elements, based on observation and investigation, into the tables takes into account each element's qualitative and quantitative contribution.

1.2 The Qualitative Modifications

1.2.1 The nature of the items (Figures 1 and 6)

Items in tables 5, 6, and 7 that comprise multiple concepts are disaggregated if each of the concepts can be used to characterize a specific behaviour. This results in the creation of new items. For example, Table 6, Column 2, Item 1 (Affectivity) comprises "coldness or anger, hatred, arousal, domination, anxiety, reassurance." In Figure 1, Column 2, this item is disaggregated into seven items:

- Coldness (Item 1)
- Anger, rage (Item 2)
- Hatred (Item 3)
- Arousal (Item 4)
- Domination (Item 5)
- Anxiety (Item 6)
- Reassurance (Item 9)

In addition, two new items are included:

- Frustration (Item 7)
- Humiliation (Item 8)

On the other hand, "Alcohol consumption" in Table 6 (Column 2, Item 2) becomes "Alcohol and/or drug consumption" in Figure 1 (Column 2, Item 12).

1.2.2 The basis of the responses to the items (Figure 4)

The responses to the items can be derived from three sources:

- observations
- suppositions (based on the first elements collected in the case)

- statements (from witnesses)

1.2.3 The table headings

1.2.3.1, "Pre-offending phase" and "Post-offending phase" (Tables 5 and 7)

As the GAC concerns itself exclusively with criminal matters (murders, sexual assaults, kidnappings, etc.), it prefers "Pre-Crime Phase" and "Post-Crime Phase".

1.2.3.2, "Modus Operandi" (Table 6)

Behavioural analysts prefer the term "acting out" to "modus operandi." In fact, the notion of acting out is broader, and comprises technical and emotional events at the crime scene immediately and very soon after the crime (from the initial contact to post-mortem activity). "Modus operandi," on the other hand, confines itself to strictly technical facts (e.g. theft of a car for transport to the crime scene, breaking into the victim's home). Therefore, actions very near the time of the crime are absent from tables 5 and 7 (concerning the pre- and post-offending periods) but present in Figure 1 (Acting Out).

For example, "High level of force during initial contact," from Table 5, Column 1, Item 7, and "High level of force during attack," from Table 6, Column 1, Item 1, are combined to form "High level of force" in Figure 1 (Acting Out), Column 1, Item 2. This relocation and change of heading results in an item that accounts the timeframe of both original items: initial contact, in the pre-offending phase, and contact during the attack *per se*. Similarly, "Post-mortem disfiguration" from Table 7, Column 1, items 1 and 2 is reclassified as "Post-mortem wounds" in Figure 1, Column 1, Item 4.

Figure 1 – Acting out

1. Violence	2. Emotions	3. Modus Operandi	4. Sexuality	5. Relationships	6. Circumstances
Aggressivity	**Affectivity**	**Technicality**	**Genitality**	**Personality**	**Contextuality**
1. Blitz attack	1. Coldness	1. Self-control	1. Undressing	1. Talks to victim	1. Place
2. High level of force	2. Anger, rage	2. High level of organisation	2. Sexual bondage	2. Negotiation with victim	2. Day
3. Ante-mortem wounds 3.1 Number 3.2 Gravity	3. Hatred	3. Surprise, violent abduction, or ruse	3. Caressing, touching, kissing, sucking, licking, biting	3. Change of aggressor's attitude during contact with victim during contact or assault	3. Time
4. Post-mortem wounds 4.1 Number 4.2 Gravity	4. Arousal	4. Burglary	4. Body shaving	4. Aggressor reacts to victim's verbal or physical resistance during initial contact or assault	4. Economical, social, cultural environment
5. Torture 5.1 Number 5.2 Gravity	5. Domination	5. Kidnapping or confinement	5. Flagellation, humiliation, psychological terror	5. Physical or verbal attention	5. Situation in which the victim was seen for the last time
6. Overkill	6. Anxiety	6. Various threats	6. Masturbation of victim	6. Execution of a mental scenario	6. Presence of witness
7. Evisceration, dismemberment	7. Frustration	7. Immobilization	7. Masturbation of aggressor		7. Modification, interruption of crime script by a third party
8. Burning of body	8. Humiliation	8. Restraints, blindfold, gag	8. Penetration of an orifice by penis, finger or object		8. Death precipitated by the assault
9. Crime-scene arson	9. Reassurance	9. Already possesses a weapon	9. Ejaculation on the body or at the scene		9. Accidental death
10. Assault involving several offenders and/or victims	10. Emotional violence	10. Nature of weapon	10. Urination, defecation on the body or at the scene		10. Murder to eliminate the victim or out of fear of being identified
11. Vandalism	11. Brief crime	11. Objects stolen	11. Sadistic mutilation		
	12. Use of alcohol and/or drugs	12. Organized crime scene	12. Vaginal washing or douching		
	13. Means found at crime scene	13. Planned crime scene	13. Fetishistic behaviour and theft		
	14. Random or disorganized crime scene	14. Planned crime	14. Verbal activity		
	15. Writing or drawings on the body	15.Crime is of long duration			
	16. Multiple weapons due to emotional charge	16.Burglary, armed robbery			
		17. Crime-scene writing or drawings for the public or the police			
		18. Multiple utilitarian weapons			

Figure 2 – Pre-crime Phase

1. Violence	2. Emotions	3. Modus Operandi	4. Sexuality	5. Relationships	6. Circumstances
Aggressivity	Affectivity	Technicality	Genitality	Personality	Contextuality
1. Crisis	1. Alcohol, drugs	1. Targeted victim (pre-selection, planning)	1. Deviant, aggressive, sexual fantasies	1. Family, marital, work, socio-cultural, criminal context	1. Favourable environment
2. Conflict and violence prior to crime	2. Primary intent: Murder	2. Contact strategy	2. Rage displaced onto victim	2. Prior aggressor-victim relationship	2. Favourable timing
3. Intimidation	3. Extremist ideology	3. Victim-hunting	3. Victim is explicitly sexually solicited	3. Media surveillance of victim	3. Chance encounter
4. Harassment	4. Anger	4. Drugging of victim	4. Rape kit	4. Victim approached fraudulently, through a ruse or abuse of authority, etc.	4. Group or gang activity
5. Obscene calls	5. Vengeance	5. Already possesses weapon	5. Bondage equipment	5. Provocation by the victim	5. Witnesses
6. Death threats	6. Jealousy	6. Equipment prepared (gloves, mask, housebreaking tools, etc.)	6. Sexual arousal	6. Victim selected on the basis of specific criteria	6. Sex, age, habits, lifestyle, behaviour of aggressor
	7. Stress	7. Vehicle used	7. Sexual frustration		7. Sex, age, habits, lifestyle, behaviour of victim
	8. Depressive state	8. Pre-selected crime scene (surveillance)			9. Victim's risk factors
	9. Feelings of injustice	9. Deserted or intimate crime scene			
	10. Loneliness	10. Accomplices			
	11. Romantic passion	11. Preparation of crime			
	12. Group excitation				
	13. Unexpressed aggressivity				
	14. Psychotic disorders				
	15. Direct confrontation				
	16. Absence of premeditation				

Figure 3 – Post-crime Phase

1. Violence	2. Emotions	3. Modus Operandi	4. Sexuality	5. Relationships	6. Circumstances
Aggressivity	**Affectivity**	**Technicality**	**Genitality**	**Personality**	**Contextuality**
1. Burning of body	1. Fear, guilt, remorse	1. Attempted or actual removal or destruction of forensic evidence	1. Sexual acts with degraded corpse	1. Oral or written conact with investigators or media	1. Aggressor attempts to escape justice
2. Crime-scene arson	2. Relief, pleasure	2. Attempted or actual removal or destruction of other material	2. Sexual positioning of corpse	2. Oral or written contact with victim's family	2. Aggressor surrenders to authorities
3. Ransacking of crime scene	3. Covering of victim's face and/or body	3.1 Removal or destruction of forensic evidence	3. Obscene signs at crime scene	3. Follows crime in the news	3. Aggressor does not change habits, does not hide
4. Violation of corpse	4. Washing of victim	3.2. Removal or destruction of bedding	4. Fetishishtic theft	4. Participates in searches or investigations	4. Secondary thefts
	5. Re-dressing of victim	3.3. Leaves with weapon	5. Masturbation on stolen items		5. Witnesses during flight or destruction of evidence
	6. Attendance at funeral or visit to cemetary	4. Moves corpse	6. Video of sexual assault or murder		
	7. Other act of reparation	5. Hides, buries, submerges corpse	7. Disorderly clothing		
	8. Many clues left at scene	6. Corpse is burned or incinerated			
	9. Corpse left at crime scene	7. Corpse is dismembered			
		8. Staging to fool investigators			
		9. Aggressor cleans scene and/or themselves			

1.2.4 Repetition of certain items

Some items are listed in more than one component, due to differences in contextual connotations. For example, in Figure 1 (Acting Out) the use of multiple weapons is included in both the emotional component (Column 2) and the modus operandi component (Column 3). However, the context differs: "due to emotional charge" in Column 2, and "utilitarian" in Column 3.

1.3 Quantitative Modifications (Figure 4)

This figure is meant to demonstrate, by the checking of "yes," "no" or "?" (unknown), the presence of items in the case.

1.3.1 Quantifiable items ("yes")

Quantifiable items related to the use of force, degree of force, duration of crime, speed of attack, or significance of the item are scored from 1 to 4.

1.3.2 Non-quantifiable items ("no," "?")

Items are considered unquantifiable when there is insufficient information in the case file to score them. For example, the number of knife wounds is unquantifiable when the corpse has decomposed so far as to make this determination impossible.

Figure 4 – Nature, origin, quantification of items

1. Violence – Aggressivity	oui	non	?			1	2	3	4
1. Blitz attack		x		...	...				
2. High level of force	x			Assessed	quantifiable	x			
3. Ante-mortem wounds		x		... Assessed Supposed Declared	... quantifiable non quantifiable				
3.1 Number		x							
3.2 Gravity		x			...				
4. Post-mortem wounds		x		...	...				
4.1 Number		x		...	...				
4.2 Seriousness		x		...	...				
5. Torture		x		...	...				
5.1 Number		x		...	...				
5.2 Gravity		x		...	...				
6. Overkill		x		...	...				
7. Evisceration, dismemberment		x		...	...				
8. Corpse incinerated		x		...	...				
9. Crime-scene arson		x		...	...				
10. Assault involving several offenders and/or victims		x		...	...				
11. Vandalism		x		...	...				
% « yes » :	7,1%								
Score/Maximum possible score:	1			/	4				
Number of unquantifiable items :	0								

Figure 5 – Existence, evaluation and quality control of items

3. Modus Operandi – Technicality	oui	non	?			1	2	3	4
1. Self-control	x			Assessed	quantifiable	x			
2. Highly organized		x		...	...				
3. Surprise, violent abduction, violence or ruse	x			Supposec	quantifiable			x	
4. Burglary		x		...	...				
5. Kidnapping or confinement		x		...	...				
6. Various threats		x		...	...				
7. Immobilization	x			Assessed	quantifiable			x	
8. Restraints, blindfold, gag		x		...	...				
9. Already possesses weapon		x		...	...				
10. Nature of weapon		x		...	...				
11. Stolen objects		x		...	...				
12. Organized crime scene		x		...	...				
13. Planned crime scene		x		...	...				
14. Crime is of long duration		x		...	...				
15. Burglary, armed robbery		x		...	...				
16. Instrumental violence	x			Assessed	quantifiable			x	
17. Crime-scene writing or drawings intended for the public or police		x		...	...				
18. Multiple utilitarian weapons		x		...	...				
% « yes » :	22,2%								
Score/Maximum possible score :	10			Sur	16				
Number of unquantifiable items :	0								

	oui	non	?			1	2	3	4
9. Already possesses weapon		x		...	...				
10. Nature of weapon		x		...	...				
11. Stolen objects		x		...	...				
12. Organized crime scene		x		...	...				
13. Planned crime scene		x		...	...				
14. Crime is of long duration		x		...	...				
15. Burglary, armed robbery		x		...	...				
16. Instrumental violence	x			Assessed	quantifiable			x	
17. Crime-scene writing or drawings intended for public or police		x		...	...				
18. Multiple Utilitarian				...	...				
% « yes » :	22,2%								
Score/Maximum possible score :	10			Sur	16				
Number of unquantifiable items :	0								

2. Experimentation

2.1 Preparation

2.1.1 Deletion of certain items

As the GAC is primarily concerned with crimes with no apparent motive, items related to motive — such as terrorism (Table 5, Column 6, Item 5) and the settling of accounts (Table 5, Column 3, Item 10) — are deleted.

2.1.2 Data processing

2.1.2.1 Quality control (Figure 5)

To ensure that the analyst has considered each listed item, we have included a quality-control component. An indicator at the bottom of each fundamental component turns from red to green once all the items in that column are checked off.

2.1.2.2 The glossary (Figure 6)

Clicking on an item takes one directly to the lexicon, which provides the definition and basis of assessment (see Paragraph 1.1).

2.1.2.3 Presence, distribution, and value of components

Phase 1: Presence and distribution of components (Figures 7 and 8)

The goal of this phase is to determine the presence and relative distribution of the components in the case. The analyst marks "yes" for each component present in the file and the program automatically transforms the "yes"s into percentages and generates a pie chart. It should be noted that while non-quantifiable items included in the behavioural analysis — as they are counted by the program — they cannot be evaluated in Phase 2.

Phase 2: Component values (Figures 7 and 9)

In this second phase, each quantifiable component present in the case is assigned a value from 1 to 4. For those items, the program compares the assigned scores to the potential scores and provides a graph of this in the form of a histogram (Figure 9). For each component, the chart shows the actual scores (in solid colours), the maximum possible score (transparent colours — see Paragraph 2.2), and the proportion of the scores (Figure 9).

2.2 Case study: Sexual Assault and Murder of a Child (Figures 7 to 10)

A child disappeared at about 10:30 p.m. at a town festival. He was found the next morning, nude and covered with earth, on a riverbank 100 meters from where he was last seen. The autopsy revealed that the attacker had sodomized the child before killing him. The cause of death was drowning.

2.2.1 Filling out the Acting Out table

Although every component was scored in this case, only the Circumstances and Sexuality components will be discussed here.

The Circumstances component immediately appears to be the dominant component in this case (Figure 9). In fact, 7 of the 10 items of this component were checked "yes" (Figure 7), for a total score of 21 out of 28 (7 x 4). The Sexuality component is weak, with only 2 of the 14 items checked "yes." However, the two items that were present received the maximum 8 points (figures 9 and 10), for a ratio of 100% (Figure 9).

2.2.2 Comparison of the Acting Out table statement to the offender's statement

When questioned a few days later, the assailant confessed to the crime. The items of the Circumstances and Sexuality components noted above were confirmed by the offender's admissions that:

- Opportunity was the primary feature of his acting out.
- He had not been seeking a victim, but saw a child alone and tricked him into coming along with him.
- Sexual assault had been his primary intention, and he killed the child to stop him from crying out. It is worth noting that the offender had a record of sexual assaults on minors.

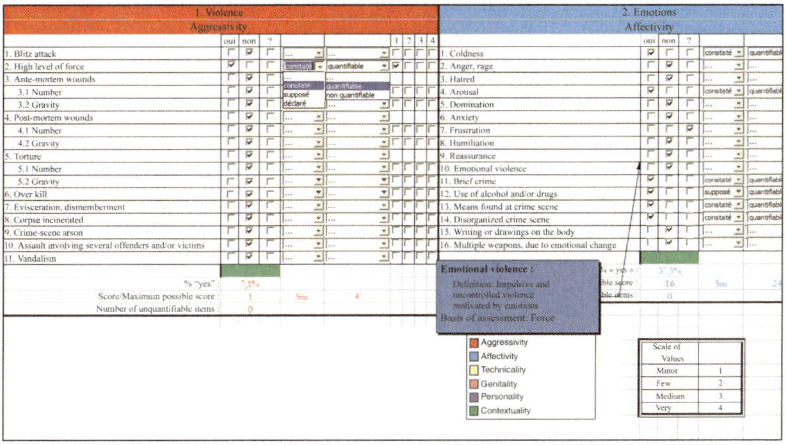

Figure 6: The Glossary

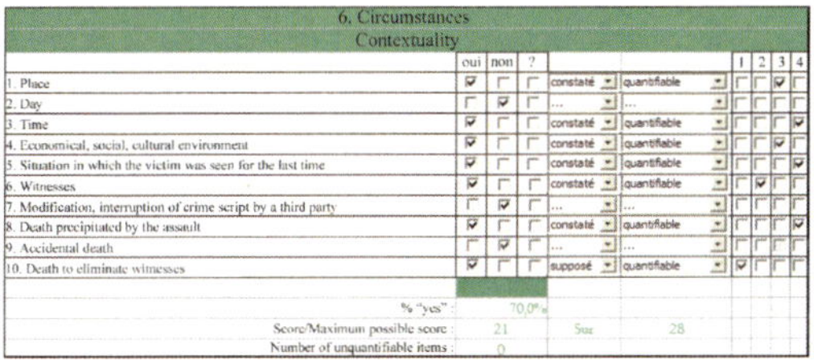

Figure 7: Checking of items

Studied files: Rape and murder of a child

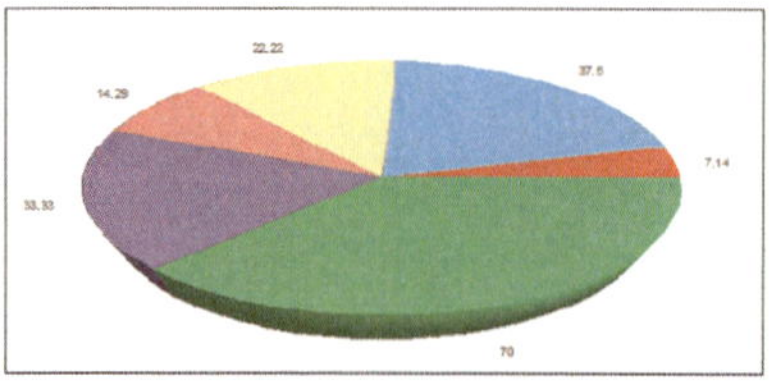

Figure 8: Presence and distribution of the components
Case Study: Sexual assault and murder of a child

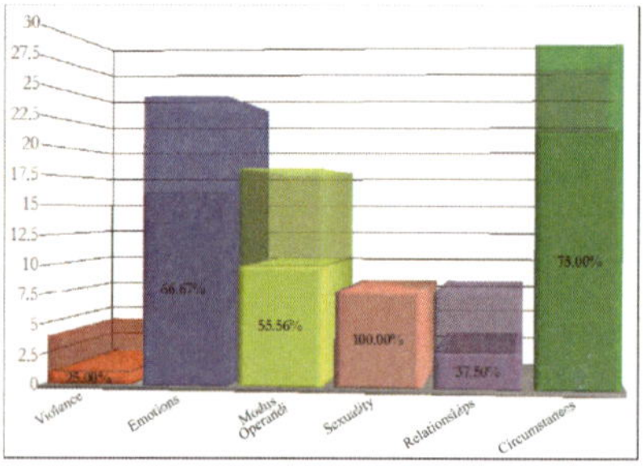

Figure 9: Value of components
Case Study: Sexual assault and murder of a child

4. Sexuality Genitality									
	oui	non	?			1	2	3	4
1. Undressing	✓			constaté	quantifiable				✓
2. Sexual bondage		✓		...	...				
3. Caressing, touching, kissing, sucking, licking, biting		✓		...	...				
4. Body shaving		✓		...	...				
5. Flagellation, humiliation, psychological terror		✓		...	...				
6. Masturbation of the victim			✓	...	...				
7. Masturbation of aggressor			✓	...	...				
8. Penetration of an orifice by penis, finger or object	✓			constaté	quantifiable				✓
9. Ejaculation on the body or at the scene		✓		...	...				
10. Urination, defecation on the body or at the scene		✓		...	...				
11. Sadistic mutilation		✓		...	...				
12. Vaginal washing or douching		✓		...	...				
				...	...				
				...	...				
% "yes" :	14.3%								
Score/Maximum possible score :	8			Sur	8				
Number of unquantifiable items :	0								

Figure 10: The sexuality component
Case Study: Sexual assault and murder of a child

2.2.3 Conclusions

Clearly, the tables generated by this computerized behavioural-analysis software allowed identification of both the dominant component of the crime (Circumstances: had the child not been alone at one point, the offender would not have committed the crime) and the sexual nature of the crime (a single sexual act reflecting long-standing deviance).

2.3 The Future

This experiment suggests that future work should include:

- A completely objective discussion among analysts of possible points of disagreement.
- Comparison of results after the case is solved in order to determine the pertinence of the analysis.
- An analysis of the results, in order to detect serial crimes. Similar conclusions about components in different crimes may suggest a common offender.
- A study of the correlation among different phases in the same or different cases.
- International comparisons, through the use of a common method of behavioural analysis.

D. FROM CRIME SCENE TO CRIMINAL PROFILE

1. A Basic Problem

At the outset of this chapter, we said that investigators' jobs would be much easier if all criminals exactly resembled their crimes. Unfortunately, this is not always the case. The gap between offenders' daily lives and the nature of their violent offences is the fundamental problem of psychological profiling, which presupposes a logical, comprehensible, and constant correlation between the profiles of the crime and the criminal. In other words: Are there cause-and-effect relationships among the offender's cognitive-emotional status, personality and modus operandi? The fact that almost no one asks this question makes it all the more pertinent! In simpler, less serious matters, such relationships can seem self-evident. The repeated theft of women's underclothes or high heels irresistibly suggests fetishism. But while the fetishist is most likely a young man, identifying him will remain difficult in the absence of a criminal, medical or anecdotal record of perverse conduct. His arrest will, in fact, no doubt be due to other facets of behavioural analysis — times and places of the thefts, skill, physical proximity to the scenes, availability of suspects at the moment of the crime, etc.

It is often the same with major crimes. Not all murderers are psychopaths with records of violent crimes that make them prime suspects. And offenders who do fit this profile may not fit the expected profile for the offence. In practice, investigators must consider four factors: a) the state of the crime scene; b) the modus operandi reconstructed from all the investigative data; c) the criminal's mental state (possibly variable) at the time of the sexual crime or the murder; d) the criminal's usual mental state in daily life.

There are often disparities — significant irrationalities — between a criminal's usual state of mind and their frame of mind at the time of the offence (Bénézech, 2001; Bénézech, 2004). Certain paranoid and dissociated schizophrenics who commit sadistic homicides or parricides can be capable of partially or totally organized criminal behaviour. On the other hand, some delusional paranoiacs, who are commonly supposed to act rationally, logically and intentionally, often commit emotional, disorganized murders (Barbara Pera and Dailliet, 2005; Bénézech, Benayoun and Hachouf, 2001; Le Bihan and Bénézech, 2004). Even where working conditions are ideal, only occasionally can profilers connect a single violent act to a personality type. The modus operandi only reveals the mental organization and behaviour of the offender in cases of identical, repeated offences of marked singularity. With the commission of emotional or sexual crimes, however, everything can depend on the circumstances.

2. The Example of Sexual Murders

In their study devoted to the psychopathology of single-victim sex murderers, Proulx and Sauvetre (2005) clearly recognized the behavioural difference between an offender's criminal and ordinary daily conduct. They note: "Here again, the clinical portrait outlined by Brittain (1970) is consistent with our results. It describes the sadistic sexual murderer as a self-effacing, shy person in daily life (avoidant and schizoid), but a predator (antisocial, narcissistic) in criminal terms... To explain this contradiction, one can hypothesize that whereas psychometric instruments assess the sexual murderer, clinicians evaluate the crime" (p. 102).

Proulx and Sauvetre (2005) suggest three explanations for the divergent observations in the literature: a) sexual murderers have a double personality — a schizoid, avoidant, dependent, borderline face in their interpersonal relations, and an antisocial, narcissistic face in their criminal acts; b) personality-disorder scales (concerning schizoid, avoidant, dependent personalities) are valuable, but clinicians, who are more focused on the crime than on its perpetrator, make erroneous diagnoses; c) there exist two types of sexual murderers — those with schizoid, avoidant, dependent, passive-aggressive personalities, and those who are antisocial and narcissistic (p. 103).

Whatever the hypothesis, it is nevertheless true that the daily conduct of an offender can be the opposite of their behaviour towards their victim.

3. Diagnostic Profiles and Violent Crime (Table 8)

Given the diversity and complexity of major crimes and the motives underlying them, it is extremely risky to attempt to predict the relationship between the personality profiles of offenders in their daily and criminal lives. We have already noted that there is no stable correlation between a psychological profile and modus operandi, although extroverted sociopaths tend to commit highly organized crimes, and introverted psychotics ("crazies") generally commit poorly or totally disorganized crimes (tables 1, 2, and 3). Experience shows in fact that apparently "normal," rational, socially integrated people can occasionally commit emotional, disordered violence, and that paranoid individuals can prepare their revenge quite thoroughly and carry it out methodically. Despite all these reservations, we provide in Table 8 what seem to us the most frequent correlations between offender-diagnostic categories and the characteristics of their crimes.

Table 8 – Principal diagnostic categories and the behaviour of violent offenders

Criminological diagnosis	Behaviour of violent aggressors			
	Typically Habitual	**Pre-crime phase**	**Crime phase**	**Post-crime phase**
Passionate	Jealous Egocentric	Depressive Highly anxious	Disorganized	Passive Suicidal
Angry Alcoholic	Impulsive Addictive	Confrontational Intoxicated	Disorganized	Variable
Chronic psychotic	Pathological Disorganized	Delusional Depressive	Disorganized	Indifferent Passive
Acute psychotic	Unremarkable	Aroused Delusional	Disorganized	Variable
Angry sexual	Impulsive	Enraged	Disorganized	Unremarkable
Sadistic sexual	Unremarkable	Paraphilic	Organized	Unremarkable
Compensatory sexual	Interiorized	Reassurance	Organized	Unremarkable
Dominating sexual	Virile	Hunter	Organized	Unremarkable

CONCLUSION

The present work does not pretend to be any more than a stepping stone toward the understanding of violent crime and its perpetrators. To this end, we have presented a personalized classification of violent homicides observed in France, and the correlation of those killings with mental disorders (Tables 1, 2, 3, 8). This was followed by a review of the six constitutive variables in criminal matters (Table 4) as well as the characteristics of the pre-offending, offending, and post-offending periods (tables 5, 6, 7). The *Groupe Analyse Comportementale* of the *Gendarmerie Nationale Française* experimentally verified this data, and modified and adapted it to their practices (Figures 1 to 6). A concrete example (Figures 7 to 10) briefly illustrated the utility of this new behavioural-analysis protocol, founded on three analytical checklists and the scoring of the case — Acting Out (Figure 1), the Pre-Crime Phase (Figure 2), and the Post-Crime Phase (Figure 3).

During the testing of this method, information technology proved invaluable both in detecting and considering possible points of disagreement, and in comparing the analytical results with the actual resolution of the case. Moreover, it is probable that the computerized protocol will be tested to determine its utility in detecting serial criminality, and even subjected to correlation analysis. We hope that it will prove useful to investigators preparing to question suspects (St- Yves and Landry, 2004) and in the preparation of treatment programs, such as the remarkably well-organized programs found in Canadian federal penitentiaries (Correctional Service of Canada, Research Division, 340 Laurier Avenue West, Ottawa, Ontario, K1A 0P9).

We would conclude by recalling that there is no absolute correlation between an offender's modus operandi and psychology: there are only tendencies — small, medium, and large statistical probabilities. In fact, it is always likely that unpredictable and circumstantial factors will intervene and disrupt the spontaneous or deliberate logic behind criminal activity. Moreover, the aggressor's mental state is not necessarily the same in their daily life and at the time of the violent offence, and can vary for many reasons (e.g. drug use, the victim's attitude). In criminology, anything, even the most improbable, is possible. These observations bring us to the limits of psychological behavioural analysis.

REFERENCES

Barbara Pera, S. and Dailliet, A. (2005). Homicide par des malades mentaux: analyse clinique et criminologique. L'Encéphale, 31, 539-549, cahier 1.

Bénézech, M. (1994). Des crimes fous commis par les fous et les autres. Forensic, 5, 41-44.

Bénézech, M. (1995). De quelques perspectives médico-psychologiques sur les homicides sexuels. Présentation de trois observations. Annales Médico-Psychologiques, 153, 501-511.

Bénézech, M. (1997). L'homicide sexuel: diagnostic et classement criminologiques. Journal de Médecine Légale Droit Médical, 40, 289-294.

Bénézech, M. (2001). Évaluation psychiatrique et scénario criminel. Forensic, 6, 1-2.

Bénézech, M. (2004). Le crime et sa scène: méthode d'analyse comportementale de l'acte homicidaire. Forensic, 19, 19-25.

Bénézech, M., Benayoun, M.D. and Hachouf, S. (2001). Homicide sadique d'un homosexuel par un schizophrène. Considérations médicolégales sur les fantasmes pervers chez les psychotiques. Annales Médico-Psychologiques, 159, 363-368.

Guttmacher, M. (1965). La psychologie du meurtrier. Paris, Presses Universitaires de France.

Jackson, J.L. and Bekerian, D.A. (1997). Offender profiling. Theory, research and practice. Chichester, John Wiley and Sons.

Le Bihan, P. and Bénézech, M. (2004). Degré d'organisation du crime de parricide pathologique: mode opératoire, profil criminologique. À propos de 42 observations. Annales Médico-Psychologiques, 162, 615-625.

MacCulloch, M., Bailey, J. and Robinson, C. (1995). Mentally disordered attackers and killers: towards a taxonomy. The Journal of Forensic Psychiatry, 6 (1), 41-61.

Proulx, J. and Sauvêtre, N. (2005). Meurtriers sexuels et violeurs: aspects psychopathologiques. Dans: Les meurtriers sexuels. Analyse comparative et nouvelles perspectives. Montréal, Les Presses de l'Université de Montréal, 81-108.

Ressler, R.K., Burgess, A.W. and Douglas, J.E. (1993). Sexual homicide. Patterns and motives. London, Simon and Schuster.

Ressler, R.K., Douglas, J.E. and Burgess, A.W. (1993). Crime classification manual. The standard system for investigating and classifying violent crimes. London, Simon and Schuster.

Salfati, C.G. and Canter, D.V. (1999). Differentiating stranger murders: profiling offender characteristics from behavioral styles. Behav Sci Law, 17, 391-406.

Santtila, P., Hakkanen, H., Canter, D. and Elfgren, T. (2003). Classifying homicide offenders and predicting their characteristics from crime scene behavior. Scandinavian Journal of Psychology, 44 (2), 107-118.

St-Yves, M. and Landry, J. (2004). Psychologie des entrevues d'enquête de la recherche à la pratique. Cowansville: Éditions Yvon Blais.

Toutin, T. (2000). Le profilage criminel. Paris, La Documentation française.

Turvey, B.E. (1999). Criminal profiling. An introduction to behavioral evidence analysis. London, Academic Press.

CHAPTER 20

Geographic Profiling and Analysis of the Hunting Process Used by Serial Sex Offenders

Eric Beauregard and Kim Rossmo

While serial crime is not a new phenomenon, only recently has it attracted much attention. The last 20 years have seen most of the research (Petee and Jarvis, 2000), originally in the wake of notorious U.S. crimes such as those by Ted Bundy and Jeffrey Dahmer. This early research was primarily descriptive and limited to analysis of a few cases (Beauregard, Proulx, and St-Yves, 2007). At the end of the 1980s, the research expanded, thanks to an increased understanding of patterns of serial criminal characteristics and behaviours. Understanding the patterns underlying serial crime, and how they vary from situation to situation, is of prime importance in helping police officers apprehend these criminals (Beauregard, Lussier and Proulx, 2005).

In this chapter, we consider the scripts of the hunting process that serial sexual aggressors employ in different contexts. To begin with, we present data from FBI studies and then discuss the prioritizing of suspects, a crucial dimension of investigating serial sex crime. We then discuss how the application of geographic profiling to such scripts is a useful investigative tool for prioritizing suspects. Finally, we provide some examples of investigative strategies using geographic profiling.

A. SERIAL SEX CRIMES

Most crimes involve people who have some sort of relationship or link. In such cases, the number of suspects is limited. As a point of departure, investigators start with the victim, then turn their attention to family members, friends, neighbours, and so on. This approach generally leads to the apprehension of a suspect and the end of a possible series of crimes. However, with most serial crimes — murders, sexual assaults, burglaries, vehicle thefts — there is no link between the perpetrator and victim (Rossmo, 2004). This lowers the probability of arrest and increases the probability that the perpetrator will continue the series.

During the 1980s and 1990s, the FBI conducted several studies of sexual aggressors (Hazelwood and Burgess, 1987; Hazelwood, Reboussin and Warren, 1989; Hazelwood and Warren, 1989; Hazelwood and Warren, 1990; Warren, Reboussin, Hazelwood, Cummings, Gibbs and Trombetta, 1998; Warren, Reboussin, Hazelwood, Gibbs, Trombetta and Cummings, 1999). The results indicate that a good number of these offenders had witnessed and experienced sexual, physical, and psychological abuse at the hands of a parent. Some exhibited deviant sexual behaviour (multiple paraphilia, prostitution, pornography collection). In most cases, they did not know their victims.

Most commonly, the serial sexual aggressor selects victims aged between 18 and 33, and attacks them in their homes. The majority of such attacks are premeditated, with manipulation the most common contact strategy. Most of the attackers use minimal or no force, but will employ verbal threats when faced with resistance (physical, verbal, or passive). The most common sexual acts perpetrated are vaginal penetration and fellatio.

According to the FBI, most serial sexual offenders appear to take no precautions to protect their identities. In addition, if the victim resists, their arousal intensifies and the attack lasts for a longer period. Attacks by white aggressors are more likely to be lengthy, violent, and injurious.

While the results such as those obtained by the FBI can be useful in the search for suspects, they have limited application in the prioritization of serial criminals. In fact, one characteristic of investigations of serial crimes, both sexual and non-sexual, is that the amount of information and the number of suspects outstrip the resources available to analyze them. For example, Project Green Ribbon, the nine-month investigation of the sexual murders of Ontario residents Leslie Mahaffy (on June 14, 1991) and Kristen French (on April 16, 1992), amassed no less than 31,000 pieces of information and a list of 3,200 suspects. However, this was modest compared to the 268,000 suspects compiled in the investigation of Peter Suttcliffe, the "Yorkshire Ripper" (Rossmo, 2004). Thus, information collected during such investigations must be intelligently and effectively managed, with prioritization of the many suspects.

B. PRIORITIZING SUSPECTS

Prioritization techniques, also known as optimal search strategies, are highly important for the management of the high volume of information in serial crime investigations. These techniques or strategies must be both valid (correct individuals receive the highest priority) and useful (the criteria are observable by, and generally known to, the police investigating serial crimes). While there are several ways to prioritize suspects, the principal methods fall into three categories: 1) physical description; 2) behaviour; 3) geography.

In some cases, victims of sexual crimes are able to provide a physical description of their attacker — for example, a white man, aged between 30 and 40, 90 to 100 kilograms in weight, 1.85 meters tall, with a tattoo on his right arm and alcohol on his breath. While investigators can make use of such information to prioritize their suspects, some indicators are more useful than others. Unfortunately, there is little research available on witness errors, which makes evaluation of the indicators problematic. Consequently, physical description tends to be the most common criterion for eliminating suspects.

Prioritizing on the basis of behaviour is associated with criminal and psychological profiling. It can be either general or specific. General profiling — sometimes called "statistical profiling" (Beauregard, 2007) — provides a summary description of the type of person likely to commit a certain type of crime, such as sexual assault on a child. The prioritization criteria are the same for all crimes in the group. For example, a study undertaken by the National Center for the Analysis of Violent Crime (NCAVC) has shown that the typical arsonist is a young white man from a middle-class background who has nocturnal habits and is of average or superior intelligence (Sapp, Huff, Gary, Icove and Horbert, 1994).

The advantage of general profiling is that it is easy and rapid, as it does not require a new analysis based on the specific crime. Its principal drawback is that it lacks precision, particularly when the statistical sample on which it is based is small or non-representative.

Specific profiling is performed following the detailed analysis of the crime under investigation. The profiles it produces are usually more precise, more detailed, and richer than general profiling. Specific profiling attempts to determine the suspect's character, as well as other characteristics, through crime-scene analysis. As a general rule, a specific profile also suggests investigative strategies geared to the crime under investigation, and can provide multiple suggestions about the offender characteristics, such as age, race, sex, socio-economic status, level of education, marital status, employability, criminal record, and mental health history. However, specific profiling requires more time and preparation, and is not possible in all cases.

Table 1: Sexual aggressor's hunting process scripts and tracks

Source	Crime	Place	Distance travelled
Aitken et al. (1996)	Sexual murder of a child	Great Britain	91.6% < 5 mi.
Alston (1994)	Serial sexual assault	British Columbia (Canada)	31.1 % < 0.5 km; 44.4 % < 1 km; 55.6 % < 1.5 km; 60 % < 2 km; 75.6 % < 3 km
Amir (1971)	Sexual assault	Philadelphia (United States)	72 % within home area (five blocks)
Boggs (1965)	Sexual assault and housebreaking	St. Louis (United States)	Most commonly outside their home territory
Canter and Hodge (1997)	Serial murder	United States	40 km; dumping: 9 km/90 km mean min./max. (25 % < 5 km and 50 % < 15 km)
Canter and Larkin (1993)	Serial sexual assault	England	mean: 1.53
Davies and Dale (1993)	Sexual assault	England	17 % < 0.5 mi; 29 % < 1 mi; 52 % < 2 mi; 60 % < 3 mi; 76 % < 5 mi.
Gabor and Gottheil (1984)	Sexual assault	Ottawa (Canada)	1.43 mi.
Hanfland (1982)	Sexual assault/sodomy	Eugene, Oregon (United States)	2.66 mi.
Lebeau (1987)	Sexual assault	San Diego (United States)	2.5 mi.
Lebeau (1987)	Serial sexual assault	San Diego (United States)	1.77 mi.

Table 1: Sexual aggressor's hunting process scripts and tracks, cont'd.

Source	Crime	Place	Distance travelled
Lebeau (1987)	Sexual assault	San Diego (United States)	3.5 mi.
Lebeau (1992)	Serial sexual assault	San Diego (United States)	25.88/1.89/0.52/3.33 km (four serial rapists)
Pyle (1974)	Sexual assault	Akron (United States)	1.34 mi.
Rhodes and Conly (1981)	Sexual assault	Washington, D.C. (United States)	1.15 mi; 0.73 mi median; 62 % < 1 mi.
Rossmo and Baeza (1998)	Serial sexual assault	New York (United States)	2.5 mi (residence); 1.0 mi. (anchor point)
Safarik et al. (2002)	Sexual murder of older women	United States	0.42 mi; 56 % within six blocks of the victim; 30 % living on the same block
Shaw (1998)	Sexual homicide	United Kingdom	2.4 mi. / 1.0 mi. median (encounter site); 2.2 mi./ 1.0 mi. median (body dump site); 25 % in offender's home and 85 % < 9.5 km
Topalin (1992)	Serial sexual assault	London (England)	2.81 mi; 20 % in or close to home
Warren et al. (1995)	Serial sexual assault	United States	3.14 mi; 1.66/4.93 mi. average closest / furthest (local offenders, travel < 20 mi.)

Geographic approaches can also be general or specific. The general approach is based mainly on journey-to-crime research. As can be seen in Table 1, the majority of sexual offenders commit their assaults close to the area in which they reside (Beauregard, Proulx and Rossmo, 2005). Thus, individuals who live very near the crime scene receive investigative priority, compared to those who live farther away. However, the limits concerning general profiling — the lack of representativity and precision — apply here, as well.

C. GEOGRAPHIC PROFILING

Specific geographic assessment, often called "geographic profiling," is based on examining the crime or crime series under investigation (Rossmo, 1997). Rather than using an offender's activity space in order to predict where crimes are likely to occur, as in the Brantingham and Brantingham model (1984; 1991; 1993), geographic profiling is an attempt to invert this premise by using the crime locations in order to predict the most probable area in which the offender resides or works. These studies have led to the development of a criminal geographic targeting (CGT) algorithm which is the basis for the computerized geographic profiling system called Rigel (Rossmo, 2000). Rigel is a strategic information management system that allows investigators to prioritize those areas most likely to contain the offender. In such a system, crime site coordinates are analyzed with a patented criminal hunting algorithm that produces a probability surface showing the likelihood of offender residence within the hunting area. This three-dimensional probability map is referred to as a jeopardy surface (see Figure 1), whereas the two-dimensional perspective integrated with a street map is termed a geoprofile (Rossmo, 1997; 2000). The geoprofile (see Figure 2) does not indicate an "x" where the offender lives, but rather describes an optimal search process.

Geographic profiling includes both an objective and a subjective component. The objective or quantitative component encompasses all the statistical methods and measures used to analyze and interpret the point pattern formed by the crime sites. Geographic profiling considers different factors related to the crime and environment, such as the locations associated with the crime, the type of offender involved, hunting style, streets and highways, psychological and physical boundaries, neighbourhood types (industrial, commercial, residential), neighbourhood demographics, and the victim's routine activities and displacement (Rossmo, 2000).

The subjective, or qualitative, component encompasses the reconstruction and interpretation of the offender's mental map. For example, sexual murderers who prey on prostitutes will find their victims in neighbourhoods frequented by these sex-workers — inner-city areas, red-light districts, etc. — rather than opulent areas in cities or suburbs.

The use of geographic profiling is subject to some conditions. To begin with, there must be a series of crimes that can be linked together with a reasonable degree of certainty. However, it is possible to construct a profile from a single crime if it is associated with several locations. For example, the investigation might identify locations at which the offender used a credit card, made a telephone call, borrowed or abandoned a car, and left objects or clues. Finally, the crime series must comprise at least five crime scenes (although it is in some cases possible to create a profile with fewer). This is not to imply that the series must include five or more *crimes*, but rather that the crime can be linked to at least five different *locations*. These may be, for example: 1) victim encounter site; 2) attack site; 3) murder or assault site; 4) body dump site; and 5) site at which vehicle or objects were left. The more locations linked to the crime, the better will be the performance of the CGT (Rossmo, 2000).

Geographic profiling is most often used in serial sex assaults and homicides, but the technique can also be effective in cases of serial arson, bombings, aggravated thefts, and kidnappings.

Geographic profiling complements traditional investigative technique when: 1) there is a series of crimes; 2) police have exhausted traditional investigative techniques; 3) linkage analysis between crimes shows that they are related; 4) investigators have prepared a psychological profile. The geographic profile is prepared after examining the investigative reports, witness statements, autopsy reports, and, where available, psychological profile and profiles of the crime scene and related venues. The person constructing the profile must discuss the case with investigators, analyze criminal and demographic statistics concerning the neighbourhood, and analyze the streets, zoning, and major arteries.

Figure 1: "Jeopardy surface" of the Southside Rapist, Lafayette, Louisiana

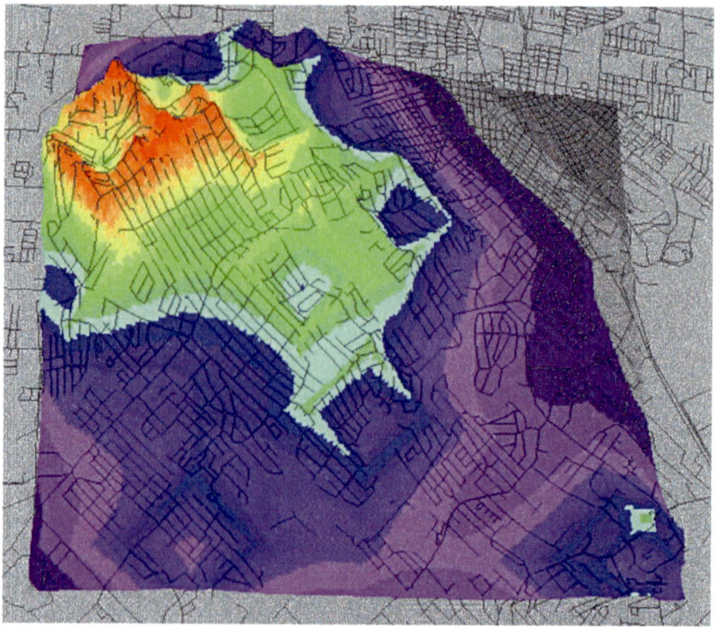

Figure 2: "Geoprofile" of the Southside Rapist, Lafayette, Louisiana

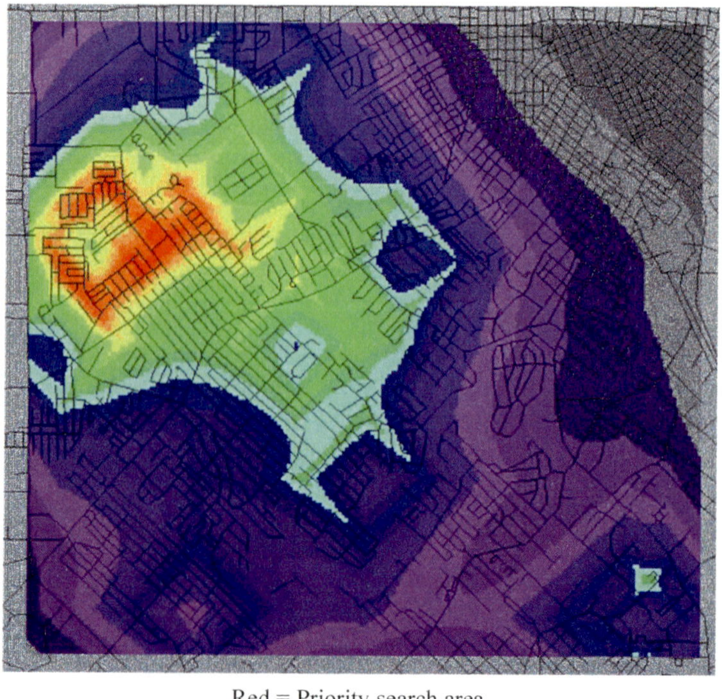

Red = Priority search area

Figure 3

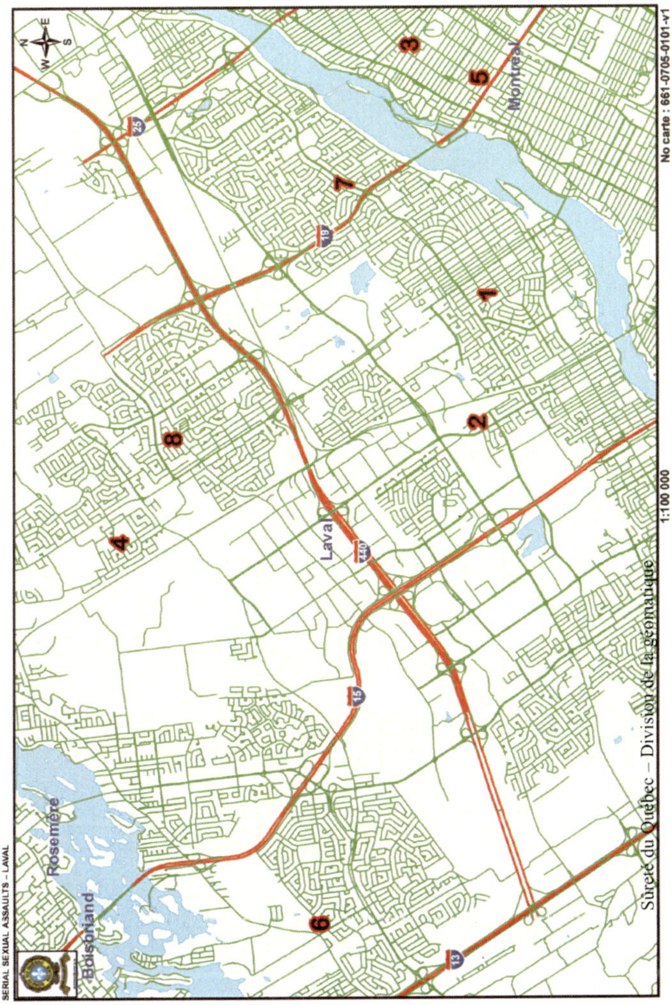
SERIAL SEXUAL ASSAULTS – LAVAL
Sûreté du Québec – Division de la géomatique
1:100 000
No carte : 661-0705-0101-v1
Montréal
Laval
Rosemère
Boisbriand
1
2
3
4
5
6
7
8
25
19
440
15
13

To measure the effectiveness of this tool, Rossmo (2001) has created the CGT "hit score percentage," which quantifies the geographic profile's performance. The CGT hit score percentage represents the area searched using a geoprofile until the offender's residence is encountered, divided by the total area covered by the crime sites (Rossmo, 2001). For example, if a sexual aggressor's residence is encountered after searching 0.6 km^2, and the assault committed by this aggressor covered 12 km^2, then the CGT hit score percentage would be of 5% (0.6/12). The smaller the CGT percentage, the better the focus of the geoprofile.

Rossmo (2001) has inventoried 1,426 crimes, involving 1,726 locations, submitted to geographic profiling by various police forces between 1991 and 2001. The average CGT hit score percentage is 4.7%, with homicides scoring 5.1%, sexual assaults 4.7%, arson 2.2%, and robberies 7.1%.

D. THE HUNTING PROCESS: FROM TYPOLOGIES TO SCRIPTS

Clinicians who evaluate and treat sexual aggressors, as well as the police, traditionally group them into different types (For sexual offender typologies used by police, see Wilson and Alison, 2005). For example, the typology of sexual aggressors of women developed by Groth, Burgess and Holmstrom (1977) has been used by the FBI to develop their own model (Hazelwood, 1995). However, when one carefully examines the behaviour of sexual aggressors, several problems emerge with the existing typologies.

To begin with, typologies of offending processes focus on the aggressor, neglecting the analysis of the criminal event as a whole — that is the offender, the victim, and the context (Meier, Kennedy and Sacco, 2001). Second, these typologies presuppose that the offending process, as well as the modus operandi, do not fluctuate in a given sexual aggressor; they assume, that is, that such offenders always act in the same way, "specializing" in a single type of victim, regardless of situational factors and opportunities.

Third, studies to date concerning the offending process have largely ignored situational factors. The majority of identified typologies suggest that individual characteristics such as personality, sexual preferences, and cognitive processes, are the principal factors influencing the offending process. Some studies, however, have demonstrated the impact of situational factors —such as alcohol consumption, pornography, anger, cognitive distortions, weapons, and resistance by the victim — on the offending process of sexual offenders. However, these studies did not take into account the geographic context of these crimes.

In light of the numerous problems with existing typologies, Rossmo (1997) developed a "hunting pattern" model for serial criminals, based on what is known about the interaction between geographic and criminal behaviours. This model was inspired by a study of Serengeti lions (Schaller, 1972). According to Rossmo, hunting patterns can be divided into two parts — the search for victims, and the attack. This model identifies four search methods and three attack methods.

1. Victim-Search Methods

The *hunter* generally commits his crimes within his city of residence. These aggressors set out from their home base and search for suitable victims. The *poacher* commits crimes by traveling outside his city of residence, or by operating from an activity node other than his home base. The *troller* is an opportunistic aggressor who encounters his victims in the course of routine activities. Although his crimes are often spontaneous, trollers may in some cases have fantasized about or planned their offences, and so are ready when opportunities present themselves. *Trappers* have an occupation or a position which brings potential victims to them, or use subterfuge (e.g. placing want ads, taking in boarders) to entice suitable victims into their home or to a location they control.

2. Victim-Attack Methods

The *raptor* attacks his victims almost immediately upon encountering them. The *stalker* follows or watches his victims, and waits for an opportune moment to attack. Finally, the attacks of the *ambusher* are committed at locations at which the aggressor has a great deal of control, such as his residence or workplace. This aggressor sometimes hides the bodies of his victims, most often on his property (Rossmo, 2000).

Rossmo's model (1997) allows evaluation of the interaction between the offender's offence-related behaviour and his geographic behaviour. The modelling of this interaction has practical implications in investigations of violent crime, and particularly for geographic profiling. Moreover, classifying hunting patterns has certain advantages over other typologies of sexual aggressors.

First, it takes into account both the behavioural components (modus operandi) and the geographic components inherent in every crime. Second, in contrast to other typologies, the concept of hunting process takes into account the dynamic nature and the adaptability of offending patterns. Moreover, it allows identification of victim-search and victim-attack methods, and — since search and attack methods are correlated — of the most common hunting styles (e.g. *hunter/raptor* and *trapper/ambusher* are more common than *hunter/ambusher* and *trapper/raptor)* (Rossmo, 2000). However, Rossmo's model of hunting patterns lacks details and does not include important parameters related to criminal decision-making (e.g. hunting field, victim selection, victim-contact strategies, offending strategies, travel methods of offenders; see Beauregard, Rossmo and Proulx, 2007). Moreover, Rossmo's model (1997) does not include certain geographic components (familiarity of locations, indoor versus outdoor locations, private versus public locations) that assist in identifying the situations in which offenders use particular methods for searching out victims, or particular methods of attack (Beauregard, Proulx, Rossmo, Leclerc, and Allaire, 2007).

To remedy these limitations in typologies and the hunting pattern model, we have developed scripts of the hunting process. These scripts are more detailed, and include a greater number of factors relevant to the investigation of serial sexual aggression. As well, combining different geographic factors with the modus operandi provides a better description of the circumstances in which the scripts of hunting process are used.

E. HUNTING SCRIPTS USED BY SERIAL SEXUAL AGGRESSORS

The script concept — borrowed from the cognitive sciences (Cornish, 1994; Schank and Abelson, 1977) — helps investigators compensate for the numerous difficulties associated with existing typologies. Scripts are acquired through social learning, and involve modeling and reinforcement. "When the behaviour associated with a script has been used repeatedly and successfully in the past, it will be activated more readily. If strong enough, an activated script will be followed by the scripted action, unless there are strong inhibitory factors present" (Tedeschi and Felson, 1994, p. 181). Serial sexual aggressors employ different hunting process scripts, depending on the situation or the type of victim they encounter.

Beauregard, Proulx, Rossmo, Leclerc, and Allaire (2007) have performed a statistical analysis of variables related to the hunting process of

72 serial sexual offenders incarcerated in different penitentiaries under the jurisdiction of the Correctional Service of Canada (Quebec region). Three scripts, comprising five different "tracks" (variations in the script), emerged from this analysis.[1] Table 2 shows the main results of this analysis.

1. The Coercive Script

The coercive script includes two different tracks:

a) The home-intrusion track

In the home-intrusion track, the aggressor uses the victim's residence as the base of his hunt. The encounter, attack, crime, and victim-release sites are the same, most often the victim's residence or somewhere in the building in which they reside (such as the stairwell, elevator, or laundry room of an apartment block). The aggressor employs physical violence when approaching the victim and in committing the crime, but uses threats to bring them to the crime scene. The relevant hunting pattern is hunter-raptor, signifying that the attacker selects a victim on the basis of their place of residence and attacks as soon as he makes contact with them.

> Paul is a serial sexual aggressor, and has committed several crimes over the years. In some cases, he rode his bicycle around his neighbourhood, taking the time to observe houses which provide a clear view of their occupants. His targets of choice were single-family residences, because of their easy access. Paul ensured that the targeted house was occupied by a single woman or a woman with children. His victims were usually young. He weighed a variety of factors, including: the home's decoration, whether a handbag was in view, the presence of a single vehicle, observable movements of the woman through the windows. He often waited until the very early hours of the morning to commit the assault, hoping to find the victim in a deep sleep. He hid his bicycle in the back yard, and entered at the back, through a window. Once inside, he went directly to the master bedroom. He immediately used physical

---

1 A general example illustrating the concepts of "script" and "track": The "restaurant script" organizes what we know about what one must do when dining at a restaurant: one enters, waits to be escorted to a table, receives a menu, orders, eats, receives the bill, pays, and leaves. The various tracks associated with this script designate the different types of restaurants (fast-food, cafeteria, gourmet), and permit individuals to follow different procedures depending on the specific circumstances.

Table 2: Sexual aggressors' hunting process scripts and tracks

Scripts	Coercive Script		Manipulative Script		Non-persuasive Script
	Home Intrusion	**Outdoor**	**Sophistication**	**Infiltration**	**Direct action**
Hunting field	Victim's residence	Ambush	Prostitution market Occupation	Family Occupation	Local visibility
Victim alone	Yes	Yes	–	No	No
Encounter site	Indoor/private Indoor/semi-public	Outdoor/public Indoor/public	Outdoor/public	Indoor/private	Indoor/public
Familiarity with encounter-site	Victim	Victim and aggressor	Victim and aggressor	Aggressor	Victim and aggressor
Contact strategy	Physical violence	Physical violence	Seduction, tricks, games	Money/gifts Drugs/alcohol	Direct action
Hunting pattern	Hunter/raptor	Hunter/raptor	Troller/ambusher	Trapper/ambusher	–/–
Victim kidnapped	No	Yes	No	No	No
Attack site	Indoor/private Indoor/semi-public	Outdoor/public	Indoor/private	Indoor/private	Indoor/public
Familiarity with attack site	Victim	Victim and aggressor	Aggressor	Aggressor	Victim and aggressor
Strategy for bringing victim to crime site	Threats	Physical violence	Seduction, trick, games	Money/gifts Drugs/alcohol	Direct Action
Familiarity with crime site	Victim	None	Offender	Aggressor	Victim and aggressor
Strategies for committing the crime	Physical violence	Physical violence Threats	Money/gifts	Money/gifts Drugs/alcohol	Direct action
Victim-release site classification	Indoor/private Indoor/semi-public	Outdoor/public Outdoor/private	Outdoor/public	Indoor/private	Indoor/public
Familiarity with victim-release-site	Victim	None or offender	Victim and offender	Aggressor	Victim and aggressor
*Crime-location set	EACVR	EA_CVR EA_C_VR E_A_CVR	E_AC_VR E_ACVR	EACVR	EACVR

* Crime-location set: E = encounter; A = attack; C = crime; VR = victim release; _ = change of location

violence to overpower the victim and prevent her from crying out. He often found it necessary to threaten the woman to lead her to the location at which he wanted to attack her. He explained that, if she resists, he would hit her or strangle her until she lost consciousness. After the sexual assault, he left the scene, without saying a word. On at least two occasions, he also assaulted children.

b) The outdoor track

In the outdoor track, the aggressor ambushes the victim in a public place familiar to both of them. Unlike the home-intrusion track, the aggressor kidnaps the victim and uses physical violence to bring them to the crime scene and to commit the crime. The crime takes place outdoors (street, alleyway, park, courtyard, etc.), as does victim release. As with the previous track, the aggressor uses a hunter-raptor hunting style.

Alex is a sexual aggressor who has wreaked havoc for approximately two years, during which time he attacked 12 women; one of his victims was 14. When he experienced the desire to sexually assault a woman, he would drive around in his car, searching for a potential victim. This "hunt" could take place in the day or night. When he identified his victim, he would park his car some distance away. He would then follow the (young) woman. Once she arrived at a place convenient for his attack (an area with trees to provide cover, an alleyway), he would grab her from behind. While strangling and threatening her, he would lead her away. His attacks —consisting of forcible fellatio or intercourse — did not last long.

2. The Manipulative Script

Like the coercive script, the manipulative script can develop along two different tracks.

a) The sophisticated track

The characteristic feature of the sophisticated track is a hunt that is based in a prostitution market or workplace (employment, volunteer work, management of activities, etc.). Contact with the victim occurs outdoors, in a public place familiar to both aggressor and victim. Unlike aggressors who use the coercive script, the aggressor here uses manipulation, games-play, or the offer of money and gifts to lead the victim to the scene where he commits the assault. He does not kidnap the victim, even if the attack takes place in an indoor or private location known to him (most often his own residence). The hunting style is troller-ambusher: the assailant meets the victim opportunistically, during his non-predatory activities, and attacks only once the victim is attracted to a place — such as a residence or workplace — where he is in power. After the attack, he usually abandons the victim where he has encountered them.

> Luc had committed three sexual assaults in a single month. He often wandered around a neighbourhood where prostitutes ply their trade. Although adult prostitutes work the area, it is also known to harbour young male prostitutes. While driving through the area, Luc noticed two young boys attempting to get into a truck parked in an alleyway. He stopped to ask the boys — that one would have expected to be in school at the time — what they were doing. After having asked the boys several questions, Luc learned that they lived in a shelter from which they had run away. Promising not to report them, he offered to take them for something to eat; the boys quickly accepted.
>
> Once in the restaurant, Luc explained to the boys that, to keep police from finding them, it now seemed to him more prudent for them to come to his apartment and order food to eat there. The group ate pizza at his apartment. Then Luc told the boys he needed to shower and invited them to do the same. The boys agreed, taking advantage of his hospitality. However, after they all had showered, Luc began playing around with the boys, who were dressed only in towels. He was highly aroused sexually, and was ready to have sexual relations with the boys, particularly as they seemed willing. He began talking about sexuality and showing them how to masturbate. To persuade them to commit sexual acts, he offered them ten dollars apiece to participate in group masturbation. In need of money, the boys agreed. After ejaculating, Luc drove the victims to a public place so as not to be further associated with the young runaways.

b) The family-infiltrator track

In this track, the aggressor mostly hunts within a family setting or through his occupation. He uses money and gifts, or alcohol and drugs, to approach the victim, lead them to the crime scene and commit the crime. The locations are private indoor places, most often the aggressor's residence. The hunting style is similar to that of the sophisticated track, except that the aggressor uses the trapper method to seek out victims: he occupies a position or creates a situation that permits him to meet potential victims on territory under his control.

> Jacques has attacked seven victims. In some cases, his preferred hunting territory were families. He contended that single-parent families, consisting of a mother and children, constitutes a pool of potential victims who are accessible and very vulnerable. In one instance, he was working as the superintendent in a public-housing apartment building. While undertaking work in an apartment, he became acquainted with the mother of two boys. Jacques was friendly and helpful to the woman, demanding nothing in return. He even offered to look after her children if she needed to go out to work. Jacques explained that, by discussing the children with her, he overcame their fears of him and began to be seen as a friend of the family. A few days later, on the pretext that he was looking after other children in any event, Jacques again offered to look after the tenant's children. He claimed that the mention of other children under his care reassured the woman. The mother went out and Jacques took the two boys home with him. Jacques quickly asked the boys if they wanted to look at comic books. The boys followed him into his bedroom, where Jacques showed them comics and said he would give them to him if they would let him do what he wanted. Jacques then touched them sexually and performed fellatio on them.

3. Non-persuasive Script

The final script comprises a single track and is very different than the others.

a) Direct-action track

In this track, the aggressor hunts in a public place but uses no particular hunting style. He acts directly (i.e. with no particular strategy) on the victim to make contact, bring her to the crime site, and commit the crime. Most often, this type of aggression takes place in indoor public places such as bars and boutiques.

> Alain had attacked 17 victims, 8 of them during a two-week period. At that time, he consumed a great deal of alcohol and drugs, and frequented various drinking establishments. When he wanted sexual contact, he would linger outside the women's washroom, and, when the opportunity presented itself, commit a more or less intrusive sexual assault on

a young woman exiting the washroom. He used no violence or particular strategy to approach his victim or commit his crimes.

F. WHAT HUNTING PROCESS SCRIPTS MEAN FOR OFFENDER PROFILING

The results described above have several implications for profiling. The results demonstrating the dynamic nature of the hunting process support the idea that offender profiling can only produce valid and realistic predictive models if it takes into consideration situational — that is, geographic — factors. The creation of geographic profiles, specifically, is greatly facilitated by the identification of the relationship between crime locations and the hunting patterns (i.e. victim-search and victim-attack methods) identified by Rossmo (1997). The scripts associated with various hunting processes and hunting fields are presented in Table 3. As can be seen, certain hunting methods are associated with specific scripts, and there is some correlation between methods.

Table 3: Matrix of hunting process scripts, victim-search methods, attack methods and hunting fields

Script	Coercive		Manipulative		Non-persuasive
Tracks	Home Intrusion	Outdoor	Sophisticated	Family Infiltration	Direct action
Victim-search method	Hunter	Hunter	Troller	Trapper	n.a.
Victim-attack method	Raptor	Raptor	Ambusher	Ambusher	n.a.
Hunting field	Residence	Ambush	Prostitution market Occupation	Family Occupation	Local visibility

Hunting style is also helpful in determining which crime locations are the best predictors of an offender's anchor point under different circumstances (Rossmo, 2000). Further, familiarity with the location associated with crime gives investigators at least a partial idea of an aggressor's awareness of space, which may help in reconstructing his mental map. The aggressor's mental map has a direct influence on the selection of a crime site, as a target cannot be victimized unless the aggressor is first aware of the site (Brantingham & Brantingham, 1991; Rossmo, 2000). Finally, the relationship between offending and geographic behaviour may serve as the basis for the development of integrated criminal-geographic profiling.

G. GEOGRAPHIC ASSESSMENT AND HUNTING PROCESS SCRIPTS IN ACTION: PROJECT WOLF

Between May 12, 2002, and October 29, 2003, a series of sexual assaults were committed in the regions of Laval and Montreal. The same individual sexually attacked eight women aged between 14 and 28. Six of them were attacked in Laval, two in Montreal (see Figure 3).

Analysis of hunting process scripts revealed that the aggressor employed a coercive script compatible with the outdoor track described above. All the attacks featured an ambush in a public place familiar to the victim and assailant. The attacker had observed most of his victims along a bus route (Figure 4, marked in yellow). When a victim got off at a stop (a public place familiar to her), he followed her until she arrived a site suitable for his attack. He then kidnapped the victim and took her to the crime site. The aggressor used some physical violence, as well as threats. The assault occurred at an outdoor public location (street, alleyway, courtyard), and the victim was usually left at the crime site. As is typical with the hunter-raptor hunting style, the aggressor searched out victims in his own residential area (where he lived with his spouse) and attacked his victims on first contact with them.

The Behavioural Sciences Unit of the Royal Canadian Mounted Police created a geographic assessment[2] of the crime scenes. This analysis was greatly influenced by a particular site associated with the assaults. After having assaulted his sixth victim, the aggressor took her handbag, which contained her cellular telephone. Forty minutes after the attack, an unanswered call was made on the phone. With the help of the cellular telephone service provider, police were able to determine the perimeter of the area in which the phone was used (Figure 4).

Subsequent analysis established that the aggressor had committed the first two sexual assaults within this perimeter. Further information suggested the attacker used a bicycle, reinforcing the thesis that he resided near the

2 There is a distinction between a geographic assessment and a geographic profile. The aim of geographic profiling is to prioritize the most likely area where the aggressor will be found, while the aim of geographic assessment is to examine the geographical characteristics associated with an investigation so as to suggest the significance of locations to the suspect. Geographic assessments are limited to the geographical examination of spatial and hunting patterns revealed by locations associated with the crimes (Corporal Carl Sesely, Behavioural Sciences Unit, Royal Canadian Mounted Police.)

crime scene.[3] Police accorded the area investigative priority, and surveillance there led to the arrest of Michael Cox, who lived in the prioritized area (marked in red) identified by the geographic profilers (see Figure 5).

H. INVESTIGATIVE STRATEGIES FOR SERIAL SEX CRIMES: APPLYING GEOGRAPHIC PROFILING

As mentioned above, investigation of serial crime often produces a long list of suspects. By predicting the likely residence of an unknown suspect, geographic profiling has proved to be useful in prioritizing suspects and clues for investigation. In 1998, investigators attributed to one aggressor a series of 11 sexual assaults extending over 35 days. Their work produced a list of 300 suspects. Geographic profiling narrowed down the investigative area to 0.03 square miles (2.2%) and thereby permitted the investigating team to prioritize the suspect list. The Peel Regional Police of Mississauga, Ontario, obtained a DNA sample of the man who turned out to be the assailant. He had been first on the revised suspect list (Rossmo, 2000).

A series of 14 sexual assaults occurred in Lafayette, Louisiana between 1984 and 1995. In 1998, refusing to close the file, police sought psychological and geographic profiles. These permitted them to circumscribe their investigation area and prioritize 2,000 clues. They obtained a DNA sample and fingerprints from a suspect, on the basis of his residence within the 0.5-mile (2.2%) region identified by the profile. The forensic evidence confirmed the suspect was the offender. He admitted to and was convicted of the rapes (Rossmo, 2000).

Geographic profiling can also be used in combination with government and commercial databases. In one case of serial sexual assault, for example, psychological profiling revealed that the suspect regularly consumed pornography. Using a CD-ROM business directory police prepared a list of all establishments at which consumers could rent or buy pornographic films. Using a geographic profile, they then prioritized the list by address. Concentrating on the prioritized establishments and investigating customers who regularly rented pornography, police prepared a sketch of the suspect, knowing that most of those who rent such films live near the stores (Rossmo, 2000).

---

3 Sexual aggressors usually commit their crimes near their place of residence. Serial sexual aggressors often commit their first crimes closer to their residences, because they are familiar with the area. The use of a bicycle suggests that an aggressor did not travel far to make contact with his victims.

Figure 4

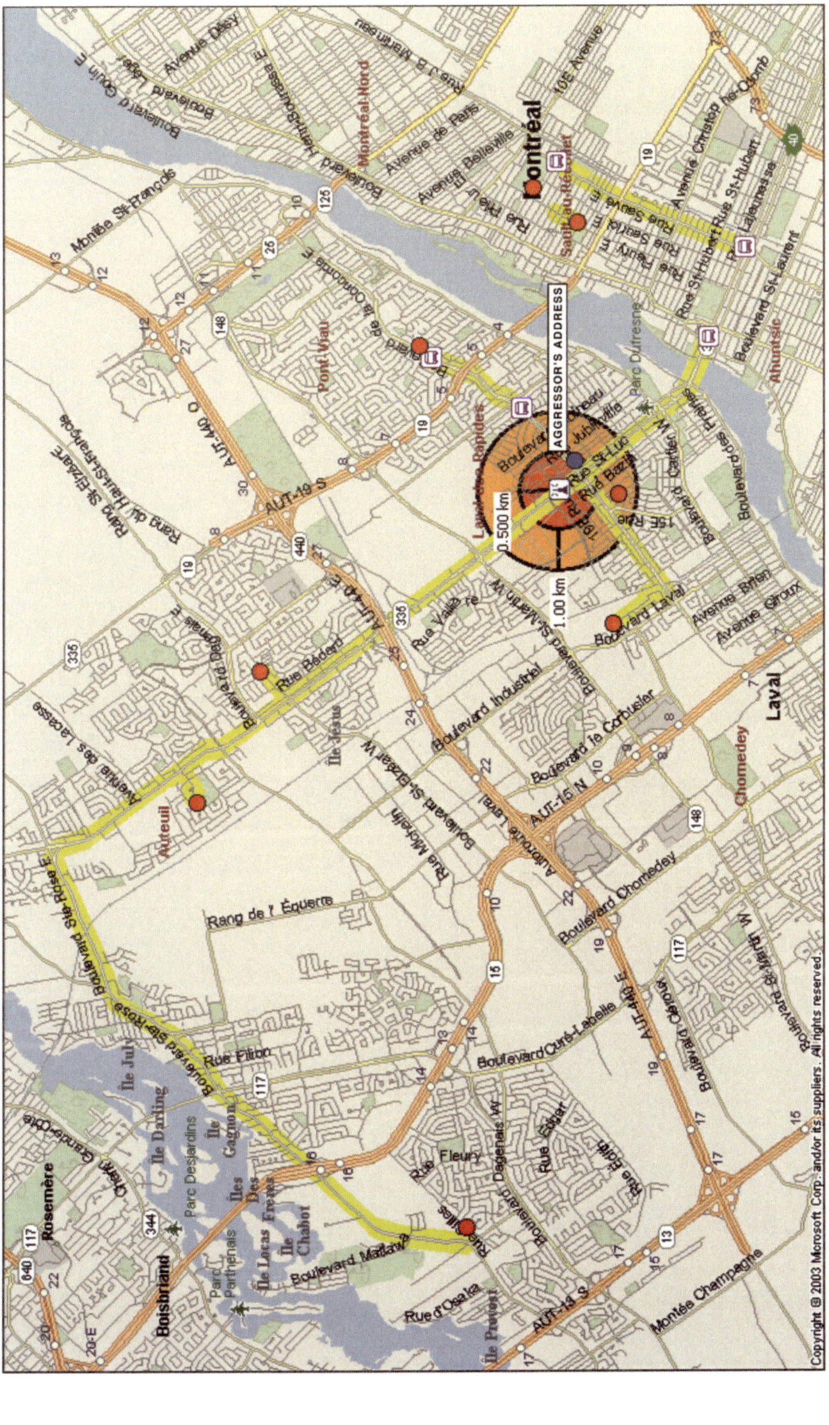

Geographic profile produced by Carl Seseley, Royal Canadian Mounted Police

Figure 5

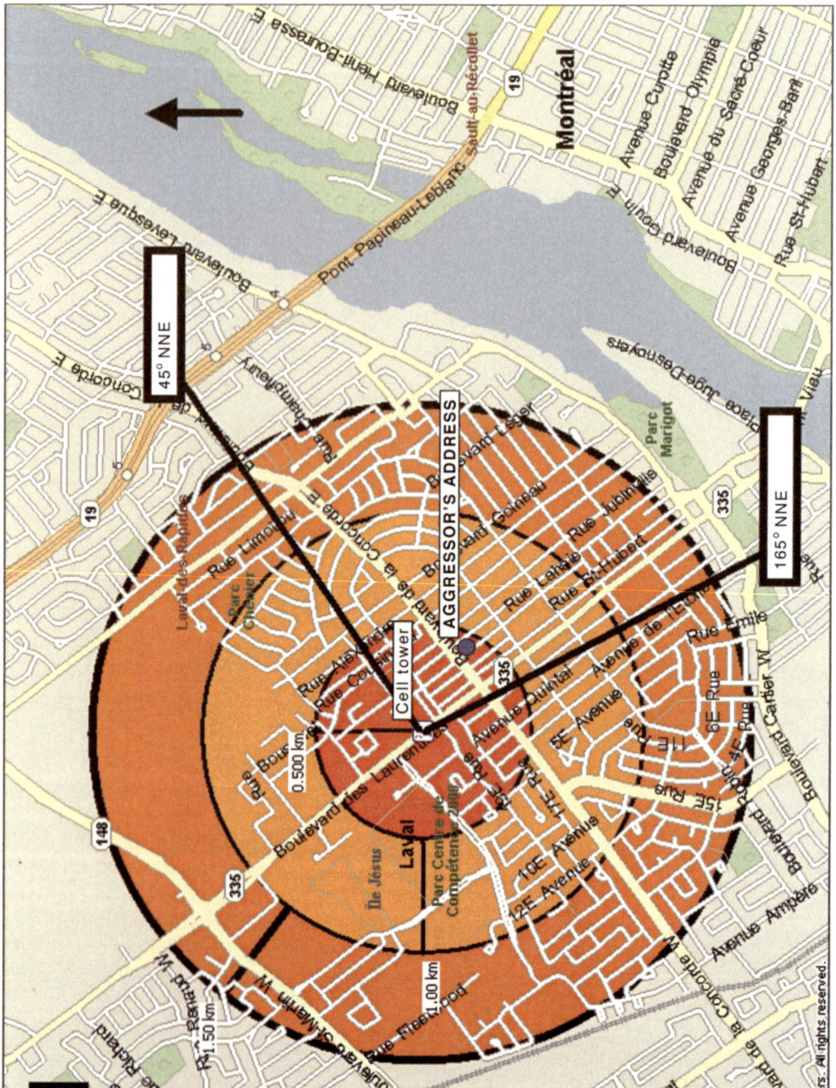

Geographic profile produced by Carl Seseley, Royal Canadian Mounted Police

Finally, geographic profiling can be useful in the search for clues and witnesses, and — in conjunction with police databases such as VICLAS (in Canada) or VICAP (in the United States), or offender registries — in the creation of task forces, in missing-persons cases, and in expert court testimony.

CONCLUSION

The investigation of serial crime requires special care in information management. Given the very large number of suspects that this type of investigation can unearth, it becomes crucial to prioritize those the police interrogate. This prioritization can be based on physical description, a criminal profile, and a geographic profile. With serial sex crimes, it has been possible to develop hunting process scripts that take into account geographic factors.

Our results show how the strategies adopted by serial sexual aggressors are shaped by the geography of the crime scene and associated locations. However, these geographic factors are often neglected in sexual-aggressor typologies, which instead put the accent on the aggressor himself, failing to consider the entire criminal event. Thus, geographic profiling can become an important tool in prioritizing suspects in serial crime investigations. Geography can prove itself an important factor in linkage analysis, given the great probability that crimes committed in the same area will be related (Bennell and Canter, 2002). Hazelwood notes that in determining the "what" and "why," reveals the "who". Henceforth, it will prove just as important to include the "where" in this equation.

REFERENCES

Beauregard, E. (2007). The role of profiling in the investigation of sexual homicide. In J. Proulx, E. Beauregard, M. Cusson, and A. Nicole (Eds.), Sexual murder: A comparative analysis and new perspectives (pp. 193-211). Winchester, UK: Wiley.

Beauregard, E., Lussier, P., and Proulx, J. (2005). The role of sexual interests and situational factors on rapists' modus operandi: Implications for offender profiling. *Legal and Criminological Psychology, 10*, 265-278.

Beauregard, E., Proulx, J., and St-Yves, M. (2007). Angry or sadistic: Two types of sexual murderers. In J. Proulx, E. Beauregard, M. Cusson, and A. Nicole (Eds.), Sexual murder: A comparative analysis and new perspectives (pp. 123-141). Winchester, UK: Wiley.

Beauregard, E., Proulx, J., and Rossmo, K. (2005). Spatial patterns of sex offenders: Theoretical, empirical, and practical issues. *Aggression and Violent Behavior, 10*, 579-603.

Beauregard, E., Proulx, J., Rossmo, D., Leclerc, B., and Allaire, J.-F. (2007). Script analysis of hunting patterns in serial sex offenders. *Criminal Justice and Behavior, 34, 1069-1084.*

Beauregard, E., Rossmo, K., and Proulx, J. (2007). A descriptive model of the hunting process of serial sex offenders: A rational choice perspective. *Journal of Family Violence, 22, 449-463.*

Bennell, C. and Canter, D.V. (2002). Linking commercial burglaries by modus operandi: Tests using regression and ROC analysis. *Science and Justice, 42*, p. 153-164.

Brantingham, P.L. and Brantingham, P.J. (1993). Environment, routine and situation: Toward a pattern theory of crime. In R.V. Clarke and M. Felson (eds.), *Routine activity and rational choice* (p. 259-294). New Brunswick, NJ.: Transaction.

Brantingham, P.J. and Brantingham, P.L. (1991). *Environmental criminology*. Prospect Heights, Illinois: Waveland Press.

Brantingham, P.J. and Brantingham, P.L. (1984). *Patterns in crime*. New

York: MacMillan.

Cornish, D.B. (1994). Crime as scripts. In D. Zahm and P. Cromwell (eds.), *Proceedings of the International Seminar on Environmental Criminology and Crime Analysis,* University of Miami, Coral Gables, Florida, 1993. Tallahassee, FL: Florida Statistical Analysis Center, Florida Criminal Justice Executive Institute, Florida Department of Law Enforcement.

Groth, A.N., Burgess, A.W., and Holmstrom, L.L. (1977). Rape, power, anger and sexuality. *American Journal of Psychiatry, 134*, 1239-1243.

Hazelwood, R.R. (1995). Analyzing the rape and profiling the offender. In R.R. Hazelwood and A.W. Burgess (eds.), *Practical aspects of rape investigation: A multidisciplinary approach* (2nd edition), (pp. 155-182). Boca Raton, FL : CRC Press.

Hazelwood, R.R. (1983). The behavior-oriented interview of rape victims. *FBI Law Enforcement Bulletin.*

Hazelwood, R.R. and Burgess, A.W. (1987). An introduction to the serial rapist. *FBI Law Enforcement Bulletin, 56*, p. 16-24.

Hazelwood, R.R., Reboussin, R., and Warren, J.L. (1989). Serial rape: Correlates of increased aggression and the relationship of offender pleasure to victim resistance. *Journal of Interpersonal Violence, 4*, p. 65-78.

Hazelwood, R.R. and Warren, J.L. (1990). The criminal behavior of the serial rapist. *FBI Law Enforcement Bulletin, 59*, p. 11-16.

Hazelwood, R.R. and Warren, J.L. (1989). The serial rapist : His characteristics and victims. *FBI Law Enforcement Bulletin, 2*, p. 19-25.

Meier, R.F., Kennedy, L.W., and Sacco, V.F. (2001). Crime and the criminal event perspective. Dans R.F. Meier, L.W. Kennedy and V.F. Sacco (eds.), *The Process and Structure of Crime : Criminal Events and Crime Aanalysis* (p. 1-27). New Brunswick: Transaction Publishers.

Petee, T.A. and Jarvis, J. (2000). Analyzing violent serial offending. *Homicide Studies, 4*, p. 211-218.

Rossmo, K. (2004). Geographic profiling as problem solving for serial crime. In Q.C. Thurman and J.D. Jamieson (eds.), *Police problem solving* (p. 121-131). Cincinnati: Anderson Publishing.

Rossmo, K. (2001). Evaluation of geographic profiling search strategies. Paper presented to the American Society of Criminology, Atlanata, GA.

Rossmo, K. (2000). *Geographic profiling*. Boca Raton: CRC Press.

Rossmo, K. (1997). Geographic profiling. In J.L. Jackson et D.A. Bekerian (eds.), *Offender Profiling : Theory, Research and Practice*, (p. 159-175). Chichester: John Wiley et Sons.

Sapp, A.D., Huff, T.G., Gary, G.P., Icove, D.J., and Horbert, P. (1994). *A report of essential findings from a study of serial arsonists*. Quantico, VA: National Center for the Analysis of Violent Crime.

Schaller, G.B. (1972). *The Serengeti lion: A study of predator-prey relations*. Chicago: University of Chicago Press.

Schank, R.C., and Abelson, R.P. (1977). *Scripts, plans, goals and understanding : An inquiry into human knowledge*. Hillsdale, NJ : Erlbaum.

Tedeschi, J.T., and Felson, R.B. (1994). *Violence, aggression, and coercive actions*. Washington, DC: American Psychological Association.

Warren, J.L., Reboussin, R., Hazelwood, R.R., Cummings, A., Gibbs, N., and Trumbetta, S. (1998). Crime scene and distance correlates of serial rape. *Journal of Quantitative Criminology, 14*, p. 35-59.

Warren, J.L., Reboussin, R., Hazelwood, R.R., Gibbs, N., Trumbetta, S., and Cummings, A. (1999). Crime scene analysis and the escalation of violence in serial rape. *Forensic Science International, 100*, p. 37-56.

Wilson, G., and Alison, L. (2005). Suspect prioritization in the investigation of sex offences: From clinical classification and profiling to pragmatism. In L. Alison (ed.), *The forensic psychologist's casebook: Psychological profiling and criminal investigation* (pp. 68-89). Cullompton, Devon, UK: Willan Publishing.

CONCLUSION

CONCLUSION

Time flies, truth flees.

Edmond Locard

Police often count on the first 24 hours to solve a crime. It is usually during those first hours that the victim contacts police (or the corpse is discovered) and the forensic services technicians examine the crime scene for concrete clues (fingerprints, DNA, fibres, projectiles, etc.) and send the clues to the forensic sciences laboratory, hoping to identify the offender.

Crime-scene and forensic-laboratory analyses are often perceived as being the heart of the investigation and the main factors in its success. Films and crime novels feed such erroneous beliefs. As criminologist Jean-Paul Brodeur notes, ". . . nothing is further from the reality of effective police work than the view that popular literature spreads among the public. The guilty are rarely discovered by the investigator's reasoning or laboratory analysis; rather, resolution is usually the result of information obtained by the police from the victim, witnesses, or informers or . . . the perpetrator themselves."[1]

To solve a crime, one must first embrace its relational dimension: approach people, question them, listen to them, collect their statements — what they saw, heard, perceived on that day and the days preceding. One must construct a portrait of the victim — their movements, their daily routine — and meet their family, friends, and work colleagues. Investigators need to go door to door and make themselves available to the public. Evidence collected this way will yield leads and working hypotheses. Then, the investigators can ask the classic, fundamental question: "Who profited from this crime?"[2] All the information must be verified, and the identified suspects more deeply investigated until there are sufficient grounds for interrogating one or more of them.

---

1 J.-P. Brodeur, (2003). *Les visages de la police. Pratiques et perceptions*, Montréal, Presses de l'Université de Montréal, p. 28.

2 L. Mucchielli (2006). L'élucidation des homicides: de l'enchantement à l'analyse du travail des enquêteurs de police judiciaire. *Déviance et Société*, vol. 30 (1), 91-119.

Numerous North American[3] and European[4] studies have established that the vast majority of criminal cases are solved on the basis of witnesses. In a study concerning the solving of murder cases in France, the sociologist and historian Laurent Mucchielli arrived at the same conclusion: "...it is in summary the perpetrator, the entourage of the perpetrator or the victim, the public's help, or rumour that usually leads investigators towards the perpetrator."[5] The principal reason for the success of criminal investigations is the quality of the relationship police establish with the public — hence the importance of community policing — not the technical quality of investigative tools. As Mucchielli points out, for material evidence such as fingerprints and DNA to be fully effective the entire population would have to be registered. But such a policy would raise serious debates about individual civil liberties and privacy.

There is no perfect crime, only imperfect investigations. And investigations are imperfect because they are performed by humans — and none of us is perfect. A police investigation is not a plot in a novel. It is demanding work that requires *savoir-faire* (knowing how to "do"), but also "*savoir-être*" — knowing how to *be*. To quote Mucchielli[6] again: "In the work of criminal investigation divisions — and more broadly in the realm of police intelligence — the human element is more important than material considerations, and relational abilities remain at least as important as technical skills."

Listening to others, being empathetic, establishing contact with someone and building a rapport with them are the hallmarks of *savoir-être*. In criminal investigations, *savoir-être* also means keeping an open mind and impartial attitude, waiting for all the necessary elements to be available before forming an impression that could otherwise distort reality. *Savoir-être* is the best protection against tunnel vision, that insidious virus that can infect all those involved in the administration of justice.

While at first blush the search for the truth in criminal investigations can appear to be a utopian enterprise, it serves daily to remind the principal

---

3 R. Ericson (1981). *Making Crime,* Scaborough, Butterworths; P. Greenwood, J. Chaiken, and J. Petersilia (1977). *The Criminal Investigation Process,* Rand Corporation, Lexington MA, Lexington Books; J. Morgan (1990). *The Police Function and the Investigation of Crime,* Aldershot, Avebury.

4 M. Innes (2003). *Investigating Murder. Detective Work and the Police Response to Criminal Homicide,* Oxford, Clarendon Press; L. Mucchielli, (2006). *Ibid.*

5 Mucchielli (2006). *Ibid,* p. 101.

6 Mucchielli (2006). *Ibid,* p. 112.

actors of their mission — to, indeed, uncover the truth. On that so-called "objective" truth, often built on a series of subjective "truths," we rely to do justice. From the first call to police to conviction of the guilty, each step in the investigation must adhere to professional standards and be performed as objectively as possible. By so doing, police ennoble their work in the public eye, and thereby help solve yet more crimes. For it is the public that most often possesses the truth we seek.

* * *

The actors are all in place. All rise. In robe and tabs, the judge enters. The clerk calls for silence and exclaims: "The court is in session!" He invites those assembled to be seated. The clerk reads the indictment and a witness comes to the stand. The process begins. "Do you swear to tell the whole truth and nothing but the truth?"

ANALYTICAL INDEX